Content Area Reading

Literacy and Learning Across the Curriculum

EIGHTH EDITION

Richard T. Vacca

Kent State University, emeritus

Jo Anne L. Vacca

Kent State University, emeritus

Boston • New York • San Francisco
Mexico City • Montreal • Toronto • London • Madrid • Munich • Paris
Hong Kong • Singapore • Tokyo • Cape Town • Sydney

Series Editor: Aurora Martínez Ramos
Development Editor: Tom Jefferies
Series Editorial Assistant: Erin Beatty
Senior Marketing Manager: Elizabeth Fogarty
Production Administrator: Michael Granger
Editorial-Production Service: Omegatype Typography, Inc.
Composition and Prepress Buyer: Linda Cox
Manufacturing Buyer: Andrew Turso
Cover Administrator: Linda Knowles
Interior Design: Carol Somberg
Electronic Composition: Omegatype Typography, Inc.

For related titles and support materials, visit our online catalog at www.ablongman.com.

Between the time Website information is gathered and then published, it is not unusual for some sites to have closed. Also, the transcription of URLs can result in typographical errors. The publisher would appreciate notification where these errors occur so that they may be corrected in subsequent editions.

Library of Congress Cataloging-in-Publication Data

Vacca, Richard T.
      Content area reading : literacy and learning across the curriculum / Richard T. Vacca,
Jo Anne L. Vacca. —8th ed.
            p. cm.
      Includes bibliographical references.
      ISBN 0-205-41031-6
        1. Content area reading. I. Vacca, Jo Anne L. II. Title.

LB1050.455.V33 2005
428.4'3—dc22

                                                                                    2004043669

Printed in the United States of America

10   9   8   7   6   5   4   3   2   1   09   08   07   06   05   04

Credits appear on page 472, which constitutes an extension of the copyright page.

We choose *friends,* not *relatives*

How blessed we are to have these
special persons who are both

Fred and Pat Vacca
Tony and Chris Vacca
Tom and Patty Schmidt
Gary and Courtney Vierstra

Brief Contents

Detailed Contents

chapter **6** **Learning with Electronic Texts** 196

chapter **9 Activating Prior Knowledge
and Interest 294**

chapter **10** Guiding Reader–Text Interactions   318

chapter **11** Writing to Learn   352

chapter **12** Studying Texts 390

Preface

When we began writing *Content Area Reading* more than twenty-five years ago, we decided to set the tone of the first edition in the opening chapter by quoting a line from Simon and Garfunkel's "Kodachrome." Although we run the risk of dating ourselves, we are reminded of the provocative line because it captures the disconnect that many students have felt in their school experience, then as well as now. The opening lyrics to "Kodachrome" are a songwriter's personal reflection on education—nothing more, nothing less. Yet the juxtaposition of having learned "crap" in school with the inability to "think" critically represents an ongoing dilemma faced by content area teachers who are wedded to an academic discipline.

We have never met a teacher who didn't believe that the essence of artful teaching is in showing students how to think deeply and critically about the content underlying an academic discipline. Yet, when *content* is taught in a vacuum without attention to the *process* by which it is learned, students are apt to make few connections between the powerful ideas underlying an academic discipline and the prior knowledge and experience that they bring to classroom learning situations. In this book, we explore the relationships between content and process by critically examining the literacy processes and strategies that students use to think and learn with texts.

Major Themes in the Eighth Edition

Influenced by the role of language, cognition, culture, and social context in learning, our goal for this edition is to inspire teachers, whether novice or veteran, to examine what it means to connect literacy and learning in a standards-based curriculum. The eighth edition continues the ambitious exploration of *content literacy*—the ability to use reading, writing, talking, listening, and viewing processes to learn subject matter across the curriculum. The major themes underlying content literacy and learning are reflected in the organizing principles described at the beginning of every chapter:

- All teachers play a critical role in helping studens comprehend and respond to information and ideas in the text.

- Instructional assessment is a process of gathering and using multiple sources of relevant information about students for instructional purposes.

- Teachers respond to the literacy needs of struggling readers and writers by scaffolding instruction so that students become confident and competent in the use of strategies that support learning.

- Teachers respond to linguistic and cultural differences in their classrooms by scaffolding instruction in the use of vocabulary and comprehension strategies and by creating classroom environments that encourage talking and working together.

- Instructional practices involving the use of informational and literary trade books in content areas help to extend and enrich the curriculum.

- Electronic texts, like trade books, extend and enrich the curriculum.

- Bringing students and texts together involves instructional plans and activities that result in active student engagement and collaboration.

- Teaching words well means giving students multiple opportunities to develop vocabulary knowledge and to learn how words are conceptually related to one another in the texts that they study.

- Activating prior knowledge and generating interest create an instructional context in which students will approach reading with purpose and anticipation.

- Teachers guide reader–text interactions through the instructional strategies and practices that they use and the reading support that they provide.

- Writing facilitates learning by helping students to explore, clarify, and think deeply about the ideas they encounter in reading.

- Looking for and using text structure in everything they read helps students to study texts more effectively.

Underlying these themes is our belief that students learn *with* texts, not necessarily *from* texts. Learning from texts suggests that a text is a body of information to be mastered by learners rather than a tool by which they construct meaning and knowledge. Learning with a text, on the other hand, implies that students have much to contribute to their own learning as they interact with texts to make meaning and construct knowledge.

Organization of the Eighth Edition

The knowledge base related to content literacy and learning has changed dramatically in the past twenty-five years, and so has thinking about what constitutes "best practice." Nevertheless, in making decisions related to changes in this edition, we ask the same question that guided the writing of the first edition twenty-five years ago: How can teachers make content literacy a visible part of their instructional routines without sacrificing high standards for content learning?

Answers to this guiding question led us to reorganize the eighth edition into three parts: Part One: Content Literacy in a Standards-Based Curriculum, Part Two: Learners and Texts, and Part Three: Instructional Strategies and Practices.

Part One situates issues and problems related to content literacy within the context of the standards-based movement and accountability systems that are changing the face of education in today's U.S. schools. Although the pressure to ensure that students meet content standards weighs heavily on instructional decisions, a teacher can make a difference in students' literacy development and knowledge acquisition by showing them how to use literacy processes and strategies to meet high standards for learning. Ongoing, authentic assessment in the classroom—when coupled with high-stakes proficiency assessment—provides the information that teachers need to inform their day-by-day instructional decisions about content literacy and learning.

In Parts Two and Three of this edition, we build an instructional framework for content literacy and learning across the curriculum. In Part Two, Learners and Texts, our emphasis is on the exploration and clarification of issues related to struggling readers and writers, culturally and linguistically diverse learners, and the use of trade books and electronic texts to extend and enrich the curriculum. Students who continually struggle with text in reading and writing situations need to build strategic knowledge, skills, and insights related to literacy and learning. Moreover, culturally and linguistically diverse students present a unique challenge to content area teachers, especially in light of the influx of immigrant students in today's classrooms. We also examine the limitations of textbooks and explain how to use trade books and information and communication technologies such as the Internet to extend and enrich a standards-based curriculum.

In Part Three, Instructional Strategies and Practices, we flesh out the instructional framework by explaining how to create active learning environments in which all students—alone and in collaboration with one another—know how to use content literacy strategies to learn with texts. To this end, Part Three offers a multitude of instructional strategies and practices that allow teachers to scaffold instruction in ways that support the following:

- development of vocabulary knowledge and concepts;
- activation of prior knowledge before, during, and after reading;
- comprehension and critical analysis of text through reader–text interactions;
- use of various writing activities to facilitate learning; and
- development of study strategies based on a search for text structure in everything that students read.

These instructional strategies and practices are designed to engage students in their strategic interactions with text and other learners. Rather than left to "sink or swim" with a text assignment, students will be more likely to know how to search for meaning in everything they talk about, listen to, and read, view, and write.

Features in the Eighth Edition

The eighth edition retains all of the features of the previous edition, while improving its overall coverage of content literacy topics and instructional strategies and practices.

New and Expanded Chapters

The text continues to emphasize a contemporary, functional approach to content literacy instruction. In a functional approach, content area teachers learn how to integrate literacy-related strategies into instructional routines without sacrificing the teaching of content. Our intent is not to "morph" a content teacher into a reading specialist or writing instructor. As a result, we expanded our discussions of topics in the previous edition by creating separate, new chapters for the following:

- Chapter 1: Reading Matters (with an emphasis on the impact of teaching to content standards);

- Chapter 3: Struggling Readers and Writers (with a renewed emphasis on writing strategies for students who struggle with the writing process);

- Chapter 4: Culturally and Linguistically Diverse Learners (with emphasis on students whose first language is other than English);

- Chapter 5: Learning with Trade Books (written by Professor Barbara Moss from San Diego State University, a leading expert in the field of informational literature for children and adolescents); and

- Chapter 6: Learning with Electronic Texts (with emphasis on learning with the Internet).

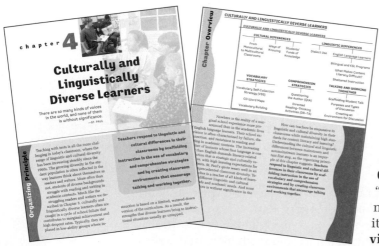

Aids to Understanding

A new design makes the text visually appealing and easy to use. Through this new, attractive design, the main features are easily identified, making the text user-friendly.

Each chapter opens with a quotation to help readers reflect on the underlying theme of each chapter. The **Organizing Principle** gives readers a "heads-up" by introducing the rationale for each chapter and highlighting its underlying theme. A **Chapter Overview** depicts the relationships that exist among the important ideas presented in each chapter. A set of questions at the start of the chapter helps readers approach the text in a critical **Frame of Mind** as they analyze and interpret information presented in each chapter.

End-of-chapter features include **Minds On** and **Hands On** activities. Minds On activities engage students individually and collaboratively in thinking more deeply about some of the important ideas that they have studied. Hands On activities engage students individually and collaboratively in applying some of the important ideas that they have studied.

New Features

New features to this edition include marginal notations and "boxed" text segments that highlight issues related to content standards and assessment, procedures for research-based best practices, and connections between chapter content and diverse learners.

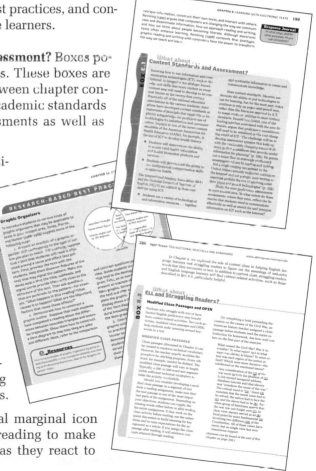

- **What about Content Standards and Assessment?** Boxes positioned throughout most of the chapters. These boxes are designed to emphasize relationships between chapter content and issues/implications related to academic standards and high-stakes state proficiency assessments as well as authentic assessments in the classroom.

- **Research-Based Best Practices.** Boxes positioned throughout most of the chapters relating to instructional strategies and practices. These boxes highlight the steps and applications involved in using high-visibility strategies that are supported by theoretically sound rationales and/or evidence-based research.

- **What About Struggling Readers and English Language Learners?** Boxes positioned occasionally in several of the chapters to augment the content presented in separate chapters on struggling readers and linguistically diverse learners.

- **Response Journal.** The Response Journal marginal icon signals readers to use a journal while reading to make personal and professional connections as they react to ideas presented in each chapter.

- **eResources.** The eResources marginal icon directs readers to the Companion Website to search for Web links, Web activities, or suggested readings to engage in further learning about the topics presented in each chapter. There are also additional eResources at the end of each chapter directing students to the Companion Website for more activities and suggested readings, as well as articles from the *New York Times.*

Supplements for Instructors and Students

Allyn and Bacon is committed to preparing the best quality supplements for its textbooks, and the supplements for the eighth edition of *Content Area Reading* reflect this commitment. For more information about the instructor and student supplements that accompany and support the text, ask your local Allyn & Bacon representative, or contact the Allyn & Bacon Sales Support Department (1-800-852-8024).

- **Instructor's Resource Manual and Test Bank** with teaching suggestions and test items for each chapter.
- **PowerPoint™ Presentation.** Ideal for lecture presentations or student handouts, the PowerPoint™ presentation created for this text provides dozens of ready-to-use graphic and text images (available for download from Supplement Central at www.suppscentral.ablongman.com).
- **Companion Website** (www.ablongman.com/vacca8e) that provides online practice tests, activities, and additional Web resources to deepen and expand understanding of the text.
- **VideoWorkshop,** a new way to bring video into your course for maximized learning! This total teaching and learning system includes quality video footage on an easy-to-use CD-ROM plus a Student Learning Guide and an Instructor's Teaching Guide. The result? A program that brings textbook concepts to life with ease and that helps your students understand, analyze, and apply the objectives of the course. VideoWorkshop is available for your students as a value-pack option with this textbook. (Special package ISBN required from your representative.) VW will eventually become part of an exciting new package online called "My Lab School" currently under construction. Watch for details.
- **My Lab School.** Discover where the classroom comes to life! From video clips of teachers and students interacting to sample lessons, portfolio templates, and standards integration, Allyn and Bacon brings your students the tools they'll need to succeed in the classroom—with content easily integrated into your existing course. Delivered within Course Compass, Allyn and Bacon's course management system, this program gives your students powerful insights into how real classrooms work and a rich array of tools that will support them on their journey from their first class to their first classroom.
- **Allyn and Bacon Digital Media Archive for Literacy.** This CD-ROM offers still images, video clips, audio clips, Web links, and assorted lecture resources that can be incorporated into multimedia presentations in the classroom.

- **Professionals in Action: Literacy Video.** This 90-minute video consists of 10-
to 20-minute segments on Phonemic Awareness, Teaching Phonics, Helping
Students Become Strategic Readers, Organizing for Teaching with Literature,
and discussions of literacy and brain research with experts. The first four segments provide narrative along with actual classroom teaching footage. The final segments present, in a question-and-answer format, discussions by
leading experts in the field of literacy.

- **Allyn and Bacon Literacy Video Library.** Featuring renowned reading scholars Richard Allington, Dorothy Strickland, and Evelyn English, this three-
video library addresses core topics covered in the literacy classroom: reading
strategies, developing literacy in multiple intelligences classrooms, developing phonemic awareness, and much more.

Acknowledgments

We are grateful to the many individuals who made this edition possible. First, we
would like to thank several of our former doctoral students who came to the res-
cue of tired and beleaguered mentors by helping us to meet deadline commitments: Dr. Barbara Moss, San Diego State University, for revising Chapter 5,
Learning with Trade Books; Dr. Christine McKeon, Walsh University, for serving
in the role of Webmaster as she updated and redesigned the Companion Website
for this edition; and Dr. Maryann Mraz, University of North Carolina, for revising
and updating the Instructor's Resource Manual.

We also wish to acknowledge the thoughtful and thought-provoking professional suggestions of those who responded to questionnaires and reviewed the
text for this edition: Vi Alexander, Stephen F. Austin State University; Mickey
Bogart, Kansas State University; Dr. Deb Carr, King's College and Hazleton Area
School District; Ann Harvey, Columbia College; Stephenie Hewett, The Citadel;
Lois E. Huffman, North Carolina State University; Luther Kirk, Longwood University; and Joyce Stallworth, The University of Alabama.

This book is only as good as the editors behind it. We owe a debt of gratitude
to our Acquisitions Editor, Aurora Martínez, whose graceful guidance and inci-
sive leadership on this project made us work harder than we wanted to. And special kudos to Tom Jefferies, the finest and steadiest developmental editor with
whom we have had the pleasure to work thus far.

A special thanks to students, colleagues, and teachers in schools throughout the United States and Canada, too numerous to list, who have contributed
immeasurably to our growth as teachers and scholars. This book has been a
marriage-of-sorts for us and it's time to celebrate our silver anniversary with
this edition's time cycle! Never in our dreams did we think it possible, and we
thank a Power greater than ourselves for making it a reality.

R. T. V.
J. L. V.

chapter 1

Reading Matters

You have to read to survive. . . .
Reading isn't fun; it's indispensable.
—WOODY ALLEN

Woody Allen, the noted film director, actor, writer, and comedian isn't joking when he declares that you have to read to survive, especially in this day and age. The ability to read—and read well—for a variety of purposes has taken on unprecedented importance for human beings in the twenty-first century.

Today's students are tomorrow's adults. As they enter the adult world, the expectation to read and write will be greater than in any other time in human history. The Commission on Adolescent Literacy of the International Reading Association asserts in its position statement that tomorrow's adults "will need advanced levels of literacy to perform their jobs, run their households, act as citizens, and conduct their personal lives. They will need literacy to cope with the flood of information they will find everywhere they turn" (1999, p. 3).

> All teachers play a critical role in helping students comprehend and respond to information and ideas in text.

Although Woody Allen may have had his tongue firmly planted in his cheek when he declared that reading isn't fun, he was right on the mark when he declared that reading is indispensable. Reading matters.

The real value of reading lies in its uses. Reading, as we will see, is a powerful means of communication. It involves putting language to

e.Resources

Read the full text of the "Adolescent Literacy Position Statement" by going to Web Destinations on the Companion Website and clicking on Professional Resources.

Chapter Overview

READING MATTERS

BEING AN ARTFUL TEACHER

| No Child Left Behind Act | Learning with Texts | Beyond Assigning and Telling |

UNDERSTANDING LITERACY

| Literacy Is Situational | Influences on Content Literacy | Incorporating Content Standards into Literacy-Based Instruction |

TEXT COMPREHENSION IN CONTENT AREAS

| Developing Research-Based Comprehension Strategies | Prior Knowledge and Comprehension | Reader Response | Levels of Comprehension | Questioning |

SCAFFOLDING INSTRUCTION

use purposefully—whether it is to enjoy and, yes Woody, to have fun; or whether it is to imagine, to solve problems, or to learn by clarifying and sharpening our thinking about a subject.

All too often students give up on reading with the expectation that teachers will impart information through lecture and recitation. When students become too dependent on teachers as their primary source of information, they are rarely in a position to engage actively in reading to learn. This need not be the case. As the organizing principle of this chapter underscores: **All teachers play a critical role in helping students comprehend and respond to information and ideas in text.**

Study the chapter overview for the chapter. It's your map to the major ideas that you will encounter in the chapter. The graphic display shows the relationships that exist among the concepts you will study. Use it as an organizer. What is the chapter about? What do you know already about the content to be presented in the chapter? What do you need to learn more about?

In conjunction with the chapter overview, take a moment or two to study the "Frame of Mind" questions. This feature uses key questions to help you think about the ideas that you will read about. Our intent is to create a mental disposition for learning, a critical "frame of mind," if you will, so that you can better interact with the ideas that we, as authors, have organized and developed in the chapter. When you finish reading, you should be able to respond fully to the "Frame of Mind" questions.

Response Journal

Write a "five-minute essay" in your response journal on your initial reaction to the organizing principle.

Frame of Mind

1. Why do "assign-and-tell" routines stifle active learning and deny students responsibility for learning on their own?

2. What is content literacy?

3. Why do content standards "crank up the pressure" for teachers as well as students? How do teachers balance the teaching of content in a standards-based curriculum with learning processes that students use to acquire information and ideas?

4. Explain the statement, "Reading is a conversation between the reader and the author of the text."

5. What roles do reader response and prior knowledge play in comprehending text?

6. What is the relationship between levels of comprehension and the types of questions teachers ask in text-related discussions?

The classroom is a crucible, a place where the special mix of *teacher, student,* and *text* come together to create wonderfully complex human interactions that stir the minds and spirits of learners. Some days, of course, are better than others. The things that you thought about doing and the classroom surprises that you didn't expect fall into place. A creative energy imbues teaching and learning.

Sometimes, however, lessons limp along. Others simply bomb—so you cut them short. The four or so remaining minutes before the bell rings are a kind of self-inflicted wound. Nothing is more unnerving than waiting for the bell to ring when students don't have anything meaningful to do.

Consider a science teacher's reflection on the way things went in one of her classes. "Something was missing," she explains. "The students aren't usually as quiet and passive as they were today. Excuse the pun, but the chemistry wasn't there. Maybe the text assignment was too hard. Maybe I could have done something differently. Any suggestions?" This teacher, like most good teachers, cares about what she does. She wants to know how to improve her craft. She knows that when the chemistry is there, teaching is its own reward.

Good teachers bring sensitivity and a spirit of reflective inquiry to their teaching. They care about what they do and how they do it. As Eliot Eisner (1985) aptly put it:

> Teaching can be done as badly as anything else. It can be wooden, mechanical, mindless, and wholly unimaginative. But when it is sensitive, intelligent, and creative—those qualities that confer upon it the status of an art—it should, in my view, not be regarded, as it so often is by some, as an expression of unfathomable talent or luck but as an example of humans exercising the highest levels of their intelligence. (p. 77)

Being an Artful Teacher

Although texts are routinely assigned in content area classrooms, helping students to learn how to learn with texts enters into the plans of teachers only infrequently. Teaching and learning with texts are challenges in today's classrooms where the demands inherent in the teaching of content standards can easily lead to "covering" information without much attention given to *how* students acquire important concepts and details.

No Child Left Behind Act

In January of 2002 President George W. Bush signed into law the No Child Left Behind (NCLB) Act, which represents the latest reauthorization of the Elementary and Secondary Education Act. There are several strong provisions of NCLB related to standards-based education, high-stakes testing, and teacher quality, which undoubtedly will impact *what* teachers do in the classroom and *how* they do it. The issue of teacher quality, for example, is an important aspect of the NCLB legislation, but the concept of what it means to be a highly qualified teacher is quickly becoming one of the most controversial aspects of NCLB. Essentially, NCLB defines a "highly qualified teacher" as someone with a strong academic background in a subject area, but not necessarily someone who enters the teaching profession with certification. Although this definition may indeed widen the pool of teaching candidates, many of these potential teachers "will not know how to work effectively with students. They will not know how to package and deliver their subjects in ways that increase student learning" (Kaplan & Owings 2003, p. 688).

Figure 1.1 depicts the results of a recent national poll on teacher quality conducted by the Educational Testing Service (Hart & Teeter 2002). Interestingly, only 19 percent of respondents believed that it was important for teachers to have "a thorough understanding of their subject." Yet, 42 percent of those surveyed indicated that it was important for teachers to have "skills to design learning experiences that inspire/interest children," and 67 percent believed that "developing the proper skills to make information interesting and understandable is a greater difficulty than developing adequate knowledge about subject matter."

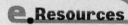

e.Resources

For a full discussion of the ETS national survey go to Web Destinations on the Companion Website, click on Professional Resources and select "A National Priority: Americans Speak on Teacher Quality."

According to Kaplan and Owings (2003):

> Overwhelmingly, Americans believe that knowing *how* to teach is at least as important as knowing *what* to teach. High quality teaching—knowing the material and how to convey it—makes the difference in student achievement. Research supports this view. (p. 687)

A strong attraction to academic content is one of the reasons teachers are wedded to a particular discipline. Yet, it is much more difficult to teach something than merely to know that something: "The teacher of the American Revolution has to

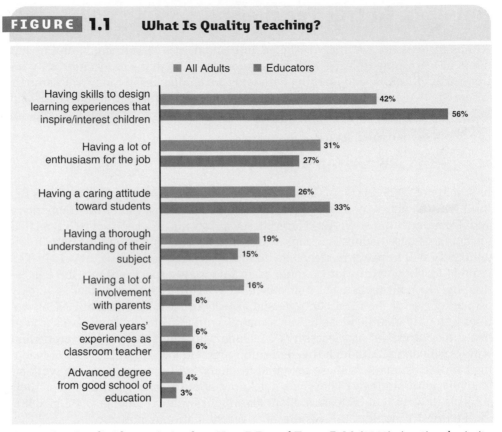

FIGURE 1.1   What Is Quality Teaching?

Source: Reprinted with permission from Hart, P. D., and Teeter, R. M. (2002). *A national priority: Americans speak on teacher quality.* Princeton, NJ: Educational Testing Service, p. 9.

know both a great deal about the American Revolution and a variety of ways of communicating the essence of the American Revolution to a wide variety of students, in a pedagogically interesting way" (Shulman 1987, p. 5). What to teach and how to teach it are nagging problems for classroom teachers. For some, using texts to teach content contributes to the problem. For others, showing students how to learn with texts is part of the solution.

Learning with Texts

Why does reading matter? Why bring students and texts together in the classroom? Texts, after all, are but one medium for learning academic content. Although we're not suggesting that texts are the only source for learning or that they should be, they will continue to be indispensable tools for constructing knowledge; sharing the experiences, ideas, and feelings of others; and developing new insights and perspectives. Learning how to teach with texts contributes significantly to the way you think about teaching, learning, and curriculum. Throughout this book, we invite you to examine content area teaching practices, and the assumptions underlying those practices, in the light of promising strategies for text learning and active student engagement.

All too often, academic texts are viewed as sacred canons, authoritative sources of knowledge by which the information in a field is transmitted from generation to generation of learners. The expression "learning *from* texts" has been used widely in content area reading, as if a text were indeed a canon to be mastered rather than a tool for learning and constructing meaning. The preposition *from* suggests a one-way act in which meaning flows from A (the text) to B (the reader). The shift in meaning from *from* to *with* is subtle but dramatic (Tierney & Pearson 1992). It places the act of reading to learn squarely in the context of a human transaction between two parties rather than being a transmission of information from one party to another. Learning *with* texts suggests that readers have much to contribute to the process as they interact with texts to make meaning and construct knowledge.

> ### Response Journal
> What do you do as a reader to make meaning and construct knowledge as you interact with a text?

Although texts come with the territory, using them to help students acquire content doesn't work well for many teachers. Teaching with texts is more complex than it appears on the surface. Whether you're a novice or a veteran teacher, using texts effectively requires the willingness to explore instructional strategies and to move beyond assigning and telling.

Beyond Assigning and Telling

Think back to when you were in school—how were you taught? Your own personal history as a student, we wager, has etched into your memory an instructional blueprint that teachers in your past probably followed: *Assign* a text to read (usually with questions to be answered) for homework; then, in subsequent lessons, *tell* students through question-and-answer routines what the material they read was about, explaining the ideas and information that the students encountered in print. The dominant interactional pattern between teacher and students during the class presentation of assigned material often involves calling on a student to answer a question, listening to the student's response, and then evaluating or modifying the student's response (Alvermann & Moore 1991). Such is the ebb and flow of assign-and-tell instructional routines in content area classrooms.

There is more to teaching with texts than assigning and telling. Assigning and telling are common but uninspired teaching practices that bog students down in the mire of passive learning. Assign-and-tell, more often than not, dampens active involvement in learning and denies students ownership of and responsibility for the acquisition of content. Teachers place themselves, either by design or by circumstance, in the unenviable position of being the most active participants during classroom interactions with students.

No wonder John Goodlad (1984) portrays textbook assignment, lecture, and recitation (a form of oral questioning in which teachers already know the answers to the questions they ask) as the dominant activities in the instructional repertoire of many content area teachers. Goodlad and his research associates conclude from a monumental study of schools that "the data from our observations in more than 1,000 classrooms support the popular image of a teacher standing in front of a class imparting knowledge to a group of students" (p. 105). His team of researchers found that the prevalence of assign-and-tell practices increases steadily from the primary to the senior high school years and that teachers often "outtalk" students by a three-to-one ratio.

Try to recall what it was like when you were in school. Well-intentioned teachers, more likely than not, assigned texts to be read as homework, only to find that for one reason or another many of the students didn't quite grasp what they were assigned to read. Some didn't read the material at all. Others read narrowly, to answer questions assigned for homework. Still others may have got tangled in text, stuck in the underbrush of facts and details. So class time was spent transmitting information that wasn't learned well from texts in the first place.

Response Journal

When you were in middle or high school, did you know students who were "informationally impaired"? Why do you think some students give up on reading and doing homework assignments?

When teachers impart knowledge with little attention to how a learner acquires that knowledge, students soon become nonparticipants in the academic life of the classroom. Assign-and-tell practices not only result in passive reading but also influence the way students view themselves in relation to texts. The accompanying "Calvin and Hobbes" cartoon has Calvin thinking of himself as "informationally impaired."

Teaching with texts requires its fair share of strategy. But it involves more than assigning pages to be read, lecturing, or using questions to check whether students have read the assigned material. To use texts strategically, you must first be aware of the powerful bonds that link literacy and learning across the curriculum.

Calvin and Hobbes   by Bill Watterson

Understanding Literacy

For many years the term *content area reading* was associated with helping students better understand what they read across the curriculum. However, the concept of content area reading has been broadened in recent years to reflect the integration of communication processes (reading, writing, talking, listening, and viewing) as students engage in text-related learning. Hence, the relatively new term *content literacy* refers to the ability to use reading, writing, talking, listening, and viewing to learn subject matter in a given discipline (Vacca 2002). Literacy is a strong cultural expectation in the United States and other technologically advanced countries. Society places a heavy premium on literate behavior and demands that its citizens acquire literacy for personal, social, academic, and economic success. To better understand what it means to be content literate in an academic subject, examine the general construct of the term *literacy* and how it is used in today's society.

Literacy is a term whose meaning fluctuates from one context to another. It may, for example, be used to describe how skillful and knowledgeable a person is in a particular subject. What do you know about computers and how to use them? Are you *computer literate?* In the same vein, the term *cultural literacy* refers to what an educated person should know about the arts, literature, and other determinants of culture.

The most common use of the term *literacy* has been to denote one's ability to read and write a language. In the past century, the term has undergone variations in meaning. It has been used to depict the level of competence in reading and writing—*functional literacy*—that one needs to survive in society; one's lack of education—*illiteracy*—manifested in an inability to read and write a language; and one's lack of a reading habit—*aliteracy*—especially among those who have the ability to read and write but choose not to.

The more researchers inquire into literacy and what it means to be literate, the more complex and multidimensional the concept becomes. Literacy is situational. In other words, a person may be able to handle the literacy demands of a task in one situation or context but not in another. Hence *workplace literacy* refers to the situational demands placed on workers to read and write effectively (Mikulecky 1990). These demands vary from job to job.

Literacy Is Situational

Reading is as situational in the content areas as it is in the workplace, where the demands placed on a reader will vary from subject matter to subject matter. Suppose you were to accompany Darryl, a sophomore at Warren Harding High, through a typical school day. Toward the end of his first-period U.S. history class, where the students have been studying the events leading up to the Bay of Pigs invasion during John F. Kennedy's presidency, the teacher calls on Darryl to read aloud to the class a textbook section describing Fidel Castro's overthrow of the Cuban dictator Fulgencio Batista:

Latin America was a special target for aid from the United States because the Soviet Union had recently gained a foothold there. In 1959 an uprising led by Fidel Castro succeeded in overthrowing the Cuban dictator, Fulgencio Batista. Many Americans applauded Castro's success, believing he would bring democracy to Cuba. Castro, however, quickly established a Communist-style dictatorship with strong ties to the Soviet Union.

When Kennedy took office, a plan to overthrow Castro was already in the works. The plan called for an invasion of Cuba by a group of anti-Castro Cuban refugees trained and financed by the Central Intelligence Agency (CIA). Kennedy gave the green light for the plan to proceed. (Boyer & Stuckey 1996, pp. 491–492)

Darryl reads the text quickly, completing the reading just as the bell rings. He grabs his stuff from the desk and hurries off to biology, where the class has been involved in a study of microorganisms. Fifteen minutes into the lesson, the teacher reinforces a point she is making during her lecture by asking Darryl to read about euglenoids:

The **euglenoids,** members of phylum Euglenophyta, are protists that have traits of both plants and animals. They are like plants because they contain chlorophyll and undergo photosynthesis. However, euglenoids have no cell walls. Instead of a cell wall, euglenoids have a layer of flexible, interlocking protein fibers inside the cell membrane. Euglenoids are similar to animals because they are responsive and move by using one or two flagella for locomotion. Euglenoids have a contractile vacuole that expels excess water from the cell through an opening. They reproduce asexually by mitosis. (Biggs, Emmeluth, Gentry, Hays, Lundgren, & Mollura 1991, p. 275)

Darryl navigates his way through the euglenoid passage, occasionally faltering on words like *flagella* as he reads. When asked to tell the class what the passage is about, he gropes for a word or two: "I dunno. Eugenoids [*sic*] or something." His teacher manages a smile, corrects the pronunciation of *euglenoids,* and proceeds to explain what Darryl read to the class.

Mercifully, the period ends. Darryl heads for algebra 2, his favorite class. The teacher assigns students to read this passage on an alternative definition of a *function:*

Since a function has the property that exactly one second component is related to each first component, an alternative definition of a function is the following. A *function* is a rule that associates with each element of one set exactly one element of another set.

Functions are often denoted by letters, such as *f, g,* and *h.* If the function defined by the rule $y = 2x$ is called *f,* the following "arrow notation" can also be used to define the *function:*

$$f: x \rightarrow 2x$$

This is read "*f* is the function that associates with a number *x* the number 2*x*." (Dolciani, Graham, Swanson, & Sharron 1992, p. 84)

Darryl handles the task with more purpose and confidence than he exhibited in the reading tasks from the previous classes. Why? you might wonder.

Darryl's scenario illustrates how demanding it is to switch gears from content area text to content area text. What demands do the various texts place on Darryl's ability to read? What demands does the task—reading aloud to the class—place on Darryl? What other factors besides the nature of the text and of the task are likely to affect his content literacy?

Influences on Content Literacy

As you might surmise, a variety of classroom-related factors influence content literacy in a given discipline, some of which include

- The learner's prior knowledge of, attitude toward, and interest in the subject;
- The learner's purpose for engaging in reading, writing, and discussion;
- The language and conceptual difficulty of the text material;
- The assumptions that the text writers make about their audience of readers;
- The text structures that writers use to organize ideas and information; and
- The teacher's beliefs about and attitude toward the use of texts in learning situations.

Shifting the burden of learning with texts from teachers' shoulders to students' is in large measure what this book is about. Yet learning with texts is all the more challenging in today's classroom where the emphasis is on standards-based learning and high-stakes assessment. The pressure to teach in a standards-based curriculum can easily lead to intense content coverage that focuses on *what* students are to learn at the expense of *how* they will learn information and concepts in a content area. What then becomes the teacher's responsibility in balancing *content* (the "what" of instruction) and *process* (the "how" of instruction) in the content areas?

Incorporating Content Standards into Literacy-Based Instruction

In April of 1983, *A Nation at Risk,* a report by the National Commission on Excellence in Education, called for widespread educational reform to stem what the commission identified as "a rising tide of mediocrity" in U.S. education. The report claimed that the United States had to reform the way it educates its children and adolescents to maintain its competitive edge in world markets with other industrialized nations such as Japan, Germany, and South Korea. Although *A Nation at Risk* advanced the position that Americans were too poorly educated to compete globally, it was not without its critics who claimed that the "crisis" in education is more manufactured than real based on an analysis of the commission's findings (Berliner & Biddle 1995; Bracey 2003). Regardless of whether one disagrees with the findings of *A Nation at Risk,* the report has led to a series of federal initiatives in the past two decades that have provided the impetus for what has become known as the "standards movement" in U.S. education.

Since the onset of the standards movement, federal initiatives have shifted from providing equal access to education for everyone to the quality of that education, especially as *quality* relates to curriculum content and student achievement. Standards, in a nutshell, are expected academic consequences defining what students should learn at designated grade levels and in content areas. Since the mid-1990s, there has been a proliferation of national, state, and local standards that provide a road map to what students *should know* and *be able to do* at each grade level and for each content area.

e.Resources

Find out how national and state content standards in your content area are similar or different. Go to Web Destinations on the Companion Website, click on Professional Resources and select "National Standards" and "State Departments of Education."

Why Have Standards?

The underlying rationale for the creation of standards is that high learning expectations—clearly stated and specific in nature—will lead to dramatic increases in student achievement. With high learning expectations comes an accountability system based on "high-stakes" assessment to determine how well students meet the standards formulated in each content area. Some states, such as Florida, California, and Texas, tie high-stakes assessment to the threat of grade-level retention for students who perform below predetermined levels of proficiency in critical areas such as reading. We explore in more detail the nature of high-stakes assessment in Chapter 2.

Pressures on Teachers

In a high-stakes educational environment, standards are bound to increase the pressure for teachers as well as students. In order for standards-based instruction to be effective in improving student performance, it needs to be aligned with the curriculum. As a result, numerous states have developed content standards, and school districts have subsequently redesigned their curricula so that it is consistent with the content area and grade-level standards outlined by the state.

The pressure to teach content standards well is omnipresent for many teachers. Yet teaching content well means helping students discover and understand the structure of a discipline (Bruner 1961). The student who discovers and understands a discipline's structure will be able to contend with its many detailed aspects. From an instructional perspective, teachers must help students see the "big picture" and develop the important concepts and powerful ideas that are part of each subject.

Teachers who are wedded to a discipline walk a tightrope between content and process. It is certainly a balancing act every time the attempt is made to influence what is learned and how it should be learned. Someone once said that teaching a set of ideas without regard to how students are to acquire those ideas is like blowing air into a punctured balloon. The effort is futile.

Balancing Content and Process

Many of the instructional strategies and practices you will learn about in this book will help you teach students to understand the structure of your discipline and the important ideas and information underlying the subject matter that you teach. Balancing content and process in a standards-based curriculum means at the very least

- Knowing the content standards for your content area and grade level;

- Making instructional decisions based on authentic assessments throughout the school year about students' abilities to use reading and writing to learn; and

- Integrating content literacy strategies into instructional plans and units.

To become literate in a content area, students must understand how to use reading, writing, viewing, and talking to learn. Integrating these communication processes helps students to better understand what they are reading about, writing about, talking about in classroom discussion, or viewing on a computer screen or video monitor. Using literacy-based learning strategies doesn't require specialized training on the part of content area teachers. And the pursuit of content literacy does not diminish the teacher's role as a subject matter specialist. To help students become literate in a content area does not mean to teach them *how* to read or write or talk as might be the case in a reading or English classroom. Instead, reading, writing, talking, and viewing are tools that learners use to comprehend texts in content areas.

Text Comprehension in Content Areas

The story of Olaudah Equiano, an African slave who lived in the 1700s, illustrates what reading is all about. Equiano kept a diary that eventually was published as a book called *The Interesting Narrative of the Life of Olaudah Equiano, or Gustavus Vassa, the African, Written by Himself.* His book was first published in London in 1789 and was later abridged and edited by Paul Edwards (1967). Equiano tells how he was kidnapped from his West African tribe as a child and sold into bondage to a ship's captain, how he educated himself, and how he eventually purchased his freedom. In his diary, Equiano describes the rather strange and mysterious activity that his master engaged in whenever he read books on long voyages across the seas. Although Equiano didn't know how to read, he was in awe of the relationship that his master had with books.

What was this thing that his master called reading? Equiano longed to be able to read books the way his master did. So when he was alone in his captain's cabin, he would pick up a book, open it, and begin *talking* to it. Then he would put his

e.Resources

Read more about text comprehension by going to Web Destinations on the Companion Website, clicking on Professional Resources, and selecting "RAND Report on Reading Comprehension."

ears near the pages of the book in hopes that the book would *talk* back to him. But the book remained silent. Equiano felt helpless in the presence of the silent text. Reading remained a mystery to him until he learned to read and write.

Much to his credit, Equiano was on the right track when he picked up a book and started talking to it in hopes that it would talk back to him. One way to think about reading is to liken it to a conversation between two parties. Reading involves a conversation between the reader and the text author. An author creates a text to communicate ideas to someone else. Readers engage in the conversation so that they can comprehend and perhaps even question and challenge the author's ideas. No wonder reading has been described as a *skillful* activity in which the reader's mind is alive with questions. Skilled readers often aren't even aware that they are raising questions while reading, because reading has become an automatic process—an activity that is second nature to the skilled reader. These questions allow readers to interact with the content of the communication: What is this text about? What is the author trying to say? What is going to happen next? What does the text mean? So what? Such questions help the reader anticipate meaning, respond to the text, search for information, and infer from and elaborate on the content of the text.

Response Journal

Describe the relationships among *reader, text,* and *activity* in the reading comprehension model described in Chapter 2 of the RAND report.

Developing Research-Based Comprehension Strategies

When skilled readers have difficulty comprehending what they are reading, they often become *strategic* in the way they approach challenging and difficult text. That is to say, good readers have developed *strategies* that they use to understand what they are reading. As Duke and Pearson (2002) explain, we know a great deal about what good readers do when they read: "Reading comprehension research has a long and rich history . . . much work on the process of reading comprehension has been grounded in studies of good readers" (p. 205). Table 1.1 delineates what good readers do when they engage in the process of comprehending text.

e.Resources

Compare the findings about comprehension instruction by going to Web Destinations on the Companion Website, clicking on Professional Resources, and selecting "National Reading Panel Report" and "RAND Report on Reading Comprehension."

The research-based findings of two recent influential reports, *The Report of the National Reading Panel* (National Reading Panel 2000) and the *RAND Report on Reading Comprehension* (RAND Study Group 2002), indicate that much is known about comprehension instruction. These reports, for example, draw several conclusions about effective comprehension instruction, including the following:

- Instruction can be effective in helping students develop a repertoire of strategies that promotes and fosters comprehension.

TABLE 1.1	What Do Good Readers Do When They Comprehend Text?
Characteristics of Good Readers	**Strategies of Good Readers**
Good readers are	Good readers
■ Active ■ Purposeful ■ Evaluative ■ Thoughtful ■ Strategic ■ Persistent ■ Productive	■ Have clear *goals* in mind for their reading and *evaluate* whether the text, and their reading of it, is meeting their goals. ■ *Look over* the text before they read, noting such things as the *structure* of the text and text sections that might be most relevant to their reading goals. ■ *Make predictions* about what is to come. ■ Read *selectively,* continually making decisions about their reading—what to read carefully, what to read quickly, what not to read, what to reread, and so on. ■ *Construct, revise,* and *question* the meanings they make as they read. ■ Try to determine the meaning of *unfamiliar words and concepts* in the text. ■ Draw from, compare, and *integrate their prior knowledge* with material in the text. ■ Think about the *authors* of the text, their styles, beliefs, intentions, historical milieu, and so on. ■ *Monitor their understanding* of the text, making adjustments in their reading as necessary. ■ *Evaluate the text's quality and value,* and react to the text in a range of ways, both intellectually and emotionally. ■ *Read different kinds of text differently.* ■ Attend closely to the setting and characters when reading narrative. ■ Frequently *construct* and *revise summaries* of what they have read when reading expository text. ■ Think about text before, during, and after reading.

Source: Adapted from Duke, N. K., & Pearson, P. D. (2001). Effective practices for developing reading comprehension. In A. E. Farstrup & S. J. Samuels (Eds.), *What research has to say about reading instruction* (pp. 205–242). Newark, DE.: International Reading Association.

- Strategy instruction, when integrated into subject matter learning, improves students' comprehension of text.

- Struggling readers benefit from *explicit instruction* in the use of strategies.

- Vocabulary knowledge is strongly related to text comprehension and is especially important in teaching English language learners.

- Effective comprehension strategies include *question generation; question answering routines; comprehension monitoring; cooperative learning; summarizing;*

visual displays known as *graphic organizers;* and knowledge of different *text structures.*

- Students benefit from exposure to different types or *genres* of texts (e.g., informational and narrative texts).

- Teachers who provide choices, challenging tasks, and collaborative learning experiences increase students' motivation to read and comprehend texts.

Learners position themselves to comprehend texts whenever they use *prior knowledge* to construct meaning for new material that they are studying. Prior knowledge reflects the experiences, conceptual understandings, attitudes, values, skills, and strategies a student brings to a text learning situation. Let's take a closer look at the role prior knowledge plays in comprehending and learning with text.

Prior Knowledge and Comprehension

In workshops for content teachers, we occasionally read the short story "Ordeal by Cheque" by Wuther Crue (first published in *Vanity Fair* magazine in 1932). The story is extraordinary in that it is told entirely through the bank checks of the Exeter family over a twenty-eight-year span. The workshop participants interact in small groups, and each group is assigned the task of constructing the meaning of the story. At first glance, the groups don't know what to make of their task. "You must be kidding!" is a typical response. At this point, we engage the groups in a *prereading activity* to activate prior knowledge, declare the purposes for reading, and arouse interest in the story. We assign them the activity in Table 1.2, which depicts in chart form the essential bits of information contained on the first nine checks of the story. Group members collaborate as they respond to the task of answering the three questions that accompany the chart: What is the story about? How would you describe the main characters? What do you think will happen in the remainder of the story? We invite you to analyze the information in the chart. Are you able to construct what has taken place so far in the story? What inferences did you make about the characters?

Your predictions and inferences are probably rooted in your "knowledge of the world" as well as your knowledge of how stories work. Some of you, for example, may have used your knowledge of *story structure* to infer a setting for "Ordeal by Cheque" and identify a problem around which the remainder of the story will unfold. Based on the information in Table 1.2, what appears to be the problem of the story? The fifteen or so minutes that it takes to complete the prereading activity is time well spent. Not only have you developed a general sense of what the story is about but also your curiosity and interest may have been aroused about the content of the remaining checks in the story.

Not only do readers activate prior knowledge *before* reading but they also use prior knowledge *during* and *after* reading to infer meaning and elaborate on the text content. You will find this to be the case as you read "Ordeal by Cheque" in

TABLE 1.2	Prereading Activity for "Ordeal by Cheque"

Here are the essential bits of information contained in the first few checks of the story:

Entry date:	Paid to:	Amount:	Signed by:
8/30/03	A baby shop	$148.50	Lawrence Exeter
9/2/03	A hospital	100.00	Lawrence Exeter
10/3/03	A physician	475.00	Lawrence Exeter Sr.
12/19/03	A toy company	83.20	Lawrence Exeter Sr.
10/6/09	A private school for boys	1,250.00	Lawrence Exeter Sr.
4/18/10	A bicycle shop	52.50	Lawrence Exeter Sr.
8/26/15	A military academy	2,150.00	Lawrence Exeter Sr.
9/3/21	A Cadillac dealer	3,885.00	Lawrence Exeter Sr.
9/7/21	An auto repair shop	288.76	Lawrence Exeter Sr.

What is the story about? How would you describe the main characters? What do you think will happen in the remainder of the story?

its entirety on pages 16–19. As you read, you will undoubtedly find yourself using your knowledge of the world as well as what you know (or think you know) about the characters, the historical era in which the story is set, and the plot to make inferences, to evaluate, and to elaborate on the story content. Why is this the case?

Schemata

Cognitive scientists use the technical term *schema* to describe how people use world or prior knowledge to organize and store information in their heads. Furthermore, *schema activation* is the mechanism by which people access what they know and match it to the information in a text. In doing so, they build on the meaning they already bring to a learning situation. Indeed, schemata (the plural of schema) have been called "the building blocks of cognition" (Rumelhart 1982) because they represent elaborate networks of information that people use to make sense of new stimuli, events, and situations. When a match occurs between students' prior knowledge and text material, schema functions in at least three ways:

First, schema provides a framework for learning that allows readers to *seek and select* information that is relevant to their purposes for reading. In the process of searching and selecting, readers are more likely to *make inferences* about the text. You make inferences when you *anticipate* content and *make predictions* about upcoming material, or you *fill in gaps* in the material during reading.

Ordeal by Cheque

Los Angeles, Calif. *Apr. 18th* 19 *10* No. ____
HOLLYWOOD STATE BANK 90-984
6801 SANTA MONICA BOULEVARD
PAY TO THE ORDER OF *City Bicycle Co.* $52.50
Fifty two ———————————— 50/ Dollars
Lawrence Exeter Sr.

Los Angeles, Calif. *Aug. 30th* 19 *03* No. ____
HOLLYWOOD STATE BANK 90-984
6801 SANTA MONICA BOULEVARD
PAY TO THE ORDER OF *Goosie Gander Baby Shoppe* $48.50
One hundred & forty eight ———— 50/ Dollars
Lawrence Exeter

Los Angeles, Calif. *Aug. 26th* 19 *15* No. ____
HOLLYWOOD STATE BANK 90-984
6801 SANTA MONICA BOULEVARD
PAY TO THE ORDER OF *Columbia Military Acad.* $2,150.00
Twenty-one hundred & fifty ———— xx Dollars
Lawrence Exeter Sr.

Los Angeles, Calif. *Sept 2nd* 19 *03* No. ____
HOLLYWOOD STATE BANK 90-984
6801 SANTA MONICA BOULEVARD
PAY TO THE ORDER OF *Hollywood Hospital* $100.00
One hundred ———————————— xx Dollars
Lawrence Exeter

Los Angeles, Calif. *Sept 3rd* 19 *21* No. ____
HOLLYWOOD STATE BANK 90-984
6801 SANTA MONICA BOULEVARD
PAY TO THE ORDER OF *Hollywood Cadillac Co.* $3,885.00
Thirty eight hundred & eighty five xx Dollars
Lawrence Exeter Sr.

Los Angeles, Calif. *Oct. 3rd* 19 *03* No. ____
HOLLYWOOD STATE BANK 90-984
6801 SANTA MONICA BOULEVARD
PAY TO THE ORDER OF *Dr. David M. McCoy* $475.00
Four hundred & seventy-five ——— xx Dollars
Lawrence Exeter Sr.

Los Angeles, Calif. *Sept. 7th* 19 *21* No. ____
HOLLYWOOD STATE BANK 90-984
6801 SANTA MONICA BOULEVARD
PAY TO THE ORDER OF *Wilshire Auto Repair Service* $288.76
Two hundred & eighty-eight ——— 76/ Dollars
Lawrence Exeter Sr.

Los Angeles, Calif. *Dec 19th* 19 *03* No. ____
HOLLYWOOD STATE BANK 90-984
6801 SANTA MONICA BOULEVARD
PAY TO THE ORDER OF *California Toyland Co.* $83.20
Eighty Three ———————————— 20/ Dollars
Lawrence Exeter Sr.

Los Angeles, Calif. *Oct. 15th* 19 *21* No. ____
HOLLYWOOD STATE BANK 90-984
6801 SANTA MONICA BOULEVARD
PAY TO THE ORDER OF *Stanford University* $339.00
Three hundred & thirty-nine ——— xx Dollars
Lawrence Exeter Sr.

Los Angeles, Calif. *Oct. 6th* 19 *09* No. ____
HOLLYWOOD STATE BANK 90-984
6801 SANTA MONICA BOULEVARD
PAY TO THE ORDER OF *Palisades School for Boys* $1,250.00
Twelve hundred & fifty ———— xx Dollars
Lawrence Exeter Sr.

Los Angeles, Calif. *June 1st* 19 *23* No. ____
HOLLYWOOD STATE BANK 90-984
6801 SANTA MONICA BOULEVARD
PAY TO THE ORDER OF *Miss Daisy Windsor* $25,000.00
Twenty-five thousand ———— xx Dollars
Lawrence Exeter Sr.

Los Angeles, Calif. June 9th 19 23 No. _____
HOLLYWOOD STATE BANK 90-984
6801 SANTA MONICA BOULEVARD
PAY TO THE ORDER OF French Line, Ile de France $585.00
Five hundred + eighty-five —————— XX Dollars
Lawrence Exeter Sr.

Los Angeles, Calif. Aug. 23rd 19 23 No. _____
HOLLYWOOD STATE BANK 90-984
6801 SANTA MONICA BOULEVARD
PAY TO THE ORDER OF Banque de France $5000.00
Five thousand —————— XX Dollars
Lawrence Exeter Sr.

Los Angeles, Calif. Feb. 13th 19 26 No. _____
HOLLYWOOD STATE BANK 90-984
6801 SANTA MONICA BOULEVARD
PAY TO THE ORDER OF University Club Florists $76.50
Seventy-six —————— 50/ Dollars
Lawrence Exeter Sr.

Los Angeles, Calif. June 22nd 19 26 No. _____
HOLLYWOOD STATE BANK 90-984
6801 SANTA MONICA BOULEVARD
PAY TO THE ORDER OF University Club Florists $312.75
Three hundred + twelve —————— 75/ Dollars
Lawrence Exeter Sr.

Los Angeles, Calif. Aug. 11th 19 26 No. _____
HOLLYWOOD STATE BANK 90-984
6801 SANTA MONICA BOULEVARD
PAY TO THE ORDER OF Riviera Heights Land Co. $56,000.00
Fifty-six Thousand —————— XX Dollars
Lawrence Exeter Sr.

Los Angeles, Calif. Oct. 30th 19 26 No. _____
HOLLYWOOD STATE BANK 90-984
6801 SANTA MONICA BOULEVARD
PAY TO THE ORDER OF Renaissance Interior Decorators $22,000.00
Twenty-two thousand —————— XX Dollars
Lawrence Exeter Sr.

Los Angeles, Calif. Nov. 18th 19 26 No. _____
HOLLYWOOD STATE BANK 90-984
6801 SANTA MONICA BOULEVARD
PAY TO THE ORDER OF Beverly Diamond + Gift Shoppe $678.45
Six hundred + seventy-eight —————— 45/ Dollars
Lawrence Exeter Jr.

Los Angeles, Calif. Nov. 16th 19 26 No. _____
HOLLYWOOD STATE BANK 90-984
6801 SANTA MONICA BOULEVARD
PAY TO THE ORDER OF Hawaii Steamship Co. $560.00
Five hundred + sixty —————— XX Dollars
Lawrence Exeter Sr.

Los Angeles, Calif. Nov. 21st 19 26 No. _____
HOLLYWOOD STATE BANK 90-984
6801 SANTA MONICA BOULEVARD
PAY TO THE ORDER OF Lawrence Exeter, Junior $200,000.00
Two hundred thousand —————— XX Dollars
Lawrence Exeter Sr.

Los Angeles, Calif. Nov. 22nd 19 26 No. _____
HOLLYWOOD STATE BANK 90-984
6801 SANTA MONICA BOULEVARD
PAY TO THE ORDER OF Ambassador Hotel $2,250.00
Twenty-two hundred + fifty —————— XX Dollars
Lawrence Exeter Sr.

Los Angeles, Calif. Dec. 1st 19 26 No. _____
HOLLYWOOD STATE BANK 90-984
6801 SANTA MONICA BOULEVARD
PAY TO THE ORDER OF University Club Florists $183.50
One hundred + eighty-three —————— 50/ Dollars
Lawrence Exeter Sr.

Los Angeles, Calif. Feb. 18 19 27 No. _____
HOLLYWOOD STATE BANK 90-984
6801 SANTA MONICA BOULEVARD
PAY TO THE ORDER OF Cocoanut Grove Sweet Shoppe $27.00
Twenty seven —————— Dollars
Lawrence Exeter Jr.

LOS ANGELES, CALIF. July 16, 19 27 No. ____
HOLLYWOOD STATE BANK 90-984
6801 SANTA MONICA BOULEVARD
PAY TO THE ORDER OF Parisian Gown Shoppe $925 00
Nine hundred twenty five —————— DOLLARS
Lawrence Exeter, Jr.

LOS ANGELES, CALIF. Dec. 1, 19 27 No. ____
HOLLYWOOD STATE BANK 90-984
6801 SANTA MONICA BOULEVARD
PAY TO THE ORDER OF Anita Lingerie Salon $750 00
Seven hundred, fifty —————— DOLLARS
Lawrence Exeter Jr.

LOS ANGELES, CALIF. April 1, 19 28 No. ____
HOLLYWOOD STATE BANK 90-984
6801 SANTA MONICA BOULEVARD
PAY TO THE ORDER OF Parisian Gown Shoppe $1,150 00
Eleven hundred fifty —————— DOLLARS
Lawrence Exeter, Jr.

LOS ANGELES, CALIF. Nov. 1, 19 28 No. ____
HOLLYWOOD STATE BANK 90-984
6801 SANTA MONICA BOULEVARD
PAY TO THE ORDER OF Moderne Sportte Shoppe $562 00
Five hundred, sixty two —————— DOLLARS
Lawrence Exeter, Jr.

LOS ANGELES, CALIF. July 1, 19 29 No. ____
HOLLYWOOD STATE BANK 90-984
6801 SANTA MONICA BOULEVARD
PAY TO THE ORDER OF The Bootery $45 25
One hundred, forty-five 25/00 DOLLARS
Lawrence Exeter, Jr.

LOS ANGELES, CALIF. Aug 23, 19 29 No. ____
HOLLYWOOD STATE BANK 90-984
6801 SANTA MONICA BOULEVARD
PAY TO THE ORDER OF Tony Spagoni $126 00
One hundred, twenty six —— DOLLARS
Lawrence Exeter Jr.

LOS ANGELES, CALIF. Aug. 30, 19 29 No. ____
HOLLYWOOD STATE BANK 90-984
6801 SANTA MONICA BOULEVARD
PAY TO THE ORDER OF Tony Spagoni $126 00
One hundred, twenty six —— DOLLARS
Lawrence Exeter, Jr.

LOS ANGELES, CALIF. May 25, 19 30 No. ____
HOLLYWOOD STATE BANK 90-984
6801 SANTA MONICA BOULEVARD
PAY TO THE ORDER OF University Club Florists $87 00
Eighty seven —————— DOLLARS
Lawrence Exeter, Jr.

LOS ANGELES, CALIF. May 28, 19 30 No. ____
HOLLYWOOD STATE BANK 90-984
6801 SANTA MONICA BOULEVARD
PAY TO THE ORDER OF Broadway Diamond Co. $575 00
Five hundred, seventy five —— DOLLARS
Lawrence Exeter, Jr.

LOS ANGELES, CALIF. Nov. 13, 19 30 No. ____
HOLLYWOOD STATE BANK 90-984
6801 SANTA MONICA BOULEVARD
PAY TO THE ORDER OF Miss Flossie Wentworth $50,000 00
Fifty thousand —————— DOLLARS
Lawrence Exeter, Jr.

LOS ANGELES, CALIF. Nov. 14, 19 30 No. ____
HOLLYWOOD STATE BANK 90-984
6801 SANTA MONICA BOULEVARD
PAY TO THE ORDER OF Wall & Smith, attys. at Law $525 00
Five hundred twenty five —— DOLLARS
Lawrence Exeter, Jr.

LOS ANGELES, CALIF. Nov. 15, 19 30 No. ____
HOLLYWOOD STATE BANK 90-984
6801 SANTA MONICA BOULEVARD
PAY TO THE ORDER OF Mrs. Lawrence Exeter, Jr. $5000 00
Five thousand —————— DOLLARS
Lawrence Exeter, Jr.

LOS ANGELES, CALIF. June 20 19 31 No. _____
HOLLYWOOD STATE BANK 90-984
6801 SANTA MONICA BOULEVARD
PAY TO THE ORDER OF Clerk Reno Municipal Court $52 00
Fifty-two —————— DOLLARS
Lawrence Exeter, Jr.

LOS ANGELES, CALIF. July 2 19 31 No. _____
HOLLYWOOD STATE BANK 90-984
6801 SANTA MONICA BOULEVARD
PAY TO THE ORDER OF Tony Spagoni $100 00
One hundred —————— DOLLARS
Lawrence Exeter, Jr.

LOS ANGELES, CALIF. June 20 19 31 No. _____
HOLLYWOOD STATE BANK 90-984
6801 SANTA MONICA BOULEVARD
PAY TO THE ORDER OF Marie Wharton Exeter $175,000 00
One hundred seventy five thousand DOLLARS
Lawrence Exeter, Jr.

LOS ANGELES, CALIF. July 3 19 31 No. _____
HOLLYWOOD STATE BANK 90-984
6801 SANTA MONICA BOULEVARD
PAY TO THE ORDER OF Peter Ventizzi $25 00
Twenty-five —————— DOLLARS
Lawrence Exeter, Jr.

LOS ANGELES, CALIF. June 20 19 31 No. _____
HOLLYWOOD STATE BANK 90-984
6801 SANTA MONICA BOULEVARD
PAY TO THE ORDER OF Walker & Walker $700 00
Seven hundred ————— DOLLARS
Lawrence Exeter, Jr.

LOS ANGELES, CALIF. July 5th 19 31 No. _____
HOLLYWOOD STATE BANK 90-984
6801 SANTA MONICA BOULEVARD
PAY TO THE ORDER OF Hollywood Hospital $100 00
One hundred ————— xx DOLLARS
Lawrence Exeter, Jr.

LOS ANGELES, CALIF. June 20 19 31 No. _____
HOLLYWOOD STATE BANK 90-984
6801 SANTA MONICA BOULEVARD
PAY TO THE ORDER OF Wall & Smith $450 00
Four hundred fifty ————— DOLLARS
Lawrence Exeter, Jr.

LOS ANGELES, CALIF. July 15th 19 31 No. _____
HOLLYWOOD STATE BANK 90-984
6801 SANTA MONICA BOULEVARD
PAY TO THE ORDER OF Dr. David M. McCoy $175 00
One hundred & seventy-five ————— xx DOLLARS
Lawrence Exeter, Jr.

LOS ANGELES, CALIF. July 1 19 31 No. _____
HOLLYWOOD STATE BANK 90-984
6801 SANTA MONICA BOULEVARD
PAY TO THE ORDER OF Tony Spagoni $100 00
One hundred ————— DOLLARS
Lawrence Exeter, Jr.

LOS ANGELES, CALIF. July 16th 19 31 No. _____
HOLLYWOOD STATE BANK 90-984
6801 SANTA MONICA BOULEVARD
PAY TO THE ORDER OF Hollywood Mortuary $1,280 00
Twelve hundred & eighty ————— xx DOLLARS
Lawrence Exeter

Source: "Ordeal by Cheque" by Wuther Crue. Reprinted by permission. Copyright © 1932 Condé Nast Publications, Inc. Originally published in *Vanity Fair*. All Rights Reserved.

Second, schema helps readers *organize* text information. The process by which you organize and integrate new information into old facilitates the ability to *retain and remember* what you read. A poorly organized text is difficult for readers to comprehend. We illustrate this point in more detail when we discuss the influences of text structure on comprehension and retention in later chapters.

Third, schema helps readers *elaborate* information. When you elaborate what you have read, you engage in a cognitive process that involves deeper levels of insight, judgment, and evaluation. You are inclined to ask, "So what?" as you engage in conversation with an author.

Not only do students engage in cognitive thinking as they read but they also respond to text on an affective level. *Reader response* helps to explain why students react to what they read with both thought *and* feeling as they engage in comprehending text.

Reader Response

Reader response theory has evolved from a literary tradition. As early as 1938, Louise Rosenblatt (1982) argued that *thought* and *feeling* are legitimate components of literary interpretation. A text, whether it is literary or informational, demands affective as well as intellectual responses from its readers. Creating an active learning environment in which students respond personally and critically to what they are reading is an important instructional goal in a response-centered classroom. Often in text-learning situations, a teacher will focus on what students have learned and how much. There is value in having what Rosenblatt calls an *efferent stance* as a reader. When readers assume an efferent stance, they focus attention on the ideas and information they encounter in a text. Reader response, however, is also likely to involve feelings, personal associations, and insights that are unique to the reader. When students assume an *aesthetic stance*, they shift attention inward to what is being created as part of the reading experience itself. An aesthetic response to text is driven by personal feelings and attitudes that are stirred by the reader's transactions with the text.

One way to encourage comprehension is to take advantage of both efferent and aesthetic stances. This works well when students actively respond to what they are reading not only by talking but also by writing. One of the instructional strategies we explore in Chapter 11, on writing to learn, is the use of *response journals.* When students combine the use of response journals with discussion, the challenge from an instructional perspective is to create an environment in which they feel free enough to respond openly. Open response is necessary to evoke students' initial feelings and thoughts. Evoking students' initial responses to a text is crucial to further exploration of the ideas they are encountering. Open responses, however, are not final responses.

For example, a history teacher divides the class into two groups and has one group read *Bearstone* (1989), by Will Hobbs, and the other read *The Cage* (1986), by Ruth Sender. These trade books have protagonists who are being held against their will in situations that are beyond their control. As the students read the books, they keep response journals in which they react to questions such as how the protagonists feel as captives of societies that discriminate against their race. When the class meets to discuss the books, students offer ideas from their response journals to generate a comparison concerning the ways in which the Jewish woman's captivity in *The Cage* during World War II differs from the contemporary Native American boy's sense of belonging in *Bearstone*. From this discussion, students go on to explore the concept of slavery and how it changes across circumstances, societies, and historical periods.

Affect, as you can see, is a catalyst for students to respond to text. Bleich (1978) suggests that response involves both the author and the reader taking active parts in the making of meaning. Thus, the initial response of "I like this" or "I hate this" becomes the springboard for other, more complex reactions. *Why* a student likes or does not like a text becomes the genesis of discussions, drama, art, and compositions that probe the reader's intentions.

Reader response questions allow students to explore their personal responses and to take those initial reactions into more analytic realms. According to Brozo (1989), the rationale behind a reader's response to text is this: "It is through a personal connection that a text becomes meaningful and memorable" (p. 141). Following are some questions that evoke student responses to informational texts:

1. *What aspect of the text interested you the most?* (The reader identifies an idea, issue, event, character, place, or any other aspect of the content that aroused strong feelings.)

2. *What are your feelings and attitudes about this aspect of the text?* (The reader describes and explains feelings and attitudes.)

3. *What experiences have you had that help others understand why you feel the way you do?* (The reader supports feelings and attitudes with personal connections.) (Brozo 1989, p. 142)

Responses to these questions help readers consciously connect their own experiences to the content of the text. The questions can be used well in combination with writing and talking.

Study a student's response to a trade book titled *Atoms, Molecules, and Quarks* (1986), by Melvin Berger, presented in Figure 1.2. Students can and do become interested in informational text when it is presented in a response-centered format.

When students are faced with challenging text, they benefit from instructional routines and strategies that engage them in a process of responding to meaning at different levels of understanding. Often teachers rely on a variety of *question answering* routines and *question generation* strategies to encourage students to think about what they read at different levels of comprehension.

Levels of Comprehension

Because reading is a thoughtful process, it embraces the idea of levels of comprehension. Readers respond to meaning at various levels of abstraction and

---

FIGURE 1.2 **Reader Response Questions for *Atoms, Molecules, and Quarks***

Student's Most Interesting Part of Text

The information about quarks was good. It was something that I didn't know before. I really thought that the names of the different types of quarks (up, down, truth, beauty, strange, and charm) were kind of weird, but these names made them easier to remember because they are so different.

Student's Feelings and Attitudes toward Subject

The author did a good job in making all of this interesting and pretty easy to read. Quarks and their flavors and colors are kind of hard to understand when you read about them in the textbook, but I could follow this book. I think it's amazing what scientists have been able to find out about atomic particles. I especially wonder about why the universe hasn't blown up already, because the book said that it should have because of the way particles and antiparticles react. Scientists don't have the answer either. But it makes you feel a little uneasy, not knowing what holds all of this together.

Student's Personal Associations

I suppose that all of us have wondered about what keeps the universe going at some time or other. I guess what started me thinking about this was a science fiction movie I saw that showed the world exploding into outer space. A lot of people see these kinds of shows and wonder if that could really happen. Then, when you read about quarks, it makes you think.

---

conceptual difficulty (Herber 1978). Figure 1.3 shows the different levels of comprehension.

At the *literal level,* students *read the lines* of the content material. They stay with print sufficiently to get the gist of the author's message. In simple terms, a literal recognition of that message determines what the author says. Searching for important literal information isn't an easy chore, particularly if readers haven't matured enough to know how to make the search or, even worse, haven't determined why they are searching in the first place. Most students can and will profit greatly from being shown how to recognize the essential information in the text.

Knowing what the author says is necessary but not sufficient in constructing meaning with text. Good readers search for conceptual complexity in material. They read at the *interpretive level—between the lines.* They focus not only on what authors say but also on what authors mean by what they say. Herber (1978) clarifies the difference between the literal and interpretive levels this way: "At the literal level readers identify the important information. At the interpretive level readers perceive the relationships that exist in that information, conceptualizing the ideas formulated by those relationships" (p. 45).

The interpretive level delves into the author's intended meaning. How readers conceptualize implied ideas by integrating information into what they already know is part of the interpretive process. Recognizing the thought relationships

FIGURE 1.3 **Levels of Comprehension**

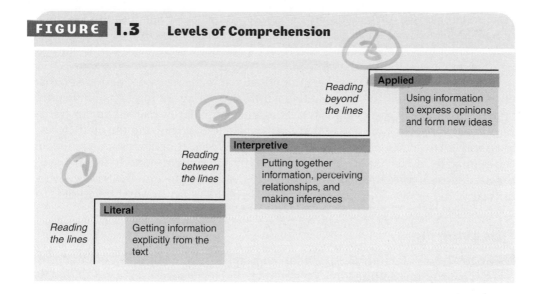

that the author weaves together helps readers make inferences that are implicit in the material.

For example, study the following passage, which is organized according to cause–effect relationships. Figure 1.4 shows how a cause combines with several effects to form a logical inference that is implicit in the text passage.

> As part of an experiment, young monkeys were taken away from their mothers when they were born and each was raised in complete isolation. When these monkeys were brought together for the first time, they didn't want to play with each other as monkeys usually do. They showed no love for each other. And in fact they never learned to live together. It seemed that living apart from their mothers and from each other from the very beginning had some unusual side effects on these growing monkeys.

From time to time throughout this chapter, you have probably been trying to read us—not our words but us. And in the process of responding to our messages,

FIGURE 1.4 **Logical Inference from Cause–Effect Relationships**

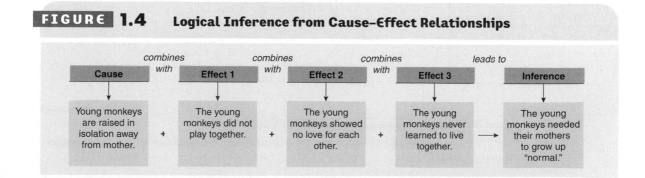

you probably raised questions similar to these: "So what? What does this information mean to me? Does it make sense? Can I use these ideas for content instruction?" Your attempt to seek significance or relevance in what we say and mean is one signal that you are reading at the *applied level.* You are reading *beyond the lines.*

Reading at the applied level is undoubtedly akin to critical reflection and discovery. It underscores the constructive nature of reading comprehension. Bruner (1961) explains that discovery "is in its essence a matter of rearranging or transforming evidence in such a way that one is enabled to go beyond the evidence so reassembled to additional new insights" (p. 21). When students respond to text at the applied level, they know how to synthesize information—and to lay that synthesis alongside what they know already—to evaluate, question the author, think critically, and draw additional insights and fresh ideas from content material.

Questioning

Using the levels of comprehension model helps teachers engage students in instructional routines that revolve around question answering and question generation. Many students do not know how to answer questions or how to make inferences. Others find it difficult to generate their own questions about text (National Reading Panel 2000). Yet orchestrating classroom discussions without asking questions is like gardening without using a hoe or a spade. Imagine a classroom without questions. It is no exaggeration to suggest that teachers often talk in questions (Dillon 1983). When they are used as tools to guide reading comprehension at different levels, questions help students not only to recall factual information but also to integrate information and put it to work for them—to make inferences, to reflect on what they have read, to make judgments, or to invent new ways of looking at the text material.

In their review of reading comprehension instruction, Duke and Pearson (2002) suggest

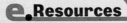

Read the full text of Duke and Pearson's paper by going to Web Destinations on the Companion Website, clicking on Professional Resources, and selecting "Effective Practices for Reading Comprehension."

We know much about the effect of asking different types of questions on students' understanding and recall of text, with the overall finding that students' understanding and recall can be readily shaped by the types of questions to which they become accustomed. . . . If students receive a steady diet of factual detail questions, they tend, in future encounters with text, to focus their effort on factual details. . . . If, by contrast, more general or more inferential understanding is desired, teachers should emphasize questions that provide that focus. When students often experience questions that require them to connect information in the text to their knowledge base, they will tend to focus on this more integrative behavior in the future. (p. 222)

The type of question asked to guide comprehension should be based on the *information readers need to answer the question.* Therefore, teachers must help students *become aware of* likely sources of information as they respond to questions (Pearson & Johnson 1978).

A reader draws on two broad information sources to answer questions: information in the text and information inside the reader's head. For example, some questions have answers that can be found directly in the text. These questions are *textually explicit* and lead to answers that are "right there" in the text.

Other questions have answers that require students to think about the information they have read in the text. They must be able to search for ideas that are related to one another and then put these ideas together in order to answer the questions. These questions are *textually implicit* and lead to "think and search" answers.

Still other questions require students to rely mainly on prior knowledge and experience. In other words, responses to these questions are more inside the reader's head than in the text itself. These questions are *schema-based* and lead to "author and you" and "on your own" answers.

"Right there," "think and search," "author and you," and "on your own" are mnemonics for the levels of comprehension discussed previously. These mnemonics signal question–answer relationships (Raphael 1982, 1984, 1986). Many kinds of responses can be prompted by textually explicit questions, by textually implicit questions, and by schema-based questions. However, the success that students experience when responding to a certain type of question depends on their ability to recognize the relationship between the question and its answer. In Chapter 3, we explore in more detail how students can be taught to be more strategic in their awareness and use of question–answer relationships.

The insights into comprehending text presented here are developed in succeeding chapters within the framework of instructional strategies related to content literacy. What these insights tell the classroom teacher is this: Learners must "work" with print in an effort to explore and construct meaning. Reading is first and foremost a conversation, a give-and-take exchange, between the reader and the text. However, the burden of learning is always on the reader. There are times when a text may be too difficult for students to handle on their own. In situations where text is difficult, teachers are in an ideal position to guide students' reading through various forms of instructional activity. *Scaffolding* learning with texts, then, is a primary responsibility of the teacher— one that we also explore throughout this book.

Scaffolding Instruction

When texts serve as tools for learning in content area classrooms, teachers have a significant role to play. That role can be thought of as "instructional scaffolding." One of the benchmarks of content-literate students, as we suggested earlier, is that they know how to learn with texts independently. Yet many students in today's diverse classrooms have trouble handling the conceptual demands inherent in text material when left to their own devices to learn. A gap often exists between the ideas and relationships they are studying and their prior knowledge, interests, attitudes, cultural background, language proficiency, or reading ability. In a nutshell, instructional scaffolding allows teachers to support students' efforts to make sense of texts while showing them how to use strategies that will, over time, lead to independent learning.

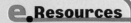
e.Resources

For additional readings related to the major ideas in this chapter, go to Chapter 1 of the Companion Website and click on Suggested Readings.

Used in construction, scaffolds serve as supports, lifting up workers so that they can achieve something that otherwise would not have been possible. In teaching and learning contexts, scaffolding means helping learners to do what they cannot do at first (Bruner 1986). Instructional scaffolds support text learners by helping them achieve literacy tasks that would otherwise have been out of reach. Applebee (1991) explains that instructional scaffolding provides the necessary support that students need as they attempt new tasks; at the same time, teachers model or lead the students through effective strategies for completing these tasks. Providing the "necessary support" often means understanding the diversity that exists among the students in your class, planning active learning environments, and supporting students' efforts to learn through the use of instructional strategies and texts beyond the textbook—all of which are explored more closely in the chapters that follow.

◄ Looking Back
Looking Forward ►

In this chapter, we invited you to begin an examination of content literacy practices, and the assumptions underlying those practices, for text learning and active student involvement. Teachers play a critical role in helping students realize a potentially powerful use of language: learning with text. Learning with text is an active process. Yet assigning and telling are still common teaching practices and often have the unfortunate consequence of dampening students' active involvement in learning. In today's standards-based educational environment, the pressure to teach content standards well can easily lead to an emphasis on content-only instruction with little attention paid to how students acquire information and develop understandings. Teachers must balance content and process as they engage students in comprehending text.

To shift the burden of learning from teacher to student requires an understanding of the importance of the relationships that exist between literacy and learning across the curriculum. As a result, we explored the role that literacy plays in the acquisition of content knowledge.

Comprehending texts is what content area reading is all about. Instead of teaching students how to read or write, we use reading, writing, viewing, and talking as tools to construct knowledge—to discover, to clarify, and to make meaning—in a given discipline.

Content literacy, then, underscores the situational demands placed on students to use communication processes to learn subject matter. Content teachers are in an ideal position to show students how to use the learning strategies that are actually needed to construct content knowledge.

Perhaps the single most important resource in learning with texts is the reader's prior knowledge. Therefore, we explored some of the influences and processes underlying reading to learn in content classrooms. In particular, we emphasized the roles that prior knowledge, reader response, and levels of comprehension play in thinking with text.

Instructional scaffolding is a concept used throughout this book. Instructional scaffolding supports text learners in achieving literacy tasks that would otherwise be out of reach.

In the next chapter, we explore another dimension of standards-based curriculum as we shift our attention to different forms of assessment in the content area classroom. Concern about assessment is one of the major issues in education in the United States today. What role do standardized "high-stakes" assessments play in the lives of classroom teachers? How do authentic forms of assessment inform instructional decisions? How can teachers use portfolios and make decisions about the texts they use? The key to assessment in content areas, as we contend in the next chapter, is to make it as useful as possible. Let's find out how and why this is the case.

 # Minds On

1. Review the passages read by Darryl in U.S. history, biology, and algebra 2 class. In small groups, create lists of the varying situational demands that each text selection places on Darryl's ability to read. Discuss possible factors besides the nature of the text and of the task that are likely to affect his content literacy. How are Darryl's attitude and willingness to be an active learner affected by these factors? What might the teachers of these various classes have done to create a more student-centered learning experience?

2. Focus on the elements of a student-centered curriculum. Obviously, the teacher's beliefs and instructional approach play a large role in permitting students to become actively involved in an ongoing lesson, but what visible signs of student involvement would exist in the physical environment of the classroom? Just by looking, would it be possible to detect a classroom where student-centered lessons are the norm? If so, what physical evidence would be present, and what would that evidence indicate to you, the observer?

3. Select a popular book, film, or song that most members of your small group know. Discuss each of the following levels of comprehension communicated in that work: (a) literal (in the lines), (b) interpretive (between the lines), (c) applied (beyond the lines).

4. Some teachers believe that because literal comprehension is necessary to answer "higher-level" questions, it is unnecessary to ask literal-level questions. Do you agree? Do you think we would agree?

5. Imagine that during lunch, several teaching colleagues comment that because many students in their courses "can't read," these teachers rarely use books. They argue that students learn content just as well through audiovisual aids and discussions.

   Divide a small group of six class members into two smaller groups of three: one representing the teachers who believe books are unnecessary and one representing those who believe books are essential. For ten minutes, role-play a lunchtime debate on the pros and cons of using reading in content areas. After the time has elapsed, discuss the arguments used by the role players. Which did you find valid, and with which did you disagree?

6. Your supervisor observes a lesson in which you use a large block of time for students to read. Afterward, the supervisor says that you should assign reading as homework, rather than "wasting" valuable class time. She adds that if you continue with lessons

like this, your students will be lucky to finish one or two books over the entire year. Consequently, you request a meeting with the supervisor. What arguments might you bring to this meeting to help convince her of the validity of your approach?

Hands On

1. With a small group, examine the following well-known passage and attempt to supply the missing words. Note that all missing words, regardless of length, are indicated by blanks in the passage.

   Besides, Sir, we shall not fight our battles alone. There is a just God, who presides over the destinies of nations, who will raise up friends to fight our _____ for us. The battle, Sir, is not to the strong alone: it is to the vigilant, the active, the _____. Besides, Sir, we have no election. If we were base enough to desire it, it is now too late to retire from the contest.

   There is no _____, but in submission or slavery. Our chains are forged. Their _____ may be heard on the plains of Boston! The war is inevitable—and let it come—I repeat, Sir, let it come! It is in vain, Sir, to extenuate the matter. Gentlemen may cry, "Peace! Peace!" But there is no peace. The war has actually begun!

   The next gale that sweeps from the North will bring to our ears the clash of resounding _____! Our brethren are already in the field! Why stand we here idle? What is it that the Gentlemen wish? What would they have? Is life so _____, or peace too _____, as to be purchased at the price of chains and _____? Forbid it, Almighty God! I know not what _____ others may take, but as for me, give me _____ or give me death!

   After you have filled in the blanks, discuss the processes by which decisions on possible responses were made and any problems encountered. How did prior knowledge of the passage's topic assist your reading process? (After you have completed this experiment, review Patrick Henry's speech at the end of the "Hands On" section in Chapter 4.)

   In what ways was your experience similar to that of a student who attempts to decipher a content passage but who has little background knowledge of its content?

2. Bring the following materials to class: a large paper bag, five paper plates, four buttons, three cardboard tubes, scraps of material, six pipe cleaners, three sheets of construction paper, scissors, tape, and a stapler. Your instructor will silently give each group a written directive to create a replica of a living creature (cat, dog, rhinoceros, aardvark, etc.) with *no* verbal communication permitted.

   After your group has constructed its creature, list the communication difficulties, and discuss how each was overcome. Finally, have a spokesperson from each group share these difficulties with the rest of the class.

3. Rewrite Lewis Carroll's poem "Jabberwocky" using "real" words.

Jabberwocky

'Twas brillig, and the slithy toves
Did gyre and gimble in the wabe;
All mimsy were the borogoves,
And the mome raths outgrabe.

"Beware the Jabberwock, my son!
The jaws that bite, the claws that catch!
Beware the Jubjub bird and shun
The frumious Bandersnatch!"

He took his vorpal sword in hand:
Long time the manxome foe he sought—

So rested he by the Tumtum tree,
And stood awhile in thought.

And, as in uffish thought he stood,
The Jabberwock, with eyes of flame,
Came whiffling through the tulgey wood,
And burbled as it came!

One, two! One, two! And through and through
The vorpal blade went snicker-snack!
He left it dead, and with its head
He went galumphing back.

Compare your efforts with those of other members of your small group, and discuss the following questions:

a. Why are there differences in the translations?

b. Does your translation change the intended meaning of the poem?

c. Do the differences affect your enjoyment of the poem?

d. What personal experiences and prior knowledge that you brought to your reading of the poem may have influenced your translation?

e.Resources extra

- Go to Chapter 1 of the Companion Website (**www.ablongman.com/vacca8e**) and click on Activities to complete the following tasks:

  1. Complete the story map outline for "Ordeal by Cheque" based on your reading of the story.

  2. Think about a highly abstract concept, such as *dream* (**www.dreamtree.com**) or *universe* (**www.handsonuniverse.org**), and go to the Websites devoted to the topics. Bring a physical object to class that represents the concept. Verbally report your criteria for choosing the object to your class.

- Go to the Companion Website (**www.ablongman.com/vacca8e**) for suggested readings, interactive activities, multiple-choice questions, and additional Web links to help you learn more about the importance of reading.

The New York Times
expect the world®
nytimes.com

Themes of the Times

Extend your knowledge of the concepts discussed in this chapter by reading current and historical articles from the *New York Times*. Go to the Companion Website and click on eThemes of the Times.

chapter 2

Assessing Students and Texts

It's not as simple as testing. It's
like thinking, if we weigh the
cow, the cow's going to get fatter.
—STATE LEGISLATOR

How effectively are students learning to use reading, writing, talking, and viewing as tools to comprehend and respond to material in content areas? Assessing students and texts to provide this kind of information means that there is a direct connection between teaching and learning, between instruction and the improvement of practice. Assessment in content area classrooms means that students and teachers are actively engaged in a process of evaluation and self-evaluation. Instead of measuring learning exclusively by a score on a standardized test or proficiency exam, the learning process includes assessment of authentic tasks.

Teachers and students want useful assessment; that is, they want to make sense of how and what is taught and learned at any given time. Teachers want to make

> **Instructional assessment is a process of gathering and using multiple sources of relevant information about students for instructional purposes.**

instructional decisions based on their students' content literacy skills, concepts, and performance. They must also deal with the very real pressure of state and federal mandates for standards-based curriculum and testing. Yet as the state legislator realized, testing alone cannot yield improvements in student learning.

To understand assessment, you need to differentiate between two major contrasting approaches: a formal, high-stakes approach and an informal, authentic approach. When standards were initially developed by professional

ASSESSING STUDENTS AND TEXTS

APPROACHES TO ASSESSMENT

HIGH-STAKES, FORMAL

ISSUES AND CONCERNS

State Standards and Accountability
Federal Legislation

STANDARDIZED TESTING

AUTHENTIC, INFORMAL

THE TEACHER'S ROLE

Portfolio Assessment

Student Work Samples
Checklists and Interviews
Rubrics and Self-Assessments

Assessing Text Difficulty

Content Area
Reading Inventories

Readability

The Fry Graph
Cloze Procedure
Checklists
FLIP Strategy

---

organizations and state governments, testing was thought to be necessary in order to ensure that schools would meet high standards of achievement. Soon, students' performances on state-mandated tests became the focus of debate among educators, policy makers, and constituency groups. The public's attention today is often on this formal, high-stakes approach to assessment. Many teachers have become adept at alternative, authentic assessment practices to help them make decisions about instruction appropriate for each student. As depicted in the graphic organizer, portfolios, observations, anecdotal records, checklists, interviews, inventories, and conferences with students are some of the methods and techniques that make authentic assessment possible.

Assessing for instruction should, first and foremost, provide the opportunity to gather and interpret useful information about students as they learn, including their prior knowledge; their attitudes toward reading, writing, and subject matter; and their ability to use content literacy to learn with texts. Through the portfolio assessment process—collecting authentic evidence of student work over time—teachers and students gather useful information about an individual's comprehension and response to content area material. The organizing principle of this chapter maintains that assessment should be useful, authentic, and responsive to teacher decision making: **Instructional assessment is a process of gathering and using multiple sources of relevant information about students for instructional purposes.**

Frame of Mind

1. How does assessment help us set instructional goals?

2. How does a formal, high-stakes approach differ from an informal, authentic approach?

3. What have state and federal legislators done to try to ensure that curriculum standards are used by school districts?

4. What are some of the informal assessment strategies teachers use in the context of their classrooms?

5. How do content area teachers involve students in the portfolio process?

6. When and how might teachers use professional judgment in analyzing the difficulty of textbooks?

7. What are predictive measures of readability, and how do they differ from performance measures?

Teachers sometimes know intuitively that what they do in class is working. More often, however, information for making decisions is best obtained through careful observation of students. Their strengths and weaknesses as they interact with one another and with texts can be assessed as they participate in small groups, contribute to class discussions, respond to questions, and complete written assignments. This approach to assessment is *informal* and *authentic*; it is student centered and classroom based. This approach, however, isn't the only one operating in schools today. If teachers are in a school district guided by standards-based curricula, they need to understand the differences between *high-stakes* and *authentic* approaches to assessment.

Response Journal

Write about a time when a teacher had an intuition about you as a student. Was it on target? Off target?

High-Stakes Testing and Authentic Approaches to Assessment

The two major views of assessment, high-stakes and authentic, are like different sides of the same coin. They represent the almost opposite perspectives of policy makers on one side, and teachers on the other. The policy makers are responding to the public and its demands for assurances that students will leave school well prepared to enter either the workforce or college. Teachers and other educators are calling for better, more authentic assessment practices that will improve instruction and result in learning. As Tierney (1998) put it, one focuses on "something you *do to* students," and the other focuses on "something you *do with* them or help them *do for themselves*" (p. 378).

Authentic methods often include some combination of observations, interviews, anecdotal records, and student-selected performances and products. The information gained from an authentic assessment can be organized into a rich description or portrait of your content area classroom or into student *portfolios.* Concerns that emerge, whether about individual students or about the delivery of instructional strategies, are likely to make sense because they come directly from the classroom context and often result from teacher–student or student–student interaction.

Consider how an authentic approach differs from a more formal, high-stakes one. In Table 2.1, the two approaches are compared in several categories. Certainly, there are many gray areas in assessment, where the formal and informal overlap. In this table, however, differences between the two approaches are emphasized. Traditional, formal assessments are product oriented. They are more tangible and can be obtained at predetermined points in time. Authentic assessments are informal and process oriented. The process is ongoing, providing as much information about the student as learner as about the product. Together, they permit a more balanced approach through a combination of traditional, formal and authentic, informal practices. The end result is an understanding of *why* particular results are obtained in formal assessment, which informs the *how* of the teacher decision-making process.

High-Stakes Testing: Some Issues and Concerns

Never have the stakes been higher. With virtually every state adopting content standards in multiple content areas, such as English, mathematics, social studies, and science, mandated, standardized testing systems have been developed and put in place throughout the United States. Thus, although standardized testing has been used to evaluate student achievement since Thorndike developed the first standardized tests in the early part of the twentieth century, the amount of mandatory testing has increased. And the stakes, significant rewards and penalties, have risen. For example, school districts must follow state regulations, which are written to comply with federal education law. When Ohio legislators recently passed its education bill, $400 million in U.S. Department of Education aid to Ohio schools was preserved!

There are several issues and concerns about the role of high-stakes testing that are being discussed widely. Proponents of high-stakes testing contend that such testing is a sound strategy to use to ensure that standards are met and students are achieving at an appropriate level of proficiency. They seek to effectively end the practice of social promotion, that is, promoting students from one grade level to the next regardless of whether the students have demonstrated on tests the potential to work successfully at the next grade level. In recent years, mandatory tests have been administered to students at younger and younger ages and with greater frequency than ever before (Hoffman et al. 1999).

> **Response Journal**
>
> When did you take your first "big" test in school? What kind of an experience was it?

As the use of mandated, high-stakes testing grows, questions have been posed about the validity of certain assessment tools. In some states, studies have called into question the reasons behind students gains on state mandated assessment, suggesting that students' improved performances on standardized tests could be attributed not only to achievement but also to factors such as the increased class

TABLE 2.1	Comparisons of Two Approaches to Assessment	
	High-Stakes, Formal	**Authentic, Informal**
Orientation	Formal; developed by expert committees and test publishers	Informal; developed by teachers and students
Administration	Testing one time performance; paper-and-pencil, multiple-choice; given to groups at one seating	Continuously evolving and intermittent throughout an instructional unit; small group, one on one
Methods	Objective; standardized reading achievement tests designed to measure levels of current attainment; state proficiency testing of content knowledge	Classroom tests, checklists, observations, interviews, and so on, designed to evaluate understanding of course content; real-life reading and writing tasks
Uses	Compare performance of one group with students in other schools or classrooms; determine funding, support for districts and schools; estimate range of reading ability in a class; select appropriate materials for reading; identify students who need further diagnosis; align curriculum; allocate classroom time	Make qualitative judgments about students' strengths and instructional needs in reading and learning content subjects; select appropriate materials; adjust instruction when necessary; self-assess strengths and weaknesses
Feedback format	Reports, printouts of subtest scores; summaries of high and low areas of performance; percentiles, norms, stanines	Notes, profiles, portfolios, discussions, recommendations that evolve throughout instructional units; expansive (relate to interests, strategies, purpose for learning and reading)

Response Journal

How do teachers squeeze more time into the day to prepare students for local or state-mandated tests?

time spent on test preparation, students' growing familiarity with test questions and procedures, and a large proportion of low-scoring students being exempted from taking tests in order to avoid the sanctions connected with low test scores (Koretz & Barron 1998; Klein, Hamilton, McCaffrey, & Stecher 2000). "Teachers are falling into line and teaching to the test not because they agree with instruction that is driven by standardized testing, but because the consequences of low test scores are so great" (Barrentine 1999, p. 5). High-stakes testing shifts decision-making authority from local personnel to central authorities (IRA 1999).

School leaders have acknowledged the challenge of blending students' needs with needed scores and have expressed additional concerns about mandated high-stakes tests. Some assert that the tests are not grounded in child development theory, pointing out that students of the same chronological age should not be expected to be at the same point in terms of cognitive development and academic achievement. Others express concern that the high-stakes nature of the tests will result in classroom instruction that focuses more on the drilling of skills and less on the application of knowledge (Mraz 2000).

In response to concerns about the use of high-stakes testing, the International Reading Association issued a position statement that advised against attaching rewards and penalties to single test scores and encouraged the use of multiple measures to inform important decisions as well as the use of assessment tools that honor the complexity of reading (Ransom et al. 1999).

> **e.Resources**
>
> Read the full text of the IRA's position statement by going to Web Destinations on the Companion Website and clicking on Professional Resources.

Additionally, no single test can meet the needs of all groups who require information about school and student performance: Different constituencies need different types of information, presented in different forms, and made available at different times. Legislators and the general public may benefit from information provided by norm-referenced tests that are administered on an annual basis. Parents, teachers, and students need information specific to individual students on a more consistent basis. Observations, portfolios, samples of student work over time, and conferences about student progress are more effective than standardized tests in providing that type of information. The purpose of the assessment selected, and the goals for its use, should be carefully considered so that the assessment tool selected will ultimately serve to provide information that can be used to improve learning opportunities for all students (Farr 1992).

A former education advisor at the state level explained, "I think that assessment is something that shouldn't be a surprise, nor should it be put up as a barrier or hurdle. It's just part of the process. We need good assessments at all times for all students, and teachers need to be trained in assessment" (Mraz 2002, p. 79).

> **Response Journal**
>
> Do you feel competent in making assessment part of teaching? What do you think is the best preparation you could receive?

In some states, initial attempts at establishing assessment programs raised concerns and resulted in programmatic and legislative adjustments. A former education advisor at the state level explained, "Initially, the thinking was that establishing high standards for all [students] would help to improve instruction. In fact, I think the proficiency test was really designed as an early warning system to decide which students needed additional assistance and intervention as they moved through the grades. So, the test was established for one purpose, and then was used for another purpose. It was designed as a warning system, but then it became a pass–fail problem, which became a political problem in that 40,000 students were not successful" (Mraz 2002, p. 81).

State Standards and Accountability

According to the Education Commission of the States (ECS), state policy makers have been actively engaged in setting standards, assessing student reading performance, and imposing consequences for students who do not meet reading standards. In some states, comprehensive plans designed to link standards with assessment have been developed. Here are snapshots of how two states took action.

North Carolina's ABCs Accountability Model is organized around the goals of ensuring strong accountability, emphasizing the basics and high educational standards, and providing schools and districts with some degree of local control. Schools are rewarded for improvements in student achievement as well as for overall percentages of students performing at or above grade level.

Under the accountability model, public school students are required to meet statewide standards, also referred to as gateways, for promotion from grades 3, 5, and 8, and for high school graduation. Students who do not meet the standards are given opportunities for retesting as well as interventions, such as additional instructional opportunities, extra support in smaller classes, personalized education plans, or increased monitoring and evaluations. The responsibility for designing strategies to reach the state standards and ensuring that constituent groups, such as educators, parents, students, and community members, understand and participate in implementing the standards is delegated to superintendents and local boards of education (North Carolina Public Schools 2003).

In Ohio, recent education reforms, based on the recommendations of the Governor's Commission on Student Success, a group of educators and community members appointed by the governor, has sought to establish an aligned system of standards, assessments, and accountability (ODE 2003). Changes were made to previous education legislation. Under the 1997 Senate Bill 55, the Fourth Grade Reading Guarantee prohibited school districts from promoting to the fifth grade any student who had not passed the reading portion of the fourth-grade off-year proficiency test (OPT), unless the student was excused from taking the test because of a documented disability or because the student's principal and reading teacher agreed that the student was academically prepared, as defined in the district's promotion policy for fifth grade (ODE 1999).

In 2001, Senate Bill 1 resulted in several revisions to the original bill, including a redefinition of the proficiency levels: "Basic" and "below basic" levels of performance were added to the original "proficient" and "advanced" levels of performance on the fourth-grade state reading test, resulting in the lowering of the required pass score from 217 to 198.

Proficiency tests given in kindergarten through eighth grade are scheduled to be replaced by achievement tests aligned to academic content standards and diagnostic tests designed to improve student comprehension of content area standards (ODE 2002). Intervention services will be provided as needed, based on a student's test scores and classroom performance. New Ohio Graduation Tests, which measure the level of reading, writing, mathematics, science, and social studies skills expected of students at the end of the tenth grade, are in the process of being implemented.

Federal Legislation

In addition to decisions made at the state level, the federal government has played a role in the standards and assessment movement. The Improving America's Schools Act and Goals 2000: Educate America Act (1994) were based on the concept of standards-based reform, that is, using federal resources to assist states in developing and implementing challenging standards for all students. Under the plan, states and school districts were granted the flexibility to implement programs in ways that met the needs of their students (*Congressional Digest* 1999). By 1998, new legislation in the form of the Reading Excellence Act included an unprecedented, and, some argued, restrictive, definition of reading and acceptable reading research (Tierney 2002).

In 2002, the No Child Left Behind Act (NCLB) instituted new accountability requirements. Schools that fail to show annual improvement on mandatory assessments risk losing part of their federal funding. Schools that fail to raise test scores over several years could risk being restaffed (Toppo 2001). Critics of the legislation fear that, although high standards of educational achievement are desirable, NCLB could unfairly penalize schools while actually lowering standards as states adjust their proficiency requirements downward in order to preserve federal funding. Additional concerns that NCLB contains a disproportionate number of mandates in relation to the funding offered to schools to fulfill those mandates have also been raised (Maguire 2001).

Standardized Testing: What Teachers Need to Know

Standardized reading tests are formal, usually machine-scorable instruments in which scores for the tested group are compared with standards established by an original normative population. The purpose of a standardized reading test is to show where students rank in relation to other students based on a single performance.

To make sense of test information and to determine how relevant or useful it may be, you need to be thoroughly familiar with the language, purposes, and legitimate uses of standardized tests. For example, as a test user, it is your responsibility to know about the norming and standardization of the reading test used by your school district. Consult a test manual for an explanation of what the test is about, the rationale behind its development, and a clear description of what the test purports to measure. Not only should test instructions for administering and scoring be clearly spelled out but also information related to norms, reliability, and validity should be easily defined and made available.

Norms represent average scores of a sampling of students selected for testing according to factors such as age, sex, race, grade, or socioeconomic status. Once a test maker determines norm scores, those scores become the basis for comparing the test performance of individuals or groups to the performance of those who were included in the norming sample. *Representativeness*, therefore, is a key concept in understanding student scores. It's crucial to make sure that the norming sample used in devising the reading test resembles the characteristics of the students you teach.

Norms are extrapolated from raw scores. A *raw score* is the number of items a student answers correctly on a test. Raw scores are converted to other kinds of scores so that comparisons can be made among individuals or groups of students. Three such conversions—percentile scores, stanine scores, and grade-equivalent scores—are often represented by test makers as they report scores.

Percentile scores describe the relative standing of a student at a particular grade level. For example, the percentile score of 85 of a student in the fifth grade means that his or her score is equal to or higher than the scores of 85 percent of comparable fifth graders.

Stanine scores are raw scores that have been transformed to a common standard to permit comparison. In this respect, stanines represent one of several types of standard scores. Because standard scores have the same mean and standard deviation, they permit the direct comparison of student performance across tests and subtests. The term *stanine* refers to a *sta*ndard *nine*-point scale, in which the distribution of scores on a test is divided into nine parts. Each stanine indicates a single digit ranging from 1 to 9 in numerical value. Thus a stanine of 5 is at the midpoint of the scale and represents average performance. Stanines 6, 7, 8, and 9 indicate increasingly better performance; stanines 4, 3, 2, and 1 represent decreasing performance. As teachers, we can use stanines effectively to view a student's approximate place above or below the average in the norming group.

Grade-equivalent scores provide information about reading-test performance as it relates to students at various grade levels. A grade-equivalent score is a questionable abstraction. It suggests that growth in reading progresses throughout a school year at a constant rate; for example, a student with a grade-equivalent score of 7.4 is supposedly performing at a level that is average for students who have completed four months of the seventh grade. At best, this is a silly and spurious interpretation: "Based on what is known about human development generally and language growth specifically, such an assumption [underlying grade-equivalent scores] makes little sense when applied to a human process as complex as learning to read" (Vacca, Vacca, & Gove 2000, p. 530).

Reliability refers to the consistency or stability of a student's test scores. A teacher must raise the question, "Can similar test results be achieved under different conditions?" Suppose your students were to take a reading test on Monday, their first day back from vacation, and then take an equivalent form of the same test on Thursday. Would their scores be about the same? If so, the test may indeed be reliable.

Validity, by contrast, tells the teacher whether the test is measuring what it purports to measure. Validity, without question, is one of the most important characteristics of a test. If the test purports to measure reading comprehension, what is the test maker's concept of reading comprehension? Answers to this question provide insight into the *construct validity* of a test. Other aspects of validity include *content validity* (Does the test reflect the domain or content area being examined?) and *predictive validity* (Does the test predict future performance?).

Standardized test results are probably more useful at the building or district, not the classroom, level. A school, for example, may wish to compare itself in reading performance to a state or national norm. Or local districtwide norms may be compared with national norms, a process that is sometimes necessary when a district is applying for federal or state funds. In general, information from standardized tests may help screen for students who have major difficulties in reading, compare general reading-achievement levels or different classes or grades of students, assess group reading achievement, and assess the reading growth of groups of students (Allington & Strange 1980).

However, you need useful information about students' text-related behavior and background knowledge. You would be guilty of misusing standardized test results if you were to extrapolate about a student's background knowledge or ability to comprehend course materials on the basis of standardized reading-test performance. Alternatives to high-stakes, formal assessments are found in an informal, authentic approach to assessment. One of the most useful tools for inquiry into the classroom is observation.

Authentic Assessment: The Teacher's Role

In a high-stakes approach to assessment, the *test* is the major tool; in an authentic approach, the *teacher* is the major tool. Who is better equipped to observe students, to provide feedback, and to serve as a key informant about the meaning of classroom events? You epitomize the process of assessing students in an ongoing, natural way because you are in a position to observe and collect information continuously (Valencia 1990). Consequently, you become an observer of the relevant interactive and independent behavior of students as they learn in the content area classroom.

Observation is one unobtrusive measure that ranges from the occasional noticing of unusual student behavior to frequent anecdotal jottings to regular and detailed written field notes. Besides the obvious opportunity to observe students' oral and silent reading, there are other advantages to observation. Observing students' appearance, posture, mannerisms, enthusiasm, or apathy may reveal information about self-image. However, unless you make a systematic effort to tune in to student performance, you may lose valuable insights. You have to be a good listener to and watcher of students. Observation should be a natural outgrowth of teaching; it increases teaching efficiency and effectiveness. Instructional decisions based on accurate observations help you zero in on what and how to teach in relation to communication tasks.

Today's teachers are expected to meet the special needs of all students. Consequently, the challenges of teaching diverse learners in the classroom may cause nonspecialist teachers to feel frustrated and unprepared. Understanding and accepting differences in students can, however, lead to effective instructional adaptations. Here's how Kim Browne, a seventh-grade teacher of language arts, used observational assessment to help deal with her "inclusion section":

One of the most frequent questions I'm asked at parent meetings and IEP [individual educational plan] meetings is, "How does my child interact with his or her peers?" I planned to collect data on each student by using a simple observation checklist when the students are participating in their literary circles after reading *Take me out to the ball game.* I keep an index card file on each student by the class period; my focus is on peer relationships, noting any overt behavior that may be indicative of boredom or confusion, as well as cooperative interactions. Additional observations can be added to a large label stuck to the back of the card.

In addition to the basic format for time sample or interval data, Kim included two other sections: *other information,* where she noted any support the student may be receiving in or out of school or if the student is on an IEP plan and asked a specific question about this student, and *tentative conclusions,* where she made comments about what she just observed and what to focus on in the next observation. Figure 2.1 illustrates Kim's recent observation on Neil, a student with special needs in her late-morning section.

To record systematic observations, to note significant teaching–learning events, or simply to make note of classroom happenings, you need to keep a notebook or index cards on hand. Information collected purposefully constitutes *field notes.* They aid in classifying information, inferring patterns of behavior, and making predictions about the effectiveness of innovative instructional procedures. As they accumulate, field notes may serve as anecdotal records that provide documentary evidence of students' interactions over periods of time.

Teachers and others who use informal, authentic tools to collect information almost always use more than one means of collecting data, a practice known as *triangulation.* This helps ensure that the information is valid and that what is learned from one source is corroborated by what is learned from another source. A fifth-grade science teacher recounted how he combined the taking of field notes with active listening and discussion to assess his students' current achievement and future needs in the subject:

> I briefly document on individual cards how students behave during experiments conducted individually, within a group, during reading assignments, during phases of a project, and during formal assessments. Knowing which students or what size group tends to enhance or distract a student's ability to stay on task helps me organize a more effective instructional environment. When students meet to discuss their projects and the steps they followed, I listen carefully for strategies they used or neglected. I sometimes get insights into what a particular student offered this group; I get ideas for topics for future science lessons and projects or mini-lessons on time management, breaking up a topic into "chunks," and so on.

Response Journal

Do you think parent–teacher conferences can make a difference in students' academic performance or are they simply educational "window dressing?"

In addition to providing valid information, informal assessment strategies are useful to teachers during parent–teacher conferences for discussing a student's strengths and weaknesses. They also help build an ongoing record of progress that may be motivating for students to reflect on and useful for their other teachers in planning lessons in different subjects. And finally, the assessments themselves may provide

| FIGURE **2.1** | **A Time Sample Observation** |

Date: Sept. 11, 1997   Time: Start: 11:15   Stop: 11:25

School: Hadley   Grade: 7

Subject: Lang. Arts   Period: 5

Other information: Neil is on an IEP that indicates A.D.D. with mild Tourette. Does Neil contribute to literary circle? Does he exhibit overt signs of Tourette or frustration?

Time interval used: 3 min.

Time: 11:15   Behavior: Neil willingly joins in a small group. He asked a question, then began to listen.

Time: 11:18   Behavior: Shrugs shoulders often. Makes a frown. Contributes orally to group.

Time: 11:21   Behavior: Put head down on desk. Pointed to text, laughing at what someone said.

Conclusions if possible: It is possible that Neil didn't fully understand what he read in Take Me Out to the Ball Game last night. Shoulder shrugging & head down may indicate confusion. He seemed to enjoy being part of literary circle.

meaningful portfolio entries from both a teacher's and a student's perspective, serving "as the essential link among curriculum, teaching, and learning" (Wilcox 1997, p. 223).

Many students want to establish a personal rapport with their teachers. They may talk of myriad subjects, seemingly unrelated to the unit. It is often during this informal chatter, however, that you find out about the students' backgrounds, problems, and interests. This type of conversation, in which you assume the role of active listener, can provide suggestions about topics for future lessons and materials and help the student's voice emerge.

Discussion, both casual and directed, is also an integral part of assessment. You need to make yourself available, both before and after class, for discussions about general topics, lessons, and assignments. For an assessment of reading comprehension, nothing replaces one-on-one discussion of the material, whether before, during, or after the actual reading. Finally, encourage students to verbalize their positive and negative feelings about the class itself as well as about topics, readings, and content area activities.

A note of caution: It's important to realize that "no matter how careful we are, we will be biased in many of our judgments" (MacGinitie 1993, p. 559). Yet teachers who observe with any sort of regularity soon discover that they are able to acquire enough information to process "in a meaningful and useful manner" (Fetterman 1989, p. 88). They can then make reliable decisions about instruction with observation and other techniques in portfolio assessment.

Portfolio Assessment

One of the most exciting and energizing developments in assessment is the emergence of portfolios. As a global, alternative, balanced practice in gathering information about students, *portfolio assessment* is a powerful concept that has immediate appeal and potential for accomplishing the following purposes:

- Providing and organizing information about the nature of students' work and achievements
- Involving students themselves in reflecting on their capabilities and making decisions about their work
- Using the holistic nature of instruction as a base from which to consider attitudes, strategies, and responses
- Assisting in the planning of appropriate instruction to follow
- Showcasing work mutually selected by students and teacher
- Revealing diverse and special needs of students as well as talents
- Displaying multiple student-produced artifacts collected over time
- Integrating assessment into the daily instruction as a natural, vital part of teaching and learning
- Expanding both the quantity and the quality of evidence by means of a variety of indicators

Portfolios are vehicles for ongoing assessment. They are composed of purposeful collections that examine achievement, effort, improvement, and, most important, processes (selecting, comparing, sharing, self-evaluation, and goal setting) according to Tierney, Carter, and Desai (1991). As such, they lend themselves beautifully to instruction in content areas ranging from math and science to English, history, and health education.

Significant pieces that go into student portfolios are *collaboratively* chosen by teachers and students. Selections represent processes and activities more than products. A distinct value underlying the use of portfolios is a commitment to students' evaluation of their own understanding and personal development.

Contrasting portfolios with traditional assessment procedures, Walker (1991) submits that instead of a contrived task representing knowledge of a subject, portfolios are an "authentic" assessment that measures the process of the construction of meaning. The *students* make choices about what to include; these choices in turn encourage self-reflection on their own development, their own evaluation of their learning, and personal goal setting. Advantages of portfolios are more easily visualized when compared with traditional assessment practices as displayed in Table 2.2, adapted from Tierney, Carter, and Desai (1991, p. 44).

Adapting Portfolios to Content Area Classes

You can, by making some individual adjustments, adapt portfolios to meet your needs. Techniques such as interviewing, observing, and using checklists and inventories provide good sources of information about students in the classroom. The use of portfolios is in many ways a more practical method of organizing this type of information. Linek (1991) suggests that many kinds of data be collected

TABLE 2.2 Portfolios versus Testing: Different Processes and Outcomes

Portfolio	Testing
Represents the range of learning activities in which students are engaged	Assesses students across a limited range of assignments that may not match what students do
Engages students in assessing their progress or accomplishments and establishing ongoing learning goals	Mechanically scored or scored by teachers who have little input
Measures each student's achievement while allowing for individual differences between students	Assesses all students on the same dimensions
Represents a collaborative approach to assessment	Assessment process is not collaborative
Has a goal of student self-assessment	Student assessment is not a goal
Addresses improvement, effort, and achievement	Addresses achievement only
Links assessment and teaching to learning	Separates learning, testing, and teaching

Source: From *Portfolio Assessment in the Reading–Writing Classroom* by Tierney, Carter, and Desai. Copyright © 1991 Christopher Gordon Publishers, Inc. Reprinted by permission of Christopher Gordon Publishers, Inc.

for a thorough documentation of attitudes, behaviors, achievements, improvement, thinking, and reflective self-evaluation. For example, students may begin a math course with poor attitudes and may constantly challenge the validity of the content by saying things such as, "What are we learning this for anyway? It's got nothing to do with me and my life." If you provide opportunities for functional application in realistic situations, comments may change over time to "Boy, I never realized how important this was going to be for getting a job in real life!"

Much more than a folder for housing daily work, a record file, or a grab bag, a portfolio is a comprehensive profile of each student's progress and growth. Most professional associations have endorsed the use of portfolios. For example, if you are preparing to teach a math class, whether it's arithmetic, algebra, or trig, consult the National Council for Teachers of Mathematics (NCTM) assessment guidelines. Then, decide with students what types of samples of student-produced work should be included. Best Practice Box 2.1 outlines a procedure for implementing portfolios.

Cherrie Jackman, a fifth-grade teacher, wanted to experiment with portfolios as an assessment tool for writing and science. Here's how she described the process of implementation that she followed:

> To begin implementing portfolios in my class, I followed certain steps:
>
> - First, I explained the concept of portfolios and discussed why they are important. We thought of how local businesses use portfolios, and how certain types of professions (architecture, art, journalism) depend on them.
>
> - Next, I explained the purposes of our portfolio: to describe a portion of students' work over the quarter, showing how it has improved; to reflect on and evaluate their own work in writing and science; and to compile a body of work that can travel with them from year to year.
>
> - Then we discussed the requirements for our portfolio: to select one or two pieces of work from science and writing that each student feels is representative of the best that he or she has done for the quarter; to add one piece for each subject area each quarter; and at the end of the school year, to evaluate students' overall progress.
>
> - I gave examples of the kinds of contributions that would be appropriate: writing samples, self-evaluations (reflections) on a particular project, semantic maps, group projects, peer evaluations—all are acceptable pieces of work to place into the portfolio.
>
> - Finally, we discussed the ongoing process of conferencing that will occur in our classroom. I will meet with students on an individual basis to discuss work in progress and assist in deciding which pieces might be placed in the portfolio. Time in class will be scheduled during the week for students to write reflections, ask for peer evaluations, or hold discussions with teachers about the portfolios. Although the actual work may be done at another time (writing, science), the assessment of the work could be done during this regularly scheduled time.
>
> Portfolios are a process! I really want students to understand that their portfolios are a work in progress. I want them to feel comfortable selecting a piece, critiquing others' work, and asking questions. I want them to feel ownership for their own work!

RESEARCH-BASED BEST PRACTICES

BOX 2.1

Steps in the Implementation of Portfolios

To get started implementing the portfolio assessment process, certain logical steps must be taken and certain decisions need to be made:

1. *Discuss with your students the notion of portfolios as an interactive vehicle for assessment.* Explain the concept and show some examples of items that might be considered good candidates for the portfolio. Provide some examples from other fields, such as art and business, where portfolios have historically recorded performance and provided updates.

2. *Specify your assessment model.* What is the purpose of the portfolio? Who is the audience for the portfolio? How much will students be involved? Purposes, for example, may be to showcase students' best work; to document or describe an aspect of their work over time (to show growth); to evaluate by making judgments by using either certain standards agreed on in advance or the relative growth and development of each individual; or to document the process that goes into the development of a single product,

such as a unit of work on the Vietnam era or the Middle East or nutrition.

3. *Decide what types of requirements will be used, approximately how many items, and what format will be appropriate for the portfolio.* Furthermore, will students be designing their own portfolios? Will they include videos or computer disks? Or will they have a uniform look? Plan an explanation of portfolios for your colleagues and the principal; also decide on the date when this process will begin.

4. *Consider which contributions are appropriate for your content area.* The main techniques for assessing students' behavior, background knowledge, attitudes, interests, and perceptions are writing samples, video records, conference notes, tests and quizzes, standardized tests, pupil performance objectives, self-evaluations, peer evaluations, daily work samples, and collections of written work, (such as vocabulary activities, graphic organizers, concept maps, inquiry/research projects, and reports).

An example of a portfolio contribution made by one of Cherrie's students is a personal reflection on an experiment done in science (see Figure 2.2).

Checklists and Interviews

Informal assessment techniques, such as checklists, interviews, and content area reading inventories (discussed later in this chapter), are different from natural, open-ended observation. They often consist of categories or questions that have already been determined; they impose an a priori classification scheme on the

FIGURE **2.2**   **A Personal Reflection for Science**

Experiment:

They're All Wet.—Determine what effect soaking seeds has on the time it takes them to sprout. In a group of four, develop an experiment using the scientific procedure. Evaluate your group from a scientific and cooperative point of view.

Reflection:

I selected the experiment "They're All Wet" as my best work in science for a number of reasons.

① My group worked very well together. Everyone was assigned a job (reader, recorder, speaker, organizer), and everyone got to talk.

② We wrote a sound hypothesis and design for our experiment because we took our time and we thought about the process.

③ We kept very good records of our observations, and then everyone participated in telling about them.

④ Even though our experiment did not prove our hypothesis, I learned many things from this experiment (see above).

Next time maybe my results will support my hypothesis, but I did learn the proper way to conduct an experiment.

observation process. A checklist is designed to reveal categories of information the teacher has preselected. When constructing a checklist, you should know beforehand which reading and study tasks or attitudes you plan to observe. Individual items on the checklist then serve to guide your observations selectively.

The selectivity that a checklist offers is both its strength and its weakness as an observational tool. Checklists are obviously efficient because they guide your observations and allow you to zero in on certain kinds of behavior. But a checklist can also restrict observation by limiting the breadth of information recorded, excluding potentially valuable raw data. Figure 2.3 presents sample checklist items that may be adapted to specific instructional objectives in various content areas.

In addition to checklists, observations, and inventories, interviews should be considered part of the portfolio assessment repertoire. There are several advantages of using interviews, "be they *formal,* with a preplanned set of questions, or *informal,* such as a conversation about a book" (Valencia, McGinley, & Pearson 1990, p. 14). First, students and teachers interact in collaborative settings. Second, an open-ended question format is conducive to the sharing of students' own

FIGURE 2.3 **Sample Checklist Items for Observing Reading and Study Behavior**

Reading and Study Behavior	Fred	Pat	Frank	JoAnne	Jerry	Courtney	Mike	Mary
Comprehension								
1. Follows the author's message	A	B	B	A	D	C	F	C
2. Evaluates the relevancy of facts								
3. Questions the accuracy of statements								
4. Critical of an author's bias								
5. Comprehends what the author means								
6. Follows text organization								
7. Can solve problems through reading								
8. Develops purposes for reading								
9. Makes predictions and takes risks								
10. Applies information to come up with new ideas								
Vocabulary								
1. Has a good grasp of technical terms in the subject under study								
2. Works out the meaning of an unknown word through context or structural analysis								
3. Knows how to use a dictionary effectively								
4. Sees relationships among key terms								
5. Becomes interested in the derivation of technical terms								
Study Habits								
1. Concentrates while reading								
2. Understands better by reading orally than silently								
3. Has a well-defined purpose in mind when studying								
4. Knows how to take notes during lecture and discussion								
5. Can organize material through outlining								
6. Skims to find the answer to a specific question								
7. Reads everything slowly and carefully								
8. Makes use of book parts								
9. Understands charts, maps, tables in the text								
10. Summarizes information								

Grading Key: A = always (excellent)
B = usually (good)
C = sometimes (average)
D = seldom (poor)
E = never (unacceptable)

views. Third, it reveals to what extent students are in touch with their internal disposition toward reading subject matter material.

In general, there are several *types of interviews:* structured, semistructured, informal, and retrospective. As described by Fetterman (1989, pp. 48–50), these types blend and overlap in actual practice.

1. *Formally structured and semistructured.* Verbal approximations of a questionnaire; allow for comparison of responses put in the context of common group characteristics; useful in securing baseline data about students' background experiences.

2. *Informal.* More like conversations; useful in discovering what students think and how one student's perceptions compare with another's; help identify shared values; useful in establishing and maintaining a healthy rapport.

3. *Retrospective.* Can be structured, semistructured, or informal; used to reconstruct the past, asking students to recall personal historical information; may highlight their values and reveal information about their worldviews.

One technique developed to interview students about the comprehension process is the Reading Comprehension Interview (RCI) (Wixson, Boskey, Yochum, & Alvermann 1984). Designed for grades 3 through 8, it takes about thirty minutes per student to administer in its entirety. The RCI explores students' perceptions of (1) the purpose of reading in different instructional contexts and content areas, (2) reading task requirements, and (3) strategies the student uses in different contexts.

The RCI's main uses are to help identify patterns of responses (in the whole group and individuals) that then serve as guides to instruction and to analyzing an individual's flexibility in different reading activities.

Several questions on the RCI are particularly appropriate for content area reading. Although the RCI was developed for grades 3 through 8, high school teachers can make good diagnostic use of some of the questions.

Rather than interviewing each student individually, we suggest the following adaptation: Have each student keep a learning log. In these logs, students write to themselves about what they are learning. For example, they can choose to focus on problems they are having with a particular reading assignment or activity. A variation on this general purpose would be to ask students to respond to some of the more pertinent questions on the RCI—perhaps one or two at any one time over several weeks.

In relation to a particular content area textbook, examine the kinds of questions students can write about from the RCI:*

*From K. Wixson, A. Boskey, M. Yochum, and D. Alvermann, "An Interview for Assessing Students' Perceptions of Classroom Reading Tasks." *The Reading Teacher,* January 1984. Reprinted with permission of K. Wixson and the International Reading Association.

1. What is the most important reason for reading this kind of material? Why does your teacher want you to read this book?

2. Who's the best reader you know in (*content area*)? What does he/she do that makes him/her such a good reader?

3. How good are *you* at reading this kind of material? How do you know?

4. What do you have to do to get a good grade in (*content area*) in your class?

5. If the teacher told you to remember the information in this story/chapter, what would be the best way to do this? Have you ever tried (*name a strategy, e.g., outlining*)?

6. If your teacher told you to find the answers to the questions in this book, what would be the best way to do this? Why? Have you ever tried (*name a strategy, e.g., previewing*)?

7. What is the hardest part about answering questions like the ones in this book? Does that make you do anything differently?

Having students respond to these questions in writing does not deny the importance of interviewing individuals. However, it does save an enormous amount of time while providing a teacher with a record of students' perceptions of important reading tasks related to comprehension.

Rubrics and Self-Assessments

Students need to play a role in the assessment of their own literacy products and processes. Teachers who want to help students get more involved in assessment invite them to participate in setting goals and to share how they think and feel. What are the students' perceptions of their achievements? McCullen (1998) described how she begins this process with middle-grade students:

> I usually start by envisioning the possible outcomes of each assignment. Then the students and I develop a standard of excellence for each facet of the process and convert the outcomes into a rubric. Thus, before the students begin their research, they know the goals of the assignment and the scope of the evaluation. (p. 7)

Rubrics are categories that range from very simple and direct to comprehensive and detailed. Some are designed to help individual students self-assess; often they are designed to be used by small groups or by an individual student and teacher. In Figure 2.4, a basic rubric serves the dual purpose of involving each student in evaluating the group's work on an inquiry project involving the Internet and in self-evaluating.

A more detailed rubric, shown in Figure 2.5, was developed in a seventh-grade life science class by the teacher and her students for a unit exploring the five senses. The teacher gave the students copies of the rubric in advance so they could monitor themselves. Using a scale of 0 to 3, students were graded individually and as part of a group by their teacher and by themselves. This rubric may be time consuming to develop.

Response Journal

Based on personal experiences, how effective have rubrics been in assessing your writing?

FIGURE 2.4 **Rubric for Self-Evaluation**

Fifth-Grade Inquiry Project Using the Internet

Name: _____

Directions: Evaluate your group's performance in each of the following categories. Be honest. Please also make comments about parts of this project you found successful and parts you found unsuccessful.

Content	Points Possible	Points Earned	Comments
Selection of topic	5		
Evidence of planning	15		
Bibliography of print resources (minimum of 3 per person)	15		
Time on task while doing research in the library computer lab	5		
Websites (minimum of 5): usefulness, appropriateness	20		
Website summaries	30		
Evidence of cooperation	10		
Total	100		

Rubrics containing less detail and those developed in partnership with students may take less time to construct. They surely help involve students in assessing their own learning in an authentic, meaningful way that keeps the focus on *why* and *how* we do *what* we do.

Assessing Text Difficulty

Evaluating texts and assessing students' interactions with texts are crucial tasks for content area teachers and students—and they call for sound judgment and decision making. One of the best reasons we know for making decisions about the quality of texts is that the assessment process puts you and students in touch with their textbooks. To judge well, you must approach text assessment in much the same manner as you make decisions about other aspects of content area instruction. Any assessment suffers to the extent that it relies on a single source or perspective on information rather than on multiple sources or perspectives.

FIGURE **2.5** **Detailed Rubric for an Inquiry Project on the Five Senses**

	Group Evaluation	Individual Evaluation
3	■ Worked well together every day ■ Thoroughly completed the lab activity ■ Developed a well-organized, very neatly presented handout that combined all group members' work, including at least one visual aid ■ Worked independently on most days	■ Used at least four sources, including one Website and one traditional source; correctly listed the sources ■ Thoroughly answered the assigned question ■ Came up with and answered thoroughly two related questions ■ Participated in an experiment and engaged in a thoughtful reflection around that experiment ■ Cooperated with and helped group members every day
2	■ Worked well together most days ■ Completed the lab activity with some effort ■ Developed a well-organized, fairly neatly presented handout that combined all group members' work; may or may not have included a visual aid ■ Worked independently on some days	■ Used at least three sources, including one Website and one traditional source; listed the sources ■ Thoroughly answered the assigned question ■ Came up with and tried to answer two related questions ■ Participated in an experiment and engaged in a thoughtful reflection around that experiment ■ Cooperated with and helped group members most days
1	■ May or may not have worked well together ■ Completed the lab activity ■ Developed a handout that combined all group members' work; did not include a visual aid ■ Did not work independently	■ Used at least two sources; listed the sources ■ Answered the assigned question ■ Came up with and tried to answer one related question ■ Participated in an experiment and engaged in a reflection around that experiment ■ Cooperated with and helped group members some days
0	■ Did not work well together ■ Did not complete the lab activity ■ Did not develop handout that combined all group members' work ■ Did not work independently	■ Used fewer than two sources ■ Did not answer the assigned question ■ Did not come up with any related questions ■ May have participated in an experiment but did not reflect on that experiment ■ May or may not have cooperated

Grading Scale

■ 70% of your grade is based on your individual score
■ 30% of your grade is based on the group score

Final Score	Letter Grade
2.5–3.0	A
2.0–2.4	B
1.4–1.9	C
0.6–1.3	D
Below 0.6	F

Therefore, it makes sense to consider evidence in the student's portfolio along with several other perspectives.

One source of information to consider is publisher-provided descriptions of the design, format, and organizational structure of the textbook along with grade-level readability designations. Another information source is your acquired knowledge of and interactions with the students in the class. A third is your own sense of what makes the textbook a useful tool. A fourth source is student perspective, so that instructional decisions are not made from an isolated teacher's perception of the students' perspectives. To complement professional judgment, several procedures can provide you with useful information: readability formulas, the Fry graph, the cloze procedure, readability checklists, and a content area framework for student analysis of reading assignments. The first order of business, then, if content area reading strategies are to involve students in taking control of their own learning, is to find out how students are interacting with the text.

Content Area Reading Inventories

Teacher-made tests provide another important indicator of how students interact with text materials in content areas. A teacher-made *content area reading inventory* (CARI) is an alternative to the standardized reading test. The CARI is informal. As opposed to the standard of success on a norm-referenced test, which is a comparison of the performance of the tested group with that of the original normative population, success on the CARI test is measured by performance on the task itself. The CARI measures performance on reading materials actually used in a course. The results of the CARI can give a teacher some good insights into *how* students read course material.

Administering a CARI involves several general steps. First, explain to your students the purpose of the test. Mention that it will be used for evaluation only, to help you plan instruction, and that grades will not be assigned. Second, briefly introduce the selected portion of the text to be read and give students an idea direction to guide silent reading. Third, if you want to find out how the class uses the textbook, consider an open-book evaluation, but if you want to determine students' abilities to retain information, have them answer test questions without referring to the selection. Finally, discuss the results of the evaluation individually in conferences or collectively with the entire class.

A CARI can be administered piecemeal over several class sessions so that large chunks of instructional time will not be sacrificed. The bane of many content area instructors is spending an inordinate amount of time away from actual teaching.

A CARI elicits the information you need to adjust instruction and meet student needs. It should focus on students' abilities to comprehend text and to read at appropriate rates of comprehension. Some authorities suggest that teachers also evaluate additional competency areas, such as study skills—skimming, scanning, outlining, taking notes, and so forth. We believe, however, that the best use of reading inventories in content areas is on a much smaller scale. A CARI should seek information related to basic reading tasks. For this reason, we recommend that outlining, note taking, and other useful study techniques be assessed through observation and analysis of student work samples.

Levels of Comprehension

Teachers estimate their students' abilities to comprehend text material at different levels of comprehension by using inventories similar to the one shown in Figure 2.6 for American history. The teacher wanted to assess how students responded at literal (getting the facts), inferential (making some interpretations), and applied (going beyond the material) levels of comprehension. At this time you can also determine a measure of reading rate in relation to comprehension.

You can construct a comprehension inventory using these steps:

1. *Select an appropriate reading selection from the second fifty pages of the book.* The selection need not include the entire unit or story but should be complete within itself in overall content. In most cases, two or three pages will provide a sufficient sample.

2. *Count the total number of words in the excerpt.*

3. *Read the excerpt, and formulate ten to twelve comprehension questions.* The first part of the test should ask an open-ended question such as, "What was the passage about?" Then develop three or more questions at each level of comprehension.

4. *Prepare a student response sheet.*

5. *Answer the questions.* Include specific page references for discussion purposes after the testing is completed.

While students read the material and take the test, the teacher observes, noting work habits and student behavior, especially of students who appear frustrated by the test. The American history teacher whose inventory is illustrated in Figure 2.6 allowed students to check their own work as the class discussed each question. Other teachers prefer to evaluate individual students' responses to questions first and then to discuss them with students either individually or during the next class session.

Rates of Comprehension

To get an estimate of students' rates of comprehension, follow these steps:

1. *Have students note the time it takes to read the selection.* This can be accomplished efficiently by recording the time in five-second intervals by using a "stopwatch" that is drawn on the board.

2. *As students complete the reading, they look up at the board to check the stopwatch.* The number within the circle represents the minutes that have elapsed. The numbers along the perimeter of the circle represent the number of seconds.

FIGURE   2.6   Sample Comprehension Inventory
in American History

General directions: Read pages 595–600 in your textbook. Then look up at the board and note the time it took you to complete the selection. Record this time in the space provided on the response sheet. Close your book and answer the first question. You may then open your textbook to answer the remaining questions.

STUDENT RESPONSE FORM

Reading time: _____ min. _____ sec.

I. *Directions:* Close your book and answer the following question: In your own words, what was this section about? Use as much space as you need on the back of this page to complete your answer.

II. *Directions:* Open your book and answer the following questions.

1. To prevent the closing of banks throughout the country, President Roosevelt declared a national "bank holiday."
   a. True
   b. False

2. The purpose of the Social Security Act was to abolish federal unemployment payments.
   a. True
   b. False

3. The National Recovery Administration employed men between the ages of 18 and 25 to build bridges, dig reservoirs, and develop parks.
   a. True
   b. False

4. President Roosevelt established the Federal Deposit Insurance Corporation to insure savings accounts against bank failures.
   a. True
   b. False

III. *Directions:* Answers to these questions are not directly stated by the author. You must "read between the lines" to answer them.

1. Give an example of how FDR's first 100 days provided relief, reform, and recovery for the nation.
_____

2. How is the Tennessee Valley Authority an example of President Roosevelt's attempt to help the poorest segment of American society?
_____

3. How did the purpose of the Civil Works Administration differ from the purpose of the Federal Emergency Relief Act?
_____

FIGURE **2.6**   **Continued**

IV. *Directions:* Answers to these questions are not directly stated by the author. You must "read beyond the lines" to answer them.

1. If FDR had not promoted his New Deal program through his fireside chats, do you think it would have been successful? Why or why not?

2. Why did FDR's critics fear the New Deal? Do you think their concerns were justified? Why or why not?

3. Which New Deal program would you call the most important? Why?

3. *Later, students or the teacher can figure out the students' rates of reading in words per minute.*

Example:
Words in selection: 1,500
 Reading time: 4 minutes 30 seconds
 Convert seconds to a decimal fraction. Then divide time into words.

$$\frac{1,500}{4.5} = 333 \text{ words per minute}$$

4. *Determine the percentage of correct or reasonable answers on the comprehension test.* Always evaluate and discuss students' rates of reading in terms of their comprehension performance.

In summary, information you glean from a CARI will help you organize specific lessons and activities. You can decide on the background preparation needed, the length of reading assignments, and the reading activities when you apply your best judgment to the information you have learned from the assessment.

Readability

There are many readability formulas that classroom teachers can use to estimate textbook difficulty. Most popular formulas today are quick and easy to calculate. They typically involve a measure of sentence length and word difficulty to determine a grade-level score for text materials. This score supposedly indicates the reading achievement level that students need to comprehend the material. Because of their ease, readability formulas are used to make judgments about materials. These judgments are global and are not intended to be precise indicators of text difficulty.

A readability formula can best be described as a "rubber ruler" because the scores that it yields are estimates of text difficulty, not absolute levels. These estimates are often determined along a single dimension of an author's writing style: sentence complexity (as measured by length) and vocabulary difficulty (also measured by length). These two variables are used to predict text difficulty. But even though they have been shown to be persistent correlates of readability, they only indirectly assess sentence complexity and vocabulary difficulty. Are long sentences always more difficult to comprehend than short ones? Are long words necessarily harder to understand than short ones? When a readability formula is used to rewrite materials by breaking long sentences into short ones, the inferential burden of the reader actually increases (Pearson 1974–1975).

Keep in mind that a readability formula doesn't account for the experience and knowledge that readers bring to content material. Formulas are not designed to tap the variables operating in the reader. Our purpose, interest, motivation, and emotional state as well as the environment that we're in during reading contribute to our ability to comprehend text.

The danger, according to Nelson (1978), is not in the use of readability formulas: "The danger is in promoting the faulty assumptions that matching the readability score of materials to the reading achievement scores of students will automatically yield comprehension" (p. 622). She makes these suggestions to content area teachers:

1. Learn to use a simple readability formula as an aid in evaluating text.

2. Whenever possible, provide materials containing the essential facts, concepts, and values of the subject at varying levels of readability within the reading range of your students.

3. Don't assume that matching readability level of material to reading achievement level of students results in automatic comprehension. Remember there are many factors that affect reading difficulty besides those measured by readability formulas.

4. Don't assume that rewriting text materials according to readability criteria results in automatic reading ease. Leave rewriting of text material to the linguists, researchers, and editors who have time to analyze and validate their manipulations.

5. Recognize that using a readability formula is no substitute for instruction. Assigning is not teaching. Subject area textbooks are not designed for independent reading. To enhance reading comprehension in your subject area, provide instruction which prepares students for the assignment, guides them in their reading, and reinforces new ideas through rereading and discussion. (pp. 624–625)

Within the spirit of these suggestions, let's examine a popular readability formula and an alternative, the cloze procedure.

The Fry Graph

The readability graph developed by Edward Fry (1977) is a quick and simple readability formula. The graph was designed to identify the grade-level score for materials from grade 1 through college. Two variables are used to predict the difficulty of the reading material: sentence length and word length. Sentence length is determined by the total number of sentences in a sample passage. Word length is determined by the total number of syllables in the passage. Fry recommended that three 100-word samples from the reading be used to calculate readability. The grade-level scores for each of the passages can then be averaged to determine overall readability. According to Fry, the readability graph predicts the difficulty of the material within one grade level. See Figure 2.7 for the graph and expanded directions for the Fry formula.

Cloze Procedure

The cloze procedure does not use a formula to estimate the difficulty of reading material. Originated by Wilson Taylor in 1953, a cloze test determines how well students can read a particular text or reading selection as a result of their interaction with the material. Simply defined, then, the *cloze procedure* is a method by which you systematically delete words from a text passage and then evaluate students' abilities to accurately supply the words that were deleted. An encounter with a cloze passage should reveal the interplay between the prior knowledge that students bring to the reading task and their language competence. Knowing the extent of this interplay will be helpful in selecting materials and planning instructional procedures. Figure 2.8 presents part of a cloze test passage developed for an art history class. Here is how to construct, administer, score, and interpret a cloze test.

1. *Construction*

   a. Select a reading passage of approximately 275 words from material that students have not yet read but that you plan to assign.

   b. Leave the first sentence intact. Starting with the second sentence, select at random one of the first five words. Delete every fifth word thereafter, until you have a total of fifty words for deletion. Retain the remaining sentence of the last deleted word. Type one more sentence intact. For children below grade 4, deletion of every tenth word is often more appropriate.

   c. Leave an underlined blank of fifteen spaces for each deleted word as you type the passage.

2. *Administration*

   a. Inform students that they are not to use their textbooks or to work together in completing the cloze passage.

   b. Explain the task that students are to perform. Show how the cloze procedure works by providing several examples on the board.

   c. Allow students the time they need to complete the cloze passage.

3. *Scoring*

   a. Count as correct every *exact* word students apply. *Do not* count synonyms even though they may appear to be satisfactory. Counting

Response Journal

How did you do on the sample cloze passage? Do you think it is a useful assessment tool?

FIGURE 2.7 Fry Readability Graph

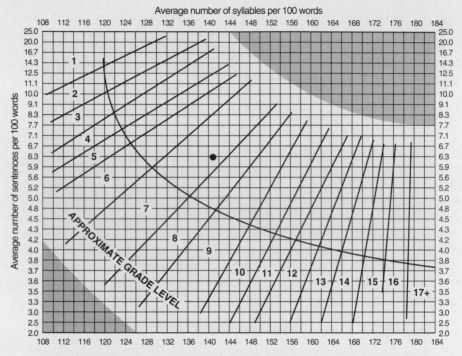

Average number of syllables per 100 words

EXPANDED DIRECTIONS FOR WORKING READABILITY GRAPH

1. Randomly select three (3) sample passages and count out exactly 100 words each, beginning with the beginning of a sentence. Do count proper nouns, initializations, and numerals.

2. Count the number of sentences in the 100 words, estimating length of the fraction of the last sentence to the nearest one-tenth.

3. Count the total number of syllables in the 100-word passage. If you don't have a hand counter available, an easy way is simply to put a mark above every syllable over one in each word; then, when you get to the end of the passage, count the number of marks and add 100. Small calculators can also be used as counters by pushing numeral 1, then pushing the + sign for each word or syllable.

4. Enter graph with *average* sentence length and *average* number of syllables; plot dot where the two lines intersect. Area where dot is plotted will give you the approximate grade level.

5. If a great deal of variability is found in syllable count or sentence count, putting more samples into the average is desirable.

6. A word is defined as a group of symbols with a space on either side; thus *1945* is one word.

7. A syllable is defined as a phonetic syllable. Generally, there are as many syllables as vowel sounds. For example, *stopped* is one syllable and *wanted* is two syllables. When counting syllables for numerals and initializations, count one syllable for each symbol. For example, *1945* is four syllables.

Source: From Edward Fry, *Elementary Reading Instruction.* Copyright © 1977 by McGraw-Hill. Reprinted by permission of The McGraw-Hill Companies.

FIGURE **2.8**   **Sample Portion of a Cloze Test**

If the symbol of Rome is the Colosseum, then Paris's symbol is without doubt the Eiffel Tower. Both are monuments unique (1) planning and construction, both (2) admiration by their extraordinary (3), and bear witness (4) man's inborn will to (5) something capable of demonstrating (6) measure of his genius. (7) tower was erected on (8) occasion of the World is (9) in 1889. These were the (10) of the Industrial Revolution, (11) progress and of scientific (12). The attempt was made (13) adapt every art to (14) new direction which life (15) taken and to make (16) human activity correspond to (17) new sensibility created by (18) changing times.

Answers to the Cloze Test sample may be found on page 67.

synonyms will not change the scores appreciably, but it will cause unnecessary hassles and haggling with students. Accepting synonyms also affects the reliability of the performance criteria, because they were established on exact word replacements.

b. Multiply the total number of exact word replacements by two to determine the student's cloze percentage score.

c. Record the cloze scores on a sheet of paper for each class. For each class, you now have one to three instructional groups that can form the basis for differentiated assignments (see Figure 2.9).

4. *Interpretation*

a. A score of 60 percent or higher indicates that the passage can be read competently by students. They may be able to read the material on their own without guidance.

b. A score of 40 to 60 percent indicates that the passage can be read with some competency by students. The material will challenge students if they are given some form of reading guidance.

FIGURE **2.9**   **Headings for a Cloze Performance Chart**

Subject _____
Period _____
Teacher _____

Below 40 percent	Between 40 and 60 percent	Above 60 percent

c. A score below 40 percent indicates that the passage will probably be too difficult for students. They will need either a great deal of reading guidance to benefit from the material or more suitable material.

The cloze procedure is an alternative to a readability formula because it gives an indication of how students will actually perform with course materials. Unfortunately, the nature of the test itself will probably be foreign to students. They will be staring at a sea of blank spaces in running text, and having to provide words may seem a formidable task. Don't expect a valid score the first time you administer the test. It's important to discuss the purpose of the cloze test and to give students ample practice with and exposure to it.

Readability Checklist

Despite the many factors to be considered in text evaluation, *teachers ultimately want texts that students will understand, be able to use, and want to use.* To help guide your assessment and keep it manageable, a checklist that focuses on *understandability, usability,* and *interestability* is useful. One such checklist is shown in Figure 2.10; it is an adaptation of the Irwin and Davis (1980) Readability Checklist.

The domain of *understandability* provides information about how likely a given group of students is to comprehend the text adequately. It helps the teacher assess relationships between the students' own schemata and conceptual knowledge and the text information. When teachers judge textbooks for possible difficulties, it is imperative to decide whether the author has considered the knowledge students bring to the text. The match between what the reader knows and the text will have a strong influence on the understandability of the material.

Armbruster and Anderson (1981) indicate that one way to judge the author's assumptions about students' background knowledge and experiences is to decide if enough relevant ideas are presented in a text to satisfy the author's purpose. Often, authors use headings to suggest their purposes for text passages. Convert the headings to questions. If the passage content answers the questions, the authors have achieved their purposes and the passage is *considerate.* If an author hasn't provided enough information to make a passage meaningful, the passage is *inconsiderate.*

The second major domain is *usability.* Is the text coherent, unified, and structured enough to be usable? Divided into two subsections on the Readability Checklist, this section provides information about the presentation and organization of content. It will help the teacher assess factors contributing to the day-to-day use of the text in teaching and the students' use in learning. These items help pinpoint for a teacher exactly what needs supplementing or what may take additional preparation time or class time.

Essentially, a teacher's response to these items is another way of deciding if a text is considerate or inconsiderate. A considerate text not only fits the reader's prior knowledge but also helps "the reader to gather appropriate information with minimal cognitive effort"; an inconsiderate text "requires the reader to put forth extra effort" to compensate for poorly organized material (Armbruster & Anderson 1981, p. 3).

| FIGURE | **2.10** **General Textbook Readability Checklist** |

In the blank before each item, indicate ✔ for "yes," + for "to some extent," or x for "no" or "does not apply."

Understandability

_____ 1. Are the assumptions about students' vocabulary knowledge appropriate?

_____ 2. Are the assumptions about students' prior knowledge of this content area appropriate?

_____ 3. Are the assumptions about students' general experiential background appropriate?

_____ 4. Does the teacher's manual provide the teacher with ways to develop and review the students' conceptual and experiential background?

_____ 5. Are new concepts explicitly linked to the students' prior knowledge or to their experiential background?

_____ 6. Does the text introduce abstract concepts by accompanying them with many concrete examples?

_____ 7. Does the text introduce new concepts one at a time, with a sufficient number of examples for each one?

_____ 8. Are definitions understandable and at a lower level of abstraction than the concept being defined?

_____ 9. Does the text avoid irrelevant details?

_____ 10. Does the text explicitly state important complex relationships (e.g., causality and conditionality) rather than always expecting the reader to infer them from the context?

_____ 11. Does the teacher's manual provide lists of accessible resources containing alternative readings for very poor or very advanced readers?

_____ 12. Is the readability level appropriate (according to a readability formula)?

Usability

External Organizational Aids

_____ 1. Does the table of contents provide a clear overview of the contents of the textbook?

_____ 2. Do the chapter headings clearly define the content of the chapter?

_____ 3. Do the chapter subheadings clearly break out the important concepts in the chapter?

_____ 4. Do the topic headings provide assistance in breaking the chapter into relevant parts?

_____ 5. Does the glossary contain all the technical terms in the textbook?

_____ 6. Are the graphs and charts clear and supportive of the textual material?

_____ 7. Are the illustrations well done and appropriate to the level of the students?

_____ 8. Is the print size of the text appropriate to the level of student readers?

_____ 9. Are the lines of text an appropriate length for the level of the students who will use the textbook?

_____ 10. Is a teacher's manual available and adequate for guidance to the teachers?

(continued)

FIGURE **2.10**   **Continued**

External Organizational Aids (continued)

_____ 11. Are the important terms in italic or boldface type for easy identification by readers?

_____ 12. Are the end-of-chapter questions on literal, interpretive, and applied levels of comprehension?

Internal Organizational Aids

_____ 1. Are the concepts spaced appropriately throughout the text, rather than being too many in too short a space or too few words?

_____ 2. Is an adequate context provided to allow students to determine the meanings of technical terms?

_____ 3. Are the sentence lengths appropriate to the level of students who will be using the text?

_____ 4. Is the author's style (word length, sentence length, sentence complexity, paragraph length, number of examples) appropriate to the level of students who will be using the text?

_____ 5. Does the author use a predominant structure or pattern of organization (compare–contrast, cause–effect, time order, problem–solution) within the writing to assist students in interpreting the text?

Interestability

_____ 1. Does the teacher's manual provide introductory activities that will capture students' interests?

_____ 2. Are the chapter titles and subheadings concrete, meaningful, or interesting?

_____ 3. Is the writing style of the text appealing to the students?

_____ 4. Are the activities motivating? Will they make the student want to pursue the topic further?

_____ 5. Does the book clearly show how what is being learned might be used by the learner in the future?

_____ 6. Are the cover, format, print size, and pictures appealing to the students?

_____ 7. Does the text provide positive and motivating models for both sexes as well as for a variety of racial, ethnic, and socioeconomic groups?

_____ 8. Does the text help students generate interest as they relate experiences and develop visual and sensory images?

Summary Rating

Circle one choice for each item.

The text rates highest in understandability / usability / interest.

The text rates lowest in understandability / usability / interest.

My teaching can best supplement understandability / usability / interest.

I would still need assistance with understandability / usability / interest.

FIGURE **2.10** **Continued**

Statement of Strengths:

Statement of Weaknesses:

Source: Adapted from Judith W. Irwin and Carol A. Davis, "Assessing Readability: The Checklist Approach"(November 1980). *Journal of Reading, 24*(2), 124–130. Copyright © 1980 by the International Reading Association. All rights reserved. Used by permission of the International Reading Association.

The third domain, *interestability,* is intended to ascertain whether features of the text will appeal to a given group of students. Illustrations and photos may have instant appeal; students can relate to drawings and photographs depicting persons similar to themselves. The more relevant the textbook, the more interesting it may be to students.

Experiment with the Readability Checklist by trying it out on a textbook in your content area. Once you've completed the checklist, sum up your ratings at the end. Does the text rate high in understandability, usability, or interestability? Is a low rating in an area you can supplement well through your instruction, or is it in an area in which you could use more help? Also, summarize the strengths and weaknesses of the textbook. If you noted two areas in which you'd still need assistance, this text is unlikely to meet your needs. Finally, decide how you can take advantage of the textbook's strengths and compensate for its weaknesses.

FLIP Strategy

Efforts to directly access student- or reader-based judgment have resulted in a strategy to provide students with the guidelines they need to assess reading tasks (Schumm & Mangrum 1991). Whereas checklists and formulas are designed for *teacher* use, a strategy such as FLIP (an acronym for *friendliness, language, interest,* and *prior knowledge*) is designed to engage the *reader* in estimating the level of difficulty of a given source or textbook. With teacher guidance, perhaps using an overhead projector and the think-aloud technique, students actually walk through FLIP and consider these factors:

Friendliness: How friendly is my reading assignment? *(Students look for text features such as index, graphs, pictures, summaries, and study questions.)*

Language: How difficult is the language in my reading assignment? *(Students estimate the number of new terms.)*

Interest: How interesting is my reading assignment? *(Students look over the title, headings, pictures, etc.)*

Prior knowledge: What do I already know about the material covered in my reading assignment? *(Students think about the title, heading, summary, etc.)* (pp. 121–122)

Figure 2.11 illustrates how Kristen Hecker uses a FLIP strategy to help her third graders assess the level of difficulty of *Under the Sea,* a book about different life forms living in the ocean, by Claire Llewellyn (1991). First, she asks the students to look at the pictures in the text and share what they think the book will be about with two of their classmates. Then, she helps the whole class examine the tools used by the author in the book: glossary, table of contents, and

---

FIGURE 2.11   A FLIP for Third-Grade Science

Friendliness:

How friendly is the book *Under the Sea*?

Is the index clearly organized? How?

What about the table of contents?

—big print —pictures
—it asks questions
—yes —space
—has page #s

Language:

How many new terms/words do you see on pages 6–10?

—lots -only 5
—not too many
—we had some

How difficult does the author's writing look to you?

—I can't tell yet
—not too hard

Interest:

In what ways does *Under the Sea* look interesting to you?

Why?/Why not?

—it's like epcot
—lots of pictures
—too many fish

Prior Knowledge:

Look at the title and the subheadings on pages 6–10. What do you already know about these topics in *Under the Sea*?

—that there are plants
  in the ocean
—kinds of fish

index. Using an overhead projector, Kristen guides her third graders through the questions on the left side of the FLIP, making sure to record their answers, including those who don't agree with the majority.

e.Resources

For additional readings related to the major ideas in this chapter, go to Chapter 2 of the Companion Website and click on Suggested Readings.

◄ Looking Back
Looking Forward ▶

Assessing students and texts is a process of gathering and using multiple sources of relevant information for instructional purposes. Two major approaches to assessment prevail in education today: a formal, high-stakes one and an informal, authentic one. Pressure from policy makers and other constituencies has resulted in the adoption of curriculum standards specifying goals and objectives in subject areas and grade levels in most states. Hence, student performance on state-mandated tests must also be considered by teachers who need to make instructional decisions based on their students' content literacy skills, concepts, and performance.

An informal, authentic approach is often more practical in collecting and organizing the many kinds of information that can inform decisions, including (1) students' prior knowledge in relation to instructional units and text assignments, (2) students' knowledge and use of reading and other communication strategies to learn from texts, and (3) assessment of materials. The use of portfolios, careful observation and documentation of students' strengths and weaknesses as they interact with one another and with content-specific material, sheds light on the *why* as well as the *what* in teaching and learning.

In this chapter, the key terms, major purposes, and legitimate uses of standardized tests were presented. Contrasts were drawn between portfolios and testing. As teachers engage learners in a process of portfolio assessment, they make adaptations appropriate for their subject matter and consider issues that have been raised about using portfolios. Suggestions for assessing students' background knowledge included interviews, pretesting, and instructionally based strategies. Interpreting interviews, surveys, scales, and observations, and developing rubrics help in assessing and students' self-assessing behaviors and views. For insights into how students interact with text material and a measure of performance on the reading materials used in a course, teacher-made content area reading inventories were suggested.

Assessing the difficulty of text material requires both professional judgment and quantitative analysis. Text assessment considers various factors within the reader and the text, the exercise of professional judgment being as useful as calculating a readability formula. Teachers, therefore, must be concerned about the quality of the content, format, organization, and appeal of the material. We supplied three types of procedures for assessing text difficulty: readability formulas, the cloze procedure, and readability checklists.

Despite efforts to assess students and to scaffold instruction in ways that facilitate text learning, some students will continually struggle with literacy. Even though the best readers and writers may struggle in certain situations, the struggling student often has given up on literacy as a way of learning. Chapter 3 takes a closer look at the literacy needs of the struggling reader and writer. As you read about struggling readers and writers, focus your attention on the role of explicit instruction in the development and use of literacy strategies.

 Minds On

1. You are planning for the new school year in a district whose scores on the statewide proficiency tests have not shown much improvement. A text has been chosen; you have a wide range of auxiliary reading and viewing materials from which to choose. As long as you don't stray from the district's curriculum standards, you may use any assessment strategies to meet the needs, abilities, and interests of your students. Outline your plan for instructional assessment.

2. For keeping records, most portfolios of student work include a cover page, one that reflects the teacher's philosophy of assessment. With a group of classmates, select a content area and design a cover page that reflects your vision of authentic assessment.

3. Imagine that you are a new teacher reviewing the required text you will be using in the fall. Initially, you find the book fascinating, and you are certain it will excite many of your students. Yet after analyzing the work, you discover that its readability appears to be above the reading level of most of your students. How might you use this text effectively?

4. Readability formulas are predictive measures. How do predictive measures differ from performance measures in helping you determine how difficult reading materials will be for your students?

 Hands On

1. In groups of three, turn to the "state standards" section of this chapter. How has your state (or region or province) taken action to put standards for curriculum content in place? Describe any recent revisions in process or testing procedures that may affect your local school district. Rewards? Consequences?

2. Develop an observation checklist for the assessment of reading and study behavior in your content area. Compare your checklist with those developed by others in the class for similar content areas. What conclusions might you draw?

3. Each member of your group should locate one sample of text material on the same topic from these sources: an elementary content area text, a secondary content area text, a newspaper, and a popular magazine. Determine the readability of a sample passage from each by using two different readability formulas. Compare your findings by using two additional readability formulas. What conclusions can you draw from the comparison?

4. Two members of your group of four should be designated as observers. The other members should collaboratively attempt to solve the following mathematics problem:

Calculate the surface area of a cylinder that is 12 inches long and 5 inches in diameter.

Note any observations that you believe might be useful in assessing the group's performance. What types of useful information do observations like these provide?

Answers

1. in	5. build	9. Fair	13. to	17. the
2. stir	6. the	10. years	14. every	18. rapidly
3. dimensions	7. The	11. of	15. had	
4. to	8. the	12. conquests	16. every	

e.Resources extra

- Go to Chapter 2 of the Companion Website (**www.ablongman.com/vacca8e**) and click on Activities to complete the following task:

  Go to the Website **www.reading.org/positions/MADMMID.html**, which contains a summary of the International Reading Association's position statement on the rights of students. Read and discuss the ten principles listed and how each relates to authentic assessment.

- Go to the Companion Website (**www.ablongman.com/vacca8e**) for suggested readings, interactive activities, multiple-choice questions and additional Web links to help you learn more about assessing students and text.

The New York Times
expect the world®
nytimes.com

Themes of the Times

Extend your knowledge of the concepts discussed in this chapter by reading current and historical articles from the *New York Times*. Go to the Companion Website and click on eThemes of the Times.

chapter **3**

Struggling Readers and Writers

If you can't read, you can't hit.
—REGGIE JACKSON

Hitting a baseball isn't easy. Neither is learning with academic texts. Students often struggle with reading and writing in the content areas in the same way that many of us might struggle with hitting a baseball. When Reggie Jackson, now a Hall of Famer, played with the New York Yankees, he wrote a book on the art of hitting a baseball. In the book, Jackson asserts, "If you can't read, you can't hit." He explains how he must be able to "read" several kinds of information in a fraction of a second to be successful as a hitter. His brain almost instantly must anticipate and process the type of pitch, its speed, and the rotation on the ball so that he can time his stride and the swing of the bat. To do this with reasonable success, Jackson has developed a repertoire of strate-

Teachers respond to the literacy needs of struggling readers and writers by scaffolding instruction so that students become confident and competent in the use of strategies that support learning.

gies for "reading" the rotation on the ball and the speed of the pitch. He has learned, for example, not to watch the pitcher's hand if he wants to see the ball early. He also knows the value of predicting the type of pitch that might be thrown in certain game situations.

Struggling readers and writers, like struggling hitters, often lack strategies—the kinds of

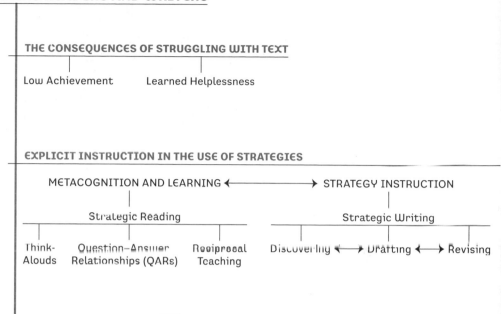

STRUGGLING READERS AND WRITERS

THE CONSEQUENCES OF STRUGGLING WITH TEXT

Low Achievement   Learned Helplessness

EXPLICIT INSTRUCTION IN THE USE OF STRATEGIES

METACOGNITION AND LEARNING ←——————→ STRATEGY INSTRUCTION

Strategic Reading   Strategic Writing

Think-   Question–Answer   Reciprocal   Discovering ←→ Drafting ←→ Revising
Alouds   Relationships (QARs) Teaching

strategies necessary to learn effectively with text. One of the realities facing teachers across all content areas today is that many students make little use of reading and writing as tools for learning. Either they read or write on a superficial level or find ways to circumvent content literacy tasks altogether. Yet the ability to read and write well is one of the keys to independent and lifelong learning.

When students struggle with content literacy tasks, teachers are in much the same position as hitting coaches. Through our instructional support, we can build students' confidence and competence as readers and writers by showing them how to read and write strategically and how to use literacy to think deeply about texts. When teachers assume the roles of coaches, they make explicit what good readers and writers do to cope with the kinds

Response Journal

What are some "first thoughts" and reactions that you have related to the organizing principle of this chapter?

of problems they encounter in academic contexts.

As teachers, how can we "step up to the plate" and be responsive to the literacy needs of struggling learners while maintaining high content standards? The organizing principle of this chapter builds on teachers' abilities to provide explicit instruction in the use of literacy strategies: **Teachers respond to the literacy needs of struggling readers and writers by scaffolding instruction so that students become confident and competent in the use of strategies that support learning.**

Frame of Mind

1. What does it mean to be a struggling reader and writer?

2. Why do students who struggle often give up when faced with content literacy tasks?

3. What is metacognition, and why is it important for struggling readers and writers to develop metacognitive knowledge and strategies?

4. Describe the various components of explicit instruction in the development and use of literacy strategies.

5. How do think-alouds, QARs, and reciprocal teaching provide instructional support for students who have difficulty comprehending text?

6. How does learning to write strategically help students monitor and develop control over the writing process?

Even skilled readers struggle with reading at some time, in some place, with some text. A good reader on occasion will get lost in the author's line of reasoning, become confused by the way the text is organized, or run into unknown words that are difficult to pronounce let alone define. Perhaps main ideas are too difficult to grasp or the reader simply lacks prior knowledge to make connections to the important ideas in the text. Regardless of the comprehension problem, often it's only temporary. The difference between good readers and poor readers is that when good readers struggle with text, they know what to do to get out of trouble. When a text becomes confusing or doesn't make sense, good readers recognize that they have a repertoire of reading strategies that they can use to work themselves out of the difficulty. Struggling readers, however, have trouble figuring out what to do.

Skilled writers, like skilled readers, have a repertoire of strategies at their command. A clean sheet of paper or a blank computer screen is the writer's call to work. Getting started, however, can be difficult, even terrifying. How do you respond to the question, "What do you do when you write?" Here's what an experienced teacher and graduate student has to say:

> When faced with the task of writing, I immediately think of all the other things I need to do. Like clean the attic. Oh and the basement, too, because it's really dirty. Then I remember that root canal surgery I've been putting off. I call the dentist. Of course, I can't write while I'm waiting for the appointment because I'm too nervous. Then certainly I can't write after the surgery, because I need to recuperate with lots of rest. Then I decide to make a list of all the animals Noah took onto the ark. Of course, I have to copy it over because they went two by two. . . . (Topping & McManus 2002, p. 104)

Many a good writer has struggled with getting started. Some procrastinate until their backs are up against the wall. Others come to grips with the blank computer screen or clean sheet of paper by performing one or more starting rituals: Pencils are sharpened; the desktop is cleared of clutter; the refrigerator is raided once or twice. Eventually, however, the first words are put on paper, and everything that has occurred to this point (all of the mental, emotional, and physical gymnastics a writer experiences) and everything that will happen toward completion of the writing task can best be described as a writing process. Good writers learn how to regulate and control the process. Struggling writers, however, have trouble figuring out what to do.

The Consequences of Struggling with Text

Throughout this book, we argue that the real value of literacy lies in its uses. Whether we use reading or writing to enter into the imaginative world of fiction; learn with academic texts; meet workplace demands; acquire insight and knowledge about people, places, and things; or understand or create a graphic on an Internet Website, readers and writers, to be successful, must use and adapt strategies to meet the demands of the task at hand. Reading and writing aren't as much a struggle as they are a challenge for those literacy users who know what to do.

For example, let's take a closer look at the act of reading as a challenge or a struggle. We developed the following passage to demonstrate how easy it is for good readers to experience what it means to struggle with reading. More often than not, a good reader will approach the passage as a challenge and use a repertoire of reading strategies to construct meaning from the text. The passage, in the form of a short parable, poses a particular problem for readers as it tells the story of a king with kind but misguided intentions.

THE KINGDOM OF KAY OSS

Once upon a time in the land of Serenity, there ruled a king called Kay Oss. The king craved approval. More than anything else, he wanted to be liked by all of his people.

So onx day thx bxnxvolxnt dxspot dxcidxd that thx bxst way to bx likxd was to frxx his pxoplx from thx swxat and toil of work. Hx dxcrxxd that no onx in Sxrxnity would xvxr again bx hxld accountablx for thxir xndxavors.

Zll of thx workxrs rxstxd from thxvr dzvly lzbors. "Blxss thx Kvng," thxy xxclzvmxd! Thx fzrmxrs dvdn't hzrvxst thx crops. Thx Kvng's zrmy dvsbzndxd. Zll of thx mxrchznts vn thx kvngdom wxnt on zn xxtxndxd vzcztvon to thx Fzr Ezst. Thx shop ownxrs hung svgns on thxvr doors thzt szvd, "Gonx Fvshvng Vndxfvnvtxly."

Xvxn thx jxstxrs, whq prqvvdxd z wxlcqmx rxspvtx frqm thx fqrmzlvtvxs qf thz kvng's cqurt, stqppxd clqwnvng zrqund. Thx kvng's knvghts, whq wxrx vxry wvsx, did nqt wznt to zct zgzvnst thx kvng's wvshxs. Sq thxy put thxvr shvnvng zrmqr vn stqrzgx znd dvsmzntlxd thx rqundtzblx. "Zt lxzst thxrx wvll bx nq mqrx bqrvng mxxtvngs," thxy svghxd wvth rxlvxf.

Wzs thx kvng whq wzntxd tq bx lvkxd by xvxryqnx z gqqd nzturxd rulxr? Qr wzs hx mxrxly fqqlhzrty? Qnly tvmx wquld txll.

(continued)

THE KINGDOM OF KAY OSS   *continued*

Zs tvmx wxnt qn, Sxrxnvty chzngxd vts nzmx to Znxvxty. Thxrx wzs tqtzl dvsqrdxr and cqnfusvqn vn thx kvngdqm, znd vt lqqkxd lvkx thvs: Bcx dqufghj klzm nqxp qqt rqst vqxwxxz bqxc dqf ghzj ythmnot kwt vmptxdl kqlxmmnxp.

And what happened to the king? He changed his name to Chaos and entered a twelve step program to regain, as you might guess, his. . . .

Serenity

Response Journal

Describe some of the reading strategies you use to successfully complete an academic reading assignment. What are some of the strategies you use for writing essays or papers that will be graded or shared with others?

In order to comprehend text successfully, skilled readers must be able to *decode* or pronounce words quickly and accurately; read with *fluency;* activate *vocabulary knowledge* in relation to the language of the text; and put into play *cognitive* and *metacognitive* strategies to understand what they are reading. As Figure 3.1 suggests decoding, reading fluency, vocabulary, and comprehension are interrelated processes. If readers have trouble decoding words quickly and accurately (e.g.,

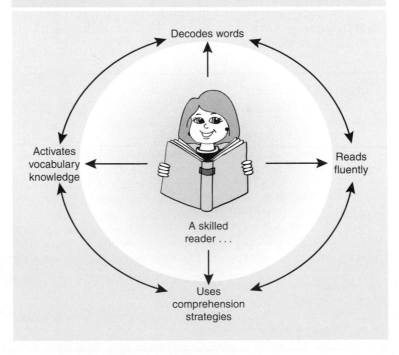

FIGURE 3.1   **Reading Involves Decoding, Reading Fluency, Vocabulary Knowledge, and Comprehension**

BOX 3.1

What about . . .
English Language Learners?

English language learners are students whose first language is other than English. They are often referred to as *language minority* students because they are nonnative speakers of English. Some English language learners struggle with reading and writing tasks in content area classrooms for a variety of complex reasons, not the least of which is their ability to use language processes such as reading, writing, speaking, and listening in academic contexts to communicate.

In *The Crosscultural, Language, and Academic Development Handbook,* Diaz-Rico and Weed (2002) capture the dilemma faced by content area teachers and schools who are unprepared to work academically with "the growing number of second language students flooding the nation's schools" (p. 115). A teacher's poignant journal entry reflects the frustration of teachers as well as students in one high school:

> School started the day after Labor Day. Our enrollment suddenly included 150 Hmong who had recently immigrated to our school district. We had neither classrooms nor teachers to accommodate such a large influx, and no one was qualified to deliver instruction in Hmong. By October, it was obvious that our policy placing these students in regular content classes was not working. The students were frustrated by their inability to communicate and keep up with the class work and teachers felt overwhelmed and inadequate to meet the needs of students who were barely literate and did not know English. A typical student was Khim, who, though better off than most Hmong because she could communicate her basic needs in English, could not cope with the reading and writing demands of eleventh-grade history, math, and science. (Diaz-Rico & Weed 2002, p. 115)

By mid-October of the school year, the high school teachers expressed their discontent at a faculty meeting and their resolve to change business as usual. The teachers recognized that they needed "a new approach" for language minority students in their school.

The discontent and frustration of these teachers is no different from that of many content area teachers who are not prepared to meet the academic and language needs of immigrant students in their classrooms. Much of what we discuss in this chapter applies to language minority as well as language majority students (native speakers) who struggle with reading and writing. In either case, students who struggle with texts cannot be left to "sink or swim" in content learning situations. They need "new" approaches—alternatives to "assign-and-tell" instructional routines—that scaffold instruction in the use of speaking, listening, reading, and writing strategies.

In the next chapter, we focus specifically on the academic and literacy needs of English language learners who struggle with literacy and learning in the core curriculum. English language learners need to develop *communicative competence* (Brown 1987; Hymes 1972) where the focus is on using language in social contexts. Our instructional emphasis will be the same as it is in this chapter. An important aspect of communicative competence is building strategic knowledge, insights, and skills related to language use in content learning situations: Knowing when, where, and how to use reading, writing, speaking, and listening strategies appropriately in instructional contexts requires students to negotiate meanings as well as interact and collaborate with other students.

analyzing and recognizing sound–letter relationships), it will slow down their ability to read fluently in a smooth, conversational manner. Moreover, if they struggle to decode words accurately, various reading errors (e.g., mispronunciations, word omissions, and substitutions), if significant, will cause cognitive confusion and limit readers' abilities to bring meaning and conceptual understanding to the words in the text.

When readers struggle, the act of reading no longer becomes automatic. As you read *The Kingdom of Kay Oss*, did the substitution of consonants *x*, *z*, *q*, and *v* for the vowels *e*, *a*, *o*, and *i* cause you to struggle as a reader? Perhaps. The progressive substitution of the consonants for vowels undoubtedly slowed down your ability to read in a smooth, conversational manner and may even have affected your accuracy in recognizing some words. Just think about some of the students in classrooms today who struggle with reading. They may experience difficulty because they read in a slow and halting manner, word-by-word, and have trouble recognizing words quickly and accurately. They spend so much time and attention on trying to "say the words" that comprehension suffers and, as a result, the reading process breaks down for them.

Did you find this the case with *The Kingdom of Kay Oss* passage? Probably not. Even though the substitution of consonants for vowels slowed down your rate of reading, chances are you were still able to comprehend the passage and construct meaning from it. This is because skilled readers do not use a single strategy to comprehend text. They know how to search for and construct meaning. Skilled readers have at their command *multiple strategies* for reading.

Moreover, skilled readers use prior knowledge to construct meaning. Take another look at the last paragraph in the passage. As you read, "As time went on Serenity changed its name to Anxiety. There was total disorder and confusion in the kingdom, and it looked like this:" did the remainder of the text confuse you? Did you comprehend the author's intent? Did you construct meaning for what seems to be a string of letters and words that make no sense? If you were reading *strategically* and *monitoring* comprehension, you probably made the inference that "it" referred to the land of Serenity and "this" referred to the string of seemingly senseless words that followed. These words convey no letter–sound or grammatical clues. They represent total confusion and disorder! By analogy, then, you may have inferred that the land of Serenity looked like it was in a state of total confusion and disorder much like the string of unknown words. Some of you may even have concluded that there is a word to describe what happened in Serenity a long time ago. The word is *chaos*.

If struggling readers can't "say the words," they usually give up on reading. But giving up on reading, or writing for that matter, is not without its consequences.

Low Achievement

The expression *struggling reader* or *struggling writer* often refers to low-achieving students who have major difficulties with reading and writing. They lack fluency; have limited vocabulary knowledge; have trouble decoding polysyllabic words;

make little sense of what they read; have difficulty getting words down on paper and organizing their thoughts; and have little control over the mechanics of writing, such as spelling, punctuation, and grammar. Struggling readers and writers typically score low on proficiency tests and are tracked in basic classes for most of their academic lives. They usually become resistant learners.

How students achieve as readers and writers reflects such factors as motivation, self-concept, prior knowledge, and the ability to use language to learn. For some struggling students, reading and writing are painful reminders of a system of schooling that has failed them. The failure to learn to read and write effectively has contributed to these students' disenchantment with and alienation from school. Although struggling readers and writers may have developed some skills and strategies, they are often inappropriate for the demands inherent in potentially difficult texts. As a result, their participation in reading-related activities, such as writing or discussion, is marginal. Getting through text assignments to answer homework questions is often the only reason to read or write, if they read or write at all.

Learned Helplessness

Learned helplessness, an expression often associated with struggling readers and writers, refers to students' perceptions of themselves as being unable to overcome failure. They usually sabotage their efforts to read or write by believing that they can't succeed at tasks that require literate behavior. Their struggles with literacy tasks result from a lack of knowledge of and control over the strategic routines needed to engage in meaningful transactions with texts. Struggling readers and writers rarely take active roles in constructing meaning; they often remain passive and disengaged.

Not only do struggling readers and writers lack competence with the use of multiple strategies but they also lack confidence in themselves as literacy learners. As a result, they are often ambivalent about reading and writing and fail to appreciate what literacy can do for them. For one reason or another, learners who struggle with literacy tasks have alienated themselves from the world of print.

Low-achieving students may not be the only ones who struggle with content literacy tasks. Average and above-average students, who are usually on track to go to college, might also struggle with reading and writing without their teachers being cognizant of it. Often these students feel helpless about their ability to engage in literacy tasks, but go through the motions of "doing" school. Since 1992 periodic national assessments of reading and writing conducted by the National Center for Education Statistics (NCES) show that the majority of U.S. students in grades 4, 8, and 12 have obtained at least basic levels of literacy. These assessments, known as the National Assessment of Educational Progress (NAEP) surveys for reading (NAEP: Reading 2003) and for Writing (NAEP: Writing 2002) reveal that most students are capable of reading and writing but have difficulty with more complex literacy tasks. For example, they may be able to read with some degree of fluency and accuracy but might not know what to do with text beyond saying the words and comprehending at what is essentially a literal level of performance. In the classroom, these students may appear *skillful* in the mechanics of reading but aren't *strategic* enough in their abilities to handle reading tasks at the interpretive and applied levels of comprehension.

Moreover, student performance on various NAEP writing tasks suggests that the majority of today's students manage to just "get by" with academic writing tasks. Their writing, by and large, includes some supporting details, an organizational structure appropriate to the writing task, and reveals sufficient command of the mechanics of writing (spelling, grammar, punctuation, and capitalization). Yet it may lack audience awareness and sufficient elaboration to clarify and enhance the central idea of the writing. In addition, the majority of writers surveyed on NAEP: Writing 2002 did not demonstrate the ability to think analytically, critically, and creatively through their writing.

Students who struggle with literacy, regardless of ability level, often get lost in a maze of words as they sit down with a text assignment, write, or word process on a computer. The text doesn't make sense to them in ways that permit them to think deeply about ideas. Reading and writing are strategic acts, which is another way of saying that successful readers and writers use *cognitive and metacognitive* strategies to understand and compose text. Explicit instruction facilitates the development and use of these strategies.

Explicit Instruction in the Use of Strategies

Teaching reading and writing explicitly in content areas builds students' confidence as text learners as well as their competence in the use of literacy-related learning strategies. Explicit instruction shows students how to use literacy to think deeply about texts. Teaching reading and writing explicitly engages students in *metacognitive learning* in the use of literacy strategies.

Metacognition and Learning

Metacognition involves awareness of, knowledge about, regulation of, and ability to control one's own cognitive processes (Brown, Bransford, Ferrara, & Campione 1983; Flavell 1976, 1981). Simply, it is our ability to think about and control our own learning. As teachers, we have metacognition in our particular subject areas. Translating our metacognition into lessons that students understand is the hallmark of effective content area teaching. Science teachers, for example, have a metacognition of science. They have knowledge about themselves as scientists; they have knowledge of the tasks of science; and they have the ability to monitor and regulate themselves when conducting experiments, writing results, or reading technical material. Science teachers can monitor and regulate themselves because they know how to perform a set of core process strategies. They know how to observe, classify, compare, measure, describe, organize information, predict, infer, formulate hypotheses, interpret data, communicate, experiment, and draw conclusions. These are the same strategies a student taking a science course is expected to learn. A science teacher's job is to get students to think like scientists. The best way for students to learn to think like scientists is to learn to read, experiment, and write like scientists (L. Baker 1991).

Showing students how to think like scientists, historians, literary critics, mathematicians, health care professionals, artists, or auto mechanics puts them on the road to independent learning. Students need to know the whats, whys, hows, and whens of strategic reading and writing. They should know enough to be able to recognize the importance of (1) using multiple strategies, (2) analyzing the literacy task before them, (3) reflecting on what they know or don't know about the topic to be read or written about, and (4) devising plans for successfully completing the literacy task and for evaluating and checking their progress in accomplishing the task (Brown 1978).

Metacognition has two components. The first is metacognitive *knowledge;* the second is *regulation.* Metacognitive knowledge includes self-knowledge and task knowledge. Self-knowledge is the knowledge students have about themselves as learners. Task knowledge is the knowledge they have about the skills, strategies, and resources necessary for the performance of cognitive tasks. The second component, self-regulation, involves the ability to monitor and regulate the reading and writing process through strategies and attitudes that capitalize on metacognitive knowledge (Baker & Brown 1984). Self- and task knowledge and self-regulation are interrelated concepts. The former are prerequisites for the latter. Together, self-knowledge, task knowledge, and self-regulation help explain how readers and writers can begin to assume responsibility for their own learning.

Self- and Task Knowledge

Teachers need to know if students know enough about their own reading and writing strategies to approach content area text assignments flexibly and adaptively. Different text assignments, for example, may pose different problems for readers to solve. For this reason, when they are assigned text material, students must be aware of the nature of the reading task and how to handle it. Is the student sophisticated enough to ask questions about the reading task? To make plans for reading? To use and adapt strategies to meet the demands of the text assignment? Or does a student who struggles with text approach every text assignment in the same manner—plowing through with little notion of why, when, or how to read the material? Plowing through cumbersome text material only once is more than students who struggle with reading can cope with. The prospect of rereading or reviewing isn't a realistic option for them. However, teachers are in a position to show students that working with the material doesn't necessarily entail the agony of slow, tedious reading.

Self-Regulation and Monitoring

To be in control of reading and writing, students must know what to do when they have trouble. This is what comprehension monitoring and self-regulation are all about. Do students have a repertoire of strategies within reach to get out of trouble if they become confused or get off track when they are reading or writing?

Linda Baker (1991) recommends six questions for students to ask themselves when they read to help monitor their comprehension:

1. Are there any words I don't understand?
2. Is there any information that doesn't agree with what I already know?
3. Are there any ideas that don't fit together because I can't tell who or what is being talked about?
4. Are there any ideas that don't fit together because I can't tell how the ideas are related?
5. Are there any ideas that don't fit together because I think the ideas are contradictory?
6. Is there any information missing or not clearly explained? (p. 10)

Strategy Instruction

Strategy instruction helps students who struggle with text become aware of, use, and develop control over learning strategies (Brown & Palincsar 1984). Explicit teaching provides an alternative to "blind" instruction. In blind instructional situations, students are taught what to do, but this is where instruction usually ends. Although directed to make use of a set of procedures that will improve reading and studying, students seldom grasp the rationale or payoff underlying a particular strategy. As a result, they attempt to use the strategy with little basis for evaluating its success or monitoring its effectiveness. Explicit instruction, however, attempts not only to show students *what* to do but also *why, how,* and *when.* Pearson (1982) concludes that such instruction helps "students develop independent strategies for coping with the kinds of comprehension problems they are asked to solve in their lives in schools" (p. 22).

Strategy instruction has several components: *assessment, explanation and awareness, modeling and demonstration, guided practice,* and *application.* By way of analogy, teaching students to be strategic readers provides experiences similar to those needed by athletes who are in training. To perform well with texts, students must understand the rules, work on technique, and practice. A coach (the teacher) is needed to provide feedback, guide, inspire, and share the knowledge and experiences that she or he possesses.

Assess What Students Know How to Do

The assessment component of strategy instruction is tryout time. It gives the teacher an opportunity to determine the degree of knowledge the students have about a strategy under discussion. Moreover, assessment yields insight into how well the students use a strategy to handle a reading task. For these reasons, assessing the use of a strategy should occur in as natural a context as possible. Assessment can usually be accomplished within a single class period if these steps are followed:

1. *Assign students a text passage of approximately 500 to 1,500 words.* The selection should take most students ten to fifteen minutes to read.

2. *Direct students to use a particular strategy.* For example, suppose the strategy involves writing a summary of a text selection. Simply ask students to do the things they normally do when they read a passage and then write a summary of it. Allow adequate time to complete the task.

3. *Observe the use of the strategy.* Note what students do. Do they underline or mark important ideas as they read? Do they appear to skim the material first to get a general idea of what to expect? What do they do when they begin actually constructing the summary?

4. *Ask students to respond in writing to several key questions about the use of the strategy.* For example, What did you do to summarize the passage? What did you do to find the main ideas? Did you find summarizing easy or difficult? Why?

Create Strategy Awareness and Explain Procedures

Assessment is a springboard to making students aware of the *why* and *how* of a study strategy. During the awareness step, a give-and-take exchange of ideas takes place between teacher and students. As a result, students should recognize the *rationale* and *process* behind the use of a strategy. To make students more aware of a learning strategy, consider the following activities:

1. *Discuss the assessment.* Use your observations and students' reflective responses to the written questions.

2. *Set the stage by leading a discussion of why the strategy is useful.* What is the payoff for students? How does it improve learning?

3. *Engage in activities that define the rules, guidelines, or procedures for being successful with the strategy.*

4. *Have students experience using the strategy.* They can practice the rules or procedures on a short selection from the textbook.

Awareness and explanation provide students with a clear picture of the learning strategy. The *why* and *how* are solidly introduced, and the road has been paved for more intensive modeling and demonstration of the strategy.

BOX 3.2

What about . . .
Content Standards and Assessment?

One way to help struggling readers self-assess and think about what they do when they read is to have them take the Metacognitive Reading Awareness Inventory (Miholic 1994). Correct responses to each item on the inventory are marked with a +, whereas "incorrect" responses are marked with a –. Teachers who use the inventory with a class should be sure to cover the + and – row. Not only does the inventory pique students' curiosity about strategic learning but it also gives them a concrete idea of important strategies.

   When struggling writers have difficulty, the teacher is in a strategic position instructionally to ask problem-solving questions that will help them monitor the writing process. These questions should model what a skilled writer—for example, the teacher—does to resolve problems related to different aspects of the writing or the process itself. These questions can help students to think about the nature of the writing task or focus on specific problems that students are having with their writing. Questions may center on the *purpose* of the writing, *content, organization, audience awareness*, or *language* and *style* issues: Where is my writing headed? Am I trying to do too much or too little? Will the reader of my writing be able to visualize the subject? Are there parts in my writing that are confusing? Are my main points in order? Is my paper interesting and readable? Is my "voice" and personality in the writing? As we will see later in the chapter, other instructional strategies, including teacher-led and peer-led conferences and response groups, are useful in showing students how to control and monitor their writing.

METACOGNITIVE READING AWARENESS INVENTORY

There's more than one way to cope when you run into difficulties in your reading. Which ways are best? Under each question here, put a checkmark beside *all* the responses you think are effective.

1. What do you do if you encounter a word and you don't know what it means?
 + a. Use the words around it to figure it out.
 + b. Use an outside source, such as a dictionary or expert.
 + c. Temporarily ignore it and wait for clarification.
 – d. Sound it out.

2. What do you do if you don't know what an entire sentence means?
 + a. Read it again.
 – b. Sound out all the difficult words.
 + c. Think about the other sentences in the paragraph.
 – d. Disregard it completely.

3. If you are reading science or social studies material, what would you do to remember the important information you've read?
 – a. Skip parts you don't understand.
 + b. Ask yourself questions about the important ideas.
 + c. Realize you need to remember one point rather than another.
 + d. Relate it to something you already know.

4. Before you start to read, what kind of plans do you make to help you read better?

− a. No specific plan is needed; just start reading toward completion of the assignment.

+ b. Think about what you know about the subject.

+ c. Think about why you are reading.

− d. Make sure the entire reading can be finished in as short a period of time as possible.

5. Why would you go back and read an entire passage over again?

+ a. You didn't understand it.

− b. To clarify a specific or supporting idea.

+ c. It seemed important to remember.

+ d. To underline or summarize for study.

6. Knowing that you don't understand a particular sentence while reading involves understanding that

+ a. the reader may not have developed adequate links or associations for new words or concepts introduced in the sentence.

+ b. the writer may not have conveyed the ideas clearly.

+ c. two sentences may purposely contradict each other.

− d. finding meaning for the sentence needlessly slows down the reader.

7. As you read a textbook, which of these do you do?

+ a. Adjust your pace depending on the difficulty of the material.

− b. Generally, read at a constant, steady pace.

− c. Skip the parts you don't understand.

+ d. Continually make predictions about what you are reading.

8. While you read, which of these are important?

+ a. Know when you know and when you don't know key ideas.

+ b. Know what it is that you know in relation to what is being read.

− c. Know that confusing text is common and usually can be ignored.

+ d. Know that different strategies can be used to aid understanding.

9. When you come across a part of the text that is confusing, what do you do?

+ a. Keep on reading until the text is clarified.

+ b. Read ahead and then look back if the text is still unclear.

− c. Skip those sections completely; they are usually not important.

+ d. Check to see if the ideas expressed are consistent with one another.

10. Which sentences are the most important in the chapter?

− a. Almost all of the sentences are important; otherwise, they wouldn't be there.

+ b. The sentences that contain the important details or facts.

+ c. The sentences that are directly related to the main idea.

− d. The ones that contain the most details.

Source: From Vincent Miholic, "An Inventory to Pique Students' Metacognitive Awareness" (1994). *Journal of Reading, 38*(2), 84–86. Reprinted with permission of the author and the International Reading Association.

Model and Demonstrate Strategies

Once the *why* and a beginning sense of the *how* are established, the students should receive careful follow-up in the use of the strategy. Follow-up sessions are characterized by demonstration through teacher modeling, explanations, practice, reinforcement of the rules or procedures, and more practice. The students progress from easy to harder practice situations and from shorter to longer text selections. The following activities are recommended:

1. *Use an overhead transparency to review the steps students should follow.*

2. *Demonstrate the strategy.* Walk students through the steps. Provide explanations. Raise questions about the procedures.

3. *As part of a demonstration, initiate a* think-aloud *procedure to model how to use the strategy.* By thinking aloud, the teacher shares with the students the thinking processes he or she uses in applying the strategy. Thinking aloud is often accomplished by reading a passage out loud and stopping at key points in the text to ask questions or provide prompts. The questions and prompts mirror the critical thinking required to apply the strategy. Once students are familiar with the think-aloud procedure, encourage them to demonstrate and use it during practice sessions. Later in the chapter we explain in more detail the role that think-alouds play in modeling strategies.

Provide Guided Practice

Use trial runs with short selections from the textbook. Debrief the students with questions after each trial run: Did they follow the steps? How successful were they? What caused them difficulty? Have them make learning-log entries. Often, a short quiz following a trial run shows students how much they learned and remembered as a result of using the study strategy.

The practice sessions are designed to provide experience with the strategy. Students should reach a point where they have internalized the steps and feel in control of the strategy.

Apply Strategies

The preceding components of strategy instruction should provide enough practice for students to know *why, how,* and *when* to use the study strategies that have been targeted by the teacher for emphasis. Once students have made generalizations about strategy use, regular class assignments should encourage its application. Rather than assign for homework a text selection accompanied by questions to be answered, frame the assignment so that students will have to apply the strategies they are learning.

e.Resources

Review the text comprehension findings of the "National Reading Panel" by going to the Companion Website and clicking on Professional Resources.

In the next section, we explain several research-based instructional practices that create frameworks for explicit instruction in the use of text comprehension strategies (Report of the National Reading Panel 2000). Throughout this book, other instructional practices will be developed in the use of text learning strategies for vocabulary, comprehension, discussion, writing, and study.

Strategic Reading

Readers who struggle with texts are usually unaware of strategies that will help them construct meaning. Teachers can use *think-alouds, reciprocal teaching,* and *question–answer relationships* (QARs) to scaffold students' use of comprehension strategies.

> **Response Journal**
>
> Think-alouds, QARs, and reciprocal teaching are research-based instructional practices. Educators often describe a research-based instructional practice as a "best practice." What does the term *best practice* mean to you?

Using Think-Alouds to Model Comprehension Strategies

In think-alouds, teachers make their thinking explicit by verbalizing their thoughts while reading orally. Davey (1983) explains that this process helps readers clarify their understanding of reading and their understanding of how to use strategies. Students will more clearly understand the strategies after a teacher uses think-alouds, because they can see how a mind actively responds to thinking through trouble spots and constructing meaning from the text.

Davey (1983) suggests five basic steps when using think-alouds. First, select passages to read aloud that contain points of difficulty, ambiguities, contradictions, or unknown words. Second, while orally reading and modeling thinking aloud, have students follow silently and listen to how trouble spots are thought through. Third, have students work with partners to practice think-alouds by taking turns reading short, carefully prepared passages and sharing thoughts. Fourth, have students practice independently. Use a checklist similar to the one shown in Figure 3.2 to involve all students while verifying use of the procedures. Finally, to encourage transfer, integrate practice with other lessons and provide occasional demonstrations of how, why, and when to use think-alouds. Five points can be made during think-alouds:

1. *Students should develop hypotheses by making predictions.*

2. *Students should develop images by describing pictures forming in their heads from the information being read.*

3. *Students should link new information with prior knowledge by sharing analogies.*

4. *Students should monitor comprehension by verbalizing a confusing point.*

5. *Students should regulate comprehension by demonstrating strategies.*

Let's look at how each of these points can be modeled in a middle school earth science class.

FIGURE 3.2   Checklist for Self-Evaluation of Think-Alouds

While I was reading, how did I do? (Put an X in the appropriate column.)

	Not very much	A little bit	Much of the time	All of the time
Made predictions	_____	_____	_____	_____
Formed pictures	_____	_____	_____	_____
Used "like-a"	_____	_____	_____	_____
Found problems	_____	_____	_____	_____
Used fix-ups	_____	_____	_____	_____

Source: From Beth Davey, "Think Aloud—Modeling the Cognitive Processes of Reading Comprehension" (1983, October). *Journal of Reading, 27*(1), 44–47. Copyright © 1983 by the International Reading Association. All rights reserved. Used by permission of the International Reading Association.

Develop Hypotheses by Making Predictions

Teachers might model how to develop hypotheses by making predictions from the title of a chapter or from subheadings within the chapter. Suppose you were teaching with an earth science text. You might say, "From the heading 'How Minerals Are Used,' I predict that this section will tell about things that are made out of different minerals." The text continues:

Some of the most valuable minerals are found in ores. An **ore** is a mineral resource mined for profit. For example, bauxite (BAWK-sight) is an ore from which aluminum is taken. Iron is obtained from the ore called hematite (HEE-muh-tight). Bauxite and hematite are metallic minerals.

Metallic minerals are metals or ores of metals. Gold, iron, and aluminum are examples of metals. Metals are important because of their many useful properties.

One useful property of many metals is malleability (mal-ee-uh-BIL-uh-tee). **Malleability** is the ability to be hammered without breaking. Malleability allows a metal to be hammered into thin sheets.

Develop Images

To model how to develop imaging, at this point you might stop and say, "I have a picture in my head from a scene I saw in a movie about the Old West. I see a blacksmith pumping bellows in a forge to heat up an iron horseshoe. When the iron turns a reddish orange, he picks it up with his tongs, and he hammers. The sparks fly, but slowly the horseshoe changes shape to fit the horse's hoof." The text continues:

Another property of many metals is ductility (duk-TIL-uh-tee). **Ductility** is the ability to be pulled and stretched without breaking. This property allows a metal to be pulled into thin wires.

Share Analogies

To model how to link new information with prior knowledge, you might share the following analogies. "This is like a time when I tried to eat a piece of pizza with extra cheese. Every time I took a bite, the cheese kept stretching and stretching into these long strings. It is also like a time when I went to the county fair and watched people make taffy. They got this glob of candy and put it on a machine that just kept pulling and stretching the taffy, but it never broke." The text continues:

> Metals share other properties as well. All metals conduct heat and electricity. Electrical appliances and machines need metals to conduct electricity. In addition, all metals have a shiny, metallic luster.

Monitor Comprehension

To model how to monitor comprehension, you can verbalize a confusing point: "This is telling me that metals have a metallic luster. I don't know what that is. I'm also confused because I thought this section was going to be about things that are made out of different minerals. This is different from what I expected."

Regulate Comprehension

To model how to correct lagging comprehension, you can demonstrate a strategy: "I'm confused about what *metallic luster* means, and I don't know why the authors are talking about this when I expected them to talk about stuff made out of minerals. Maybe if I ignore the term *metallic luster* and keep on reading, I'll be able to make some connections to what I expected and figure it all out." The text continues:

> Very shiny metals, like chromium, are often used for decorative purposes. Many metals are also strong. Titanium (tigh-TAY-nee-um), magnesium (mag-NEE-zee-um), and aluminum are metals that are both strong and lightweight. These properties make them ideal building materials for jet planes and spacecraft.

"Oh, they're talking about properties of metals that make them especially good for making certain things, like aluminum for jets because it is strong and lightweight. Now I understand why they're talking about properties. I'll bet chrome and chromium are just about the same, because I know chrome is the shiny stuff on cars. I think *metallic luster* must mean something like shiny because chromium reminds me of chrome."

Think-alouds are best used at the beginning of lessons to help students learn the whats and hows of constructing meaning with text. The next teaching strategy, *reciprocal teaching,* is an excellent follow-up to think-alouds. Reciprocal teaching helps students learn how to apply the strategy learned during a think-aloud so that they can understand the author's message.

Using Reciprocal Teaching to Model Comprehension Strategies

When using reciprocal teaching, you model how to use four comprehension activities (generating questions, summarizing, predicting, and clarifying) while leading a dialogue (Palinscar & Brown 1984). Then students take turns assuming the teacher's role. A key to the effectiveness of this strategy is adjusting the task demand to support the students when difficulty occurs. That is, when students experience difficulty, you provide assistance by lowering the demands of the task. As the process goes on, you slowly withdraw support so that students continue learning. When planning a reciprocal teaching lesson, there are two phases. The first phase has five steps:

1. *Find text selections that demonstrate the four comprehension activities.*

2. *Generate appropriate questions.*

3. *Generate predictions about each selection.*

4. *Locate summarizing sentences and develop summaries for each selection.*

5. *Note difficult vocabulary and concepts.*

In the second phase, decisions are made about which comprehension activities to teach, based on the students' needs. It also helps determine students' present facility with the activities so that you are prepared to give needed support during the process. Once students are familiar with more than one strategy, reciprocal teaching can be used to model the decision-making process about which strategy to use.

Using Question–Answer Relationships (QARs) to Model Comprehension Strategies

In Chapter 1, we highlighted the importance of prior knowledge in text comprehension as well as the match between the types of questions asked and levels of comprehension. As an instructional practice, question–answer relationships (QARs) make explicit to students the relationships that exist among the type of question asked, the text, and the reader's prior knowledge. In the process of teaching QARs, you help students become aware of and skilled in using learning strategies to find the information they need to comprehend at different levels of response to the text (Raphael 1982, 1984, 1986).

The procedures for learning QARs can be taught directly to students by reading teachers and can be reinforced by content area specialists. Keep in mind, however, that students may come to your class totally unaware of what information sources are available for seeking an answer, or they may not know when to use different sources. In this case, it is worth several days' effort to teach students the relationship between questions and answers. It may take up to three days to show students how to identify the information sources necessary to answer questions. The following steps, which we have adapted for content area situations, are suggested for teaching QARs:

1. *Introduce the concept of QARs.* Show students a chart or an overhead transparency containing a description of the four basic question–answer relationships. (We recommend a chart that can be positioned in a prominent place in the classroom. Students may then refer to it throughout the content area lessons.) Point out the two broad categories of information sources: "In the text" and "In your head." Figure 3.3 is adapted from a chart recommended by Raphael (1986).

2. *Begin by assigning students several short passages from the textbook.* (These should be no more than two to five sentences in length.) Follow each reading with one question from each of the QAR categories on the chart. Then discuss the differences between a "right there" question and answer, a "think and search" question and answer, an "on your own" question and answer, and an "author and you" question and answer. Your explanations should be clear and complete. Reinforce the discussion by assigning several more short text passages and asking a question for each. Students will soon begin to catch on to the differences among the four QAR categories.

3. *Continue the second day by practicing with short passages.* Use one question for each QAR category per passage. First, give students a passage to read along with questions *and* answers *and* identified QARs. Why do the questions and answers represent one QAR and not another? Second, give students a passage along with questions and answers; this time they have to identify the QAR for each. Finally, give students passages, decide together which strategy to use, and have them write their responses.

4. *Review briefly on the third day.* Then assign a longer passage (75 to 200 words) with up to six questions (at least one each from the four QAR categories). First, have students work in groups to decide the QAR category for each question and the answers for each. Next, assign a second passage, comparable in length, with five questions for students to work on individually. Discuss their responses either in small groups or with the whole class. You may wish to work with several class members or colleagues to complete the QAR activity in Box 3.3. It was developed by a high school English teacher as part of a short story unit.

5. *Apply the QAR strategy to actual content area assignments.* For each question asked, students decide on the appropriate QAR strategy and write out their answers.

FIGURE 3.3 **Introducing QARs**

Where Are Answers to Questions Found?

In the Text:

Right There

The answer is in the text. The words used in the question and the words used for the answer can usually be found in the same sentences.

Think and Search

The answer is in the text, but the words used in the question and those used for the answer are not in the same sentence. You need to think about different parts of the text and how ideas can be put together before you can answer the question.

In Your Head:

Author and You

The answer is not in the text. You need to think about what you know, what the author says, and how they fit together.

On Your Own

The text got you thinking, but the answer is inside your head. The author can't help you much. So think about it, and use what you know already about the question.

Source: Adapted from T. E. Raphael (1986). "Teaching question-answer relationships." *Reading Teacher, 39,* 516–520.

RESEARCH-BASED BEST PRACTICES

BOX 3.3

QAR Awareness in a High School English Class

A high school English teacher develops students' awareness of QARs with the following guided practice activity. The teacher selects an excerpt from Richard Wilbur's *A Game of Catch* and asks students to answer a set of questions about the excerpt. The students are also asked to identify the QAR associated with each question.

"Got your glove?" asked Glennie after a time. Scho obviously hadn't.

"You could give me some easy grounders," said Scho. "But don't burn 'em."

"All right," Glennie said. He moved off a little, so the three of them formed a triangle, and they passed the ball around for about five minutes, Monk tossing easy grounders to Scho, Scho throwing to Glennie, and Glennie burning them into Monk. After a while, Monk began to throw them back to Glennie once or twice before he let Scho have his grounder, and finally Monk gave Scho a fast, bumpy grounder that hopped over his shoulder and went into the brake on the other side of the street.

"Not so hard," called Scho as he ran across to get it.

"You should've had it," Monk shouted.

It took Scho a little while to find the ball among the ferns and dead leaves, and when he saw it, he grabbed it up and threw it toward Glennie. It struck the trunk of the apple tree, bounced back at an angle, and rolled steadily and stupidly onto the cement apron in front of the firehouse, where one of the trucks was parked. Scho ran hard and stopped it just before it rolled under the truck, and this time he carried it back to his former position on the lawn and threw it carefully to Glennie. (*From "A Game of Catch," copyright 1953 by Richard Wilbur. Reprinted by permission of Harcourt, Inc. Originally appeared in* The New Yorker, *1953.*)

1. *Question:* What are the three boys doing?

   Answer: _____

   QAR: _____

2. *Question:* Why did Monk throw the ball so hard to Scho?

   Answer: _____

   QAR: _____

3. *Question:* Who was throwing the ball to Monk?

   Answer: _____

   QAR: _____

4. *Question:* How would you describe Scho's throwing ability?

   Answer: _____

   QAR: _____

5. *Question:* How would you characterize Monk?

   Answer: _____

   QAR: _____

6. *Question:* Why do friends sometimes get frustrated with one another?

   Answer: _____

   QAR: _____

Once students are sensitive to the different information sources for different types of questions and know how to use these sources to respond to questions, variations can be made in the QAR strategy. For example, you might have students generate their own questions to text assignments—perhaps two for each QAR strategy. They then write down the answers to the questions as they understand them, except that they leave one question unanswered from the "think and search" category and one from the "on your own" or "author and you" category. These are questions about which the student would like to hear the views of others. During the discussion, students volunteer to ask their unanswered questions. The class is invited first to identify the question by QAR category and then to contribute answers, comments, or related questions about the material.

A second variation involves discussions of text. During question-and-answer exchanges, preface a question by saying, "This question is *right there* in the text," or "You'll have to *think and search* the text to answer," or "You're *on your own* with this one," or "The answer is a combination of the *author and you.* Think about what the author tells us and what we already know to try and come up with a reasonable response." Make sure that you pause several seconds or more for "think time." Think time, or "wait time," is critical to responding to textually implicit and schema-based questions. Gambrell (1980) found that increasing think time to five seconds or longer increases the length of student responses as well as the quality of their speculative thinking.

Once students are familiar with QARs, they can be used in combination with a variety of interactive strategies that encourage readers to explore ideas through text discussions.

Modeling comprehension strategies through think-alouds, reciprocal teaching, and QARs provides the instructional support that will help students do more than simply read the words on a page. These procedures scaffold students' use of strategies that will help them read texts in a more thoughtful and thought-provoking manner.

Another dimension of strategy instruction involves showing students how to think strategically about the writing process as they engage in content area activities that culminate in finished written products. Strategic instruction helps struggling writers to develop "ownership" as they work collaboratively with the teacher and other students to solve problems that they are experiencing during the various stages of writing (Collins 1997).

Strategic Writing

One of the teacher's first instructional tasks is to make students aware that the writing process occurs in stages (Kirby, Liner, & Vinz 1988). It's the rare writer who leaps in a single bound from an idea-in-head to a finished product on paper. In this book, writing strategies are defined broadly within stages of writing. The stages may be defined broadly as *discovery, drafting,* and *revising* (Maxwell 1995). Table 3.1 presents an overview of these stages.

TABLE 3.1	Stages in the Writing Process

Discovery

- Exploring and generating ideas
- Finding a topic
- Making plans (Audience? Form? Voice?)
- Getting started

Drafting

- Getting ideas down on paper
- Sticking to the task
- Developing fluency and coherence

Revising

- Revising for meaning
- Responding to the writing
- Organizing for clarity
- Editing and proofreading for the conventions of writing, word choice, syntax
- Polishing

Within each of these stages, there are strategies at the command of writers that they can use to facilitate the process. As teachers, we can make struggling writers aware of these strategies, demonstrate how to use them, and provide students with guided practice in their use. There is a catch, however. Strategic writing instruction is not as simple as "giving" strategies to students (Collins 1997). Learning to write strategically involves a transaction between teacher and student, not a transmission from teacher to student. Students who struggle with writing must construct writing strategies that will work for them as they confront real problems in real writing situations. This is best facilitated under the watchful eye and coaching of the teacher. If this is the case, then, students will need time to write in class—and they must write often—for strategy instruction to make a difference in their control of the writing process.

As we make instruction explicit in the use of writing strategies, keep in mind that the stages in the writing process are by no means neat and orderly. Few writers proceed from stage to stage in a linear sequence. Instead, writing is a *recursive* process; that is to say, writing is a back-and-forth activity. As teachers we want to engage students in the use of discovery strategies to explore and generate ideas and

e.Resources

Read a chapter excerpt from James Collins's book *Strategies for Struggling Writers* by going to the Companion Website, clicking on Professional Resources, and selecting "Struggling Writers."

make plans before writing a draft, but once they are engaged in the physical act of composing a draft, writers often discover new ideas, reformulate plans, rewrite, and revise.

The Discovery Stage: Generating Ideas, Planning, and Organizing

What students do before writing is as important as what they do before reading. Discovery strategies involve planning, building and activating prior knowledge, setting goals, and getting ready for the task at hand. In other words, discovery refers to everything that students do before putting words on paper for a first draft. The term *prewriting* is often used interchangeably with *discovery,* but it is somewhat misleading because students often engage in some form of writing before working on a draft.

Response Journal

What kinds of discovery strategies do you use to get started with an important writing assignment?

Discovery is what the writer consciously or unconsciously does to get energized—to get ideas out in the open, to explore what to say and how to say it: What will I include? What's a good way to start? Who is my audience? What form should my writing take? Scaffolding the use of discovery strategies in a classroom involves any support activity or experience that motivates a student to write, generates ideas for writing, or focuses attention on a particular subject. Students can be guided to think about a topic in relation to a perceived audience and the form that a piece of writing will take. A teacher who recognizes that the writing process must slow down at the beginning will help students discover that they have something to say and that they want to say it.

Getting started on the right foot is what the discovery stage is all about. Generating talk about an assignment before writing buys time for students to gather ideas and organize them for writing. Discussion before writing is as crucial to success as discussion before reading. In preparing seniors to write letters to the editor concerning the legal age for drinking in Ohio, the teacher of a course called "Problems in Democracy" asked students for their opinions: "At what age do you think people in Ohio should be permitted to drink alcoholic beverages?" The discussion among the senior students, as you might anticipate, was animated. The teacher followed the discussion with an assignment of a newspaper article on the legal age issue. Further discussion generated more ideas and helped students formulate a stand on the issue. In addition to talk, several strategies that will help students make discoveries for writing by gathering and organizing ideas include *brainstorming, clustering,* and *concept matrix charting.*

Brainstorming

Brainstorming permits students to explore and examine ideas as a quick way to get started for writing. It helps them set purposes for writing because it gives students problems to solve. Examine how the following two variations on brainstorming can be easily adapted to writing situations:

1. Present a concept or problem to students based on some aspect of what they have been studying. Set a time limit for brainstorming ideas or solutions. The teacher calls, "Stop," but allows *one more minute* for thinking to continue. Creative ideas are often produced under time pressure.

In a high school special education class for students with learning problems, several weeks had been spent on a unit dealing with the Civil War era. As part of their study of the Reconstruction period, students explored issues such as the rebuilding of the South and the dilemma presented by the freed slaves. One of the culminating learning experiences for the chapter on freed slaves concerned a writing activity designed to help students synthesize some of the important ideas that they had studied. As part of her introduction to the writing assignment, the teacher began the discovery phase of the lesson with a lead-in: "Using any information that you can recall from your text or class discussion, think about what might have been some of the problems or concerns of a freed slave immediately following the Civil War. Let's do some brainstorming." As the students offered ideas related to prejudice and lack of money, homes, and food, the teacher listed them on the board. Getting ideas out in the open in this manner was the first step in the discovery strategy. (In the next subsection, on clustering, we discuss how the teacher used brainstorming as a stepping stone for students to organize ideas and make decisions about the writing assignment.)

2. Engage students in "brainwriting" (Rodrigues 1983). Here's how it works. Divide the class into cooperative groups of four or five students. Each group member is directed to jot down ideas about the writing assignment's topic on a sheet of paper. Each student then places his or her paper in the center of the group, chooses another's list of ideas, and adds to it. The group compiles the best ideas into a single list and shares them with the class. Two advantages of brainwriting are that every student contributes and there is time given to consider ideas.

Brainstorming techniques allow students to become familiar with a topic and, therefore, to approach writing with purpose and confidence. Often teachers combine brainstorming with another discovery strategy: clustering.

Clustering

To introduce the concept of clustering, write a keyword on the chalkboard and then surround it with other associated words offered by the students. In this way, students learn not only how to gather ideas for writing but also how to connect the ideas within categories of information. Teacher-led clustering provides students with an awareness of how to use clustering as a writing strategy. Once they are aware of how to cluster their ideas around a topic, students should be encouraged to create their own clusters for writing. Box 3.4 provides steps in the clustering strategy for students to follow.

In our discussion of brainstorming, we described how a special education teacher used the list of ideas generated by her students to explore the concerns

RESEARCH-BASED BEST PRACTICES

BOX 3.4

How Clustering Works

(Nucleus word)

Student Directions:

1. Choose a nucleus word and circle it on a blank sheet of paper.

2. Cluster, circling each new thought and connecting it. Cluster quickly and freely until you have exhausted a line of thought.

3. When a different line of thought strikes you, start again at the nucleus and con-

tinue until those connections are exhausted.

4. Cluster until you feel a sense of direction or purpose. This often happens within two or three minutes.

5. Write spontaneously as soon as you finish clustering. The length can range from a few sentences to a page.

of freed slaves during the post–Civil War period. This was a first step in the rehearsal phase of the writing activity. The second step was to cluster the words into meaningful associations based on student suggestions. The teacher modeled the activity by choosing as the keyword the concept of *freed slaves.* She then drew a line to the upper right corner of the chalkboard and connected the keyword to the word *problems.* She connected some of the words generated by students during brainstorming to the cluster. The teacher then asked what some of the results of the freed slaves' problems would be. One student volunteered the word *suffering.* The teacher wrote *suffering* in the upper left corner of the cluster and asked the students to brainstorm some examples. These examples were then connected to the cluster.

The remainder of the clustering session centered on discussion related to the *aid* freed slaves received and the *opportunities* that resulted from the Reconstruction years. Figure 3.4 depicts the completed cluster that the teacher and students produced on the chalkboard.

With the cluster as a frame of reference, the students were assigned to write what it would have been like to be a freed slave in the 1860s and 1870s. They were asked to consider what the form of the writing should be. Because the textbook presented a variety of primary sources (including diary entries, newspaper clippings, and death notices), the students could, if they wanted, write in one of those forms. Or they could approach the writing activity as a historian would and write an account that might be read by other students as a secondary source of information.

FIGURE **3.4**   **Free Slaves Immediately after Civil War**

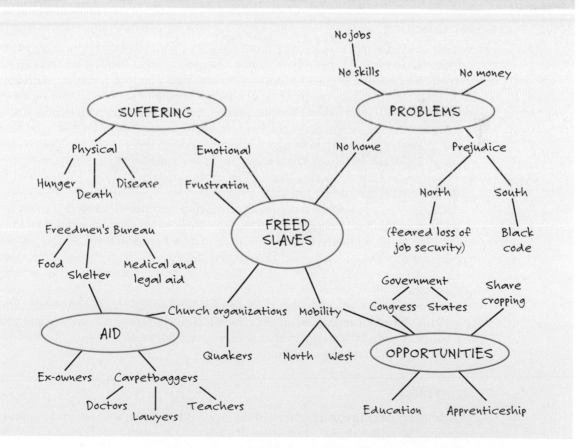

Students should begin to develop their own clusters for writing as soon as they understand how to use the strategy effectively. They should feel comfortable enough to start with a basic concept or topic—written in the center of a sheet of paper—and then to let go by making as many connections as possible on the paper. Connections should develop rapidly, "radiating outward from the center in any direction they want to go" (Rico 1983, p. 35). Because there is no right or wrong way to develop a cluster, students should be encouraged to play with ideas based on what they are studying and learning in class.

The value of clustering in writing shouldn't be sold short. Gabriele Rico (1983), a leading proponent of this discovery strategy, maintained that it not only "unblocks and releases" information stored in the student writer's mind but that it also generates inspiration for writing. Moreover, clustering becomes a self-organizing process. According to Rico (1983), "As you spill out seemingly random words and phrases around a center, you will be surprised to see patterns forming until a moment comes—characterized by an 'Aha!' feeling—when you suddenly sense a focus for writing" (p. 35). Students can discuss their clusters in small groups and share their plans for writing. Or, as Rico recommended, they can begin to write immediately after clustering.

Jot-Charting

Similar to clustering, jot-charting provides a way for students to organize information. However, it doesn't rely on freely associating ideas to a key concept word. Instead, jot-charting helps students to collect and connect ideas by outlining them on a matrix. The strategy is especially appropriate for writing that relies on explanation and description of ideas, people, events, characters, or processes.

Across the top of the matrix, list some of the main ideas that are to be analyzed or described in the writing assignment. Along the side of the matrix, list some of the areas by which these ideas are to be considered. Students complete the chart by jotting notes and ideas from course material, class lectures, and so on in the spaces created by the matrix.

A language arts teacher used jot-charting as a planning tool for a writing activity that compared famous heroes from the stories that the class had read. The activity directed students to write about how the heroes (David, Hercules, Beowulf) approached and handled challenges. The jot-chart in Figure 3.5 helped students to reread selectively and to take notes in preparation for the writing assignment.

Students in the language arts class discussed their jot-charts before engaging in writing. Jot-charting can be an effective outlining strategy for writing and also has value as a study strategy in that it provides a framework on which students can organize and relate information.

Drafting

The drafting stage involves getting ideas down on paper in a fluent and coherent fashion. The writer drafts a text with an audience (readers) in mind.

FIGURE **3.5**	**Jot-Chart for "Stories about Heroes"**

	David	Hercules	Beowulf
Each hero's feelings when confronted with his challenge			
How did each hero handle his challenge?			
How did each hero react after conquering his challenge?			

If students are primed for writing through discovery strategies, first drafts should develop without undue struggle. The use of in-class time for drafting is as important as alotting in-class time for reading. In both cases, teachers can regulate and monitor the process much more effectively. For example, while students are writing, a teacher's time shouldn't be occupied grading papers or attending to other unrelated chores. Teachers can do much to influence the quality of writing and learning *as* students are writing:

> When students are writing during class time, the teacher can take an active role. For example, monitor facial expressions—they often tell when a student is starting to get in a jam and needs help. Float around the class during a writing assignment, glancing at first paragraphs and rough beginnings, offering advice if it seems needed—in other words, help students get it right *while* they are writing and encourage them to solve problems the first time around. (Tchudi & Yates 1983, pp. 12–17)

The drafting stage, then, should be a time to confer individually with students who are having trouble using what they know to tackle the writing task. Serve as a sounding board or play devil's advocate: "How does what we studied in class for the past few days relate to your topic?" or "I don't quite understand what you're getting at. Let's talk about what you're trying to say." Students should also have the opportunity to confer with one another: "There are great benefits from such forms of peer collaboration as encouraging writers to bounce ideas off one another, reading draft paragraphs aloud to seek advice, pumping their friends for new advice" (Tchudi & Yates 1983, p. 17). Teacher feedback and peer collaboration underscore the importance of *response* in the writing process.

Revising

Revising a text is hard work. Struggling writers often think that *rewriting* is a dirty word. They mistake it for recopying—emphasizing neatness as they painstakingly transcribe from pencil to ink. They need to recognize that revising strategies help them to "take another look"—to rethink a paper. This is why good writing often reflects good rewriting. From a content area learning perspective, rewriting is the catalyst for clarifying and extending concepts under study. Revising text hinges on the feedback students receive between first and second drafts.

Response Journal

When you write a draft of an academic writing assignment, do you seek feedback before revising it? If not, why not? As a skilled writer, do you need feedback from a peer or an instructor?

Teacher feedback is always important, but it's often too demanding and time consuming to be the sole vehicle for response. It may also lack the *immediacy* that student writers need to "try out" their ideas on an audience—especially if teachers are accustomed to taking home a stack of papers and writing comments on each one. The "paper load" soon becomes unmanageable and self-defeating. An alternative is to have students respond to the writing of other students. By working together in "response groups," students can give reactions, ask questions, and make suggestions to their peers. These responses to writing-in-progress lead to revision and refinement during rewriting.

Student Response Groups

The purpose of peer response groups is to provide a testing ground for students to see how their writing influences a group of readers. Writers need response to sense the kinds of changes they need to make.

There's an important difference between *response* and *evaluation*. Response involves an initial reaction to a first draft. The reaction is usually in the form of questions to the writer about the content and organization of the writing. Both teacher and student share responsibility for responding. Evaluation, however, involves a final assessment of a piece of writing that has progressed through drafts. The teacher has primary responsibility for evaluating a finished product.

Learning to respond to writing in peer groups requires training. Response groups must be "phased in" gradually—students can't be expected to handle response tasks in groups without extensive modeling and coaching. Moreover, response groups shouldn't be initiated too early in the school year. After a month or two of regular writing activity, students will be more confident in their writing ability and will, in all probability, have developed some fluency in their writing. It is at this point that they are ready to be introduced to responding and rewriting situations.

The following steps provide enough structure to shift the burden of feedback from teacher to students:

Step 1. Discuss students' attitudes toward school writing and attempt "to shape new ones if existing attitudes are constricting or counterproductive" (Healy 1982, p. 268). For example, talk about writing as a process that occurs in stages. When students are engaged in an important writing task that will be presented to others ("published"), they shouldn't expect a finished product in one sitting. A first draft is often rough around the edges. It usually needs focus and clarity. Let students know what you value in their writing. Moreover, emphasize the importance of "trying out" writing on an audience before tackling a final draft. Tryouts are a time to react as readers to writing, not nitpick over errors or correct writing as evaluators.

Step 2.   Use the whole class as a response group to demonstrate how to give feedback to a writer. On an overhead transparency, show a paper that was written by an "anonymous" student from a different class. Read the paper aloud and talk about it. The goal is to practice talking about writing without posing a threat to any of the students. Camp (1982) suggested kicking off discussion with the question: "If you were the teacher of this student, and you received this paper, what would you decide to teach the student *next,* so that the next paper he or she writes will be better than this one?" (p. 21). Let the class brainstorm responses. List their suggestions on the chalkboard, and then ask the students to reach a consensus as to the most important points for improvement. Conclude the discussion by acknowledging that responses to content and organization have a higher priority than to mechanics. Writers-in-progress need feedback on how to set their content and organize it before attending to concerns related to spelling, capitalization, punctuation, and grammar.

Step 3.   On an overhead transparency, project another paper from a different class and ask students to respond as the writing by making comments or raising questions. Write these on the transparency next to the appropriate section of the paper. You may find that students have difficulty with this task, so demonstrate several responses that tell what is positive about the paper. What do you as a reader like about it? What is done well?

   Note the differences between *useful* and *useless* feedback. The response "This section is confusing" is of little help to the writer because it isn't specific enough. A useful response, however, is one in which the writer learns what information a reader needs: "I was confused about the Bay of Pigs invasion. Did Kennedy fail to give backup support to the commandos?" Students will soon catch on to the idea that a response gives information that helps the writer get a clear sense of the needs of the audience.

Step 4.   Form cooperative groups of three or four students. Distribute copies of a paper that was written in a different class. Also pass out a response sheet to guide the group discussion. The response sheet should contain several questions that pattern what to look for in the writing. Figure 3.6 illustrates a response sheet.

Step 5.   Form response groups to discuss first drafts that the students have written. Healy (1982, p. 274) recommends the following conditions for working in small groups:

   • Keep the groups small—two to five at first.

   • Have groups sit as far away as possible from other groups for noise control.

   • Have students write the names of their response partners at the top of their original drafts.

FIGURE **3.6**   **Sample Response Sheet**

Response Sheet: Personal Experience Writing

Writer _____

Responder _____

A. What did you like best about this paper? What worked really well?
   _____
   _____
   _____

B. What questions would you ask the writer about things in this paper that were confusing
   or unclear to you?
   _____
   _____
   _____

C. Where in the paper would you like more details? Where could the writer show instead
   of tell?
   _____
   _____
   _____

D. Rate each of the following on a scale from 1 to 4. 4 is tops.

    1. Beginning _____   3. Ending _____

    2. Use of conversation _____   4. Title _____

Source: Adapted from Gerald Camp, *A Success Curriculum for Remedial Writers.* Berkeley: National Writing Project, University of California, 1982, p. 28.

- After response partners have heard a paper read, have them make any comments or ask the writer any questions that occur to them. The writer will note these on the paper.

- Encourage writers to ask for help with different sections of their papers.

- Have writers make all revisions on their original drafts before doing the final one. Have them staple both copies together.

A variation on these conditions is to use response sheets to guide the group discussions. They are particularly useful in the beginning, when the task of responding is still new to students. However, with enough modeling and practice, response sheets will probably not be necessary.

Once feedback is given on the content and organization of a draft, response group members should work together to edit and proofread their texts for spelling, punctuation, capitalization, word choice, and syntax. Accuracy counts.

Cleaning up a text shouldn't be neglected, but struggling writers in particular must recognize that concern about proofreading and editing comes toward the end of the process.

e.Resources

For additional readings related to the major ideas in this chapter, go to Chapter 3 of the Companion Website and click on Suggested Readings.

◄ Looking **Back**
Looking **Forward** ►

Struggling readers and writers exhibit a learned helplessness characterized by a lack of control over literacy strategies and an ambivalent attitude toward anything that has to do with classroom activities involving reading and writing. As a result, they tend to avoid reading and writing or being held accountable for content literacy tasks in school. Students who struggle with text challenge the teacher to look for and experiment with instructional practices that actively involve them in the academic life of the classroom.

Teachers reach struggling readers and writers by scaffolding instruction in ways that support content literacy and learning. Throughout this chapter, we explore scaffolded instruction designed to help all students develop the ability to read and write strategically. To achieve this, we concentrated on the role of explicit instruction in the development and use of literacy strategies.

Strategic classrooms are places where students learn how to learn. We explored how to teach for metacognition so that students will be more aware of, confident in, and competent in their use of literacy strategies. Explicit strategy instruction includes assessing students' knowledge of and use of strategies, explaining the rules and procedures involved in strategy use, modeling and demonstrating how to use a strategy, providing guided practice, and application in the use of strategies. Think-alouds, reciprocal teaching, and question–answer relationships (QARs) are

three research-based instructional practices that help students develop text comprehension strategies.

Moreover, writing should be thought of and taught as a process. When students develop process-related writing strategies, they will be in a better position to generate ideas, set goals, organize, draft, and revise. The writing process occurs in stages; it is not necessarily in a linear sequence of events but more of a recursive, back-and-forth activity. The stages of writing explored in this chapter were defined broadly as discovery, drafting, and revising. Discovery-related writing strategies discussed in this chapter include brainstorming, clustering, jot-charting, and discussion. These help students to explore and generate ideas for the writing, set purposes, and do some preliminary organizing for writing. As students discover what to write about, they draft ideas into words on paper or on the computer screen. Drafting itself is a form of discovery and may lead to new ideas and plans for the writer. Revising strategies help students to rethink what they have drafted, making changes that improve both the content and organization of the writing. Response is essential for students while writing is in progress to develop revising strategies.

In the next chapter, we take a closer look at one type of student that often struggles with content literacy tasks—the English language learner. With every passing year, the United States becomes more linguistically and culturally diverse. English language learners struggle with academic language and are often tracked in lower ability classes than language majority students. The dropout rate among English language learners is alarmingly high. How can content area teachers plan instruction to account for cultural and linguistic differences in their classrooms? Let's read to find out.

Minds On

1. Picture a science class of twenty-five students from very diverse backgrounds—different social classes, different ethnicity, and varying achievement levels. Many of the students struggle with text materials. Describe some classroom strategies you might use to respond to struggling readers and writers while maintaining high standards of content learning.

2. What strategies do you feel would be most useful in helping to make writing assignments meaningful for struggling writers?

3. Your group should divide into two teams, one pro and one con. Review each of the following statements, and discuss from your assigned view the pros and cons of each issue.

   a. We write to discover meaning (to understand) as much as we write to communicate meaning to others (to be understood).

   b. Students need to know the purpose and audience for a writing assignment if they are going to write effectively.

   c. The stages of the writing process are so interrelated that a knowledge of them is of little practical value for students.

Hands On

1. Bring several copies of a favorite poem or short text to class. Following the "think-aloud" guidelines in the chapter, model the checklist for self-evaluation by (a) developing hypotheses by making predictions, (b) developing images, (c) sharing analogies, (d) monitoring comprehension, and (e) regulating comprehension.

2. Using a passage from a content area text, develop one example of each of the four QAR categories: (a) "right there," (b) "think and search," (c) "on your own," and (d) "author and you."

3. In the center of a blank sheet of paper, write the name of the first color that comes to your mind. Circle that color. Let your mind wander, and quickly write down all descriptive words or phrases that come to your mind that are related to that color word. Connect the words logically, creating clusters. Next, see what images these relationships suggest to you. Write a piece (e.g.,

a poem, a story, or an essay) based on your clusters. Exchange papers, and in pairs, comment on the following:

a. What is the best phrase in your partner's piece?

b. What needs explanation or clarification?

c. What is the central idea of the piece?

With your partner, discuss how this exercise illustrates some of the characteristics of the discovery stage of writing.

4. Work with a partner to better understand the strategies you use during writing. Each partner is to observe the other during the following activity and to record the characteristics of the other's process. For ex-

ample, you might describe the writer pausing, sighing, gazing off, writing hurriedly, scratching out, and erasing. At the end of the activity, share your written description with the partner you observed to see if your observations match the writer's own perceptions of the process.

For this activity, write down seven pairs of rhyming words, and then recopy the pairs, alternating words (e.g., *hot, see, not, me*). Next, give your list of rhymes to your partner, and have him or her write lines of poetry, using each word on the list as the final word in a line of the poem.

What did you learn from both observing and being observed as a writer in process?

e.Resourcesextra

- Go to Chapter 3 of the Companion Website (**www.ablongman.com/vacca8e**) and click on Activities to complete the following task:

  The following site contains a wealth of material for struggling students in all content areas. **www.sparknotes.com**. The site includes review concepts, story summaries, math problems, and much more. Browse the various content areas and locate helpful information to assist struggling learners. Share your findings in small groups.

- Go to the Companion Website (**www.ablongman.com/vacca8e**) for suggested readings, interactive activities, multiple-choice questions, and additional Web links to help you learn more about struggling readers.

The New York Times
nytimes.com
expect the world®

Themes of the Times

Extend your knowledge of the concepts discussed in this chapter by reading current and historical articles from the *New York Times*. Go to the Companion Website and click on eThemes of the Times.

chapter 4

Culturally and Linguistically Diverse Learners

There are so many kinds of voices
in the world, and none of them
is without significance.
—ST. PAUL

Teaching with texts is all the more challenging in today's classroom, where the range of linguistic and cultural diversity has been increasing steadily since the 1960s. The growing diversity in the student population is often reflected in the way learners think about themselves as readers and writers. More often than not, students of diverse backgrounds struggle with reading and writing in academic contexts. Much like the struggling readers and writers we described in Chapter 3, culturally and linguistically diverse learners often are caught in a cycle of school failure that contributes to marginal achievement and high dropout rates. Typically, they are placed in low-ability groups where in-

Teachers respond to linguistic and cultural differences in their classrooms by scaffolding instruction in the use of vocabulary and comprehension strategies and by creating classroom environments that encourage talking and working together.

struction is based on a limited, watered-down version of the curriculum. As a result, the strengths that diverse learners bring to instructional situations usually go untapped.

CULTURALLY AND LINGUISTICALLY DIVERSE LEARNERS

CULTURALLY AND LINGUISTICALLY DIVERSE LEARNERS

CULTURAL DIFFERENCES

- From Monocultural to Multicultural Classrooms
- Ways of Knowing
- Students' Funds of Knowledge

LINGUISTIC DIFFERENCES

- Dialect Use
- English Language Learners
- Bilingual and ESL Programs
- What Makes Content Literacy Difficult?
- Sheltered Instruction

VOCABULARY STRATEGIES

- Vocabulary Self-Collection Strategy (VSS)
- CD Word Maps
- Vocabulary Building

COMPREHENSION STRATEGIES

- Questioning the Author (QtA)
- Directed Reading–Thinking Activities (DR–TA)

TALKING AND WORKING TOGETHER

- Scaffolding Student Talk
- Purposes and Types of Discussion
- Creating an Environment for Discussion

Nowhere is the reality of a marginal school experience more pronounced than in the academic lives of English language learners. Their school experience is often characterized by failure, disconnection, and resistance to reading and writing in academic contexts. The increasing number of learners whose first language is one other than English demands literacy related instruction that is strategic and culturally responsive, with high learning expectations for all students. St. Paul's quote wears well in an era of unprecedented classroom diversity. Today's teacher is a teacher of all kinds of learners, with different linguistic and cultural backgrounds and academic needs. And none of their voices is without significance in the classroom.

How can teachers be responsive to linguistic and cultural diversity in their classrooms while maintaining high standards for content literacy and learning? Understanding the cultural and linguistic differences between mainstream and nonmainstream learners is an important first step, as the organizing principle of this chapter suggests: **Teachers respond to linguistic and cultural differences in their classrooms by scaffolding instruction in the use of vocabulary and comprehension strategies and by creating classroom environments that encourage talking and working together.**

Frame of Mind

1. Why are today's classrooms more diverse than they were several decades ago?

2. What are some of the cultural and linguistic differences that students from various racial and ethnic backgrounds bring to classroom learning situations?

3. Why do English language learners struggle with content literacy tasks, and how does sheltered instruction make content more accessible to them while providing additional language support?

4. How can teachers scaffold instruction to develop vocabulary-building strategies for diverse learners?

5. How are the questioning the author (QtA) strategy and the directed reading–thinking activity (DR–TA) similar? How are they different?

6. Why is classroom talk especially important to English language learners, and how can teachers create an environment for discussion in their classrooms?

We began our teaching careers in the 1960s in a suburban high school just outside of Albany, New York, during the height of the civil rights movement and the Vietnam War. The times were tumultuous in the wake of great social change. Practically every facet of American society was open to critical examination, if not reform, including the nation's schools. The landmark 1954 U.S. Supreme Court case *Brown* v. *Board of Education of Topeka* ruled that "separate but equal" schools were unconstitutional and laid the groundwork for educational reform in the 1960s. The civil rights movement fueled the legislative agenda of President Lyndon Johnson's Great Society. The Civil Rights Act of 1964 prohibited discrimination in public institutions on the basis of race, color, religion, or national origin. Also in 1964, the Economic Opportunity Act resulted in educational programs, such as Head Start and Upward Bound, that are still in existence today. In 1965, the Elementary and Secondary Education Act (ESEA) established compensatory educational programs (Title 1) to provide educational opportunities for low-income students from minority backgrounds. In addition, the Bilingual Education Act of 1967 made it possible for schools to receive federal funding for minority groups who were non-English speaking.

Despite the social and educational reforms taking place in the 1960s, it was business as usual at the high school where we taught. The school seemed impervious to change. In a student body of more than 1,000 students, no more than 1 or 2 percent of the students were people of color or immigrants whose first language was one other than English. One of our students during our first year of teaching, Johnny, was the oldest son of Hungarian immigrants. He worked after school at his uncle's garage where he pumped gas and did minor repairs on cars. He used to work on our beat-up, old Chevy Impala whenever it broke down and needed repair. Anyone who took the time to get to know him could tell that Johnny was a bright young man, but in school he was mostly a quiet student who kept to himself. Some would call him a loner, but at the garage he was so-ciable, even outgoing, with his uncle's customers.

In retrospect, the school's culture did not reflect or even recognize Johnny's cul-ture. He was one of the "forgotten" students at school who went largely unnoticed, except when he got into trouble. To this day, we still recall how he would do every-thing in his power to avoid literacy, even disrupt a class, whenever reading and writ-ing became the focus of instruction. As novice teachers, we didn't have a clue about how to deal with his resistance to reading and writing activities. Neither did many of the other teachers. As it turned out, Johnny dropped out of school at the age of nineteen and went to work for his uncle.

Teachers who have worked with students are no strangers to resistant learners. Mary Krogness (1995), a veteran teacher of twenty-nine years, wrote a book about the resistant adolescent learners she taught in a metropolitan area school district. These seventh and eighth graders were all too often overage, underprepared, and weighted down with emotional baggage. Nearly all were students of color. They scored low on achievement tests and were tracked in basic skills classes for most of their academic lives. Yet Krogness observed that her students were smart in ways not recognized or valued in school: They could "read" people—gauge their feelings and interpret attitudes, actions, reactions, tone of voice, and body language. The challenge for Krogness became that of showing her students how to use their "street smarts" to analyze texts and interpret current events. Her aim, as she put it, was "to hook my students on talking, reading, and writing, to immerse them in language and give them plenty of practice in doing what they'd learned not to like or feel good about" (p. 5).

Krogness's students are noticeably different from those she taught two decades earlier. Changes in the racial and ethnic composition of the public school population in the United States have been dramatic. Significant demographic shifts in the pop-ulation have resulted in a society that is increasingly diverse. For whatever reason, students of diverse backgrounds—that is to say, students who may be distinguished by their ethnicity, social class, language, or achievement level—often struggle in their academic programs. As Wang, Reynolds, and Walberg (1994–1995) put it, these students challenge teachers to the limits of their commitment, insights, and skill. However, the more that teachers develop understanding, attitudes, and strategies related to student diversity, the better equipped they will be to adapt instruction to the differences in their classrooms.

Cultural Differences in Today's Schools

Most people, other than those who study culture, probably don't think much about what it means to be immersed in a culture, just as fish probably don't think much about what it means to be immersed in water. The term *culture* is a com-plex and multidimensional concept at best. Culture has been defined by Peregoy

What about . . .

Content Standards and Assessment?

BOX 4.1

Standards-based education and high-stakes assessment are realities for all of today's students, including culturally and linguistically diverse learners. Proficiency assessments, based on statewide content standards in reading and mathematics (and science in 2007–2008), must be in compliance with provisions of the No Child Left Behind (NCLB) Act. NCLB requires that all students, including English language learners, be held accountable for achievement in a standards-based curriculum based on statewide assessments regardless of language proficiency.

The NCLB Act exerts enormous pressure on states and school districts to meet the academic and linguistic needs of second-language learners. The goals of NCLB in relation to statewide proficiency assessments are to ensure that limited English proficient and immigrant students meet state content standards, attain English proficiency, and achieve high levels of academic competence in English.

Ironically, the lack of appropriate, valid, and reliable assessments for culturally and linguistically diverse students has been a major educational issue for more than two decades. Critics contend that assessments have been culturally insensitive; that they often overlook the cultural traditions of underrepresented groups. As a result, test scores may not reflect student achievement or ability level but the cultural traditions not considered in testing (Lapp, Fisher, Flood, & Cabello 2001; Lipsky & Gartner 1997; Valdes & Figueroa 1994).

NCLB provides for accommodations on statewide assessments for English language learners. It list examples of accommodations that may be made by states, including the following: native language assessments, small-group administration, extra time for flexible scheduling, simplified instructions, the availability of dictionaries, recorded native language instructions, and allowing students to record responses in their native language. Moreover, English language learners may take reading/language assessments in a language other than English only for the first three years that they are in school in the United States. School districts, however, may determine on a case-by-case basis that a native language assessment would yield more accurate and reliable information. In such cases, an additional two-year exemption may be given. There is no limit in NCLB on how long students can take math or science assessments in their native language.

Will NCLB make a difference in the academic and English language proficiency of limited English proficient and immigrant students? Will statewide proficiency assessments contribute to an already alarming school dropout rate for English language learners? Only time will tell.

and Boyle (2001) as the shared beliefs, values, and rule-governed patterns of behavior that define a group and are required for group membership. On one level are the surface features of a culture—its foods, dress, holidays, and celebrations. On another level are deeper elements, which include not only values and beliefs systems but also "family structures and child-rearing practices, language and non-verbal communication, expectations, gender roles, biases—all the fundamentals of life that affect learning" (Diaz-Rico & Weed 2002, p. 197).

Language and culture are inextricably connected. Native speakers learn language in social settings, and in the process, they also learn their culture's norms for using language. As you might expect, different cultures have different rules that are always culturally defined and culturally specific. When a student's norms differ from the teacher's expectations, communication is often hindered. Suppose a high school teacher overheard two friends, Lily and Sugar, talking in the school cafeteria during lunch time:

Sugar:	How was your weekend?
Lily:	I had a money time! The bomb and me put on our finest bling bling and went partying Saturday night. Let me tell you Suge, he's no chickenhead. He's a real fly!
Sugar:	No kidding. I bet you two looked really cizool.
Lily:	We had a crunk time until we ran into Jasmine and her do boy.
Sugar:	What happened?
Lily:	Well one thing led to another. Jasmine starting hissing and her do boy stabbed the bomb. So we decided to jet and click up with some classier folks.

Lily and Sugar are using language and slang expressions that have made their way from rap music and the hip-hop cultural scene into the vernacular of today's youth. About what are the two friends talking? Who is the bomb? What's does it mean to be a chickenhead? A do boy? What does it mean to have a money time? A crunk time? To stab? To jet? To click up? Suppose you were the teacher in the cafeteria and were unfamiliar with the language that the friends were using. You might jump to unwarranted conclusions about what happened Saturday night. Did someone get stabbed in the literal sense of the word as it is used in mainstream culture? Because language use is culturally specific, it is easy for teachers not to recognize that language rules are indeed in effect for speakers of other dialects or speakers with different cultural norms for communicating.

> **Response Journal**
>
> Brainstorm a list of words and idiomatic expressions that are specific to a cultural group with whom you identify. Why would someone outside of your cultural group have difficulty understanding these words and expressions?

From Monocultural to Multicultural Classrooms

The school memories of many teachers are most likely to be of *monocultural* classrooms like ours when we began teaching in the 1960s. The monoculture represents the mainstream culture in U.S. society, a culture that is rooted in European American beliefs, standards, and values. The rapidly changing demography of the United States and its schools, however, is transforming the country into a society that is increasingly *multicultural*.

Sturtevant (1992) studied content literacy practices in a multicultural context in a northern Virginia high school. An American history teacher in her study began the school year with twenty-nine students, but by May, the size of the class had dwindled to eighteen. Most of the Hispanic students in this class had moved from the school district, many returning to their home countries. Of the remaining students, there were five African Americans, two whites, three Asians (a Chinese, a Korean, and a Cambodian), two Africans (one from Ethiopia and the other from Zambia), one European (from Germany), and five Latin Americans (four from El Salvador and one from Peru). All of the immigrant students spoke English with limited proficiency but well enough to be mainstreamed into the regular classroom.

The American history teacher, born in a small all-white Ohio town, drew on his own experiences in the Peace Corps to build positive social relationships in the classroom. While in the Peace Corps, he had learned what it meant to be a member of a minority cultural group on a small Caribbean island of almost entirely black inhabitants. In class, he was sensitive to cultural and language differences, and his willingness to understand these differences enabled him to teach more effectively. For example, he recognized that "kids become distrustful" if the teacher views their culture as inferior or their language as deficient. In class discussions, he avoided correcting students' English, believing that it was more important for them to explore ideas openly and critically without fear of humiliation than to speak "correct" English. His sensitivity to cultural and dialect differences allowed his students to interact with one another and with him in the way they spoke to peers and adults in their home or community. Sturtevant (1992) concluded that the teacher's response to student diversity in his classroom made a difference in the academic lives of his students. In diverse classrooms, cultural and linguistic sensitivity is a crucial first step in working with students to achieve academic standards. Teaching for cultural understanding will also make a difference in the way diverse learners respond to instruction.

Teaching for Cultural Understanding

Various instructional perspectives reflect different belief systems related to the teaching of multicultural concepts in today's classrooms. Diaz (2001) describes these perspectives within the context of four distinct instructional approaches. In the *contributions approach*, teachers typically emphasize culturally specific celebrations and holidays within the curriculum, such as Martin Luther King Day. The contributions approach reflects the surface level of a culture but does not make provisions for in-depth study of its deeper elements.

Somewhat related to the contributions approach is an instructional perspective that is additive in nature. The *additive approach* underscores the teaching of various themes related to multicultural concepts and issues. These concepts and issues are integrated into the curriculum through the development of a thematic unit of study, but on the whole the curriculum remains relatively the same throughout the year.

When teachers attempt to help students understand diverse ethnic and cultural perspectives by providing them with ongoing opportunities to read about concepts and events, make judgments about them, think critically, and generate their own conclusions and opinions, they are using a *transformative approach.* This approach, combined with the next one, lends itself well to content literacy strategies that emphasize critical analysis and interpretation. According to Diaz (2001), an extension of the transformative approach involves project learning. The *decision-making/social action approach* provides learners with opportunities to engage in activities and projects related to cultural concepts and issues, particularly those issues and problems dealing with social action.

Teachers need to go beyond limiting the content of instructional lessons to celebrations or one-time only thematic units related to multicultural concepts. Today's teacher needs to provide students with literacy and learning experiences that will provide them with the cross-cultural knowledge and skills they will need as future adults in a nation that has become increasingly diverse. Multicultural literature helps students develop cross-cultural knowledge and skills.

Integrating Multicultural Literature across the Curriculum

In the next chapter, we discuss the role of literature across the curriculum and suggest multicultural book titles and strategies for classroom use. When teachers use multicultural literature in the classroom, they provide students with texts that are not only engaging but also recognize the unique contributions of each culture and the similarities of the human experience across cultures. At the same time, they help nonmainstream cultures appreciate and value their heritage and give all students the benefits of understanding ways of knowing about the world that are different from their own. Choosing multicultural texts to integrate into the curriculum is no easy task. Asking several questions can help you select those books that will be most useful to students in your classroom (Yokota 1993):

Resources

There are many Websites for you and your students to visit related to multicultural issues and themes. Go to Web Destinations on the Companion Website, click on Professional Resources, and search for Multicultural Resources for Teachers and Students.

- Is this book good literature? Is the plot strong? Is characterization true to experience?

- Are setting, theme, and style well developed?

- Is this book culturally accurate? Will it help readers gain a true sense of the culture?

- Is the book rich in cultural details? Do details that give readers insight into the nuances of daily life enhance the story? Or is the culture overgeneralized?

- Are cultural issues presented comprehensively? Do they have enough depth and realism for readers to get a true sense of how culture affects the lives of people?

- Are minorities relevant? Are members of a minority group present for a reason, or could the story be told as easily about any cultural group? Token involvement of minority characters gives little sense of their unique, culturally rooted experience.

- Are dialogue and relationships culturally authentic?

Teaching for cultural understanding and using multicultural literature create a community of learners within the four walls of the classroom. Within such learning communities, it is important for teachers to understand the ways in which diverse learners "come to know" and to tap into students' "funds of knowledge."

Ways of Knowing

Heath (1983) reminds us that it is crucially important to be aware that students from diverse cultural backgrounds may bring different ways of knowing, different styles of questioning, and different patterns of interaction to school. For example, different cultures may have different attitudes, expectations, and assumptions about the value of reading and writing and what it means to be a reader and writer. Alicia, a Latino student, didn't want to be a "schoolgirl." To be a schoolgirl meant always having her head in a book, always doing homework. However, Alicia had little trouble getting involved in school activities that revolved around meaningful, collaborative literacy activities, such as tutoring younger students and writing social studies texts for them (Heath & Mangiola 1989).

Different cultures may place a different emphasis and value on various cognitive activities and styles of questioning. Some societies, for example, emphasize memorization and analytical thinking over the ability to experiment or to make predictions (Fillmore 1981). The cognitive styles of culturally diverse students may differ. Heath (1983) discovered that African American students experienced academic difficulty in their classrooms partly because of their lack of familiarity with the kinds of questions they were expected to answer in school. For example, based on family interaction patterns in the African American community that she studied, Heath found that students were not familiar with school questions, asking them to describe or identify the attributes of objects or concepts. The students were much more familiar with analogy-type questions comparing one object or concept with another. When teachers became aware of the differences between the kinds of questions they asked and the kinds of questions familiar to the students, they were able to make adjustments in their questioning style. As a result, the teachers noticed a marked contrast in their students' participation and interest in lessons.

Ways of knowing are intertwined with ways of interacting and learning. Rather than place emphasis on individual competition, some cultural groups prize group interaction, helping one another, and collaborative activity. Reyes and Molner (1991), for example, suggest that cooperative learning is 'more "culturally congruent" with students from Mexican American backgrounds. The research support for cooperative classroom strategies, especially in diverse learning situations, is impressive (Little Soldier 1989; Slavin 1987).

Students' Funds of Knowledge

The powerful role that culture plays in shaping students' behaviors and their knowledge of the world often goes unnoticed in classrooms. Understanding the sociocultural dynamics of home and community, gives us a broader perspective on the worldviews students bring to school. Culturally and linguistically diverse students typically come from working-class families where their individual lives are inseparable from the social dynamics of the household and community in which they live. A teacher who makes a point of understanding the home culture, ethnic background, and community of students is in a better position (1) to understand the kinds of knowledge that culturally diverse students bring to learning situations and (2) to adjust the curriculum to their sociocultural strengths.

Luis Moll (1994) contends that much is to be gained from understanding the "social networks" of the households in a cultural group. These networks are crucial to families, who often engage in exchanging "funds of knowledge." These funds of knowledge may represent occupationally related skills and information that families share with one another as a means of economic survival. Moll argues that the social and cultural resources that students bring to school—their funds of knowledge—are rarely tapped in classroom learning contexts. Using the community's rich resources and funds of knowledge builds on one of students' greatest assets: the social networks established within a cultural group. One such resource is its people. Moll (1994) puts it this way: "One has to believe that there are diverse types of people that can be helpful in the classroom even though they do not have professional credentials. Wisdom and imagination are distributed in the same way among professional and nonprofessional groups" (p. 194).

> **Response Journal**
>
> Think about the funds of knowledge that you possess based on your cultural background and heritage. Describe how you make use (or will make use) of such knowledge in your teaching.

In a middle-level classroom, Mexican American students in Tucson, Arizona, engage in a study of construction which includes inquiry into the history of dwellings and different ways of building structures. The students have access to a wide array of reading materials from the library to focus their investigation: trade books; magazines, newspapers, and reference resources, to name a few. The teacher builds on students' reading by inviting parents and community members to speak to them about their jobs in the construction industry. For example, a father visits the class to describe his work as a mason.

Showing interest in students' home cultures and ethnic backgrounds builds trust in the classroom. Jackson (1994) believes that building trust with students of diverse backgrounds is a culturally responsive strategy that is often overlooked. One way to create trust may be as simple as learning students' names and pronouncing them correctly, and perhaps having them share the unique meanings and special significance of their first names. Teachers may also invite them to research and share information about their family's ethnic background, using questions suggested by Covert (1989): What generation in the United States do you represent? Are you and your siblings the first of your family to be born in this country? Were you foreign born? From where did you or your ancestors migrate? What made them wish to come here? Does your immediate or extended family practice ethnic or cultural customs which you or they value or with which you or they identify? Do you or your relatives speak your ethnic group's language? What occupations are represented in your family background?'

Linguistic Differences in Today's Schools

Linguistic differences among today's student population are strikingly evident in many school districts throughout the United States. From the East Coast to the West Coast, and from the Gulf to the Northern Great Lakes, the increasingly large number of immigrants from non-European nations is influencing how content area teachers approach instruction. It is no exaggeration to suggest that in some urban school districts more than fifty languages are spoken (Banks 2001).

When immigrant students maintain a strong identification with their culture and native language, they are more likely to succeed academically, and they have more positive self-concepts about their ability to learn (Banks 2001; Diaz 2001; Garcia 2002). Schools, however, tend to view linguistically diverse students whose first language is one other than English from a deficit model, not a difference model. For these English language learners, instructional practices currently are compensatory in nature: "That is, they are premised on the assumption that language diversity is an illness that needs to be cured" (Diaz 2001, p. 159).

In addition, regional variations in language usage, commonly known as dialects, are a complicated issue for teachers. In truth, all English language users speak a dialect of English, which is rooted in such factors as age, gender, socioeconomic status, and the region of the country where one was born and grew up. Even presidents of the United States speak a dialect! The difficulty with dialect differences in the classroom is the *value* assigned to dialects—the perceived goodness or badness of one particular language variation over another. Roberts (1985), however, suggests that language variations are neither good nor bad, and that such judgments are often about the people who make them rather than about clarity or precision. Delpit (1988) argues quite convincingly that teachers need to respect and recognize the strengths of diverse learners who use dialect in the classroom.

Dialect Use in the Classroom

Cultural variation in the use of language has a strong influence on literacy learning. Even though students whose first language is not English do not have full control of English grammatical structures, pronunciation, and vocabulary, they can engage in reading and writing activities (Goodman & Goodman 1978). When students use their own culturally acceptable conversational style to talk and write about ideas they read in texts, they are likely to become more content literate and to improve their literacy skills. Au and Mason (1981), for example, describe how minority Hawaiian learners improved their reading abilities when they were allowed to use their home language to talk about texts.

Language *differences* should not be mistaken for language *deficits* among culturally diverse students. Many of the low-achieving high school students in the rural Georgia classroom that Dillon (1989) studied were African Americans who spoke a dialect commonly referred to as black English vernacular. Black dialect is acquired through family interactions and participation in the culture of the community. The teacher in Dillon's study had much success in leading text-related discussions because of his sensitivity to his students' dialect as a tool for communication in the class. As Dillon put it, the teacher "allowed students to use dialect in his classroom because they were more comfortable with it and more effective communicators" (p. 245).

Shouldn't students from minority backgrounds learn to use standard American English? The question is a rhetorical one. As teachers, our stance toward the use of standard American English is critical. Standard American English, often thought of as the "news broadcast—type" English used in the conduct of business, is the language of the dominant mainstream culture in U.S. society—the "culture of power," according to Delpit (1988). Delpit explains that the rules and codes of the culture of power, including the rules and codes for language use, are acquired by students from mainstream backgrounds through interaction with their families. Minority students, however, whose families are outside the mainstream culture, do not acquire the same rules and codes. If students are going to have access to opportunities in mainstream society, schools must acquaint students from minority backgrounds with the rules and codes of the culture of power. Not making standard American English accessible to students from minority backgrounds puts them at a disadvantage in competing with their mainstream counterparts.

Although it is important for culturally diverse learners to receive explicit instruction in the use of standard American English, *when* and *under what circumstances* become critical instructional issues. All students should understand how cultural contexts influence what they read, write, hear, say, and view. Language arts classes are probably the appropriate place to provide explicit instruction in the functional use and conventions of standard American English. Although becoming proficient in standard American English may be an important school goal for all students, it should not be viewed as a prerequisite for literate classroom behavior (Au 1993). When it is viewed as a prerequisite, teachers deny students the opportunity to use their own language as a tool for learning. Increasing their command of standard American English, in and of itself, will not improve students' abilities to think critically, "since students' own languages can serve just as well for verbal expression and reasoning" (p. 130).

English Language Learners

English language learners are those students who speak English as a nonnative language. Because their home language is that of a minority group—for example, Spanish, Navajo, or Vietnamese—they are considered to be *language minority* students. English language learners are, for the most part, the children of immigrants who left their homelands for one reason or another. Some English language learners, however, are born in the United States. As Peregoy and Boyle (2001) explain,

> Many recent immigrants have left countries brutally torn by war or political strife in regions such as Southeast Asia, Central America, and Eastern Europe; others have immigrated for economic reasons. Still others come to be reunited with families who are already here or because of the educational opportunities they may find in the United States. Finally, many English language learners were born in the United States and some of them, such as Native Americans of numerous tribal heritages, have roots in American soil that go back for countless generations. (p. 3)

Immigration patterns have changed dramatically in the past one hundred years. At the onset of the twentieth century, the vast majority of immigrants (87 percent) were from Europe (Lapham 1993). At the beginning of the twenty-first century, however, the majority of immigrants have come from Latin America (57 percent). Based on the most recent data from the U.S. Bureau of the Census (2000), as displayed in Table 4.1, there are approximately 25,800,000 foreign born living in the United States as of December 1999 (Tse 2001).

Bilingual and ESL Programs

English language learners vary in their use of English. Some may have little or no proficiency in the use of English. Others may have limited English skills; still others may use English proficiently and are mainstreamed into the regular curriculum. What is language proficiency? It has been defined as "the ability to use a language effectively and appropriately throughout the range of social, personal, school, and work situations required for daily living in a given society" (Peregoy & Boyle 2001, p. 29). Language proficiency, therefore, encompasses both oral and written language processes, including speaking, listening, reading, and writing.

e.Resources

For professional and student ESL Websites, go to Web Destinations on the Companion Website, click on Professional Resources, and search for ESL Resources for Teachers and Students.

In the United States, there is an array of instructional programs for English language learners. Programs vary greatly, depending on the number of English language learners enrolled in a school district. Many with limited English proficiency are placed in bilingual and English as a second language (ESL) programs. Bilingual and ESL programs are designed specifically to meet the academic, cultural, and linguistic needs of English language learners until they are proficient enough in English to be mainstreamed into the regular curriculum.

Bilingual programs are designed to teach English and to provide instruction in the core curriculum using the home language of the English learner. Bilingual programs reach only a small percentage of students, despite a growing body of research

TABLE **4.1** **Number and Percentage of U.S. Foreign Born and Country of Origin**

Country of Origin	Foreign Born March 1997 Number (percentage)
All Countries	25,779,000 (100.0%)
Mexico	7,017,000 (27.2%)
Philippines	1,132,000 (4.4%)
China and Hong Kong	1,107,000 (4.3%)
Cuba	913,000 (3.5%)
Vietnam	770,000 (3.0%)
India	748,000 (2.9%)
Dominican Republic	632,000 (2.5%)
El Salvador	607,000 (2.4%)
Great Britain	606,000 (2.4%)
Korea	591,000 (2.3%)

Source: Reprinted with permission from Tse, L. (2001). *Why don't they learn English? Separating fact from fallacy in the U.S. language debate.* New York: Teachers College Press, p. 11.

that suggests when immigrant students maintain a strong identification with their culture and native language, they are more likely to succeed academically and have more positive self-concepts about their abilities to learn (Banks 2001; Diaz 2001; Garcia 2002). ESL programs differ from bilingual programs in that they are taught entirely in English in schools where there are many language-minority groups represented, making it difficult to implement bilingual instruction.

Bilingual and ESL teachers provide invaluable compensatory services for language minority students with limited English proficiency. When these students are mainstreamed into the regular curriculum, however, they often struggle with content literacy tasks. Let's take a closer look at some of the reasons diverse learners struggle with reading and writing in content area classrooms.

What Makes Content Literacy Difficult for English Language Learners?

Once they are mainstreamed into the regular curriculum, English language learners often struggle with content area texts. In schools where tracking is used as an organizational tool, a disproportionate number of English language learners have been placed in lower-track classrooms, even though the notion that students learn best with others of similar achievement levels has not been supported by research (Allington 2001; Oakes 1985). In mainstream classes, reading textbooks is one of the most cognitively demanding, context-reduced tasks that language-minority students will encounter (Cummins 1994). Some students may become frustrated by texts because of issues related to background knowledge. According to Kang (1994),

> Some information or concepts in textbooks may presuppose certain background knowledge that native speakers may take for granted but that may be different or lacking in some ESL students. Culture-specific background knowledge developed in students' native country, community, or home may affect their comprehension, interpretation, and development of social, cultural, historical, and even scientific concepts. Even if students possess the background knowledge presumed for a particular text, they may not be able to activate it to relate and organize new information. (p. 649)

The vocabulary load of content area textbooks is also a problem for some second-language learners. The academic language of texts is not the language of conversational speech. If students have limited literacy skills in their own native language, they will obviously experience a great deal of frustration and failure with English texts. Moreover, if students are good readers in their native language but have minimal proficiency in English, the language barrier may inhibit them from making effective use of their literacy skills.

Sheltered Instruction

When English language learners struggle with content literacy tasks, instruction should be specially designed to meet their academic and linguistic needs, which often include (1) learning grade-appropriate and academically demanding content; (2) learning the language of academic English as reflected in content subjects, texts, and classroom discourse; (3) engaging in appropriate classroom behavior and understanding participation rules and expectations in small groups and whole class instructional routines; and (4) mastering English vocabulary and grammar (Echevarria, Vogt, & Short 2000). *Sheltered instruction,* also known as SDAIE (specially designed academic instruction in English), is an approach to content area learning and language development that provides the instructional support needed to making grade-level content more accessible for English language learners while promoting English development (Echevarria & Graves 2003). Although the concept of "sheltering" English language learners is similar to the concept of scaffolding instruction for all learners who need instructional support to be successful with content literacy tasks, it has been adapted for use in two types of instructional contexts: (1) in mainstreamed, core curriculum classrooms made up of native speakers and nonnative speakers who are at an *intermediate* level of language proficiency and (2) in ESL classrooms made up of nonnative speakers who are at similar levels of language proficiency. Content area teachers are in a strategic position to make adaptations in the way they design and deliver instruction in classrooms with native and nonnative speakers. These adaptations in instructional design and delivery lead to additional lan-

Response Journal

What does the term *sheltered* suggest to you? Why do you think it is used to describe an instructional approach for English language learners?

guage support for English language learners, as well as increased learning opportunities in the core curriculum.

One model for sheltered instruction, SIOP (sheltered instruction observation protocol), provides a comprehensive instructional framework that can be used in several ways to scaffold instruction for English language learners. First, the SIOP model serves as a blueprint for designing lessons that integrate content learning with additional language support for English language learners. Second, the SIOP model enhances instructional delivery by making teachers aware of highly effective practices and behaviors that will make a difference in the academic and language development of students. And third, the SIOP model provides an observational framework for rating teachers in sheltered classrooms. Figure 4.1 depicts the major components within the SIOP model: lesson preparation, instruction, strategies, interaction, practice/application, lesson delivery, and assessment (Echevarria, Vogt, & Short 2000).

Sheltered instruction is a powerful approach to content area learning and language development. The literacy strategies described throughout this book may be incorporated into instructional routines for students in sheltered or nonsheltered classrooms. Many of the instructional practices, for example, that we developed in the previous chapter on struggling readers and writers, and those that we will develop in subsequent chapters, have been recommended by English language educators for use with language minority students (Diaz-Rico & Weed 2002; Echevarria & Graves 2003; Echevarria, Vogt, & Short 2000; Peregoy & Boyle 2001). As we turn our attention to vocabulary, comprehension, and discussion strategies in the remainder of this chapter, keep in mind that the instructional practices we describe can make a difference in the academic lives of all learners, depending on how thoughtful teachers adapt them to meet the academic and language needs of students in their classrooms.

Vocabulary Strategies

Linguistically diverse learners, whether they are good or poor readers, will encounter unfamiliar content area vocabulary during reading that may pose comprehension problems for them. In a study of bilingual readers, researchers discovered that good readers focused on increasing vocabulary (Jimenez, Garcia, & Pearson 1995, 1996). In addition, English language learners who struggle as readers benefited from vocabulary strategy instruction (Jimenez & Gamez 1996). Vocabulary strategy instruction is effective when a teacher helps English language learners to develop a few key terms in depth rather than attempting to have them learn many words superficially (Gersten & Jimenez 1994). Such instruction should take into account strategies and procedures that will help students build meaning for important concept terms. *Vocabulary self-collection strategy (VSS)*, *concept of definition (CD) word maps*, and *vocabulary-building strategies* scaffold students' abilities to define concepts in the context of their use.

FIGURE **4.1**   **The Sheltered Instructional Observation Protocol (SIOP)**

Observer: _____

Date: _____

Grade: _____

Class: _____

Teacher: _____

School: _____

ESL level: _____

Lesson: Multi-day   Single-day

I. Preparation

1. Clearly defined *content objectives* for students
2. Clearly defined *language objectives* for students
3. *Content concepts* appropriate for age and educational background level of students
4. *Supplementary materials* used to a high degree, making the lesson clear and meaningful (graphs, models, visuals)
5. *Adaptation of content* (e.g., text, assignment) to all levels of student proficiency
6. *Meaningful activities* that integrate lesson concepts (e.g., surveys, letter writing, simulations, constructing models) with language practice opportunities for reading, writing, listening, and/or speaking

II. Instruction

(1) Building Background

7. *Concepts explicitly linked* to students' background experiences
8. *Links explicitly made* between past learning and new concepts
9. *Key vocabulary emphasized* (e.g., introduced, written, repeated, and highlighted for students to see)

(2) Comprehensible

10. *Speech* appropriate for students' proficiency level (e.g., slower rate, enunciation, and simple sentence structure for beginners)
11. *Explanation* of academic tasks clear
12. Uses a variety of *techniques* to make content concepts clear (e.g., modeling, visuals, hands-on activities demonstrations, gestures, body language)

(3) Strategies

13. Provides ample opportunities for student to use *strategies*
14. Consistent use of *scaffolding* techniques throughout lesson, assisting and supporting student understanding
15. Teacher uses a variety of *question types throughout the lesson including those that*

promote higher-order thinking skills throughout the lesson (e.g., literal, analytical, and interpretive questions)

(4) Interaction

16. Frequent opportunities for *interactions* and discussion between teacher/student and among students, which encourage elaborated responses about lesson concepts
17. *Grouping configurations* support language and content objectives of the lesson
18. Consistently provides sufficient *wait time for student response*
19. Ample opportunities for students to *clarify key concepts in L1*

(5) Practice/Application

20. Provides *hands-on* materials and/or manipulatives for students to practice using new content knowledge
21. Provides activities for students to *apply content and language knowledge* in the classroom
22. Uses activities that integrate all *language skills* (i.e., reading, writing, listening, and speaking)

(6) Lesson Delivery

23. *Content objectives* clearly supported by lesson delivery
24. *Language objectives* clearly supported by lesson delivery
25. *Students engaged* approximately 90–100% of the period
26. *Pacing* of the lesson appropriate to the students' ability level

III. Review/Assessment

27. Comprehensive *review* of key vocabulary
28. Comprehensive *review* of key content concepts
29. Regularly provides *feedback* to students on their output (e.g., language, content, work)
30. Conducts *assessment* of student comprehension and learning of all lesson objectives (e.g., spot checking, group response) throughout the lesson

Source: From Jana Echevarria, Maryellen Vogt, and Deborah Short, *Making content comprehensible for English language learners: The SIOP model.* Published by Allyn & Bacon, Boston, MA. Copyright © 2000 by Pearson Education Inc. Reprinted with permission of the publisher.

Vocabulary Self-Collection Strategy

Vocabulary self-collection strategy (VSS) promotes the long-term acquisition of language in an academic discipline (Haggard 1986). As a result of the repeated use of the strategy, students learn how to make decisions related to the importance of concepts and how to use context to determine what words mean. VSS begins once students read and discuss a text assignment. The teacher asks students, who are divided into teams, to nominate one word that they would like to learn more about. The word must be important enough for the team to share it with the class. The teacher also nominates a word. Here are several suggested steps in VSS:

1. *Divide the class into nominating teams of two to five students.* Together the students on a nominating team decide which word to select for emphasis in the text selection.

2. *Present the word that each team has selected to the entire class.* A spokesperson for each team identifies the nominated word and responds to the following questions:

   a. *Where is the word found in the text?* The spokesperson reads the passage in which the word is located or describes the context in which the word is used.

   b. *What do the team members think the word means?* The team decides on what the word means in the context in which it is used. They must use information from the surrounding context and may also consult reference resources.

   c. *Why did the team think the class should learn the word?* The team must tell the class why the word is important enough to single out for emphasis.

To introduce VSS to the students, the teacher first presents his or her nominated word to the class, modeling how to respond to the three questions. During the team presentations, the teacher facilitates the discussion, writes the nominated words on the board with their meanings, and invites class members to contribute additional clarifications of the words.

To conclude the class session, students record all the nominated words and their meanings in a section of their learning logs or in a separate vocabulary notebook. These lists may be used for review and study. As a consequence of VSS, the teacher has a set of student-generated words that can be incorporated into a variety of follow-up extension activities, as suggested in Chapter 8.

Concept of Definition Word Maps

Although VSS provides opportunities to define and explore the meanings of words used in text readings, many students are not aware of the types of information that contribute to the meaning of a concept. Nor have they internalized a strategy for defining a concept based on the information available to them. In addition, words in a text passage often provide only partial contextual information for defining the meaning of a concept.

Concept of definition (CD) word maps provide a framework for organizing conceptual information in the process of defining a word (Schwartz 1988; Schwartz & Raphael 1985). Conceptual information can be organized in terms of three types of relationships: the general class or category in which the concept belongs, the attributes or properties of the concept and those that distinguish it from other members of the category, and examples or illustrations of the concept. Students from elementary school through high school can use CD to learn how to construct meaning for unknown words encountered in texts.

CD instruction supports vocabulary and concept learning by helping students internalize a strategy for defining and clarifying the meaning of unknown words. The hierarchical structure of a concept has an organizational pattern that is reflected by the general structure of a CD word map (see Figure 4.2).

In the center of the CD word map, students write the concept being studied. Working outward, they then write the word that best describes the general class or superordinate concept that includes the target concept. The answer to "What is it?" is the general class or category. Students then provide at least three examples of the concept as well as

> **Response Journal**
>
> Select a concept from your content area and develop a CD word map for it.

FIGURE 4.2   General Structure for a CD Word Map

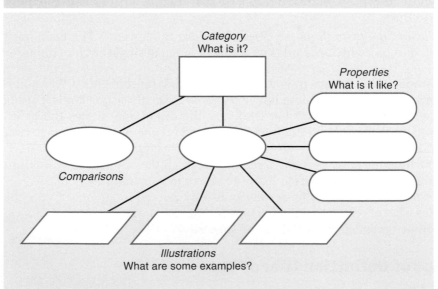

Source: From Robert Schwartz, "Learning to Learn: Vocabulary in Content Area Textbooks" (1988, November). *Journal of Reading, 32*(2), 108–118. Copyright © 1988 by the International Reading Association. All rights reserved. Used by permission of the author and the International Reading Association.

three properties by responding, respectively, to the questions, "What are some examples?" and "What is it like?" Comparison of the target concept is also possible when students think of an additional concept that belongs to the general class but is different from the concept being studied. Figure 4.3 provides an example of a CD word map for the word *tiger*.

Because students use the general CD word map as a framework for defining unknown concepts that they encounter during reading, a teacher can easily combine CD instruction with VSS. Schwartz (1988) recommends a detailed plan for modeling CD with students. The plan includes demonstrating the value of CD by connecting its purpose to how people use organizational patterns to aid memory and interpretation; introducing the general structure of a CD word map, explaining how the three probes define a concept, and walking students through the completion of a word map; and applying CD to an actual text selection.

Two caveats are relevant to CD instruction: CD works best with concept words that function as nouns, but the procedure may be used, with some adaptation, with action words as well. Also, a potential misuse of CD occurs when teachers reproduce the general CD word map on the copier and expect students

FIGURE 4.3 **CD Map for the Word *Tiger***

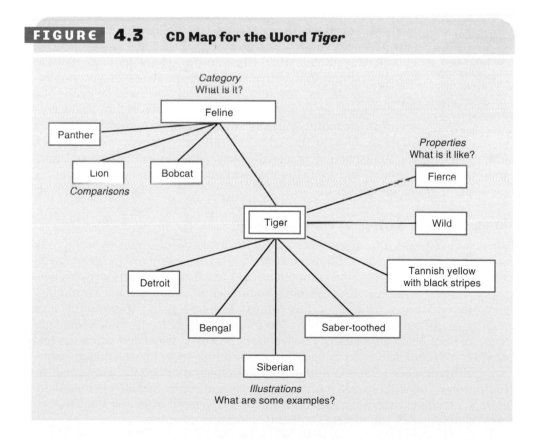

to define lists of words at the end of a text chapter. This is not the intent of CD instruction. Instead, students should internalize the process through demonstration and actual use, applying it as they need it in actual text learning. Ultimately, the goal of CD instruction is to have students own the strategy of defining unknown words in terms of category, property, and example relationships.

Vocabulary-Building Strategies

Showing diverse learners how to construct meaning for unfamiliar words encountered during reading helps them develop strategies needed to monitor comprehension and increase their own vocabularies. Demonstrating how to use *context, word structure,* and the *dictionary* provides students with several basic strategies for vocabulary learning that will last a lifetime. With these strategies, students can search for information clues while reading so that they can approximate the meanings of unknown words. These clues often reveal enough meaning to allow readers who struggle with text to continue reading without "short-circuiting" the process and giving up because the text does not make sense.

You can scaffold the use of vocabulary-building strategies before assigning material to be read. If one or more words represent key concepts—and the words lend themselves to demonstration—you can model the inquiry process necessary to construct meaning. The demonstration is brief, often lasting no more than five minutes. There are three types of demonstrations that will make students aware of vocabulary-building strategies. The first is to model how to make sense of a word in the context of its use, the second involves an analysis of a word's structure, and the third combines context and word structure. Usually these demonstrations require the use of visuals, such as an overhead transparency or a chalkboard. After the brief demonstration, guide students to practice and apply the strategy that you just modeled so that they can become proficient in its use.

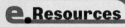

e.Resources

Use the keywords, "vocabulary + lessons + (content area)" to search for vocabulary-building strategy applications in your content area.

Using Context to Approximate Meaning

Constructing meaning from context is one of the most useful strategies at the command of proficient readers. Showing readers who struggle how to make use of context builds confidence and competence and teaches the inquiry process necessary to unlock the meaning of troublesome technical and general vocabulary encountered during reading. Using context involves using information surrounding a difficult word to help reveal its meaning. Every reader makes some use of context automatically. Strategy instruction, however, is needed when the text provides a *deliberate context* to help the reader with concept terms that are especially difficult. Often the text author will anticipate that certain words will be troublesome and will provide information clues and contextual aids to help readers with meaning. In these instances, students will benefit from a strategy that allows them to use the deliberate context to construct meaning.

Even though textbook authors may consciously or unconsciously use deliberate contexts for unknown words, constraints in the material itself or the reader's own background limit the degree to which context reveals word meaning. The teacher and students must know how context operates to limit meaning as well as to reveal it.

Deighton (1970) identified several factors that limit the use of context: (1) What a context may reveal to a particular reader depends on the reader's experience, (2) the portion of context that reveals an unfamiliar word must be located reasonably close to the word if it is to act effectively, and (3) there must be some clear-cut connection between the unfamiliar term and the context that clarifies it.

The use of context, as you have probably concluded, is mostly a matter of inference. Inference requires readers to see an explicit or implicit relationship between the unfamiliar word and its context or to connect what they know already with the unknown term. It can't be assumed that students will perceive these relationships or make the connections on their own. Most students who struggle with text simply don't know how to use a deliberate context provided by an author. Three kinds of information in particular are useful to struggling readers: *typographic, syntactic,* and *semantic* clues.

TYPOGRAPHIC CLUES   Typographic or format clues make use of footnotes, italics, boldface print, parenthetical definitions, pictures, graphs, charts, and the like. A typographic clue provides a clear-cut connection and a direct reference to an unknown word. Many students tend to gloss over a typographic aid instead of using it to spotlight the meaning of a difficult term. The teacher can rivet attention to these aids with minimal expenditure of class time.

For example, consider the way a science teacher modeled a strategy for revealing the meaning of the word *enzymes,* which was presented in boldface type in the text. Before assigning a text section titled "Osmosis in Living Cells," the teacher asked students to turn to page 241. Then he asked, "Which word in the section on osmosis stands out among the others?" The students quickly spotted the word *enzymes.* "Why do you think this word is highlighted in boldface type?" he asked. A student replied, "I guess it must be important." Another student said, "Maybe because it has something to do with osmosis—whatever that is." The teacher nodded approvingly and then asked the class to see if they could figure out what *enzymes* meant by reading this sentence: "Chemical substances called **enzymes** are produced by cells to break down large starch molecules into small sugar molecules."

The science teacher continued the demonstration by asking two questions: "What are enzymes?" and "What do they do?" The students responded easily. The teacher concluded the walk-through with these words: "Words that are put in large letters or boldfaced print are important. If you pay attention to them as we just did, you will have little trouble figuring out what they mean. There are four other words in boldfaced type in your reading assignment. Look for them as you read and try to figure out what they mean."

TABLE 4.2 Syntactic and Semantic Contextual Clues

Type of Clue	Explanation	Examples[a]
1. Definition	The author equates the unknown word to the known or more familiar, usually using a form of the verb *be*.	*Entomology* **is** the study of insects, and biologists who specialize in this field **are called** *entomologists*. A *critical review* **is** an attempt to evaluate the worth of a piece of writing.
2. Linked synonyms	The author pairs the unknown word with familiar synonyms or closely related words in a series.	Kunte Kinte was the victim of **cruel, evil,** *malevolent,* and **brutal** slave traders. The senator from Connecticut possessed the traits of an honest and just leader: **wisdom, judgment,** *sagacity.*
3. Direct description: examples, modifiers, restatements	The author reveals the meaning of an unknown word by providing additional information in the form of appositives, phrases, clauses, or sentences.	*Example clue:* Undigested material **such as fruit skins, outer parts of grain, and the stringlike parts of some vegetables** forms *roughage.* *Modifier clues:* Pictographic writing, **which was the actual drawing of animals, people, and events,** is the forerunner of written language. *Algae,* **nonvascular plants that are as abundant in water as grasses are on land,** have often been called "grasses of many waters." *Restatement clue:* A billion dollars a year is spent on *health quackery.* **In other words, each year in the United States, millions of dollars are spent on worthless treatments and useless gadgets to "cure" various illnesses.**

[a]Italics denote the unknown words. Boldface type represents information clues that trigger context revelation.

SYNTACTIC AND SEMANTIC CLUES Syntactic and semantic clues in content materials should not be treated separately. The grammatical relationships among words in a sentence or the structural arrangement among sentences in a passage often helps clarify the meaning of a particular word.

Syntactic and semantic clues are much more subtle than typographic clues. Table 4.2 presents a summary of the most frequently encountered syntactic and semantic clues.

Type of Clue	Explanation	Examples[a]
4. Contrast	The author reveals the meaning of an unknown word by contrasting it with an antonym or a phrase that is opposite in meaning.	You have probably seen animals perform tricks at the zoo, on television, or in a circus. Maybe you taught a dog to fetch a newspaper. **But learning tricks— usually for a reward—is very different from** *cognitive problem solving.*
		It wasn't a *Conestoga* like Pa's folks came in. **Instead, it was just an old farm wagon drawn by one tired horse.**
5. Cause and effect	The author establishes a cause-and-effect relationship in which the meaning of an unknown word can be hypothesized.	The *domestication* of animals probably began when young animals were caught or strayed into camps. **As a result, people enjoyed staying with them and made pets of them.**
		A family is *egalitarian* **when both husband and wife make decisions together and share responsibilities equally.**
6. Mood and tone	The author sets a mood (ironic, satirical, serious, funny, etc.) in which the meaning of an unknown word can be hypothesized.	A sense of *resignation* engulfed my thoughts as **the feeling of cold grayness was everywhere around me.**
		The *tormented* animal **screeched with horror and writhed in pain as it tried desperately to escape** from the hunter's trap.

The chalkboard or an overhead transparency is valuable for helping students visualize the inquiry process necessary to reveal meaning. For example, if a *definition clue* is used, as in this example from Table 4.2: "Entomology is the study of insects, and biologists who specialize in this field are called entomologists," it may be appropriate first to write the sentence on the board. During the modeling discussion, you can then show how *is* and *are called* provide information clues that reveal meaning for *entomology* and *entomologists*. A simple strategy

127

would be to cross out *is* and *are called* in the sentence and replace them with equal signs (=):

> Entomology ~~is~~ = the study of insects, and biologists who specialize in this field ~~are called~~ = entomologists.

A brief discussion will reinforce the function of the verb forms *is* and *are called* in the sentence.

The definition clue is the least subtle of the syntactic and semantic clues. However, all the clues in Table 4.2 require students to make inferential leaps. Consider one of the examples from the mood and tone clue: "The tormented animal screeched with horror and writhed in pain as it tried desperately to escape from the hunter's trap." Suppose this sentence came from a short story about to be assigned in an English class. Assume also that many of the students would have trouble with the word *tormented* as it is used in the sentence. If students are to make the connection between *tormented* and the mood created by the information clues, the teacher will have to ask several effective clarifying questions.

The demonstration begins with the teacher writing the word *tormented* on the board. She asks, "You may have heard or read this word before, but how many of you think that you know what it means?" Student definitions are put on the board. The teacher then writes the sentence on the board. "Which of the definitions on the board do you think best fits the word *tormented* when it's used in this sentence?" She encourages students to support their choices. If none fits, she will ask for more definitions now that students have seen the sentence. She continues questioning, "Are there any other words or phrases in the sentence that help us get a feel for the meaning of *tormented*? Which ones?"

The inquiry into the meaning of *tormented* continues in this fashion. The information clues (*screeched with horror, writhed in pain, desperately*) that establish the mood are underlined and discussed. The teacher concludes the modeling activity by writing five new words on the board and explaining, "These words are also in the story that you are about to read. As you come across them, stop and think. How do the words or phrases or sentences surrounding each word create a certain feeling or mood that will allow you to understand what each one means?"

When modeling the use of context in Table 4.2, it's important for students to discover the information clues. It's also important for the teacher to relate the demonstration to several additional words to be encountered in the assignment. Instruction of this type will have a significant cumulative effect. If students are shown how to use contextual clues for two or three words each week, over the course of an academic year they will have 80 to 120 applications in the process.

Cognate Relationships and Context

Whenever the opportunity presents itself, it's important to help students recognize and use the relationship between *cognates* and the context in which they are used. Cognates are words that are culturally and linguistically related in both the nonnative speaker's language and in English. As part of cognitive strategy instruction for struggling readers, Latina/o students in a middle school special education classroom were shown how to approximate word meaning through the cognate relationships they encountered in the texts that they were reading. The researchers used a "think-aloud" strategy, as discussed in the previous chapter, to scaffold instruction (Jimenez & Gamez 1996, p. 88):

Researcher: You know the word in Spanish, so we can use a Spanish clue to help us figure out what it means. Victor, what does *espectacular* mean?

Victor: That it's useful?

Researcher: It's something very . . .

Sara: Special?

Researcher: Special, you got it! I like this. So (for) something very special, you can say wonderful, *maravilloso*. The Spanish clue helped us with *spectacular* because that is exactly the same in English and Spanish. Have you guys heard that word on the radio, *spectacular*? (The researcher writes this on the chalkboard.) That's English, and here's Spanish *espectacular*. The only difference between English and Spanish is that we put an *e* in the front in Spanish. That's exactly the same word. It almost sounds exactly the same, only a little bit different. But when you guys can do this you're taking advantage of your bilingualism and you're using what you already know to help you understand. OK? I think it's really cool when Latino kids do that. That makes a lot of sense to me.

In addition to emphasizing cognate-related vocabulary building, showing linguistically diverse learners how to approximate word meaning through *word structure* and context is another important aspect of vocabulary building.

Word Structure

A word itself provides information clues about its meaning. The smallest unit of meaning in a word is called a *morpheme*. Analyzing a word's structure, *morphemic analysis*, is a second vocabulary-building strategy that students can use to predict meaning. When readers encounter an unknown word, they can reduce the number of feasible guesses about its meaning considerably by approaching the whole word and identifying its parts. When students use morphemic analysis in combination with context, they have a powerful strategy at their command.

Student readers often find long words daunting. Olsen and Ames (1972) put long or polysyllabic words into four categories:

1. *Compound words made up of two known words joined together.* Examples: *commonwealth, matchmaker.*

2. *Words containing a recognizable stem to which an affix (a prefix, combining form, or suffix) has been added.* Examples: *surmountable, deoxygenize, unsystematic, microscope.*

3. *Words that can be analyzed into familiar and regular pronounceable units.* Examples: *undulate, calcify, subterfuge, strangulate.*

4. *Words that contain irregular pronounceable units so that there is no sure pronunciation unless one consults a dictionary.* Examples: *louver, indictment.*

Content vocabulary terms from categories 1 and 2 (compound words and recognizable stems and affixes) are the best candidates for instruction. You can readily demonstrate techniques for predicting the meanings of these words because each of their isolated parts will always represent a meaning unit.

In some instances, a word from category 3 may also be selected for emphasis. However, there is no guarantee that students will bring prior knowledge and experience to words that comprise the third category. Long phonemically regular words lend themselves to syllabication. Syllabication involves breaking words into pronounceable sound units or syllables. The word *undulate*, for example, can be syllabicated (un-du-late). However, the syllable *un* is not a meaning-bearing prefix.

Many words from category 3 are derived from Latin or Greek. Students who struggle with texts will find these words especially difficult to analyze for meaning because of their lack of familiarity with Latin or Greek roots. Occasionally, a word such as *strangulate* (derived from the Latin *strangulatus*) can be taught because students may recognize the familiar word *strangle*. They might then be shown how to link *strangle* to the verb suffix *-ate* (which means "to cause to become") to hypothesize a meaning for *strangulate*. Unfortunately, the verb suffix *-ate* has multiple meanings, and the teacher should be quick to point this out to students. This procedure is shaky, but it has some payoff.

Words from category 2 warrant instruction, because English root words are more recognizable, obviously, than Latin or Greek ones. Whenever feasible, teach the principles of structural word analysis using terms that have English roots. Certain affixes are more helpful than others, and knowing which affixes to emphasize during instruction will minimize students' confusion.

The most helpful affixes are the combining forms, prefixes, or suffixes that have single, invariant meanings. Deighton's (1970) monumental study of word structure has helped identify affixes that have single meanings. (See Appendix A for a summary of Deighton's findings.)

Many other commonly used prefixes have more than one meaning or have several shades of meaning. Because of their widespread use in content terminology, you should also consider these variant-meaning prefixes for functional teaching. (See Appendix B for a list of prefixes with varying meanings.)

The tables of affixes are resources for you. Don't be misled into thinking that students should learn long lists of affixes in isolation to help in analyzing word structure. This approach is neither practical nor functional. We recommend instead that students be taught affixes as they are needed to analyze the structure of terms that will appear in a reading assignment.

For example, an English teacher modeled how to analyze the meaning of *pandemonium* before students were to encounter the term in an assignment from *One Flew over the Cuckoo's Nest*. She wrote the word on the board—pan*demonium*—

underlining the English base word *demon*, and asked students for several synonyms for the word. Student responses included *witch, devil, monster*, and *wicked people.*

Then she explained that *-ium* was a noun suffix meaning "a place of." "Now let's take a look at *pan*. Sheila, have you ever heard of the Pan American Games? They are similar to the Olympics, but what do you think is a major difference between the Olympics and the Pan American Games?" Sheila and several students responded to the question. A brief discussion led the students to conclude the Pan American Games, like the Olympics, are a series of athletic contests; however, unlike the Olympics, only countries in North, Central, and South America and the Caribbean participate in the Pan American Games. The teacher affirmed the students' conclusions and noted that Pan American means quite literally, "all the Americas." Further discussion centered around the word *panoramic.* Through this process, relating the known to the unknown, students decided that *pan* meant "all."

"Now, back to *pandemonium*. 'A place of all the demons.' What would this place be like?" Students were quick to respond. The demonstration was completed with two additional points. The teacher asked the class to find the place in *One Flew over the Cuckoo's Nest* where *pandemonium* was used and read the paragraph. Then she asked them to refine their predictions of the meaning of *pandemonium*. Next the teacher discussed the origin of the word—which the English poet John Milton coined in his epic poem *Paradise Lost*. Pandemonium was the capital of hell, the place where all the demons and devils congregated—figuratively speaking, where "all hell broke loose."

Using the Dictionary as a Strategic Resource

The use of context and word structure are strategies that give struggling readers insight into the meanings of unknown words. Rarely does context or word structure help learners derive precise definitions for keywords. Instead, these vocabulary-building strategies keep readers on the right track so that they are able to follow a text without getting bogged down or giving up.

There are times, however, when context and word structure reveal little about a word's meaning. In these instances, or when a precise definition is needed, a dictionary is a logical alternative and a valuable resource for students.

Knowing when to use a dictionary is as important as knowing how to use it. A content teacher should incorporate dictionary usage into ongoing plans but should avoid a very common pitfall in the process of doing so. When asked, "What does this word mean?" the teacher shouldn't automatically reply, "Look it up in the dictionary."

To some students, "Look it up in the dictionary" is another way of saying "Don't bug me" or "I really don't have the time or the inclination to help you." Of course, this may not be the case at all. However, from an instructional perspective, that hard-to-come-by teachable moment is lost whenever we routinely suggest to students to look up a word in the dictionary.

One way to make the dictionary a functional resource is to use it to verify educated guesses about word meaning revealed through context or word structure.

For example, if a student asks you for the meaning of a vocabulary term, an effective tactic is to bounce the question right back: "What do you think it means? Let's look at the way it's used. Are there any clues to its meaning?" If students are satisfied with an educated guess because it makes sense, the word need not be looked up. But if students are still unsure of the word's meaning, the dictionary is there.

When students go into a dictionary to verify or to determine a precise definition, more often than not they need supervision to make good decisions. Keep these tips in mind as you work on dictionary usage.

1. *Help students determine the "best fit" between a word and its definition.* Students must often choose the most appropriate definition from several. This poses a real dilemma for young learners. Your interactions will help them make the best choice of a definition and will provide a behavior model for making such a choice.

2. *If you do assign a list of words to look up in a dictionary, choose them selectively.* A few words are better than many. The chances are greater that students will learn several key terms thoroughly than that they will develop vague notions about many.

3. *Help students with the pronunciation key in a glossary or dictionary as the need arises.* This does not mean, however, that you will teach skills associated with the use of a pronunciation key in isolated lessons. Instead, it means guiding and reinforcing students' abilities to use a pronunciation key as they study the content of your course.

Vocabulary development is a gradual process, "the result of many encounters with a word towards a more precise grasp of the concept the word represents" (Parry 1993, p. 127). If this is the case, students who struggle with demanding text material will benefit from vocabulary-building strategies that make use of context clues, word structure, and appropriate uses of reference tools such as the dictionary. Johnson and Steele (1996) found that with English language learners, the use of *personal word lists* provided excellent strategy practice and application in the use of vocabulary-building strategies.

The use of personal word lists would be of value not only to English language-minority students but also to all students who need explicit support in the use of vocabulary-building strategies. The personal word list technique emphasizes the need for students to self-select important concept words and incorporates key principles learned from the VSS strategy discussed earlier in the chapter. Students then complete a personal word list, which may be part of a vocabulary notebook or learning log. The personal word list is divided into four columns as illustrated in Figure 4.4. For each word entry, students list (1) the word, (2) what the word means, (3) the clues used to construct meaning for the word (context, word structure, or a combination of the two), and (4) a dictionary definition, when it is appropriate to consult the dictionary for a definition. Figure 4.4 illustrates an English language learner's personal word list entries (Johnson & Steele 1996).

FIGURE 4.4   An English Language Learner's Personal Word List

Word	What I Think It Means	Clues (context or structure)	Dictionary Definition (if needed)
sacred	religious	they were entering a sacred building that loomed out of the night to give them what haven and what blessing they yearned for.	
vexation	displeasure	but something would come up some vexation that was like a fly buzzing around their heads.	
lurch	movement	she took a step toward the porch lurching	a sudden movement forward or sideways

Source: From Denise Johnson, "So Many Words, So Little Time: Helping College ESL Learners Acquire Vocabulary-Building Strategies" (1996, February). *Journal of Adolescent and Adult Literacy, 39*(5), 351. Copyright © 1996 by the International Reading Association. All rights reserved. Used by permission of the author and the International Reading Association.

Comprehension Strategies

In Chapter 3, we discussed question–answer relationships (QARs) and reciprocal teaching as two research-based comprehension strategies used to show learners how to generate and answer questions (NRP 2000; Pearson & Duke 2001). In this section, we extend our discussion of comprehension strategies by exploring two additional research-based practices that are integral parts of strategy instruction for students who might struggle with texts in content literacy situations: *Questioning the author (QtA)* and the *directed reading–thinking activity (DR–TA)*. Both of these comprehension strategies involve students in a process of asking and answering questions about a text, making inferences, and thinking critically. Because QtA and DR–TA are highly interactive strategies that rely on active engagement and student talk, we recommend them for use in sheltered classrooms.

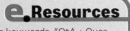

e.Resources

Use the keywords, "QtA + Questioning the author" to search for additional information about and classroom applications of the QtA strategy.

Questioning the Author (QtA)

Questioning the author (QtA) is a comprehension strategy that models for students the importance of asking questions while reading. Beck, McKeown, Hamilton, and Kucan (1997) devised the QtA strategy to demonstrate the kinds of questions students need to ask in order to think more deeply and construct meaning about segments of text as they read. Good readers act on the author's message. If what they are reading doesn't make sense to them, they generate questions about what the author says and means. When students struggle with text, however, they often do not have a clue about generating questions, let alone interacting with the author of text. Enter QtA instruction.

The QtA strategy shows students how to read text closely as if the author were there to be challenged and questioned. QtA places value on the quality and depth of students' responses to the author's intent. It is important that students keep their minds active while reading as they engage in a dialogue with an author. Good readers monitor whether the author is making sense by asking questions such as, "What is the author trying to say here?" "What does the author mean?" "So what? What is the significance of the author's message?" "Does this make sense with what the author told us before?" "Does the author explain this clearly?" These questions, according to Beck and colleagues (1997), are posed by the teacher to help students "take on" the author and understand that text material needs to be challenged.

Through QtA, students learn that authors are fallible and may not always express ideas in the easiest way for readers to understand. QtA builds metacognitive knowledge by making students aware of an important principle related to reading comprehension: *Not comprehending what the author is trying to say is not always the fault of the reader.* As a result, students come to view their roles as readers as "grappling with text" as they seek to make sense of the author's intent.

Planning a QtA Lesson

Planning QtA lessons for narrative or informational texts involves a three-stage process that requires the teacher to (1) identify major understandings and potential problems with a text prior to its use in class, (2) segment the text into logical stopping points for discussion, and (3) develop questions, or *queries,* that model and demonstrate how to "question the author." Box 4.2 examines the planning process.

RESEARCH-BASED BEST PRACTICES

BOX 4.2

Steps in a QtA Lesson

1. Analyze the text
   - *Identify major understandings and potential problems that students may encounter during reading.*
   - *Read the text closely and note the author's intent, the major ideas and themes, and any areas or potential obstacles in the material that could affect comprehension.*
   - *Reflect on your own comprehension as you read the text.* Note any passages that you reread or pause to think about, knowing that these sections will most likely be problematic for students.

2. Segment the text
   - *Determine where to stop the reading to initiate and develop discussion.* The text segments may not always fall at a page or paragraph break. You may want to stop reading after one sentence to ask a question.

3. Develop questions
   - *Plan questions that will help students respond to what the author says and means.* These generic questions prompt students' responses to the text and encourage them to dig deeper and make sense of what they are reading. The following question guide will help you frame initiating and follow-up questions at different points in the lesson. Initiating questions at the beginning of the reading draws students' attention to the author's intent, whereas follow-up queries focus the direction of the discussion and assist students as they integrate and connect ideas. Follow-up questions help students determine why the author included certain ideas.

QtA QUESTION GUIDE

Initial questions at the beginning of the lesson:

- What is the author trying to say?
- What is the authors's message?
- What is the author talking about?

Follow-up questions during reading help students make connections and inferences about the text:

- This is what the author says, but what does it mean?
- How does this text segment connect with what the author has already said?

Follow-up questions during reading help students with difficulties and confusions with the way the author presents information:

- Does the author make sense here?
- Did the author explain this clearly?
- What's missing? What do we need to find out?

Follow-up questions during reading clarify misinterpretations or make students aware that they made an inference (reinforce QARs):

- Did the author tell us that?
- Did the author say that or did you "think and search" to get the answer?

When using QtA to comprehend stories, pose *narrative queries*. Through the use of narrative queries, students become familiar with an author's writing style as they strive to understand character, plot, and underlying story meaning. The following queries help students think about story characters: "How do things look for this character now?" "Given what the author has already told us about this character, what do you think the author is up to?" Understanding the story plot can be accomplished with queries such as these: "How has the author let you know that something has changed?" "How has the author settled this for us?"

Guiding the QtA Discussion

Beck and colleagues (1997) recommend the use of a variety of "discussion moves" to guide students:

Marking: Draw attention to certain ideas by either paraphrasing what a student said or by acknowledging its importance with statements such as "Good idea" or "That's an important observation."

Turning back: Make students responsible for figuring out ideas and turning back to the text for clarification.

Revoicing: Assist students as they express their ideas; filter the most important information and help students who are struggling to express their ideas by rephrasing their statements.

Modeling: Think aloud about an issue that is particularly difficult to understand, one that students are unable to reach without assistance.

Annotating: Provide information that is not in the text so that students can understand the concepts fully.

Recapping: Summarize the main ideas as a signal to move on in the lesson. Recapping can be done by either the teacher or the students.

The thoughtful use of questions is vital for classroom discussion. As learners actively explore and clarify meaning, guide the discussion as you progress from one text segment to the next. Another research-based comprehension strategy also centers around the use of segmented text while modeling comprehension processes. It is called the directed reading–thinking activity (DR–TA).

Directed Reading–Thinking Activity (DR-TA)

The DR–TA fosters critical awareness and thinking by engaging learners in a process that involves prediction, verification, interpretation, and judgment. Much like the QtA, the teacher guides the reading and stimulates thinking through the frequent use of open-ended questions such as "What do you think?" "Why do you think so?" "Can you prove it?" The learning environment for a DR–TA lesson is critical to its success as an instructional practice. The teacher must be supportive and encouraging so as not to inhibit students' participation in the activity. As a rule, avoid inhibiting participation by refuting students' predictions. Wait time is also important. When posing an open-ended question, it is not unusual to pause for two, three, five, or even ten seconds for students to respond. Too often, the tendency is to slice the original question into smaller parts. Sometimes a teacher starts slicing too quickly out of a sense of frustration or anxiety rather than because of students' inability to respond. Silence may very well be an indication that hypothesis formation or other cognitive activities are taking place in the students' heads. So wait—and see what happens.

To prepare for a DR–TA with an informational text, analyze the material for its superordinate and subordinate concepts. What are the relevant concepts, ideas, relationships, and information in the material? The content analysis will help you decide on logical stopping points as you direct students through the reading.

For short stories and other narrative material, determine the key elements of the story: the *setting* (time and place, major characters) and the *events in the plot* (the initiating events or problem-generating situation, the protagonist's reaction to the event and his or her goal to resolve the problem, the set of attempts to achieve the goal, outcomes related to the protagonist's attempts to achieve the goal and resolve the problem, the character's reaction).

Once these elements have been identified, the teacher has a framework for deciding on logical stopping points within the story. In Figure 4.5, we indicate a general plan that may be followed or adapted for specific story lines. Notice that the suggested stopping points come at key junctures in a causal chain of events in the story line. Each juncture suggests a logical stopping point in that it assumes that the reader has enough information from at least one preceding event to predict a future happening or event. Box 4.3 outlines steps in a DR–TA lesson for narrative and informational texts.

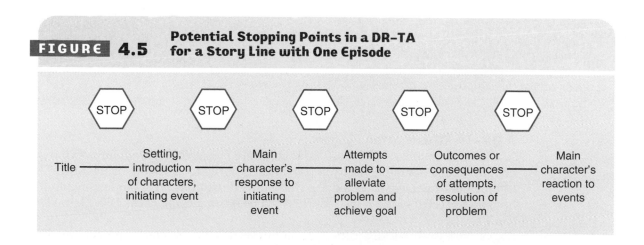

FIGURE 4.5 **Potential Stopping Points in a DR–TA for a Story Line with One Episode**

STOP	STOP	STOP	STOP	STOP
Title —	Setting, introduction of characters, initiating event —	Main character's response to initiating event —	Attempts made to alleviate problem and achieve goal —	Outcomes or consequences of attempts, resolution of problem — Main character's reaction to events

RESEARCH-BASED BEST PRACTICES

BOX 4.3

Steps in a DR–TA Lesson for Narrative and Informational Texts

NARRATIVE TEXT

1. *Begin with the title of the narrative or with a quick survey of the title, sub-heads, illustrations, and other expository material.* Ask, "What do you think this story (or section) will be about?" Encourage predictions. Ask, "Why do you think so?"

2. *Ask students to read silently to a predetermined logical stopping point in the text.* Have students use a 5-by-8-inch index card or a blank sheet of paper placed on the page to mark the place to which they are reading. This will also slow down those who want to read on before answering the questions.

3. *Repeat questions as suggested in step 1.* Some predictions will be refined; new ones will be formulated. Ask, "How do you know?" to encourage clarification or verification. Redirect questions.

4. *Continue silent reading to another suitable point.* Ask similar questions.

5. *Continue in this way to the end of the material.* A note of caution: Too frequent interruption of reading may detract from the focus of attention, which needs to be on larger concepts. As readers move through the DR–TA process,

encourage reflection and thoughtful responses to the text.

INFORMATIONAL TEXT

1. *Set the purposes for reading.* Individual or group purposes are set by students based on some limited clues in material and their own background experience.

   a. "From reading only the chapter title (subtitles, charts, maps, etc.), what do you think the author will present in this chapter (passage, next pages, etc.)?"

   b. Record speculations on the chalkboard and augment them by the query, "Why do you think so?"

   c. Encourage a guided discussion. If speculations and statements of proof yield an inaccurate or weak knowledge base, review through discussion. Frequently, terminology will be introduced by students (especially those who are more knowledgeable) in their predictions. The teacher may choose to capitalize on such situations by further clarifying significant concepts in a way that enhances pupil discussion and inquiry through discovery techniques.

A DR–TA Illustration

In an eighth-grade science class, students were engaged in a study of a textbook chapter about the light spectrum (Davidson & Wilkerson 1988). Using a DR–TA framework, the teacher guided the students' interactions with the text material. Study an excerpt of the transcript from the beginning cycle of the DR–TA in Figure 4.6.

As you examine the transcript, note that teacher–student interactions are recorded in the left column of the box. The teacher's questions and comments are

d. A poll can be taken to intensify the predictive process, and a debate may naturally ensue. Additional proof may be needed from available reference books.

2. *Adjust the rate to the purposes and the material.* The teacher should adjust the amount of reading, depending on the purposes, nature, and difficulty of the reading material; skimming, scanning, and studying are involved. Students are told, "Read to find out if your predictions were correct." The reading task may be several pages, a few passages, or some other amount of the text. If the teacher designates numerous stopping points within the reading task, the same procedures as noted in step 1 should be executed at each stopping point.

3. *Observe the reading.* The teacher observes the reading by assisting students who request help and noting abilities to adjust rate to purpose and material, to comprehend material, and to use word recognition strategies.

4. *Guide reader–text interactions.* Students check the purposes by accepting, rejecting, or redefining them. This can be accomplished during discussion time after students have read a predetermined number of pages or by encouraging students to rework their predictions as they read, noting their revised predictions and hypotheses.

5. *Extend learning through discussion, further reading, additional study, or writing.* Students and teacher identify these needs throughout the strategy.

a. After reading, students should be asked (1) if their predictions were inaccurate, (2) if they needed to revise or reject any predictions as they read, (3) how they knew revision was necessary, and (4) what their new predictions were.

b. Discussion in small groups is most useful in this step. A recorder, appointed by the group, can share the groups' reading–thinking processes with the whole class. These should be compared with original predictions.

c. The teacher should ask open-ended questions that encourage generalization and application relevant to students' predictions and the significant concepts presented. In any follow-up discussion or questioning, proof should always be required: "How do you know that? Why did you think so? What made you think that way?" Encourage students to share passages, sentences, and so on for further proof (Homer 1979).

printed in capital letters, followed by the students' responses in lowercase letters. An analysis of the DR–TA lesson as it evolved is printed in the right column.

The transcript shows how the students used prior knowledge to anticipate the information that the text would reveal. As they shared what they expected to find, the students engaged in analyzing their pooled ideas. Their interactions with the teacher illustrate how a DR–TA instructional framework creates a need to know and helps readers declare purposes through anticipation and prediction making.

Excerpt of a DR–TA Transcript from a Science Lesson on the Light Spectrum

Teacher–Student Interactions	Analysis of Lesson
I'D LIKE FOR YOU TO BEGIN BY JUST READING THIS ACTIVITY IN THIS SECTION. THEN TELL ME WHAT YOU EXPECT TO FIND IN THIS PASSAGE. YOU KNOW IT'S ABOUT LIGHT AND COLOR AND SPECTRUMS. WHAT ELSE DO YOU EXPECT THAT YOU WILL FIND?	The teacher directs students to read a description of an activity designed to produce a sun's spectrum with a prism. The activity includes holding a thermometer in the spectrum produced, placing a fluorite substance near the spectrum, and anticipating changes.
s: Heat	
WHY DO YOU SAY HEAT?	
s: Well, some of the colors are cooler.	The student's response is based on prior knowledge which she judges will be relevant.
DO YOU KNOW WHICH ONES WILL BE COOLER?	The teacher encourages the student to extend the response.
s: I think the darker ones.	
WHY DO YOU SAY THAT?	Teacher asks for justification.
s: They look cooler.	
THEY LOOK COOLER? OKAY.	Teacher accepts response, recognizing that the student has, in fact, generated a question to be answered in reading the text.
WHAT ELSE? DO YOU AGREE OR DISAGREE?	The teacher encourages other students to analyze this hypothesis or generate a different one.
s: Well, I agree with her on infrared and ultraviolet. They are probably the hottest colors you can get of the spectrum.	The student's response shows that he is evaluating the other student's response. Also, he uses specific vocabulary from his prior knowledge to extend the prediction.
ALL RIGHT. ANYBODY ELSE?	The teacher does not make a judgment about the validity of the predictions since that is the responsibility of the students as they read and discuss.

Once the purposes were established, the teacher assigned a section of the text chapter to be read. According to Davidson and Wilkerson (1988), two observers of the lesson:

When students read the portion of the text they were directed to read, they read that infrared waves are invisible and that they are heat waves. Discussion, involving text ideas, students' previous ideas, and their reasoning abilities, showed that they dis-

FIGURE **4.6** **Continued**

Teacher–Student Interactions	Analysis of Lesson
s: I think he is wrong.	A student disagrees.
WHY?	Teacher asks for justification.
s: Because whenever you melt steel, steel always turns red before it turns white. When it turns white, it melts completely.	The student analyzes the prior student's prediction and explains in terms of his own experience.
OKAY.	
s: You can't see infrared.	As stated, the student's response is a literal statement.
AND HOW WOULD THAT MAKE A DIFFERENCE IN WHAT HE JUST SAID?	The teacher assumes that there is a connection with the discussion and asks for explanation.
s: Well, he just said that it turned red before it turned white. And you can't see white, it's just a shade. Infrared you can't see—which would be just like sunlight. You can't see sunlight. So, I think it would be hotter.	In his extended response the student disagrees with the prior student's conclusion and explanation and uses an illustration from his prior knowledge which he feels is relevant to "prove" his point.
YOU THINK IT WOULD BE HOTTER?	
OKAY.	The teacher does not point out the validity or lack of validity of either student's logic. She recognizes that both students are thinking critically and that they and others in the group will read to find clues to justify the concepts they are hypothesizing. She is consistent in her role as a facilitator of student discussion.
ANYBODY ELSE?	
WELL, LET ME GIVE YOU THIS WHOLE FIRST PARAGRAPH. I WANT YOU TO READ TO THE BOTTOM OF THE PAGE AND THEN I WANT YOU TO GO TO THE TOP OF THE NEXT PAGE. IT WILL BE THE VERY TOP PARAGRAPH. COVER UP WHAT'S BELOW IT WITH YOUR PAPER. READ THAT FAR AND THEN STOP.	
(Students read silently.)	

Source: Reprinted with permission of Jane L. Davidson and Bonnie C. Wilkerson.

covered that infrared light is *not* one of the hottest colors because it is not a color. They also discovered that infrared waves are hot, since they are heat waves. The text supplied literal information. The discussion facilitated concept development and critical thinking. (p. 37)

Although the students' predictions were amiss in the initial cycle of questioning, the teacher chose not to evaluate or judge the predictions. She recognized that as readers interact with the text, more often than not they are able to clarify their misconceptions for themselves.

Instructional practices such as the QtA and DR–TA not only model comprehension strategies but also engage learners in meaningful talk and discussion. Teachers can make strong connections between content learning and literacy development when they link classroom talk to reading and writing. The predominant type of talk in content areas classrooms usually revolves around instructional routines known as *recitations,* in which students take turns answering questions with bits and pieces of information. In these turn-taking exchanges, the social context for learning is dominated by teacher talk with little opportunity for students to explore and clarify ideas. Discussions that emphasize student talk are an alternative to recitations.

Talking and Working Together

Talking is critical to the success of linguistically diverse learners in content area classrooms. Instructional routines that revolve around discussion provide the support that native and nonnative speakers need to engage in meaningful activities that involve talking and working together. Classroom talk, however, can easily become teacher dominated rather than student centered. When a teacher does most of the talking, asks mostly factual questions, and controls who takes turns answering questions, learners quickly perceive their roles as passive nonparticipants in the academic life of the classroom. Lou, a Chinese American student in a northern California high school, describes what it is like to be in classrooms where teachers dominate talk: "When a teacher runs the show, it's just, just kind of up to him. He has like a lecture written out and, you know, point by point. . . . A teacher kind of intimidates the students. 'Cause' he's up there, you know, talking, making these complicated points and, you know, [students] just taking notes or something" (Knoeller 1994, p. 578). Let's take a closer look at the veracity of Lou's words, the role that talk plays in diverse classrooms, and some alternatives to teacher-dominated classroom talk.

Scaffolding Student Talk

The talk that students engage in during class discussions supports content literacy and learning in powerful ways. As we showed in the previous chapter, talk shapes what students learn about their own reading processes. Metacognitive discussions, if you will, make students aware of reading strategies and how to use those strategies to learn with text. The modeling of strategies through thinkalouds and other types of metacognitive talk reveals what otherwise would be the "secrets" of text comprehension to which only good readers have access.

Talk also helps students to explore and clarify concepts they encounter during reading. As Douglas Barnes (1995) explains, "The kinds of participation in the classroom conversation that are supported and encouraged by a teacher signal to students what learning is required of them" (p. 2). At times, teachers unwittingly intimidate learners through the questions they ask. Samples (1977) likens questions to conversational acts of aggression when they put students on the spot. Do you recall ever being put on the spot by a question? In that interminable second or two between question and response, between pounding heart and short gasps for air, do you remember asking yourself, "What's *the* right answer—the one this instructor expects?" When questions are used to foster a right-answer-only atmosphere in class, they will not focus thinking about what has been read, and they will not prompt the processes by which diverse learners construct knowledge. Instead, they make the response—the correct answer—the all-important concern.

When students are on the spot, they often resort to guessing what is inside the teacher's head. One need only read Judy Blume's devastating parody of a music teacher's question to her class in Figure 4.7 to appreciate how nonproductive it is playing "Guess What's in My Head."

Turn-Taking Instructional Routines

Seeking right answers only, putting students on the spot, and reinforcing Guess What's in My Head behavior are tied to what some consider the prevalent instructional model in U.S. schooling, *turn taking* (Duffy 1983). Turn taking occurs whenever the teacher asks a question or assigns a turn, the student responds, and the teacher gives feedback by correcting or reinforcing the response. Teachers often depend on turn taking to "discuss" the content of textbook assignments. Yet what results is hardly a discussion at all. During turn-taking routines, questions usually forestall or frustrate classroom talk. Question–answer exchanges are brief, usually three to five seconds in duration, sometimes less, sometimes more. Rather than to characterize these question–answer exchanges as discussion, it is more appropriate to view them as recitation.

The striking feature of recitation is that the teacher's talk consists of questions. To illustrate this point, Dillon (1983, pp. 10–11) provides a transcript from a typical recitation conducted by a high school teacher of U.S. history:

Teacher: OK, so we've kind of covered leadership and some of the things that Washington brought with it. Why else did they win? Leadership is important, that's one.

Student: France gave 'em help.

Teacher: OK, so France giving aid is an example of what? France is an example of it, obviously.

Student: Aid from allies.

Teacher: Aid from allies, very good. Were there any other allies who gave aid to us?

Student: Spain.

Teacher: Spain. Now, when you say aid, can you define that?

Student: Help.

FIGURE **4.7** **Guess What's in My Head**

When she finished her song she was right next to Wendy. "Wendy . . . can you tell me what was coming out of my mouth as I sang?"

"Out of your mouth?" Wendy asked.

"That's right," Miss Rothbelle told her.

"Well . . . it was . . . um . . . words?"

"No . . . no . . . no," Miss Rothbelle said.

Wendy was surprised. She can always give teachers the answers they want.

Miss Rothbelle moved on. "Do you know, Caroline?"

"Was it sound?"

"Wrong!" Miss Rothbelle said, turning. "Donna Davidson, can you tell me?"

"It was a song," Donna said.

"Really Donna . . . we all know that!" Miss Rothbelle looked around. "Linda Fischer, do you know what was coming out of my mouth as I sang to the class?"

Linda didn't say anything.

"Well, Linda . . ." Miss Rothbelle said.

"I think it was air," Linda finally told her. "Either that or breath."

Miss Rothbelle walked over to Linda's desk. "That was not the correct answer. Weren't you paying attention?" She pulled a few strands of Linda's hair. . . .

She walked up and down the aisles until she stopped at my desk. . . .

"We'll see if you've been paying attention . . . suppose you tell me the answer to my question."

I had no idea what Miss Rothbelle wanted me to say. There was just one thing left that could have been coming out of her mouth as she sang, so I said, "It was spit."

"What?" Miss Rothbelle glared at me.

"I mean, it was saliva," I told her.

Miss Rothbelle banged her fist on my desk. "That was a very rude thing to say. You can sit in the corner for the rest of the period." . . .

At the end of the music period Robby Winters called out, "Miss Rothbelle . . . Miss Rothbelle . . ."

"What is it?" she asked.

"You never told us what was coming out of your mouth when you sang."

"That's right," Miss Rothbelle said. "I didn't."

"What was it?" Robby asked.

"It was melody," Miss Rothbelle said. Then she spelled it. "M-e-l-o-d-y. And every one of you should have known." She blew her pitchpipe at us and walked out of the room.

Teacher: Define "help." Spell it out for me.

Student: Assistance.

Teacher: Spell it out for me.

Student: They taught the men how to fight the right way.

Teacher: Who taught?
Student: The allies.
Teacher: Where? When?
Student: In the battlefield.
Teacher: In the battlefield?

In the preceding exchanges, the students take turns answering questions about the success of Washington's revolutionary army. The eight question–answer exchanges lasted a little more than thirty seconds, or four to five seconds per exchange. Each student addressed a response to the teacher, not to other students. The nature of turn taking is such that it is *verboten* for another student to jump into the exchange unless first recognized by the teacher to take a turn.

In turn taking, as you can infer, certain rules accompany classroom talk. One was alluded to earlier: The teacher speaks in questions; the students speak in answers. And the form of their answers indicates another rule of turn taking: Give just enough information specified by the question to satisfy the teacher. No wonder question–answer exchanges are brief. Interestingly, as part of the exchange, students invariably address their responses to the teacher. The implicit rule is never to address other students because only the teacher gives feedback. Each respondent thus awaits his or her turn to answer further questions. Any attempts at conversation or discussion are stifled.

A teacher's language and actions signal to students what their roles are to be within a lesson. Although recitation may serve legitimate educational purposes (quizzing, reviewing), it may negatively affect students' cognitive, affective, and expressive processes. Given the rules that operate during turn taking, teachers may very well increase student passivity and dependence. Furthermore, turn taking leads to a limited construction of meaning with text. Because the pace of questions is often rapid, readers hardly have the time to think about or to clarify or explore their understanding of the text material. When we ask predominantly "quiz show" questions, students soon engage in fact finding rather than in thinking about the ideas the author communicates. The inherent danger to text learners is subtle but devastating: Mistaken signals may be telegraphed to students about what it means to comprehend text and what their role is as comprehenders. Finding bits and pieces of information becomes the end-all and be-all of reading.

Discussion as an Alternative to Turn Taking

Discussion allows teacher and students to renegotiate authority, or as Lou, the English language learner quoted earlier, put it, renegotiate who "runs the show." Teachers lead, but do not dominate, classroom talk. The "show" belongs to both the teacher and the students. In discussion-centered classrooms, the burden of responsibility for learning shifts from the teacher's shoulders to the students'. Scaffolding talk through discussions creates an environment where students have opportunities to participate more fully by talking more, and by sharing their understanding, interpretations, and perspectives related to the ideas and concepts under discussion. Each classroom is a community, and talk is at its heart. As John Barnitz (1994) explains, it is talk that "connects people, that enables them to negotiate meaning in a situation or from text, that enables a teacher to lead a class in new directions" (p. 586).

Lou's English teacher, Joan Cone, teaches in a culturally diverse high school that reformed its tracking policies by opening up senior-level English classes to all students by self-selection (Knoeller 1994). Regardless of their academic history, students could choose to take college preparatory courses "and even AP classes." Cone's AP class, for example, was ethnically diverse, balanced in terms of gender and levels of achievement (Scholastic Assessment Test scores ranged from 750 to 1350). Given the broad range of student differences, Cone's challenge was responding to diversity while maintaining the high standards of a rigorous AP class. She experimented with a variety of instructional strategies, including student-led discussions of literature.

Christian Knoeller (1994), who studied Cone's class, notes that she allowed students to volunteer as discussion leaders. A discussion leader was responsible for raising questions and keeping the discussion moving. At times, when discussions got bogged down or students had to be coached into using the text to justify their interpretations, Cone would step into the discussion to get it back on track. But she did so as a participant rather than as an authority figure. The goal was to have students engage with the text and with one another. In Cone's words:

> Besides assisting students with understanding sophisticated text, talk can create a classroom atmosphere in which the most able reader and least able reader can collaborate in making meaning and can learn from each other by sharing their insights, experiences, questions, and interpretations. . . . The emphasis (during student-led discussions) was always on asking questions, looking back in the text for substantiation, trying out interpretations, coming to agreement or living with disagreement: students creating meaning together, students teaching each other. . . . A sense of community had been established. (Knoeller 1994, p. 574)

Whether student-led or teacher-led, a discussion has certain characteristics that distinguish it from a recitation. First, discussions represent an open exchange of ideas. Second, both students and teacher ask questions. Third, students are just as likely to talk to other students as they are to respond to the teacher. And fourth, students learn to use their texts to substantiate their responses and support their interpretations.

Discussion can best be described as conversational interactions between teacher and students as well as between students and other students. In teacher-led discussions, the teacher doesn't ask questions over long stretches of time, although questions are used judiciously throughout most discussions. As a result, discussion signifies an exchange of ideas and active participation among all parties involved.

Asking questions, even those designed to get students to open up and share their understanding of text, doesn't always result in a good discussion or, for that matter, a bad discussion; only nondiscussion whenever students do not make sense of what they are doing or what is happening. Students stand a better chance of participating in discussion when they have a clear sense of purpose, understand the discussion task, and are given explicit directions and clear explanations.

Different types of discussion have different purposes. Let's explore some of these purposes and the types of discussion that are likely to unfold when students talk about what they have read.

Purposes and Types of Discussions

Many of the instructional strategies and alternatives in this book are necessarily tied to discussion of one kind or another. Discussion allows students to respond to text, build concepts, clarify meaning, explore issues, share perspectives, and refine thinking. But effective discussions don't run by themselves. For a discussion to be successful, a teacher has to be willing to take a risk or two.

Whenever you initiate a discussion, its outcome is bound to be uncertain, especially if its purpose is to help students think critically and creatively about what they have read. Often a teacher abandons discussion for the safety of recitation, where the outcome is far more predictable. A text discussion, however, should be neither a quiz show nor, at the opposite end of the continuum, a bull session (Roby 1987). Yet, when discussions aren't carefully planned, students often feel an aimlessness or become easily threatened by the teacher's questions. Both being quizzed about text material and simply shooting the bull are apt to close doors on active text learning.

Different purposes for text discussion lead to the use of different types of discussions by content area teachers. *Guided discussions* and *reflective discussions* provide varying degrees of structure for students to talk about text as they interact with one another.

Guided Discussion

If your aim is to develop concepts, clarify meaning, and promote understanding, the most appropriate discussion may be *informational*. The main objective of an informational discussion is to help students grapple with issues and understand important concepts. When the discussion task is information centered, teachers use a *guided discussion*.

In a guided discussion, a teacher provides a moderate amount of scaffolding as he or she directs students to think about what they have read through the use of questions and/or teacher-developed guide material. Because the emphasis is on content understanding and clarification, it is important to recognize the central role of the teacher in a guided discussion. Your responsibilities lie in asking questions, in probing student responses because clarifications are needed to extend thinking, in encouraging student questions, and in providing information to keep the discussion on course. The potential problem, however, is domination of the discussion. Alvermann, Dillon, and O'Brien (1988) caution that, when overused, this role "can result in a discussion that more nearly resembles a lecture and frequently may confuse students, especially if they have been encouraged to assume more active roles in discussion" (p. 31).

A guided discussion can easily take a *reflective turn*. When teachers consciously shift gears from guided discussion to reflective discussion, their roles in the discussion shift.

Reflective Discussion

A reflective discussion is different from a guided discussion in several respects. The purpose of a reflective discussion is to require students to engage in critical and creative thinking as they solve problems, clarify values, explore controversial issues, and form and defend positions. A reflective discussion, then, presumes that students have a solid understanding of the important concepts they are studying. Without a basic knowledge and understanding of the ideas or issues under discussion, students cannot support opinions, make judgments, or justify and defend positions.

The teacher's role during a reflective discussion is that of participant. As a participant, you become a group member, so that you can contribute to the discussion by sharing ideas and expressing your own opinions: "Teachers can guide students to greater independence in learning by modelling different ways of responding and reacting to issues, commenting on others' points of view, and applying critical reading strategies to difficult concepts in the textbooks" (Alvermann et al. 1988, p. 31).

e.Resources

For additional guidelines, go to Web Destinations, click on Professional Resources, and search for Classroom Discussions and Collaborative Learning.

Creating an Environment for Discussion

Discussion is one of the major process strategies in the content area classroom. Because many of the strategies in this text revolve around discussion of some sort, we offer several suggestions for creating an environment in which discussion takes place, whether in small groups or in the whole class.

Support English Language Learners by Providing Comprehensible Input

Support nonnative speakers in your classroom by showing sensitivity to their language needs. An important component of the SIOP model for sheltered instruction is to provide *comprehensible input* for English language learners (Echevarria & Graves 2003). Make content learning comprehensible by simplifying your language when giving directions, leading whole-class discussions, or facilitating small-group interactions. When talking to a class that includes English language learners, especially students at a beginning or intermediate level of language proficiency, it may be necessary to speak clearly and use a slightly slower speech rate than you normally would if you had native speakers only in your classroom. During discussions, it may also be necessary to repeat yourself, define new words in a meaningful context, or paraphrase when you use more sophisticated language than English language learners can understand. Providing comprehensible input also means being aware of your use of idiomatic expressions and limiting them when students find idiomatic expressions difficult to understand. Moreover, keep in mind that gestures and facial expressions help to dramatize what you are saying during discussion. Barton (1995) reminds teachers not only to simplify and clarify the language they use but also to check for understanding frequently throughout classroom conversations. As we explained earlier in the chapter, scaffold instruction during discussion by supporting students' in their use of home languages and their own culturally acceptable conversational styles.

Arrange the Classroom to Facilitate Discussion

Arrange the room so that students can see each other and huddle in conversational groupings when they need to share ideas. A good way to determine how functional a classroom is for discussion is to select a discussion strategy that does not require continuous question asking. For example, in Chapter 9 we will see that brainstorming involves a good mixture of whole-class and small-group discussion. Students need to alternate their attention between the chalkboard (where the teacher or another student is writing down all the ideas offered within a specified time) and their small groups (where they might categorize the ideas) and back to the front of the room (for comparison of group categories and summarization). If students are able to participate in the various stages of brainstorming with a minimum of chair moving or other time-consuming movements, to see the board, and to converse with other students without undue disruption, the room arrangements are adequate or conducive to discussion.

Encourage Listening

Encourage a climate in which everyone is expected to be a good listener, including the teacher. Let each student speaker know that you are listening. As the teacher begins to talk less, students will talk more. Intervene to determine why some students are not listening to each other or to praise those who are unusually good role models for others. Accept all responses of students positively.

Try starting out with very small groups of no more than two or three students. Again, rather than use questions, have students react to a teacher-read statement ("Political primaries are a waste of time and money"). In the beginning, students may feel constrained to produce answers to questions to satisfy the teacher. A statement, however, serves as a possible answer and invites reaction and justification. Once a statement is given, set a timer or call time by your watch at two-minute intervals. During each interval, one student in the group may agree or disagree *without interruption*. After each group member has an opportunity to respond, the group summarizes all dialogue, and one person presents this summary to the class (Gold & Yellin 1982, pp. 550–552).

Establish a Goal for Discussion

Establish the meaning of the topic and the goal of the discussion: "Why are we talking about railroad routes and how do they relate to our unit on the Civil War?" Also, explain directions explicitly, and don't assume that students will know what to do. Many of the content area reading strategies in this book involve some group discussion. Frequently, strategies progress from independent, written responses to sharing, to comparing those responses in small groups, and then to pooling small-group reactions in a whole-class discussion. Without the guidance of a teacher who is aware of this process, group discussion tends to disintegrate.

Focus the Discussion

Keep the focus of the discussion on the central topic or core question or problem to be solved. Teachers may begin discussions by asking a question about a perplexing situation or by establishing a problem to be solved. From time to time, it may be necessary to refocus attention on the topic by piggybacking on comments made by particular students: "Terry brought out an excellent point about the Underground Railroad in northern Ohio. Does anyone else want to talk about this?" During small-group discussions, one tactic that keeps groups on task is reminding them of the amount of time remaining in the discussion.

Keeping the focus is one purpose for which teachers may legitimately question to clarify the topic. They may also want to make sure that they understood a particular student's comment: "Excuse me, would you repeat that?" Often, keeping the discussion focused will prevent the class from straying away from the task.

Avoid Squelching Discussion

Give students enough think time to reflect on possible answers before calling on someone or rephrasing your question. Moreover, try to avoid answering your own question. (One way to prevent yourself from doing this is to resist having a preset or "correct" answer in your own mind when you ask a question beyond a literal level of comprehension.) Do not interrupt students' responses or permit others to interrupt students' responses. Do, however, take a minute or two for you or a student to summarize and bring closure to a group discussion just as you would in any instructional strategy.

Both guided and reflective discussions may be conducted with the whole class or in small groups. A small-group discussion, whether guided or reflective, places the responsibility for learning squarely on students' shoulders. Because of the potential value of collaborative student interactions, we underscore the invaluable contribution of cooperative learning in diverse classrooms.

Cooperative learning, as we explain in detail in Chapter 7, allows students to work together to pursue academic objectives. The goals of cooperative learning, therefore, are to foster collaboration in a classroom context, to develop students' self-esteem in the process of learning, to encourage the development of positive group relationships, and to enhance academic achievement (Johnson, Johnson, & Holubec 1990). Small-group learning opportunities help diverse learners to contribute ideas to a discussion and take chances in the process. The students can try out ideas without worrying about being wrong or sounding dumb—a fear that often accompanies risk taking in a whole-class situation.

e.Resources

For additional readings related to the major ideas in this chapter, go to Chapter 4 of the Companion Website and click on Suggested Readings.

◄ Looking Back
Looking Forward ▶

Changes in the racial and ethnic composition of our student population have been dramatic. Today's classrooms are more linguistically and culturally diverse than they were in the 1960s. The linguistic, cultural, and achievement differences of students contribute to the complexities of classroom diversity. Students of diverse backgrounds (who may be distinguished by their ethnicity, social class, language, or achievement level) often struggle in classrooms. English language learners especially challenge teachers to look for and experiment with instructional strategies that will actively involve them in the life of the classroom. Sheltered instruction makes a difference in the academic and language development of English language learners.

Teachers reach diverse learners by scaffolding instruction in ways that support content literacy and learning. Throughout this book, we explore scaffolded instruction designed to help all students learn with texts. In this chapter, we concentrated on two aspects of classroom strategy instruction: vocabulary and comprehension.

Not only are classrooms strategic but they are also interactive and collaborative. Talk is the heart of classroom learning. Scaffolding instruction that capitalizes on classroom conversations shapes what diverse students learn and signals to them what teachers value in their classroom community. Classroom talk about texts is effective in a collaborative environment where team learning is valued.

In the next chapter, we change our focus from learners to texts. If teachers are going to meet the academic, linguistic, and cultural needs of students, they need to reconsider the roles that textbooks play in classroom learning. How do teachers move beyond the use of textbooks to provide students with authentic reading experiences by using a variety of "real-world" texts? Literature is an alternative to textbook study. We argue that literature should be used interchangeably with textbooks to give students an intense involvement with subject matter. We explore not only the rationale for literature across the curriculum but also the wide array of text possibilities and the role that critical perspectives play in learning with literature.

Minds On

1. Picture a content area class of twenty-five students from very diverse backgrounds—different native languages, different ethnicities, and varying achievement levels. Describe some classroom strategies you might use to respond to individual differences while maintaining high standards of content literacy and learning.

2. According to the latest census projections, by the year 2020 one of two public school students will be from minority backgrounds. How do you believe this change will influence learning strategies in the classroom?

3. In some classes, teachers do most of the talking, and students recite one- or two-word answers. What learning strategies are denied to students in this type of classroom design? How can teachers share their knowledge with students and still avoid overlecturing?

4. Think of the concept of *class discussion*. Try to visualize in your mind an example of a prior classroom situation in which enjoyable, lively discussions occurred. Look closely at this scene, and jot down as many descriptive or sensory words as you can to paint this picture verbally. Now try to recall a prior classroom situation that was not conducive to meaningful or enjoyable class discussions. Follow the same recording procedure. Share your lists with other members of the group, and collaboratively define the components of effective and ineffective class discussions. Finally, ask each group to share its lists with the entire class.

5. Picture a content area class of twenty-five to thirty students (your choice of grade level and subject) from diverse backgrounds. Describe how you would use the QtA and DR–TA strategies while maintaining high standards of content literacy and learning.

Hands On

1. For fifteen minutes in a four-member small group, discuss the topic "how technology might transform popular sports by the year 2121." After the discussion, reflect on how the unique background of each member of the group contributed to the views expressed. Did any of the following factors influence individual participation: background knowledge of sports or technology, past experience playing sports, individual understanding of sports language or technological applications, or personal definitions of "popular" sports? What parallels might you draw with classroom lessons in which students bring cultural and linguistic differences to the learning activities?

2. Come to class prepared to share a piece of your personal "fund of knowledge"—knowledge and information that your family has passed on—with your small group. For example, you might share a passed-on craft, a skill, a family hobby, or a recipe. How did this sharing "connect" you to the group and the group to your culture?

3. Select a short informational article in a magazine or book, and bring copies for each member of your group. Have each member of the group discuss the merits of one of the following instructional strategies: (1) guided discussion, (2) a directed reading–thinking activity (DR–TA), (3) questioning the author (QtA), and (4) a reflective discussion. If there are more than four members in your group, duplicate strategies as needed.

Using the same article, design a lesson around the strategy you have discussed and make copies to share with the members of the group. As you review the four different lessons prepared by your colleagues, what comparisons and contrasts can you make between these instructional strategies.

e.Resources extra

- Go to Chapter 4 of the Companion Website (**www.ablongman.com/vacca8e**) and click on Activities to complete the following task:

  The following site is filled with ideas for engaging English language learners of all levels: **www. eslpartyland.com**. The site includes vocabulary development ideas, activities that use music, and more. Browse this site for engaging activities and adapt them to content area lessons.

- Go to the Companion Website (**www. ablongman.com/vacca8e**) for suggested readings, interactive activities, multiple-choice questions, and additional Web links to help you learn more about culturally and linguistically diverse learners.

expect the world®

The New York Times
nytimes.com

Themes of the Times

Extend your knowledge of the concepts discussed in this chapter by reading current and historical articles from the *New York Times*. Go to the Companion Website and click on eThemes of the Times.

chapter 5

Learning with Trade Books

Books are not made for furniture . . .
—HENRY WARD BEECHER

Instructional practices involving the use of trade books in content areas help to extend and enrich the curriculum.

Organizing Principle

Books are familiar fixtures in classrooms. They are as much a part of the physical makeup of most classrooms as desks, tables, chairs, chalkboards, and bulletin boards. Although they are highly visible in a well-furnished classroom, books, as Henry Ward Beecher reminds us, are not made for furniture. Books are made to read for a variety of purposes, not the least of which is to learn. Textbooks, although they certainly have an important role in content area learning, have been scrutinized by educational critics who express concerns about their quality in terms of accuracy, read-

ability, and appeal. These criticisms remind us that some textbooks may as well be made for furniture rather than learning.

In this chapter we explore the uses and limitations of textbooks. We make the case that in today's rapidly changing classrooms, textbooks by themselves are not enough. Students

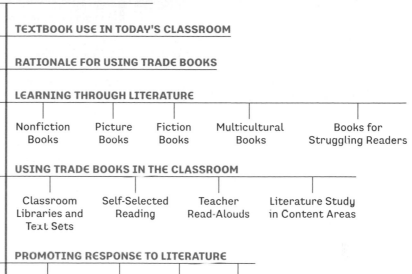

LEARNING WITH TRADE BOOKS

TEXTBOOK USE IN TODAY'S CLASSROOM

RATIONALE FOR USING TRADE BOOKS

LEARNING THROUGH LITERATURE

Nonfiction Books | Picture Books | Fiction Books | Multicultural Books | Books for Struggling Readers

USING TRADE BOOKS IN THE CLASSROOM

Classroom Libraries and Text Sets | Self-Selected Reading | Teacher Read-Alouds | Literature Study in Content Areas

PROMOTING RESPONSE TO LITERATURE

Making Connections | Process Drama | Readers Theatre | Idea Circles

need access to a range of reading materials, and trade books provide a veritable mother lode of fiction and nonfiction works that connect to most curricular areas. Trade books, as distinguished from textbooks, are published for distribution to the general public through booksellers. Trade books are informative, entertaining, and have built-in appeal for people of all ages. Trade books, whether picture books, fiction, nonfiction, or poetry, have the potential to provide students with intense involvement in a subject and the power to develop in-depth understanding in ways not imagined a few years ago. Furthermore, by engaging students in active response to trade books, we heighten their interest and understanding of text content.

Should textbooks be abandoned? Certainly not. Our point in this chapter (and the next chapter on the use of electronic texts in content areas) is to underscore the value of integrating a variety of print and multimedia environments into the curriculum. The organizing principle for this chapter looks beyond the ofttimes limiting role of textbooks in content areas: **Instructional practices involving the use of trade books in content areas help to extend and enrich the curriculum.**

Frame of Mind

1. What are some problems associated with textbook use?

2. Why use trade books to learn subject matter?

3. How can teachers create classroom libraries in content area classrooms?

4. What should the roles of self-selected reading and teacher read-alouds be in the content area classroom?

5. What are some ways that teachers can engage students in responding to the trade books they read?

6. How can teachers involve students in inquiry-related activities?

In the beginning of his book *The Winter Room,* Gary Paulsen, the author of popular fiction books for adolescents, appeals to readers to engage actively in the reading of his book. *The Winter Room* is the story of two brothers, Eldon and Wayne, growing up on a farm in northern Minnesota. In the prologue to the story, Paulsen makes it clear to his readers that the book they are about to read can't have the smells of old farms or cooking in the kitchen. It can't have the sounds of farm life. Finally, books can't have light to create the images that readers will construct in their heads. As Paulsen (1989) puts it

> If books could have more, give more, show more, they would still need readers, who bring to them sound and smell and light and all the rest that can't be in books. The book needs you. (p. 3)

Just as books need readers, readers need books, and they need them in their content area classrooms. Readers need books that take them different places, let them live different lives, and be different people. They need books that captivate them, that nurture their souls and capitalize on their interests. Readers need books that let them see themselves and satisfy their need to know about the world around them.

In many ways, the content area classroom is the perfect place for students to connect with books because it affords students opportunities to build webs of meaning about a topic through a variety of sources. Through these experiences, students engage in meaning making by evaluating information, connecting ideas across sources, comparing and contrasting information, and reflecting on meaning. In this chapter, we explore the complementary roles of textbooks and trade books in the classroom as well as the unique ways in which responses to trade books can enhance and extend content learning experiences.

BOX 5.1

What about . . .
Content Standards and Assessment?

The ability to read literary and informational texts is an important component of all statewide proficiency assessments in reading and language arts. In addition, most proficiency assessments outside of reading are in actuality assessments of literacy. In order to respond to content-specific assessment questions, students need to be able to read and write effectively. No wonder, then, that the first two content standards of the *Standards for the English Language Arts* (IRA/NCTE 1996) have broad implications for the use of literary and informational texts in all content areas:

■ Students read a wide range of print and nonprint texts to build an understanding of texts, of themselves, and of the cultures of the United States and the world; to acquire new information; to respond to the needs and demands of society and the workplace; and for personal fulfillment. Among these texts are fiction and nonfiction, classic and contemporary works.

■ Students read a wide range of literature from many periods in many genres to build an understanding of the many dimensions (e.g., philosophical, ethical, aesthetic) of human experience.

As you read this chapter on learning with trade books, also analyze national and state standards, where they exist, in your content area. What are the implications of these standards for reading "a wide range of literature" in your content area?

Textbook Use in Today's Classrooms

A familiar ritual occurs in classrooms practically everywhere at the beginning of each school year. The ritual, of course, is the "distribution of textbooks" captured brilliantly in the accompanying Funky Winkerbean cartoon.

Source: © NAS. Reprinted with special permission of King Features Syndicate.

Textbooks are more the rule than the exception in most classrooms. Estimates suggest that 75 to 90 percent of classrooms in the United States use textbooks almost exclusively (Palmer & Stewart 1997). Les Moore, the teacher in the cartoon, mouths the words that many teachers have either spoken aloud or thought about as part of the "distribution of textbooks" ritual. Textbooks, after all, are expensive. School districts, depending on their size, invest hundreds of thousands of dollars on a textbook adoption. Textbooks are purchased to last several years or more before the next adoption period. Mr. Moore expects his course textbooks to be returned at the end of the year in the same condition as the beginning of the year: "Although," he says somewhat wryly, "some signs of use would be nice!"

The cartoon hits home. Textbooks remain unread by too many students, even though teachers attempt to use textbooks with the best of intentions. Often we have heard teachers note with regret that students "simply don't read assigned textbook material anymore." Yet, it's not that the majority of students can't read. Most choose not to, primarily because they have never been shown how to think and learn with textbooks.

Reasons Teachers Use Textbooks

Textbooks are, for most teachers, essential classroom tools. They act as blueprints for learning in particular content areas. And in today's standards-driven environment, they provide coverage of content in particular disciplines that may well appear on high-stakes tests of some kind. Time constraints in a standards-driven curriculum are real. Teachers feel enormous pressure to cover a certain amount of content in a specified amount of time before students move on to the next chapter or unit of study. Teachers who operate under time constraints often view textbooks as efficient informational resources that support what students are studying in a particular subject at a particular time. Textbook-driven instruction relies on lecturing and other means of information giving when content coverage is the primary purpose. For these reasons and others, content area teaching often involves the use of one type of text—the textbook, often at the exclusion of other types of texts.

Problems with Using Textbooks

Textbooks are not without problems, though. Because of their comprehensive and encyclopedic nature, most textbooks do not treat subject matter with the breadth and depth necessary to fully develop ideas and concepts. The very nature of textbooks may often restrict their use in content area classrooms.

The textbook, *History of the United States*, for example, tells the U.S. story in two volumes (DiBacco, Mason, & Appy 1992). The first volume is more than 700 pages long; the second is more than 800 pages. The design of the two volumes is attractive and the texts are full of eye-catching and instructionally helpful features, including black and white and color photos; colorful visual aids such as maps, tables, graphs, and

Response Journal

Based on your own school experiences, what do you believe are some of the problems associated with textbook-only instruction?

cartoons; and a wide variety of instructional aides, such as key terms, questions, objectives, and a capsule main idea statement for each chapter section. All of these design features serve several purposes: to support students' reading, to make learning more visual and appealing, and to break up written text into manageable chunks of writing that won't overwhelm students. The authors of *History of the United States* write in an appealing manner to capture students' interest and hold their attention. Take, for example, a passage from a subsection of text describing the Holocaust:

> People had known all along that the war was taking a terrible toll, still the full agony only became apparent when Allied forces entered Nazi territory and liberated dozens of concentration camps. Soldiers could not believe their eyes. They found prisoners so emaciated that they resembled living corpses. The found gas chambers, crematoriums (ovens in which bodies were burned), and thousands of corpses stacked like cordwood in boxcars and open pits. One soldier recalled:
>
>> The odors, well there is no way to describe the odors. Many of the boys I am talking about now—these were tough soldiers, there were combat men who had been all the way through the invasion—were ill and vomiting, throwing up, just at the sight of this. (DiBacco, Mason, & Appy 1992, p. 433)

This passage is graphic in its description and creates a sense of horror for the atrocities that are described. Yet despite the magnitude of the Holocaust as a historical event and its profound human and moral implications, the authors' coverage of the Holocaust is limited to eight brief paragraphs as part of a comprehensive chapter on World War II. Eight paragraphs! Even though coverage of the Holocaust is cursory at best, the authors accomplish their purposes for the chapter: to chronicle events and people and to describe the major political, economic, and social forces underlying World War II.

This example illustrates a major problem with textbooks in general. They aren't designed to provide in-depth coverage. A textbooks conveys a body of knowledge and casts a wide net in an effort to cover as much information as possible. No wonder textbooks are often described as being "a mile wide and an inch deep."

As state standards require even more content coverage, textbooks must include an even greater number of topics. Space limitations require that textbooks merely mention people or topics, often omitting important background information on particular topics. This can result in students with superficial knowledge of many topics, but little in-depth knowledge of any.

Experts have identified at least four other concerns with textbooks: (1) They are often "inconsiderate" of their readers, (2) they may contain inaccuracies, (3) they are often written at high levels of difficulty, and (4) they lack appeal for students.

Inconsiderate Texts

"Inconsiderate texts" contain writing that may be confusing and lack clear organization. Textbooks tend to jump from topic to topic, rather than using generally accepted patterns of exposition, such as cause–effect, sequence, or comparison contrast. Many of these texts are often written in a descriptive mode—which makes retention of material more difficult.

Inaccuracy

A second concern about textbooks is that of accuracy. A recent edition of the television news show *20/20* focused on this issue. It reported that today's textbooks are rife with errors. In fact, it featured a concerned parent who found 113 errors in a recent edition of a best-selling science textbook! Further concerns about accuracy relate to the fact that students in many schools are using outdated textbooks because of budget constraints.

Inappropriate Reading Level

Another critical concern is that textbooks are often written well above the reading level of their intended audiences. Of today's students, 25 to 40 percent are reading, or attempting to read, textbooks that are well beyond their reading levels (Schoenbach, Greenleaf, Cziko, & Hurwitz 1999). For struggling readers or English language learners, the gap between reader and textbook can be as great as three to five years. This coupled with students' lack of prior knowledge for text content can create a situation where the textbook becomes little more than furniture.

Negative Student Reactions

Finally, students themselves express reservations about their textbooks. When eleventh- and twelfth-grade students in physics classes were queried about the use of their textbooks, one student in the course said flatly, "I don't mess with the textbook. It's confusing." Another responded, "I should be telling you that the text is the best way to learn information. I would tell you that for all my other classes. I learn by reading, and I read a lot. But I just can't understand this textbook. It's way above my head." These revealing comments came from interviews that were part of a study on the use of texts in science classes (Hynd, McNish, Guzzetti, Lay, & Flower 1994). The researchers, who interviewed a mix of students in general and college prep science classes, were struck by the similarities in the students' comments, despite assumed differences in ability, motivation, and background. Various student comments revealed insightful perspectives, including the beliefs that textbooks assume too much student knowledge, that textbooks need fuller explanations and more relevant examples, and that textbooks should be better organized.

As these examples illustrate, when reading merely chronicles events, students dismiss (and miss) the power of text to inform and transform their lives. When the textbook is the only source of information in a particular content area class, students come to connect the content of a particular subject with what are sometimes dull, lifeless textbooks. When the textbook becomes the curriculum, students are denied the range of perspectives and opportunities for critical thinking that multiple texts can provide. Rather than viewing the body of knowledge of a discipline like a scientist or a historian, for example, students simply see facts to be memorized.

Increasing numbers of teachers, however, are moving beyond the exclusive use of textbooks to incorporate trade books, electronic texts, and other authentic alternatives to textbooks. In order to motivate students and meet the needs of an increasingly diverse student population, they are filling their classrooms with magazines, newspapers, films, and any number of other print and nonprint learning tools.

Rationale for Using Trade Books

Trade books, rich in narrative and informational content, can provide a valuable complement to most textbooks. Trade books can take students to different places and times in ways that textbooks can't. Learning with trade books involves exposure to many different genres, all of which are potential sources of information for the active learner. A nonfiction or fiction trade book has the potential to act as a magnifying glass that enlarges and enhances the reader's personal interactions with a subject. When teachers use textbooks and trade books in tandem, they help learners think critically about content.

Today's trade books can provide an effective complement to textbooks in virtually any subject. The best trade books overcome many of the limitations of content area texts discussed in the previous section. They provide depth, considerate and accurate information, material at a variety of reading levels, and motivation for learning. High-quality trade books can, for example, provide depth of information that space limitations prevent textbooks from providing. Consider the earlier example of the textbook treatment of the Holocaust. Many outstanding trade books provide in-depth personal accounts of that terrible event in history. Titles such as *I Have Lived a Thousand Years* (Bitton-Jackson 1997) or *Number the Stars* (Lowry 1989) not only help students develop understanding of the events of the Holocaust and World War II but also help them connect emotionally with the sufferings of victims who were themselves young at the time. Trade books can fill the need for story and provide the emotional dimension so lacking in textbooks. Unlike textbooks, they can move not only students' minds but also their hearts.

In addition, trade books, nonfiction titles in particular, are written and organized in ways that make information interesting and accessible. The best nonfiction authors are more than "baskets of facts"; they speak to young readers personally through informal, engaging writing styles. Their clear, reader-friendly explanations of scientific principles or processes can be extremely helpful to students. In addition, authors of trade books take enormous pains to ensure accuracy. In a speech in Columbus, Ohio, Jim Murphy explained that *each fact* in his award-winning nonfiction title *The Great Fire* (Murphy 1998) was checked for accuracy at least three times.

Response Journal

How can trade books help you address the needs of struggling readers or English language learners in the classroom? What advantages might they have over textbooks?

Trade books can help teachers meet the range of reading levels in their classrooms. By using a variety of trade books in a range of reading levels, teachers can match students with books they can read. Instead of having all students read the same textbooks, students can read a variety of trade books about a particular topic. This allows teachers the opportunity to give students books at their independent reading levels, a practice that has been associated with gains in achievement.

Furthermore, exposure to nonfiction literature gives students much needed practice reading expository text, which unlike narrative, does not typically involve characters, plots, or settings. This type of text is typically less familiar to students than narrative and more difficult for them to read. The reality is that many students do not know how to read to learn with informational texts because their school experiences have been limited to textbook-only reading. For some students the only historical, mathematics, or science materials they will ever read in a lifetime are in textbooks.

Trade books help readers at all levels develop greater understanding of content-related concepts. Historical fiction titles, for example, provide a framework for remembering and understanding historical content. The same holds for content in science and in other subject areas. Popular science books, both fact and fiction, provide background knowledge for science concepts covered in class and help students relate these concepts to their everyday lives.

Finally, trade books have the power to motivate students to read more. The compelling visual qualities of today's nonfiction books make them many students' favorite out-of-school reading. Authors of nonfiction not only provide information but also entertain. Consider, for example, *Phineas Gage: A Gruesome but True Story about Brain Science* (Fleischman 2002). In 1848, Phineas Gage had a three-and-a-half-foot long iron rod blasted through his head and survived. Despite his recovery, Gage's personality underwent a drastic transformation. He changed from a reliable, respected supervisor to an unpredictable and temperamental man who eventually lost his job. The focus of the book is not only on what happened to Gage but also what neurologists learned and continue to learn today about the workings of the human brain. This amazing book, because of its lively writing and extraordinary visuals, provides background information about the human brain in a format sure to motivate even those students who have little initial interest in the topic.

Authors of fiction engage students through characters that remind them of themselves and their peers. Many titles address students' emotional needs because they are written from the viewpoint of students. People of all ages are attracted to books that reflect themselves in some personal way. For many female students, for example, Ann Brashares's (2001) best-selling *Sisterhood of the Traveling Pants* considers the powerful bonds of friendship and its power to transform lives.

The primary motivation for including trade books in any classroom should be to capture students' attention and engagement in learning. When students are given opportunities to interact with quality trade books, they have a better chance of becoming lifelong readers. Textbooks alone cannot motivate students to continue their learning, particularly in the case of reluctant or academically diverse readers, who are often frustrated and defeated by textbooks in the first place.

Learning through Literature

When students have opportunities to learn with trade books, they can explore and interact with many kinds of texts, both fiction and nonfiction. Today's trade books are better than ever. They are written by authors who relate to the emotions and experiences of today's young people and address an enormous range of themes and genres. They present characters and events from virtually every ethnic and cultural group in accurate and meaningful circumstances and settings.

The variety of genres available in today's trade books offers teachers a vast array of titles from which to choose, ranging from easy-to-read titles using engaging formats to extremely sophisticated treatments of complex topics. Trade books are available to serve the needs of every student in every academic area. The greatest challenge for teachers is deciding which books to choose from the enormous possibilities available. Figure 5.1 provides a list of references to help teachers select good books for their classrooms.

Nonfiction Books

Nonfiction trade books have, in recent years, moved from the shadows into the spotlight of literary excellence. Nonfiction books, which include informational books and biographies, are no longer glorified textbooks; they connect with readers through writing that is not strictly objective in tone and literal in content but that provides entertainment to contemporary readers. They contain elements of fiction that flesh out details and provide a component of entertainment. This "new journalism" (Donelson & Nelson 1997) represents the kind of meaty material that entertains students at the same time as it informs.

For many students, nonfiction is the literature of choice for out-of-school reading. Many students report a fascination with facts and a "need to know" about information that drives their reading choices. Despite its popularity, nonfiction seldom makes its way into content area classrooms. Because of this, nonfiction trade books are a largely untapped resource with great potential for motivating readers. By using nonfiction trade books in the classroom, teachers can bridge the gap between students' in- and out-of-school reading and capitalize on their interest in this genre.

The endless array of nonfiction books available for the classroom can help teachers enliven classroom instruction in every content area, including art, music, science, health, and mathematics. No single book will satisfy all readers, but teachers will find many titles that can spark student learning in these content

FIGURE 5.1   Trade Book Selection Guide for Children and Adolescents

The Alan Review (Assembly on Literature for Adolescents, National Council of Teachers of English). Published three times a year; articles and "Clip and File" reviews. Urbana, IL: National Council of Teachers of English.

Appraisal: Children's Science Books for Young People. Published quarterly by Children's Science Book Review Committee. Reviews written by children's librarians and subject specialists.

Association for Library Service to Children. (1995). *The Newbery & Caldecott Awards: A guide to the medal and honor books.* Chicago: American Library Association. Provides short annotations for the winners and runners-up of ALA-sponsored awards.

Book Links: Connecting Books, Libraries, and Classrooms. Published six times a year by the American Library Association to help teachers integrate literature into the curriculum; bibliographies in different genres and subjects; suggestions for innovative use in the classroom.

Booklist. Published twice monthly by the American Library Association. Reviews of children's trade books and nonprint materials (video, audio, and computer software). Approximate grade levels are given; separate listing for nonfiction books.

Books for the Teen Age. Published annually by the Office of Young Adult Services, New York Public Library. Recommendations from young adult librarians in the various branches of the New York Public Library.

Bulletin of the Center for Children's Books. Published monthly by the University of Chicago Press; detailed reviews and possible curriculum uses are noted.

Children's books: Awards and prizes. New York: Children's Book Council. Award-winning titles as well as state "Children's Choice" awards for exemplary trade books.

Christenbury, L. (Ed.). (1995). *Books for you: A booklist for senior high students* (11th ed.). Urbana, IL: National Council of Teachers of English. Provides annotations for both fiction and nonfiction written for students, organized into fifty categories.

Friedberg, J. B. (1992). *Portraying persons with disabilities: An annotated bibliography of nonfiction for children and teenagers* (2nd ed.). New Providence, NJ: Bowker. Provides comprehensive listings of nonfiction dealing with physical, mental, and emotional disabilities.

Gillespie, J. T. (1991). *Best books for junior high readers.* New Providence, NJ: Bowker. Lists more than 6,000 books for young adolescents; fiction is listed by genre, nonfiction by subject.

Helbig, A., & Perkins, A. R. (1994). *This land is your land: A guide to multicultural literature for children and young adults.* Westport, CT: Greenwood Press. Provides an extensive listing of titles featuring African Americans, Asian Americans, Hispanic Americans, and Native Americans.

The Horn Book Magazine. Published six times a year by Horn Book, Inc.; articles by noted children's authors, illustrators, and critics on aspects of children's literature, including its use in the classroom. Nonfiction books are reviewed in a separate section.

International Reading Association. "Children's Choices," a list of exemplary, "reader-friendly" children's literature, is published every October in *The Reading Teacher.*

Jensen, J. L., & Roser, N. (Eds.). (1993). *Adventuring with books: A booklist for pre-K–grade 6* (9th ed.). Urbana, IL: National Council of Teachers of English. Summaries of nearly 1,800 books published between 1988 and 1992, Books arranged by genre and topics within content areas.

FIGURE 5.1 **Continued**

Montenegro, V. J., O'Connell, S. M., & Wolff, K. (Eds.). (1986). *AAA's science book list, 1978–1986.* Reviews science and math books for middle and high school students. Books reviewed by experts.

Montenegro, V. J., O'Connell, S. M., & Wolff, K. (Eds.). (1988). *The best science books and materials for children.* Washington, DC: American Association for the Advancement of Science. Reviews more than 800 science and math books, grades K–9. Books reviewed by experts.

Notable children's trade books in the field of social studies. National Council for the Social Studies. Published yearly in the spring issue of *Social Education;* annotates notable fiction and nonfiction books, primarily for children in grades K–8.

Outstanding Science Trade Books for Children. National Science Teachers Association. Published each year in the spring issue of *Science and Children;* contains information consistent with current scientific knowledge; is pleasing in format; illustrated; and is nonsexist, nonracist, and nonviolent.

Rudman, M. K. (1995). *Children's literature* (3rd ed.). New York: Longman. Includes extensive annotated bibliographies of books that promote children's understanding of sensitive issues (e.g., divorce, death, siblings, heritage).

School Library Journal. Published by R. R. Bowker; articles on all aspects of children's literature, including its use in content areas; reviews by school and public librarians.

Totten, H. L., & Brown, R. W. (1995). *Culturally diverse library collections for children.* New York: Neal-Schuman. Includes annotations on Native Americans, Asian Americans, Hispanic Americans, and African Americans.

Walker, E. (Ed.). (1988). *Book bait: Detailed notes on adult books popular with young people* (4th ed.). Chicago: American Library Association. Extensive annotations of 100 books, including plot summaries and discussions of appeal for adolescents.

Williams, H. E. (1991). *Books by African-American authors and illustrators for children and young adults.* Chicago: American Library Association. Provides bibliographical information and annotations of quality literature.

Winkel, L. (Ed.). (1996). *Elementary school library collection: A guide to books and other media.* Williamsport, PA: Bordart Books. Reviews of books and other media in all subject areas for elementary and middle school students. Books rated by interest level and reading level.

areas as well as others. Using nonfiction in the classroom has further advantages. It can

- *deepen student knowledge* of real people, places, and phenomena of the present and the past;

- *provide in-depth, up-to-date information;*

- *help students see how knowledge in different domains is organized, used, and related;*

- *develop student familiarity with the language and vocabulary of a discipline;*

- *improve student comprehension of expository text,* a skill required for survival in the information age; and

- *provide insights into contemporary issues* of interest to teens that get little attention in textbooks.

The range of topics available, the variety of formats, and the varying levels of difficulty make these books indispensable resources for content area classrooms. Topics addressed in nonfiction trade books range from art museums to zoology. Formats range from encyclopedic treatments of topics, such as David Macaulay's (1998) *The New Way Things Work,* to tightly focused, narrowly defined topics, such as Beil's (1999) *Fire in Their Eyes: Wildfires and the People Who Fight Them.*

There are outstanding biographies and autobiographies of all sorts of people, including rock stars, writers (*Jack London, A Biography,* Dyer 1997), athletes such as Lance Armstrong and Sally Jenkins' (2001) *It's Not about the Bike: My Journey Back to Life,* composers (*This Land Was Made for You and Me: The Life and Songs of Woody Guthrie,* Partridge 2002), scientists (*Carl Sagan: Superstar Scientist,* Cohen 1987), artists (*Chuck Close, Up Close,* Greenberg & Jordan 1998), and ordinary and not-so-ordinary teens (*Rocket Boys,* Hickam 1998). There are books that recount real-life adventures such as *Shipwreck at the Bottom of the World: The Extraordinary True Story of Shackleton and the Endurance* (Armstrong 1998) and *Exploring the Titanic* (Ballard 1998). Other titles address contemporary issues of concern to everyone the world over, including AIDS, global warming, and homelessness. There are collections of essays written with young readers in mind, such as *New Kids in Town: Oral Histories of Immigrant Teens* (Bode 1989), which presents the voices of teen immigrants from places such as Afghanistan, El Salvador, India, Cuba, and China; or *Busted Lives: Dialogues with Kids in Jail* (1982), by Ann Zane Shanks, which offers first-person perspectives of prison life. Figure 5.2 lists additional nonfiction titles useful for various content areas.

Perhaps the greatest difficulty teachers face when selecting nonfiction for the classroom is deciding which books to choose from the large number available. An important thing to keep in mind is that variety is truly the spice of life where reading and learning are concerned. No one book will satisfy all readers. The point of using nonfiction trade books in the classroom is to expose students to more than one point of view in a form that is both informational and readable. Although many nonfiction books sound like textbooks packaged in pretty covers, teachers can select quality books by considering the five As (Moss 1995).

1. The *authority* of the author

2. The *accuracy* of text content

3. The *appropriateness* of the book for its audience

4. The literary *artistry*

5. The *appearance* of the book (pp. 123–124)

FIGURE 5.2 **Nonfiction Trade Books for Content Area Classrooms**

Science

Cone, M., & Wheelwright, S. (1992). *Come Back Salmon: How a Group of Dedicated Kids Adopted Pigeon Creek and Brought It Back to Life.* San Francisco: Sierra Club.

Dash, J. (2000). *The Longitude Prize.* New York: Farrar Straus & Giroux.

Epstein, S., & Epstein, B. (1978). *Dr. Beaumont and the Man with a Hole in His Stomach.* New York: Coward, McCann & Geoghegan.

Fleischman, J. (2002). *Phineas Gage: A Gruesome but True Story about Brain Science.* Boston: Houghton Mifflin.

Giblin, J. (1995). *When Plague Strikes: The Black Death, Smallpox, AIDS.* New York: HarperCollins.

Hickam, H. (1998). *Rocket Boys.* New York: Delacorte.

Lauber, P. (1986). *Volcano: The Eruption and Healing of Mount St. Helen's.* New York: Bradbury Press.

Thimmesh, C. (2000). *Girls Think of Everything: Stories of Ingenious Inventions by Women.* New York: Houghton Mifflin.

Social Studies

Bartoletti, S. C. (2001). *Black Potatoes: The Story of the Great Irish Famine, 1845–1850.* Boston: Houghton Mifflin.

Bitton-Jackson, L. (1997). *I Have Lived a Thousand Years: Growing Up in the Holocaust.* New York: Simon & Schuster

Bode, J. (1989). *New Kids on the Block: Oral Histories of Immigrant Teens.* New York: F. Watts.

Calabro, M. (1999). *The Perilous Journey of the Donner Party.* New York: Clarion Books.

Freedman, R. (2000). *Give Me Liberty! The Story of the Declaration of Independence.* New York: Holiday House.

Giblin, J. (2002). *The Life and Death of Adolf Hitler.* New York: Clarion Books.

Hoose, P. M. (2001). *We Were There, Too! Young People in U.S. History.* New York: Farrar Straus & Giroux.

Murphy, J. (1990). *The Boys' War: Confederate and Union Soldiers Talk about the Civil War.* New York: Clarion Books.

Art and Music

Ames, L. J. (1986). *Draw 50 Cars Trucks, and Motorcycles* (1st ed.). Garden City, NY: Doubleday.

Aronson, M. (1998). *Art Attack: A Short Cultural History of the Avant Garde.* New York: Clarion.

Greenberg, J., & Jordan, S. (1998). *Chuck Close: Up Close.* New York: DK Inc.

Marsalis, W. (1995). *Marsalis on Music.* New York: Norton.

Mühlberger, R. (1993). *What Makes a Monet a Monet?* New York: Metropolitan Museum of Art and Viking.

Zhensun, Z., & Low, A. (1991). *A Young Painter: The Life and Paintings of Wang Yani.* New York: Scholastic.

Table 5.1 suggests questions teachers can consider in relationship to each of the five As as they select nonfiction books.

Classroom uses for nonfiction are limitless but are most often thought of in reference to student report writing or inquiry projects. Nonfiction trade books have many other excellent uses as well. Nonfiction trade books can help students consider multiple perspectives related to a particular issue. One interesting way to use nonfiction involves pairing fiction with non-fiction. For example, teacher Judy Hendershot involved her middle graders in reading the historical fiction novel *Out of the Dust* (Hesse 1997) as part of a social studies unit on the depression. During this time she read aloud the nonfiction title *Children of the Dust Bowl: The True Story of the School at Weedpatch Camp* (Stanley 1992). Through this pairing of fiction with nonfiction, students developed deeper understanding of the experiences of the Okies who came to California during the era of the Dust Bowl. The first title exposed students to the harsh experiences of the female narrator during this time. The second provided a somewhat wider view; it described factual information about the enormous prejudice against the Okie children and a man who was determined to provide them with a school of their own.

Response Journal

Select several nonfiction trade books related to your discipline. Use the five As to evaluate the books, and identify one title that you think represents a quality book. Explain why you made the choice you did, what content-related objectives the book could help you meet, and how you might use the book in your classroom.

TABLE 5.1	The Five As for Evaluating Nonfiction Trade Books (Moss 2003)

Criteria	Questions to Ask
Authority	Does the author identify and credit experts consulted during the research process?
Accuracy	Is text content accurate?
	Are maps, graphs, charts, and other visual aids presented clearly?
	Does the author distinguish between facts and theories?
Appropriateness	Is information presented in ways appropriate to the intended audience?
	Does the author show respect for the reader?
	Is information effectively organized?
Literary artistry	Does the book have literary artistry?
	Does the author use literary devices to make information come alive?
	Is the author's style engaging?
Attractiveness	Is the appearance and layout of the book likely to entice readers?

Source: Reprinted by permission of Guilford Press. B. Moss (2003). *Exploring the Literature of Fact: Children's Nonfiction Trade Books in the Elementary Classroom.* New York: Guilford Press.

RESEARCH-BASED BEST PRACTICES

BOX 5.2

Appreciating Art and Artists through the Use of Trade Books

Today's nonfiction trade books offer teachers rich opportunities to involve students in learning about artists and analyzing their works. Art teacher Carole Newman has found many ways to create literacy activities that serve to extend student learning in her middle school art classes. One project that she typically involves her students in is the study of the life and work of famous artists. This project combines reading, writing, and artistic expression. She begins this project by providing her students with a wide array of artists' biographies. These include books from the Lives of the Artists series, artists' biographies by Jan Greenberg and Diane Stanley, and many others. Some of the artists students study include Diego Rivera, Freda Kahlo, Marc Chagall, Pablo

Picasso, Jackson Pollack, Edgar Degas, Claude Monet, Georgia O'Keefe, and so on.

Students identify an artist they wish to learn about, and select and read a book about the artist's life. Students are required to identify five important facts about the artist's life and prepare an in-depth analysis of two of the artist's works. As part of this analysis, students record their observations about the works in a learning log. Finally, students create their own artwork, employing the style and media used by the artist under study. They share their findings through group presentations where they present information about the artists and their works as well as their original artistic creations.

Picture Books

All too often, middle and high school teachers think picture books are suitable only for the primary grades. The picture book format is, however, an elastic one, that has, particularly recently, been adapted for students of all ages and in various ways. Picture books encompass every genre and cover a wide range of subject matter. They can be used to enhance instruction in every content area.

Picture books are books where pictures and texts work together to tell a story. They typically average about thirty-two pages in length, and their illustrations represent a wide range of media from collage to cut paper. These books are works of art that can represent an area of study in and of themselves. Picture books are more than visual feasts though; they contain the rich vocabulary and lyrical language characteristic of the finest literature. Picture books fall into four general categories: wordless books, picture storybooks, picture books with minimal text, and illustrated books.

- *Wordless books* carry the story completely; no text is involved. Tom Feelings's *The Middle Passage: White Ships Black Cargo* (1995) portrays the cruel experience of slavery through powerful illustrations that transcend the need for words.

- *Picture storybooks* provide interdependent story and illustrations; both are central to the telling of the tale. *Pink and Say* (Polacco 1994) is an excellent example of a picture storybook where illustration and text work together to create a seamless whole.

- *Picture books with minimal text* have illustrations that carry the story, but a few words are used to enhance the pictures. *Mysteries of Harris Burdick* (Van Allsburg 1984) is an example of a book with minimal text.

- *Illustrated books* have more words than pictures, but the illustrations are still important to the text. An example is *Kashtanka* (1991) by Anton Checkhov, illustrated by Barry Moser.

Many picture books suitable for middle and high school students are written to appeal to all age groups. Increasingly, however, picture books are written specifically with older readers in mind. Walter Dean Myers's (2002) *Patrol: An American Soldier in Vietnam* is a vivid example of this trend. This unusual and gripping book combines mixed-media collages with a riveting poem about a young soldier's fear, confusion, and fatigue. Its in-depth focus on its topic and emotional content help readers connect with the realities of war for the typical foot soldier.

Picture books can scaffold student understanding of a range of topics through formats that intrigue rather than intimidate. Picture books provide students with background knowledge about people, places, events, and experiences. They can ground students in cognitive concepts critical for understanding a variety of content area subjects. In addition, they can provide rich opportunities for promoting cultural diversity because picture books with a multicultural focus are increasing in availability.

Picture books can be a particularly rich resource for struggling readers or English language learners. The rich support provided by the illustrations serves as an aid to comprehension. Their manageable length and limited amounts of print enhances their appeal to students for whom reading is a challenge. Because of their accessible format, picture books can provide motivation and enjoyment for reading. This independent reading can lead to reading that continues after the bell has rung, an important correlate to increased reading achievement.

Picture books lend themselves to use in virtually every content area. Math and science concepts can come alive through nonfiction picture books such as *G is for Googol* (Schwartz 1998), an engaging math alphabet book that uses cartoons to explain complex concepts such as network theory and probability. *Anno's Math Games II* (Anno 1989) inspires critical analysis of the notion of sets and logical possibilities presented in the detailed illustrations. Science-related biographies such as *The Man Who Made Time Travel* (Lasky 2003), for example, relate the story of John Harrison, who devoted thirty-five years of his life to solving the problem of tracking longitude in shipboard navigation.

Picture books can also build bridges between the past and present. Many excellent titles focus on events surrounding World War II. *Rose Blanche* (Innocenti 1985) uses realistic drawings of the Nazi occupation to portray a young girl caught up in the horrors of the Holocaust. *Home of the Brave* (Say 2002) presents an enigmatic, haunting view of the internment of the Japanese during World War II. In *The Butter Battle Book* (1984), Dr. Seuss explores the illogical nature of war and poses the question, Which country will "push the button" first?

Picture books have many uses in the English classroom as well. Bruce Coville's (1997) *William Shakespeare's Macbeth* provides an easy-to-read picture book complement to Shakespeare's original work. A similar picture book adaptation of *The Necklace* is also available. Picture book versions of poems are increasingly popular and combine traditional texts with dramatic illustrations. The vivid illustrations in *Cremation of Sam McGee* (Service 1986), for example, provide an interesting visual counterpart to this tale of the Yukon during the gold rush.

Picture books also address those individuals who have made significant contributions to the arts. Kathleen Krull's (1993) *Lives of the Musicians: Good Times, Bad Times (and What the Neighbors Thought)* and *Lives of the Artists: Masterpieces, Messes (and What the Neighbors Thought)* (1995) give lighthearted, amusing glimpses of well-known musicians and artists. Each thumbnail sketch is only a few pages long, making them ideal for short read-alouds in music and art classes respectively.

These picture books and countless others can be integrated into your curricular area. They can be used with older students as interesting schema builders, anticipatory sets to begin lessons, models for quality writing, motivators for learning, read-alouds, and springboards into discussion and writing. Figure 5.3 provides examples of picture books useful for content area classrooms at all grade levels.

Fiction Books

Fiction entices readers to interact with texts from a number of perspectives that are impossible to achieve in nonfiction alone. Fantasy and traditional works (e.g., folktales and myths) and historical and realistic fiction, for example, help readers step outside their everyday world for a while to consider a subject from a different point of view. By doing so, they learn something about what it means to be a human being on this planet of ours.

Ray Bradbury (1989), an acclaimed contemporary author, likens the ability to fantasize to the ability to survive. Although fantasy seems an unlikely addition to the required reading list in a content area classroom, consider the possibilities for a moment. Robert C. O'Brien's *Z for Zachariah* (1975) and Louise Lawrence's *Children of the Dust* (1985) contemplate the aftermath of a nuclear holocaust and the fate of the people who are left alive. Can students really know enough about nuclear issues without considering the crises described in these books? Probably not. The facts concerning the effects of nuclear war are too large and too disconnected from our present reality to understand. Only by focusing on the possible experiences of a small group of people can readers begin to understand the ramifications of such an event.

FIGURE **5.3**   **Picture Books for Secondary Classrooms**

Aliki. (1999). *William Shakespeare and the Globe.* New York: HarperCollins.

Aliki. (1986). *A Medieval Feast.* New York: HarperCollins.

Anno, M. (1989). *Anno's Math Games II.* New York: Philomel.

Bunting, E. (1984). *Smoky Night.* Ill. D. Diaz. Orlando: Harcourt Brace.

Burleigh, R. (1997). *Hoops.* Ill. S. T. Johnson. San Diego: Silver Whistle.

Chekhov, A. (1991). *Kashtonka.* Trans. R. Povear. Ill. B. Moser. New York: Putnam.

Coville, B. (1997). *William Shakespeare's Macbeth.* Ill. G. Kelly. New York: Dial.

deMaupassant, G. (1993). *The Necklace.* Ill. G. Kelly. New York: Creative Editions.

Feelings, T. (1995). *The Middle Passage: White Ships, Black Cargo.* New York: Dial.

Fox, M. (2000). *Feathers and Fools.* Ill. N. Wilton. San Diego: Voyager.

Garland, S. (1993). *The Lotus Seed.* Ill. T. Kiuchi. San Diego: Harcourt.

Giblin, J. (1994). *Thomas Jefferson: A Picture Book Biography.* Ill. M. Dooling. New York: Scholastic.

Golenbock, P. (1990). *Teammates.* Ill. P. Bacon. San Diego: Harcourt.

Goodall, J. (1979). *The Story of an English Village.* New York: Atheneum.

Hoyt-Goldsmith, D. (1994). *Day of the Dead: A Mexican-American Celebration.* Ill. L. Migdale. New York: Holiday House.

Innocenti, R. (1985). *Rose Blanche.* San Diego: Creative Editions.

Krull, K. (1995). *Lives of the Artists: Masterpieces, Messes (and What the Neighbors Thought).* Ill. K. Hewitt. San Diego: Harcourt.

Krull, K. (2000). *Wilma Unlimited: How Wilma Rudolph Became the World's Fastest Woman.* Ill. D. Diaz. San Diego: Harcourt.

Krull, K. (1993). *Lives of the Musicians: Good Times, Bad Times (and What the Neighbors Thought).* Ill. K. Hewitt. San Diego: Harcourt.

Krull, K. (1997). *Lives of the Athlete: Thrills, Spills (and What the Neighbors Thought).* Ill. K. Hewitt. San Diego: Harcourt.

Lasky, K. (1994). *The Librarian Who Measured the Earth.* Ill. K. Hawkes. Boston: Little, Brown.

Lasky, K. (2003). *The Man Who Made Time Travel.* Ill. K. Hawkes. New York: Farrar Straus & Giroux.

Lauber, P. (1996). *Hurricanes: Earth's Mightiest Storms.* New York: Scholastic.

Lindbergh, R., & Brown, R. (1992). *A View from the Air: Charles Lindbergh's Earth and Sky.* New York: Viking.

Lowe, S. (1990). *Walden.* Ill. R. Sabuda. New York: Philomel.

Macauley, D. (1973). *Cathedral: The Story of Its Construction.* Boston: Houghton Mifflin.

Macauley, D. (1998). *The New Way Things Work.* Boston: Houghton Mifflin.

Maruki, T. (1980). *Hiroshima No Pika.* New York: Lothrop, Lee & Shepard.

FIGURE **5.3**   **Continued**

Myers, W. D. (2002). *Patrol: An American Soldier in Vietnam.* New York: HarperCollins.

Noyes, A. (1983). *The Highwayman.* Ill C. Mikolaychak. New York: Lothrop, Lee & Shepard.

Peacock, L. (1998). *Crossing the Delaware: A History in Many Voices* Ill. W. L. Krudop. New York: Atheneum.

Polacco, P. (1994). *Pink and Say.* New York: Scholastic.

Price, L. (1990). *Aida.* Ill. L. & D. Dillon. San Diego: Harcourt.

Rappaport, D. (2001). *Martin's Big Words: The Life of Dr. Martin Luther King, Jr.* Ill. B. Collier. New York: Hyperion.

Raschka, C. (1997). *Mysterious Thelonious.* New York: Orchard.

Ryan, P. M. (1998). *When Marian Sang: The True Recital of Marian Anderson.* Ill. B. Selznick. New York: Scholastic.

Rylant, C. (1984). *Waiting to Waltz: A Childhood.* Ill. S. Gammell. New York: Bradbury.

Say, A. (2002). *Home of the Brave.* Boston: Houghton Mifflin.

Service, R. (1986). *The Cremation of Sam McGee.* Ill. T. Harrison. New York: Greenwillow.

Seuss, Dr. (1984). *The Butter Battle Book.* New York: Random House.

Simon, S. (1990). *Oceans.* New York: Morrow Junior Books.

Stanley, D. (1996). *Leonardo da Vinci.* New York: Morrow.

Stanley, D. (2000). *Michelangelo.* New York: HarperCollins.

Tsuchiya, Y. (1988). *Faithful Elephants: A True Story of People, Animals and War.* Trans. T. Kykes. Ill. T. Lewin. Boston: Houghton Mifflin.

Van Allsburg, C. (1984). *Mysteries of Harris Burdick.* Boston: Houghton Mifflin.

Wisniewski, D. (1996). *Golem.* New York: Clarion.

Yolen, J. (1992) *Encounter.* Ill. D. Shannon. San Diego: Harcourt.

Jane Yolen's fantasy series, which takes place on a planet called Austar IV, has much to offer readers about social conditions of modern life that need to be examined and changed. We can see ourselves more objectively when we consider our lives from the distance of these stories.

Perhaps even more unlikely in a middle or high school curriculum would be the inclusion of traditional or folk literature because of its associations with younger children; however, the protagonists of most folktales are adolescents who have much to say to today's young adults. Robin McKinley's *Beauty* (1978) and Robert Nye's *Beowulf* (1968) continue to teach readers that strength of character is the crucial ingredient in changing the world. The human dimension of slavery is powerfully told in *The People Could Fly* (1985), by Virginia Hamilton, and true multicultural understanding is enhanced by her compilation of creation myths, *In the Beginning* (1988). Also, John Langstaff's *Climbing Jacob's Ladder* (1991), a compendium of African American spirituals richly illustrated by Ashley Bryan, offers young people a further understanding of African American history. A host of folktale collections from around the world is also readily available to add insight to the study of history, social studies, and geography. Folk literature is the "cement" or "mirror" of society (Sutherland & Arbuthnot 1986, p. 163) and thus gives readers an insider's view of a culture's beliefs and attitudes that is not found in the study of population density and manufacturing trends.

Poetry and drama provide fascinating insights into a myriad of topics. From Mel Glenn's (1991) classic work of poetry about the lives of students in *Class Dismissed! High School Poems* to Naomi Sihab Nye's (2002) *19 Varieties of Gazelle: Poems of the Middle East,* this genre provides personal glimpses into the human experience of everyday life.

Using drama in the classroom can be particularly engaging for teens. Gary Soto's (1997) *Novio Boy: A Play* is a lighthearted story about young love in a Mexican American community. It describes realistic characters and familiar situations with which students will identify. For teachers who don't want to tackle group plays, Chamber Stephens's (2002) *Magnificent Monologues for Teens* provides single-character sketches covering a range of topics of interest to teens.

Fiction books run the gamut from problem realism to sports stories, mysteries, adventures, romance, and historical fiction. Books of any and all of these types can be related to classroom content. Historical fiction can be associated with history in ways that textbooks can't. Through vicarious involvement in the lives of characters who never actually existed, but who are placed in times and places that actually did, teens can participate in the most triumphant or the most terrible moments in history. Laurie Anderson's (2000) *Fever 1793* is a dramatic account of a little known historical event—the yellow fever epidemic in Philadelphia; it demonstrates how a young woman's strength of character helps her survive events that turn her world upside down.

Although many fiction books have formulized plots, stereotypical characters, and overly sentimental themes, a large body of quality literature is also available. Many worthy works are found on the annual *Young Adults' Choices List,* established with research sponsored by the International Reading Association. This list reflects the diversity of young adult literature, including titles dealing with social and political issues, such as drunk driving, women's rights, death, and war. The host of fiction books available can do much to enhance and clarify the content curriculum. An author's ability to bring lifelike characters into sharp focus against a setting that smacks of real places results in compelling reading.

Multicultural Books

Multicultural books provide today's diverse students with rich opportunities to associate with the books they read. Multicultural books portray members of a wide variety of cultures, including African and African American, Asian and

RESEARCH-BASED BEST PRACTICES

BOX 5.3

Exploring Different Points of View toward Historical Events

The use of trade books can help expose students to a variety of perspectives in relationship to particular historical events. Students typically study world explorers as part of social studies at both the middle and high school levels. The use of trade books can offer perspectives about historical events beyond those provided in the textbook. By providing students with a wide variety of texts, they can reflect on the ways in which history is not only reported but also interpreted by writers. Consider, for example, the events surrounding Christopher Columbus's discovery of the New World. Trade books from the historical fiction, nonfiction, and picture book genres provide dramatically different portrayals of that event.

Social studies teacher Robert Wells involves his students in examining these different points of view. He uses six different biographies and historical fiction titles for this lesson. Two of these are *Pedro's Journal* (Conrad 1991), a fictionalized account of Columbus's voyage, narrated by Pedro, a ship's boy who accompanied Columbus on his journey, and Jane Yolen's *Encounter* (1992), an account of Columbus's arrival told from the point of view of a Taino Indian boy.

Robert divides students into groups based on the books they are reading and directs students to looks at each book's account of the events of October 12, 1492. He focuses groups' reading, asking them to think about the following questions as they read: What are the events that take place as Columbus lands? What is the author's point of view toward Columbus? How does the author describe the native people Columbus meets? What is Columbus's attitude toward the natives?

After students have read their books, Robert leads the whole class in completing a data chart that compares the answers to the questions found in each of the books. The students then engage in a discussion about why the accounts of the same events are different. They reflect on the sources each author used to create the account, as well as the reasons authors who consulted the same sources might provide different accounts. Through this discussion, students gain understanding of the idea of history as interpretation, rather than fact.

Asian American, Native American, and Latino. They include picture books, poetry, fiction, and nonfiction. Multicultural books can help all students learn about the unique cultures in today's classrooms. Through literature they can develop understanding of cultural norms related to family, morality, sex roles, dress, and values. Most importantly, however, multicultural literature brings the people of a particular group into focus and can help students realize that in spite of our differences all people share many common emotions, dreams, and hopes for the future. Through interactions with characters representing a variety of cultures, young people begin to view members of parallel cultures as individuals who are unique and yet have universal feelings and experiences.

Fiction titles, such as Suzanne Fisher Staples's (1991) *Shabanu: Daughter of the Wind* draw the reader into the life of a girl growing up among camel-dealing nomads in modern Pakistan. Pam Munoz Ryan's (2000) *Esperanza Rising* is a wonderful coming-of-age novel focused on a "riches-to-rags" story of a wealthy young Mexican girl and her mother who end up becoming migrant workers in the fields of California. The book is based on the real-life experiences of the author's grandmother.

Nonfiction titles realistically address the struggles encountered by people of color. Walter Dean Myers's (1991) *Now Is Your Time: The African-American Struggle for Freedom* profiles African Americans who have made important contributions to the development of the United States. Loung Ung's (2000) *First They Killed My Father: A Daughter of Cambodia Remembers* graphically portrays one family's struggle to survive the horrors of the Khmer Rough in Cambodia. In *Voices from the Fields: Children of Migrant Farm Workers Tell Their Stories* (Atkin 1993), ten Mexican American children of migrant farm workers describe their lives in their own words. One of the young people featured is a gang member, one is an unmarried teenage mother, and another is making plans to attend college to become a physician. The author portrays the uncertainty of their lives, at the same time recognizing the strong bonds that bind them to their families.

Books for Struggling Readers

Meeting the needs of reluctant readers is a perennial challenge for all teachers. Now more than ever before, however, there are easy-to-read titles on a range of topics relevant to today's content area classrooms. In addition to picture book titles, reluctant readers often respond positively to short books (books fewer than 100 pages), series books, and comic books or cartoons.

Short but intriguing fiction titles, such as *Stuck in Neutral* (Trueman 2001) are sure to captivate those readers who simply will not connect to books. Shawn Mc-Daniel, the main character and narrator of the story, has cerebral palsy and can neither walk, talk, nor focus his eyes. As the story progresses, the reader comes to understand the strange world that Shawn inhabits; a world rich with experiences that he is unable to communicate to others. As the story progresses, Shawn becomes increasingly concerned about his father's attitude toward him, and he panics when he begins to think that his father is considering killing him to stop his suffering. This moving book raises a number of issues related to euthanasia and is sure to provoke interesting discussions.

Series books continue to have great appeal for reluctant readers. Popular series for students include historical fictional series, such as the *Dear America* books, which describe young people's experiences from America's past. Gary Paulsen's *World of Adventure* series books are short and easy to read, and draw students into dramatic adventures ranging from forest fires to Iditarod dog-sled races across Alaska. Series books, such as the Dorling Kinder-

e Resources

There are many Websites that will help you locate books of interest to your students. To get started, go to Web Destinations on the Companion Website. Go to Professional Resources and search for either of these sites: The Children's Literature Web Guide or The Assembly on Literature for Adolescents Review (ALAN Review).

sley *Eyewitness Books,* are extremely appealing for students whose favorite reading is informational.

Even cartoons have their place in the classroom, particularly when they are as well written as is Art Spiegelman's *Maus: A Survivor's Tale* (1986). In this book, the story of the Holocaust is vividly told with the Nazis depicted as cats and the Jewish people as mice. Rather than detracting from the seriousness of the subject, the cartoon format lends force to the Nazi victims' plight.

Using Trade Books in the Classroom

A recent study of exemplary content area instruction found a key commonality among effective teachers: All of them used multiple texts with a range of formats and difficulty levels (Allington & Johnston 2002). These teachers capitalized on the myriad uses for trade books in the content area classroom and used them to enhance and extend students' content area literacy learning. This section addresses uses for trade books, including creating classroom libraries, developing text sets, student self-selected reading, and teacher read-alouds. In addition, it identifies how teachers can organize students for literature study. Virtually all of these ways of using literature can enhance objectives for student learning in every content area.

> **e.Resources**
>
> To find lesson plans and resources for using literature, go to Web Destinations on the Companion Website. Go to Professional Resources and search for this site: Lesson Plans and Resources for Adolescent and Young Adult Literature.

There are several key components necessary to creating a multitext content area classroom. First, and foremost, content area teachers need to acquire books related to their content area. These books can be used to stock classroom libraries for large- and small-group reading of trade books and for individual inquiry. Locating books for these purposes is always challenging, but resourceful teachers have found that library book sales, garage sales, and book clubs, such as Scholastic and Trumpet, are good resources for obtaining inexpensive books.

Creating Classroom Libraries and Text Sets

A classroom library is a critical component of a multitext classroom. By creating a classroom library of books in a range of reading levels and in a variety of genres, including picture books, poetry, historical fiction, biography, and information, teachers increase student access to books and contribute to their motivation for learning. Other resources, such as magazines and newspapers, are equally appropriate for inclusion in a content area classroom library. To meet the diverse reading needs and interests of today's students, as well as the variety of ways that trade books can be used in content area classrooms, classroom libraries should include a wide range of titles, addressing a variety of topics and reading levels.

What kinds of books might be found in a classroom library in a U.S. history class, for example? Good choices might include survey books about history such as *A History of Us* (Hakim 1999), the highly acclaimed series by Joy Hakim that speaks directly to adolescents about historical events using a conversational style. Historical fiction titles by authors such as Ann Rinaldi and biographies by authors such as Russell Freedman could enhance this collection. Easy-to-read picture book biographies by James Cross Giblin, such as *The Amazing Life of Benjamin Franklin* (Giblin 2000), can also be added to the classroom library. Hundreds of informational titles could round out such a collection, including books by renowned young adult authors such as Jim Murphy and many others.

However, these titles, as excellent as they are, might not be terribly appealing to less-motivated students. Middle and high school students enjoy books with humor and comic books. For that reason, titles such as *Cartoon History of the United States* (Gonick 1991), a satirical vision of U.S. history, might be included. Other amusing titles, such as *So You Want to Be President?* (St. George 2000) or *Explorers Who Got Lost* (Sansevere-Dreher, Dreher, & Renfro 1994), debunk some of the myths about U.S. presidents and famous explorers of the past. Magazines, such as *National Geographic World, Cobblestone,* or *Time for Kids,* could complement such a collection.

> **Response Journal**
>
> Create a text set of six books related to your discipline. Be sure to select books from a variety of genres and difficulty levels. Describe the books you selected and why you chose those particular books. What kinds of connections exist across the texts? How might you use the books to capitalize on those connections?

In addition to a range of titles broadly related to a content area discipline, teachers will want to create text sets related more specifically to particular units of study within a content area. Text sets are a variety of titles that span a range of difficulty levels and a range of resources, including books as well as magazines, Internet sources, newspaper articles, and so on. A sample text set related to the Civil War appears in Figure 5.4. These text sets can be used in myriad ways: for independent reading, self-selected reading, individual inquiry, or idea circles.

Student Self-Selected Reading

The more time students spend reading, the higher their reading achievement. To encourage reading and demonstrate its importance, many schools provide uninterrupted sustained silent reading time, sometimes referred to as USSR time or DEAR (drop everything and read). At one San Diego high school, a separate twenty-five minute period is allocated each day for sustained silent reading time. During this time, everyone—teachers, students, and even construction workers at the school site—reads. Uninterrupted sustained silent reading time lets students practice reading and read for their own purposes and pleasure. Students self-select materials other than their textbooks. They can read books or magazines from home or obtain books from the school or classroom library that relate to personal interests.

Providing students with opportunities to choose their own books and time to read during content area classes allows students to engage with interesting texts that they themselves have chosen. This has a number of benefits:

- *It increases the amount of time students spend reading during the school day.*

- *It helps students develop interest in a subject.*

FIGURE 5.4   Text Set on the Civil War

Picture Books

Ackerman, N. (1990). *The Tin Heart*. Ill. Michael Hays. New York: Atheneum.
This picture book describes the effect of the Civil War on the friendship of two young girls who
   live on opposite sides of the Mason–Dixon line.

Lyon, G. E. (1991). *Cecil's Story*. Ill. P. Catalanotto. New York: Orchard.
Picture book that describes the apprehensions of a young boy whose father may need to leave
   home to serve in the Civil War.

Turner, A. (1987). *Nettie's Trip South*. Ill. Ron Himler. New York: Macmillan.
A young girl travels south during the 1850s and discovers the horrors of slavery firsthand.

Play

Davis, O. (1978). *Escape to Freedom: A Play about Frederick Douglass*. New York: Viking Penguin.
This compelling play exposes young readers to the incredible life of Frederick Douglass.

Folktales

Hamilton, Virginia. (1985). *The People Could Fly*. Ill. Leo and Diane Dillon. New York: Knopf.
A collection of African American folktales narrated in authentic dialect.

Historical Fiction

Beatty, P. (1987). *Charley Skedaddle*. New York: Morrow.
This novel describes the experiences of a young drummer boy for the Union Army during the
   American Civil War.

Hansen, J. (1986). *Which Way Freedom?* New York: Walker.
Describes the life of an escaped slave who serves in the Civil War.

Hunt, I. (1964). *Across Five Aprils*. New York: Follett.
Describes how the Creighton family of southern Illinois struggles with the impact of the Civil War.

Reeder, C. (1989). *Shades of Gray*. New York: Macmillan.
Twelve-year-old Will Page, the orphaned son of a Confederate soldier, must live with his Uncle Jed,
   who refused to fight for the Confederacy.

Nonfiction

Fleming, T. (1988). *Band of Brothers: West Point in the Civil War*. New York: Walker.
Describes men who were friends and classmates at West Point and later served in the Civil War,
   often fighting against one another.

Lester, J. (1968). *To Be a Slave*. Ill. T. Feelings. New York: Dutton.
Using the actual words of his subjects, Lester presents life as it existed for slaves in the United
   States.

Murphy, J. (1990). *The Boys' War*. New York: Clarion.
Diaries, letters, and original photographs tell the stories of young boys who participated in the
   Civil War.

Websites

American Memory–Primary Source Photographs of the Civil War: http://memory.loc.gov/

The Civil War Home Page–Comprehensive Web Site Related to the Civil War: www.civilwar.com

- *It builds knowledge* that helps students read and learn more about a topic.

- *It can provide a basis for researching a particular topic.*

- *It familiarizes students with different formats and genres* used to report information, that can be models for their own research and writing. (Worthy, Broaddus, & Ivey 2001)

Teacher Read-Alouds

Students in teacher Maria Prieto's ninth-grade English class read excerpts from *The Diary of Anne Frank* (Frank 1967) in their literature anthology every year. This year Maria decided to enrich her students' study of the diary by reading aloud the informational *Anne Frank: Beyond the Diary* (van der Rol & Verhoeven 1993). The text contains background on the Frank family, including their move from Germany to Amsterdam, photographs of the diary itself and other artifacts, maps of the "secret annex," and a copy of a primary source document—the Nazi's typewritten list of Frank family members targeted for arrest.

Maria described her use of the book in the following way:

> Before my students start reading the diary, I read aloud Chapters 1 and 2. These chapters provide important background about Anne's life and information about Hitler's rise to power. I put the map of the "secret annex" that appears in the book on the document camera to give students a spatial understanding of the place where the Franks and the van Dams lived. Then my students read the diary. After they've completed their reading of the diary, I read chapters which describe how the Frank family was arrested and the later discovery of the diary. Finally, I read the section of the book that describes Anne's life after the arrest at the concentration camp at Bergen Belsen. After each reading, I passed the book around so that students could more closely examine the photographs. They were very interested in the book, and several of them read it on their own after reading the diary.

This example demonstrates a number of purposes that content area read-alouds can accomplish. First, read-alouds can provide important background information that will enhance student understanding of assigned readings. Maria's use of the map of the secret annex, for example, helped students visualize the setting for Anne Frank's experiences. In addition, the read-aloud extended and enhanced the content in the diary itself by describing the rest of Anne Frank's tragic story. Finally, reading aloud can generate student interest in a topic. After hearing books read aloud, students are much more likely to pick them up on their own.

Reading aloud is considered by many experts to be the single most important activity in developing student literacy ability, regardless of age. Reading aloud provides literary experiences in a supportive context and exposure to the various forms of written language, both narrative and expository. As students listen to literature, they subconsciously absorb its rhythms, structures, and cadences. Read-alouds give struggling readers access to information in the more difficult texts commonly used in content area classrooms.

In addition, read-alouds provide a format whereby teachers can demonstrate for students the mental processes used to make sense of what they are reading. These processes can become evident to students through many of the strategies described in this book, including think-alouds, directed reading–listening activities, and many others. Some read-aloud experiences should go beyond brief isolated experiences during which the teacher reads and students listen. These "bigger" read-aloud experiences should be interactive; with students actively engaged in thinking, questioning, clarifying, and summarizing texts (Ivey 2002). Finally, read-alouds provide opportunities for responses to literature that can lead to engagement and further understanding of content. These are described in the following section.

Based on her experiences with hundreds of read-aloud experiences, Erickson (1996) offers guidelines for middle and high school teachers who wish to incorporate reading aloud in their classes:

She recommends selecting books that

hold students interest;

stimulate discussion;

reflect authors from many cultures; and

match the social and emotional levels of the listeners.

She suggests that teachers prepare for read-alouds carefully by first practicing the work. Initially, she recommends that read-alouds last no longer than fifteen minutes. She also suggests using pictures and props that can heighten student interest and increase understanding of text content.

Read-alouds can include books from a variety of genres, including poetry, short stories, fiction, nonfiction, magazine articles, or even plays. Short stories such as Chris Crutcher's (1989) *Athletic Shorts*, for example, are perfect read-alouds for physical education classes.

At the beginning of a science lesson, an excerpt from a book read aloud to the class or a picture book can serve as an enjoyable preview of the lesson's contents. Trade books, thus, play a supporting role by introducing a part of or a perspective on the lesson that may entice students to want to know more. The verbal imagery of a text and the visual stimuli of picture books appeal to all age groups and help to activate schemata that are crucial to further learning. For example, an excellent introduction to a study of the building instincts of animals and birds would be Kitchen's *And So They Build* (1993). Students might look at the detailed drawings before starting the unit and predict how each type of shelter is constructed. They might speculate on comparisons of the animals' and birds' building strategies to those of people. In addition, the teacher might read several of the examples in the book to the class and conduct a discussion of how they will be used in the forthcoming unit.

Every read-aloud need not be cover to cover. Reading excerpts from books, magazines, or newspaper articles can sometimes be more effective than longer

> **Response Journal**
> Identify a read-aloud book that you might use to introduce a unit or topic of study. Plan a lesson around the book, identifying follow-up discussion questions that you might use after you have read the book aloud.

read alouds. "Bits and pieces" read alouds could include reading picture captions from nonfiction titles to provide "sneak previews" of books or brief profiles from any of the Kathleen Krull "*Lives of . . .*" books mentioned earlier.

Literature Study in Content Areas

As teachers become increasingly convinced of the value of using literature in the content area classrooms, they will want students to experience literature in increasingly varied ways. They may decide that students can benefit from "breaking out" of the textbook to engage in reading trade books, or they may use literature in connection with units of study. Many teachers use the additional time provided by block scheduling to engage students in reading and discussing trade books.

One of the most challenging aspects of using literature in the classroom—whether fiction or nonfiction—is grouping students for instruction. The grouping pattern of choice depends on teacher and students' goals and purposes for using the literature. The following section explains three different grouping models that teachers might wish to use as they involve students in studying content-related literature.

Whole-Group/Single-Book Model

Sometimes teachers want all students in a class to have a common reading experience centered on the same book. On these occasions they may use a whole-group model where all students read the same book. Science teacher Ken Blake wanted to extend his textbook's treatment of outer space and space travel. He decided to involve his students in reading Sally Ride and Susan Okie's (1986) *To Space and Back,* a wonderful account of Ride's experiences on the space shuttle.

Because this was the first time he had used literature to supplement the textbook, he decided to use the whole-group/single-book model. He purchased twenty-five paperback copies of the book. Each student read the book and participated in large- and small-group discussions about a variety of topics, including everyday life in a space capsule. Students also compared and contrasted information in their textbook to that found in Ride and Okie's book. They considered the challenges posed by life in a space capsule and debated the importance of sending astronauts into space.

Small-Groups/Multiple-Books Model

A second model for using literature is the small-groups/multiple-books model. With this model, students work in small groups reading different books related to a common theme. Alan Trent, for example, used multiple copies of several nonfiction titles to supplement textbook content and enrich his students' study of the

RESEARCH-BASED BEST PRACTICES

BOX 5.4

Linking Physical Education with Literacy Learning

Teacher Tona Wilson at Monroe Clark Middle School in San Diego makes literacy learning an integral part of her physical education classes. She uses read-alouds on a regular basis, for example, to teach students concepts related to health and physical education. She often reads aloud from books such as *Wilma Unlimited* or *Chicken Soup for the Sports Fan's Soul* (Canfield 2000). She regularly reads short newspaper and magazine articles about current events related to sports. These read-alouds provide a rich source for discussion and help students recognize the importance of health and physical education in their everyday lives.

Tona uses her strong knowledge of trade books related to sports to encourage her students to read in school and out of school. In order to become better acquainted with her students' sports-related interests, Tona has each student complete a survey about their sports-related preferences and extracurricular activities. This provides her with information that enables her to recommend particular titles to her students that relate to their interests in soccer, baseball, dance, or field hockey. She regularly consults with reading teachers at the school who provide assistance in locating books for students with particular interests.

Another literacy-related activity Tona involves her students in is a research project she calls "bioboards." Bioboards involve her students in using trade books to research sports figures from the past or present. Students are required to locate information related to the person's life and (1) create a time line of the sport figure's life (2) identify great sports moments in his or her life, (3) research the schools the person attended and sports participation in school, and (4) create color pictures depicting selected events and write captions explaining each picture. Each student displays his or her information on an 11-by-17-inch board and presents it to the other members of the class.

As they learn about different types of games, students regularly engage in shared and guided reading activities that teach them about the history, rules, and methods of scoring. They then work with partners incorporating what they have learned about these games to create their own new games, such as racquetball soccer. In these and many other ways, Tona Wilson helps her students see the many values of literacy as their learn about health and physical education.

Civil War. Students formed groups based on their selection of one of four different books: *The Long Road to Gettysburg* (Murphy 1992), *A Separate Battle: Women and the Civil War* (Chang 1991), *A Nation Torn* (Ray 1990), and *Boy's War: Confederate and Union Soldiers Talk about the Civil War* (Murphy 1990). Students read and discussed each title in their small groups over a two-week period. Using the jigsaw strategy, students then formed new groups in which they shared their information. They then shared the information obtained from one another with the larger group through creative extensions including projects, dramatic presentations, and debates.

Individual Inquiry

As we discuss in Chapter 7, inquiry involves students in conducting research on a variety of topics. As part of inquiry experiences, students generate ideas and questions and pose problems. They gather information from a variety of sources and communicate this information in a variety of ways. Individual inquiry is an increasingly popular way to involve students in research by letting students explore issues of personal interest. Through these research projects students investigate topics and collect, analyze, and organize information. Students later present this information as a project or report. By using several sources about the same topic, students can examine multiple points of view and evaluate the accuracy of information.

Inquiry projects can combine fiction with nonfiction. In an inquiry project with high school students, English teacher Joan Kaywell (1994) linked fiction and nonfiction books. Her class first generated a list of problems affecting today's teens such as anorexia nervosa, stress, suicide, pregnancy, sexual abuse, and so on. The class narrowed the number of topics to five and formed inquiry groups based on each topic. At this point, each student in a group selected and read a different young adult novel related to the identified problem.

After reading their novels, students used nonfiction materials to conduct research about the problem posed in their novel. Each student found at least one nonfiction source and cited a minimum of ten facts related to the topic. At this point, students reconvened in small groups where they pooled these facts. They then selected the best twenty-five facts to be included in an information sheet about the problem. They discussed source credibility, recency, and relevancy of information as they narrowed down their lists. They then presented this information to the larger group.

Promoting Response to Literature

As discussed in Chapter 1, reader response refers to the way a person reacts to hearing or reading a piece of literature. It describes the unique interaction that occurs between a reader's mind and heart and a particular literary text (Hancock 2000). You may recall from Chapter 1 that readers seek to construct meaning from the text and these responses are dynamic, fluid, and varied. Different readers construct different meanings from texts; no two readers may interpret the same work in the same way.

Why should content area teachers be interested in response to literature? Research suggests that students grow in several different areas when engaged in response-based activities:

- *They develop ownership of their reading and their responses.*

- *They make personal connections with literature.*

- *They gain appreciation for multiple interpretations and tolerance for ambiguity.*

- *They become more critical readers* and attain higher levels of thinking and richer understandings of literature.

- *They increase their repertoire of responses to literature.*

- *They begin to view themselves as successful readers.*

- *They develop greater awareness of the literary quality of a work.* (Speigel 1998)

Involving students in response to literature can help content area teachers meet many important goals they have in terms of developing students' thinking skills. Responsive activities can help to develop critical thinkers, students who can examine different sides of an argument, respond thoughtfully to texts, and heighten their understandings of the ways texts work.

Response-centered classrooms can help students grow in their understanding and appreciation of nonfiction just as surely as fiction. Teachers often assume that nonfiction literature will elicit only efferent responses, but studies have found that readers do respond aesthetically to nonfiction (Vardell & Copeland 1992). Effective teachers guide students' responses to both biography and informational books in ways that encourage both efferent and aesthetic responses. By providing a supportive context and engaging activities that promote both oral and written responses, teachers can extend and deepen students' literary experiences with both nonfiction and fiction.

The rest of this chapter is devoted to examples of instructional strategies teachers can use to promote responses to literature. Strategies for promoting responses range from writing to drama to inquiry-driven idea circles. All of the strategies described are designed to help teachers encourage meaningful student responses, both aesthetic and efferent, to the excellent literature available today. Through these experiences, students can make personal connections between these texts and their lives and reflect on what these texts have to teach them. In this way students deepen their involvement with literature and become more aware of its possibilities.

Making Connections: Text-to-Self, Text-to-Text, Text-to-World

Writing in response to literature, whether fiction or nonfiction, allows learners to share their thoughts and feelings about a text. It can help students construct meanings of texts at the same time it improves writing fluency. Writing in response to nonfiction literature can both involve the evocation of feelings and enhance learning of text content. As we explained in the previous chapter, "writing to learn" can help students think about what they will be reading or reflect on what has been read. It can improve understanding of difficult concepts, increase retention of information, prompt learners to elaborate on and manipulate ideas, and help them gain insight into the author's craft. Several of the response activities described in this section help students connect personally to texts, whereas others help them process information or record what they have learned. Some of the activities are formal, whereas others are informal in nature.

Text Connections

One of the many excellent ideas presented in Stephanie Harvey and Anne Goudvis's (2000) *Strategies That Work* is the idea of asking students to use writing to reflect on the personal connections they make between the texts they are reading and their own lives. As students grow in sophistication, they develop the ability to recognize the connections they make between the texts they read and other texts, as well as between the texts they are reading and the wider world. Harvey and Goudvis refer to these connections as *text-to-self, text-to-text,* and *text-to-world* connections respectively. It is possible for students to make these connections with books from any genre.

Text-to-self connections involve instances when readers feel personal connections with text events or character's emotions. Harvey recommends using memoirs or realistic fiction to help students develop skills in making text-to-self connections because reader identification with characters can be particularly strong in these types of texts. "It reminds me of . . ." can help students reflect on these types of connections.

Text-to-text connections involve connecting ideas across texts. The concept of texts can be a broad one here; students might connect text content to a movie or song for example. These can include comparing characters' personalities and actions; story events and plot lines; lessons, themes, or messages in stories; finding common themes, writing styles, or perspectives in an author's work; or comparing the treatment of common themes by different authors.

Text-to-world connections are the most sophisticated connections students can make. With these types of connections, students reflect on the relationship between the content of the text and the wider world. This could include connections related to world events, issues, or concerns.

Post-It Notes

Harvey recommends that teachers use think-alouds and other text demonstrations to model for students how readers naturally create these connections. After this modeling occurs, students can begin to record the various kinds of connections on Post-it notes as they read. On the notes, they will want to record a word or phrase that explains the thought or feeling that occurs to them as they read. As they read and record these connections, students can code text-to-self connections as T–S, text-to-text connections as T–T, or text-to-world connections as T–W. Students should focus not only on recording and categorizing their connections but also should reflect on how the connection has led them to a greater understanding of the text. These Post-it notes can serve as the basis for rich postreading discussions about the kinds of thinking students have done as they read. In addition, these notes can often evolve into longer written pieces in response journals or essays.

Expository Texts as Models for Writing

Students need a variety of writing experiences in the classroom, including experience in writing nonnarrative types of texts. One way to involve students in informational-type writing is by having them use information trade books as models for their own writing. These books can serve as models for brief, shortterm writing experiences, or extended, long-term experiences.

The Important Book (Brown 1949), although not a nonfiction book, can serve as a model for information writing in many content areas. Each paragraph of this book states an important characteristic, or main idea, about a common object. This trait is followed by supporting details that further enhance the description of the object, and each paragraph concludes with a restatement of the main idea. Leslie Hughes, a middle school science teacher, used this text structure during a review of a unit on oceans. The teacher read the model to the class and provided students with the *text frame* "the important thing about _____ is _____." Students formed writing groups and were assigned particular topics related to oceans. They identified the main ideas related to their topic and inserted it into the text frame. They provided supporting details and concluded the writing with a restatement of the main idea. An example of one students' effort follows:

> The important thing about a tide pool is that it contains a community of plants and animals. Tidepools are left in rocky basins and shallow hollows as low tide causes ocean water to go back out to sea. These basins of sea water contain plants, crabs, periwinkles and other plant and animal life. But the important thing about tide pools is that they contain a community of plants and animals.

As we show in Chapter 11, many different types of text frames can be used to scaffold expository and narrative writing experiences. Moreover, dozens of nonfiction books can provide models for inquiry-related writing. A book such as *My Season with Penguins: An Antarctic Journal* (Webb 2000) is, in actuality, a field journal maintained by biologist Sophie Webb. This title could serve as a model for students' own field journals to be used in a science class. Examples of books that model the use of interviews and oral history abound. One of the finest is *Oh Freedom: Kids Talk about the Civil Rights Movement* (King & Osborne 1997). This book was actually created by young people; the students interviewed thirty-one friends, family members, and neighbors who each told the story of the civil rights movement from their own perspective. The result is an amazing oral history of that turbulent time. Teachers could involve students in conducting their own oral history interviews related to topics of study in a social studies class.

Process Drama as a Heuristic Response

Responding to literature through drama provides a wealth of opportunities for enhancing student engagement in learning. *Process drama* experiences allow students to establish an imaginary world in which students experience fictional roles and situations. Process drama differs from other forms of drama in that it does not involve the use of scripts, but it includes episodes that students themselves compose and rehearse, it continues over time, and audience is integral (O'Neill 1995). Like reading, drama requires that students make meaning based on the reading that they have done. However, with drama, meaning-making takes on a visual component. That is, students externalize the visual images they create from a text and incorporate thought, language, and movement to demonstrate their learning. Through drama they enter the world of the text, whether fiction or nonfiction, which lets them observe and reflect on that world.

Many struggling readers have difficulty creating mental images as they read. Dramatic activities scaffold this image-making in a motivating and meaningful way. These activities can generate interest at the same time they help students enter a text, seeing and feeling the emotions of the characters or experiencing the events described. By combining reading with dramatic experiences, teachers help students enhance their oral language skills through listening and speaking, thereby developing vocabulary and reading fluency. Dramatic activities encourage learners to listen for cues and learn to use their voices to convey emotion. In addition, they help students develop self-confidence and cooperative learning skills. These activities also offer a natural entry point into the world of writing; students can move from simply dramatizing the words of others to creating their own scripts that can be performed.

For many students, drama can heighten understanding of the often dense and complex expository material found in today's nonfiction. It can enhance student understanding of both technical vocabulary and specific content-related concepts. It can motivate students to explore the content of these books more deeply. Most of all, it can bring abstract information to life, making it concrete and, therefore, comprehensible, which can be particularly helpful for struggling readers or second-language learners.

Dramatic responses to literature have other benefits as well. Responses of this type require in-depth familiarity with the text to be dramatized. Generally, learners need repeated exposure to a text before they can formulate a response to it. This repeated exposure could be particularly beneficial for struggling readers.

Spontaneous Drama

Spontaneous drama involves students in active response to literature and allows them to invoke their imaginations. It can be very beneficial for students of all ages, many of whom often find dramatic play extremely motivating. Spontaneous responses to nonfiction can help students mediate texts in ways that make them interesting, memorable, and comprehensible. For example, students can create spontaneous dramatizations in response to fiction and nonfiction read-alouds. Students not only enjoy these activities but also appear to retain much of the information presented as a result of the dramatizations.

Other more structured forms of dramatic response can sensitize students to expository text organization. For example, after reading *The Heart and Blood (How Our Bodies Work)* (Burgess 1988) a middle grade teacher involved her students in a dramatic activity designed to demonstrate the sequence by which blood flows through the heart. One-half of the class carried red sheets of construction paper (to represent oxygenated blood) and the other half carried blue to represent deoxygenated blood. Then eight students paired up to act as the valve gatekeepers. Student desks were arranged in the shape of the heart, and stations represented the lungs and other body parts. After that the students moved around the room, simulating the flow of blood through the heart and other organs. Then students wrote about the activity in their learning logs (Moss 2003).

Pantomime

Pantomime is another form of response useful with content-related texts. It requires learners to communicate through their bodies without relying on verbal communication. Students might enjoy creating pantomimes in response to Aliki's (1983) *A Medieval Feast.* This particular book contains many scenes that students could pantomime, including depictions of turning boars on the spit, fencing in the fields, and sounding the trumpets (Stewig & Burge 1994). Nicholas Reeves's (1992) *Into the Mummy's Tomb,* for example, could stimulate dramatizations including the building of the pyramids, the burial of Tutankhamen, the process of mummification, or the purposes of the artifacts found in the tomb.

Tableau

Tableau, or snapshot drama, is another motivating dramatic response activity. Tableau is a dramatic activity that involves a still, silent performance that involves three-dimensional representations. A tableau typically involves no movement, talk, or props, only gestures. Students depict the freezing of moments in time and demonstrate physical or emotional relationships and character gestures or activities. Typically, teachers give students time to plan their tableau in small groups. Each group comes in front of the class and the teacher gives a "one, two, three, freeze" cue. The audience then discusses what they see in the tableau, offering interpretations of what they see.

This activity works extremely well with all kinds of texts, including poetry, fantasies, realistic fiction, biographies, or other informational books. Using Cynthia Rylant's (1984) *Waiting to Waltz*, for example, small groups could create tableau related to selected poems from that work. Or, small groups of students could select and read a biography. After they have read the book, the teacher could distribute a three- or four-sentence scene from the story that could form the basis for a tableau. The biography *El Chino* (Say 1990), which describes the life of Billy Wong, the first Chinese matador, includes scenes that could be dramatized in this way. These could include Billy's years as a basketball player, his efforts to become a matador, or his first bullfight. Each person in the group would assume a role in the drama. After practicing, students could create their "frozen moments." The other students in the class could then attempt to identify the scene portrayed.

Readers Theatre

Readers theatre differs from process drama in that it involves oral presentation of a script by two or more readers. No props, costumes, or memorization of lines is required. Students must, however, read their parts fluently, with appropriate dramatic flair. Readers theatre is often used with folktales or narrative text, but it can be adapted easily to nonfiction as well.

Informational books and biographies with dialogue are easily adapted to this format, but picture books or excerpts from longer books can also be effective. The following guidelines can help teachers adapt nonfiction texts to a readers theatre script:

1. *Select an interesting section of text* containing the desired content.

2. *Reproduce the text.*

3. *Delete lines not critical to the content being emphasized,* including those that indicate that a character is speaking.

4. *Decide how to divide the parts for the readers.* Assign dialogue to appropriate characters. With some texts, it will be necessary to rewrite text as dialogue or with multiple narrators. Changing third-person point of view to first person (*I* or *we*) can create effective narration.

5. *Add a prologue to introduce the script in storylike fashion.* If needed, a postscript can be added to bring closure to the script.

6. *Label the readers' parts* by placing the speaker's name in the left-hand margin, followed by a colon.

7. *After the script is finished, ask others to read it aloud.* Students can then make revisions based on what they hear. Give students time to read and rehearse their parts. (Young & Vardell 1993)

An obvious next step is to involve students in selecting books from which they can develop their own readers theatre scripts. Through this activity, learners develop critical-thinking skills, make decisions, work cooperatively, and engage in the process of revision.

Idea Circles

Another excellent way for students to respond to literature is by using idea circles. Idea circles represent the small-group/multiple-books model of organizing the classroom for literature study. They involve students in small-group peer-led discussions of concepts fueled by reading experiences with multiple texts (Guthrie & McCann 1996). Idea circles are an ideal way to promote peer-directed conceptual understanding of virtually any aspect of content area learning. This conceptual learning involves three basic ingredients: facts, relationships between facts, and explanations.

Idea circles not only engage students in learning about science or social studies but they also require engagement in a variety of literacy activities, including locating information, evaluating the quality and relevance of information, summarizing information for their peers, and determining relationships among information found in a variety of sources. They require that students learn to integrate information, ideas, and view points. In addition, they involve students in a variety of important collaborative processes, including turn-taking, maintaining group member participation, and coaching one another in the use of literacy strategies (Guthrie & McCann 1996).

Idea circles share some things in common with literature circles (Daniels 1994). Like literature circles, they involve three to six students in directed small-group discussions. Like literature circles, idea circles are peer led and involve student-generated rules. However, idea circles involve students in discussion surrounding the learning of a particular concept rather than a discussion centering on a single literary text. In literature circle discussions, students may have conflicting interpretations of a piece of literature. With idea circles, students work together to create a common understanding of a concept by constructing abstract understanding from facts and details. Another difference between literature circles and idea circles is in the use of texts. With literature circles, students all read and respond to a single text. With idea circles, every student may interact with a different text in preparation for the group discussion. Then during the discussion, students share the unique information that they have found. Furthermore, idea circle discussions require the use of informational, rather than literary, texts.

The teacher begins the idea circle experience by presenting students with a goal in the form of a topic or question. An example of a question might be "What is a desert?" Before the idea circle meets, students can either read extensively from relevant informational trade books or read and discuss their findings concurrently. Information that students bring to the group may come from prior experiences, discussions with others, as well as from their readings. In their groups, students exchange facts, discuss relationships among ideas, and offer explanations. As this linking together of facts continues, students create a conceptual framework around a topic or question. Individuals offer information, check it against the information found by others, and discuss more deeply. Students continually challenge one another regarding the accuracy and relevance of their information. Through this checking, students are encouraged to search for information, comprehend the texts being used, and synthesize information from multiple sources. When discrepancies arise, students search their sources to clarify conflicting information. Ultimately, the group must weave together the important details that all students contribute. Try to keep the following tips in mind as you plan idea circle experiences:

Response Journal

What are some of the challenges you might face as you involve students in using idea circles? How might you go about solving some of those problems?

1. *Decide whether to engage the entire class* in idea circles simultaneously or to start with a single team and gradually add more.

2. *Identify appropriate topics of study.* The topic should be interesting, explanatory, and expansive. In addition, the topic should contain natural categories or subtopics.

3. *Set clear goals* about what each group should accomplish during their discussions. Students may complete data charts, semantic maps, or other graphic organizers.

4. *Provide students with a rich array of trade books and other resources* at a variety of levels related to the topic under study.

5. *Students should have read and learned about the topic before participating in the idea circle.*

6. *Post student-generated interaction rules* so that students know how to function in their groups. When used as part of a unit of study, idea circles are most effective when placed at the middle or end of a unit.

During a social studies study of the mound-building tribes in Ohio, teacher Ann Craig involved her students in using idea circles for an inquiry project. She divided the students into three groups, and each was assigned to study a different mound-building tribe—the Hopewells, the Adenas, and the Fort Ancient. The teacher focused student inquiry through questions like these: "What were some of the purposes of the mounds?" "Where did each tribe live in Ohio?" and "Why are they no longer in existence?" Students consulted a variety of sources, including trade books, textbooks, Websites, and so on to locate answers to these questions. Finally, the groups were reconfigured so that each contained an Adena expert, a Hopewell expert, and a Fort Ancient expert. The final product for the idea circle was for each group to complete a data chart comparing and contrasting each of the three different tribes.

e.Resources

For additional readings related to the major ideas in this chapter, go to Chapter 5 of the Companion Website and click on Suggested Readings.

◀ Looking Back
Looking Forward ▶

Trade books in content area classrooms can extend and enrich information across the curriculum. Textbooks generally are unable to treat subject matter with the depth and breadth necessary to develop ideas and concepts fully and engage students in critical inquiry. Trade books have the potential to capture students' interests and imaginations in people, places, events, and ideas.

Whereas textbooks compress information, trade books provide students with intensive and extensive involvement in a subject. Trade books offer students a variety of interesting, relevant, and comprehensible text experiences. With trade books, students are likely to develop an interest in and an emotional commitment to the subject. Trade books are schema builders. Reading books helps students generate background knowledge and provides them with vicarious experiences. Many kinds of trade books, both nonfiction and fiction, can be used in tandem with textbooks.

By giving students access to books within the content area classroom, teachers help to ensure that students gain exposure to content in a variety of formats. By creating classroom libraries, providing time for reading, and reading aloud to students, teachers increase the likelihood that students will become lifelong readers.

By involving students in reading and responding to trade books through writing, drama, and inquiry activities such as idea circles, teachers move students from the solitary act of reading to building community around texts through peer interaction. Through the sharing of their responses to literature, whether written or oral, students learn to reflect more deeply on the meanings of texts and connect more personally to the texts that they read. They begin to see that reactions to texts are as varied as the students in a particular classroom, and that by understanding each person's response to a text we come to understand our humanity and ourselves more fully.

Whereas textbooks compress information, electronic texts, like trade books, provide students with intensive and extensive involvement in a subject.

Electronic texts, as you will study in the next chapter, are highly engaging and interactive. Hypertext and hypermedia make it possible to interact with text in ways not imaginable a short while ago. Text learning opportunities in electronic environments are interactive, enhance communication, engage students in multimedia, create opportunities for inquiry through information searches and retrieval, and support socially mediated learning. Whether students are navigating the Internet, interacting with innovative educational software, or, for that matter, popular media such as video games, an array of electronic text learning experiences await them.

Minds On

1. Read this statement: "One way of thinking about a textbook is that it takes a subject and distills it to its minimal essentials. In doing so, a textbook runs the risk of taking world-shaking events, monumental discoveries, profound insights, intriguing and

faraway places, colorful and influential people, and life's mysteries and processes and compressing them into a series of matter-of-fact statements." Can you think of a book you have read that opened new or more perspectives on a topic of which you had previously had only textbook knowledge? What do you believe is the ideal balance between the use of textbooks and the use of fiction books, nonfiction books, and picture books in a content classroom?

2. To what extent do you believe students should participate in the selection of documents from Websites for use in a content course? Would you answer this question differently for students of various ages?

3. You are one of only a few content area teachers in your school that regularly reads aloud to their students. After observing you, your principal suggests that teacher read-alouds represent a waste of instructional time that might be used more profitably. Write a letter to the principal that provides a thoughtful response to this criticism.

4. Reflect on some of the response-to-literature activities you have experienced as a student, either in middle school, high school, or college. These could include discussions, dramatic activities, writing, or other types of activities. How did participation in these kinds of activities influence your understanding of or reaction to the text you were studying?

 # Hands On

1. Select two nonfiction trade books that you are considering for use in the classroom. The two titles should relate to the same topic—preferably one your students are actually studying. Read the two books, and analyze them in terms of their quality, using the criteria identified in Table 5.1. Which book do you think is most appropriate for use in the classroom and why? Then compare the two titles in terms of their treatment of the topic. How are they alike? How are they different? In what ways do they support or extend information provided in the textbook? Come to class prepared to share your analysis.

2. Select two picture books that you might coordinate with a particular unit you now teach or with a unit you have planned or observed. Explain why you chose these particular books and how you will use them with your students. Describe the activities that will follow the initial use or reading of the book.

3. Create a text set consisting of at least six titles related to a topic of study in your classroom. Select at least one of the books from the text set and plan a read-aloud lesson using the book. Then, decide how your students might respond to the book through discussion, writing, or drama. Come to class prepared to read the book and have your classmates participate in the response activity.

e.Resourcesextra

- Go to Chapter 5 of the Companion Website (**www.ablongman.com/vacca8e**) and click on Activities to complete the following task:

  Visit the Children's Literature Web Guide (**www.acs.ucalgary.ca/ ~dkbrown/index.html**). Browse this site for useful information about children's literature, including award-winning books. Share your findings in small groups and discuss the ways teachers might use the site.

- Go to the Companion Website (**www.ablongman.com/vacca8e**) for suggested readings, interactive activities, multiple-choice questions, and additional Web links to help you learn more about learning with trade books.

The New York Times
expect the world®
nytimes.com

Themes of the Times

Extend your knowledge of the concepts discussed in this chapter by reading current and historical articles from the *New York Times.* Go to the Companion Website and click on eThemes of the Times.

chapter 6

Learning with Electronic Texts

The revolution that I envision
is of ideas, not technology.
—SEYMOUR PAPERT

Organizing Principle

The speed at which the world of the classroom is mutating requires teachers to rethink business as usual. Students are changing. Texts are changing. The very face of literacy is changing. Technological advances, brought on by the digital forces of the computer, are transforming the way we communicate and construct knowledge. And therein lies the revolution that Seymour Papert (1980), a pioneer in the fields of artificial intelligence and computer science, envisioned in his groundbreaking book, *Mindstorms: Children, Computers, and Powerful Ideas.*

Papert was right. The revolution that he foresaw has not been about romancing

Electronic texts, like trade books, extend and enrich the curriculum.

the technology, as impressive as it might be. It is about radical changes in the way we communicate with one another, access information, and interact with big ideas. Papert's revolution of ideas "consists of new understandings of specific subject domains and in new understandings of the process of learning. . . . It consists of a new and much more ambitious setting of the sights of educational aspiration" (p. 186). When Johann Gutenburg invented movable type in the fifteenth century, it too resulted in a revolution of ideas. Printed texts in

LEARNING WITH ELECTRONIC TEXTS

RATIONALE FOR ELECTRONIC TEXTS

Interactivity | Communication and Information Search/Retrieval | Multimedia Environments | Socially Mediated Learning

ELECTRONIC TEXTS IN THE CLASSROOM

Word Processors and Authoring Systems | E-Mail and Discussion Groups | ← ⟩ Internet ⟷ → Hypertext and Hypermedia | Electronic Books | Software Programs

STRATEGIES FOR ONLINE LEARNING

Internet Workshops | Internet Inquiries | Internet Projects | WebQuests

the hands of the masses changed the face of literacy and learning in much the same way that information and communication technologies (ICT) are creating "new literacies" and new ways of learning today.

Electronic texts, constructed and displayed on a computer screen, are not fixed entities cast in typesetter's print. In today's posttypographic world, highly interactive and engaging digitally created texts are becoming an integral part of today's classroom. So is it good-bye Johann Gutenburg, hello Seymour Papert? Mass-produced printed texts have been a dominant part of the cultural landscape in literate societies for about 600 years and are likely to be around for a long time to come. As teachers, how will we integrate the print and electronic resources that are quickly working their way into the curriculum? How will our roles and interactions with students change as the nature and kinds of texts change in our classrooms? In the previous chapter, we argued that trade books enrich and extend learning by pushing us beyond the boundaries of what was once considered to be the exclusive domain of textbooks for content area study. The organizing principle for this chapter is similar to the chapter on learning with trade books: **Electronic texts, like trade books, extend and enrich the curriculum.**

Frame of Mind

The potential for technology to make a difference in students' literacy development and learning was evident in the early 1980s when computers began to play an increasingly more important role in classrooms. However, computer-related technologies two decades ago were primitive compared to the powerful technologies that are available today. The Internet as a technology for communication and information had little or no impact on classroom learning until recently (Mike 1996). In the 1980s, the computer's potential for classroom learning revolved mainly around its uses as a tool for word processing and as a teaching machine for computer-assisted instruction (CAI).

CAI entails the use of instructional software programs to help students to learn. CAI programs in the 1980s included the use of drills, tutorials, games, and simulations. Some computer programs, mainly simulations such as *Oregon Trail* (MECC), were engaging and interactive. But many weren't. Drill and tutorial software, for example, often provided students with dull, uninviting "electronic worksheets" to practice skills and reinforce concepts.

Times have changed, however, with the development of powerful technologies that make learning with electronic texts highly engaging and interactive. CD-ROMs, for example, permit much larger storage capacity for text, graphics, and sound and offer tremendous retrieval capabilities not possible with floppy disks. Moreover, online learning opportunities on the Internet allow students to communicate with others throughout the world and to access significant and relevant content in ways not imagined only a few short years ago. As Rose and Fernlund (1997) explain

> We have come a long way since those early years. We talk more about work stations than computers. A contemporary work station might combine a powerful computer with a high-resolution color monitor, CD-ROM drive, a high-speed modem, scanner, speech synthesizer, digital camera/recorder, videodisc player, as well as a telecommunications link to on-line services and the Internet. (p. 160)

Today computer-related technologies create complex electronic learning environments. Reading and writing with computers allow students to access and retrieve information, construct their own texts, and interact with others. Reinking (1995) argues that computers are changing the way we communicate and disseminate information, how we approach reading and writing, and how we think about people becoming literate. Although electronic texts often enhance learning, Reinking (1998) contends that posttypographic reading and writing with computers have the power to transform the way we teach and learn.

> **Response Journal**
>
> In what ways, and for what purposes, do you use computers?

What about . . .
Content Standards and Assessment?

BOX 6.1

Knowing how to use information and communication technologies (ICT), such as the Internet, is integral to the strategic knowledge and skills that every student in every content area will need to develop to be content literate in the twenty-first century. Practically all of the national education associations in the various academic disciplines have developed content standards or statements of principle that implicitly or explicitly acknowledge the proficient use of technologies for information and communication. Implicit in two of the seven content standards of the American Association for Health Education (AAHE), for example, is the use of ICT to develop health literacy:

- Students will demonstrate the ability to access valid health information and health promotion products and services.
- Students will demonstrate the ability to use interpersonal communication skills to enhance health.

The International Reading Association (IRA) and the National Council of Teachers of English (NCTE) are explicit in their standard for using ICT:

- Students use a variety of technological and information resources . . . together

and synthesize information to create and communicate knowledge.

State content standards, likewise, underscore the ability to put technologies to use for learning, but for the most part, states continue to rely on paper-and-pencil tests, rather than the literacies required by ICT, to assess students' abilities to meet content standards. Donald Leu (2002), one of the leading scholars associated with the new literacies, argues that proficiency assessments will need to be redefined in the ever changing world of ICT: "The challenge will be to develop assessment systems that keep up with the continually changing nature of literacy so that assessment data provide useful information for planning" (p. 326). He points out a major flaw in statewide proficiency assessments related to reading and writing: "not a single reading assessment in the United States currently evaluates reading on the Internet and not a single state writing assessment permits the use of anything other than paper and pencil technologies" (p. 326).

Study the state proficiency assessments in your content area. To what extent do these assessments, where they exist, reflect the literacies that students need to communicate effectively as well as search for and interpret information on ICT such as the Internet?

With continuously emerging information and communication technologies (ICT) a reality in today's world, *new literacies* are necessary to use ICT effectively and to fully exploit their potential for learning (Leu 2000). The new literacies are grounded in students' abilities to use reading and writing to learn but require new strategic knowledge, skills, and insights to meet the conceptual and technological demands inherent in complexly networked environments. To be sure, the Internet is one of the most powerful ICTs extant, and it depends on literacy. Without content literacy as we defined it in Chapter 1, students will not have a solid foundation on which to build new literacies. They will struggle with learning on the Internet, for example, or with other ICT that require reading and writing in much the same way they struggle with printed texts.

Leu (2002) underscores several classroom implications for the development of new literacies. First and foremost, teachers need to help students to "learn how to learn" new technologies. From a new literacies perspective, knowing how to learn continuously changing technologies is more critical than learning any particular ICT. Moreover, teachers need to provide instructional support in the development and use of strategies that, among other things, help students critically evaluate information. According to Leu (2002), learners will need to know how to put into play

<table>
<tr><td>

Response Journal

How proficient are you with the use of new literacies associated with ICT? Are you proficient enough to help students "learn how to learn" ICT such as the Internet? Elaborate.

</td><td>

new forms of strategic knowledge necessary to locate, evaluate, and effectively use the extensive resources available within complexly networked ICT such as the Internet. The extent and complexity of this information is staggering. . . . How do we best search for information in these complex worlds? How do we design a Web page to be useful to people who are likely to visit? How do we communicate effectively with videoconference technologies? Strategic knowledge is central to the new literacies. (p. 314)

</td></tr>
</table>

Scaffolding strategy instruction in the use of ICT begs the question, "Why use ICT and electronic texts in content learning situations?" Aren't textbooks and trade books and other print resources adequate? Aren't many of today's children and adolescents already strategic in their use of ICT such as the Internet—even more so than some of their teachers and parents are? Our position is that print resources in combination with electronic texts create powerful environments for learning. Moreover, the very nature of electronic texts is such that there are some powerful and compelling reasons for their use in content learning situations.

Rationale for Electronic Texts

Some of the reasons for the use of electronic texts across the curriculum parallel those associated with trade books: variety, interest, relevance, and comprehensibility. Highly engaging and interactive computer software programs—many of which provide multimedia learning environments—and the Internet make it possible for students to have access to thousands of interesting and relevant information resources. Not only is there wide access to information but electronic texts on a relevant topic of study also can help students read extensively and think critically about content central to the curriculum. In addition, text that students construct electronically can help them examine ideas, organize and report research findings, and communicate with others. *Word processing* and *authoring software* programs, for example, allow students to develop content and multimedia presentations relevant to curriculum objectives. Moreover, *electronic mail (e-mail)* has the potential to engage students in learning conversations with others within the same community or throughout the world.

We suggest a rationale for integrating electronic texts into the curriculum based on the following concepts as they apply to technology-based learning:

- *Interactivity.* Students are capable of manipulating texts, and text is responsive to student's interests, purposes, and needs.

- *Communication.* Telecommunication networks enhance electronic text interaction with others throughout the world.

- *Information search and retrieval.* A wide range of information resources and search capabilities enhance student research and information gathering.

- *Multimedia environments.* Images, sound, and text are highly engaging and extend students' understanding.

- *Socially mediated learning.* Students collaboratively construct meaning as part of literacy learning.

Interactivity

Throughout this book, we use the word *interaction* to refer to the reader's active role in learning with text. Recall from Chapter 1 that active readers engage in meaning-making whenever they interact with texts. Reinking (1995), however, points to the imprecision of the term *interaction* as it applies to printed texts. He correctly notes that the interaction between reader and printed text has a metaphorical, not literal, meaning. Reinking's point is well taken: "Printed texts are fixed, inert entities that stand aloof from the influence and needs of a particular reader" (p. 22). Yet this is not the case with electronic texts. An interactive literacy event in an electronic environment is one in which a text is responsive to the actions of the reader. Electronic texts differ from printed texts in that they have the capability to be modified and manipulated by readers according to their individual needs, interests, and purposes for reading.

Communication and
Information Search/Retrieval

What better way is there to establish authentic communication than through reading and writing with computers? Digitalized technologies make it possible for students to participate in communication exchanges, search for information, and retrieve information from a multitude of resources throughout the world. One such technology, the Internet, offers users "a natural blend of communication and information retrieval functions incorporated within a framework that literally encompasses the world" (Mike 1996, p. 4). The Internet—also called *cyberspace,* the *information superhighway,* the *infobahn,* or simply the *Net* in popular culture—consists of a worldwide collection of computers able to communicate with each other with little or no central control. Through computers, the Internet connects people and resources. All you need to access this vast collection of computer networks is a computer, appropriate communication software, a modem, and an account with an Internet provider.

One of the most compelling rationales for using the Internet and CD-ROM software programs is that they create multimedia environments for learning.

Multimedia Environments

Sound, graphics, photographs, video, and other nonprint media may be linked to electronic text to create a learning environment far beyond the limitations of printed texts. If students want to find out about space exploration, for example, they can access a site on the World Wide Web. They can click on the term *space shuttle* for a definition and a computer-generated model of the space shuttle, click on the highlighted word *history* for a brief overview and history of the space program, digress to an audio recording and video-clip of Neil Armstrong as he sets foot on the moon, or engage in a live interview with a NASA scientist or astronaut. Later in the document, they might click on the word *projects* to find out about many of the on-line projects that NASA offers to students.

> **Response Journal**
>
> To what extent has a hypertext environment made a difference in your ability to read for information? On a personal level, do you prefer linear reading experiences or nonlinear? Elaborate.

The concepts of hypertext and hypermedia are crucial to understanding the interactions between reader and text in a multimedia environment. *Hypertext* differs from printed text in that its structure is much less linear. If you were reading a document in a hypertext environment, you could scroll through it on a screen in a linear fashion, much as you would read a printed text paragraph by paragraph. But the hypertext format also offers a "web" of text that allows you to link to other related documents and resources on demand. When sound, graphics, photographs, video, and other nonprint media are incorporated into the hypertext format, the electronic environment is called *hypermedia.*

Socially Mediated Learning

Electronic texts create a medium for social interactions—whether we have students use the Internet to communicate or assign them to learning teams as they share a computer to access information on a CD-ROM or the Web. Literacy learning with computers is social and collaborative. Students learn with electronic texts by sharing their discoveries with others. Leu (1996) underscores this type of literacy learning: "Multimedia environments, because they are powerful and complex, often require us to communicate with others in order to make meaning from them. Thus, learning is frequently constructed through social interactions in these contexts, perhaps even more naturally and frequently than in traditional print environments" (p. 163). What are the implications of socially mediated learning events in the classroom? As teachers, we need to support and encourage social interactions in electronic environments and have our students take the lead in making discoveries and sharing knowledge with other students and with us.

Electronic Texts in the Classroom

There are unlimited possibilities for learning with electronic texts. Access to the Internet means, quite literally, that students have at their fingertips a virtual library of electronic texts for subject matter learning. People use reading and writing almost entirely to interact with information or with other people on the Internet. With the Internet, it is possible, as suggested by Williams (1995), to engage in a variety of communication and information search-and-retrieval activities through use of the following: electronic mail (e-mail) to send and receive messages from others and to participate in discussion groups and "live" conferences; *telnet* to connect to another computer at another location and work interactively with it as if your computer were directly connected to it; *file transfer protocol (FTP)* to move files and information data from one computer to another; and the *World Wide Web*, a system for point-and-click knowledge navigation around the world to access text documents, video, images, and sound.

The Internet also provides students with CAI software, particularly CD-ROM programs, that can create multimedia environments for learning. Let's examine several of the opportunities that students have for learning with electronic texts.

Learning with Hypertext and Hypermedia

Hypertext enriches and extends any literacy learning event in the content areas. With hypertext and hypermedia, highlighted and linked texts, called *hyperlinks* (or simply *links*), enable you to move between documents in a nonlinear manner. This process is possible because in hypertext there are many "branches" or pathways that readers may choose to follow in many different orders, depending on their interests and purposes. If your students were to make a cyberspace visit to the home page of one of best science museums for young people, San Francisco's Exploratorium (www.exploratorium.edu/), they would be able to participate in a variety of interactive exhibits simply by selecting the links in which they were interested. Suppose that several students clicked on the link *Cow's Eye Dissection*. In a second or two, the students would be transported to the cow's eye dissection demonstration site (see Figure 6.1), where they would be invited to select from several "banners" to begin the demonstration. The students may decide to link to

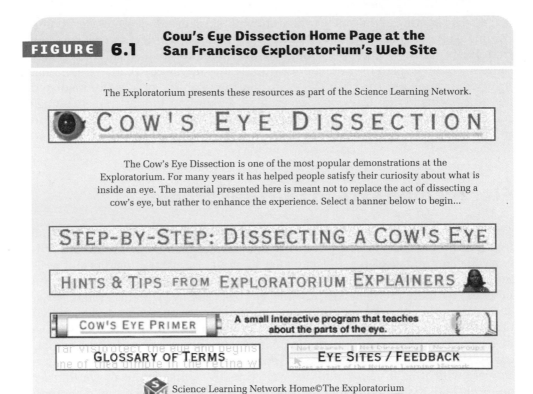

FIGURE 6.1   Cow's Eye Dissection Home Page at the San Francisco Exploratorium's Web Site

The Exploratorium presents these resources as part of the Science Learning Network.

COW'S EYE DISSECTION

The Cow's Eye Dissection is one of the most popular demonstrations at the Exploratorium. For many years it has helped people satisfy their curiosity about what is inside an eye. The material presented here is meant not to replace the act of dissecting a cow's eye, but rather to enhance the experience. Select a banner below to begin...

STEP-BY-STEP: DISSECTING A COW'S EYE

HINTS & TIPS FROM EXPLORATORIUM EXPLAINERS

COW'S EYE PRIMER   A small interactive program that teaches about the parts of the eye.

GLOSSARY OF TERMS   EYE SITES / FEEDBACK

Science Learning Network Home©The Exploratorium

Source: © 2000 Exploratorium, www.exploratorium.edu/learning_studio/cow_eye/index.html.

the banner marked "Cow's Eye Primer" to participate in an interactive lesson that teaches about the parts of the eye. Or they might choose to click on "Step-by-Step: Dissecting a Cow's Eye" to begin the demonstration.

Using hyperlinks, students can move to other related text or nonprint media simply by clicking on a highlighted word or icon in the document. As a result, they can "jump around" or digress to explore related branches of text at their own pace, navigating in whatever direction they choose. Jumping around in a hypertext gives a sense of freedom with the text that is unattainable with printed text. The possibility for multiple digressions, according to Reinking (1997), is the defining attribute of hypertext. As he puts it, "Trying to write a hypertext means being free to digress and to assume that readers will willingly share in that same freedom. Digression can be positive and enjoyable in a hypertext because there is no compulsion to stick closely to only one main idea" (p. 629).

From an instructional perspective, the branching options offered in hypertext and hypermedia serve two important functions: to scaffold students' learning experiences and to enhance and extend thinking. For readers who may struggle with text or with difficult concepts, the resources available on demand in a hypertext environment include pronunciations of keywords and terms, definitions and explanations, audio versions of the text, video recordings, quick-time movies, photographs, graphics, interactive exercises, and student-centered projects. These links have the potential to arouse curiosity, stimulate interest, and reinforce and extend students' thinking about a subject.

Keep in mind, however, a cautionary note about hypertext and hypermedia learning environments. Computer software programs and the Internet are technologies that lend themselves to *extensive* explorations of information resources. A key instructional concern is to avoid the more superficial experiences with technology that are fun but do not necessarily support students' literacy learning or critical thinking about content central to the curriculum (Leu 1996). Because multimedia environments are highly engaging, student discoveries, in Leu's words, "spread like wildfire" in the classroom. Whenever you plan a lesson or unit that involves students in multimedia learning environments, you run the risk of having them ignore substantive content in favor of superficial discoveries. As a result, students might navigate multimedia environments to explore topics extensively at only a superficial level of understanding without reading and thinking deeply about a specific or single topic. How teachers scaffold intensive literacy experiences and in-depth explorations of electronic and printed texts remains a key instructional issue that we explore throughout this book.

Learning with Software Programs

The proliferation of educational software programs can make it difficult for teachers to choose appropriate CAI programs for classroom use. Most of the major publishers of printed textbooks have entered the educational software market. Prentice Hall, for example, has developed highly interactive multimedia CD-ROM software in most of the content areas. One Prentice Hall program, Multimedia Math, appropriate for use in the middle grades, allows students to interact with and experience math concepts through engagement in "math investigations" and "hot pages" using a rich, three-dimensional, multisensory environment. Another of its software programs, Chemedia, designed for use in high school chemistry courses, combines videodisks with simulation software to engage students in visual explorations of interesting phenomena otherwise not available in the classroom.

In addition to software development by major publishing houses, hundreds of smaller companies, specializing exclusively in technology-related programs, have mushroomed in the past decade, inundating the educational landscape with innovative software in all content areas for all age levels. Because of the prolific development of educational software, most of the major content area educational associations and societies offer program reviews in their professional journals.

Making decisions about educational software is no easy task. Rose and Fernlund (1997), speaking directly to social studies teachers, suggest asking a set of reflective questions related to CAI and multimedia use that is applicable to all content teachers who are interested in using educational software to enhance instruction. To guide the evaluation of computer-based instructional products, consider the questions posed in Figure 6.2.

FIGURE 6.2 | **Evaluating Computer-Based Educational Software: Questions to Consider**

Hardware-Related Questions to Consider

1. What are the instructional tasks and levels of complexity? Do I have the necessary technology?

2. Do my computers have enough memory to run the desired software application?

3. What type of technical delivery system will be used: single computer(s) or computers attached to a local area network (LAN), a wide area network (WAN), and/or the Internet?

4. Is the speed of the network sufficient to accomplish the instructional task in an efficient and timely manner?

Software-Related Questions to Consider

1. How does this computer program help achieve my objectives for this unit of study? Can I modify the program to fit my plans better?

2. Does my computer system have the right hardware to run this program (required memory, printers, speech synthesizer, other peripherals)?

3. Is the program easy for students to use? What preparation do students need? What preparation do I need?

4. Does the publisher offer technical assistance, free or inexpensive updates, network licenses?

5. Does the program offer multiple options for delivery? For example, can the program be used over the Internet or linked to sites on the World Wide Web (the Internet's hypertext-based environment)?

Multimedia-Use Questions to Consider

1. Do I have the necessary technology to use this multimedia package, including sufficient computer memory, a videodisk player/CD-ROM drive if needed, a large screen monitor or projection device for large class viewing?

2. What is the perspective of this commercial package? How does this viewpoint differ from other resources that I plan to have students use?

3. Is this product to be used by teachers or students? Do I want to use the entire package or select particular parts?

4. In what ways will this use of technology enhance my students' learning? How can I assess the impact on learning?

Source: From "Using Technology for Powerful Social Studies Learning," by S. A. Rose and P. M. Fernlund, *Social Education*, March 1997. Copyright © National Council for the Social Studies. Reprinted with permission.

Learning with Electronic Books

The recent innovations in educational software have led to the development of what has been called the *electronic book*. Anderson-Inman and Horney (1997) use stringent criteria to distinguish electronic books from other forms of educational software:

- *Electronic books must have electronic text presented to the reader visually.*

- *They must use the metaphors of a book* by adapting some of the conventions associated with books, such as a table of contents, pages, and a bookmark, so that readers will feel that they are reading a book.

- *They must have an organizing theme* of an existing book or a central focus if it is not based on an equivalent printed book.

- *They must be primarily text centered.* When media enhancements other than text are available in the software, they are incorporated primarily to support the text presentation.

Many electronic books, available on CD-ROM, make excellent reference resources. *The Grolier Multimedia Encyclopedia* (Grolier) gives readers more than 33,000 articles and easy-to-use features that make searching and retrieving information uncomplicated. Many CD-ROM books are informational and focus on in-depth studies of subjects. *In the Company of Whales* (Discovery Communications), intended for use in middle and high schools, provides students with well-organized informative text, pictures, action footage, and sound. The electronic text shows how whales are studied and introduces students to some of the people who study them. Still other electronic books are for recreational reading. Highly interactive storybooks such as *Afternoon* (Eastgate Systems) and Walt Disney's *Animated Storybooks* are suitable for younger as well as older readers. In studies of interactive electronic books, researchers find that children generally respond positively to CD-ROM stories over printed versions (Matthew 1996) and that reading from electronic books increases comprehension when students read longer and more difficult narratives (Greenlee-Moore & Smith 1996).

e.Resources

Visit an electronic book library by going to Web Destinations on the Companion Website and clicking on Professional Resources. Search for The Book Page link.

There are many electronic book venues online on the Internet that give students and teachers nearly instant access to libraries. For online electronic books, it would be worth your while to visit The Book Page (www.cs.cmu.edu/books.html), The Classic Archive at MIT (http://classics.mit.edu), or The English Server (English-www.hss.cmu.edu/). In addition, "expanded" electronic books provide students with digital texts that join a main work of print with film or video. These multimedia-enhanced electronic books extend the possibilities for intertextual studies.

Learning with Word Processors and Authoring Systems

Reading and writing on the Internet play important roles in learning. But merely using computer-related technologies in your classrooms doesn't guarantee more effective or meaningful learning. As one teacher put it,

> Students must be good communicators. In my classroom, students whose writing skills are lacking will not spend nearly as much time on the computer as those with more competency. Does this make some students strive to be more competent so they can use the computers? Yes indeed, and that brings up a positive aspect of computers; they provide incentive and encouragement for improvement. (Jasper 1995, p. 17)

Not only do computers provide incentive for improvement but they can also be important tools for developing students' writing abilities.

Computers as word processors allow writers to create a text and change it in any way desired. Word processing software programs have the potential to make students more active in brainstorming, outlining, exploring and organizing ideas, revising, and editing a text.

Academic-related writing is one of the most cognitively as well as physically demanding tasks required of students in school. Computers can make writing easier by taking away some of the sheer physical demands of putting ideas on paper with a pen or pencil. This is not to say that communicating with paper and pen is less effective than with a computer. A computer, however, frees students from the laborious physical tasks associated with drafting, editing, and revising a text so that they can expend more cognitive energy on the communication itself. One of the best reasons people use computers to write and communicate with others is that it takes a complex activity such as writing and expedites the process. Suid and Lincoln (1989), somewhat "tongue in cheek," draw this analogy: "You can cook terrific meals on a wood-burning stove. But if you're like most people, you prefer a modern range. It's easier. It's faster. And it lets you do more" (p. 318). One of the things that a computer lets you do in a classroom is generate a finished and attractive text that others can read.

Student-generated texts and reports shouldn't be for the teacher's eyes only. They should be read by other students and can become "minibooks" for classroom learning. *Desktop publishing* programs, which combine text and graphics in varied arrangements, can help students produce attractive reports as part of thematic and topical units of study. Students can also design multimedia projects using hypermedia programs such as Hyperstudio, Linkway, or Hypercard. Hypermedia programs encourage active engagement with information and extend the composing process through the interaction of various media. These programs are called *authoring systems* and are often used in research projects designed by students as part of a thematic or topical unit of study.

Lapp and Flood (1995), for example, describe a middle grade classroom where they observed small groups of students using Hyperstudio to design geology-related science projects. The students used the authoring software to help them organize their multimedia reports on a unit dealing with the causes and effects of tornadoes. One group of students located a National Geographic Society *laser disk* containing some footage of an actual tornado and used the authoring software program to incorporate the footage into their presentation. A laser disk is a computer peripheral on which large amounts of video and audio are stored. A student in another group found some photographs taken by his aunt of a tornado and the destruction it left in its wake. The student used a *scanner* to incorporate the photos into the multimedia presentation. A scanner is another peripheral used to convert pictures, texts, graphs, or charts into an image that can then be used in a computer presentation.

Authoring software allows students to develop multimedia projects and presentations that wed visual images, sound, graphics, and text. The premise underlying authoring systems is not as complicated as it may appear if you're a novice with the use of hypermedia technologies. Authoring software programs facilitate multimedia compositions and encourage students to communicate what they are learning through the construction of computer "cards" and "buttons." The student (or small group of students) creates the multimedia presentation by filling in computer cards with information (referred to as textual "fields") and with pictures, drawings, graphics, photographs, video, music, and voice messages. Buttons are then created to link the network of completed cards.

Students not familiar with authoring systems need to learn how to use hypermedia tools and peripherals to scan in photographs, create pictures and graphics, and record video and sounds. They will also need instructional support in planning, researching, and designing projects and in learning how to use authoring software effectively.

Learning with the Internet

The Internet is one of the most powerful technologies for information and communication today. The potential for integrating literacy and learning on the Internet as well as other technologies for information and communication brings to fruition Seymour Papert's visionary use of computers as a revolution of ideas. To use the Internet to its fullest potential, students will need to develop strategic knowledge, skills, and insights that will take them beyond trivial and superficial learning on the Internet, despite recent patterns that show multimedia and networked environments generate increased interest and motivation for reading among today's students (Leu 2002; Reinking 2003).

Harry Noden (1995), a middle school teacher, describes an electronic conversation that he had with a teacher, Ken Blystone, from Texas. Blystone explained that he was having difficulty securing funding for Internet connections in his school district because some school administrators considered the Internet a high-tech frill rather than a substantive tool for literacy and learning. According to Noden, Blystone "approached his principal early one morning before school and asked him how much it would be worth investing to get students so excited about reading and writing that they would stand in line for the opportunity." The principal chuckled at the notion until Blystone "invited him to walk to the library. There, a half an hour before school had started, gathered around the one computer connected to the Internet, stood a large group of students . . . standing in line waiting for the opportunity to read and write" (p. 26).

The Internet as an Information Resource

The Internet has been described by some as providing the "textbooks of tomorrow." And then some! The World Wide Web of the Internet is fertile ground for learning with electronic texts on every subject imaginable. Access to the Web on the Internet means access to a hypermedia system. The Web represents the universe of servers (computers) that allows text, graphics, sound, and images to be mixed together.

> **e.Resources**
>
> For Websites related to your content area, go to Web Destinations on the Companion Website and click on your content area.

Alvarez (1996) describes a project called Explorers of the Universe for high school students in grades 9 through 12 enrolled in an astronomy class. In this class, the Web on the Internet became an important tool for gathering information and communicating ideas. Students worked in teams of two and three, conducting research using library resources as well as resources on the Web. The Internet was also used as a medium to publish students' research reports, broaden their knowledge base in specific areas, and make inquiries to other students and astronomers in the field.

Alvarez notes that the Web serves a function similar to the library except that access to information resources is nearly instantaneous and students are able to contact authors of Web documents directly to clarify information or ask additional questions. The teachers involved in Explorers of the Universe used textbooks in tandem with Internet connections. They found that the textbook became a resource as opposed to a singular source of science information. Preliminary findings of the project show that students related new information to their existing world knowledge, analyzed their sources more carefully, and attempted to identify new sources of information (Alvarez 1996).

To use the Web effectively, students will need to develop expertise at navigating through the hypertext world of the Web. For students not experienced with browsing or surfing the Web, try scaffolding activities, such as guided tours and scavenger hunts, to familiarize beginners with how to navigate. Also, use bookmarks that take students directly to locations that you want them to visit on the Web. One of the most useful resource books for literacy and learning, *Teaching with the Internet: Lessons from the Classroom* (Leu & Leu 2000), provides many suggestions for developing navigation skills and numerous Website locations for content area study.

Figure 6.3 lists some frequently visited Websites by content area. A visit to several of these Websites gives you insight into the possibilities for subject matter learning that await students. Information resources and Web sites can easily be integrated into units of study in your content area.

FIGURE 6.3   Selected Websites across the Curriculum

The Websites that we have selected illustrate some of the possibilities for locating information resources on the Internet in various content areas. Because the Web is a fluid and continually changing medium, some of the locations listed here may no longer be in operation. For additional Websites go to Web Destinations on the Companion Website.

The Arts
The Kennedy Center's ArtsEdge
www.artsedge.kennedy-center.org/
   artsedge.html

Asian Arts
www.asianart.com/

The Provincial Museum of Alberta Virtual
   Exhibits, Genghis Khan
http://pma.edmonton.ab.ca/vexhibit/
   genghis/intro.htm

The National Endowment for the Arts
www.arts.endow.gov/

English Language Arts
Literature Resources
http://vos.ucsb.edu/shuttle/eng-mod.html

The English Server
http://eserver.org/

National Public Radio
www.npr.org/

PBS Web Site
www.pbs.org/

Computer-Assisted Language Learning (CALL)
www.ohiou.edu/opie/index.html

Foreign Language
Elementary Spanish Curriculum
www.veen.com/veen/leslie/curriculum/

Web 66 International School Registry
www.web66.coled.umn.edu/schools/ES/
   Spain.html

Links to Language Arts Educator Websites
www.waterloo.k12.wi.us/whs/infocenter/
   edlang.htm

Health: Ideas for Health Lessons
Health Lesson Plans, Ideas, and Activities
www.lessonplanspage.com/PE.htm

Ideas for Developmentally Appropriate Physical
   Education
www.pecentral.org/

The California Healthy Kids Initiative
www.hkresources.org/

The Surgeon General's Official Website
www.surgeongeneral.gov/

Mathematics
MathEd: Mathematics Education Resources
www-hpcc.astro.washington.edu/scied/
   math.html

Twenty-first Century Problem Solving
http://www2.hawaii.edu/suremath/
   home1.html

MathMagic
http://forum.swarthmore.edu/mathmagic/

McNair Scholar's Program
http://www.sci.sdsu.edu/usp/mcnair/

Science
Environmental Education
www.eelink.net/

A User-Friendly Frog Dissection Guide
http://george.lbl.gov/ITG.hm.pg.docs/
   dissect/info.html

The Official Website of NASA
www.nasa.gov/

Social Studies
Benjamin Franklin
www.fi.edu/franklin/

(continued)

FIGURE **6.3**   **Continued**

Russian History
www.friends-partners.org/oldfriends/mes/
   russia/history.html

Interactive Egyptian History Site
www.iwebquest.com/egypt/ancientegypt.htm

A Massive History Database Online
www.thehistorynet.com/

The Photography of a Vietnam Veteran
www.woodlot.com/vietnam/start.html

Vocational Education
Career Magazine
http://careermag.com/

U.S. Department of Labor Career Outlook
   Website
http://stats.bls.gov/ocohome.htm

Links to the Top 100 Internet Job Websites
www.100hot.com/directory/business/
   jobs.html

Office of Vocational and Adult Education (OVAE)
www.ed.gov/offices/OVAE/

Links to Vocational Education Resources
http://pegasus.cc.ucf.edu/~sorg/vocation.html

The Internet as a Communication Resource

On the Internet, students (and teachers) can send and receive messages anywhere in the world via e-mail. E-mail messages are sent electronically from one computer to another through the use of special software. E-mail communication can generate important learning connections for students by making "reading and writing across the planet" a reality. Imagine the possibilities: On Monday, two students from Yakeala, Finland, talk to your students about minority groups in their country—the Gypsies and the Lapps. On Tuesday, students discuss the environmental problems of the Amazon jungle with students in Lima, Peru. On Wednesday, a student who is wheelchair bound from Palatka, Florida, drops in to give his one- to five-star reviews of the latest video games. On Thursday, teenage refugees from Bosnia tell how most of their relatives "just disappeared" and how the young people managed to escape. On Friday, a student from Keene, New Hampshire, shares a visit from a Holocaust survivor.

These are only some of the e-mail learning events that occurred in Harry Noden's eighth-grade class in the course of a week. To allow this to happen, Noden first made e-mail connections with other teachers through the use of *electronic bulletin boards,* sites where students and teachers can post ideas for exchanges and Internet projects. Leu and Leu (2000) recommend the following sites as "jumping-off points" for Internet projects, a strategy for Internet learning that we describe in the next section.

NickNack's Telecollaborations
http://home.talkcity.com/academydr/nicknacks/
This site provides summaries of many projects.

Kidlink
www.kidlink.org/english/general/sub.html
E-mail–based projects aimed at students ages ten to fifteen
are featured.

The GLOBE Program
www.globe.gov/
This site highlights environmental science projects that connect students and scientists around the world.

e.Resources

Visit one of the electronic bulletin
boards for teachers and students.
Go to Web Destinations on the
Companion Website and click
on Professional Resources.
Search for Kidlink or NickNack's
Telecollaborations.

In one Internet project, preservice teachers from Walsh University in Ohio engaged in e-mail exchanges with fourth graders from a local elementary school (McKeon 2001). The collaborative project revolved around
"booktalks" and literature discussions. Each preservice teacher was paired with
a student. Throughout the semester, the e-mail partners discussed the books they
were reading. These electronic conversations provided natural opportunities for
the partners to engage in authentic talk about books and for the preservice teachers to blend instructional strategies into the discussion. For example, in one cor-
respondence just prior to reading the book *A Taste of Blackberries* (Smith 1973),
a preservice teacher invites his partner to make predictions about the book:

> Just to let you know before you start reading, the book is very sad and it involves peo-
> ple dying. I would like you to brainstorm a little bit about the name of the book and
> give me some guesses of what you think the story may be about. Then we will take
> your guesses, and after we read the book, we can find out how close you were with
> some of your guesses. I am really looking forward to hearing from you.

Not only was the e-mail project successful in making important learning connections during the literature discussions, but also in the course of a semester, the
e-mail partners got to know each other socially as they shared information and
asked questions about college life, hobbies, interests, and family life.

In addition to individual messages, a person can send messages to and receive
messages from groups of people by subscribing to a *mailing list* or *listserv.* These
groups, often called *discussion groups,* allow students and teachers to ask questions, share information, and locate resources. In Noden's class, students received
a collection of memoirs compiled by students at Hiroshima Jogakuin High School.
The memoirs, written by survivors of the atomic bomb, stimulated a great deal of
discussion among students, prompting them to investigate additional information
sources in the library and on the Web. Several of the most popular mailing lists
for discussion groups include these:

Liszt Select
www.liszt.com/
This comprehensive site contains more than 50,000 lists. You can either do
a search for lists in your interest area or click the Liszt Select box for a
much smaller annotated list of sites.

Pitsco's Launch to Lists
www.pitsco.com/thecause2k/thecause.htm
This site does not have search capabilities, but the list is focused on education.

EdWeb
http://edweb.gsn.org/
This smaller list focuses on K–12 issues, educational technology, and education reform.

Whether they are engaged in communication or searching for information, there are many learning opportunities awaiting students on the Internet. However, teachers cannot assume that students, if left to their own devices, will engage in deep thinking and critical literacy online simply because they are adept at the mechanics of surfing the Net. Too often, random acts of surfing lead to superficial learning and amassing bits and pieces of information. Instructional strategies embedded in well-planned lessons can make a difference in developing the kinds of strategic knowledge and literacy skills that learners need to think deeply about electronic texts.

Strategies for Online Learning

There are at least four instructional strategies, as indicated in Figure 6.4, that teachers use to influence the nature and depth of online learning in their classrooms. Detailed descriptions, examples, and teachers' reflections on these practices may be found in the invaluable instructional resource for Internet teaching and learning *Teaching with the Internet: Lessons from the Classroom* (Leu & Leu 2000). Instructional strategies for online learning include the following: Internet workshops, Internet inquiries, Internet projects, and WebQuests.

Internet Workshops

An Internet workshop is characterized by its flexibility. In some respects, it is similar in purpose to a writing workshop or a reading workshop in an English/ language arts classroom (Atwell 1998). In writing and reading workshops, teachers who use a workshop model in their classrooms set aside regularly scheduled time for students to engage in reading and writing activities. In the process of doing so, students share their reading and writing with others in the class, typically in small-group book discussions or writing response groups. During workshop time, teachers often conduct "minilessons" to respond to content and process-related issues and problems students are having during reading or writing sessions. Minilessons may also be designed for strategy instruction. In these explicit instructional situations, a teacher may take several minutes or more of workshop

FIGURE 6.4   Literacy and Learning on the Internet

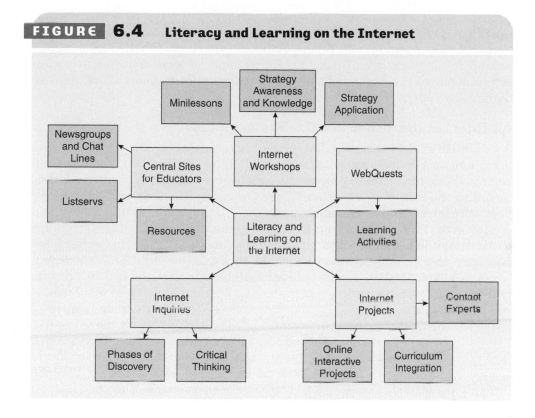

time to show students how to use a set of procedures that will help them become more skillful as readers and writers.

Like reading and writing workshops, an Internet workshop provides an instructional framework for students allowing for regularly scheduled time to engage in activity on the Internet. The activity may range from specific electronic text assignments to individual or group research to collaborative projects on the Internet. For example, a teacher might assign a Website or several Websites for students to visit. With younger learners, the Website(s) are bookmarked in advance by the teacher so that the class has easy access to them. Students are directed to the Website(s) to engage in a content literacy activity in much the same way as they would in a textbook or other print resources. Many of the content literacy activities in this book can be adapted for this purpose.

On other workshop occasions, students may work individually or in collaboration with one another on WebQuests, Internet inquiries, or Internet projects. These instructional strategies are much more extensive than specific assignments on the Internet and may take one to several weeks to accomplish. Regardless of the type of instructional focus, teachers should bring students together intermittently during workshops to share their work or to build strategic knowledge and skills related to the effective use of the Internet as a tool for learning. In these situations, workshop time is devoted to problems students are having searching for information or communicating with others. Internet workshops can also be designed around explicit strategy instruction. For example, a workshop might revolve around using search engines effectively, thinking critically about information, or designing a Web page.

An Internet Workshop in a U.S. History Class

A U.S. high school history teacher brought his students together in a workshop to explore an informational database related to the Vietnam War. The class had been studying the Vietnam War using a variety of print and electronic resources, including the trade book *The Things They Carried* by Tim O'Brien, and the Vietnam War television documentary produced by the Public Broadcast System (PBS). On the PBS Website (www.pbs.org), the students, working in small groups in the computer lab, were asked to click on the American Experience series' Vietnam War link. They then were directed to click on For the Record, which pro-

> **Response Journal**
>
> What conclusions do you draw when you compare the statistical information for U.S. combat soldiers in World War II and the Vietnam War?

vided a statistical database for various categories related to the U.S. soldiers who participated in the war. The introduction to the database included statistical information related to such factors as number of Americans in the military during the years of the Vietnam conflict (8,744,000), number of Americans in the military during World War II (16,354,000), number of Americans who served overseas during World War II (11,938,420), number of Americans who served in Vietnam (2,700,000), average age of U.S. combat personnel in Vietnam (19), and average age of U.S. combat personnel in World War II (27). These statistics obviously invited broad comparisons to be made about U.S. combat personnel in World War II and in the Vietnam War.

Other categories of information included a demographic breakdown of the men who actually fought in Vietnam—for example, the percentage of men who fought in Vietnam from below the Mason–Dixon line (28), the number of soldiers from Puerto Rico sent to Vietnam (34,700), the percentage of soldiers in combat platoons who were African American (20), and the percentage of U.S. soldiers from working class or poor backgrounds (80). Screen after screen on the For the Record link dealt with categories of statistical information, including casualties, refusing to fight, fragging and friendly fire, and South Vietnamese military personnel.

The teacher did not want students to superficially gloss over the statistics but rather to think critically about the information. So he invited each group to study the database carefully, looking for relationships among the different pieces of information within and across categories, and then to develop a written profile of the "typical U.S. soldier fighting in Vietnam." As part of a minilesson, the teacher illustrated how the profiles could be written within the context of different "writing forms," such as a hometown newspaper article, a personal diary, a letter to a loved one, or an obituary column (see Chapter 11 for a discussion of *discourse forms* used in writing-to-learn activities).

Throughout the week, students spent parts of each class session analyzing the data and working on the development of their profiles. Toward the end of the

FIGURE 6.5   Excerpts from Several Vietnam War Soldier Profiles

A letter to a former high school teacher:

Dear Mrs. Baker,

When I graduated from high school last year I thought it was the last place I wanted to be. Boy was I wrong. My dad was helping me get a job in the foundary [sic]. We didn't have the money to send me to college right away, but many of my buddies were going to Kent State in the fall. Now I wish I was back there with them. They don't know how lucky they are; they didn't have to end up here. I'm in a VA hospital with an amputated leg, and my best friend here, Rodney, was killed right next to me. . . .

Notes from a GI's diary:

December 7, 1967

I never dreamed things would turn out this way. Me, Michael Freeman, here in the middle of a jungle in Vietnam. Viet Cong all around, mines all over the place. To tell you the truth, we're all really scared. Tempers flare up like nothing I seen before. What a place to celebrate my 19th birthday. I still remember the birthday Poppa took me downtown to work with him. He's a janitor there in the Terminal Tower and has keys to all the rooms. . . .

Obituary column:

Local Boy Dies in Vietnam

Birmingham, Alabama

Darnell "Junior" Washington, nineteen, lost his life fighting for his country in Vietnam on May 25, 1970. Darnell was a second-generation laborer for the Dole Family Acres Farm. He was drafted into the U.S. Army in 1968, shortly after graduating from high school. According to his platoon leader, Michael Kennedy, Darnell was fighting on the front lines when he was ambushed by Viet Cong sniper fire. He will be sadly missed by his six brothers and sisters and parents, Millie and Darnell Sr. He served his country well.

week, the groups shared their profiles, discussed them with the class as a whole, and related them to the texts that they were reading as part of the Vietnam War unit. Figure 6.5 illustrates parts of several profiles students developed in their small groups.

Internet Inquiries

The Internet inquiry engages students in research using information sources on the Internet. Inquiries can be conducted individually or collaboratively and often take one or more weeks to complete. Internet inquiries are typically part of larger thematic units and are used in conjunction with Internet workshops. The Internet inquiry broadly follows the tenets of a discovery model for investigating hypotheses or questions. Students are invited to (1) generate questions about a topic or theme under discussion in class, (2) search for information on the Internet to answer the questions, (3) analyze the information, (4) compose a report or some other form of dissemination related to findings, and (5) share findings with the whole class.

Question generation is one of the keys to conducting a successful Internet inquiry. Many teachers use the *K–W–L* strategy (see Chapter 10) to help students raise questions. Others use brainstorming techniques to generate a list of questions. Whatever strategy is used for generating questions, the questions should come from the students whenever possible rather than the teacher. An Internet workshop minilesson might focus on asking good questions to guide the information search. A teacher may also use workshop time to scaffold instruction on how to use search engines effectively or how to record and analyze information through the use of "inquiry charts" (I-charts) and other tools for recording and analyzing findings (Hoffman 1992; Randall 1996). In Chapter 7, we provide steps to guide the various phases of any type of inquiry or research investigation.

An Internet Inquiry in Elementary Science

Students in a third-grade elementary classroom have been engaged in a thematic unit related to the study of monarch butterflies. As part of the unit, the class developed a plan for raising monarch butterflies and visited several Websites on the Internet related to specific workshop activities that the teacher had planned. The students also read trade books such as *Discovering Butterflies* by Douglas Florian, *Monarch Butterfly* by Gail Gibbons, and *Animal World: Butterflies* by Donna Bailey. As a result of these classroom learning experiences, the class embarked on an Internet inquiry designed around the students' "personal questions" regarding monarch butterflies. The class first brainstormed a list of questions that the teacher recorded on chart paper. Some of the questions included "Do monarch butterflies eat anything besides milkweed?" "Are monarch butterflies found all over the world?" "How long do monarch butterflies live?" and "How many eggs can one monarch butterfly lay?" Using the list of questions on chart paper as a guide, each student selected three questions to research. The questions did not have to come from the brainstormed list but could be generated by students as they engaged in their information search on the Internet and from trade books that were available in the classroom.

The teacher conducted an Internet workshop on how to use the search engine Ask Jeeves (www.askjeeves.com). She also explained to students how to use I-charts to record information they found on individual Websites or in trade books related to each of their questions. Across the top of the I-chart, each student recorded his or her name and a personal question about monarch butterflies. The remainder of the I-chart was divided into two columns. The left column provided space for a student to record the name of the Website or trade book that was used to gather information. The right column was used to record information that students found to answer their questions. Across the bottom of the I-chart was space for students to record "new questions" based on their research.

When students completed their information searches, they collected their I-charts and began analyzing the information to answer their questions. The teacher facilitated the analysis by walking around the room helping individuals as needs arose. Students used the analysis to create a poster portraying the answers to their questions. The inquiry culminated with a "poster session" in which students shared the information related to their questions.

Internet Projects

An Internet project involves collaborative approaches to learning on the Internet. Often students engage in project learning with other students who may be from different schools in different parts of the country or the world. Other types of projects may involve collaborative interactions between students and experts from various fields. For example, Internet projects are regularly posted on Websites such as NASA Quest, where students have the opportunity to discuss space science and many other topics with one another and with NASA personnel. Figure 6.6 displays the home page for NASA Quest as of October 2003. The home page highlights several of the projects and events awaiting students' collaborative interactions.

> **e.Resources**
>
> Study several project descriptions of Internet projects in your content area. Go to Web Destinations on the Companion Website and click on Professional Resources. Search for the Global SchoolNet's Internet Projects Registry link.

Many Internet projects are designed by teachers as part of thematic units. Advanced planning is essential for teacher-designed projects. Generally the following steps need to be considered:

- *Plan a project for an upcoming unit and write a project description.*

- *Post the project description and time line several months in advance* seeking classroom partnerships with other teachers.

- *Post the project at a location on the Internet where teachers advertise their projects,* such as Global SchoolNet's Internet Project Registry (www.gsn.org/pr/index.cfm).

- *Arrange collaboration details* with teachers in other classrooms who agree to participate.

- *Complete the project using Internet workshop sessions* for project-related activities and e-mail information exchanges with students and teachers in other classrooms involved in the project.

Leu and Leu (2000) provide numerous examples at different grade levels of Internet projects for various content areas that are posted on Websites or have been designed by teachers. Figure 6.7 depicts a basic math project for high school students featured on the Global SchoolNet's Internet Project Registry.

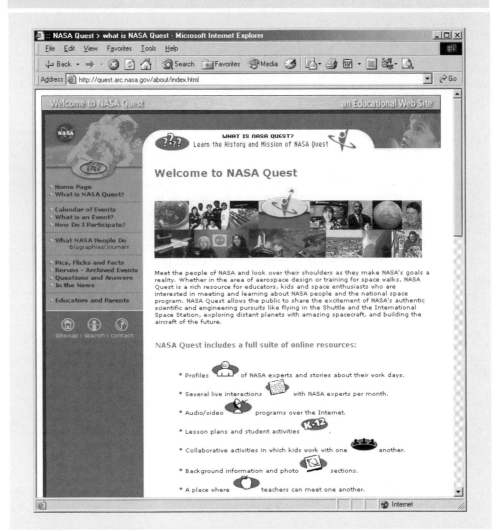

FIGURE 6.6   **NASA Quest Home Page**

WebQuests

WebQuests have become a popular instructional model for engaging learners on the Internet. A WebQuest is a teacher-designed Web page that packages various learning tasks and activities for students to complete using Internet resources. WebQuests are typically organized around several components: introduction, task, process, resources, learning advice, and conclusion.

The introduction to a WebQuest provides an overview of the learning opportunity available to the students. Often the introduction places the learner(s) in a hy-

| FIGURE | **6.7** | **Example of a Project Description** |

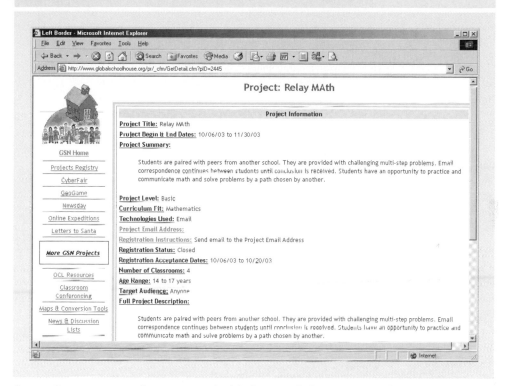

pothetical situation somewhat similar to RAFT writing activities (see Chapter 11). As a result, students are assigned a role and a purpose for engaging in the learning activity. The task component of the WebQuest describes the task(s) students will complete and lists the questions that guide the information search. The process component outlines the steps and procedures students will follow to complete the learning task. The resources component of a WebQuest provides links to information resources on the Internet that students will need to access to complete the learning task. The "learning advice" component provides directions to students on how to organize information, whether in outlines, time lines, graphic organizers (see Chapter 12), notebook entries such as the double entry journal format (see Chapter 11), or I-charts. And finally, the conclusion to the WebQuest brings closure to the activity and summarizes what students should have learned from participation in the WebQuest. Figure 6.8 provides an example of a WebQuest for middle grade students designed by students at New Mexico State University.

e.Resources

Find out more about the Web-Quest strategy by going to Web Destinations on the Companion Website and clicking on Professional Resources. Search for the WebQuest page.

FIGURE 6.8   WebQuest Example

FIGURE 6.8   WebQuest Example

Titanic WebQuest

Introduction

You have been given the opportunity to appear on a game show called "One Thing I Know About."
You could win up to one-million dollars on this game show. You and your classmates will learn
everything there is to know about a topic. The topic chosen by your class was the Titanic disaster.

This WebQuest should answer any question you have about the Titanic disaster.

Good luck and enjoy the learning.

The Task

Working in a group of three, you will research and document information on the Titanic. You will
need to visit all the online and book resources and document your findings as part of your research.

Divide the resources equally among members of your group.

As the group members are reviewing the resources, use the following questions to guide you
as you document your findings:

- In 1912, what did a 3 room suite with a promenade cost on the Titanic?
- What class of people were allowed to occupy a 3 room suite?
- How many decks did the Titanic have? How many stories?
- How many elevators did the Titanic have in each class?
- What was used to slide the Titanic into the water?
- How long did it take to slide the Titanic into the water?
- What items, including food, were taken on Titanic's maiden voyage?
- How many rich people were in first class?
- Who was the richest person aboard the Titanic? Did he/she survive?
- What was the total wealth of the rich people on the Titanic?
- What are the coordinates of the Titanic wreakage using latitude and longitude?
- What date did Titanic sink?
- What caused the Titanic to sink?
- How many people survived? How many people died?
- From which class did more people die? Live?

Each group will create 10 questions that will stump other members of the class based on your
findings about the Titanic.

The Process

1. Divide the resources equally among the members of the group.
2. Each member will be responsible for visiting the resources assigned.
3. Some of the questions provided should be addressed by each group member.
4. Each group member will keep a notebook on research findings.
5. Organize the findings from each member into 10 questions to stump class.
6. Groups will participate in the game show and answer questions asked by other groups.
7. The final group notebook should be turned in after the game show activity.

FIGURE **6.8**   **Continued**

The Resources

On Line Resources
- Titanic Facts Page
- Complete List of Resources
- James Cameron's New Movie
- Encyclopaedia Britannica Presents Titanic
- Titanic: Legacy of the World's Greatest Ocean Liner
- Titanic in Cyberspace
- The Titanic Exhibition
- RMS, Titanic Inc. Online

Books and Other Resources
- *Titanic, an illustrated history* by Don Lynch & Ken Marschell, 1992
- *A Night to Remember,* by Walter Lord, 1955
- *The Night Lives On,* by Walter Lord, 1986
- *The Story of the Titanic as Told by Its Survivors,* 1960
- *Titanic, Triumph, & Tragedy,* by John P. Eaton & Charles Haas, 1988
- *Titanic: The Death & Life of a Legend,* by Michael Davie, 1987
- *Titanic: Destination Disaster,* by John P. Eaton & Charles A. Haas, 1996
- *Titanic Legacy: Disaster as Media Event & Myth,* by Paul Heyer, 1995
- *Down with the Old Canoe: A Cultural History of the Titanic Disaster,* by Steven Biel, 1996
- *The Discovery of the Titanic,* by Robert D. Ballard, 1995

Learning Advice
It is very important that you keep track of the information you are learning. Organize a notebook into four sections with all your findings:

a. Most interesting information.
b. Most important facts.
c. Other information about the Titanic.
d. Resources about the Titanic.

Make sure and write down where you found each document in your notebook. Include name of author, title of document, site address if it was an online source, and date.

The Conclusion
Now that you have appeared on the game show "One Thing I Know About," you and your team have learned everything there is to know about the Titanic.

   This activity should have given you an opportunity to learn how to organize information into a meaningful document to answer facts and questions on any topic assigned.

Page created by James R. McGehee, Christine Bove, and Laura Ramirez for EDUC 528 NMSU—Spring 1998.

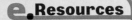

e.Resources

For additional readings related to the major ideas in this chapter, go to Chapter 6 of the Companion Website, and click on Suggested Readings.

Learning with electronic texts can be just as challenging for students as learning with print resources. The various instructional strategies that we described in this chapter provide students with opportunities for online learning. How teachers bring students and texts together in well-designed content literacy lessons and units is the subject of the next chapter.

◄ Looking Back
Looking Forward ►

Electronic texts are highly engaging and interactive. Hypertext and hypermedia make it possible to interact with text in ways not imaginable a short while ago. Text learning opportunities in electronic environments are interactive, enhance communication, engage students in multimedia, create opportunities for inquiry through information searches and retrieval, and support socially mediated learning. Reading and writing with computers has changed the way we think about literacy and learning. Whether students are navigating the Internet or interacting with innovative educational software, an array of electronic text learning experiences await them.

Various instructional strategies, including Internet workshops, Internet inquiries, Internet projects, and WebQuests were discussed as approaches to online learning in various content areas. In the next chapter, we explore the design of content literacy lessons and units of study. These lessons and units bring students and texts together in content learning situations. In a well-designed lesson, there are instructional provisions that teachers make *before*, *during*, and *after* reading to ensure that students will use strategies effectively for reading and writing. Moreover, units of study help teachers to organize lessons around themes and concepts that make use of multiple print and electronic information resources.

Minds On

1. To what extent do you believe students should participate in the selection of documents from Websites for use in a content course? Would you answer this question differently for students of various ages?

2. How often have you used electronic texts as part of subject matter learning? In your estimation, did the teacher use an electronic text assignment to its full potential? If not, in what additional ways might the electronic text resource have been explored?

3. Why do many students seem to dislike doing research in a library but are enthusiastic about surfing the Net for information resources?

Hands On

1. Select a recent news event and conduct a search for information resources on the Web. Select several resources and compare them for treatment, reliability, and accuracy. What does it mean to develop a healthy skepticism when interacting with texts on the Web?

2. Using the keywords, "Examples of WebQuests," conduct a search on the Internet for teacher-designed WebQuests in the content area of your choice. Evaluate three or four of the WebQuest Websites. Based on your search, what are some of the strengths of a WebQuest instructional model? What are some of the weaknesses? Discuss the strengths and weaknesses of these WebQuests in a small group.

3. Search the Global SchoolNet's Internet Projects Registry or other locations similar to it for Internet project descriptions in your content area. Use these project descriptions to guide the development of a project description that you have in mind at a grade level of your choice. Share your project descriptions with others in your group.

e Resources extra

- Go to Chapter 6 of the Companion Website (**www.ablongman.com/vacca8e**) and click on Activities to complete the following task:

  Visit the Children's Literature Web Guide (**www.acs.ucalgary.ca/ ~dkbrown/index.html**). Browse this site for useful information about children's literature, including award-winning books. Share your findings in small groups and discuss the ways teachers might use the site.

- Go to the Companion Website (**www.ablongman.com/vacca8e**) for suggested readings, interactive activities, multiple-choice questions, and additional Web links to help you learn more about learning with electronic texts.

The New York Times
expect the world®
nytimes.com

Themes of the Times

Extend your knowledge of the concepts discussed in this chapter by reading current and historical articles from the *New York Times*. Go to the Companion Website and click on eThemes of the Times.

chapter 7

Bringing Students and Texts Together

In our culture, TV—above all—dominates
literacy. The authority of literature—
if not the number of readers—has
declined. But books need readers.
—SUSAN SONTAG

Organizing Principle

Notions of what constitutes a text are
changing. For many of today's students, a
text quite legitimately may represent a favorite television show, movie, or video
game (Neilsen 1998). Various types of media, as well as computers, are quickly redefining what counts as literacy. Yet, the
rapid growth of the trade book industry for children and adolescents suggests that books are not obsolete
among our student population. Although the number of readers may

**Bringing students and texts
together involves instructional
plans and activities that result
in active student engagement
and collaboration.**

have declined in contemporary society, as
noted author and critic Susan Sontag reminds
us, books—actually all forms of texts—still

need readers. Bringing students and texts together may very well be one of the most important functions of teachers in content area learning situations.

Bringing students and texts together, however, is not without its risks or its rewards. Without risks, teaching often lacks innovation. Teachers who take risks have enough confidence in themselves to experiment with instructional practices, even if they are uncertain of the outcomes. They are willing to go out on a creative limb and then reflect on what they do

and why. Showing students how to use literacy to learn is worth the risks. The time it takes to connect literacy and learning will get you the results you want: active and purposeful engagement with texts. The organizing principle underscores the importance of active text learning in content area classrooms: **Bringing students and texts together involves instructional plans and activities that result in active student engagement and collaboration.**

Frame of Mind

1. How can content area teachers plan and design instruction so that students will become actively engaged in literacy-related activities?

2. How does sociocultural context in classrooms affect literacy and learning?

3. What is involved in designing a text lesson based on a B–D–A lesson structure?

4. How does designing a unit of study help teachers plan a variety of instructional activities that connect literacy and learning?

5. How do teachers create an inquiry/research emphasis within units of study?

6. How can teachers incorporate collaborative/cooperative learning activities within lessons and units of study?

"Doing school" is deeply rooted in the culture of content area classrooms where assign-and-tell practices dominate. Teachers assign students a text to read and questions to answer for homework as they hustle out the door at the end of a period more often than we would like to admit. Under these conditions, the reading assignment is often purposeless. Why read it? The answer students give all too frequently is "Because it's assigned." The only reason for reading, if students read at all, is to get through the material to answer homework questions.

Response Journal

Describe what it was like to "do school" when you were a student in a middle or high school class.

From a cultural perspective, students implicitly understand the "rules of the game." Because they are immersed in the culture of an assign-and-tell classroom, they recognize that plodding through the text to find answers to the questions at the end of an assignment is one of the expectations of doing school. Regardless of whether students answer questions fully or thoughtfully, handing in homework assignments is one of the rituals associated with the classroom culture. The class discussion that follows the homework assignment quickly becomes an exercise in futility as the teacher's questions are met with silence—another cultural expectation whose mantra is, "Don't respond unless called on." The older students become, the more prevalent the cultural expectation is in assign-and-tell classrooms to sit back and let a handful of students respond to the teacher's questions. Often the result of doing school is a disconnect between reader and text that leads to passive, non-engaged learning.

Teachers and students can change the classroom culture of doing school by changing the *sociocultural context* in which teaching and learning occurs. The sociocultural context refers to the dynamic interactions that occur between reader, text, and the instructional activity of which reading is a part. These interactions form the very basis for classroom communication, comprehension, and learning (Rand Reading Study Group 2002).

Sociocultural Context for Reading Comprehension

Teachers often are aware of the physical context underlying classroom instruction. Physical space in a classroom, for example, may restrict social interaction and student participation, depending on how a teacher interprets the learning situation. A science teacher once explained why she permitted small-group work in one class but not in another: "There are several overly rambunctious students in my third period class and not enough room to spread them apart." In addition to space considerations, the physical arrangement of the classroom also contributes to the nature and types of social interactions that occur in a classroom. Whereas an arrangement of straight rows of desks lends itself to classroom lectures and turn-taking routines, desks or tables arranged in clusters facilitate face-to-face interactions and small-group work. Of course, some teachers remain oblivious to the physical environment that they and students inhabit together. A room, after all, is only a room.

Nevertheless, the physical arrangement of the room makes a cultural statement. It contributes to a classroom environment that signals to students whether they are to be passive or engaged learners. A room isn't simply a room for teachers who seek to make the learning environments in their classrooms compatible with social interactions that support active participation in various instructional activities. From a sociocultural perspective, such interactions may be between reader and text as the class participates in content literacy activities. Or the interactions may be among teacher and students (or students and other students) as they engage in text-related discussions. Let's take a closer look at the sociocultural context underlying reading comprehension in content classrooms.

The Reader–Text–Activity Dynamic

The Rand Reading Study Group (2002) defines reading comprehension in terms of the dynamic interplay between "the *reader* who is doing the comprehending, the *text* that is to be comprehended, and the *activity* in which comprehension is a part" (p. 11). Figure 7.1 illustrates the reader–text–activity dynamic within the larger sociocultural context of underlying reading comprehension.

Readers, as we explained in previous chapters, comprehend text by using all of their capacities for learning—their prior knowledge, experiences, attitudes, beliefs, and the cognitive and metacognitive strategies that they have developed. Reading comprehension is affected not only by these reader variables but also by the text itself. Text-related variables such as the *genre*, the *text structure*, and the *readability* or *conceptual level* of the text influence comprehension. In classroom learning situations, reader–text interactions do not occur in a vacuum. Reading is a purposeful activity. Students read text to achieve some end, whether it is to answer questions at the end of a textbook chapter or to think deeply about

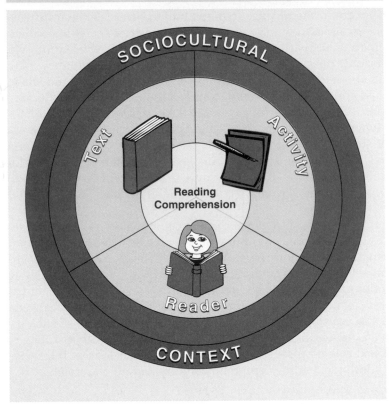

FIGURE 7.1   **The Reader–Text–Activity Dynamic in Reading Comprehension**

Source: Adapted with Permission from RAND Reading Study Group (2002). *Reading for Understanding: Toward an R&D Program in Reading Comprehension.* Santa Monica, CA: RAND, p. 12.

subject matter. Reading activity, therefore, takes into account the *purposes* for reading, the *processes* that readers engage in to accomplish the task at hand, and *consequences* of the reading activity.

For example, a math teacher assigns a chapter section on the topic "angles," as well as several problems to be solved using information from the text. The context includes the students' purpose, the reading task, the set of relationships established over time between the math teacher and the students, the relationship of the students to the textbook, and all the conditions surrounding the learning situation. The sociocultural context affects the way students interact with the text and the quality of that interaction. The students' purpose, for example, will influence how they read the material. The task—reading to solve problems—also affects how students approach the text and tackle the assignment.

Collaborative Interactions

The sociocultural context has a tremendous effect on what happens in the class-room. The learning environment depends on what the teacher and students do together. Classroom learning is as much collaborative as it is individual. It often involves on-the-spot decision making: Who gets to do what? With whom? When? Where? Because most learning situations in the classroom are face-to-face en-counters, they necessarily entail language. Most instructional routines, therefore, build on a series of conversational acts between teacher and students and between students and students. These acts are governed by rules (Wilkinson & Silliman 2000). Students quickly learn the rules and interact with the teacher or with other students accordingly.

> **Response Journal**
>
> What do you think are some of the rules and ex-pectations associated with classrooms where there is a *high level* of student engagement and active/interactive learning?

Engaged Minds

The social and cultural factors that influence the classroom learning en-vironment contribute heavily to the intellectual climate of content area classrooms. As we have suggested in earlier chapters, content literacy practices promote student engagement. Engaged readers and writers are knowl-edgeable, strategic, motivated, and socially interactive. Engaged readers are ar-chitects of their own learning. They use prior knowledge and a variety of strategies to construct meaning with texts. Furthermore, they are internally mo-tivated to succeed in learning tasks that involve literacy and choose to read and write as a way of knowing and enjoying (Guthrie & Wigfield 2000).

Teachers make content literacy visible in the context of classroom instruction through the design of well-planned text lessons and units of study. Someone in the world of business once said that 90 percent of your results come from activ-ities that consume 10 percent of your time. When this saying is applied to edu-cation, the time teachers take to plan and organize active learning environments is time well spent. Planning appropriate frameworks for instruction may include the design of *text lessons* and *units of study* revolving around student-centered in-quiry and self-selection from an array of text possibilities.

Designing and Planning Text Lessons

A text lesson revolves around all of the students in a class reading the same text. Text lessons usually evolve from textbook assignments and whole-class readings of a trade book, frequently referred to as a *core book study.* These lessons provide a blueprint for action. Having a blueprint or a plan in advance of actual practice is simply good common sense. A lesson plan is essential because students re-spond well to structure. When reading text material, they need to sense where they are going and how they will get there. Classroom experiences without rhyme or reason lack the direction and stability that students need to grow as readers.

Lessons should be general enough to include all students and flexible enough to allow the teacher to react intuitively and spontaneously when a particular plan is put in actual practice. In other words, lessons shouldn't restrict decisions about the instruction that is in progress; instead, they should encourage flexibility and change.

B–D–A Lesson Structure

What a teacher does *before reading, during reading,* and *after reading* (B–D–A) is crucial to active and purposeful reading.

The B–D–A lesson structure can help teachers design a single lesson involving reading. A lesson doesn't necessarily take place in a single class session; several class meetings may be needed to achieve the objectives of the lesson. Nor do all the components of a B–D–A lesson necessarily receive the same emphasis in any given reading assignment; the difficulty of the material, students' familiarity with the topic, and your judgment all play a part when you decide on the sequence of activities you will organize. What the structure of a B–D–A lesson tells you is that readers need varying degrees of guidance. As we show throughout this book, there are before-reading, during-reading, and after-reading activities that support students' efforts to extract and construct meaning. The components of a B–D–A lesson can be examined in Figure 7.2.

Before Reading

A B–D–A lesson that includes activity and discussion before reading reduces the uncertainty that students bring to an assignment. Before-reading activities get stu-

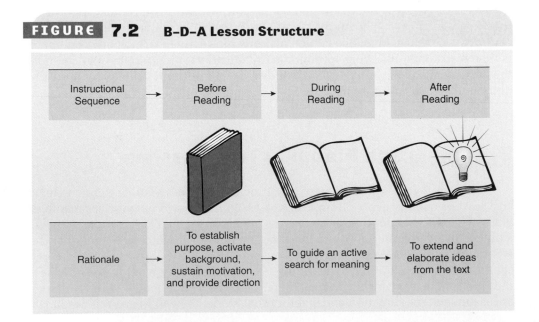

FIGURE 7.2   B–D–A Lesson Structure

Instructional Sequence	Before Reading	During Reading	After Reading
Rationale	To establish purpose, activate background, sustain motivation, and provide direction	To guide an active search for meaning	To extend and elaborate ideas from the text

dents ready to read, to approach text material critically, and to seek answers to questions they have generated about the material. The before-reading dimension of a text lesson has also been called the *prereading* phase of instruction. During this instructional phase, a teacher often places emphasis on one or more of the following: (1) motivating readers, (2) building and activating prior knowledge, (3) introducing key vocabulary and concepts, and (4) developing metacognitive awareness of the task demands of the assignment and the strategies necessary for effective learning.

A key factor related to motivation is activating students' interest in the text reading. However, conerning how to motivate students, we must first raise a fundamental question: Why should students be interested in this lesson? A teacher may even wish to consider whether he or she is interested in the material! If teachers are going to be models of enthusiasm for students, then the first step is to find something in the material about which to get really excited. Enthusiasm—it is almost too obvious to suggest—is contagious.

Building and activating prior knowledge for a lesson and presenting key vocabulary and concepts are also essential to preparation before reading. In making decisions related to prior knowledge, it's important to review previous lessons in light of present material. What does yesterday's lesson have to do with today's? Will students make the connection to previously studied material? Sometimes several minutes of review before forging into uncharted realms of learning can make all the difference in linking new information to old. Furthermore, when deciding which vocabulary terms to single out for instruction, we emphasize three questions that should be considered: What keywords will students need to understand? Are all the terms equally important? Which new words carry heavy concept loads?

Before-reading activities may also include discussions that develop an awareness of the reading task at hand and of the strategies needed to handle the task effectively. These are metacognitive discussions. Providing direction is another way of saying that students will develop task knowledge and self-knowledge about their own learning strategies. Helping students analyze the reading task ahead of them and modeling a learning strategy that students will need during reading are two metacognitive activities that quickly come to mind. Here are some general questions to ask in planning for a metacognitive discussion: What are the most important ideas in the lesson? What strategies will students need to learn these ideas? Are the students *aware* of these strategies?

A B–D–A lesson also includes provisions for guiding the search for meaning during reading. In other words, students need to be shown how to think with texts as they read.

During Reading

Teachers easily recognize the important parts of a text assignment. Most students don't. Instead, they tend to read every passage in every chapter in the same monotonous way. Each word, each sentence, each paragraph is treated

> **Response Journal**
>
> Reflecting on your school experience, how did some of your teachers create interest in text readings in the "before-reading" phase of a text lesson?

with equal reverence. No wonder a disconnect often exists between the text and the reader.

The disconnect between text and reader is especially noticeable in content areas where readers must interact with highly specialized and technical language. Nowhere, for example, is content literacy more challenging for students than in the reading of mathematics texts. Math texts are tersely written in highly condensed language. Students must perceive and decode mathematical symbols, construct meanings for specialized and technical vocabulary and concepts, analyze and interpret relationships, and apply interpretations to the solution of problems.

Study how two mathematics teachers adapt the B–D–A lesson structure to scaffold reader–text interactions during reading. The first teaches prealgebra classes in a middle school. The students are studying probability, and the objective of the teacher's lesson is to ensure that the class will be able to determine the probability of a simple event. During the before-reading phase of the lesson, the students explore the questions: Why do some sporting events, such as football, use the flipping of a coin to begin a game? Is the coin flip a fair way to decide which team will kick off? The questions tap into the students' prior knowledge and their conceptions (some naive, some sophisticated) of probability.

As part of the lesson, the teacher asks the students to use their math journals to write definitions of several terms associated with probability: *odds, chances, outcomes, events,* and *sample space.* The students' definitions are discussed as the teacher builds on what they know to arrive at a set of class definitions of the terms. He then pairs the students in "study buddy" teams and asks them to use what they already know about probability to read the assigned section from the textbook. The "study buddies" read the text section and complete the "selective reading guide" illustrated in Figure 7.3.

Together, the study buddies discuss the assigned material as they work through the guide. Selective reading guides are one way of scaffolding reader–text interactions during reading by providing a "road map" to the important concepts in the material. These guides are discussed more fully in Chapter 10.

The second teacher, a high school mathematics teacher, also adapts the structure of the B–D–A lesson to guide students' interactions with the text and to help them make important connections between reading and mathematics. When she first started teaching, she noticed with some dismay that students almost never read the text. Nor did they talk about mathematics with one another. Therefore, she makes a conscious effort to incorporate literacy and cooperative learning principles whenever instructional situations warrant them.

One such situation occurred when her students were studying the concepts of ratio, proportion, and percentage. The focus of the lesson was a section that dealt with the development of scale drawings as an application of proportion. She initiated the lesson by having students take five minutes to write "admit slips." Admit slips are students' "tickets of admission" to the lesson. The teacher can use them in a variety of ways to find out what students are feeling and thinking as they begin the class period. A more detailed discussion of admit slips occurs in

---

FIGURE 7.3   **Using a Selective Reading Guide in Math to Guide Reader–Text Interactions during Reading**

Page 236. Before reading, think about the ways in which we have defined *probability* in class discussion. Now compare our definitions with the one in the book. Develop in your own words a definition of *probability* based on what you know and what you have read.

Probability: _____

Page 236. Now read and define other key terms in this section.

Outcomes: _____

Events: _____

Sample space: _____

Page 236, Example 1. Read the example and answer the following:

What is the probability of rolling a 5? _____

How do you know? _____

Page 237, Example 2. Read this example slowly, and when you finish:

Define odds in favor: _____

Page 238, Example 3. Put on your thinking caps to answer the following:

What are the odds? _____

What is the difference between finding the probability and finding the odds? _____

_____

Pages 238–240. You're on your own!

Complete problems 1–31 with your study buddy.

Chapter 11 within the larger context of using writing as a tool for learning subject matter.

The teacher triggered admit slip writing with the prompt: "If you had a younger brother or sister in the sixth grade, how would you describe a scale drawing in words that he or she would understand?" Using half-sheets of paper distributed by the teacher, the students wrote freely for several minutes until instructed to "wind down" and complete the thoughts on which they were working. The teacher collected the admit slips and shared a few of the students' descriptions with the class. The discussion that followed revolved around the students' conceptions of scale drawings and what it means to be "in proportion."

The teacher then formed four-member cooperative groups to guide students' interactions with the text section on scale drawings. Each team was assigned to draw a scale model of the recreation room in its "dream house." First, the teams had to decide what facilities would be included in the recreation room. Once they developed the list of facilities, the team members read the text section and discussed how to develop a scale that would fit all of the facilities into the space provided for each team at the chalkboard. The lesson concluded with the teams' describing their scale drawings. The teacher then asked the students to regroup and develop a list of the important ideas related to scale models.

After Reading

Guidance during reading bridges the gap between students and text so that students learn how to distinguish important from less important ideas, to perceive relationships, and to respond actively to meaning.

Ideas encountered before and during reading may need clarification and elaboration after reading. Postreading activities create a structure that refines emerging concepts. For example, a social studies teacher who was nearing completion of a unit on Southeast Asia asked her students to reflect on their reading by using the activity in Figure 7.4. The writing prompt in part II of the after-reading activity is based on an instructional practice called RAFT, which is described in Chapter 11. The writing and follow-up discussion refined and extended the students' thinking about the ideas under study. The questions "Who is really best qualified?" and "Who is the specialist in each field?" prompted students to sort out what they had learned. The teacher provided just enough structure by listing topics from various facets of Southeast Asian culture to focus students' thinking and help them make distinctions.

Activities such as the one in Figure 7.4 extend thinking about ideas encountered during reading. Writing activities, study guides, and other after-reading practices are springboards to thinking and form the basis for discussing and articulating ideas developed through reading.

Some Examples of Text Lessons

The B–D–A text lesson structure is a generic framework for planning content literacy lessons. How teachers adapt the B–D–A lesson depends on the students in the class, the text that they are studying, and the kinds of activities that will be reflected in the lesson. Following are some examples of text lessons in different content areas at different grade levels. As you study these lessons, notice how the teachers adapt the B–D–A structure in their lessons.

e.Resources

Access useful ideas for content literacy lesson plans in your subject area by conducting a search using the keywords, "content literacy + lesson plans." Also, go to Web Destinations on the Companion Website; click on Professional Resources, and look for Ask ERIC, the Ohio Resource Center, and the Content Literacy Information Consortium (CLIC).

Middle School Science Class

Middle-level students were assigned a text selection on how bees communicate. The text told the story of Karl von Frisch, an entomologist who had studied bees for years, and focused on his experimental observations leading to the discovery of bees' communication behaviors. The teacher's objectives were to (1) involve students in an active reading and discussion of the text

FIGURE 7.4   **Postreading Activity for a Southeast Asia Lesson**

I. *Directions:* A rice farmer, a Buddhist monk, a government official, and a geographer all feel competent to speak on any of the following topics. Who is really best qualified? Who is the specialist in each field? On the blank line preceding each topic, place the letter of the correct specialist.

A. Rice farmer

B. Buddhist monk

C. Government official

D. Geographer

_____ 1. The forested regions of Thailand

_____ 2. The life of Siddhãrtha Gautama

_____ 3. The amount of rice exported each year

_____ 4. The monsoon rains in Southeast Asia

_____ 5. Harvesting rice

_____ 6. The causes of suffering

_____ 7. The art of meditation

_____ 8. The Me Nam River Basin

_____ 9. The amount of rice produced per acre

_____ 10. The pagodas in Thailand

_____ 11. The number of Buddhists living in Bangkok

_____ 12. The virtues of a simple life

_____ 13. The rice festival in Bangkok

_____ 14. The Temple of the Emerald Buddha

_____ 15. The attainment of Nirvana (perfect peace)

II. *Directions:* Pretend you are the rice farmer, the Buddhist monk, the government official, or the geographer. Write a "guest editorial" for the local newspaper revealing your professional attitude toward and opinion about the approaching monsoon season.

assignment and (2) have them experience some of the steps scientists go through when performing laboratory or field experiments. Study how she planned her instructional activities in Best Practice Box 7.1.

High School French Class

By way of contrast, study how a high school French teacher taught Guy de Maupassant's short story "L'Infirme" to an advanced class of language students. The

BOX 7.1

A B–D–A Lesson in a Sixth-Grade Science Class

I. Before Reading
   A. Before introducing the text, determine what students now know about bees.
      1. Who has observed bees close up?
      2. What do you notice about bees that seems unique to them?
      3. When you see a bee, is it usually by itself or in a group?
      4. Why do you think bees swarm?
   B. Connect students' responses to these questions to the text assignment. Introduce the story and its premise.
   C. Form small groups of four students each, and direct each group to participate in the following situation:

Karl von Frisch worked with bees for many years. He was puzzled by something he had observed again and again. When he set up a table on which he placed little dishes of scented honey, he attracted bees. Usually, he had to wait hours or days for a bee to discover the feeding place. But as soon as one bee discovered it, many more came to it in a short time. Evidently, the first bee was able to communicate the news of food to the other bees in its hive.

   Pretend that you are a scientist helping von Frisch discover how bees communicate. How do they tell each other where food is located? List ten things you could do to find out the answers to this question.

   D. Have the students share their group's top five ideas with the class, and write them on the chalkboard.
II. During Reading
   A. Assign the selection to be read in class.
   B. During reading, direct students to note the similarities and differences between their ideas on the board and von Frisch's experimental procedures.

III. After Reading (Day 2)
   A. Discuss the previous day's reading activity. How many of the students' ideas were similar to von Frisch's procedures? How many were different?
   B. Extend students' understanding of the inquiry process that scientists, such as von Frisch, follow. Divide the class into groups of four students to work on the following exercise:

All scientists follow a pattern of research to find answers to the questions they have about different subjects. For example, von Frisch wanted to know about how bees communicated. He (1) formed a question, (2) formulated an experiment to answer the question, (3) observed his subjects in the experiment, and (4) answered the question based on his observations.

   Now it's your turn! Tomorrow we are going on a field trip to the park to experiment with ants and food. Your first job as a scientist is to devise a question and an experiment to fit your question. After we return, you will write your observations and the answer to your question. You will be keeping notes on your experiment while we are in the park.

Question: _____

Experiment: _____

Observations: _____

Answer: _____

   C. Conduct the experiment the next day at the park. Each group will be given a small amount of food to place near an existing anthill. The students will make notes and take them back to the classroom. Each group's discoveries will be discussed in class.

story is about two men riding in a train. Henri Bonclair is sitting alone in a train car when another passenger, Revalière, enters the car. This fellow traveler is handicapped, having lost his leg during the war. Bonclair wonders about the type of life he must lead. As he looks at the handicapped man, Bonclair senses that he met him a few years earlier. He asks the man if he is not the person he met. Revalière is that man. Now Bonclair remembers that Revalière was to be married. He wonders if he got married before or after losing the leg or at all. Bonclair inquires. No, Revalière has not married, refusing to ask the girl to put up with a deformed man. However, he is on his way to see her, her husband, and her children. They are all very good friends. The French teacher formulated five objectives for the lesson:

1. To teach vocabulary dealing with the concept of "infirmity"

2. To foster students' ability to make inferences about the reading material from their own knowledge

3. To foster students' ability to predict what will happen in the story in light of the background they bring to the story

4. To foster students' ability to evaluate their predictions once they have read the story

5. To use the story as a basis for writing a dialogue in French

Two of the activities, the *graphic organizer* and the *inferential strategy,* used in the French teacher's plan are explained in depth in Chapters 8 and 10, respectively. The steps in the plan are outlined in Best Practice Box 7.2.

Middle School Music Class

In an ambitious B–D–A text lesson, a sixth-grade music teacher, Donna Mitchell, combines literacy-related practices within the context of studying the components of an opera and engaging students in the understanding and appreciation of Richard Wagner's opera, *The Flying Dutchman.* As part of the before-reading component of the lesson, students worked in teams to complete a *cloze activity sheet* (see Figure 7.5) in the form of a playbill. (We described the cloze procedure as an assessment tool in Chapter 2.) Cloze as an instructional activity is described in Chapter 6.

The playbill serves to activate students' prior knowledge about opera. Students fill in the playbill with the words and names provided at the bottom of the playbill activity sheet in Figure 7.5. When the student teams complete the activity, they share their answers with the class. Mrs. Mitchell then reads to the class a brief biographical sketch of Richard Wagner. She directs the student teams to check their playbills after listening to some of the events and highlights in Wagner's life to determine if the biographical sketch cleared up any of the teams' questions related to the cloze activity. Students then brainstorm what the opera, *The Flying Dutchman,* is about.

BOX 7.2

RESEARCH-BASED BEST PRACTICES

A B–D–A Lesson in a High School French Class

I. Before Reading

A. Begin the lesson by placing the title of the story on the board: "L'Infirme." Ask students to look at the title and compare it to a similar English word (or words). Determine very generally what the story is probably about. (A handicapped person.)

B. On the overhead, introduce keywords used in the story by displaying a *graphic organizer*:

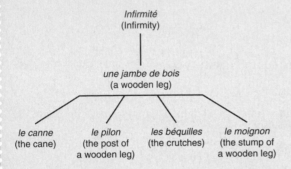

C. Use the *inferential strategy*. Ask and discuss with the class the following three sets of questions. Have the students write down their responses.

1. *Vous avez peut-être vu quelqu'un qui est très estropié à cause de la perte d'une jambe ou d'un bras. Qu'est-ce qui traverse votre es-prit? De quoi est-ce que vous vous demandez?*

(You may have seen someone who is very crippled because of the loss of a leg or an arm. When you see such a person, what crosses your mind? What do you wonder about?)

2. *Dans l'histoire, Bonclair voit ce je-une infirme qui a perdu la jambe. Qu'est-ce que vous pensez tra-verse son esprit?*

(In the story, Bonclair sees this crippled young man who has lost his leg. What do you think crosses his mind?)

3. *Quand vous voyez quelqu'un qui a l'air vaguement familier, qu'est-ce que vous voulez faire? Qu'est-ce que vous faites? Quels sont sou-vent les résultats?*

(When you see someone who looks vaguely familiar, what do you want to do? What do you do? What are often the results?)

4. *Dans cette histoire, Bonclair se souvient vaguement qu'il a fait la connaissance de cet infirme. Prédites ce qu'il fera et prédites les résultats.*

(In this story, Bonclair remembers vaguely having met this cripple.)

As part of the during-reading phase of the lesson, Mrs. Mitchell dims the lights in the classroom and invites students to close their eyes as they listen to the over-ture to *The Flying Dutchman*. In this context, the term *overture* is redefined by the class. After establishing the mood of the opera, students rethink their ideas about

Predict what he does and the results.)

5. *Imaginez que vous êtes fiancé(e) à un jeune homme ou à une jeune femme. Puis vous avez un accident qui vous rend estropié(e). Qu'est-ce que vous feriez? Voudriez-vous se marier? Pourriez-vous compter sur l'autre de vous aimer encore?*
(Imagine that you are engaged to a young man or woman. Then you have an accident that leaves you crippled. What would you do? Would you still want to marry? Could you still expect the other to love you?)

6. *Dans notre histoire, Revalière a eu un accident juste avant son marriage. Prédites ce qu'il fera et ce qu'il comptera de la jeune fille. Prédites les résultats.*
(In our story, Revalière has had an accident just before his marriage. Predict what he did and what he expected of the young woman. Predict the results.)

II. During Reading
   A. Assign the reading, instructing the students to keep in mind their prior knowledge and predictions.
   B. Ask them to note possible changes in their predictions.

III. After Reading
   A. After the reading, conduct a follow-up discussion with the class. Relate their predictions to what actually happened, noting how our background knowledge and experience of the world lead us to think along certain lines.
   B. Have the class form groups of four with at least one male and one female in each group. Establish the following situation:

   Une jeune fille vient d'être estropiée dans un accident de natation. Son fiancé lui a téléphoné. Il veut lui parler. Qu'est-ce qu'il veut lui dire? On frappe à la porte. C'est lui.
   (A young lady was recently crippled in a swimming accident. Her fiancé has called her. He wants to talk to her. What does he want to talk about? There is a knock at the door. It is he.)

   1. Think together, drawing on your past knowledge or experience of situations like this. Write a fifteen- to twenty-line group dialogue in French between the girl and her fiancé. What might he have to tell her? How might she react?
   2. Select a male and female student to present the group's dialogue to the class.

the story. During the next several class sessions, Mrs. Mitchell reads the story, stopping each day at a turning point of the story to pique students' curiosity. She ends each read-aloud with an enthusiastic, "To be continued!" and then engages students in a discussion of the story that has occurred thus far. Toward the end of each

FIGURE 7.5   Cloze Playbill for the Opera, *The Flying Dutchman*

The Flying Dutchman

An _____ by _____

_____ in _____ with _____

subtitles on overhead screen

_____—Taken from a Norwegian legend

_____—The shores of Norway

_____—Maestro George Szell

Chorus—_____

_____—Constructed and designed by Marc Chagall

_____—Designed by Mademoiselle Choé

· ·

_____—The Cleveland Orchestra

_____—Aboard the ship

Dutchman—Sung by _____

Daland—Sung by _____

_____—On Shore

Senta—Sung by _____

German	Act II	Setting	Spoken	Sung
Costumes	Choreographer	Conductor	libretto	Scenery
Opera	Richard Wagner	Overture	Tenor	Baritone
English	Townspeople	Soprano	Sailors	Act I

Source: Donna Kowallek Mitchell © 2000. Reprinted with permission.

discussion, she elicits predictions about what the students think will happen next. Throughout this process excerpts of the music are played at appropriate places in the lessons.

At the conclusion of the story, students enter the after-reading phase of the lesson. Mrs. Mitchell follows procedures associated with the discussion web strategy (see Chapter 10). The discussion web is a collaborative strategy that requires students to explore multiple perspectives around a key question. First, the students work in "think-pair-share" dyads to respond to the question, "Did Senta need to throw herself off the cliff into the sea?" from yes/no perspectives. They then form groups of four to share their perspectives in a larger forum and to reach a conclusion, which the groups share with the class.

These text lessons all have the same underlying structure. Each plan provides a set of experiences designed to move readers from preparation to interaction with the text to extension and elaboration of the concepts in the material under study. The lessons show how teachers translate knowledge about content area reading into plans for active learning.

How teachers plan instructional activities for text lessons varies by grade level and the sophistication of the students. The same is true of developing plans for a unit of study. In the next section, we go beyond designing and planning text lessons to decisions related to thematic learning involving multiple literacy experiences.

Designing and Planning Units of Study

Units of study organize instruction around objectives, activities, print and non print resources, and inquiry experiences. A unit may be designed for a single discipline or may be interdisciplinary, integrating two or more content areas. In middle schools, where content area teachers are teamed in learning "communities" or "families," opportunities abound to develop interdisciplinary units. Interdisciplinary units require coordination and cooperation by all of the content area teachers teamed within a learning community. Team planning helps students make connections not otherwise possible among many knowledge domains. Noden and Vacca (1994), for example, describe how a middle school teaching team organized an interdisciplinary unit around the theme of "Native Americans." They developed a four-week unit in which 130 seventh graders were "born" into one of sixteen Native American tribes. The students inquired into tribal lifestyles from many disciplinary perspectives and participated in a variety of activities to understand life as Native Americans both emotionally and intellectually.

Components of a Well-Designed Unit

The unit of study is a planning tool that includes (1) a title reflecting the theme or topic of the unit, (2) the major concepts to be learned, (3) the texts and information sources to be studied by students, (4) the unit's instructional activities, and (5) provisions for assessing what students have learned from the unit.

Content Objectives

Content analysis is a major part of teacher preparation in the development of a unit of study. Content analysis results in the *what* of learning—the major concepts and understandings that students should learn from reading the unit materials. Through content analysis, the major concepts become the objectives for the unit. It doesn't matter whether these content objectives are stated in behavioral terms. What really matters is that you know which concepts students will interact with and develop. Therefore, it's important to decide on a manageable number of the most important understandings to be gained from the unit. This means setting priorities; it's impossible to cover every aspect of the material that students will read or to which they will be exposed.

A unit on spatial relationships for a high school art class provides an example of how a teacher planned content objectives, activities, and materials. First, she listed the major concepts to be taught in the unit:

1. Humans are aware of the space about them as functional, decorative, and communicative.

2. Space organized intuitively produces an aesthetic result, but a reasoned organization of space also leads to a pleasing outcome if design is considered.

3. Occupied and unoccupied space have positive and negative effects on mood and depth perception.

4. The illusion of depth can be created on a two-dimensional surface.

5. The direction and balance of lines or forms create feelings of tension, force, and equilibrium in the space that contains them.

6. Seldom in nature is the order of objects so perfect as to involve no focal point or force or tension.

Instructional Activities and Text Resources

The high school art teacher then developed the activities and identified the texts to be used in the unit (see Figure 7.6). As you study the figure, keep in mind that some of the text-related activities suggested are explored later in this book.

The actual framework of units will vary. For example, you might organize a unit entirely on a sequence of lessons from assignments in a single textbook. This type of organization is highly structured and is even restrictive in the sense that it often precludes the use of various kinds of other literature rich in content and substance. However, a unit of study can be planned so that the teacher will (1) use a single textbook to begin the unit and then branch out into multiple-text study and differentiated activities, (2) organize the unit entirely on individual or group inquiry and research, or (3) combine single-text instruction with multiple-text activities and inquiry.

Branching out provides the latitude to move from a single text lesson to independent learning activities. The move from single- to multiple-information sources exposes students to a wide range of texts that may be better suited to their needs and interests. (See Figure 7.7.)

FIGURE 7.6   **Activities and Texts**

Text-Related Activities	Texts
1. Graphic organizer	Graham Collier, Form, Space, and Vision
2. Vocabulary and concept bulletin board	
3. Prereading	Chapter 3, Collier
4. Prereading	chapters 6 and 7
5. Art journal	chapters 6 and 7
6. K-W-L	Chapter 11
7. Vocabulary exercise	Chapter 3
8. Vocabulary exercise	chapters 6 and 7
9. Vocabulary exercise	Chapter 11
10. Student's choice (list of projects for research study)	H. Botten, Do You See What I See?
	H. Helfman, Creating Things That Move
	D. McAgy, Going for a Walk with a Line
	L. Kaumpmann, Creating with Space and Construction
	G. LeFrevre, Junk Sculpture
11. Hands-On	J. Lynch, Mobile Design
Ink dabs	
Straw painting	
Dry seed arrangement	
Cardboard sculpture	
Positive–negative cutouts	
Perspective drawing	Calder's Universe
Large-scale class sculpture	
Mobiles	
Space frames	Displays of artist's works with questionnaires to be filled out
12. Filmstrip	about them
13. Field trip to studio of a sculptor	
14. Field trip to museum	
15. Learning corner	

Although units of study may include multiple-text opportunities, the textbook is not necessarily excluded from the unit. Unit planning simply provides more options to coordinate a variety of information sources. In single-discipline units, B–D–A activities become an integral part of unit teaching.

Listing texts and resources is an important part of the preparation for a single-discipline unit. One reason a unit is so attractive as a means of organization is that the teacher can go beyond the textbook—or, for that matter, bypass it. A wide array of literature, both narrative and informational, gives students opportunities for an intense involvement in the theme or topic under study. Trade

e.Resources

Access useful ideas for integrating electronic texts into units by conducting a search using the keywords, "integrated technology + thematic units." Also, go to Web Destinations on the Companion Website; click on Professional Resources, and look for Enhancing Thematic Units with Technology

FIGURE 7.7 "Branching Out" in a Thematic Unit: Using a Wide Range of Texts

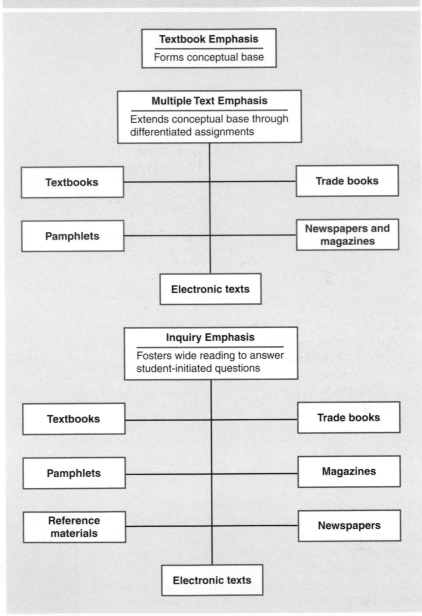

books, electronic texts, pamphlets, periodicals, reference books, newspapers, magazines, and audiovisual materials are all potential alternative routes to acquiring information.

Moreover, the Internet has become a valuable planning resource for teachers in the development of units. You can access many useful ideas for integrating electronic texts into units of study.

An Inquiry/Research Emphasis in Units of Study

Gathering, organizing, and sharing information are crucial to both academic success and success in our information-rich society. Inquiry should, therefore, play a major role in learning important content, and the process of inquiry should be woven into thematic units of study. *Standards for the English Language Arts* (1997) developed by IRA and NCTE describes the fundamental characteristics of inquiry reading as follows: "Students conduct research on issues and interests by generating ideas and questions and by posing problems. They gather, evaluate, and synthesize data from a variety of sources (e.g., print and non-print texts, artifacts, and people) to communicate their discoveries in ways that suit their purpose and audience" (p. 7).

Steps and Stages Involved in Inquiry Projects

How teachers guide inquiry/research projects is the key to a successful unit. The process of inquiry, like the process of writing that we describe in Chapter 11, works best when it occurs in steps and stages. Clark (1987) draws on his experience as a former journalist to ease his middle grade students into the inquiry process. The students use human resources from the community to conduct their inquiries. The students must decide whom they will interview and what the focus of the inquiry will be. They collect data for their projects through interviews. Clark then encourages his budding researchers to write about their inquiries using information they gathered from the interviews. He identifies the following stages as part of the inquiry process in which his students engage: searching for ideas, gathering and sifting, finding a focus, building momentum, rethinking and revising, and reaching an audience. For students to be successful, Clark realizes that he must encourage inquiry through learner choice and teacher guidance.

Each stage of an inquiry/research project requires careful support by a teacher. In Best Practice Box 7.3, we outline the stages and procedures for guiding inquiry/research.

When teachers simply assign and evaluate research reports, students often paraphrase whatever sources come to hand rather than actively pursuing information

e.Resources

Access useful ideas for inquiry projects in your subject area by conducting a search using the keywords, "inquiry projects + lessons + units." Also, go to Web Destinations on the Companion Website; click on Professional Resources, and look for Teacher Resources and Education Planet.

RESEARCH-BASED BEST PRACTICES

Procedures for Guiding Inquiry/Research Projects

I. Raise questions, identify interests, organize information.
  A. Discuss interest areas related to the unit of study.
  B. Engage in goal setting.
    1. Arouse curiosities.
    2. Create awareness of present levels of knowledge.
  C. Pose questions relating to each area and/or subarea.
    1. "What do you want to find out?"
    2. "What do you want to know about _____?"
    3. Record the questions or topics.
    4. "What do you already know about _____?"
  D. Organize information; have students make predictions about likely answers to gaps in knowledge.
    1. Accept all predictions as possible answers.
    2. Encourage thoughtful speculations in a nonthreatening way.

II. Select materials.
  A. Use visual materials.
    1. Trade books and encyclopedias
    2. Magazines, catalogs, directories
    3. Newspapers and comics
    4. Indexes, atlases, almanacs, dictionaries, readers' guides, computer catalogs
    5. Films, filmstrips, slides
    6. Videotapes, television programs
    7. Electronic texts: CD-ROMs, Website documents, videodisks
  B. Use nonvisual materials.
    1. Audiotapes
    2. Records
    3. Radio programs
    4. Field trips
  C. Use human resources.
    1. Interviews
    2. Letters
    3. On-site visits
    4. Discussion groups
    5. E-mail
    6. Listservs

that they are eager to share with others. Genuine inquiry is always a messy endeavor characterized by false starts, unexpected discoveries, changes in direction, and continual decision making. Too much guidance can be as dangerous as too little.

In an in-depth study of two middle school research projects, Rycik (1994) found that teachers may lose their focus on genuine inquiry as they establish procedures for guiding all students to complete a project successfully. The teachers in the study were very concerned with providing sufficient guidance, so they broke down their projects into a series of discrete steps (such as making note cards) that could be taught, completed, and evaluated separately. As the projects

  D. Encourage self-selection of materials.
     1. "What can I understand?"
     2. "What gives me the best answers?"
III. Guide the information search.
  A. Encourage active research.
     1. Reading
     2. Listening
     3. Observing
     4. Talking
     5. Writing
  B. Facilitate with questions.
     1. "How are you doing?"
     2. "Can I help you?"
     3. "Do you have all the materials you need?"
     4. "Can I help you with ideas you don't understand?"
  C. Have students keep records.
     1. Learning log that includes plans, procedures, notes, and rough drafts
     2. Book record cards
     3. Record of conferences with the teacher

IV. Consider different forms of writing.
  A. Initiate a discussion of sharing techniques.
  B. Encourage a variety of writing forms.
     1. Essay or paper
     2. Lecture to a specific audience
     3. Case study
     4. Story: adventure, science fiction, other genre
     5. Dialogue, conversation, interview
     6. Dramatization through scripts
     7. Commentary or editorial
     8. Thumbnail sketch
V. Guide the writing process.
  A. Help students organize information.
  B. Guide first-draft writing.
  C. Encourage responding, revising, and rewriting.
  D. "Publish" finished products.
     1. Individual presentations
     2. Classroom arrangement
     3. Class interaction

moved forward, the teachers gradually came to believe that mastering the procedure for each step was the primary outcome of the project, even more important than learning content information.

Rycik (1994) concluded that inquiry should not be confined to one big research paper because teachers cannot introduce and monitor the wide range of searching, reading, thinking, and writing skills that students need to complete such projects. Good researchers, like good writers, must learn their craft through frequent practice in a variety of contexts. This means that students should research from a variety of sources and express their findings for a variety of audiences in a variety of forms. Some recommendations for integrating research into the class-room routine include the following:

- *Make identifying questions and problems as important in your classroom as finding answers.*

- *Provide frequent opportunities to compare, contrast, and synthesize information from multiple sources.*

- *Present findings of research in a variety of products and formats,* including charts, graphs, and visual or performing arts.

- *Discuss possible sources for information* presented in the class or for answering questions posed by the teacher or students (e.g., personal interviews, diaries, experiments).

The teacher must carefully plan inquiry-centered projects, giving just the right amount of direction to allow students to explore and discover ideas on their own. The research process isn't a do-your-own-thing proposition; budding researchers need structure. Many a project has been wrecked on the shoals of nondirection. The trick is to strike a balance between teacher guidance and student self-reliance. A research project must have just enough structure to give students (1) a problem focus, (2) physical and intellectual freedom, (3) an environment in which they can obtain data, and (4) feedback situations in which to report the results of their research.

A Multiple Text Emphasis in Units of Study

The literature-based movement in elementary schools serves as a prototype for the use of trade books in middle and high school classrooms. In addition, technology makes it possible to access and explore information sources through CD-ROM programs, electronic books, and the Internet. Although textbooks may be used to provide an information base, the foundation for individual and group inquiry into a theme or topic is built on students' use of multiple-information resources, both printed and electronic. Trade books and electronic texts are geared to students' interests and inquiry needs.

Say that in a middle grade classroom, students are engaged in a thematic unit on the environment. What might you observe over several weeks? For starters, the teacher may conduct several whole-class lessons at the beginning of the unit using the textbook to develop a conceptual framework for individual and group investigation. As the weeks progress, however, whole-class activity is less prevalent. Instead, small groups work on research projects or in discussion teams using Gary Paulsen's *Woodsong* (1990) and *Hatchet* (1987) and Roy Gallant's *Earth's Vanishing Forests* (1991). Individual students are also working on inquiries with books such as Paul Goble's *I Sing for the Animals* (1991) and Peter Parnall's *Marsh Cat* (1991) and *The Daywatchers* (1984).

In addition, the students are conducting research online, tapping into the rich information resources of the World Wide Web. Several students investigate the Websites of Environmental Science, the Rainforest Action Network, and the Global Recycling Network. Others explore software programs: Ozzie's World (Digital Impact), Zug's Adventures on Eco-Island (Zugware), Zurk's Rainforest (Soliel), and Imagination Express: Rainforest (Edmark). One or two students navigate the pages of electronic reference books, such as Grolier's Multimedia Encyclopedia (Grolier).

Toward the end of the unit, the class completes culminating activities, which may involve panel discussions, report writing, and oral presentations in which individuals or groups share knowledge gleaned from the various activities and texts. In this class, what you would observe is that everyone has something to contribute.

Steps Involved in the Use of Multiple Texts

Brozo and Tomlinson (1986) define several steps that facilitate the uses of trade books in thematic units. We have expanded their plan to include electronic texts.

1. *Identify salient concepts that become the content objectives for the unit.*

   a. What are the driving human forces behind the events?

   b. What patterns of behavior need to be studied?

   c. What phenomena have affected or may affect ordinary people in the future?

2. *Identify appropriate trade books, Websites, and software that will help in the teaching of these concepts.*

3. *Teach the unit.*

   a. Use the textbook, trade books, and electronic texts interchangeably.

   b. Use strategies, such as read-alouds, in which a trade book or electronic text becomes a schema builder before students read the textbook.

   c. Use trade books and electronic texts to elaborate and extend content and concepts related to the unit.

4. *Follow up.*

   a. Engage students in strategies and activities that involve collaboration, inquiry, and various forms of expression and meaning construction.

   b. Evaluate students' learning by observing how they interpret and personalize new knowledge.

Active learning environments within units of study integrate whole-class, small-group, and individual learning activities. Whole-class presentation is an economical means of giving information to students when the classroom context lends itself to information sharing. A whole-class activity, for example, may be used to set the stage for a new thematic unit. The unit introduction, discussion of objectives, and background building can all take place within whole-class structure. However, the chief drawback of whole-class presentation is that it limits active participation among students. Although whole-class interaction provokes discussion to an extent, it cannot produce the volume of participation necessary to engage students in active learning situations. A viable alternative supported by a substantial body of research lies in the use of collaborative interactions between teacher and students and students and other students. These collaborative interactions are grounded in the principles underlying cooperative learning and small-group processes.

Designing and Planning Collaborative Interactions

Cooperative learning allows groups of students to pursue academic goals through collaboration in classroom instructional activities. The goals of cooperative learning, therefore, are to foster collaboration in a classroom context, to develop students' self-esteem in the process of learning, to encourage the development of positive group relationships, and to enhance academic achievement (Johnson, Johnson, & Holubec 1990). Cooperative groups facilitate active participation and should be a primary form of classroom organization when teachers bring students together to comprehend texts. The National Reading Panel's (NRP) review of research on text comprehension identifies cooperative learning as a scientifically supported comprehension strategy (NRP 2000). We agree with Duke and Pearson (2002), however, who view cooperative learning as an "instructional medium" that facilitates reading comprehension rather than an individual instructional strategy. Within the learning environment created by cooperative groups, students produce more ideas, participate more, and take greater intellectual risks. A cooperative group, with its limited audience, provides more opportunity for students to contribute ideas to a discussion and take chances in the process. The students can try out ideas without worrying about being wrong or sounding dumb—a fear that often accompanies risk taking in a whole-class situation.

e.Resources

Access useful ideas about cooperative learning by conducting a search using the keywords, "cooperative learning + lesson plans." Also, go to Web Destinations on the Companion Website; click on Professional Resources and look for Education World.

Cooperative Learning Groups

Bringing readers and texts together in social collaboration to engage in discussions may be achieved through the use of cooperative learning groups. Many variations on cooperative group learning are possible. Several cooperative grouping patterns, in particular, work well within the context of content literacy practices and text-related discussions. The cooperative groups described in the following sections give you a feel for how students might collaborate in their interactions with texts and with one another as they extract and construct meaning to make sense out of what they are reading.

Jigsaw Groups

Interdependent team learning with texts may be achieved through *jigsaw groups* (Aronson 1978). Jigsaw teaching requires students to specialize in a content literacy task that contributes to an overall group objective. Jigsaw groups are composed of students divided heterogeneously into three- to six-member teams. Each student on a team becomes an expert on a subtopic of a theme or topic about which the class is reading. Not only is the student accountable for teaching the other members of the group about his or her subtopic but he or she is also responsible for learning the information other group members provide during the jigsaw discussions.

> **Response Journal**
>
> Describe how you would use the jigsaw strategy in your content area.

For example, a life science teacher in a middle school engages students in a thematic unit on the topic "birds." As part of the unit of study, he divides the class into five six-member jigsaw groups. Each member of a group is expected to become an expert on one of the following concepts in the unit: the relationship between birds and reptiles, the adaptation of various species of birds to their environment, the migration patterns of birds, the adaptation of birds for flight, the economic importance of birds, and the identification of various families and species.

As part of the jigsaw strategy, members of the different teams who share the same subtopic meet in temporary "expert groups" to discuss what they are reading and learning. Each of the expert groups has a variety of resource materials and texts made available by the teacher to help them explore and clarify their subtopics. When the members in each of the expert groups complete their tasks, They return to their jigsaw teams to teach and share what they have learned. As a jigsaw member presents his or her findings, the other members listen and take notes in preparation for a unit exam the teacher will give on the overall topic.

Student Teams Achievement Divisions (STAD)

Student teams lend themselves well to content area learning situations that combine whole-class discussion with follow-up small-group activity. The originator of STAD groups, Robert Slavin (1988), emphasizes the importance of achieving team learning goals but also recognizes that individual performance is important in cooperative groups.

STAD groups work this way: The teacher introduces a topic of study to the whole class, presents new information, and then divides the class into heterogeneous four-member groups of high-, average-, and low-achieving students to engage in follow-up team study. The goal of team study is to master the content presented in the whole-class discussion. The team members help each other by discussing the material, problem solving, comparing answers to guide material, and quizzing one another to ensure that each member knows the material. The students take periodic quizzes, prepared by the teacher, following team study. A team score is determined by the extent to which each member of the team improves over past performance. A system of team awards based on how well students perform individually ensures that team members will be interdependent for learning.

Learning Circles

Johnson and colleagues (1990) underscore the importance of positive interdependence through a cooperative learning model. Similar to STAD, learning circles mesh whole-group study with small-group interactions and discussion. Learning circles may comprise two to six members of varying abilities who come together to share text resources and help each other learn. All of the content literacy activities that we present in this book can be adapted to the type of interdependent learning teams that are suggested by Johnson and colleagues. However, cooperative groups don't run by themselves. You have to plan for the success of positive interdependence by teaching students how to use collaboration skills to work interdependently in teams and then facilitating the group process as students engage in discussion and interaction.

Johnson and colleagues (1990) suggest eighteen steps for structuring learning circles, some of which include specifying content objectives, deciding on the size of the group, assigning students to groups, arranging the room, planning instructional activities and guide material to promote interdependent learning, explaining the academic task, explaining the criteria for success, structuring the division of labor within the groups, structuring individual accountability and intergroup cooperation, monitoring students' behaviors, teaching the skills of collaboration, providing task assistance as needed, evaluating student learning, and assessing how well the teams functioned.

Group brainstorming, prediction, problem solving, mapping, and study strategies, all of which are discussed in Part 3, are easily woven into the fabric of cooperative learning circles. Coming to a group consensus on a variety of discussion tasks is an important outcome in cooperative learning groups. Students need to be shown how to engage cooperatively in consensus building as they decide what conclusions they can or cannot support as a result of their interactions with texts and one another.

Group Investigation

As we explained earlier in this chapter, students can be combined in teams of two to six to collaborate on inquiry topics that interest them within the context of a thematic unit and the major concepts of study. Each group selects a topic and cooperatively plans the inquiry in consultation with the teacher. Each research team, for example, decides how to investigate the topic, which tasks each member will be responsible for, and how the topic will be reported. The groups then conduct the investigation, synthesize their findings into a group presentation, and make their presentation to the entire class. The teacher's evaluation includes individual performance and the overall quality of the group presentation. In Figure 7.8, study how an American history teacher in high school sets up a group investigation project on the Revolutionary War.

Group Retellings

Group retellings underscore the importance of *conceptually related reading* in which each member of a cooperative group reads a different text on the same topic. For example, Wood (1987) illustrates the use of group retellings in a health class. Students of different abilities work in groups of three or more, reading timely articles or brochures on the topic of safety in the home. A magazine article might describe an eyewitness account of a home fire resulting from an electrical overload. A brochure from the local fire department might outline the precautions to take to avoid such a mishap, perhaps emphasizing the hazards associated with an overloaded circuit. A newspaper editorial might warn parents against leaving their children unattended and unfamiliar with safety hazards in the home.

> **Response Journal**
> Describe how you would use the group retellings strategy in your content area.

After reading, each member of the group shares what he or she has read while the other members of the team listen and, at any point, share additional information and insights into the topic based on their reading. According to Wood (1987), group retellings capitalize on the pleasure derived from sharing newly learned information with a friend.

Small-Group Processes Underlying Cooperative Learning

Small-group learning is complex, and cooperative teams don't run by themselves. Students must know how to work together and how to use techniques they have been taught. The teacher, in turn, must know about small-group processes. The practical question is, "How will individual students turn into cooperative groups?" Anyone who has ever attempted small-group instruction in the classroom knows the dilemma associated with the question. Many conditions can confound team learning if plans are not made in advance; in particular, teachers must scaffold instruction around such matters as the size, composition, goals, and performance criteria of small groups and the division of labor within a group.

Group Size

The principle of "least group size" operates whenever you form learning teams. A group should be just large enough to include all the skills necessary to solve a

FIGURE 7.8   **A Group Investigation Project for a Unit on the Revolutionary War**

Directions: Congratulations! You have been chosen to anchor the new series *TimeLine.* This show features the same type of in-depth interview as *NightLine,* except you have a time machine. You can go back in time and interview someone from the Revolution. To prevent changing the future, here are the rules:

1. Work in pairs. Both of you will do research and write the interview. Decide who will be the interviewer and who the interviewee. Decide on a historical interview date.

2. Your interviewee may be an actual historical figure (e.g., Paul Revere), or you may create a fictional eyewitness to a historical event (e.g., the Boston Tea Party).

3. Your research must be based on at least two sources, only one of which may be an encyclopedia. A bibliography must be included in the written interview turned in after the presentation.

4. Presentation

   a. Introduce the interviewee and briefly tell why this person is important or interesting.

   b. Your questions must stay within your time frame. You can't ask George Washington if he wants to be president; the office doesn't exist yet. You may ask him if he would like a political office in the future.

   c. The interviewee's answers must be reasonable and based on historical facts from your research.

   d. You are encouraged to include visual aids: pictures, cartoons, maps, props, and costumes.

   e. The interview should last no less than four minutes and no more than ten minutes.

Here is a list of possible subjects, or you may choose your own.

George Washington	Haym Solomon (financier)	David Bushnell (submarine inventor)
Samuel Adams	George Rogers Clark	Boston Massacre
Crispus Attucks	John Dickinson	Boston Tea Party
Thomas Jefferson	Thomas Paine	Reading and responding to the Declaration of Independence as a wealthy merchant or planter, a poor artisan or farmer, or a slave
John Adams	John Locke	
Benjamin Franklin	Jean-Jacques Rousseau	
Benedict Arnold	Abigail Adams	
Francis Marion, the "Swamp Fox"	James Arnistead (spy)	
Marquis de Lafayette	Deborah Sampson Gannett (soldier)	Revolutionary battle or campaign of your choice
Charles Cornwallis (British general)	Patrick Henry	Treaty of Paris
Frederick North (British prime minister)	John Hancock	
King George III	Ethan Allen	
	Peter Zenger	

problem or complete a task. A group that's larger than necessary provides less chance for individual participation and greater opportunity for conflict. If too many students are grouped together, there's bound to be a point of diminishing returns. The group size for content area reading should range from two to six members (depending, of course, on the type of reading task). Because most small-group activities involve discussion, three- or four-member groups are probably best.

Group Composition

Homogeneous grouping is often not necessary for discussion tasks. Both intellectual and nonintellectual factors influence a small group's performance, and the relationship between intelligence and small-group performance is often surprisingly low. Experiential and social background, interests, attitudes, and personality contribute greatly to the success of a cooperative group. Grouping solely by reading or intellectual ability shortchanges all students and robs discussion of diversity.

Students who struggle with reading shouldn't be relegated to tasks that require minimal thinking or low-level responses to content material. There is no quicker way to initiate misbehavior than to put students who find reading difficult together in a group. People learn from one another. A student whose background is less extensive than other students' can learn from them. The student who has reading difficulties needs good readers as models. Furthermore, the student who has trouble reading may in fact be a good listener and thinker who will contribute significantly to small-group discussion.

Group Goals and Tasks

Group learning is goal oriented. How the goals and the paths to task completion are perceived affects the amount and quality of involvement of the team members. If group goals are unclear, members' interest quickly wanes. Goals must also be directly related to the task. The conditions of the task must be clearly defined and must be understood by the individual members of the group.

Therefore, you should explain the criteria for task performance. For example, when students work with reading guides, such as those that are suggested in this book, they should attempt to adhere to such criteria as the following:

1. *Each student should read the selection silently and complete each item of the guide individually or with others in the group,* depending on the teacher's specific directions.

2. *Each item should be discussed by the group.*

3. *If there is disagreement on any item, a group member must defend his or her position and show why there is disagreement.* This means going back into the selection to support one's position.

4. *No one student should dominate a discussion or boss other members around.*

5. *Each member should contribute something to each group discussion.*

As students work on literacy activities in their groups, the teacher can facilitate performance by reinforcing the criteria that have been established.

Positive Interdependence

Groups lack cohesiveness when learning is not cooperative but competitive and when students aren't interdependent in learning but work independently. However, since the 1970s, social scientists and instructional researchers have made great strides in understanding the problems of the competitive classroom. Researchers (Johnson & Johnson 1987; Slavin 1988) have studied the practical classroom applications of cooperative principles of learning. The bulk of their research suggests that cooperative small-group learning has positive effects on academic achievement and social relationships. Positive interdependence can be achieved through a variety of schemes in which students are rewarded for collaborative effort (Johnson & Johnson 1990). For example, a social studies teacher attempted to have students adhere to discussion behaviors during their interactions in small groups (these discussion behaviors were basically the same as those we discussed under performance criteria). Each small group earned a performance grade for discussing text assignments in a six-week thematic unit. Here's how the group members earned their grades.

> **Response Journal**
>
> What is your reaction to the point system that the social studies teacher used to create positive interdependence among the small groups in his class?

1. The teacher observed each member in the group to monitor the use of the desired discussion behaviors.

2. On Fridays, each group earned a color reward worth a given number of points: green = 1 point, blue = 2 points, black = 3 points, and red = 4 points. The color that a group earned was based on how well it had performed according to the criteria for discussion.

3. Each member of the group received the color (and the points that went with it) that the whole group earned. Therefore, if one or two members of the group did not use the appropriate discussion behaviors, the entire group got a lower point award.

4. The color for each student in the class was noted on a learning incentive chart.

5. Each week, the small groups changed composition by random assignment.

6. The points attached to each color added up over the weeks. When the unit was completed, so many points resulted in a performance grade of A, B, C, or D.

What happened as a result of the reward system? On the Monday of each week that students were randomly assigned to new groups, they immediately went to the learning incentive chart to check the color received the previous week by each of the other members in their new group. Motivation was high. Group pressure caused individual students who had not received high points the previous week to become intent on improving their performance in the new group.

Group Roles and Division of Labor

If cooperative groups are to be successful, members must divide the work of the group and understand their different roles within the group. Therefore, consider specifying complementary and interconnected responsibilities that the group must undertake to accomplish a joint task. Johnson and Johnson (1990) define several roles, which may vary by the nature of the task, for example:

Leader: The group leader facilitates the work of the group. Leadership skills may include *giving directions* (reviewing instructions, restating the goals of the group, calling attention to time limits, offering procedures on how to complete the task most effectively), *summarizing* aloud what has been read or discussed, and *generating responses* by going beyond the first answer or conclusion and producing a number of plausible answers from which to choose.

Reader: The reader in the group is responsible for reading the group's material aloud so that the group members can understand and remember it.

Writer-recorder: The writer recorder records the responses of the group on paper, edits what the group has written, and makes sure the group members check this work for content accuracy and completeness.

Checker: The checker makes sure the group is on target by checking on what is being learned by the members. The checker, therefore, may ask individuals within the group to explain or summarize the material being discussed.

Encourager: The encourager watches to make sure that all the members in the group are participating and invites reluctant or silent members to contribute.

If students are to understand the roles and the responsibilities of each role, you will need to develop in them a knowledge and an awareness of each. Discuss each role, demonstrate appropriate behavior and responses, role-play with students, coach, and provide feedback during actual group discussions.

We believe that the main reason for the infrequent use of small groups is the frustration that teachers experience when teams lack cohesion and interdependence. Uncooperative groups are a nightmare. No wonder a teacher abandons or is hesitant to use small groups in favor of whole-class instruction, which is

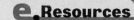

e.Resources

For additional readings related to the major ideas in this chapter, go to Chapter 7 of the Companion Website and click on Suggested Readings.

easier to control. Small-group instruction requires risk taking by the teacher as much as it encourages risk taking by the students.

◀ **Looking Back**
Looking Forward ▶

Content area teachers can design and plan instruction that will lead to active text learning. The reader–text–activity dynamic must be taken into consideration when designing and planning content literacy-related lessons and units of study. The dynamic interplay between reader, text, and activity occurs within the sociocultural context of content classrooms. Within the sociocultural context, readers interact with texts, and also with one another, as they engage in activity that considers the purposes, processes, and consequences of reading.

The B–D–A text lesson helps teachers to design and plan instructional activities at critical periods within the reading and discussion of a text that has been assigned to the whole class. This particular lesson structure focuses on what students do *before*, *during*, and *after* reading to facilitate text comprehension. A unit of study, however, helps teachers to organize instructional activities around inquiry projects and multiple texts. Unit planning gives the teacher much more latitude to coordinate resource materials and activities. Unit activities can be organized around the whole class, small groups, or individuals. An effective content classroom, organized around text lessons and units of study, thrives on collaborative interactions between teacher and students and students and other students. These interactions are grounded in the principles of small-group processes and cooperative learning.

In the next chapter we examine the relationships between the vocabulary of a content area—its special and technical terms—and its concepts. How can a teacher help students to interact with the language of a content area and, in the process, show them how to define, clarify, and extend their conceptual knowledge?

 ## **Minds On**

1. You have probably seen some variation of the bumper sticker "If you can read this, thank a teacher." In a small group, sitting in a circle, discuss how you feel about seeing this sticker and what you think it means. Select one member of your group to act as an observer, and use the questions that follow to record group interactions. Allow ten to fifteen minutes for discussion, and then ask the observer to share her or his list of questions and answers with the group.

Observer's questions:

a. Who raised questions during group discussion?

b. Could most of the questions be answered yes or no, true or false?

c. Who answered the questions?

d. Who decided who would answer and when they would answer?

e. Who kept the group on task?

f. Did your seating arrangement change before or after the discussion?

As a group, discuss the following:

a. Did the discussion process described by the observer involve the sharing of ideas by group members with no one person asking or answering all the questions?

b. What were the advantages and disadvantages of having the discussion progress without the rigid protocol of one person deciding who would answer and when?

c. How would you contrast the effect of the seating in rows used in lecture question-and-answer sessions with the effect of the circle seating used in this discussion?

2. Join together with four or five other individuals who either teach or are planning to teach at approximately the same grade level. Imagine that you have just attended a cooperative learning workshop and you plan to incorporate what you learned into your teaching. What do you consider the single best cooperative activity for your grade level and why? Discuss how you would implement this approach with a selected topic. List any problems you expect might arise, and explain how you would solve them.

3. Recognizing that students with different abilities and interests learn differently, to what extent should a teacher attempt to organize a class so that all the students in the class will learn the same concepts and information? Would your answer be the same for a third-grade science class and a high school advanced physics class? What general guidelines can you develop as a group to help a new teacher organize learning to balance course content with individual differences? Also, what type of physical classroom design do you think would best facilitate your philosophy?

 Hands On

1. Try the following experiment. Roll a standard 8½-by-11-inch sheet of paper into a tube 11 inches long and approximately 1 inch in diameter. Then hold the tube in your left hand and, keeping both eyes open, look through the tube with your left eye. Next, place your right hand, palm toward your face, against the side of the tube approximately half the distance from your eye to the end of the tube. Angle the tube slightly so that the far end of the tube is behind your palm, and a hole should appear in your hand.

With a small group or individually, brainstorm how you might use this experiment as a prereading activity for a science lesson on the eye.

2. Team up with two other individuals. Designate one member of your group "observer," one "reader," and one "artist." The observer's task will be to make a written record of the actions of the reader and the artist. The artist will draw a triangle described by the reader in the following instructions:

Draw a triangle so that one side is twice as long as one of the other two. Use one of the small sides as the base, and construct the triangle so that the longest side faces the left side of the paper. Design your triangle so that the longest side is three inches long. Make it exactly three inches if you have a ruler available, or estimate the length if you do not. Finally, assign the letters a, b, and c to each side of the triangle, designating the longest side as c.

After the reader and the artist have completed the drawing, review the notes by the observer, and develop a written record of the intentions or reasons for each action previously recorded. For example, if the observer recorded that the reader turned back to reread the instructions, you might explain that the artist had forgotten a fact that he or she needed to understand. Finally, compare observations, make a class list of the learning strategies used by each group, and discuss which are successful approaches for a number of people. From this activity, what conclusions can you draw about the role of metacognition in reading to learn?

3. Bring your favorite book, magazine, poem, or drama to class. Develop a prereading activity that would provide the rationale for using this material, and introduce this piece. (This activity can be done in small groups of five or six or with the entire class.)

Before your presentation, plan a series of entry questions and comments to match what you think others will say in response. Also, because you are introducing this material with a purpose in mind, the discussion should lead your small group to a particular point from which the next activity might begin.

Be prepared to reach that departure point by a number of alternate routes. Prereading activities and discussions often remain detached from the reading/content activity, so that a novice is tempted to say, "That's enough talking. Let's get to the real lesson." The discussion or activity must be integral to the "real" lesson.

Here is the complete passage from the exercise at the conclusion of Chapter 1:

Besides, Sir, we shall not fight our battles alone. There is a just God, who presides over the destinies of nations, who will raise up friends to fight our battles for us. The battle, Sir, is not to the strong alone: it is to the vigilant, the active, the brave. Besides, Sir, we have no election. If we were base enough to desire it, it is now too late to retire from the contest.

There is no retreat, but in submission or slavery. Our chains are forged. Their clanking may be heard on the plains of Boston! The war is inevitable—and let it come—I repeat, Sir, let it come! It is in vain, Sir, to extenuate the matter. Gentlemen may cry, "Peace! Peace!" But there is no peace. The war has actually begun!

The next gale that sweeps from the North will bring to our ears the clash of resounding arms! Our brethren are already in the field! Why stand we here idle? What is it that the Gentlemen wish? What would they have? Is life so dear, or peace too sweet, as to be purchased at the price of chains and slavery? Forbid it, Almighty God! I know not what course others may take, but as for me, give me liberty or give me death!

e.Resourcesextra

- Go to Chapter 7 of the Companion Website (**www.ablongman.com/vacca8e**) and click on Activities to complete the following task:

     Review several of the award-winning educational Websites, for example, **www.education-world.com/ awards/**. Brainstorm how you could use them to enhance student learning with texts.

- Go to the Companion Website (**www. ablongman.com/vacca8e**) for suggested readings, interactive activities, multiple-choice questions, and additional Web links to help you learn more about bringing students and texts together.

expect the world®

The New York Times
nytimes.com

Themes of the Times

Extend your knowledge of the concepts discussed in this chapter by reading current and historical articles from the *New York Times*. Go to the Companion Website and click on eThemes of the Times.

chapter 8

Developing Vocabulary Knowledge and Concepts

I am a Bear of Very Little Brain
and long words Bother me.
—A. A. MILNE, FROM *WINNIE-THE-POOH*

Organizing Principle

There is a strong connection between vocabulary knowledge and reading comprehension. If students are not familiar with most words they meet in print, they will undoubtedly have trouble understanding what they read. Long words bothered Pooh, probably as

Teaching words well means giving students multiple opportunities to learn how words are conceptually related to one another in the texts they are studying.

e.Resources

For a research review on the relationship between vocabulary and comprehension, go to Web Destinations on the Companion Website; click on Professional Resources, and look for "NRP Report," then select Part IV, Vocabulary.

much as technical vocabulary—words unique to a content area—bother students who are not familiar with the content they are studying in an academic discipline. The more experience students have with unfamiliar words

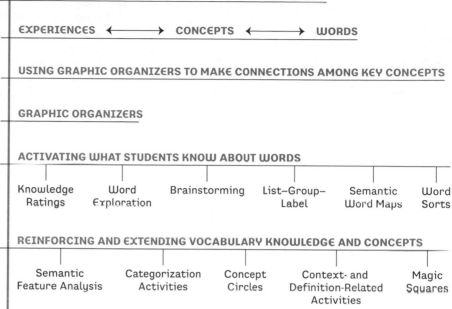

DEVELOPING VOCABULARY KNOWLEDGE AND CONCEPTS

EXPERIENCES ←——→ CONCEPTS ←——→ WORDS

USING GRAPHIC ORGANIZERS TO MAKE CONNECTIONS AMONG KEY CONCEPTS

GRAPHIC ORGANIZERS

ACTIVATING WHAT STUDENTS KNOW ABOUT WORDS

| Knowledge Ratings | Word Exploration | Brainstorming | List–Group–Label | Semantic Word Maps | Word Sorts |

REINFORCING AND EXTENDING VOCABULARY KNOWLEDGE AND CONCEPTS

| Semantic Feature Analysis | Categorization Activities | Concept Circles | Context- and Definition-Related Activities | Magic Squares |

and the more exposure they have to them, the more meaningful (and less bothersome) the words will become.

Vocabulary is as unique to a content area as fingerprints are to a human being. A content area is distinguishable by its language, particularly the technical terms that label the concepts undergirding the subject matter. Teachers know they must do something with the language of their content areas, but they often reduce instruction to routines that direct students to look up, define, memorize, and use content-specific words in sentences. Such practices divorce the study of vocabulary from an exploration of the subject matter. Learning vocabulary becomes an activity in itself—a separate one—rather than an integral part of learning academic content. Content area vocabulary must be taught *well enough* to remove potential barriers to students' understanding of texts in content areas. The organizing principle underscores the main premise of the chapter: **Teaching words well means giving students multiple opportunities to learn how words are conceptually related to one another in the texts they are studying.**

Frame of Mind

1. Why should the language of an academic discipline be taught within the context of concept development?

2. What are the relationships among experiences, concepts, and words?

3. How can a teacher activate what students know about words and help them make connections among related words?

4. How do activities for vocabulary extension help students refine their conceptual knowledge of special and technical vocabulary?

5. How do magic squares for vocabulary reinforcement help students associate words and definitions?

Fridays always seemed to be set aside for quizzes when we were students. And one of the quizzes most frequently given was the vocabulary test: "Look up these words for the week. Write out their definitions and memorize them. Then use each word in a complete sentence. You'll be tested on these terms on Friday."

Our vocabulary study seemed consistently to revolve around the dull routines of looking up, defining, and memorizing words and using them in sentences.

Such an instructional pattern resulted in meaningless, purposeless activity—an end in itself, rather than a means to an end. Although there was nothing inherently wrong with looking up, defining, and memorizing words and using them in sentences, the approach itself was too narrow for us to learn words in depth. Instead, we memorized definitions to pass the Friday quiz—and forgot them on Saturday.

Response Journal

What were some of your experiences with vocabulary instruction in content areas?

Having students learn lists of words is based on the ill-founded notion that the acquisition of vocabulary is separate from the development of ideas and concepts in a content area. Teaching vocabulary often means assigning a list of words rather than exploring word meanings and relationships that contribute to students' conceptual awareness and understanding of a subject. Once teachers clarify the relationship between words and concepts, they are receptive to instructional alternatives.

Teaching words well removes potential barriers to reading comprehension and supports students' long-term acquisition of language in a content area. Teaching words well entails helping students make connections between their prior knowledge and the vocabulary to be encountered in the text, and providing them with multiple opportunities to clarify and extend their knowledge of words and concepts during the course of study.

To begin, let's explore the connections that link direct experience to concepts and words. Understanding these connections lays the groundwork for teaching words, with the emphasis on learning concepts. As Anderson and Freebody (1981) suggest, "Every serious student of reading recognizes that the significant aspect of vocabulary development is in the learning of concepts, not just words" (p. 87).

Experiences, Concepts, and Words

Response Journal

What are some words related to your content area that didn't exist ten years ago? One year ago? Why do you think these words are now in use?

Words are labels for concepts. A single concept, however, represents much more than the meaning of a single word. It may take thousands of words to explain a concept. However, answers to the question, "What does it mean to know a word?" depend on how well we understand the relationships among direct experiences, concepts, and words.

Concepts are learned by acting on and interacting with the environment. Students learn concepts best through direct, purposeful experiences. Learning is much more intense and meaningful when it is firsthand. However, in place of using direct experience (which is not always possible), we develop and learn concepts through various levels of contrived or vicarious experience. According to Dale (1969), learning a concept through oral or written language is especially difficult because this kind of learning is so far removed from direct experience.

What Are Concepts?

Concepts create mental images, which may represent anything that can be grouped together by common features or similar criteria: objects, symbols, ideas, processes, or events. In this respect, concepts are similar to schemata. A concept hardly ever stands alone; instead, it is bound by a hierarchy of relationships. As a result, "most concepts do not represent a unique object or event but rather a general class linked by a common element or relationship" (Johnson & Pearson 1984, p. 33).

Bruner, Goodnow, and Austin (1977) suggest that we would be overwhelmed by the complexity of our environment if we were to respond to each object or event that we encountered as unique. Therefore, we invent categories (or form concepts) to reduce the complexity of our environment and the necessity for constant learning. For example, every feline need not have a different name; each is known as a *cat*. Although cats vary greatly, their common characteristics cause them to be referred to by the same general term. Thus, to facilitate communication, we invent words to name concepts.

Concept Relationships: An Example

Consider your concept for the word *ostrich*. What picture comes to mind? Your image of an ostrich might differ from ours, depending on your prior knowledge

BOX 8.1

What about . . .
Content Standards and Assessment?

The development of vocabulary knowledge and concepts is essential for students to comprehend and think critically about texts across the curriculum. Although most state and national content standards in the various academic disciplines do not explicitly state a standard for vocabulary learning, it is more broadly implied in content standards that relate to comprehension, interpretation, inquiry, and critical thinking. As a result, some state proficiency assessments may not have direct measures of word meaning related to a specific discipline other than on reading and language arts assessments.

Informal, authentic assessments are an important aspect of content area instruction and should be used, as we explained in Chapter 2, in conjunction with high stake measures of proficiency. Blachowicz and Fisher (1996), for example, recommend Knowledge Rating as a self-assessment/instructional strategy before students read a chapter or engage in a unit of study. The steps in Knowledge Rating include the following:

1. *Develop a Knowledge Rating sheet to survey students' prior knowledge of vocabulary they will encounter in a text assignment or unit of study* (see the following examples from a middle grade language arts class and a high school mathematics class).

2. *Invite students to evaluate their level of understanding of the keywords on the Knowledge Rating sheet.*

3. *Engage in follow-up discussion,* asking the class to consider questions such as, "Which are the hardest words? Which do you think most of the class doesn't know? Which words do most of us know?" Encourage the students to share what they know about the words and to make predictions about their meanings.

4. *Use the self-assessment to establish purposes for reading.* Ask, "About what do you think this chapter/unit is going to be?"

5. *As students engage in chapter/unit study, refer to the words on the Knowledge Rating sheet as they are used in text.* Have students compare their initial word meaning predictions with what they are learning as they read.

of the ostrich or the larger class to which it belongs, generally referred to as *land birds.* Moreover, your direct or vicarious experiences with birds may differ significantly from someone else's. Nevertheless, for any concept, we organize all our experiences and knowledge into conceptual hierarchies according to *class, example,* and *attribute* relations.

EXAMPLES

From a newspaper unit in a middle school language arts class:

How much do you know about these words?

	A Lot!	Some	Not Much
Wire service		X	
AP		X	
Copy		X	
Dateline	X		
Byline	X		
Caption	X		
Masthead			X
Jumpline			X
Column	X		

From a unit on quadratic functions and systems of equations in a high school math class:

How much do you know about these words?

	Can Define	Have Seen/Heard	?
Exponent	X		
Intersection	X		
Domain			X
Intercept			X
Slope		X	
Parabola			X
Origin		X	
Vertex		X	
Irrationals	X		
Union		X	
Coefficient		X	

The concept *ostrich* is part of a more inclusive class or category called *land birds,* which is in turn subsumed under an even larger class of animals known as *warm-blooded vertebrates.* These class relations are depicted in Figure 8.1.

In any conceptual network, class relationships are organized in a hierarchy consisting of superordinate and subordinate concepts. In Figure 8.1, the superordinate

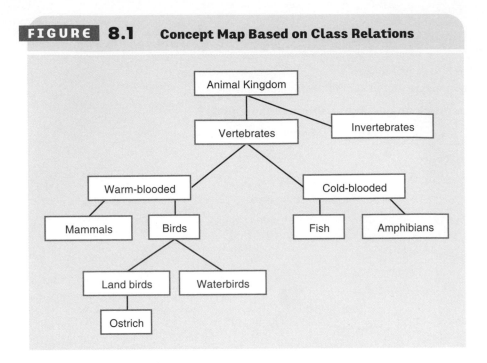

FIGURE 8.1   Concept Map Based on Class Relations

concept is *animal kingdom*. *Vertebrates* and *invertebrates* are two classes within the animal kingdom; they are in a subordinate position in this hierarchy. *Vertebrates*, however—divided into two classes, *warm-blooded* and *cold-blooded*—are superordinate to *mammals*, *birds*, *fish*, and *amphibians*, which are types or subclasses of vertebrates. The concept *land birds*, subordinate to *birds* but superordinate to *ostrich*, completes the hierarchy.

For every concept, there are examples. An *example* is a member of any concept being considered. Class–example relations are complementary: Vertebrates and invertebrates are examples within the *animal kingdom*; mammals, birds, fish, and amphibians are examples of *vertebrates*; land birds are one example of *birds*; and so on.

Let's make *land birds* our target concept. What are some other examples of land birds in addition to the ostrich? *Penguin, emu,* and *rhea* are a few, as shown in Figure 8.2. We could have listed more examples of land birds. Instead, we now ask, "What do the ostrich, penguin, emu, and rhea have in common?" This question allows us to focus on their *relevant attributes*, the features, traits, properties, or characteristics common to every example of a particular group. In this case, the relevant attributes of land birds are the characteristics that determine whether the ostrich, penguin, emu, and rhea belong to the class of birds called *land birds*. An attribute is said to be *critical* if it is a characteristic that is necessary to class membership. An attribute is said to be *variable* if it is shared by some but not all examples of the class.

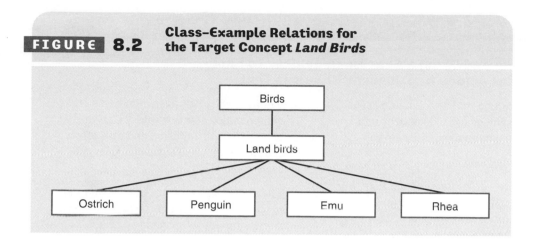

FIGURE 8.2 **Class–Example Relations for the Target Concept *Land Birds***

Thus, we recognize that certain physical and social characteristics are shared by all land birds but that not every land bird has each feature. Virtually all land birds have feathers, wings, and beaks. They hatch from eggs and have two legs. They differ in color, size, habitat, and size of feet. Some land birds fly, and others, with small wings that cannot support their bodies in the air, do not. In what ways is the ostrich similar to other land birds? How is the ostrich different?

This brief discussion illustrates an important principle: **Teachers can help students build conceptual knowledge of content area terms by teaching and reinforcing the concept words in relation to other concept words.** This key instructional principle plays itself out in content area classrooms whenever students are actively making connections among the keywords in a lesson or unit of study.

Using Graphic Organizers to Make Connections among Key Concepts

At the start of each chapter, we have asked you to use a "chapter overview" to organize your thoughts around the main ideas in the text. These ideas are presented within the framework of a *graphic organizer,* a diagram that uses content vocabulary to help students anticipate concepts and their relationships to one another in the reading material. These concepts are displayed in an arrangement of key technical terms relevant to the important concepts to be learned.

Graphic organizers may vary in format. One commonly used format to depict the hierarchical relationships among concept words is a "network tree" diagram. Keep in mind, network tree graphic organizers always

> **Response Journal**
>
> How useful do you find the chapter overviews at the beginning of each chapter in preparing to study a chapter? Why? Why not?

RESEARCH-BASED BEST PRACTICES

BOX 8.2

Constructing and Using a Graphic Organizer to Show Relationships among Key Concept Words in Text

Barron (1969) suggests the following steps for developing the graphic organizer and introducing the vocabulary diagram to students:

1. *Analyze the vocabulary of the learning task.* List all the words that you believe are important for the student to understand.

2. *Arrange the list of words until you have a scheme that shows the interrelationships among the concepts particular to the learning task.*

3. *Add to the scheme vocabulary.* Add terms that you believe the students understand in order to show the relationships between the learning task and the discipline as a whole.

4. *Evaluate the organizer.* Have you clearly shown major relationships? Can the organizer be simplified and still effectively communicate the idea you consider crucial?

5. *Introduce the students to the learning task by showing them the scheme.* Tell them why you arranged the terms as you did. Encourage them to contribute as much information as possible to the discussion of the organizer.

6. *As you complete the learning task, relate new information to the organizer where it seems appropriate.*

---

show concepts in relation to other concepts. Let's take a closer look at how to construct and apply graphic organizers in the classroom. Box 8.2 outlines several steps to follow for developing and using a graphic organizer as a before-reading activity.

A Graphic Organizer Walk-Through

Suppose you were to develop a graphic organizer for a text chapter in a high school psychology course. Let's walk through the steps involved.

1. *Analyze the vocabulary, and list the important words.* The chapter yields these words:

hebephrenia	neurosis	personality disorders
psychosis	schizophrenia	catatonia
abnormality	mental retardation	phobias

2. *Arrange the list of words.* Choose the word that represents the most inclusive concept, the one superordinate to all the others. Then choose the words

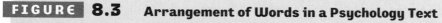

FIGURE 8.3   **Arrangement of Words in a Psychology Text**

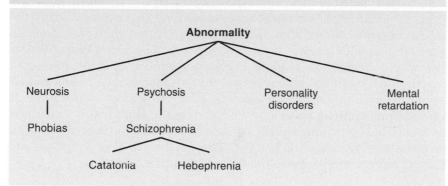

classified immediately under the superordinate concept, and coordinate them with one another. Then choose the terms subordinate to the coordinate concepts. Your diagram may look like Figure 8.3.

3. *Add to the scheme vocabulary terms that you believe the students understand.* You add the following terms: *antisocial, anxiety, intellectual deficit, Walter Mitty, depression, paranoia.* Where would you place these words on the diagram?

4. *Evaluate the organizer.* The interrelationships among the key terms may look like Figure 8.4 once you evaluate the vocabulary arrangement.

FIGURE 8.4   **Arrangement of Psychology Words after Evaluation of Organizer**

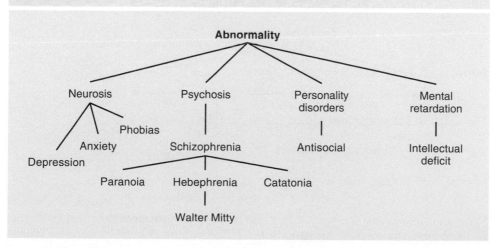

5. *Introduce the students to the learning task.* As you present the vocabulary relationships shown on the graphic organizer, create as much discussion as possible. Draw on students' understanding of and experience with the concepts the terms label. You might have students relate previous study to the terms. For example, *Walter Mitty* is subsumed under *hebephrenia.* Students who are familiar with James Thurber's short story "The Secret Life of Walter Mitty" would have little trouble bringing meaning to *hebephrenia:* a schizophrenic condition characterized by excessive daydreaming and delusions. The discussion might also lead to a recognition of the implicit comparison-and-contrast pattern of the four types of abnormality explained in the text. What better opportunity to provide direction during reading than to have students visualize the pattern? The discussions you will stimulate with the organizer will be worth the time it takes to construct it.

6. *As you complete the learning task, relate new information to the organizer.* This step is particularly useful as a study and review technique. The organizer becomes a study guide that can be referred to throughout the discussion of the material. Students should be encouraged to add information to flesh out the organizer as they develop concepts more fully.

Use a graphic organizer to show the relationships in a thematic unit, in a chapter, or in a subsection of a chapter. Notice how the graphic organizer in Figure 8.5, developed for a high school class in data processing, introduced students to the different terms of data processing, delineating causes and effects.

An art teacher used Figure 8.6 to show relationships among types of media used in art. She used an artist's palette rather than a tree diagram. After com-

FIGURE **8.5**   **A Graphic Organizer for Data Processing**

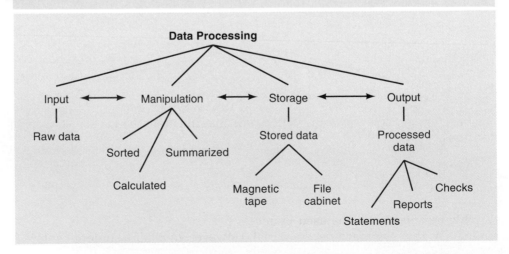

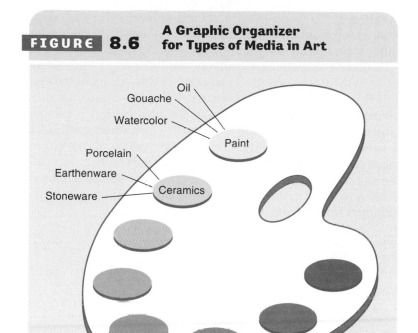

FIGURE 8.6   **A Graphic Organizer for Types of Media in Art**

pleting the entries for paint and ceramics herself, the teacher challenged her students to brainstorm other media that they had already used or knew about and to provide examples; she used the open areas on the palette to record students' associations.

Graphic organizers are easily adapted to learning situations in the elementary grades. For class presentation, elementary teachers often construct organizers on large sheets of chart paper or on bulletin boards. Other teachers introduce vocabulary for content units by constructing mobiles they hang from the ceiling. Hanging mobiles are an interest-riveting way to attract students' attention to the hierarchical relationships among the words they will encounter. Still other elementary teachers draw pictures with words that illustrate the key concepts under study.

Showing Students How to Make Their Own Connections

Graphic organizers may be used by teachers to build a frame of reference for students as they approach new material. However, in a more student-centered adaptation of the graphic organizer, the students work in cooperative groups and organize important concepts into their own graphic representations.

To make connections effectively, students must have some familiarity with the concepts in advance of their study of the material. In addition, student-constructed graphic organizers presume that the students are aware of the idea behind a graphic organizer. If they are not, you will need to give them a rationale and then model the construction of an organizer. Exposure to teacher-constructed graphic organizers from past lessons also creates awareness and provides models for the instructional strategy.

To introduce students to the process of making their own graphic organizers, follow these steps, adapted from Barron and Stone (1973):

1. *Type the keywords and make copies for students.*

2. *Have them form small groups of two or three students each.*

3. *Distribute the list of terms and a packet of 3-by-5-inch index cards to each group.*

4. *Have the students write each word from the list on a separate card.* Then have them work together to decide on a spatial arrangement of the cards that depicts the major relationships among the words.

5. *As students work, provide assistance as needed.*

6. *Initiate a discussion of the constructed organizer.*

Before actually assigning a graphic organizer to students, you should prepare for the activity by carefully analyzing the vocabulary of the material to be learned. List all the terms that are essential for students to understand. Then add relevant terms that you believe the students already understand and will help them relate what they know to the new material. Finally, construct your own organizer.

The form of the student-constructed graphic organizer will undoubtedly differ from the teacher's arrangement. However, this difference in and of itself should not be a major source of concern. What is important is that the graphic organizer support students' abilities to anticipate connections through the key vocabulary terms in content materials.

Activating What Students Know about Words

Graphic organizers may be used to (1) activate students' prior knowledge of the vocabulary words in a text assignment or unit of study and (2) clarify their understanding of concepts as they study text. From a strategy perspective, students need to learn how to ask the question, "What do I know about these words?" When you use graphic organizers before reading or talking about key concepts, help the students build strategy awareness by exploring key terms before assigning text to read. In addition, consider the use of a quasi-instructional/informal assessment strategy known as Knowledge Rating (Blachowitz & Fisher 1996). For an explanation of the Knowledge Rating strategy, see Box 8.1. In addition to graphic organizers and knowledge ratings, there are several instructional activities that you can use to scaffold student's exploration of words.

Word Exploration

Word exploration is a *writing-to-learn* strategy that works well as a vocabulary activity. Before asking students to make connections between the words and their prior knowledge, a biology teacher asked them to explore what they knew about the concept of *natural selection* by writing in their learning logs.

A word exploration activity invites students to write quickly and spontaneously, a technique called *freewriting*, for no more than five minutes, without undue concern about spelling, neatness, grammar, or punctuation. The purpose of freewriting is to get down on paper everything that students know about the topic or target concept. Students write freely for themselves, not for an audience, so the mechanical, surface features of language, such as spelling, are not important.

Word explorations activate schemata and jog long-term memory, allowing students to dig deep into the recesses of their minds to gather thoughts about a topic. Examine one of the word explorations for the target concept *natural selection:*

> Natural selection means that nature selects—kills off—does away with the weak so only the strong make it. Like we were studying in class last time things get so competitive even among us for grades and jobs etc. The homeless are having trouble living with no place to call home except the street and nothing to eat. That's as good an example of natural selection as I can think of for now.

The teacher has several of the students share their word explorations with the class, either reading them verbatim or talking through what they have written, and notes similarities and differences in the students' concepts. The teacher then relates their initial associations to the concept and asks the students to make further connections: "How does your personal understanding of the idea *natural selection* fit in with some of the relationships that you see?"

Brainstorming

An alternative to word exploration, brainstorming is a procedure that quickly allows students to generate what they know about a key concept. In brainstorming, the students can access their prior knowledge in relation to the target concept.

Brainstorming involves two basic steps that can be adapted easily to content objectives: (1) The teacher identifies a key concept that reflects one of the main topics to be studied in the text, and (2) students work in small groups to generate a list of words related to the concept in a given number of seconds.

These two steps help you discover almost instantly what your students know about the topic they are going to study. Furthermore, Herber (1978) suggests

> The device of having students produce lists of related words is a useful way to guide review. It helps them become instantly aware of how much they know, individually and collectively, about the topic. They discover quickly that there are no right or wrong answers. . . . Until the students reach the point in the lesson where they must read the passage and judge whether their predictions are accurate, the entire lesson is based on their own knowledge, experience, and opinion. This captivates their interest much more than the more traditional, perfunctory review. (p. 179)

List–Group–Label

Hilda Taba (1967) suggests an extension of brainstorming that she calls "list–group–label." When the brainstorming activity is over, and *lists* of words have been generated by the students, have the class form learning teams to *group* the words into logical arrangements. Then invite the teams to *label* each arrangement. Once the list–group–label activity is completed, ask the students to make predictions about the content to be studied. You might ask, "Given the list of words and groupings that you have developed, about what do you think we will be reading and studying? How does the title of the text (or the thematic unit) relate to your groups of words? Why do you think so?"

A teacher initiated a brainstorming activity with a class of "low-achieving learners." The students, working in small groups, were asked to list in two minutes as many words as possible that were related to the Civil War. Then the groups shared their lists of Civil War words. The teacher then created a master list on the board from the individual entries of the groups. He also wrote three categories on the board—"North," "South," and "Both"—and asked the groups to classify each word from the master list under one of the categories. Here's how one group responded:

NORTH	SOUTH	BOTH
blue	gray	soldiers
Lincoln	farms	armies
Grant	Rebel	guns
factories	Booth	cannons
Yankee	slavery	Gettysburg Address
Ford Theater		roots
victory		death
		horses
		assassination

Note that in this example, the teacher provided the categories. He recognized that students needed the additional structure to be successful with this particular task. The activity led to a good deal of discussion and debate. Students were put in the position of "authority," sharing what they knew and believed already with other class members. As a result of the activity, they were asked to raise questions about the Civil War that they wanted to have answered through reading and class discussion.

Semantic Word Maps

Semantic word maps spatially depict relationships among words. The use of semantic word maps may include brainstorming and the use of collaborative small groups. Semantic word maps allow students to cluster words belonging to categories and to distinguish relationships among words. Here's how semantic mapping works:

1. *The teacher or the students decide on a key concept to be explored.*

2. *Students suggest related terms and phrases.* Once the key concept is determined, the students, depending on what they have been studying and on their background knowledge and experiences, offer as many words or phrases as possible related to the concept term. These are recorded by the teacher on the chalkboard.

Once the list of terms is generated, the teacher may form small groups of students to create semantic maps and then to share their constructions in class discussion. Such was the case in a woods technology class exploring the concept of *solvents* in relation to choosing different kinds of wood finishes. The semantic map created by one of the small groups in the class is shown in Figure 8.7.

Teachers will need to model the construction of semantic maps once or twice so that students will get a feel for how to develop their own in small groups or individually. In Chapter 12, we expand on the use of semantic maps as an after-reading learning strategy used by students to outline content material as they study texts.

Word Sorts

Like brainstorming, word sorts require students to classify words into categories based on their prior knowledge. However, unlike brainstorming, students do not generate a list of words for a target concept. Instead, the teacher identifies the keywords from the unit of study and invites the students to sort them into logical arrangements of two or more.

A word sort is a simple yet valuable activity. Individually or in small groups, students literally sort out technical terms that are written on cards or

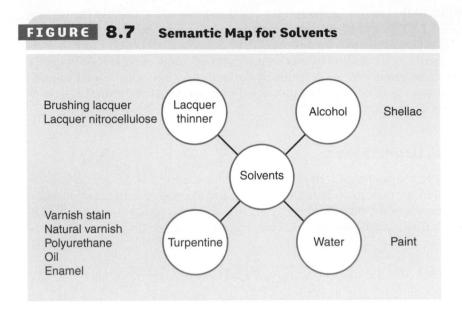

FIGURE 8.7   **Semantic Map for Solvents**

listed on an exercise sheet. The object of word sorting is to group words into different categories by looking for shared features among their meanings. According to Gillet and Kita (1979), a word sort gives students the opportunity "to teach and learn from each other while discussing and examining words together" (pp. 541–542).

Gillet and Kita (1979) also explain that there are two types of word sorts: the *open sort* and the *closed sort.* Both are easily adapted to any content area. In the closed sort, students know in advance of sorting what the main categories are. In other words, the criterion that the words in a group must share is stated. In a middle grade music class, students were studying the qualities of various "instrumental families" of the orchestra. The music teacher assigned the class to work in pairs to sort musical instruments into four categories representing the major orchestral families: strings, woodwinds, brass, and percussion. Figure 8.8 represents the closed sort developed by one collaborative "think–pair–share" group.

Open sorts prompt divergent and inductive reasoning. No category or criterion for grouping is known in advance of sorting. Students must search for meanings and discover relationships among technical terms without the benefit of any structure.

Study how an art teacher activated what students knew about words associated with pottery making by using the open word sort strategy. She asked the high school students to work in collaborative pairs to arrange the following words into possible groups and to predict the concept categories in which the words would be classified:

| FIGURE **8.8** | **Closed Sort for Musical Instruments** |

Strings (Bow or Struck)	Woodwinds (Single or Double Reed)	Brass (Lips Vibrate in Mouthpiece)	Percussion (Sounds of Striking)
Violin	Flute	Trumpet	Timpani
Viola	Piccolo	Trombone	Bass drum
Cello	Oboe	French Horn	Chimes
Harp	Clarinet		Xylophone
	Saxophone		Bells
	Bassoon		Triangle
			Snare drum

Jordan	lead	Cornwall stone	sgraffito
ball	chrome	cone	roka
antimony	slip	wheel	leather
cobalt	scale	bisque	hard
mortar	kaolin	stoneware	oxidation

Three categories that students formed were *types of clay, pottery tools,* and *coloring agents.*

Open word sorts can be used before or after reading. Before reading, a word sort serves as an activation strategy to help learners make predictive connections among the words. After reading, word sorts enable students to clarify and extend their understanding of the conceptual relationships.

Reinforcing and Extending Vocabulary Knowledge and Concepts

Students need many experiences, real and vicarious, to develop word meanings and concepts. They need to use, test, and manipulate technical terms in instructional situations that capitalize on reading, writing, speaking, and listening. In having students do these things, you create the kind of natural language environment that is needed to extend vocabulary and concept development. Various vocabulary extension activities can be useful in this respect.

e.Resources

For more examples of vocabulary activities and useful ideas in your content area, go to Web Destinations on the Companion Website; click on Professional Resources, and select "Vocabulary University."

These activities should be completed individually by students and then discussed either in small groups or in the class as a whole. The oral interaction in team learning gives more students a chance to use terms. Students can exchange ideas, share insights, and justify responses in a nonthreatening situation.

Semantic Feature Analysis (SFA)

Semantic feature analysis (SFA) establishes a meaningful link between students' prior knowledge and words that are conceptually related to one another. The strategy requires that you develop a chart or grid to help students analyze similarities and differences among the related concepts. As the SFA grid in Figure 8.9 illustrates, a topic or category (in this case, properties of quadrilaterals) is selected, words related to that category are written across the top of the grid, and features or properties shared by some of the words in the column are listed down the left side of the grid.

Students analyze each word, feature by feature, writing Y (yes) or N (no) in each cell of the grid to indicate whether the feature is associated with the word. Students may write a question mark (?) if they are uncertain about a particular feature.

FIGURE 8.9   **An SFA for Geometry**

Directions: Determine which of these properties is found in the four quadrilaterals listed. Mark "Y" or "N" in each box.

	Parallelogram	Rectangle	Rhombus	Square
Diagonals bisect each other.				
Diagonals are congruent.				
Each diagonal bisects a pair of opposite angles.				
Diagonals form two pairs of congruent triangles.				
Diagonals form four congruent triangles.				
Diagonals are perpendicular to each other.				

As a teaching activity, SFA is easily suited to before- or after-reading instructional routines. If you used it before reading to activate what students know about words, recognize that they can return to the SFA after reading to clarify and reformulate some of their initial responses on the SFA grid.

Categorization Activities

Vocabulary extension exercises involving categorization require students to determine relationships among technical terms much as word sorts do. Students are usually given four to six words per grouping and asked to do something with them. That something depends on the format used in the exercise. For example, you can give students sets of words and ask them to circle in each set the word that includes the others. This exercise demands that students perceive common attributes or examples in relation to a more inclusive concept and to distinguish superordinate from subordinate terms. Following is an example from an eighth-grade social studies class.

Directions: Circle the word in each group that includes the others.

1. government
   council
   judges
   governor

2. throne
   coronation
   crown
   church

A variation on this format directs students to cross out the word that does not belong and then to explain in a word or phrase the relationship that exists among the common items, as illustrated in the following example.

Directions: Cross out the word in each set that does not belong. On the line above the set, write the word or phrase that explains the relationship among the remaining three words.

1. _____
   drama
   comedy
   epic
   tragedy

2. _____
   time
   character
   place
   action

Concept Circles

One of the most versatile activities we have observed at a wide range of grade levels is the concept circle. Concept circles provide still another format and opportunity for studying words critically—for students to relate words conceptually to one another. A concept circle may simply involve putting words or phrases in the sections of a circle and directing students to describe or name the concept relationship among the sections. The example in Figure 8.10 is from a middle grade science lesson.

In addition, you might direct students to shade in the section of a concept circle containing a word or phrase that *does not relate* to the words or phrases in the other sections of the circle and then identify the concept relationships that exist among the remaining sections (see Figure 8.11).

Finally, you can modify a concept circle by leaving one or two sections of the circle empty, as in Figure 8.12. Direct students to fill in the empty section with a word or two that relates in some way to the terms in the other sections of the concept circles. Students must then justify their word choice by identifying the overarching concept depicted by the circle.

As you can see, concept circles serve the same function as categorization activities. However, students respond positively to the visual aspect of manipulating the sections in a circle. Whereas categorization exercises sometimes seem like tests to students, concept circles are fun to do.

Context- and Definition-Related Activities

Artley (1975) captured the role that context plays in vocabulary learning: "It is the context in which the word is embedded rather than the dictionary that gives

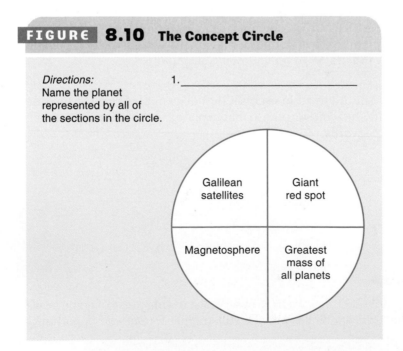

FIGURE **8.10** **The Concept Circle**

Directions:
Name the planet represented by all of the sections in the circle.

1._____

- Galilean satellites
- Giant red spot
- Magnetosphere
- Greatest mass of all planets

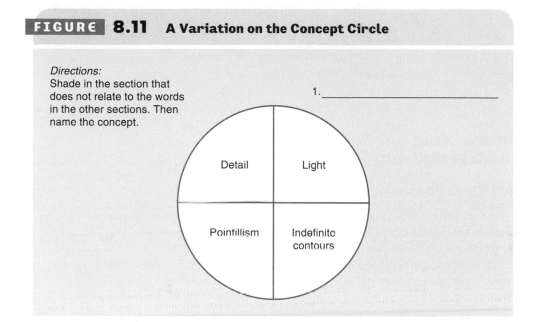

FIGURE **8.11**   **A Variation on the Concept Circle**

Directions:
Shade in the section that does not relate to the words in the other sections. Then name the concept.

1._____

Detail | Light

Pointillism | Indefinite contours

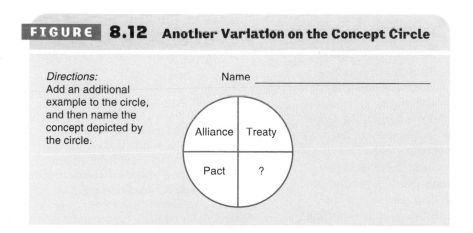

FIGURE **8.12**   **Another Variation on the Concept Circle**

Directions:
Add an additional example to the circle, and then name the concept depicted by the circle.

Name _____

Alliance | Treaty

Pact | ?

it its unique flavor" (p. 1072). Readers who build and use contextual knowledge are able to recognize fine shades of meaning in the way words are used. They know the concept behind the word well enough to use that concept in different contexts.

In Chapter 4, we explored the role of context clues in helping English language learners and struggling readers to figure out the meanings of unknown words that they encounter in text. In addition to context clues, struggling readers and English language learners will find context-related activities, such as those described in Box 8.3, particularly helpful.

BOX 8.3

What about . . .
ELL and Struggling Readers?

Modified Cloze Passages and OPIN

Students who struggle with text or have limited English proficiency may benefit from context-related activities. Two such activities, modified cloze passages and OPIN, help students make meaning around keywords in a text.

MODIFIED CLOZE PASSAGES

Cloze passages (discussed in Chapter 2) can be created to reinforce technical vocabulary. However, the teacher usually modifies the procedure for teaching purposes. Every *n*th word, for example, needn't be deleted. The modified cloze passage will vary in length. Typically, a 200- to 500-word text segment yields sufficient technical vocabulary to make the activity worthwhile.

Should you consider developing a modified cloze passage on a segment of text from a reading assignment, make sure that the text passage is one of the most important parts of the assignment. Depending on your objectives, students can supply the missing words either before or after reading the entire assignment. If they work on the cloze activity before reading, use the subsequent discussion to build meaning for key terms and to raise expectations for the assignment as a whole. If you assign the cloze passage after reading, it will reinforce concepts attained through reading.

On completing a brief prereading discussion on the causes of the Civil War, an American history teacher assigned a cloze passage before students read the entire introduction for homework. See how well you fare on the first part of the exercise.

What caused the Civil War? Was it inevitable? To what extent and in what ways was slavery to blame? To what extent was each region of the nation at fault? Which were more decisive—the intellectual or the emotional issues?

Any consideration of the (1) of the war must include the problem of (2). In his second inaugural address, Abraham Lincoln said that slavery was "somehow the cause of the war." The critical word is "(3)." Some (4) maintain that the moral issue had to be solved, the nation had to face the (5), and the slaves had to be (6). Another group of historians asserts that the war was not fought over (7). In their view, slavery served as an (8) focal point for more fundamental (9) involving two different (10) of the Constitution. All of these views have merit, but no single view has won unanimous support.

(Answers can be found at the end of this chapter on page 292.)

Magic Squares

The magic square activity is by no means new or novel, yet it has a way of reviving even the most mundane matching exercise. We have seen the magic square used successfully in elementary and secondary grades as well as in graduate courses. Here's how a magic square works. An activity sheet has two columns, one for content area terms and one for definitions or other distinguishing statements

OPIN

OPIN provides another example of context-based reinforcement and extension. *OPIN* stands for *opinion* and also plays on the term *cloze*.

Here's how OPIN works. Divide the class into groups of three. Distribute exercise sentences, one to each student. Each student must complete each exercise sentence individually. Then each group member must convince the other two members that his or her word choice is the best. If no agreement is reached on the best word for each sentence, each member of the group can speak to the class for his or her individual choice. When all groups have finished, have the class discuss each group's choices. The only rule of discussion is that each choice must be accompanied by a reasonable defense or justification. Answers such as "Because ours is best" are not acceptable.

OPIN exercise sentences can be constructed for any content area. Here are sample sentences from science, social studies, and family and consumer studies:

SCIENCE

1. A plant's _____ go into the soil.
2. The earth gets heat and _____ from the sun.
3. Some animals, such as birds and _____, are nibblers.

SOCIAL STUDIES

1. We cannot talk about _____ in America without discussing the welfare system.
2. The thought of _____ or revolution would be necessary because property owners would fight to hold on to their land.
3. Charts and graphs are used to _____ information.

FAMILY AND CONSUMER STUDIES

1. Vitamin C is _____ from the small intestine and circulates to every tissue.
2. Washing time for cottons and linens is eight to ten minutes unless the clothes are badly _____.

(Answers can be found at the end of the chapter on page 292.)

OPIN encourages differing opinions about which word should be inserted in a blank space. In one sense, the exercise is open to discussion, and as a result, it reinforces the role of prior knowledge and experiences in the decisions that each group makes. The opportunity to "argue" one's responses in the group leads not only to continued motivation but also to a discussion of word meanings and variations.

such as characteristics or examples (see Figure 8.13). Direct students to match terms with definitions. In doing so, they must take into account the letters signaling the terms and the numbers signaling the definitions. The students then put the number of a definition in the proper space (denoted by the letter of the term) in the "magic square answer box." If their matchups are correct, they will form a magic square. That is, the numerical total will be the same for each row across and

---

FIGURE 8.13 Magic Square on Care of Clothing

Directions: Select the best answer for each of the laundering terms from the numbered definitions. Put the number in the proper space in the magic square box. If the totals of the numbers are the same both across and down, you have found the magic number!

Terms

A. Durable press
B. Soil release
C. Water repellent
D. Flame retardant
E. Knitted fabrics
F. Simulated suede leather
G. Pretreating
H. Sorting
I. Care labeling

Definitions

1. Federal Trade Commission ruling that requires permanently attached fabric care instructions.
2. Fabric must maintain finish for up to fifty machine washings.
3. Ability to protect against redeposition of soil on fabrics.
4. Turn inside out to avoid snags.
5. Resists stains, rain, and dampness.
6. Special treatment of spots and stains before washing.
7. Resists wrinkling during wear and laundering.
8. Separate clothes into suitable washloads.
9. Washable suedelike fabric made from polyester.

Answer Box

A	B	C
D	E	F
G	H	I

Magic number = _____

each column down the answer box. This total forms the puzzle's "magic number." Students need to add up the rows and columns to check if they're coming up with the same number each time. If not, they should go back to the terms and definitions to reevaluate their answers.

The magic square exercise in Figure 8.13 is from a family and consumer studies class. Try it. Its magic number is 15. Analyze the mental maneuvers that you went through to determine the correct number combinations. In some cases, you undoubtedly knew the answers outright. You may have made several educated guesses on others. Did you try to beat the number system? Imagine the possibilities for small-group interaction.

Many teachers are intrigued by the possibilities offered by the magic square, but they remain wary of its construction: "I can't spend hours figuring out number combinations." This is a legitimate concern. Luckily, the eight combinations in Figure 8.14 make magic square activities easy to construct. You can generate many more combinations from the eight patterns simply by rearranging rows or columns (see Figure 8.15).

Notice that the single asterisk in Figure 8.14 denotes the number of foils needed so that several of the combinations can be completed. For example, the

FIGURE 8.14 **A Model of Magic Square Combinations**

7	3	5
2	4	9
6	8	1

0^* 15^{**}

10	8	6
2	9	13
12	7	5

4^* 24^{**}

7	11	8
10	12	4
9	3	14

5^* 26^{**}

9	2	7
4	6	8
5	10	3

1^* 18^{**}

9	7	5
1	8	12
11	6	4

3^* 21^{**}

16	2	3	13
5	11	10	8
9	7	6	12
4	14	15	1

0^* 34^{**}

19	2	15	23	6
25	8	16	4	12
1	14	22	10	18
7	20	3	11	24
13	21	9	17	5

0^* 65^{**}

2	7	18	12
8	5	11	15
13	17	6	3
16	10	4	9

0^* 39^{**}

* Foils needed in answer column
** Magic number

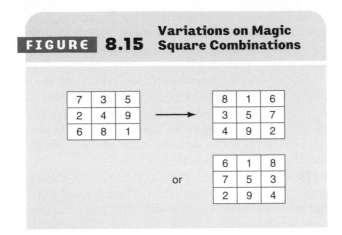

FIGURE 8.15   Variations on Magic Square Combinations

magic number combination of 18 requires one foil in the number 1 slot that will not match with any of the corresponding items in the matching exercise. To complete the combination, the number 10 is added. Therefore, when you develop a matching activity for combination 18, there will be ten items in one column and nine in the other, with item 1 being the foil.

◀ Looking Back
Looking Forward ▶

A strong relationship exists between vocabulary knowledge and reading comprehension. In this chapter, we provided numerous examples of what it means to teach words well: giving students multiple opportunities to build vocabulary knowledge, to learn how words are conceptually related to one another, and to learn how they are defined contextually in the material that students are studying. Vocabulary activities provide students the multiple experiences they need to use and manipulate words in different situations. Conceptual and definitional activities provide the framework needed to study words critically. Various types of concept extension activities, such as semantic feature analysis, semantic maps, concept of definition, word sorts, categories, concept circles, word puzzles, and magic squares, reinforce and extend students' abilities to perceive relationships among the words they are studying.

In the next chapter, our emphasis turns to kindling student interest in text assignments and preparing them to think positively about what they will read. The importance of the role of prereading preparation in learning from text has often been neglected or underestimated in the content area classroom. Yet prereading activity is in many ways as important to the text learner as warm-up preparation is to the athlete. Let's find out why.

Minds On

1. A few of your students come to you and ask why they aren't using dictionaries to help them learn vocabulary words as they did last year. What is your response? Justify your response.

2. Each of the following statements should be randomly assigned to members of your group. Your task with your drawn statement is to play the "devil's advocate." Imagine that you are in a conference with other teachers, all of whom have the same child in their classes. One member of the teaching team, represented by the other members of your discussion group, makes the statement you've selected, and you totally disagree. Argue to these teachers why you believe this statement is false. Members of the teaching team must respond with counterarguments, using classroom examples for support whenever possible.

   a. Students who are interested and enthusiastic are more likely to learn the vocabulary of a content area subject.

   b. Students need to know how to inquire into the meanings of unknown words by using context analysis and dictionary skills.

   c. An atmosphere for vocabulary reinforcement is created by activities involving speaking, listening, writing, and reading.

   d. Vocabulary reinforcement provides opportunities for students to increase their knowledge of the technical vocabulary of a subject.

   e. Vocabulary taught and reinforced within the framework of concept development enhances reading comprehension.

   f. Vocabulary knowledge and reading comprehension have a strong relationship.

   Were there any statements that you had difficulty defending? If so, pose these to the class as a whole, and solicit perspectives from other groups.

3. Your principal notices that your history class spends a lot of time working in pairs and groups on vocabulary, and she doesn't understand why this is necessary "just to learn words." As a group, compose a letter to her explaining the importance of student interaction in learning the vocabulary of any content area.

Hands On

1. The class should be organized into four groups. Two groups will represent alien life forms, and two will represent human beings. Each group meets for fifteen to twenty

minutes. Working separately, each alien group will create five or six statements in their own "alien" language. The humans will organize strategies for decoding the messages they will receive.

After the time has elapsed, each alien group meets with a human group, and the aliens make their statements. If possible, the aliens will attempt to respond to the humans' questions with keywords or phrases. Next, with the alien and human groups switched, the process is repeated. Finally, as a whole class, discuss your success or lack of success in translating in relation to what you have learned about vocabulary and concepts.

2. Examine the following list of vocabulary words taken from this chapter:

general vocabulary

technical vocabulary

special vocabulary

concept

word sorts (open, closed)

brainstorming

semantic word maps

knowledge ratings

syntactic and semantic contextual aids

semantic feature analysis

freewriting

modified cloze passages

context

comprehension

conceptual level

concept circles

OPIN

word puzzles

magic squares

prior knowledge

target concept

cognitive operations

joining

excluding

selecting

implying

Team with three other members of the class, and with this list of words, each create one of the following:

a. Two conceptually related activities, such as a set of concept circles and a closed word sort

b. A context activity that presents the key concept words in meaningful sentence contexts

c. A semantic word map or a semantic feature analysis

Follow this activity with a discussion of the advantages and disadvantages of each approach and of the appropriate time during a unit to use each.

Answers to cloze passage
1. causes, 2. slavery, 3. somehow, 4. historians, 5. crisis, 6. freed, 7. slavery, 8. emotional, 9. issues, 10. interpretations.

Possible answers to OPIN exercises
Science: 1. roots, 2. radiation, 3. rodents; Social Studies: 1. poverty, 2. violence, 3. organize; Family and Consumer Studies: 1. absorbed, 2. soiled.

e.Resources extra

- Go to Chapter 8 of the Companion Website (**www.ablongman.com/vacca8e**) and click on Activities to complete the following task:

    The following site allows users to create all sorts of word puzzles: **http://puzzlemaker.com/**. Design a puzzle based on vocabulary words from a chapter of a content area text.

- Go to the Companion Website (**www. ablongman.com/vacca8e**) for suggested readings, interactive activities, multiple-choice questions, and additional Web links to help you learn more about developing vocabulary knowledge and concepts.

expect the world®

The New York Times
nytimes.com

Themes of the Times

Extend your knowledge of the concepts discussed in this chapter by reading current and historical articles from the *New York Times*. Go to the Companion Website and click on eThemes of the Times.

chapter 9

Activating Prior Knowledge and Interest

When the student is ready,
the teacher appears.
—ANONYMOUS

Content area teachers are perplexed on occasion by the behaviors of learners who are capable of acquiring content through lecture and discussion but appear neither ready nor willing to learn with text. The wisdom in the saying, "When the student is ready, the teacher appears," is self-evident, yet teachers who want students to use text often find themselves wondering, "When will my students be ready?"

Certainly, preparing students for the vocabulary of a content area, as we discussed in Chapter 6, readies them

Activating prior knowledge and generating interest create an instructional context in which students will read with purpose and anticipation.

for learning with texts. The more learners connect what they know to the vocabulary of a content area, the more familiar and confident they are likely to be with the text being studied. To be ready is a state of mind, a mental

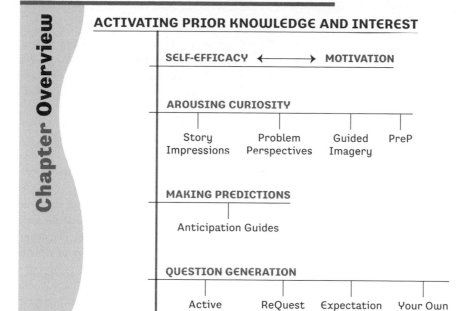

ACTIVATING PRIOR KNOWLEDGE AND INTEREST

SELF-EFFICACY ←——→ MOTIVATION

AROUSING CURIOSITY

Story Impressions Problem Perspectives Guided Imagery PreP

MAKING PREDICTIONS

Anticipation Guides

QUESTION GENERATION

Active Comprehension ReQuest Expectation Outlines Your Own Questions

preparation for learning, a psychological predisposition. But readiness also entails an emotional stake in the ideas under scrutiny and a willingness on the part of the students to *want* to engage in learning. Most students, we believe, would like to use reading to learn but don't believe that they have much chance of success.

Students *will* want to read when they have developed a sense of confidence in their ability to use reading to learn. As Virgil, the ancient Roman poet, mused, "They can because they think they can." All things are within the realm of human possibility, including learning with text, when readers have confidence in their ability to succeed. Confident readers connect what they already know to what they are reading. They generate interest in the reading task at hand, even when the text is inherently dry or difficult. Preparing students to think positively about what they will read is implicit in the organizing principle for this chapter: **Activating prior knowledge and generating interest create an instructional context in which students will read with purpose and anticipation.**

Frame of Mind

1. Why do prereading strategies that activate prior knowledge and raise interest in the subject prepare students to approach text reading in a critical frame of mind?

2. How can meaningful learning be achieved with content area reading?

3. What are the relationships among curiosity arousal, conceptual conflict, and motivation?

4. How and why does a prediction strategy such as use of an anticipation guide facilitate reading comprehension?

5. What is the value of student-generated questions, and how might teachers help students ask questions as they read?

Explanations of reading tend to be complex. Yet as intricate a process as reading may be, it's surely just as mysterious to most of us. After all, who ever really knows a covert process—one that takes place in the head?

Huey (1908) tells a fascinating tale about the adventurer David Livingstone in Africa:

> Livingstone excited the wonder and awe of an African tribe as he daily perused a book that had survived the vicissitudes of travel. So incomprehensible, to these savages, was his performance with the book, that they finally stole it and *ate* it, as the best way they knew of "reading" it, of getting the white man's satisfaction from it. (p. 2)

The preliterate natives wanted what Livingstone had. They were so motivated by his sense of pleasure and satisfaction with texts that they wanted to exercise some control over the rather mysterious process of which they had little concept. Eating Livingstone's book was a somewhat magical response to their uncertainty and lack of control over the process that we call reading. Teachers should be so fortunate as to have students who want to devour texts, metaphorically speaking, in the pursuit of knowledge!

Magic and uncertainty go hand in hand. According to Malinowski (1954), people resort to magic in situations where they feel they have limited control over the success of their activities. This is so in primitive cultures or in highly technological societies such as ours.

We believe an element of mystery will always be a part of reading, even though

it appears to be automatic and second nature to many of us. For most teachers, reading just happens, particularly when there is a strong purpose or a need to read in the first place. However, a great deal of uncertainty pervades reading for many students. The reading process remains a mystery to students who believe they have limited control over their chances of success with a reading assignment.

You can do a great deal to reduce the lack of control and the uncertainty that students bring to text learning situations. You can take the mystery out of learning with texts by generating students' interest in what they are reading, convincing them that they know more about the subject under study than they think they do, helping them actively connect what they do know to the content of the text, and making them aware of the strategies they need in order to construct meaning.

The challenge content area teachers face with reading to learn is not necessarily related to students' inability to handle the conceptual demands of academic texts. What students can do and what they choose to do are related but different instructional matters. Therefore, you need to create conditions that not only allow students to read effectively but also motivate them to want to read purposefully and meaningfully.

Self-Efficacy and Motivation

When students engage in content literacy activities, some feel confident in their ability to achieve success with reading and writing tasks. Others feel unsure and uncertain. Confident learners exhibit a high level of *self-efficacy* in content literacy situations; unsure learners, a low level. Self-efficacy refers to an "I can" belief in self that leads to a sense of competence. Bandura (1986) explains that self-efficacy refers to "people's judgment of their abilities to organize and execute courses of action required to attain designated types of performance (p. 391)." Self-efficacy is not as concerned with the skills and strategies students bring to content literacy situations as with their estimations of what they can do with whatever skills and strategies they do bring to learning situations requiring literacy.

Self-efficacy and motivation are interrelated concepts. If students believe, for example, that they have a good chance to succeed at a reading task, they are likely to exhibit a willingness to engage in reading and to complete the task. Guthrie and Wigfield's (2000) model of reading engagement calls for instruction that not only underscores the importance of students' growth in conceptual knowledge, their use of comprehension strategies, and social interaction in the classroom but also student motivation. Bruner (1970), a pioneer in the field of cognitive psychology, suggested that the mind doesn't work apart from feeling and commitment. The learner makes meaning when he or she exhibits an "inherent passion" for what is to be learned. That is to say, *if* knowledge is to be constructed, it must be put into a context of action and commitment. Willingness is the key; action, the instrument for learning.

In his book *Acts of Meaning*, Bruner (1990) champions a renewed cognitive revolution that is sensitive to meaning-making

> **Response Journal**
>
> Think about your own self-efficacy as a learner. In which subject, if any, in your academic background have you judged yourself unable to succeed? How has low self-efficacy in the subject affected academic performance?

> **e.Resources**
>
> Find out more about self-efficacy and motivation by going to Web Destinations on the Companion Website, clicking on Professional Resources, and selecting "Motivation."

What about . . .
Content Standards and Assessment?

BOX 9.1

The prior knowledge and experience that students bring to any learning situation is one of the most important conditions underlying reading comprehension and learning in general. For example, in the document, *Principles and Standards for School Mathematics,* the role of prior knowledge and experience in learning mathematics is underscored (National Council of Teachers of Mathematics [NCTM] 2000). The NCTM principles and standards document acknowledges that students bring a considerable base on which to build mathematical concepts and skills. Although some of the text comprehension questions in statewide proficiency assessments take into account students' use of prior knowledge, authentic classroom assessment/instructional strategies are needed for teachers to make effective instructional decisions and to plan literacy experiences accordingly. The PreP strategy is an excellent way to assess students' prior knowledge in any type of teaching situation requiring text.

Brainstorming is a key feature of the pre-reading plan (PreP), which may be used to es-timate the levels of background knowledge that students bring to the text assignments.

Before beginning the PreP activity, the teacher should examine the text material for keywords (which represent major concepts to be developed), phrases, or pictures and then introduce the topic that is to be read, following the three-phase plan outlined by Langer (1981, p. 154):

1. *Initial associations with the concept.* In this first phase the teacher says, "Tell anything that comes to mind when . . ." (e.g., ". . . you hear the word *Congress*"). As each student tells what ideas initially came to mind, the teacher jots each response on the board. During this phase, the students have their first opportunity to find associations between the key concept and their prior knowledge. When this activity was carried out in a middle school class, one student, Bill, said, "Important people." Another student, Danette, said, "Washington, D.C."

within a cultural context. How people construct meaning depends on their be-liefs, mental states, intentions, desires, and commitments. Likewise, Eisner (1991) calls us to celebrate thinking in schools by reminding us that brains may be born, but minds are made. Schools do not pay enough attention to students' curiosity and imagination. As a result, students disengage from active participation in the academic life of the classroom because there is little satisfaction to be gained from it. Unless the student receives satisfaction from schoolwork, Eisner argues, there is little reason or motive to continue to pursue learning: "Thinking . . . should be prized not only because it leads to attractive destinations but because the jour-ney itself is satisfying" (p. 40).

In exploring matters of the mind, cognitive activity cannot be divorced from emotional involvement. Meaningful learning with texts occurs when students reap satisfaction from texts and a sense of accomplishment.

Two of the most appropriate questions that students can ask about a text are "What do I need to know?" and "How well do I already know it?" "What do I need

2. *Reflections on initial associations.* During the second phase of PreP, the students are asked, "What made you think of . . . [the response given by a student]?" This phase helps the students develop awareness of their network of associations. They also have an opportunity to listen to each other's explanations, to interact, and to become aware of their changing ideas. Through this procedure, they may weigh, reject, accept, revise, and integrate some of the ideas that came to mind. When Bill was asked what made him think of important people, he said, "I saw them in the newspaper." When Danette was asked what made her think of Washington, D.C., she said, "Congress takes place there."

3. *Reformulation of knowledge.* In this phase, the teacher says, "Based on our discussion and before we read the text, have you any new ideas about . . . [e.g., Congress]?" This phase allows students to verbalize associations that have been elaborated or changed through the discussion. Be-cause they have had a chance to probe their memories to elaborate on their prior knowledge, the responses elicited during the third phase are often more refined than those from the first. This time, Bill said, "Lawmakers of America," and Danette said, "U.S. government part that makes the laws."

Through observation and listening during PreP, content area teachers will find their students' knowledge can be divided into three broad levels. On one level are students who have *much* prior knowledge about the concept. These students are often able to define and draw analogies, make conceptual links, and think categorically. On the second level are students who may have *some* prior knowledge. These students can give examples and cite characteristics of the content but may be unable to see relationships or make connections between what they know and the new material. On the third level are students who have *little* background knowledge. They often respond to the PreP activity by making simple associations, often misassociating with the topic.

to know?" prompts readers to activate their prior knowledge to make predictions and set purposes. It gets them thinking positively about what they are going to read. "How well do I already know it?" helps readers search their experience and knowledge to give support to tentative predictions and to help make plans for reading.

As simple as these two questions may seem on the surface, maturing readers rarely *know enough* about the reading process to ask them. "What do I need to know?" and "How well do I already know it?" require *metacognitive awareness* on the part of learners. However, these two questions, when consciously raised and reflected on, put students on the road to regulating and monitoring their own reading behavior. It is never too early (or too late) to begin showing students how to set purposes by raising questions about the text.

In Chapter 1, we underscored the important role that prior knowledge plays in meaningful learning, so we won't belabor the point here, other than to reaffirm that prior knowledge activation is inescapably bound to one's purposes for reading and learning. As students ready themselves to learn with texts, they need to approach upcoming material in a critical frame of mind for potentially meaningful but new material that they will encounter while reading. Instructional scaffolding should make readers receptive to meaningful learning by creating a reference point for connecting the given (what one knows) with the new (the material to be learned). A frame of reference signals the connections students must make between the given and the new. They need to recognize how new material fits into the conceptual frameworks they already have.

Conceptual conflicts are the key to creating motivational conditions in the classroom (Berlyne 1965). Should students be presented with situations that take the form of puzzlement, doubt, surprise, perplexity, contradiction, or ambiguity, they will be motivated to seek resolution. Why? The need within the learner is to resolve the conflict. As a result, the search for knowledge becomes a driving motivational force. When a question begins to gnaw at a learner, searching behavior is stimulated; learning occurs as the conceptual conflict resolves itself.

Arousing Curiosity

Arousing curiosity and activating prior knowledge are closely related instructional activities. Curiosity arousal gives students the chance to consider what they know already about the material to be read. Through your guidance, they are encouraged to make connections and to relate their knowledge to the text assignment. And further, they will recognize that there are problems—conceptual conflicts—to be resolved through reading. Arousing curiosity helps students raise questions that they can answer only by giving thought to what they read.

Creating Story Impressions

Story impressions is an instructional strategy that arouses curiosity and allows students to anticipate story content. Although teachers use story impressions with narrative text, it may also be used to create "text impressions" in content areas other than English language arts.

Story impressions uses clue words associated with the setting, characters, and events in the story to help readers write their own versions of the story prior to reading. McGinley and Denner (1987), originators of the strategy, describe it this way: "Story impressions get readers to predict the events of the story that will be read, by providing them with fragments of the actual content. After reading the set of clues, the students are asked to render them comprehensible by using them to compose a story of their own in advance of reading the actual tale" (p. 249).

Fragments from the story, in the form of clue words and phrases enable readers to form an overall impression of how the characters and events interact in the story. The clue words are selected directly from the story and are sequenced with arrows or lines to form a descriptive chain. The chain of clue words triggers impressions about the story. Students then write a "story prediction" that anticipates the events in the story.

Response Journal
How might you adapt story impressions to a content area other than English or history?

Study the story impressions example in Figure 9.1. It is based on *The Wretched Stone* by Chris Van Allsburg. The book was used as a read-aloud to introduce middle-level learners to a unit on "supernatural happenings."

FIGURE **9.1**   **Story Impression for *The Wretched Stone***

Story Chain	Story Prediction
harbor ↓ voyage ↓ crew ↓ books, instruments ↓ adventure ↓ island, water, fruit ↓ strange ↓ textured, glowing ↓ heavy, aboard ↓ fascinated, peculiar ↓ stone ↓ clumsy ↓ shrieks, fever ↓ deserted, locked ↓ danger, storm ↓ horrifying, beasts ↓ doomed ↓ lightning ↓ rescue, discovery, alert ↓ normal	A ship's crew left the harbor ~~for their~~ on a voyage. Some of the crew brought along books and instruments ~~to make it though the~~ for While sailing across the ocean, long journey. They discovered an island with strange water and fruit. They drank the water and ate the fruit. One of the crew members found a glowing stone and took it with him to the ship. They set sail, and every time the stone would glow they heard shrieks and saw horrifying beasts. The crew was doomed. Then a terrible storm hit the ship. The stone stopped glowing and everything went back to normal.

McGinley and Denner (1987) explain. "The object, of course, is not for the student to guess the details or the exact relations among the events and characters of the story, but to simply compare his or her own story guess to the author's actual account" (p. 250). Research-Based Best Practice Box 9.2 outlines the steps to follow in the story impression strategy.

Notice in Figure 9.2 how a U.S. history teacher adapted story impressions to have students predict events leading up to the Boston Tea Party. In the space provided for a "text prediction," try writing what you think the text will be about. Compare your prediction with the one appearing on page 317.

Establishing Problematic Perspectives

Creating problems to be solved or perspectives from which readers approach text material provides an imaginative entry into a text selection. For example, the

RESEARCH-BASED BEST PRACTICES

BOX 9.2

Story Impressions

McGinley and Denner (1987) suggest the following steps to introduce story impressions to the class for the first time:

1. *Introduce the strategy.* Say to the students, "Today we're going to make up what we think this story *could* be about."

2. *Use large newsprint, a transparency, or a chalkboard to show students the story chain.* (See the left side of Figure 9.1 for an example.) Say, "Here are some clues about the story we're going to read." Explain that the students will use the clues to write their own version of the story and that after reading, they will compare what they wrote with the actual story.

3. *Read the clues together, and explain how the arrows link one clue to another in a logical order.* Then brainstorm story ideas that connect all of the clues in the

order that they are presented saying, "What do we think this story could be about?"

4. *Demonstrate how to write a story guess.* Use the ideas generated to write a class-composed story that links all of the clues. Use newsprint, the chalkboard, or a transparency for this purpose. Read the story prediction aloud with the students.

5. *Invite the students to read the actual story silently, or initiate a shared reading experience.* Afterward, discuss how the class-composed version is similar to and different from the author's story.

6. *For subsequent stories, use story impressions to have students write individual story predictions.* Or have them work in cooperative teams to write a group-composed story guess.

> **FIGURE 9.2**   **Chain of Events Leading to the Boston Tea Party**

Chain of Events	Text Prediction
French and Indian War ↓ Stamp Act ↓ rights ↓ took away ↓ Parliament ↓ petitions ↓ repeal ↓ Sons of Liberty ↓ Townshend Acts ↓ boycott ↓ repeal ↓ tea tax ↓ Mohawk Indians ↓ Boston Tea Party	

teacher's role in creating problematic perspectives is (1) providing the time to discuss the problem, raising questions, and seeking possible solutions before reading and then (2) assigning the reading material that will help lead to resolution and conceptual development.

A social studies teacher and her students were exploring the development of early American settlements in a unit on colonial life. She presented the problem situation to her students as shown in Figure 9.3. The series of questions promoted an interest-filled discussion, putting students in a situation in which they had to rely on prior knowledge for responses.

Asking the students in the social studies class to approach reading by imagining that they were early European settlers placed them in a particular role. With the role came a perspective. Creating such a perspective has its underpinnings in a schema-theoretical view of the reading process.

FIGURE **9.3**   **A Problem Situation in a U.S. History Class**

The time is 1680, and the place is Massachusetts. Imagine that you are early European settlers. You will want to try to think as you believe they may have thought and act as they might have acted. You and your group have petitioned the Great and General Court to be allowed to form a new town. After checking to make sure you are of good character and the land is fertile and can be defended, the court says yes. It grants you a five-mile-square plot of land. As proprietors of this land, you must plan a town. What buildings would you put in first? Second? Third? Later? Why? How would you divide the land among the many people who want to live there? Why? As proprietors, would you treat yourselves differently from the others? Why? How would you run the government?

Response Journal

Create a problematic perspective on some topic of study in your content area.

One of the early studies of the Center for the Study of Reading at the University of Illinois pointed to the powerful role of perspective in comprehending text (Pichert & Anderson 1977). The researchers showed just how important the reader's perspective can be. Two groups of readers were asked to read a passage about a house from one of two perspectives: a burglar or a house buyer. When readers who held the perspective of a house burglar read the story about going through the house, they recalled different information from those readers who approached the story from the perspective of a house buyer.

Creating a perspective (a role) for the student is one way to get into reading. Students in these roles find themselves solving problems that force them to use their knowledge and experience.

In Figure 9.4, a high school teacher created a perspective for students before assigning a reading selection from an auto mechanics manual.

In preparation for reading the short story "Alas Babylon," an English teacher set up a perspective in which students' curiosity was aroused and their expectations of the story raised:

> The year is 2015. We are on the verge of a nuclear disaster. Through inside sources, you hear that the attack will occur within five days. What preparations will you consider making before the nuclear attack occurs?

The class considered the orienting question. After some discussion, the teacher initiated the activity in Figure 9.5. The students formed small groups, and each group was directed to come to a consensus on the twelve activities they would choose. Those items were chosen from the list in Figure 9.5.

From the small-group discussions came the recognition that the values, beliefs, and attitudes readers bring to a text shape their perspective as much as their background knowledge of a topic. For this reason, we suggest that building the

FIGURE 9.4 **Creating a Perspective in an Auto Mechanics Class**

You are the only mechanic on duty when a four-wheel-drive truck with a V-8 engine pulls in for repair. The truck has high mileage, and it appears that the problem may be a worn clutch disk. What tools do you think you will need? What procedures would you follow? Put your answers to these questions under the two following headings.

Tools Needed   **Procedures**

_____   _____

_____   _____

_____   _____

_____   _____

FIGURE 9.5 **Creating a Perspective in an English Class**

Assuming that your town and house will not be destroyed by the bomb and that you have enough time to prepare for the attack, which twelve activities from the following list will you choose?

_____ 1. Buy a gun and ammunition to protect against looters.

_____ 2. Cash in all savings bonds and take all the money out of your checking and savings accounts.

_____ 3. Build a fireplace in your house.

_____ 4. Buy firewood and charcoal.

_____ 5. Buy extra tanks of gasoline and fill up your car.

_____ 6. Purchase antibiotics and other medicines.

_____ 7. Dig a latrine.

_____ 8. Buy lumber, nails, and various other supplies.

_____ 9. Plant fruit trees.

_____ 10. Notify all your friends and relatives of the coming nuclear attack.

_____ 11. Invest in books on canning and making candles and soap.

_____ 12. Buy a few head of livestock from a farmer.

_____ 13. Buy fishing equipment and a boat.

_____ 14. Buy seeds of several different kinds of vegetables for a garden.

_____ 15. Make friends with a farmer who has a horse and wagon.

_____ 16. Shop at antique stores for kerosene lamps and large cooking pots.

_____ 17. Buy a safe in which to hide your money.

_____ 18. Buy foodstuffs.

motivation for a text to be read take into account, where appropriate, an examination of values, attitudes, and controversial issues related to the subject matter.

Guided Imagery

Guided imagery allows students to explore concepts visually. Samples (1977) recommends guided imagery, among other things, as a means of

- Building an experience base for inquiry, discussion, and group work
- Exploring and stretching concepts
- Solving and clarifying problems
- Exploring history and the future
- Exploring other lands and worlds

Read the example in Figure 9.6; then close your eyes and do what it says.

You may wish to have students discuss their "trips," which, of course, should parallel in some way the content of the reading selection to be assigned. In the classroom where this example was devised, students in a literature class participated in the imagery discussion before reading a short story on space travel. Discussion questions included, "How did you feel just before entering the space capsule? What were the reactions of your companions? Where did your exploration take you? Were there things that surprised you on the trip? Colors? Sounds?"

Some teachers will find themselves uncomfortable using guided imagery as an instructional strategy; others will not. However, it gives you an additional instructional option that will help students connect, in this case, what they "see" in their mind's eye to what they will read.

> **Response Journal**
>
> Create a guided imagery scenario on a topic of study in your content area.

FIGURE 9.6   A Guided Imagery Illustration

Close your eyes . . . tell all your muscles to relax. You are entering a space capsule ten minutes before takeoff. Soon you feel it lift off . . . you look over at your companions and check their reactions. Now you are ready to take a reading of the instrument panel. As you relay the information to ground control, it is eleven minutes into the flight . . . you settle back into your chair and tell your fellow astronauts about your thoughts . . . about what you hope to see when the vehicle lands . . . about what you might touch and hear as you explore your destination. Finally, you drift off to sleep . . . picturing yourself returning to earth . . . seeing once again your friends and relations. You are back where you started . . . tell your muscles to move . . . open your eyes.

Content area teachers assess students' prior knowledge of and interest in a topic to be studied through authentic instructional practices. Box 9.1 describes an instructional strategy, PreP, designed by Langer (1981) to assess students' prior knowledge within an instructional context.

Making Predictions

Prediction strategies activate thought about the content before reading. Students must rely on what they know through previous study and experience to make educated guesses about the material to be read.

Why an educated guess? Smith (1988) defines predicting as the prior elimination of unlikely alternatives. He suggests:

> Readers do not normally attend to print with their minds blank, with no prior purpose and with no expectation of what they might find in the text. . . . The way readers look for meaning is not to consider all possibilities, nor to make reckless guesses about just one, but rather to predict within the most likely range of alternatives. . . . Readers can derive meaning from text because they bring expectations about meaning to text. (p. 163)

You can facilitate student-centered purposes by creating anticipation about the meaning of what will be read.

Anticipation Guides

An anticipation guide is a series of statements to which students must respond individually before reading the text. Their value lies in the discussion that takes place after the exercise. The teacher's role during discussion is to activate and agitate thought. As students connect their knowledge of the world to the prediction task, you must remain open to a wide range of responses. Draw on what students bring to the task, but remain nondirective in order to keep the discussion moving.

Anticipation guides may vary in format but not in purpose. In each case, the readers' expectations about meaning are raised before they read the text. Keep these guidelines in mind in constructing and using an anticipation guide:

1. *Analyze the material to be read.* Determine the major ideas—implicit and explicit—with which students will interact.

2. *Write those ideas in short, clear declarative statements.* These statements should in some way reflect the world in which the students live or about which they know. Therefore, avoid abstractions whenever possible.

3. *Put these statements in a format that will elicit anticipation and prediction.*

4. *Discuss the students' predictions and anticipations before they read the text selection.*

5. *Assign the text selection.* Have the students evaluate the statements in light of the author's intent and purpose.

6. *Contrast the readers' predictions with the author's intended meaning.*

Adapting Anticipation Guides in Content Areas

A middle school social studies teacher prepared students for a reading assignment that contrasted the characteristics of the northern and southern soldiers in the Civil War. She began by writing "Johnny Reb" and "Billy Yank" in separate columns on the chalkboard. She asked students to think about what they already knew about the two soldiers, "How do you think they were alike? How were they different?" After some discussion, the teacher invited the students to participate in the anticipation activity in Figure 9.7.

Of course, each of the points highlighted in the statements was developed in the text selection. Not only did the students get a sense of the major ideas they would encounter in the text selection but they also read to see how well they had

FIGURE 9.7   Anticipation Guide for a Civil War Lesson

Johnny Reb and Billy Yank were common soldiers of the Civil War. You will be reading about some of their basic differences in your textbook. What do you think those differences will be? Before reading your assignment, place the initials JR in front of the phrases that you think best describe Johnny Reb. Place the initials BY in front of the statements that best describe Billy Yank. Do not mark statements common to both.

_____ 1. More likely to be able to read and write

_____ 2. Best able to adjust to living in open areas

_____ 3. More likely to be from a rural setting

_____ 4. More interested in politics

_____ 5. More deeply religious

_____ 6. Often not able to sign his name

_____ 7. More apt to dislike regimentation of army life

_____ 8. More likely to speak slowly

_____ 9. More probably a Native American

_____ 10. More likely to be a common man in the social order predicted which statements more accurately represented soldiers from the South and the North during the Civil War.

A science teacher began a weather unit by introducing a series of popular clichés about the weather. He asked his students to anticipate whether the clichés had a scientific basis (see Figure 9.8).

The before-reading discussion led the students to review and expand their concepts of scientific truth. Throughout different parts of the unit, the teacher returned to one or two of the clichés in the anticipation guide and suggested to the class that the textbook assignment would explain whether there was a scientific basis for each saying. Students were then directed to read to find out what the explanations were.

A health education teacher raised expectations and created anticipation for a chapter on the human immunodeficiency virus (HIV) and AIDS. Rather than prepare written statements, she conducted the anticipatory lesson as part of an introductory class discussion. She raised curiosity about the topic by asking students to participate in a strategy known as the "every-pupil response." She told the students that she would ask several questions about becoming infected with HIV. Every student was to respond to each question by giving a "thumbs up" if they agreed or a "thumbs down" if they disagreed. The class had to participate in unison and keep their thumbs up or down. After each question, the students

---

FIGURE 9.8   Anticipation Guide for Clichés about Weather

Directions: Put a check under "Likely" if you believe that the weather saying has any scientific basis; put a check under "Unlikely" if you believe that it has no scientific basis. Be ready to explain your choice.

Likely   Unlikely

_____   _____   1. Red sky at night, sailors delight; red sky at morning, sailors take warning.

_____   _____   2. If you see a sunspot, there is going to be bad weather.

_____   _____   3. When the leaves turn under, it is going to storm.

_____   _____   4. If you see a hornet's nest high in a tree, a harsh winter is coming.

_____   _____   5. Aching bones mean a cold and rainy forecast.

_____   _____   6. If a groundhog sees his shadow, six more weeks of winter.

_____   _____   7. Rain before seven, sun by eleven.

_____   _____   8. If a cow lies down in a pasture, it is going to rain soon.

_____   _____   9. Sea gull, sea gull, sitting on the sand; it's never good weather while you're on land.

shared their reasons for responding thumbs up or thumbs down. The questions were framed as follows: "Is it true that you can contract HIV by

- Having unprotected sex with an infected partner?"
- Kissing someone with HIV?"
- Sharing needles with an HIV-infected drug user?"
- Sharing a locker with an infected person?"
- Using a telephone after someone with HIV has used it?"
- Being bitten by a mosquito?"

The "oral anticipation guide" created lively discussion as students discussed some of their preconceived notions and misconceptions about HIV and AIDS.

Mathematics teachers also have been successful in their use of anticipation guides. In a precalculus class, the teacher introduced the activity in Figure 9.9 to begin the trigonometry section of the textbook. She created the anticipation guide to help students address their own knowledge about trigonometry and to create

FIGURE **9.9** **Anticipation Guide for Preconceived Notions about Trigonometry**

Directions: Put a check under "Likely" if you believe that the statement has any mathematical truth. Put a check under "Unlikely" if you believe that it has no mathematical truth. Be ready to explain your choices.

Likely   Unlikely

_____   _____ Trigonometry deals with circles.

_____   _____ Angles have little importance in trigonometry.

_____   _____ Sailors use trigonometry in navigation.

_____   _____ Angles can be measured only in degrees.

_____   _____ Calculators are useless in trigonometry.

_____   _____ Trigonometry deals with triangles.

_____   _____ Trigonometry has no application in the real world.

_____   _____ Radians are used in measuring central angles.

_____   _____ Trigonometry has scientific uses.

_____   _____ Radians can be converted to degrees.

conceptual conflict for some of the more difficult sections of the chapter they would be studying.

Question Generation

e.Resources

Find out more about question-generation as a research-based comprehension strategy. Go to Web Destinations on the Companion Website, click on Professional Resources, and look for "Question-Generation."

Teaching students to generate their own questions about material to be read is an important prereading instructional goal. Harry Singer (1978) contends that whenever readers are involved in asking questions, they are engaged in "active comprehension."

Active Comprehension

Teachers can use an active comprehension strategy when they *ask questions that beget questions in return*. You might, for example, focus attention on a picture or an illustration from a story or book and ask a question that induces student questions in response, "What would you like to know about the picture?" In return, invite the students to generate questions that focus on the details in the picture or its overarching message.

Or you might decide to read to students an opening paragraph or two from a text selection, enough to whet their appetites for the selection. Then ask, "What else would you like to know about _____?" Complete the question by focusing attention on some aspect of the selection that is pivotal to students' comprehension. It may be the main character of a story or the main topic of an expository text.

Active comprehension questions not only arouse interest and curiosity but also draw learners into the material. As a result, students will read to satisfy purposes and resolve conceptual conflicts that they have identified through their own questions. Let us examine several additional instructional strategies for engaging students in asking questions for reading.

ReQuest

ReQuest was originally devised as a one-on-one procedure for a remedial instructional context. Yet this strategy can easily be adapted to content area classrooms to help struggling readers think as they read. The strategy also is appropriate for English language learners (see Box 9.3). ReQuest encourages students to ask their own questions about the content material under study. Self-declared questions are forceful. They help students establish reasonable purposes for their reading. Betts (1950) describes a "highly desirable learning situation" as one in which the student does the questioning: "That is, the learner asks the questions, and sets up the problems to be solved during the reading activity" (p. 450).

What about . . .
ELL and Struggling Readers?

BOX 9.3

ReQuest

When ReQuest is used as a small-group or whole-class activity for struggling readers or English language learners, follow these steps:

1. *Both the students and the teacher silently read the same segment of the text.* Manzo (1969) recommends one sentence at a time for students who have trouble comprehending what they read. However, text passages of varying length are suitable in classroom applications. For example, both teacher and students begin by reading a paragraph or two.

2. *The teacher closes the book and is questioned about the passage by the students.*

3. *Next, there is an exchange of roles.* The teacher queries the students about the material.

4. *On completion of the student–teacher exchange, the class and the teacher read the next segment of text.* Steps 2 and 3 are repeated.

5. *Stop questioning and begin predicting.* At a suitable point in the text, when the students have processed enough information to make predictions about the remainder of the assignment, the exchange of questions stops. The teacher then asks prediction questions, "What do you think the rest of the assignment is about? Why do you think so?" Speculation is encouraged.

6. *Students are then assigned the remaining portion of the selection to read silently.*

7. *The teacher facilitates a follow-up discussion of the material.*

ReQuest fosters an active search for meaning. Manzo (1969) describes the rules for ReQuest:

> The purpose of this lesson is to improve your understanding of what you read. We will each read silently the first sentence. Then we will take turns asking questions about the sentence and what it means. You will ask questions first, then I will ask questions. Try to ask the kind of questions a teacher might ask, in the way a teacher might ask them. You may ask me as many questions as you wish. When you are asking me questions, I will close my book (or pass the book to you if there is only one between us). When I ask questions, you close your book. . . . Any question asked deserves to be answered as fully and honestly as possible. It is cheating for a teacher to withhold information or play dumb to draw out the student. It is unacceptable for a student to answer with "I don't know," since he can at least attempt to explain why he cannot answer. If questions are unclear to either party, requests for rephrasing or clarification are in order. The responder should be ready (and make it a practice) to justify his answer by reference back to the text or to expand on background that was used to build or to limit an answer. Whenever possible, if there is uncertainty about an answer, the respondent should check his answer against the text. (pp. 124–125)

Although the steps for ReQuest outlined in Box 9.3 were devised for one-on-one instruction, they can be adapted for the content area classroom where students struggle with texts.

You can modify the ReQuest procedure to good advantage. For example, consider alternating the role of questioner after each question. By doing so, you will probably involve more students in the activity. Once students sense the types of questions that can be asked about a text passage, you might also try forming ReQuest teams. A ReQuest team composed of three or four students can be pitted against another ReQuest team. Your role is to facilitate the multiple actions resulting from the small-group formations.

Our own experiences with ReQuest suggest that students may consistently ask factual questions to stump the teacher or other students. Such questions succeed brilliantly because you are subject to the same restrictions imposed by short-term memory as the students. That you miss an answer or two is actually healthy—after all, to err is human.

However, when students ask only verbatim questions because they don't know how to ask any others, the situation is unhealthy. The sad fact is that some students don't know how to ask questions that will stimulate interpretive or applied levels of thinking. Therefore, your role as a good questioner during ReQuest is to provide a model from which students will learn. Over time, you will notice the difference in the quality of the student questions formulated.

Expectation Outlines

Spiegel (1981) suggests the use of an expectation outline to help students ask questions about text. She recommends the expectation outline for factual material, but the strategy can be adapted to narrative studies as well. The expectation outline is developed on the chalkboard or an overhead projector transparency as students simply tell what they expect to learn from a reading selection.

If students are reading a factual selection, you may have them first take several minutes to preview the material. Then ask, "What do you think your assignment is going to be about?" Ask students to state their expectations in the form of questions. As they suggest questions, group related questions on the chalkboard or transparency. You also have the opportunity to ask students what prompted them to ask these questions in the first place. At this point, students may be encouraged to refer to the text to support their questions.

Once questions have been asked and grouped, the class labels each set of questions. Through discussion, students begin to see the major topics that will emerge from the reading. Help them to recognize that gaps may exist in the expectation outline of the assignment. For example, you may add a topic or two to the outline about which no questions were raised. On completion of the expectation outline, students read to answer the questions generated.

For narrative materials, students may formulate their questions from the title of the selection or pictures or keywords and phrases in the selection. For example, direct students to preview a story by skimming through it quickly, studying the pictures and illustrations (if any), and jotting down five to ten key-words or phrases that appear to indicate the main direction of the story. As students suggest keywords and phrases, write them on the board and categorize them. Then ask students to state what they expect to find out from the story. Have them raise questions about its title, setting, characters, plot, and theme. As an alternative to questions, students may summarize their expectations by writing a paragraph about the story using the keywords and phrases that were jotted down and categorized.

Your Own Questions

A variation on the expectation outline is a strategy called your own questions. Here's how it works:

1. *Have students listen to or read a portion of the text from the beginning of a selection.*

2. *Ask students to write five to ten questions that they think will be answered by the remainder of the selection.*

3. *Discuss some of the questions asked by the students before reading.* Write the questions on the board.

4. *Have students read to determine whether the questions are answered.*

5. *After reading, ask the students to explain which questions were answered, which weren't, and why not.*

e.Resources

For additional readings related to the major ideas in this chapter, go to Chapter 9 of the Companion Website and click on Suggested Readings.

Strategies such as an expectation outline or your own questions teach students how to approach reading material with an inquisitive mind. These instructional strategies and the others presented in this chapter form a bridge between teacher-initiated guidance and independent learning behavior by students.

◀ Looking Back
Looking Forward ▶

Meaningful learning with texts occurs when students experience a sense of satisfaction with text and a feeling of accomplishment. In this chapter, the role that self-efficacy and motivation play in purposeful learning was em-

phasized. Although some students may be skilled in reading and knowledgeable about the subject, they may not bring that skill and knowledge to bear in learning situations. It takes motivation, a sense of direction and purpose, and a teacher who knows how to create conditions in the classroom that allow students to establish their own motives for reading. One way to arouse curiosity about reading material is to encourage students to make connections among the key concepts to be studied. Another is to create conceptual conflict. Students will read to resolve conflicts arising from problem situations and perspectives and will use guided imagery to explore the ideas to be encountered during reading.

To reduce any uncertainty that students bring to reading material, you can help them raise questions and anticipate meaning by showing them how to connect what they already know to the new ideas presented in the text. The questions students raise as a result of predicting will guide them into the reading material and keep them on course. Anticipation guides, ReQuest, expectation outlines, and self-questioning are strategies for stimulating predictions and anticipation about the content.

In the next chapter, we explore ways to guide reader–text interactions in the curriculum. A classroom teacher who encourages reader–text interactions brings learners and texts together to explore and construct meaning.

 # Minds On

1. Suppose you go to the library looking for a good book to read. You see a cart with a sign: "Current Best-Sellers." Because you have little familiarity with any of the books, how will you make a selection? How will you anticipate which book is for you? Because students rarely have the opportunity to select their course textbook, what can teachers do to help students make the book "fit"?

2. Divide your discussion group into two subgroups: individuals who are willing to take the position that all of the following statements are correct and those willing to argue that all of the statements are inaccurate. Discuss the pros and cons of each topic for five minutes. After you have finished, bring any items to the class as a whole that you believe could truly have been defended from either view, and be prepared to explain why or under what circumstances.

   a. Students are not qualified to ask their own questions about difficult content material.

   b. The old but still common practice of assigning reading in preparation for a discussion is, unfortunately, backward.

   c. Just as athletes need to warm up before a contest, readers need to warm up to get ready for text.

   d. Analyzing content vocabulary before reading is a sound instructional practice.

   e. Having students read a variety of materials on the subject matter will only confuse them.

   f. It is pointless to discuss most subjects with students before they read the text, because the varied social and economic backgrounds of the students make it possible for only a few to connect any relevant personal experience to the text subject.

3. Eliot Eisner believes that brains are born but minds are made. What do you believe is the teacher's role in a classroom filled with twenty-five brains waiting to be made into minds? Is the teacher the molder,

shaper, and maker—that is, the only active partner? Is the teacher to serve as a model learner, a guide through knowledge, or a facilitator—that is, an equal or superior partner? Or do you see some happy medium? In your group, attempt to reach a consensus on what you consider the best role for a teacher to be in relation to these prompts.

Hands On

1. Try the following science experiment to activate prior knowledge and to stimulate interest in reading an explanation of the formula, *force equals pressure times area.* Bring the following materials to class: one thirty-gallon garbage bag, duct tape, and a dozen straws. Flatten the trash bag on a table large enough for a volunteer to lie on with his or her upper body resting on the bag. Cut four small holes about nine inches apart along each of the edges of the two sides of the flattened bag that are perpendicular to the open end. Insert one straw in each opening. Next, tape each hole airtight. Tape the open end of the bag airtight as well. Ask a volunteer to lie on his or her back on top of the garbage bag on the table.

   Next, have eight individuals each select one straw, and explain that they will be attempting to lift the volunteer by blowing through the straws into the sealed bag. Before proceeding, however, invite the group to pose questions, draw on their prior knowledge, and anticipate why this experiment may succeed or fail. After the group has theorized about and discussed the problem, mention that the bag will break at a pressure of one pound per square inch, and ask if that fact changes their predictions. Finally, have the eight individuals attempt to inflate the bag by blowing into the straws simultaneously. As they do, be sure that someone stabilizes the volunteer so that he or she does not roll off the bag.

   If the experiment works, the volunteer should rise several inches from the table. Break into small groups of five or six, and imagine that a science instructor has just used this experiment as an introduction to a chapter on the relationship between air pressure, force, and surface area. How motivated are the group members to read this chapter? As a group, discuss how science experiments may be used with anticipation guides, ReQuest, expectation outlines, and graphic organizers.

2. Team with a group of four or five other students. Before the next class, each member should collect three political cartoons, each using a different newspaper, magazine, or book. These cartoons may represent current or historical political issues.

   When you return to class, share the cartoons you found, and discuss the knowledge the reader must already have in order to understand the humor. Select the one cartoon you found most enjoyable, and list the background knowledge needed to understand it. When all groups have finished discussing and selecting, have each group read and explain its favorite cartoon to the whole class. As a large group, discuss how this activity illustrates the concept of prior knowledge when reading text. If there are art majors in the class, ask them to share the role of prior knowledge in viewing works of art.

3. Bring to class a nonfiction book or magazine article on a subject you enjoy. With a partner, practice the ReQuest strategy. On completion of the activity, join with two other pairs, and as a small group, discuss the effectiveness of the questioning, the successfulness of the learning that occurred, and your perceptions of the usefulness of this activity in a content area classroom.

Text prediction (by a student) for story impressions activity in Figure 9.2

Following the French and Indian War, England passed the Stamp Act to recover some of its war debts. Colonists complained that their right to vote on their own taxes had been taken away by Parliament. The Americans wrote petitions asking for the Stamp Act to be repealed. It was. Groups of colonists called the Sons of Liberty formed and carried on some rather rowdy activities. The Stamp Act was replaced by the Townshend Acts. Angry Americans boycotted all taxed products until England once again repealed the taxes—all except the tax on tea. One night a group of colonists, led by the Sons of Liberty, dressed as Mohawk Indians and threw tea overboard into the Boston Harbor. This event was known as the Boston Tea Party

---

e.Resources extra

- Go to Chapter 9 of the Companion Website (**www.ablongman.com/vacca8e**) and click on Activities to complete the following task:

    Select an article from the Teen Newsweek Website: **www.msnbc. com/news/NW-TEENNEWSWEEK_ Front.asp** and develop an anticipation guide. These can be shared in small groups with copies of the stories.

- Go to the Companion Website (**www.ablongman.com/vacca8e**) for suggested readings, interactive activities, multiple-choice questions, and additional Web links to help you learn more about activating prior knowledge and interest.

The New York Times
expect the world®
nytimes.com

Themes of the Times

Extend your knowledge of the concepts discussed in this chapter by reading current and historical articles from the *New York Times*. Go to the Companion Website and click on eThemes of the Times.

chapter 10

Guiding Reader–Text Interactions

Reading transcends the mere transmission of information. It fosters an imaginative dialogue between the text and the reader's mind that actually helps people to think.

—STRATFORD P. SHERMAN

Organizing Principle

Behind every text is an author—a real person doing real work. Authors work at their craft because they believe that they have something worthwhile to say and reasons for saying it. Some write to entertain, others to inform. Authors like us do the latter. When writers of informational texts talk directly to readers as we're doing now, text linguists have labeled the process *metadiscourse,* a mouthful of a word that describes what a writer does to engage the reader in thinking about the text. Most readers don't consciously think about what a writer does

Teachers guide reader–text interactions through the instructional strategies that they use and the reading guidance that they provide.

to draw them into thoughtful interaction with the text. But an effective writer of informational texts knows that when readers engage in the process, they think about what they are reading. As Stratford Sherman points out in the chapter-

GUIDING READER–TEXT INTERACTIONS

INSTRUCTIONAL STRATEGIES

KWL   Discussion   Guided Reading   Intra-Act
       Webs   Procedure (GRP)

READING GUIDES

Three-Level   Selective
Reading Guides   Reading Guides

opening quote, an imaginative dialogue takes place in the mind.

Students have much to contribute to the learning conversation as they interact with text to extract and construct meaning, but they may not be skillful and strategic enough to do so on their own. In today's diverse classrooms, many students have trouble handling the conceptual demands of potentially difficult texts. How does a content area teacher guide instruction in ways that engage and sustain students in text-related learning, especially if the ideas they encounter during reading are complex and perhaps just beyond their level of knowledge and experiential grasp? As we suggested in the previous chapter, building and activating prior knowledge before, during, and after reading is a critical instructional component of content literacy lessons. In this chapter, we extend the dialogue on instructional practices and strategies as we explore ways to scaffold reader–text interactions. As the organizing principle of this chapter highlights: **Teachers guide reader–text interactions through the instructional strategies that they use and the reading guidance that they provide.**

Frame of Mind

1. Why do the instructional strategies described in this chapter guide reader–text interactions?

2. Describe the procedures associated with each of these instructional strategies: KWL, Guided Reading Procedure (GRP), Intra-Act, and Discussion Web.

3. Why and when should you use reading guides?

4. What is a three-level guide?

5. What is a selective reading guide and how can you use it to model flexible reading behaviors?

6. How can you use and adapt reading guides in your content area?

Although metaphors come and go, one that has been around since the ancient Greeks is as powerful today as it was centuries ago. In Plato's *Theaetetus*, written more than 2,000 years ago, Socrates is asked to explain what it means to think. He responds to his questioner by explaining that when the mind is thinking it is merely talking to itself, asking questions and answering them. Thinking is a conversation. It is a dialogue that you have with yourself in your mind. When a reader engages in a dialogue with text, the conversation metaphor puts an incredibly complex process—reading—into the context of what happens inside the minds of readers.

Response Journal

What is your reaction to Socrates' explanation of what it means to think?

The conversations that take place between readers and texts transcend time and space. Texts make it possible to bring readers and authors together in content area classrooms. There is a catch, however. Thinking with texts requires students to participate actively in the conversation. A conversation works only when participants are involved and interacting with one another. Everyday conversations, for example, involve an exchange of ideas between two or more parties—a give-and-take dialogue—around topics of mutual interest and relevance.

Learning conversations in content area classrooms have similar characteristics, unless they break down or never get started. Dialogues easily turn into monologues when the transmission of information becomes more important than the sharing of ideas among students, teachers, and texts. Guiding the learning conversations that occur between the reader and the text is the subject of this chapter. Teachers guide reader–text interactions through the instructional strategies that they use so that students can engage the text and each other *before, during,* and *after* reading.

What about . . .
Content Standards and Assessment?

BOX 10.1

Practically every national and state standards document, regardless of content domain, highlights the importance of comprehension, inquiry, and critical thinking. The words used to signify standards may vary from academic discipline to academic discipline, but at the heart of content standards is the student's ability to comprehend, inquire, and think critically. Critical thinking, interpretation, and analysis are highly valued in American education. In the national science standards developed by the National Science Teachers Association (NSTA), for example, science as inquiry is a critical dimension of what students should know and be able to do. The science as inquiry standards acknowledge that students at every grade level must have opportunities to engage in scientific inquiry and to think and act in ways that support inquiry, including asking questions, planning and conducting investigations, gathering data, thinking critically, constructing and analyzing alternative explanations, and communicating scientific arguments.

Moreover, the content standards that guided the writing of this chapter, as well as other chapters in this book, are reflected in IRA/NCTE's standards documents, including the following standard on the use of strategies:

> Students apply a wide range of strategies to comprehend, interpret, evaluate, and appreciate texts. They draw on their prior experience, their interactions with other readers and writers, their knowledge of word meaning and of other texts, their word identification strategies, and their understanding of textual features.

To the extent that state proficiency assessments measure students' abilities to comprehend and think critically, they provide useful and valuable information for teachers, parents, school districts, and policy makers. However, critics argue that proficiency assessments aren't measuring what they are supposed to measure: critical thinking in academic domains. According to Monte Neill, the executive director of the National Center for Fair and Open Testing, "Even the test-promoting organization Achieve, Inc., recognizes that most state exams are weak and acknowledges that much higher-order thinking . . . cannot be adequately assessed through standardized paper-and-pencil tests" (Neill 2003, p. 225).

Improving proficiency assessments, no doubt, will be an ongoing challenge for states as they refine their accountability systems. From our perspective, however, authentic classroom assessments and high-stakes assessments, when combined, build a corroborative framework for ensuring that students meet the standards associated with high levels of thinking before, during, and after reading academic texts. As you read about the instructional strategies in this chapter, note the many opportunities teachers will have to assess comprehension and critical thinking through observation, student work samples, and classroom interactions within the context of instruction.

Instructional Strategies

In this section, we describe several instructional strategies that prepare students for reading, guide their interactions with texts, and help them to clarify and extend meaning. Underlying these strategies is a B–D–A lesson structure that allows teachers to integrate activities before, during, and after reading. The instructional strategies that follow include (1) **KWL,** which stands for What do you **K**now? What do you **W**ant to know? What did you **L**earn? (2) **discussion webs,** (3) **Guided Reading Procedure (GRP)**, and (4) **intra-act.** Note the differences as well as the similarities of various instructional strategies emphasized in this section. Each can be adapted to serve any subject matter material. Think about the kinds of adaptations you will have to make with each instructional strategy to meet the particular needs of your content area.

The KWL Strategy

KWL is an instructional strategy that engages students in active text learning. The strategy begins with what students *know* about the topic to be studied, moves to what the students *want to know* as they generate questions about the topic, and leads to a record of what students *learn* as a result of their engagement in the strategy. Follow-up activities to KWL include discussion, the construction of graphic organizers, and summary writing to clarify and internalize what has been read.

e.Resources

Use the keywords "KWL + reading comprehension" to search for useful ideas about KWL as a comprehension strategy.

KWL may be initiated with small groups of students or the whole class. When they develop confidence and competence with the KWL strategy, students may begin to use it for independent learning. KWL uses a strategy sheet, such as the one in Figure 10.1. The procedures to follow in KWL revolve around the completion of the strategy sheet as part of the dynamics of student response and discussion.

Procedures for KWL

Here's how the KWL strategy works.

1. *Introduce the KWL strategy in conjunction with a new topic or text selection.* Before assigning a text, explain the strategy. Donna Ogle (1992), the originator of KWL, suggests that dialogue begin with the teacher saying

> It is important to first find out what we think we know about this topic. Then we want to anticipate how an author is likely to present and organize the information. From this assignment we can generate good questions to focus on reading and study. Our level of knowledge will determine to some extent how we will study. Then as we read we will make notes of questions that get answered and other new and important information we learn. During this process some new questions will probably occur to us; these we should also note so we can get clarification later. (p. 271)

FIGURE **10.1** **A KWL Strategy Sheet**

K—What I Know	W—What I Want to Know	L—What I Learned and Still Need to Learn

Categories of Information
I Expect to Use

A.

B.

C.

D.

E.

F.

G.

Source: From Donna M. Ogle, "K-W-L: A Teaching Model That Develops Active Reading in Expository Text" (February 1986). *The Reading Teacher,* *39*(6), 564–570. Copyright © 1986 by the International Reading Association. All rights reserved. Used by permission of the author and International Reading Association.

In the process of explaining KWL, be sure that students understand *what* their role involves and *why* it is important for learners to examine what they know and to ask questions about topics that they will be reading and studying.

The next several steps allow you to model the KWL strategy with a group of learners or the entire class. Some students will find it difficult to complete the KWL strategy sheet on their own. Others will avoid taking risks or revealing what they know or don't know about a topic. Others simply won't be positively motivated. Modeling the KWL strategy reduces the initial risk and creates a willingness to engage in the process. Students who experience the modeling of the strategy quickly recognize its value as a learning tool.

2. *Identify what students think they know about the topic.* Engage the class in brainstorming, writing their ideas on the board or on an overhead transparency. Use the format of the KWL strategy sheet as you record students' ideas on the chalkboard or transparency. It's important to record everything that the students *think* they know about the topic, including their misconceptions. The key in this step is to get the class actively involved in making associations with the topic, not to evaluate the rightness or wrongness of the associations. Students will sometimes challenge one another's knowledge base. The teacher's role is to help learners recognize that differences exist in what they think they know. These differences can be used to help students frame questions.

3. *Generate a list of student questions.* Ask, "What do you want to know more about? What are you most interested in learning about?" As you write their questions on the chalkboard or transparency, recognize that you are again modeling for students what their role as learners should be: to ask questions about material to be studied.

When you have completed modeling the brainstorming and question-generation phases of KWL, have the students use their own strategy sheets to make decisions about what they personally think they know and about what they want to know more. Students, especially those who may be at risk in academic situations, may refer to the chalkboard or the overhead transparency to decide what to record in the first two columns.

4. *Anticipate the organization and structure of ideas that the author is likely to use in the text selection.* As part of preparation for reading, have students next use their knowledge and their questions to make predictions about the organization of the text. What major categories of information is the author likely to use to organize his or her ideas?

The teacher might ask, "How do you think the author of a text or article on _____ is likely to organize the information?" Have students focus on the ideas they have brainstormed and the questions they have raised to predict possible categories of information. As students make their predictions, record these on the board or transparency in the area suggested by the KWL strategy sheet. Then have students make individual choices on their own strategy sheets.

5. *Read the text selection to answer the questions.* As they engage in interactions with the text, the students write answers to their questions and make notes for new ideas and information in the L column of their strategy sheets. Again, the teacher's modeling is crucial to the success of this phase of KWL. Students may need a demonstration or two to understand how to record information in the L column.

Debrief students after they have read the text and have completed writing responses in the L column. First, invite them to share answers, recording these on the chalkboard or transparency. Then ask, "What new ideas did you come across that you didn't think you would find in the text?" Record and discuss the responses.

6. *Engage students in follow-up activities to clarify and extend learning.* Use KWL as a springboard into postreading activities to internalize student learning. Activities may include the construction of graphic organizers to clarify and retain ideas encountered during reading or the development of written summaries.

KWL Examples

In Christa Chaney's U.S. history class, students were beginning a study of the Vietnam War. Christa realized that her students would have some, if not much, prior knowledge of and attitudes toward the Vietnam War because it has remained "a strong part of our national consciousness." The students, in fact, were acutely aware of the war from recent popular movies and also from fathers and other relatives who had participated in it.

e.Resources

Use the keywords "KWL + lesson plans + (content area)" to search for KWL strategy applications in your content area.

However, Christa realized that although students might know something about the Vietnam War, they had probably had little opportunity to study it from the perspective of historians. This, then, was Christa's objective as a teacher of history: to help students approach the study of the Vietnam War—and understand the social, economic, and political forces surrounding it—from a historian's perspective.

Therefore, Christa believed that the KWL strategy would be an appropriate way to begin the unit. She believed that it would help students get in touch with what they knew (and didn't know) about the Vietnam War and raise questions that would guide their interactions with the materials that they would be studying.

Christa began KWL knowing that her students were familiar with its procedures, having participated in the strategy on several previous occasions in the class. Following the six steps, the class as a whole participated in brainstorming what they knew about the war and what they wanted to know. Christa recorded their ideas and questions on an overhead transparency and encouraged students' participation by asking such questions as, "What else do you know? Who knows someone who was in the war? What did he or she say about it? Who has read about the Vietnam War or seen a movie about it? What did you learn?"

As ideas and questions were recorded on the transparency, Christa asked the students to study the K column to anticipate categories of information that they might study in their textbook and other information sources that they would be using: "Do some of these ideas fit together to form major categories we might be studying?" She also asked the students to think about other wars they had studied—World Wars I and II, the U.S. Civil War, and the American Revolution: "When we study wars, are there underlying categories of information on which historians tend to focus?"

On completion of the whole-class activity, Christa invited her students to complete their strategy sheets, recording what they knew, what they wanted to find out more about, and what categories of information they expected to use.

Then, for homework, she assigned several sections from a textbook covering the Vietnam War and asked students to work on the L column on their own. Figure 10.2 shows how one student, Clayton, completed his strategy sheet.

As part of the next day's class, Christa asked the students to work in groups of four to share what they had found out about the war. They focused on the questions they had raised, as well as on new ideas they had not anticipated. When the groups completed their work, Christa brought the class together. She directed them to open their learning logs and write a summary of what they had learned from participating in KWL. Students used the L column on their strategy sheets to compose the summary. Clayton's summary is shown in Figure 10.3.

FIGURE 10.2 Clayton's KWL Strategy Sheet on the Vietnam War

K—What I Know	**W**—What I Want to Know	**L**—What I Learned and Still Need to Learn
U.S. lost war protest marches and riots movies made in 1960s jungle fighting POWs guerrilla fighting North and South fighting each other U.S. soldiers suffered the wall in Washington	Why did we go to war? Why did we lose? How many soldiers died? Who helped us? Who was president during war? On whose side were we?	Gulf of Tonkin Resolution made it legal for war but was not legally declared French helped U.S. Nixon withdrew troops because of fighting at home Lottery used to draft soldiers Antiwar movement at home 55,000 Americans died plus thousands of innocent people Kennedy, Johnson, and Nixon were the presidents Fought war to stop communism

Categories of Information I Expect to Use

A. cause   E.
B. results   F.
C. U.S. involvement G.
D. type of fighting

FIGURE **10.3** **Clayton's Summary in the Learning Log**

We fought the Vietnam War to stop communism. The U.S. Congress passed the Gulf of Tonkin Resolution, which said it was OK to go to war there, but the war was never declared a war—it was only called a conflict. The French and South Vietnamese people helped us, but it didn't matter. 55,000 Americans died fighting. People protested in the United States. Nixon withdrew the troops because of pressure to end the war at home.

In Christa's class, the learning logs serve as a history notebook, where students can record what they are learning, using a variety of writing-to-learn activities. (We explain learning logs and their uses more fully in Chapter 11.)

A high school math teacher adapted the KWL strategy to support his students' study of the Fibonacci numbers. Fibonacci numbers (a famous sequence of numbers that have been shown to occur in nature) are the direct result of a problem posed by a thirteenth-century mathematician, Leonardo of Pisa, on the regeneration of rabbits. The teacher used a math text from an enrichment unit to clarify and extend students' understanding of the Fibonacci numbers. The text selection, "Mathematics in Nature," illustrates the properties of the Fibonacci numbers and requires students to determine the relationships between these numbers and various phenomena in nature—for example, the leaves on a plant, the bracts on a pinecone, the curves on a seashell, or the spirals on a pineapple.

Before initiating the KWL strategy, the teacher used three props (a toy rabbit, a plant, and a pineapple) to arouse students' curiosity and to trigger their responses to the question, "What do these items have to do with mathematics?" After some exploratory talk, he then asked students, "What do you know about mathematics and nature?" The strategy sheet in Figure 10.4 illustrates the reader–text interactions that occurred as the teacher guided students through the steps in KWL.

FIGURE 10.4   A KWL Strategy Sheet in a Math Class

K—What I Know	W—What I Want to Know	L—What I Learned and Still Need to Learn
planetary motion spirals 4 seasons landscaping geometric designs multiplying populations phases of the moon	What does a pineapple have to do with math? How are growth patterns in plants related to math? How is mathematics specifically related to nature? Where do bees fit?	Pineapples have hexagons on the surface that are arranged in sets of spirals. These spirals are related to Fibonacci numbers. Fibonacci numbers are found in leaf arrangements on plants. The rate that bees regenerate males is related to Fibonacci numbers.
Categories of Information I Expect to Use 1. Animals 2. Plants 3. Solar System 4. Laws of Nature		Who is this Fibonacci guy? What's the big deal about the "golden ratio"?

Discussion Webs

Discussion webs encourage students to engage the text and each other in thoughtful discussion by creating a framework for students to explore texts and consider different sides of an issue in discussion before drawing conclusions. Donna Alvermann (1991) recommends discussion webs as an alternative to teacher-dominated discussions.

The strategy uses cooperative learning principles that follow a "think–pair–share" discussion cycle (McTighe & Lyman 1988). The discussion cycle begins with students' first thinking about the ideas they want to contribute to the discussion based on their interactions with the text. Then they meet in pairs to discuss their ideas with a partner. Partners then team with a different set of partners to resolve differences in perspective and to work toward a consensus about the issue under discussion. In the final phase of the discussion cycle, the two sets of partners, working as a foursome, select a spokesperson to share their ideas with the entire class.

The discussion web strategy uses a graphic display to scaffold students' thinking about the ideas they want to contribute to the discussion based on what they have read. The graphic display takes the shape of a web, as illustrated in Figure 10.5. In the center of the web is a question that is central to the reading. The question is posed in such a way that it reflects more than one point of view. Students explore the pros and cons of the question in the "no" and "yes" columns of the web—in pairs, and then in groups of four. The main goal of the four-member teams is to draw a conclusion based on their discussion of the web.

Response Journal

Why do you think discussion webs would help students read critically in your content area?

FIGURE 10.5 A Discussion Web for "Where the Red Fern Grows" by Wilson Rawls

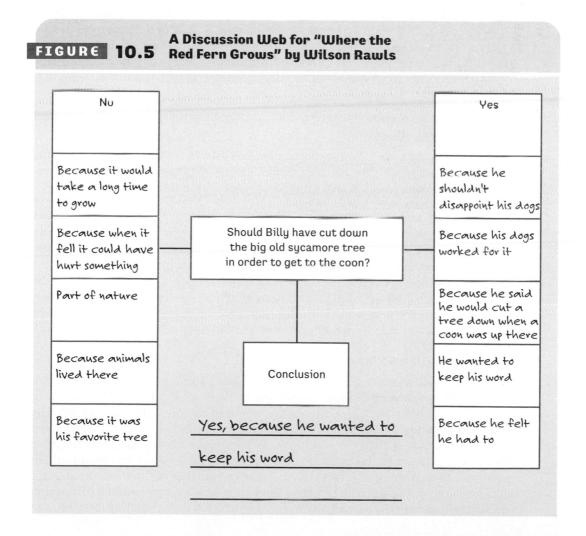

No		Yes
Because it would take a long time to grow		Because he shouldn't disappoint his dogs
Because when it fell it could have hurt something	**Should Billy have cut down the big old sycamore tree in order to get to the coon?**	Because his dogs worked for it
Part of nature		Because he said he would cut a tree down when a coon was up there
Because animals lived there	**Conclusion**	He wanted to keep his word
Because it was his favorite tree	*Yes, because he wanted to keep his word*	Because he felt he had to

Procedures for the Discussion Web

Alvermann (1991) suggests an integrated lesson structure for the discussion web strategy that includes the following steps:

1. *Prepare your students for reading by activating prior knowledge, raising questions, and making predictions about the text.*

2. *Assign students to read the selection and then introduce the discussion web by having the students work in pairs to generate pro and con responses to the question.* The partners work on the same discussion web and take turns jotting down their reasons in the "Yes" and "No" columns. Students may use keywords and phrases to express their ideas and need not fill all of the lines. They should try to list an equal number of pro and con reasons on the web.

3. *Combine partners into groups of four to compare responses, work toward consensus, and reach a conclusion as a group.* Explain to your students that it is OK to disagree with other members of the group, but they should all try to keep an open mind as they listen to others during the discussion. Dissenting views may be aired during the whole-class discussion.

4. *Give each group three minutes to decide which of all the reasons given best supports the group's conclusion.* Each group selects a spokesperson to report to the whole class.

5. *Have your students follow up the whole-class discussion by individually writing their responses to the discussion web question.* Display the students' responses to the question in a prominent place in the room so that they can be read by others.

The level of participation in discussion web lessons is usually high. The strategy encourages students' individual interpretations of what they are reading and also allows them to formulate and refine their own interpretations of a text in light of the points of view of others. As a result, students are eager to hear how other groups reached a consensus and drew conclusions during whole-class sharing. The strategy works well with informational or narrative texts and can be adapted to the goals and purposes of most content area subjects.

Discussion Web Examples

Donna Mitchell, a music teacher, introduced her middle grade students to components of an opera by having them listen to Wagner' *The Flying Dutchman*. In Chapter 7, we discussed Mrs. Mitchell's lesson in detail. In the discussion, she activated students' prior knowledge of opera using a playbill that she constructed in the form of a modified cloze activity. As part of the lesson, Mrs. Mitchell also had students listen to the overture of the opera to set a mood and read to them portions of the story over several days. At the conclusion of the read-alouds, students entered the postreading stage of the lesson as they engaged in a discussion web activity. Study the discussion web in Figure 10.6 completed by one group of students in her class as they grappled with the question, "Did Senta need to throw herself off the cliff into the sea?"

Math teachers might also use the discussion web to help students consider relevant and irrelevant information in story problems. Study the discussion web in Figure 10.7, noting the adaptations the teacher made. In this illustration, the students worked in pairs to distinguish relevant and irrelevant information in the story problem. They then formed groups of four to solve the problem.

Guided Reading Procedure (GRP)

The guided reading procedure (GRP) emphasizes close reading (Manzo 1975). It requires that students gather information and organize it around important ideas,

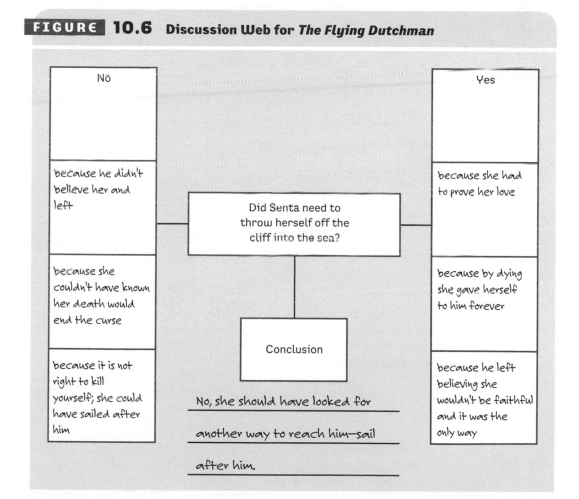

FIGURE **10.6** **Discussion Web for *The Flying Dutchman***

No

because he didn't believe her and left

because she couldn't have known her death would end the curse

because it is not right to kill yourself; she could have sailed after him

Did Senta need to throw herself off the cliff into the sea?

Conclusion

No, she should have looked for another way to reach him—sail after him.

Yes

because she had to prove her love

because by dying she gave herself to him forever

because he left believing she wouldn't be faithful and it was the only way

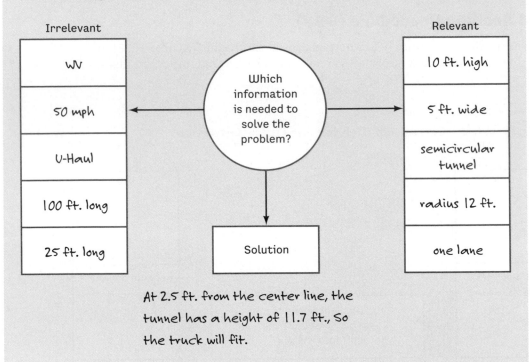

FIGURE 10.7   Discussion Web for a Story Problem

A U-Haul truck is driving through West Virginia. It is approaching a one-lane semicircular tunnel at a rate of fifty miles per hour. The truck is ten feet high, five feet wide, and twenty-five feet long. The tunnel has a radius of twelve feet and is 100 feet long. Will the truck fit through the tunnel?

Irrelevant

WV

50 mph

U-Haul

100 ft. long

25 ft. long

Which information is needed to solve the problem?

Solution

Relevant

10 ft. high

5 ft. wide

semicircular tunnel

radius 12 ft.

one lane

At 2.5 ft. from the center line, the tunnel has a height of 11.7 ft., so the truck will fit.

and it places a premium on accuracy as students reconstruct the author's message. With a strong factual base, students will work from a common and clear frame of reference. They will then be in a position to elaborate thoughtfully on the text and its implications.

Procedures for GRP

Here's how the GRP works.

1. *Prepare students for reading.* Clarify key concepts; determine what students know and don't know about the particular content to be studied; build appropriate background; give direction to reading.

2. *Assign a reading selection.* Assign 500 to 900 words in the middle grades (approximately five to seven minutes of silent reading); 1,000 to 2,000 words for high school (approximately ten minutes). Provide general purpose to direct reading behavior. Direction: Read to remember all you can.

3. *As students finish reading, have them turn books face down.* Ask them to tell what they remember. Record it on the chalkboard in the fashion in which it is remembered.

4. *Help students recognize that there is much that they have not remembered or have represented incorrectly.* Simply, there are implicit inconsistencies that need correction and further information to be considered.

5. *Redirect students to their books and review the selection to correct inconsistencies and add further information.*

6. *Organize recorded remembrances into some kind of an outline.* Ask guiding, nonspecific questions: "What were the important ideas in the assigned reading? Which came first? What facts on the board support it? What important point was brought up next? What details followed?"

7. *Extend questioning to stimulate an analysis of the material and a synthesis of the ideas with previous learnings.*

8. *Provide immediate feedback, such as a short quiz, as a reinforcement of short-term memory.*

A GRP Example

Eighth graders were assigned a reading selection from the music education magazine *Pipeline*. The selection, "Percussion—Solid as Rock," concerns the development and uses of percussion instruments from ancient to modern times.

The teacher introduced the selection by giving some background. She then began a guided discussion by asking students to remember as much as they could as they read the assignment silently. The teacher recorded the collective memories of her students on a transparency, projecting responses onto an overhead screen. Then she asked, "Did you leave out any information that might be important?" Students were directed to review the selection to determine whether essential information was missing from the list on the screen. The teacher also asked, "Did you mix up some of the facts on the list? Did you misrepresent any of the information in the author's message?"

These questions are extremely important to the overall GRP procedure. The first question—"Did you leave out any information that might be important?"—encourages a review of the material. Students sense that some facts are more important than others. Further questioning at this point will help them distinguish essential from nonessential information. The second question—"Did you mix up some of the facts on the list?"—reinforces the importance of selective rereading and rehearsal because of the limitations imposed by short-term memory.

Next, the teacher asked the class to study the information recorded on the screen. The teacher requested the students to form pairs and then assigned the following task: "Which facts on the overhead can be grouped together? Organize the information around the important ideas in the selection. You have five minutes to complete the task."

On completion of the task the teacher encouraged students to share their work in whole-group discussion. Their groupings of facts were compared, refined, and extended. The teacher served as a facilitator, keeping the discussion moving, asking clarifying questions, and provoking thought. She then initiated the next task: "Let's organize the important ideas and related information. Let's make a map." Figure 10.8 shows what the students produced.

Outlining the mass of information will make students aware of the text relationships developed by the author. In Chapter 12 we explore several outlining procedures, such as semantic mapping, which help students produce the author's main ideas in relation to one another. Producing the author's organizational structure leads to more efficient recall at a later time and lays the groundwork for interpreting and applying the author's message. Once this common framework is developed, your questioning should lead to more divergent and abstract responding by the students.

FIGURE 10.8   Semantic Map of "Percussion—Solid as Rock"

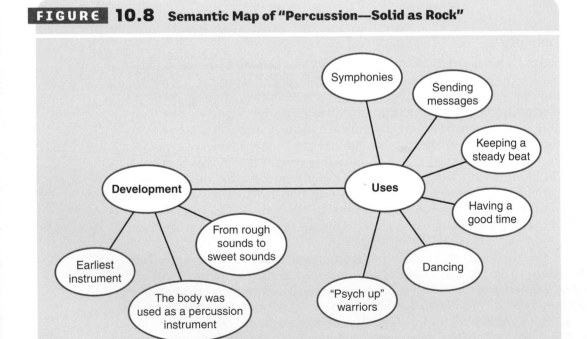

The discussion "took off" after the outline was completed. The teacher asked several reflective questions that helped students associate their previous experiences and beliefs about drumming to the content under discussion. Cognitive performance centered on evaluation and application as students linked what they knew to what they were studying.

The final suggested step in the GRP is a short quiz—mainly to demonstrate in a dramatic way how successful the students can be with the reading material. The quiz should be viewed as positive reinforcement, not an interrogation check. Most of the students in this class earned perfect or near-perfect scores on the quiz—and this is as it should be.

Response Journal
How is the GRP similar to KWL? How is it different?

Intra-Act

Intra-act lays the groundwork for reflective discussion. Pivotal to the intra-act strategy is the notion that students engage in a process of valuing as they reflect on what they have read. Hoffman (1979) suggests intra-act to provide readers with "the opportunity to experience rather than just talk about critical reading" (p. 608). According to Hoffman, students are more likely to read critically when they engage in a process of valuing. The valuing process allows students to respond actively to a text selection with thought and feeling.

The intra-act procedure can be used with a variety of reading materials— content area text assignments, historical documents, newspaper and magazine articles, narrative, and poetic material. The procedure requires the use of small groups whose members are asked to react to value statements based on the content of the text selection.

Procedures for Intra-Act

There are four phases in the intra-act procedure.

1. *Comprehension.* The comprehension phase promotes an understanding of the reading material to be learned. To begin this phase, the teacher follows effective prereading procedures by introducing the text reading, activating and building prior knowledge for the ideas to be encountered during reading, and inviting students to make predictions and speculate on the nature of the content to be learned. Building a frame of reference for upcoming text information is crucial to the overall success of the intra-act procedure.

Before inviting students to read the selection individually, the teacher forms small groups—intra-act teams—of four to six members. Assign a student from each group to serve as the team leader. The comprehension phase depends on the team leader's ability to initiate and sustain a discussion of the text. The team leader's responsibility is to lead a discussion by first summarizing what was read. The group members may contribute additional information about the selection or ask questions that seek clarification of the main ideas of the selection.

The comprehension phase of the group discussion should be limited to seven to ten minutes.

2. *Relating.* The team leader is next responsible for shifting the discussion from the important ideas in the selection to the group's personal reactions and values related to the topic. Many times, this shift occurs naturally. However, if this is not the case, members should be encouraged by the team leader to contribute their own impressions and opinions. Discussion should again be limited to seven to ten minutes.

3. *Valuation.* Once group members have shared their personal reactions to the material, they are ready to participate in the valuation phase of the discussion. The teacher or team leader for each group distributes a game sheet. This game sheet contains a valuing exercise—a set of four declarative statements based on the selection's content. These value statements reflect opinions about the text selection and draw insights and fresh ideas from it. The purpose of the valuing exercise is to have students come to grips with what the material means to them by either agreeing (A) or disagreeing (D) with each statement. Figure 10.9 shows such a game sheet.

Study the game sheet in Figure 10.9. Note that students must first indicate on the game sheet their own reactions to the four value statements. Then, based on the previous discussion, they must predict how each of the other members of their group would respond. In the example of Figure 10.9, Joe disagreed with three of the statements. His predictions as to how other team members would respond are indicated by the circled letters underneath the individual names. Once the responding is complete, the students are ready for the reflective phase of the intra-act procedure.

4. *Reflection.* Begin the reflection phase of intra-act by scoring the game sheet. Group members take turns revealing how each responded to the four statements. As each member tells how he or she responded, the other members check whether their predictions agreed with that member's actual responses. During this phase, the teacher acts as a facilitator, noting how students responded but refraining from imposing a particular point of view on students. Instead, encourage students to reflect on what they have learned. According to Hoffman (1979), "It is very important that during this period students be allowed ample time to discuss, challenge, support and question one another's response. This interaction serves to separate opinions quickly arrived at from sound evaluative thinking" (p. 607).

Intra-act will require several classroom applications before students become accustomed to their roles during discussion. Repeated and extensive participation in intra-act will help students become fully aware of the task demands of the procedure. In the beginning, we recommend that on completion of an intra-act discussion, students engage in a whole-class discussion of the process in which they

FIGURE 10.9   **Joe's Game Sheet**

Name _____
Date _____
Total Score _____
Percentage
of Correct Predictions _____

Names	Joe		Sharon		Paul		Katie	
1. Tobacco companies should be held responsible for the deaths of smokers from heart attacks and lung cancer.	A	(D)	A + D		A + D		A − D	
2. Smokers should be able to quit. They just need to really want to.	(A)	D	A + D		A + D		A + D	
3. The sale of cigarettes should be illegal just like the sale of cocaine or heroin.	A	(D)	A + D		A + D		A + D	
4. The government should spend money on programs to help people stop smoking.	A	(D)	A − D		A + D		A − D	

+: Joe's predictions were correct.
−: Joe's predictions were incorrect.

participated. Help students debrief: "What did we learn from our participation in intra-act? Why must all members of a group participate? How might discussion improve the next time we use intra-act?" Questions such as these make students sensitive to the purpose of the intra-act procedure (problem solving) and the role of each reader (critical analysis).

An Intra-Act Example

After students in a health education class read the article "Getting Hooked on Tobacco," four students, Joe, Sharon, Paul, and Katie, met as a group to discuss their impressions. Joe, who was the group's team leader, began with a summary of the article and then gave his own reactions. Here's how Joe summarized the article's main ideas: "Well, basically the article says that the government says that tobacco makes you, you know, a drug addict, or something like that. It's like using cocaine or heroin. They say that people can't quit and they need more and more, so cigarettes should be like liquor and you have to get a license to sell them. The cigarette companies don't agree. Me too. I don't think a guy is going to go out and rob people just to get cigarettes. I mean, if he is that hard up, he would just quit."

After some clarifying discussion of what the article was about, the discussion shifted gears into the relating phase. Sharon reacted to the article this way: "Well, I don't think that a company should be allowed to sell stuff that kills people. And if all the people quit, the company would go out of business anyway, so it should just go out of business now because of a law."

Paul entered the conversation: "I think the guy was right that said if cigarettes were illegal the gangs would have gang wars to see who would get to sell them—just like they do with crack and cocaine right now. Besides, if people really want to kill themselves with smoking, they should be allowed. And if they don't, they should just quit. Right on the pack it says *quit*."

Katie replied, "It ain't so easy to quit. My dad tried, like, five times, and he finally had to get hypnotized to quit. And he wouldn't have started if he had to buy them from some gang or something. You get them from a store, and nobody ever asks you how old you are. Besides, who reads the warnings?"

When time for discussion was over, the valuation phase was initiated. Students were given a game sheet with these four value statements:

1. Tobacco companies should be held responsible for the deaths of smokers from heart attacks and lung cancer.

2. Smokers should be able to quit. They just need to really want to.

3. The sale of cigarettes should be illegal just like the sale of cocaine or heroin.

4. The government should spend money on programs to help people stop smoking.

Each student was asked to respond individually to the statements and then predict whether the other members of the group would agree or disagree with each statement. Joe's sheet is reproduced in Figure 10.9. From the discussion, he was pretty sure that Sharon would agree with the first statement because she had said that they "shouldn't be allowed to kill people." Similarly, he thought Paul would disagree because he thought people should "just quit." He was also pretty sure that Katie would agree because she seemed to think it was bad that you could just go into a store and buy cigarettes. He used similar reasons to predict the group members' reactions to the other statements.

As part of the reflection phase of intra-act, the group members shared what they had learned. Joe found that most of his predictions were correct. He was surprised to find out that Katie did not agree with statement 1, but she explained that, "It's not the companies' fault that they sold something that's not illegal. First, they should make it illegal; then it's the companies' fault." Other members argued that her reasoning "didn't make sense" because the tobacco companies know that cigarettes are

Response Journal

How is the intra-act strategy similar to discussion webs? How is it different?

harmful. That debate was typical of the discussion that went on in all the groups as students worked out the ways in which the ideas presented in the text fit in with their own attitudes and beliefs.

Teachers, as you can see, are in a strategic position to influence readers' interaction with texts, especially when students have trouble handling hard-to-read assignments. This is often the case when they have difficulty thinking about what they're reading at high levels of comprehension. In addition to the instructional strategies illustrated in this section, various kinds of reading guides also provide instructional support that allows students to interact with difficult texts in meaningful ways.

Reading Guides

What exactly is a reading guide? It has sometimes been compared to a "worksheet"—something students complete after reading, usually as homework. But reading guides do more than give students work to do. Guides, like worksheets, may consist of questions and activities related to the instructional material under study. The difference is that students respond to the questions and activities in the reading guide *as* they read the text, not after. Because a reading guide accompanies reading, it provides instructional support as students need it. Moreover, a well-developed guide not only influences content acquisition but also prompts higher-order thinking.

Guides help students comprehend texts better than they would if left to their own resources. Over time, however, text learners should be weaned from this type of scaffolding as they develop the maturity and the learning strategies to interact with difficult texts without guide material. With this caveat in mind, let's explore the use of two types of reading guides that scaffold learning at different levels of understanding: three-level guides and selective reading guides.

> **Response Journal**
>
> When you were a student, how helpful were worksheets in comprehending a text assignment?

Three-Level Reading Guides

The levels-of-comprehension model that we introduced in Chapter 1 lends itself well to the development of guide material to scaffold reader–text interactions. A three-level reading guide provides the framework in which students can interact with difficult texts at different levels of comprehension. One of the best ways to become familiar with the three-level guide is to experience one. Therefore, we invite you to participate in the following demonstration.

Preview the three-level guide in Figure 10.10; next, read "The Case of the Missing Ancestor" (pp. 340–341). Then complete the three-level guide as you read the text or after reading.

FIGURE **10.10** **Three-Level Guide for "The Case of the Missing Ancestor"**

I. *Directions:* Check the statements that you believe say what the author says. Sometimes, the exact words are used; at other times, other words may be used.

_____ 1. The Germans discovered the fossilized remnants of the Neanderthal man and the Heidelberg man.

_____ 2. Charles Dawson found a human skull in a gravel pit in Piltdown Common, Sussex.

_____ 3. Charles Dawson was a professional archaeologist.

_____ 4. The fossil, labeled *Eoanthropus dawsoni,* became known as the Piltdown man.

_____ 5. The discovery of the Piltdown man was acclaimed as an important archaeological find.

_____ 6. Dental evidence regarding the Piltdown man was ignored.

II. *Directions:* Check the statements that you believe represent the author's *intended* meaning.

_____ 1. The English scientific community felt left out because important fossils had been found in other countries.

_____ 2. Good scientific practices were ignored by the people working with the Piltdown fossils.

_____ 3. Many scientists said that Piltdown was important because they wanted England to be important.

_____ 4. Dawson wanted to make himself famous, so he constructed a hoax.

III. *Directions:* Check the statements you agree with, and be ready to support your choices with ideas from the text and your own knowledge and beliefs.

_____ 1. Competition in scientific research may be dangerous.

_____ 2. Scientists, even good ones, can be fooled by poorly constructed hoaxes.

_____ 3. People often see only what they want to see.

_____ 4. A scientific "fact" is not always correct simply because many scientists believe strongly in it; theories are always open to question.

THE CASE OF THE MISSING ANCESTOR

From the mid-1800s to the early 1900s, Europeans were actively searching for early ancestors. The Germans dug up the fossilized remnants of Neanderthal man and Heidelberg man. The French discovered not only ancient bones but also cave paintings done by early humans.

England, Charles Darwin's home, had no evidence of ancient ancestors. English scientists—both professionals and amateurs—began searching for fossils. Scarcely a cave was left unexplored, scarcely a stone was left unturned. Many scientists asked workers in gravel pits to watch for fossils.

In 1912, Charles Dawson, a part-time collector of fossils for the British Museum, wrote to Dr. Arthur Smith Woodward, keeper of the Natural History Department at the British Museum. Dawson claimed that a human skull he had found in a gravel pit in Piltdown Common, Sussex, "would rival Heidelberg man." Soon Woodward was digging in the gravel pit with Dawson and other eager volunteers. They found a separate jaw that, though apelike, included a canine tooth and two molars, worn down as if by human-type chewing. Flints and nonhuman fossils found at the same dig indicated that the finds were very old.

Despite arguments by some scientists that the jaw came from a chimpanzee or an orangutan, the discoverers reconstructed the skull and connected the jaw to it. They named the fossil *Eoanthropus dawsoni*, Dawson's "Dawn man," and said that it was much older than Neanderthal man. The find came to be known as Piltdown man.

The finds were X-rayed. One dental authority was suspicious of the canine; he said it was too young a tooth to show such wear. However, such contrary evidence was ignored in the general surge of enthusiasm. So the Piltdown man was acclaimed as an important find, a human in which the brain had evolved more quickly than the jaw.

Beginning in the 1940s, the bones were subjected to modern tests. It is now believed that the skull was from a modern human and the jaw was from a modern ape, probably an orangutan. The animal fossils and flints were found to be very old, but not the types that have been found in England. Apparently, they had been placed in the gravel pit to make the finds more convincing. Why were the scientists and others fooled so easily? Perhaps the desire to find an "ancestor" may have interfered with careful scientific observation.

Source: From *Silver Burdett Biology,* 1986.

Several comments are in order on your participation in the three-level guide demonstration. First of all, note that the three-level format gave you a "conscious experience" with comprehension levels as a process (Herber 1978). Note also that as you proceded through the process, you responded to and manipulated the important explicit and implicit ideas in the material. You may have sensed the relatedness of ideas as you moved within and among the levels.

Why did we direct you first to preview the guide and then to read the material? Because surveying helps create a predisposition to read the material. Previewing helps reduce the reader's uncertainty about the material to be read. You know what is coming. When we asked you to read the guide first, we hoped to raise your expectations about the author's message. By encountering some of the ideas before reading, you are in a better position to direct your search for information in the reading material that may be relevant.

You probably noted also that the declarative statements did not require you to produce answers to questions. Rather, you had to make decisions among likely alternatives; it's easier to recognize possible answers than to produce them.

Notice, too, that in a very positive way, the statements can serve as springboards for discussion and conversation about the content. Were students to react to guides *without* the opportunity to discuss and debate responses, the instructional material would soon deteriorate into busy-work and paper shuffling.

Response Journal

What do you think is the difference between responding to statements at different levels of comprehension versus responding to questions?

A final comment: Your maturity as a reader is probably such that you didn't need structured guidance for this selection, particularly at levels I and II. If you make the decision that certain segments of your text can be handled without reading guidance, don't construct guide material. A three-level guide is a means to growth in reading and growth through reading. It is not an end in itself.

Constructing Three-Level Guides

Don't be misled by the apparent discreteness of comprehension levels. Don't, as Dale (1969) pronounced, suffer from "hardening of the categories." The term *levels* implies a cognitive hierarchy that may be more apocryphal than real. A reader doesn't necessarily read first for literal recognition, then interpretation, and finally application—although that may appear to be a logical sequence. Many readers, for instance, read text for overarching concepts and generalizations first and then search for evidence to support their inferences.

It is very important to recognize that in reading, levels are probably interactive and inseparable. Nevertheless, the classroom teacher attempts to have students experience each aspect of the comprehension process as they read content material. In doing so, students adapt strategies as they interact with the material. They get a feel for the component processes within reading comprehension. They come to sense in an instructional setting what it means to make inferences, to use information as the basis for those inferences, and to rearrange or transform acquired understandings into what they know already in order to construct knowledge.

If reading guides were to be used with every text assignment every day, it would become counterproductive. One math teacher's evaluation of a three-level guide crystallizes this point: "The students said the guide actually helped them organize the author's ideas in their minds and helped them understand the material. I think the guide was successful, but I would not use it all the time because many of the assignments don't lend themselves to this type of activity." The three-level guide is only one instructional aid that helps students grow toward mature reading and independent learning.

Finally, we urge you also to consider guides as tools, not tests. Think of each statement in a three-level guide as a prompt that will initiate student discussion and reinforce the quality of the reader's interaction with text.

Before constructing a guide, the teacher has to decide the following: What important ideas should be emphasized? What are the students' competencies? What depth of understanding are the students expected to achieve? What is the difficulty of the material? Having made these decisions, consider these guidelines:

1. *Begin construction of the guide at level II, the interpretive level.* Analyze the text selection, asking yourself, "What does the author mean?" Write down in your own words all inferences that make sense to you and that fit your content objectives. Make sure your statements are written simply and clearly. (After all, you don't want to construct a guide to read the guide.)

2. *Next, search the text for the propositions and explicit pieces of information needed to support the inferences you have chosen for level II.* Put these into statement form. You now have level I, the literal level.

3. *Decide whether you want to add a distractor or two to levels I and II.* We have found that a distractor maintains an active response to the information search, mainly because students sense that they cannot indiscriminately check every item and, therefore, must focus their information search more carefully.

4. *Develop statements for level III, the applied level.* Such statements represent additional insights or principles that can be drawn when relationships established by the author are combined with other ideas outside the text selection itself but inside the heads of your students. In other words, help students connect what they know already to what they read.

5. *Be flexible and adaptive.* Develop a format that will appeal to you and your students. Try to avoid crowding too much print on the reading guide.

Three-Level Guide Examples

The format of the three-level guides should vary. The classroom examples that follow serve only as models. As you study them, think of ways that you will be able to adapt and apply the three-level construct to your content materials.

Guides are extremely useful adjuncts in the study of literature. A three-level guide can be easily adapted to dramatic, narrative, and poetic forms of literature. For example, note in Figure 10.11 how a ninth-grade English teacher used a three-level guide for Shakespeare's *Romeo and Juliet*. The class was at the tail end of its study of the play, and the guide helped students pull together some of the important points related to the climactic action of the final act. Moreover, the statements at levels II and III of the guide helped students reflect on possible inferences and themes that emerge from the action.

A middle grade teacher constructed the three-level guide in Figure 10.12 as part of a health unit. Notice how she uses Question–Answer Relationships (QARs) as cues to direct students' responses. Students completed the guide individually and then discussed their responses in small groups.

As we have shown, one important way to guide comprehension is through three-level guides, which a teacher constructs to bridge the gap between students' competences and the difficulty of the text material. As you consider adapting three-level guides to content area materials, keep these summarizing points in mind. First, the three-level guide stimulates an active response to meaning at the literal, interpretive, and applied levels. It helps readers acquire and construct knowledge from content material that might otherwise be too difficult for them to read. Second, levels of comprehension interact during reading; in all probability, the levels are inseparable in mature readers. Nevertheless, for instructional purposes, it is beneficial to have students experience each level in order to get a feel for the component

FIGURE 10.11   **Three-Level Guide for *Romeo and Juliet***

I. *Literal level:* Check the items that explicitly represent some of the important details and actions in the last part of the play.

_____ 1. The reason Friar Laurence marries Romeo and Juliet is to bring the families of the Montagues and Capulets together.

_____ 2. Friar Laurence believes words of wisdom will help Romeo deal with his banishment.

_____ 3. Juliet gives the ring to the Nurse to give to Romeo as a sign of her love.

_____ 4. Lady Capulet believes marriage to Paris will take care of all of Juliet's sorrows.

_____ 5. Paris goes to Juliet's grave nightly to place flowers there.

_____ 6. Prince Escalus says that he is the one to blame for the deaths because he did not act decisively enough.

II. *Interpretive level:* Several statements follow that may represent what the playwright means. If you think any of the statements are reasonable inferences and conclusions, put a check on the line provided. Be prepared to support your answers by citing parts of the play.

_____ 1. Romeo would be alive if the apothecary had obeyed the law.

_____ 2. Lord and Lady Capulet are to blame for Juliet's death because they forced her into marriage.

_____ 3. If Prince Escalus had punished the Montagues and Capulets earlier, the entire tragedy would not have happened.

_____ 4. Romeo's impulsiveness, rashness, immaturity, and emotionalism caused him problems.

_____ 5. A fourteen-year-old is not capable of true love.

_____ 6. Romeo did not want to kill Paris.

III. *Applied level:* To apply what you read means to take information and ideas from what you have read and connect them to what you already know. If you think the following statements are supported by statements in section II and by your own previous experience or study, place a check in the blank provided. Be sure you have good reasons to justify your answers if you are called on to do so.

_____ 1. People who live by the sword die by the sword.

_____ 2. People in positions of power must take responsibility for the actions of those under them.

_____ 3. A person cannot change the role that fate has ordained for him or her.

_____ 4. The most important thing in life is love. It is even worth dying for.

_____ 5. No person has the right to take his or her own life.

_____ 6. Nothing is worth dying for.

_____ 7. Our own personalities shape our lives, and we can shape our personalities by the choices we make.

_____ 8. Events outside our control shape our lives.

FIGURE 10.12 Three-Level Guide for a Health Lesson

I. Right There! What did the author say?

   Directions: Place a check on the line in front of the number if you think a statement can be found in the pages you read.

   _____ 1. Every human being has feelings or emotions.

   _____ 2. Research workers are studying the effects on the body of repeated use of marijuana.

   _____ 3. You should try hard to hide your strong emotions, such as fear or anger.

   _____ 4. Your feelings affect the way the body works.

   _____ 5. You are likely to get angry at your parents or brothers or sisters more often than at other people.

II. Think and Search! What did the author mean?

   Directions: Check the following statements that state what the author was trying to say in the pages you read.

   _____ 1. Sometimes you act in a different way because of your mood.

   _____ 2. Your emotional growth has been a continuing process since the day you were born.

   _____ 3. The fact that marijuana hasn't been proved to be harmful means that it is safe to use.

   _____ 4. Each time you successfully control angry or upset feelings, you grow a little.

III. On Your Own! Do you agree with these statements?

   Directions: Check each statement that you can defend.

   _____ 1. Escaping from problems does not solve them.

   _____ 2. Decisions should be made on facts, not fantasies

   _____ 3. Getting drunk is a good way to have fun.

processes involved in comprehending. And third, three-level guides will help students develop a good sense of the conceptual complexity of text material.

In the next section, we consider another type of reading guide: selective reading guides.

Selective Reading Guides

Selective reading guides show students how to think with print. The effective use of questions combined with signaling techniques helps model how readers interact with text when reading and studying.

Response Journal

Which reading guide— three-level or selective— is more appropriate for your content area? Why?

Cunningham and Shablak (1975) were among the first to discuss the importance of guiding students to respond selectively to text. They indicate that content area teachers can impart tremendous insight into *how* to acquire text information through a selective reading guide:

> The teacher begins . . . by determining the overall purpose for a particular reading assignment. Second, he selects those sections of the reading which are necessary to achieve this purpose.
>
> Most important . . . he eliminates from the assignment any and all sections that are irrelevant to the purpose. Third, for those relevant sections that remain, the teacher determines, *based on his own model reading behaviors,* what a student must operationally do to achieve the purpose—step by step, section by section. (p. 381; emphasis added)

The premise behind the selective reading guide is that teachers understand how to process information from their own subject matter areas. Figure 10.13 illustrates how an English teacher developed a selective reading guide that mixes written questions with appropriate signals for processing the material.

In elementary and middle school situations, selective reading guides have been called reading road maps (Wood 1988). For maturing readers, teachers add a visual dimension to the guide. Study the reading road map in Figure 10.14 developed by a middle school science teacher. Notice how he guides students through the life functions of bacteria by using various kinds of cues, signals, and statements. The guide provides location cues to focus students' attention on relevant segments of text, speed signals to model flexibility in reading, and mission statements that initiate tasks that help students think and learn with texts.

e.Resources

For additional readings related to the major ideas in this chapter, go to Chapter 10 of the Companion Website and click on Suggested Readings.

The examples presented in this chapter should give you some idea of how guides may be used and developed for different instructional purposes across a wide range of texts. We encourage you to develop and experiment with several study guides for potentially difficult text assignments in your content area.

◀ Looking Back
Looking Forward ▶ ——————

When readers are not able to handle difficult texts on their own, a teacher supports their efforts to make meaning by guiding their in-

teractions with texts. Various kinds of instructional strategies may be used to guide reader–text interactions. In this chapter, sev-

| FIGURE 10.13 | Selective Reading Guide for "Advertising: The Permissible Lie" |

Page 128. Read the title. Write a definition of a permissible lie. Give an example of this type of lie.

Page 128, par. 1. Do you agree with this quotation? Why or why not?

Pages 128–129. Read paragraphs 2–6 slowly and carefully. What aspects of TV were borrowed from radio? Write them down. From personal experience, do you think TV reflects reality? Jot an answer down, and then continue reading.

Pages 129–130. Read paragraphs 7–15 quickly. What specific types of commercials are being discussed?

Pages 130–131. Read paragraphs 16–26 to find out the author's opinion of this type of commercial.

Page 131. Read paragraph 7. The author gives an opinion here. Do you agree?

Pages 131–133. Read to page 133, paragraph 45. You can skim this section, slowing down to read parts that are especially interesting to you. What are some current popular phrases or ideas in advertising? Think of some commercials you've seen on TV. List another word or idea or fad that's used in a lot of advertising.

Pages 133–134. Read paragraphs 45–50 quickly. Give your own example of a sex-based advertisement.

Page 134, par. 51. According to the author, what is a good test for an advertisement? Do you agree? Would most advertisements pass or fail the test? Try out a few.

Page 134, par. 52. Restate Comant's quote in your own words.

After reading the assignment, summarize what you read in 100 words or less.

eral strategies that prepare students for reading, guide their interaction with texts, and help them to clarify and extend meaning were described.

KWL is a meaning-making strategy that engages students in active text learning and may be used with small groups of students or with the whole class. KWL comprises several steps that help students examine what they know, what they want to know more about, and what they have learned from reading. The guided reading procedure (GRP) encourages close read-ing of difficult text, whereas the discussion web and intra-act strategies are based on the notion that students engage in a process of consensus building and valuing as they reflect on what they have read. The GRP, the discussion web, and intra-act lay the groundwork for reflective discussion following the reading of text material.

In addition to instructional strategies, teachers develop reading guides to scaffold reader–text interactions. With the use of guides, teachers provide instructional support to allow students

FIGURE **10.14 A Reading Road Map**

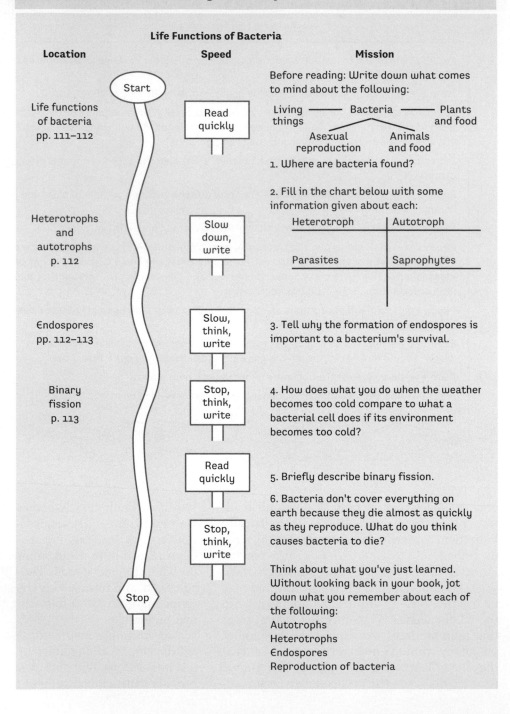

Life Functions of Bacteria

| Location | Speed | Mission |

Location   **Speed**   **Mission**

Start

Life functions of bacteria pp. 111–112 — Read quickly

Before reading: Write down what comes to mind about the following:

Living things —— Bacteria —— Plants and food

Asexual reproduction   Animals and food

1. Where are bacteria found?

2. Fill in the chart below with some information given about each:

Heterotroph	Autotroph
Parasites	Saprophytes

Heterotrophs and autotrophs p. 112 — Slow down, write

Endospores pp. 112–113 — Slow, think, write

3. Tell why the formation of endospores is important to a bacterium's survival.

Binary fission p. 113 — Stop, think, write

4. How does what you do when the weather becomes too cold compare to what a bacterial cell does if its environment becomes too cold?

Read quickly

5. Briefly describe binary fission.

6. Bacteria don't cover everything on earth because they die almost as quickly as they reproduce. What do you think causes bacteria to die?

Stop, think, write

Think about what you've just learned. Without looking back in your book, jot down what you remember about each of the following:
Autotrophs
Heterotrophs
Endospores
Reproduction of bacteria

Stop

to interact with and respond to difficult texts in meaningful ways. We explored and illustrated two types of guides: three-level guides and selective reading guides. Three-level guides allow readers to interact with text, constructing meaning at different levels of abstraction and conceptual complexity: literal, interpretive, and applied levels. Selective reading guides show students how to think with text by modeling reading behaviors necessary to read effectively.

In the next chapter we underscore the interrelationships among reading, thinking, and writing processes as we explore the role of writing in content area learning. The ideas presented in the chapter are intended to show how writing activity can and must go beyond "mechanical uses" in the content classroom.

Minds On

1. Why and how will the instructional strategies that you have studied help you facilitate reader–text interactions?

2. With a small group, create an intra-act guide sheet for this chapter. After you have finished, discuss any insights into reading gained from this activity.

3. The basic premise of a reading guide is to provide instructional support for students for whom the text is too difficult to handle independently. How might guides be especially well suited to below-level students who have low self-esteem and little confidence in their ability to meet success with content material? In what ways will the purpose of meeting the individual needs of academically at-risk students be better served through their use? Provide specific examples when possible.

4. Reflect on the use of reading guides in each of the content areas. Do you agree or disagree with the following statements:

   a. Reading guides provide students with direction and organization for their reading.

   b. Reading guides give students the chance to respond to texts in meaningful ways.

   c. Reading guides are not meant to be used every day or with every reading assignment; that would reduce their effectiveness.

   d. Levels of comprehension are not as discrete as they may seem, but their division and treatment as separate entities is necessary to address each aspect of comprehension.

   e. If students become used to the support reading guides offer, they will always be teacher dependent.

5. If a reading guide is offered as an independent activity, students will get little out of it; failure will be just as frequent as with the traditional question-laden worksheet. Students need to be led through the use of study guides, sometimes working independently, sometimes working together. Reflect on the role of the content teacher in designing and using reading guides for learning.

Hands On

1. Without sharing perceptions, each member of your group should read this short paragraph and follow the directions that follow it.

   An artist was talking enthusiastically about one of her favorite paintings to several people visiting the gallery when a woman approached her and offered to purchase the work. The owner of the gallery removed the painting from the wall. The painting was snatched from her hands, and the woman bolted through the front door into a waiting van, which sped down the street through a nearby red light and vanished into the night.

   Using the paragraph as a reference, respond to each of the following statements, in the order presented, by circling T (for true), F (for false), or ? (for unable to determine from the paragraph). Once you have characterized a statement as true, false, or questionable, you cannot change your answer.

   a. The artist talked about one of her paintings. T   F   ?

   b. The thief was a woman. T   F   ?

   c. The crime appeared to be premeditated. T   F   ?

   d. This type of theft seems unlikely. T   F   ?

   e. The owner removed the painting from the wall. T   F   ?

   f. The owner was the artist. T   F   ?

   g. The woman who bolted through the door stole the painting. T   F   ?

   h. The person who snatched the painting from the owner's hands was the artist. T   F   ?

   i. A robbery didn't occur. T   F   ?

Discuss the variety of possible answers based on your responses. What does this activity tell you about reader–text interactions?

2. Select a short informational article in a magazine or book, and make copies for each member of your group. Have each member of the group choose one of the following instructional strategies: (1) KWL (What do you *know*? About what do you *want to know* more? What did you *learn*?), (2) GRP (guided reading procedure), (3) intra-act, and (4) a discussion web. If there are more than four members in your group, duplicate strategies as needed.

   Using the same article, design a lesson around the strategy you have chosen and make copies to share with the members of the group. As you review the four different lessons prepared by your colleagues, what comparisons and contrasts can you make between these instructional strategies?

3. Choose a brief content area reading selection. Working as two groups, one group should prepare a selective reading guide, and the other a three-level guide on the material. Meet together to share the completed products and to discuss the ways in which they are similar and dissimilar and the advantages and disadvantages of each.

4. Work together to create a three-level guide for an article from an electronic media source, a newspaper, or an educational journal. Follow the guidelines for construction presented in this chapter.

e.Resources extra

- Go to Chapter 10 of the Companion Website (**www.ablongman.com/vacca8e**) and click on Activities to complete the following task:

  The following Website explores oral language: **http://pw1.netcom.com/ ~rlederer/index.htm**. Browse this site and work with language play in small groups. Use the activity as a springboard for talking about language in the classroom.

- Go to the Companion Website (**www.ablongman.com/vacca8e**) for suggested readings, interactive activities, multiple-choice questions, and additional Web links to help you learn more about guiding reader–text interactions.

expect the world®

The New York Times
nytimes.com

Themes of the Times

Extend your knowledge of the concepts discussed in this chapter by reading current and historical articles from the *New York Times.* Go to the Companion Website and click on eThemes of the Times.

chapter 11

Writing to Learn

We do not write in order to be understood;
we write in order to understand.
—C. DAY LEWIS

Writing is not without its rewards and surprises. The surprises come from discovering what you want to say about a subject; the rewards lie in knowing that you crafted to satisfaction what you wanted to say. C. Day Lewis didn't sit down at his desk to write about things that were already clear in his mind. If he had, there would have been little incentive to write. Lewis used writing first to discover and clarify meaning—*to understand*—and second, to communicate meaning to others—*to be understood*.

Writing facilitates learning by helping students explore, clarify, and think deeply about the ideas and concepts they encounter in reading.

In other chapters, we recommend various kinds of writing activities to scaffold students' interactions with texts. In this chapter, however, our intent is to highlight and reaffirm the powerful learning opportunities that arise

INTEGRATING READING AND WRITING

EXPLORATORY WRITING ACTIVITIES

Unsent Letters   Biopoems   Dialogues   Admit Slips and Exit Slips   Brainstorming and Clustering

JOURNAL WRITING

Response Journals   Double-Entry Journals   Learning Logs

RAFTING ACTIVITIES

Creating Contexts for Writing

whenever teachers link reading and writing in the lessons that they create. A classroom environment that supports reading and writing invites students to explore ideas, clarify meaning, and construct knowledge. When reading and writing are taught in tandem, the union influences content learning in ways not possible when students read without writing or write without reading. When teachers invite a class to write before or after reading, they help students use writing to think about what they will read and to explore and think more deeply about the ideas they have read.

Reading and writing have been taught in some classrooms as if they bear little relationship to each other. The result has often been to sever the powerful bonds for meaning-making that exist between reading and writing. There's little to be gained from teaching reading apart from writing. The organizing principle reflects this notion: **Writing facilitates learning by helping students explore, clarify, and think deeply about the ideas and concepts they encounter in reading.**

Frame of Mind

1. Why emphasize writing to learn in content areas?

2. Why integrate writing and reading?

3. How might teachers create occasions for students to write to read and to read to write?

4. How can teachers use exploratory writing activities to connect reading and writing?

5. How can teachers use journals to connect writing and reading?

6. How can teachers develop RAFT writing activity assignments?

Sinclair Lewis, the first American author to win a Nobel Prize for literature, said that writing is just work. It doesn't matter if "you dictate or use a pen or type or write with your toes—it is still just work." Computers notwithstanding, writing isn't easy for most people. Yet for those who are successful, the process of writing—sweat and all—is enormously challenging and rewarding.

Perhaps for this reason, Allyse's mother was a bit perplexed by her daughter's writing. Allyse was thirteen years old and, by all accounts, a bright student. Yet her mother was bewildered by her daughter's writing activities both in and out of school: "She'll spend hours slaving over pages to mail to an out-of-state friend but writes skimpy, simpleminded paragraphs for school assignments." When Allyse was questioned about the discrepancy in her writing, her reply was all the more confusing: "But, Mom, that's what my teachers want."

Allyse may never win a Nobel Prize for literature. But she does have a need to write. Most children and adolescents do. Often, just out of sight of teachers, students will write continually to other students during the course of a school day—about classmates, teachers, intrigues, problems, parents, or anything else that happens to be on their minds. The topics may not be academically oriented, but they are both real and immediate to students.

In Allyse's case, writing to an out-of-state friend was so important that she was willing to struggle with a blank page to keep in touch. However, as far as school writing was concerned, she had probably psyched out what her teachers expected from her. She knew what she needed to do to get by and, most likely, to be successful. Allyse intuitively understood the role of writing in her classes and operated within that context.

Although students often engage in some form of writing in content area classrooms, few teachers use writing to its fullest potential as a tool for learning. Allyse's response to her mother's question reflects what researchers such as Judith Langer and Arthur Applebee (1987) have consistently observed to be the role

> ## Response Journal
> What do the "hidden writing" activities of students suggest about their need to communicate with others?

of writing in content classrooms: It is mainly restricted to short responses to study questions or to taking notes in class. For example, examine in Figure 11.1 the worksheet responses of a student in a high school biology class. The students have been studying a unit on viruses. The worksheet is designed to have the class think about the life characteristics of viruses in relation to other living organisms. Notice how the spacing on the worksheet restricts the student's responses to short one- or two-sentence answers. The student provides accurate information but only enough to satisfy the requirements of the assignment.

Even though the purpose of the worksheet writing may be legitimate, students need varied and frequent experiences with writing as a tool for learning. According to Langer and Applebee (1987), "Put simply, in the whole range of academic course work, American children do not write frequently enough, and the reading and writing tasks they are given do not require them to think deeply enough" (p. 4). There are

FIGURE 11.1 **A Biology Student's Written Responses on a Worksheet**

Characteristics of Life

1. CELLS: All living things are composed of cells.
   VIRUSES: Viruses are constructed of compounds usually associated with cells but they are not considered cells.

2. ORGANIZATION: All organisms are organized at both the molecular and the cellular levels. They take in substances from the environment and organize them in complex ways.
   VIRUSES: No, they aren't organized because they don't take in substances from the environment. They just replicate, using a host cell.

3. ENERGY USE: All organisms use energy for growth and maintenance.
   VIRUSES: Viruses don't use energy until they are in a cell; they do not grow; they use host cells for energy.

4. RESPONSE TO THE ENVIRONMENT: All organisms respond to a stimulus. A complex set of responses is called a behavior.
   VIRUSES: They only respond when they are affecting a cell.

5. GROWTH: All living things grow. Growth occurs through cell division and cell enlargement.
   VIRUSES: They don't grow.

6. REPRODUCTION: All species of organisms have the ability to reproduce on their own.
   VIRUSES: They require a host cell to reproduce.

at least three good reasons for teachers to take a second look at the role of writing in their classrooms. First, writing improves thinking. Second, it facilitates learning. Third, writing is intimately related to reading.

Content area teachers usually have second thoughts about assigning writing in their classrooms because of preconceived notions of what the teaching of writing may entail. Writing isn't generally thought of as basic to thinking and learning about content fields. Nancie Atwell (1990) is quick to point out that although the role of language arts teachers is to guide students' development as writers, teachers of every discipline share in the responsibility of showing students how to think and write as scientists, historians, mathematicians, and literary critics do. When students engage in writing as a way of knowing, they are thinking on paper.

Integrating Reading and Writing

There is no better way to think about a subject than to have the occasion to read and write about it. However, reading and writing don't necessarily guarantee improved thinking or learning. Students can go through the motions of reading and writing, lacking purpose and commitment, or they can work thoughtfully to construct meaning, make discoveries, and think deeply about a subject. Classrooms that integrate reading and writing lend encouragement to students who are maturing as readers and writers and provide instructional support so that readers and writers can play with ideas, explore concepts, clarify meaning, and elaborate on what they are learning.

Reading and Writing as Composing Processes

Reading and writing are acts of composing because readers and writers are involved in an ongoing, dynamic process of constructing meaning (Tierney and Pearson 1983). Composing processes are more obvious in writing than in reading: The writer, initially facing a blank page or screen, constructs a text. The text is a visible entity and reflects the writer's thinking on paper. Less obvious is the "text"—the configuration of meanings—that students compose or construct in their own minds as they read.

Think of reading and writing as two sides of the same coin. Whereas the writer works to make a text sensible, the reader works to make sense from a text. As a result, the two processes, rooted in language, are intertwined and share common cognitive and sociocultural characteristics. Both reading and writing, for example, involve purpose, commitment, schema activation, planning, working with ideas, revision and rethinking, and monitoring. Both processes occur within a social, communicative context. Skilled writers are mindful of their content (the subject about which they are writing) and also of their audiences (the readers for whom they write). Skilled readers are mindful of a text's content and are also aware that they engage in transactions with its author.

The relationships between reading and writing have been a source of inquiry by language researchers since the mid-1970s (Tierney & Shanahan 1991). Several broad conclusions about the links between reading and writing can be drawn: Good readers are often good writers, and vice versa; students who write well tend to read more than those who do not write well; wide reading improves writing; and students who are good readers and writers perceive themselves as such and are more likely to engage in reading and writing on their own.

Why connect reading and writing in instructional contexts? According to Shanahan (1990), the combination of reading and writing in a classroom improves achievement and instructional efficiency. From a content area perspective, writing about ideas and concepts encountered in texts will improve students' acquisition of content more than simply reading without writing. When reading and writing are taught in concert, the union fosters communication, enhances problem solving, and makes learning more powerful than if reading or writing is engaged in separately.

Reading and Writing as Exploration and Clarification

When teachers integrate writing and reading, they help students use writing to *think about what they will read* and to *understand what they have read.* Writing may be used to catapult students into reading. It is also one of the most effective ways for students to understand something they have read. Teachers can put students into writing-to-read or reading-to-write situations because the writing process is a powerful tool for exploring and clarifying meaning.

Donald Murray (1980) explains that writers engage in a process of exploration and clarification as they go about the task of making meaning. In Figure 11.2, Murray suggests that writers progress from exploring meaning to clarifying it as they continue to draft and shape a piece of writing. A writer's first draft is an initial attempt to think on paper or screen. The more writers work with ideas put on paper or screen, the more they are able to revise, rethink, and clarify what they have to say about a subject.

> **Response Journal**
> Why should exploratory writing be encouraged in content area classrooms?

Santa and Havens (1991) illustrate the power of writing before and after reading with an example from a biology class. Before reading a textbook assignment on flower reproduction, students wrote before-reading entries in *learning logs* (a student resource we explain shortly), telling what they knew about the subject they would be reading and studying. Here's an example of a student's entry:

> In this chapter I am going to learn about flower reproduction. I know that flowers have male and female parts. I think that these parts are in the inside of the flower. To see them you have to pull aside the petals. I think petals probably protect the reproductive parts, but I am not sure. I remember something about separate flowers for males and females, but I think many flowers have both parts on the same flower. I'm pretty sure you need to have at least two plants before they can reproduce. (p. 124)

What about . . .
Content Standards and Assessment?

BOX 11.1

The ability to write clearly and effectively is an important content standard for students to meet in a variety of writing situations in academic, job-related, and nonacademic contexts. Proficiency assessments, especially in test situations where students must respond to open-ended questions or write extended essays, evaluate both the content and the process by which students produced a piece of writing. In these situations, student writing often is evaluated through *holistic scoring* procedures. In holistic scoring, a *rubric* or guide (a set of standards against which the writing is evaluated) is used to assess the quality of the written response or essay. Rubrics, as we explained in Chapter 2, provide a scale by which to evaluate the writing.

For example, in holistic scoring a *general impression* rubric allows teachers or test evaluators to judge a piece of writing quickly and accurately based on a "general impression" of its overall effectiveness. As a result, holistic scoring permits the teacher/evaluator to sort, rank, and grade written pieces rather efficiently and effectively. Rubrics based on an overall impression of a piece of writing usually contain either a 9-point, 6-point, or 4-point scoring scale. The 9-point scale allows the evaluator to make detailed distinctions about the effectiveness of the writing, whereas a 4-point scale permits "pass/fail" type broader judgments of a written response.

Another holistic scoring measure is the *primary trait scoring* rubric. Primary trait scoring focuses on the characteristics in a piece of writing that are crucial to completion of a writing activity that establishes a context for writing. For example, how effectively did students handle the writing activity in rela-

tion to role, audience, form, or topic? (In this chapter, you will read about RAFT [which stands for *role, audience, form, topic*] writing activities that provide students with a specific context for writing.)

The completed writing activity is evaluated typically for these primary traits or characteristics: (1) accurate content in support of a position statement, (2) a logical and coherent set of ideas in support of a position statement, and (3) a convincing and persuasive position statement aimed at a specific audience. With primary trait scoring, a rubric provides several levels of writing quality/effectiveness in which to assess the piece of writing:

- *Level 4: High-quality writing.* The position statement is clearly stated. Lines of argument and evidence are presented in systematic and convincing fashion.

- *Level 3: Medium-quality writing.* The position statement is both clearly stated and supported with several lines of argument. The lines of evidence and support are moderately well developed.

- *Level 2: Lower-quality writing.* The position statement is clear, but the writing offers minimal evidence for support and falls short of unifying arguments.

- *Level 1: Lowest-quality writing.* The position statement is unclearly and inappropriately stated. Evidence is illogical, emotional, or nonexistent. Paper lacks clear sense of organization. (adapted from Lapp, Fisher, Flood, & Cabello 2001)

The accompanying rubric was developed by Pearce (1983) based on the following writing activity: *You are a newspaper reporter who covered the civil rights movement during the 1960s. Write a time capsule document analyzing Martin Luther King Jr.'s approach to civil rights during the 1960s. Compare this approach to one taken by other African American leaders during this period.* For this writing activity, papers were evaluated for the following primary traits: (1) accurate and adequate content about civil disobedience, (2) a comparison of Dr. King's approach to civil disobedience with at least one other African American leader's approach, and (3) a logical and organized presentation that provides evidence for any generalization made. The rubric guides the teacher/evaluator in making decisions about the quality of the writing:

Paper topic: 1960s approaches to civil rights in the United States

High-quality papers contain:

An overview of civil rights or their lack during the 1960s, with three specific examples.

A statement defining civil disobedience, with three examples of how it was used and Martin Luther King's role.

At least one other approach to civil rights, with specific examples, and a comparison of this approach with King's civil disobedience that illustrates differences or similarities in at least two ways.

Good organization, well-developed arguments, few mechanical errors (sentence fragments, grammatical errors, spelling errors).

Medium-quality papers contain:

An overview of Black civil rights during the 1960s, with two specific examples.

A statement defining civil disobedience, with two examples of its use and Martin Luther King's involvement.

One other approach to civil rights, with examples, and a comparison of it with King's civil disobedience by their differences.

Good organization, few mechanical errors, moderately developed arguments.

Lower-quality papers contain:

A general statement defining civil disobedience with reference to Martin Luther King's involvement and at least one example.

One other approach to civil rights and how it differed from civil disobedience.

Fair organization, some mechanical errors.

Lowest-quality papers contain:

A general statement on who Martin Luther King was or a general statement on civil disobedience.

A general statement that not all Blacks agreed with civil disobedience.

A list of points, poor organization, many mechanical errors.

Source: From Daniel L. Pearce, "Guidelines for the Use and Evaluation of Writing in Content Classrooms" (December 1983). *Journal of Reading, 27*(3), 212–218. Copyright © 1983 by the International Reading Association. All rights reserved. Used by permission of the author and the International Reading Association.

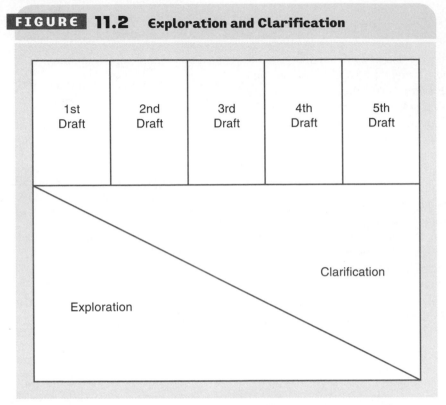

FIGURE 11.2   Exploration and Clarification

Source: From "Writing as Process: How Writing Finds Its Own Meaning," by Donald M. Murray in *Eight Approaches to Teaching Composition,* Donovan and McClelland (Eds.). Copyright © 1980 by the National Council of Teachers of English. Reprinted with permission.

In the biology class, students also had an occasion to write about flower reproduction after reading. In an after-reading entry, writing helps the students continue to explore and clarify meaning by focusing on what they learned and noting their misconceptions in their before-reading entries. Study the after-reading entry written by the same student:

> I learned that stamens are the male parts of the flower. The stamen produces the pollen. The female part is the pistil. At the bottom of the pistil is the ovary. Plants have eggs just like humans. The eggs are kept in the ovary. I still am not sure how pollen gets to the female part. Do bees do all this work, or are there other ways to pollinate? I was right, sometimes male and female parts are on separate flowers. These are called incomplete flowers. Complete flowers have both male and female parts on the same flower. I also learned that with complete flowers just one plant can reproduce itself. So, I was partially wrong thinking it always took two plants to reproduce. (p. 124)

Occasions to write on content subjects, such as the before-reading and after-reading entries just shown, create powerful opportunities to learn content in concert with reading. Students who experience the integration of writing and reading are likely to learn more content, to understand it better, and to remember it longer. This is the case because writing, whether before or after reading, promotes thinking, but in different ways. Writing a summary after reading (see Chapter 12), for example, is likely to result in greater understanding and retention of important information. However, another type of writing—let's say an essay—may trigger the analysis, synthesis, and elaboration of ideas encountered in reading and class discussion.

Because writing promotes different types of learning, students should have many different occasions to write. Let's look at some ways that teachers can create occasions for students to think and learn by writing.

Exploratory Writing Activities

Exploratory writing is first-draft writing. Often, it is messy, tentative, and unfinished. Exploration of ideas and concepts may be pursued before or after reading. Writing activities that help students tap into their storehouses of memories—their prior knowledge—make excellent springboards into reading. Exploratory writing helps students collect what they know and connect it to what they will be reading. For example, some teachers combine brainstorming, a topic to be studied, with five or so minutes of spontaneous freewriting in which students tell what they know about the subject to be studied.

Gere (1985) describes exploratory writing as unfinished. In her words, unfinished writing is "writing that evinces thought but does not merit the careful scrutiny which a finished piece of writing deserves" (p. 4). There is value in planning unfinished writing activities in the content area classroom.

Unsent Letters

The writing-to-learn activity known as *unsent letters* establishes a role-play situation in which students are asked to write letters in response to the material they are studying. The activity requires the use of imagination and often demands that students engage in interpretive and evaluative thinking. Following is Jeremy's unsent letter to the president of the United States, written after he studied the effects of nuclear war in his social studies text. It reflects both personal and informative writing.

Dear Mr. President,
How is life in the White House? In school we have been studying the horrible effects of a nuclear war. The United States alone has enough nuclear weapons to wipe out 1 million Hiroshimas. The earth doesn't even have that many cities that big.

In a nuclear war 1.1 billion people would be killed outright, and they are the lucky ones. Another 1.1 billion would suffer from burns and radiation sickness.

1 nuclear warhead or 2 megatons is 2 million tons of TNT, imagine 15 megatons. . . .

During a nuclear war buildings and people would be instantly vaporized. The remaining people would starve to death. The radiation would be 250 rads or 1,000 medical x-rays which is enough to kill you.

After all this I hope you have learned some of the terrible facts about nuclear war. (Levine 1985, p. 44)

Unsent letters direct students' thinking with particular audiences in mind. Biopoems, by contrast, require students to play with ideas using precise language in a poetic framework.

Biopoems

Response Journal

What is your reaction to the use of a biopoem as a writing to learn activity?

A *biopoem* allows students to reflect on large amounts of material within a poetic form. The biopoem follows a pattern that enables writers to synthesize what they have learned about a person, place, thing, concept, or event under study. For example, study the pattern suggested by Gere (1985) for a person or character:

Line 1. First name

Line 2. Four traits that describe character

Line 3. Relative ("brother," "sister," "daughter," etc.) of _____

Line 4. Lover of _____ (list three things or people)

Line 5. Who feels _____ (three items)

Line 6. Who needs _____ (three items)

Line 7. Who fears _____ (three items)

Line 8. Who gives _____ (three items)

Line 9. Who would like to see _____ (three items)

Line 10. Resident of _____

Line 11. Last name

Notice how a health education teacher adapted the preceding pattern to a writing activity in her course. The lesson was part of a unit on HIV and AIDS awareness. After the class spent several days studying the topic, the teacher introduced the biopoem strategy and explained how it could be useful in learning. She shared several biopoems from previous years that students had written on various topics. She then discussed the biopoem format and clarified any questions that students might have about writing a biopoem. She invited the students to write a biopoem using what they learned about AIDS. They could apply what they learned to a person they "invented" or to a real-life person who had HIV.

Here are two of the biopoems the students wrote. The first deals with an invented person; the second, with Earvin "Magic" Johnson, a former All-Star professional basketball player who tested positive for HIV at the height of his career.

Valerie,
Thin, tired, sad, confused.
She asks: "Why me?"
             "How will I deal with this?"
             "Will I be alone?"

Valerie,
She needs love,
              support,
              care,
              and advice.

Valerie,
She fears dying,
              being alone,
              feeling rejected.

Valerie,
She would like to see a cure,
                         Her family's approval,
                         Friends who care.

Valerie,
Your neighbor next door
A resident of Anywhere, U.S.A.
Valerie

The Magic Man,
Born Earvin Johnson.
Strong, Brave, Outspoken, Respected
Why you?
You "the Man!" But how do you feel now:
Stupid? Confused? Lonely?
Even the Magic Man needs love, support, family.
You fear dying, rejection, loss.
Would you like to see another ten years?
Your children grow up?
Your place in the Hall of Fame?
Resident of the world
Magic Johnson
You still "the Man!"

Dialogues

In a dialogue activity, students are asked to create an exchange between two or more persons, historical figures, or characters being studied. Beaman (1985), a high school social studies teacher, illustrated the use of dialogue as a writing-to-learn assignment. He asked his students to write a dialogue between themselves and a "friend" who wanted them to do something they were opposed to but were unsure of how to respond to because of peer pressure. Beaman suggested that students write about awkward teenage situations of peer pressure. Here's a sample dialogue between Mary and Betty:

Mary: Let's skip class and go out on the parking lot. I have some awesome dope and a new tape by the Scorpions.

Betty: I can't. I've skipped second period one too many times, and I really want to graduate. Contemporary Problems is required, and I'm afraid I may fail.

Mary: Get serious, one class missed is not going to get you an F. You need the relaxation, and besides, the Scorpions . . .

Betty: I wish I could say "yes" to you.

Mary: Say "yes" then, or are you turning into a real "school" girl?

Betty: You are pressuring me, Mary!

Mary: No pressure, just fun, come on . . .

Betty: No, I'm going to class, I do want to graduate. You can go, but I'm going to class. (Beaman 1985, p. 63)

A dialogue such as this one permits writers to think about conflicts and possible solutions. As an unfinished writing activity, a dialogue also provides an opportunity for students to react to ideas and to extend their thinking about the material being studied.

Foreign-language teachers adapt the use of dialogues to help their students converse in writing and then to role-play their conversations in front of the class. In the dialogue that follows, high school Spanish students wrote about a concert they would like to see. The teacher gave them the option of working in pairs or groups of three. As part of the dialogue writing, each student had to contribute at least four lines to the conversation. The teacher also directed the students to use at least three new verbs in their dialogue and at least ten new vocabulary words. The students practiced reading their dialogues to each other while working in their groups. The teacher evaluated students on their pronunciation during the role-play of the dialogues (individual accountability) and on originality, sentence structure, and grammar usage in the written dialogue (group accountability). The dialogue, as drafted by the students, follows:

> **Response Journal**
>
> Write a dialogue between you and the authors of this text in which you discuss the value of informal writing activities in the content areas.

Rául: ¿Te gustas el cantante Elvis Presley?

Joa Quìn: Sì, Yo fui a concìerto de Elvis. Él tenió un grande Voz.

Rául: Yo no voy. Son Agotado.

Joa Quìn: Yo tengo un cartel y una entrada de concierto.

Rául: Yo sìempre canto la canción "Blue suede shoes."

Joa Quìn: Aqui vení Senorita Holtman.

Rául: ¡Hola Senorita Holtman!

Lucía: ¡Hola, muchachos!

Joa Quìn: Senorita Holtman, E te quedas ver la fonción de Elvis año pasado.

Lucía: Sì, Yo me reuní muchos los jovencitos. Ellos queneron entrevistar él. Fue mucho grande. Hasta Luego.

Admit Slips and Exit Slips

Admit slips and exit slips involve anonymous writing and, therefore, shouldn't be part of the permanent record of learning that builds over time in students' learning logs. Thus, these activities should be introduced as a separate assignment and not as part of a learning-log entry.

Admit slips are brief comments written by students on index cards or half-sheets of paper at the very beginning of class. Gere (1985) recommends that these written responses be collected as tickets of admission to class. The purpose of the admit slip is to have students react to what they are studying or to what's happening in class. Students are asked to respond to questions such as

What's confusing you about _____?

What problems did you have with your text assignment?

What would you like to get off your chest?

What do you like (dislike) about _____?

The admit slips are collected by the teacher and read aloud (with no indication of the authorship of individual comments) as a way of beginning class discussion. Admit slips build a trusting relationship between teacher and students and contribute to a sense of community in the classroom.

In an advanced algebra class, where students had been studying complex numbers, the teacher asked the class to use admit slips to explain difficulties students had with one of their homework assignments. One student wrote, "I didn't know where to start." Several other students made similar comments. The teacher was able to use the written feedback to address some of the problems that students had with the assignment.

An *exit slip*, as you might anticipate, is a variation on the admit slip. Toward the end of class, the teacher asks students for exit slips as a way of bringing closure to what was learned. An exit slip question might require students to summarize, synthesize, evaluate, or project.

In the advanced algebra class, exit slips were used toward the end of the class to introduce a new unit on imaginary numbers. The teacher asked students to write for several minutes as they reflected on the question "Why do you think we are studying about imaginary numbers after we studied the discriminant?" One student wrote, "Because the discriminant can be negative and I didn't know what kind of a number $\sqrt{-1}$ was. I guessing [*sic*] it must be imaginary. Right?" The teacher was able to sort through the exit slip responses and use them to introduce the new unit.

The several minutes devoted to exit-slip writing are often quite revealing of the day's lesson and establish a direction for the next class.

Brainstorming and Clustering

Brainstorming and clustering are related instructional strategies that permit students to examine ideas as rehearsal for reading and writing. Brainstorming and clustering are exploratory strategies for prereading or prewriting because they help students to establish purpose as they think about ideas and concepts to be studied. Teachers usually begin a brainstorming session by presenting an idea or concept to students based on some aspect of the subject they will be studying. A time limit is then set for brainstorming, which involves listing as many ideas as possible about the topic.

Clustering may be viewed as both a variation and an extension of brainstorming. Rather than list ideas, students "cluster" them around a nucleus word

FIGURE 11.3 **Sample Cluster**

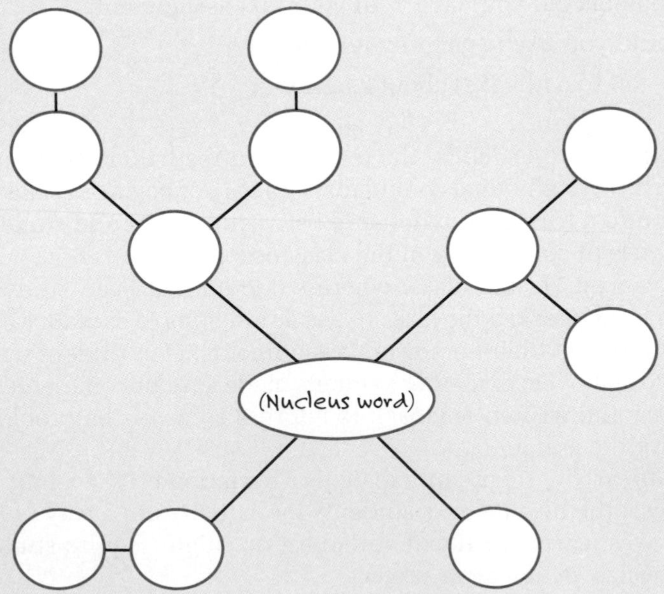

or concept, as in Figure 11.3. When introducing clustering to students, first model the strategy by writing a key or nucleus word on the chalkboard or overhead transparency and then surround it with other associated words that are offered by the students. In this way, students not only gather ideas for writing but also connect the ideas within categories of information. Teacher-led clustering provides students with opportunities to practice the strategy. As they become aware of the strategy and how to use it, students will be able to cluster ideas quickly on their own.

Notice in Figure 11.4 how a special education teacher used brainstorming and clustering to help her students explore the topic of "freed slaves" as part of a unit on the Civil War and its aftermath. As part of their study of the Reconstruction period, students explored issues such as the rebuilding of the South and the dilemma presented by the freed slaves. One of the learning experiences for the

FIGURE 11.4   Cluster on the Lives of Freed Slaves in the Years after the Civil War

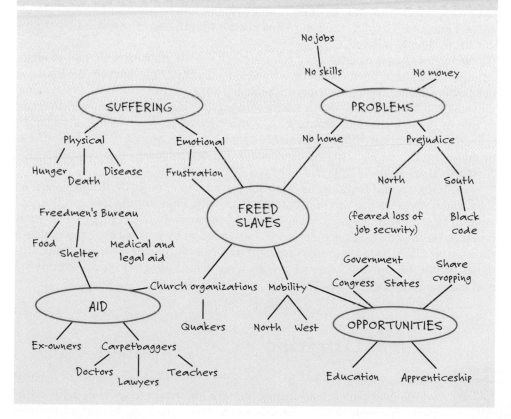

chapter on freed slaves concerned a writing activity designed to help students examine some of the important ideas that they had studied. The teacher began the lesson with a lead-in: "Using any information that you can recall from your text or class discussion, think about what might have been some of the problems or concerns of a freed slave immediately following the Civil War. Let's do some brainstorming." As the students offered ideas related to prejudice and lack of money, homes, and food, the teacher listed them on the board.

Getting ideas out in the open through brainstorming was the first step in the lesson. The second step was to cluster the words into meaningful associations based on student suggestions. The teacher modeled the activity by choosing as the keyword the concept of *freed slaves*. She then drew a line to the upper right corner of the chalkboard and connected the keyword to the word *problems*. She connected some of the words generated by students during brainstorming to the cluster. The teacher then asked what some of the results of the freed slaves' problems would be. One student volunteered the word *suffering*. The teacher wrote *suffering* in the upper left corner of the cluster and asked the students to brainstorm some examples. These examples were then connected to the cluster.

The remainder of the class session centered on discussion related to the *aid* freed slaves received and the *opportunities* that resulted from the Reconstruction years. Figure 11.4 depicts the completed cluster that the teacher and students produced on the chalkboard.

With the cluster as a frame of reference, the students were assigned to write what it would have been like to be a freed slave in the 1860s and 1870s. Because the textbook presented a variety of primary sources (including diary entries, newspaper clippings, and death notices), many of the students decided to write in one of those forms (see Figure 11.5). One member of the class became so involved in the activity that he wanted his historical document to appear authentic by aging the paper. This he did by burning the edges so that it would look "historic."

Students should begin to develop their own clusters for writing as soon as they understand how to use the strategy effectively. They should feel comfortable enough to start with a basic concept or topic—written in the center of a sheet of paper or on the computer screen—and then to let go by making as many connections as possible. Because there is no right or wrong way to develop a cluster, students should be encouraged to play with ideas based on what they are studying and learning in class.

Journal Writing

Response Journal
Why do people journal?

Because journals serve a variety of real-life purposes, not the least of which is to write about things that are important to us, they have withstood the test of time. Artists, scientists, novelists, historical figures,

FIGURE 11.5 A Student's Writing Sample on What It Would Be Like to Be a Freed Slave

May 3, 1866

My mane is Toby and I had been a slave for eight years before we were freed. It was good at first but them we realized there were problems.

We had great prolblems. Prejudice kept us from doing what we wanted to do. Black Codes which were suppose to help didn't help us at all. We weren't allowed to be out after dark. We weren't allowed to carry a gun. We weren't allowed to go out without a pass.

We had no food. My family had no food. My kids were all sick and there was nothing I could do to help them.

But there was some nice people. The army and Quakers helped my kids get better and they helped us get some land and food for my family. then we started a farm we grew crops and got money.

We had some opertunites. We could move to another state for a Job. We could also get an education. Some Blacks even gained Goverment positions.

mathematicians, dancers, politicians, teachers, children, athletes—all kinds of people—have kept journals. Some journals—diaries, for example—are meant to be private and are not intended to be read by anyone but the writer. Sometimes, however, a diary makes its way into the public domain and affects readers in powerful ways. Anne Frank, probably the world's most famous child diarist, kept a personal journal of her innermost thoughts, fears, hopes, and experiences while hiding from the Nazis during World War II. Having read her diary, who hasn't been moved to think and feel more deeply about the tragic consequences of the Holocaust?

Other journals are more work related than personal in that writers record observations and experiences that will be useful, insightful, or instructive. In more than forty notebooks, Leonardo da Vinci recorded artistic ideas, detailed sketches of the human anatomy, elaborate plans for flying machines, and even his dreams. Novelists throughout literary history have used journals to record ideas, happenings, and conversations that have served to stimulate their imaginations and provide material for their writing. Even in a professional sport such as baseball, it is not unusual for hitters to keep a log of their at-bats: who the pitcher was, what the situation was (e.g., runner on base or bases empty), what types of pitches were thrown, and what the outcome of each at-bat was.

Academic journals also serve a variety of purposes. They help students generate ideas, create a record of thoughts and feelings in response to what they are reading, and explore their own lives and concerns in relation to what they are reading and learning. Academic journals create a context for learning in which students interact with information personally as they explore and clarify ideas, issues, and concepts under study. These journals may be used as springboards for class discussion or as mind stretchers that extend thinking, solve problems, or stimulate imagination. All forms of writing and written expression can be incorporated into academic journal writing, from doodles and sketches to poems and letters to comments, explanations, and reactions.

Three types of journals in particular have made a difference in content literacy situations: *response journals, double-entry journals,* and *learning logs.* Each of these can be used in an instructional context to help students explore literary and informational texts. Teachers who use academic journals in their classes encourage students to use everyday, expressive language to write about what they are studying, in the same way that they encourage students to use talk to explore ideas during discussion. When expressive or exploratory language is missing from students' journal writing, the students do not experience the kind of internal talk that allows them to explore and clarify meaning in ways that are personal and crucial to thinking on paper (Britton 1970) or on screen.

When writing in academic journals, students need not attempt to sound "academic," even though they are writing about ideas and information of importance in various disciplines. Like the exploratory writing activities previously discussed in this chapter, journal entries need to be judged on the writer's ability to communicate and explore ideas, not on the quality of handwriting or the number of spelling and grammatical errors in the writing. Journal writing underscores informal learning. It relieves teachers of the burden of correction so that they can focus on students' thinking, and it creates a nonthreatening situation for students who may be hesitant to take risks because they are overly concerned about the mechanics of writing (e.g., handwriting, neatness, spelling, and punctuation).

Response Journals

Response journals create permanent records of what readers are feeling and thinking as they interact with literary or informational texts. A response journal allows students to record their thoughts about texts and emotional reactions to them. Teachers may use prompts to trigger students' feelings and thoughts about a subject or may invite students to respond freely to what they are reading and doing in class. Prompts may include questions, visual stimuli, read-alouds, or situations created to stimulate thinking. An earth science teacher, for example, might ask students to place themselves in the role of a water molecule as they describe what it's like to travel through the water cycle. Examine how Mike, a low-achieving ninth grader who didn't like to write, responded in his journal entry:

> My name is Moe, its short for Molecule. I was born in a cloud when I was condensed on a dust particle. My neverending life story goes like this.
>
> During Moes life he had a great time boncing into his friends. He grew up in the cloud and became bigger and heavier. Moe became so heavy that one night lightning struck and he fell out of his cloud as a raindrop. He landed in a farmers field where this leavy plant sucked him up. Moe became a small section of a leave on the plant and then he absorbed sunlight and other things. One day a cow came by and ate Moes leave. He was now part of the cow.
>
> Well you can guess the rest. The farmer ate the cow and Moe became part of the farmer. One day the farmer was working in the field, he started sweating and thats when Moe escaped. He transpired into the air as a molecule again. Free at last he rejoined a group of new friends in a cloud and the cycle went on.

Mike's teacher was pleased by his journal entry, mechanical errors and all. On homework questions, he usually wrote short, incoherent answers. In this entry, however, he interacted playfully with the information in the text and demonstrated his understanding of the water cycle.

Historical Character Journals

Role playing is an excellent prompt for response journal writing. A history teacher may invite students to assume the role of a historical character and to view events and happenings from the character's perspective. In Claudia Finley's U.S. history class, students keep journals of events that took place in American history from the perspective of a fictitious historical family that each student created. The families witness all of the events that take place in American history and write their reactions to these events. Finley scaffolds the journal writing assignment with the guidesheet in Figure 11.6. Study the guidesheet, and then read several entries from one student's journal in Figure 11.7.

Sketchbooks in Art

A high school art teacher incorporates a sketchbook into his courses to guide students' thinking and responses to what they are learning and studying in

FIGURE **11.6** **A Guidesheet for Historical Character Journals**

To help you develop your historical character, use the information that you have gained about the American colonies and your own background knowledge.

Who is your character?

1. What is your character's name? How old is your character? Is he or she married? (*Note:* How old were people when they married during his or her time?)
   _____
   _____

2. Who else is in your character's family? How old is each of these people? (*Note:* What happened to a lot of children during this time?)
   _____
   _____

3. Where does your character live?
   _____
   _____

4. What does your character do for a living? Is he or she rich or poor?
   _____
   _____

5. What religion is your character? What attitude does he or she have toward religion?
   _____
   _____

6. How much education does your character have?
   _____
   _____

7. Was your character born in the United States, Europe, or Africa? If he or she was born in Europe, in what country?
   _____
   _____

8. How does your character feel about people who are "different" in skin color, religion, social or economic class, or nationality?
   a. Skin color? (*Note:* This may depend on where he or she lives.)
   _____
   b. Religion?
   _____
   c. Social or economic class?
   _____
   d. Nationality?
   _____

9. How does your character feel about being part of a colony instead of living in an independent country?
   _____
   _____

FIGURE 11.7   Historical Character Journal Entries

1770

My name is Victoria Black and I'm thirteen years old. We are a
Protestant family and we attend church regularly. It's a social as well
as religious occasion for us. We stay all day and my mother gossips with
all of the neighbors. I've made a few friends there but usually I stay
with my sister. I have long blond hair and sparkling blue eyes in my
mother's words. I'm learning how to take care of the home and cook
lately. My mother says it's important because soon enough I'll be
married. I think she wants me to marry one of the boys from town
whose father is a popular lawyer. I have an older sister Sarah who is
fifteen and has just gotten married. My parents are Mathew and
Elizabeth Black, they are becoming older and mother has been sick
lately. We worry very much for them and say prayers daily. We live on
Mander Plantation in Trenton, Pennsylvania, where my father grows
cotton and some tobacco. We have many indentured servants which
we treat very nicely. I've become close with a couple of them. Usually
when the servants' time has expired my father will give them some
land to start up their lives. Because we are more north we haven't any
African slaves yet. My father is planning a trip out east to buy some
slaves later this month. I'm still not sure if buying people is the right
thing to do but my brother told me he doesn't think they're real
people. I don't know how my father feels on this, he must think it's
alright. My father is very confused about what's going on with the
British. He doesn't understand why the colonists think they even have
a chance at fighting and winning with the British. He thinks the war
will be over in no time.

1778

I'm married now to William Brown, a new lawyer for Pennsylvania. We
have two children, Mary and Richard Brown. They are still both very
young, Mary is six and Richard is four and I'm expecting another soon!
William is for the Revolutionary War. He feels the British are not being
sensible with their laws for us. The taxation has bothered us greatly.
Each week we scramble for money. Even though William is a lawyer,
it's still hard to get started and receive reasonable wages. The
British have also gone too far with the quartering act. We had British

(continued)

FIGURE **11.7** **Continued**

soldiers knock on our door last week asking for food. William was outraged. He says we have to have a revolution and win, if we want to survive and live happily. William said things are just going to get worse and worse. I don't think things could get any worse. I do worry about this war, for my brothers and William. Hopefully neither of them will be in the militia. We are already hearing of some battles, which sound awful. We are starting to go to church and pray every day now for our family and country.

1779–1781
William and my brothers are going to be in the militia. I'm very worried for them. William feels what he's doing is right for the country. We seem to be winning some of the battles, which is surprising. The women and children from our church gather every day and pray for our brothers and husbands. We all try our hardest to stay on our feet and have enough food for everyone. Some weeks it's difficult. We feel that all of our money is going to taxes. We pray that the end will be here soon. I had a baby boy which we named Daniel Brown. It will be hard to raise these children alone. Before William goes to the militia I'm going to visit my mother, she's dying and I'd like to say goodbye to her.

class. As an introduction to the sketchbook, the class discusses reasons for keeping a sketchbook, which the teacher adapted from a model used by McIntosh (1991):

● *What should you include in your sketchbook?*

New ideas, sketches, concepts, designs, redesigns, words, notes from class, drawings to show understanding, reflections on the class, questions that you have, and new things you've learned.

● *When should you include entries in your sketchbook?*

(1) After each class; (2) anytime an insight or a design idea or question hits you; (3) anytime, so keep the sketchbook handy and visible in your work area.

- *Why should you draw and write in your sketchbook?*

  (1) It will record your ideas and ideas you might otherwise forget; (2) it will record and note your growth; (3) it will facilitate your learning, problem solving, idea forming, research, reading, and discussion in class.

- *How should you write and draw entries in your sketchbook?*

  You can express yourself in sketches and drawings; in single words, questions, or short phrases; in long, flowing sentences; in designs and redesigns; in diagrams, graphs, and overlays; or in colors.

- *Remember, the sketchbook is yours, and it reflects how perceptive you are with your ideas and how creative you are in your thought processes!*

Examine several of the students' sketchbook entries in Figure 11.8.

Math Journals

Math teachers use response journals in a variety of ways. They may invite students to write a "math autobiography" in which they describe their feelings and prior experiences as math learners. Rose (1989) suggests the following prompt for a biographical narrative in math:

> Write about any mathematical experiences you have had. The narratives should be told as stories, with as much detail and description as possible. Include your thoughts, reactions, and feelings about the entire experience. (p. 24)

If students need more scaffolding than the prompt, Rose recommends having them complete and write elaborations on sentences, such as

My most positive experience with math was _____

My background in math is _____

I liked math until _____

Math makes me feel _____

If I were a math teacher, I'd _____

The content of math journals may also include exploratory writing activities, summaries, letters, student-constructed word problems and theorem definitions, descriptions of mathematical processes, calculations and solutions to problems, and feelings about the course. Examine, for example, the journal entries in Figures 11.9 and 11.10.

Freewriting Response Journals

In addition to prompts, consider having students engage in "freewriting" in their journals. Hancock (1993) provides a set of guidelines for writing freely in response journals in literature. These guidelines, with some modification, can easily be

FIGURE **11.8** **Entries from a Sketchbook**

<u>Van Gogh vs. Gauguin</u>

—I like Van Gogh much better
—Gauguin is nice but too showy
—I like elegance of Van Gogh
—Self-portraits are really challenging
—Van Gogh—master directionalist
—Unbelievable that he (Van Gogh) had no training!

—I like looking at different artists. Even though I know these people are masters,
   I love their work.
—I could never do that without lots of training!!

<u>Impressionists</u>

—Pretty
—Watercolory
—Really masterful handling of paint (watercolor)
—Saw them at Smithsonian

<u>Question</u>
 When am I going to work larger?
I liked what we did on the Amiga—hope I get a chance to work with it again.

<u>Questions</u>
Why is it that I always draw late at night or early in the morning?
Shouldn't I start thinking about painting?
Will I ever understand color mixing?
Will I ever understand doing pencil directions?
Will I learn to stretch a canvas?

<u>Looking to the future</u>
—I don't use this sketchbook to do sketches—I like it more as a log
—Paint!! (probably a final problem)

| FIGURE **11.9** | **Journal Entry in Response to the Prompt, "What Goes through Your Mind When You Do a Proof?"** |

October 7

When I look at something I have to prove, the answer is always so obvious to me, I don't know what to write. This confuses me more because then I just write down one thing. Even though I understand it, no one else could. I don't use postulates & theorems because I have no idea which is which. So if you gave me a proof, I could probably prove it, but just not mathematically using big words.

| FIGURE **11.10** | **Journal Entry in Response to the Prompt, "Explain to Someone How to Bisect an Angle"** |

9/4

How to Draw a Bisected Angle

Make an acute angle. Label it $\angle ABC$—making Point A on one ray, B at the vertex, or point where rays meet, and C on the other ray. Now, with a compass, draw an arc of any measurement which will cross both rays. Next, use your compass to measure the distance between the two points you made by making the arc and keep the measurement locked on your protractor. Now, put the point of your compass on one of the arc points and make a slash in the middle of the angle. Do the same from the other dot on the other ray. The slash marks should cross in the center. Make a point where the slashes cross. Label it Point D. Draw a ray starting at Point B going through Point D. $\overrightarrow{BD}$ now bisects $\angle ABC$.

adapted to informational text. Some of the guidelines for students to consider when using response journals are the following:

- *Write your innermost feelings, opinions, thoughts, likes, and dislikes.* This is your journal. In it, feel the freedom to express yourself and your personal responses to reading.

- *Write down anything that you are thinking about while you read.* The journal is a way of recording those fleeting thoughts that pass through your mind as you interact with the book.

- *Don't worry about the accuracy of spelling and mechanics in the journal.* The content and expression of your personal thoughts should be your primary concern.

- *Record the number of the page you were reading when you wrote your response.* You might want to look back to reread and verify your thoughts.

- *Write on only one side per page of your spiral notebook.* Expect to read occasional interested comments from your teacher or another student on the other side.

- *Relate what you are reading to your own experiences.*

- *Ask questions while reading.* This will help you make sense of the story or characters.

- *Make predictions about what you think will happen as the plot unfolds.* Validate or change those predictions as you proceed in the text. Don't worry about being wrong.

- *Praise or criticize the book, the author, the style.*

- *Talk to the characters as you begin to know them.* Give them advice to help them. Put yourself in their place and tell them how you would act in a similar situation.

- *There is no limit to the types of responses you can write.* These guidelines are meant to trigger, not limit, the kinds of things you write.

Teachers often make students aware of how and why to use response journals through metacognitive discussions and demonstrations. One way to demonstrate how to write an effective entry is to share with the class some past students' responses of different types. Use these demonstrations to build confidence and procedural knowledge in the use of the journal.

Double-Entry Journals (DEJs)

A double-entry journal (DEJ) is a versatile adaptation of the response journal. As the name implies, DEJs allow students to record dual entries that are conceptually related. In doing so, students juxtapose their thoughts and feelings according to the prompts they are given for making the entries. To create a two-column format for the DEJ, have students divide sheets of notebook paper in half lengthwise. As an alternative, younger writers may need more room to write their entries than a divided page allows. They find that it is easier to use the entire left page of a notebook as one column and the right page as the other column.

Purposes for Using DEJs

DEJs serve a variety of functions. In the left column of the journal, students may be prompted to select words, short quotes, or passages from the text that interest them or evoke strong responses. In this column, they write the word, quote, or passage verbatim or use their own words to describe what is said in the text. In the right column, the students record their reactions, interpretations, and responses to the text segments they have selected. As part of a science unit on the solar system, for example, middle level students used double-entry journals as an occasion to explore their own personal meanings for the concept of the solar system. In the left column, they responded to the question, "What is it?" In the right column, the students reflected on the question, "What does it mean to you?" Study the entries that three of the students wrote in the, "What is it?" column. Then compare the three corresponding entries from the right column, "What does it mean to you?"

e.Resources

Find out more about using double-entry journals in content areas by conducting a search using the keywords "double entry journal + classroom lessons."

"WHAT IS THE SOLAR SYSTEM?"

It is nine planets, along with asteroid belts, stars, black holes, and so on.

"WHAT DOES IT MEAN TO YOU?"

The solar system is a mystery to me. I know the planets and stuff, but how did it come into being? Galileo had something to do with the solar system, but I'm not sure exactly what. I would like to find out more about it.

It is planets and stars. Earth is the third planet from the sun. It is the only planet with water. Stars are huge many much greater than the sun in size.

The solar system reminds me of a white haired scientist who is always studying the big vast opening in the sky. When I look at the sky at night I see tiny twinkling lights. People tell me that they're planets but I think they're stars. I see constellations but I don't recognize them. I am not a white haired scientist yet.

(continued)

"WHAT IS THE SOLAR SYSTEM?"

The nine planets are not very interesting to me and I won't bother to go through them. But I did memorize the order of the planets by this sentence. *My very eager mother just served us nine pizzas.* Take the beginning letters to remind you of each planet.

"WHAT DOES IT MEAN TO YOU?"

When I think about what the solar system means to me, I think about an unknown universe, which could be much larger than we think it is. I start to think about science fiction stories that I have read, alien beings and creatures that are in the universe some place.

Examples of DEJs in English and Math Classrooms

In an eighth-grade language arts class, Harry Noden and his students were engaged in a unit on the Yukon and Jack London's *Call of the Wild* (Noden & Vacca 1994). As part of the core book study of London's classic novel about the adventures of a sled dog named Buck, Noden arranged for a sled dog team demonstration by a group of local residents who participate in dog sledding as a hobby. His class was excited by the demonstration, which took place on the school's grounds. The next day, the class used double-entry journals to reflect on the experience. In the left column, they responded to the question, "What did you learn from the demonstration?" In the right column, they reflected on the question, "How did the demonstration help you better understand the novel?" Examine some of the students' entries in Figure 11.11.

Mathematics teachers have also been encouraged to use double-entry journals to help students solve word problems (Tobias 1989). In the left column, a teacher might direct students to engage in "thinking out loud" as they work on a word problem. In the right column, the students go about solving the problem, providing a layout of their sketches and calculations. Tobias noticed that as students began to use the two-column format to think about their problem-solving processes, they focused on posing two kinds of questions: "What is making the problem difficult for me? What could I do to make it easier for myself?" Here is one student's "thinking out loud" entry in response to this problem: *A car goes 20,000 miles on a long trip, rotating its five tires (including the spare) regularly and frequently. How many miles will any one tire have driven on the road?*

I assume there is a formula for solving this problem, but I have forgotten (if I ever knew) what it is.

I am being confused by the word "rotate." Simply by driving, we cause our tires to turn or "rotate" on the road. But "rotate" means something else in this problem. I had better concentrate on that.

I wonder how many miles each tire will have gone while in the trunk? Is this a useful approach? Let me try. (p. 52)

FIGURE	11.11	Entries from a Double-Entry Journal Assignment for *The Call of the Wild*

What did you learn from the demonstration?	How did the demonstration help you better understand the novel?
I learned that although dogs just look big and cuddly they really can work. When people take the time they can teach their dog anything. Yet that saying also applies to life. [Alex]	I never realized how hard it was for Buck to pull the sled. It takes a lot of work.
It was excellent. I learned that the owners and the dogs were a family and extremely hard workers. I learned how hard a race could be and the risk involved. I'm glad I got to see the dogs and their personalities. [Marcus]	It proved to me how Buck needed to be treated with praise and discipline and equality. That way you get a wonderful dog and a companion for life.
I learned about how they trained their dogs and that they need as much or more love and attention as they do discipline. [Jennifer]	It helped me understand the book better because it showed how unique Buck is compared to the other dogs. Also what a dog sled looks like and what Buck might have looked like. It made the story come alive more.

Tobias explains that using this unorthodox approach, trying to find the number of miles that any one tire will have traveled in the trunk of the car, is a productive way to solve the problem. In the right column, the student calculated the correct answer by dividing 5 tires into 20,000 miles to get 4,000 miles per tire in the trunk. He then subtracted 4,000 miles from the total 20,000 miles driven, yielding the correct answer: Each tire, rotated onto the four on-road positions, traveled a total of 16,000 miles.

Learning Logs

Learning logs add still another dimension to personal learning in content area classrooms. The strategy is simple to implement but must be used regularly to be effective. As is the case with response and double-entry journals, students keep an ongoing record of learning *as it happens* in a notebook or loose-leaf binder. They write in their own language, not necessarily for others to read but to themselves, about what they are learning. Entries in logs influence learning by revealing problems and concerns.

There is no one way to use learning logs, although teachers often prefer allowing five or ten minutes at the end of a period for students to respond to process questions such as, "What did I understand about the work we did in class today? What didn't I understand? At what point in the lesson did I get confused? What did I like or dislike about class today?" The logs can be kept in a box and stored in the classroom. The teacher then reviews them during or after school to see what the students are learning and to recognize their concerns and problems. Let's take a look at how several teachers integrate logs into their instructional contexts.

Learning Logs in Math Classrooms

Two math teachers report using learning logs with much success in their classrooms. Kennedy (1985), a middle school teacher, has designed what he calls a "writing in math" program in which learning logs are a key feature. In addition to the preceding process questions, he likes to ask students about what they're wondering. What specific questions do they have about the material being studied? He also finds that logs are effective for "making notes." According to Kennedy, the distinction between *taking* and *making* notes is central to the use of learning logs: "Taking notes is copying someone else's information; *making notes* is writing interpretive comments and personal reminders such as 'Ask about this' or just 'Why?' " (p. 61).

A high school algebra teacher introduces learning logs to her class this way:

> From time to time, I'll be asking you to write down in your logs how you went about learning a particular topic in this class. In other words, can you capture that moment when things finally made sense to you and how you felt? And can you express the frustration that might have preceded this moment? (Pradl & Mayher 1985, p. 5)

Students may at first be tentative about writing and unsure of what to say or reveal—after all, journal writing is reflective and personal. It takes a trusting atmosphere to open up to the teacher. However, to win the trust of students, teachers, such as the algebra teacher, refrain from making judgmental or evaluative comments when students admit a lack of understanding of what's happening in class. If a trusting relationship exists, students will soon recognize the value of logs, although perhaps not as enthusiastically as one high school student:

> This journal has got to be the best thing that's hit this chemistry class. For once the teacher has direct communication with every member of the class. No matter how shy the student is they can get their lack of understanding across to the teacher. . . . These journals act as a "hot line" to and from the teacher. I feel this journal has helped me and everyone that I know in class. The only thing wrong is we should have started these on the first day of school!! In every class! (Pradl & Mayher 1985, p. 6)

The algebra teacher's students probably feel the same way about their algebra class. Here are some of the things that they do in their logs. For starters, the teacher likes to introduce a new topic by asking students to jot down their predictions and expectations of what the topic may involve. She also has her students write down their understanding of any new theorem that is introduced. After students believe that they have learned a theorem well, they use their logs to imagine how they might explain the theorem to another, less well informed person, such as a younger sister or brother.

Both Kennedy and the algebra teacher use logs to have students create word problems that are then used to challenge other members of the class. Kennedy (1985) likes to have students write different kinds of word problems in their learning logs: "Sometimes I have them supply the data (for example, 'Write a problem involving the use of percent'); other times I supply the data (for example, 'Write a problem using the numbers 200, 400, and 600')" (p. 61).

Most journal activities require thinking but do not demand a finished product. Students soon learn to write without the fear of making errors. However, there are times when students should know in advance that their journal entries will be read aloud in class. According to Levine (1985), this is when students often produce their best writing because they are composing for an audience of peers. Josh, for example, an eighth grader, wrote about a lab experiment this way:

> Today in class we did a demo to try and find effective ways of recovering the solute from a solution.
>
> Several people came up with ideas as to how we could do this. A few people suggested filtering the solution, and others thought heating the solution so it evaporated would bring the solute back.
>
> First we tried filtering a copper sulfate solution but found that process didn't work. Evidently the crystals had dissolved to such an extent, that they were too small to be gathered by the filter paper.

We then heated the solution and found we were far more successful than in our first try. Approximately thirteen minutes after we began heating the solution, a ring of copper sulfate crystals appeared in the bowl where the solution was. Eventually all the liquid evaporated leaving only the crystals. Quite obviously I learned that to recover the solute from a solution you can heat the solution. I also learned not to bother trying to filter the solution. (p. 45)

Journal writing allows students such as Josh to express what's on their minds honestly and without pretense. RAFTing activities, likewise, help students to express themselves by creating a context for writing.

RAFTing Activities

RAFT is an acronym that stands for *role*, *audience*, *form*, and *topic*. RAFT allows teachers to create writing prompts for essay writing assignments (Holston & Santa 1985). What constitutes an effective writing prompt for academic assignments? Suppose you were assigned one of the following topics to write on, based on text readings and class discussion:

- Batiking
- The role of the laser beam in the future
- Victims of crime

> **Response Journal**
>
> Develop a RAFT writing activity for a topic in your content area.

No doubt, some of you would probably begin writing on one of the topics without hesitation. Perhaps you already know a great deal about the subject, have strong feelings about it, and can change the direction of the discourse without much difficulty. Others, however, may resist or even resent the activity. Your questions might echo the following concerns: "Why do I want to write about any of these topics in the first place? For whom am I writing? Will I write a paragraph? A book?" The most experienced writer must come to grips with questions such as these, and with even more complicated ones: "How will I treat my subject? What role will I take?" If anything, the questions raise to awareness the *rhetorical context*—the *writer's role*, the *audience*, the *form* of the writing, and the writer's *topic*—that most writing assignments should provide. A context for writing allows students to assess the writer's relationship to the subject of the writing (the topic) and to the reader (the audience for whom the writing is intended).

Establish a Context for Writing

A good writing activity, then, *situates* students in the writing task. Instead of assigning an essay on how to batik, give students a RAFT.

To show that you understand how batiking works, imagine that you are giving a demonstration at an arts-and-crafts show. Describe the steps and procedures involved in the process of batiking to a group of onlookers, recognizing that they know little about the process but are curious enough to find out more.

This example creates a context for writing. It suggests the writer's role (the student providing a batiking demonstration), the writer's audience (observers of the demonstration), the form of the writing (a how-to demonstration), and the topic (the process of batiking). RAFT writing prompts contrived situations and audiences in the context of what is being read or studied. However, they are far from trivial, nonacademic, or inconsequential. Instead, when students "become" someone else, they must look at situations in a nontraditional way. After writing, they can compare different perspectives on the same issue and examine the validity of the viewpoints that were taken.

e.Resources

Find out more about using RAFT writing activities by conducting a search using the keywords "RAFT writing strategy."

Use Discourse Forms in RAFTing Activities

Although some RAFT writing activities may contrive situations and audiences, others should reflect real situations and audiences outside the classroom. For example, letters to the editor of the local newspaper and to political leaders, authors, and scientists can be an important part of classroom study. Furthermore, a variety of writing forms can be easily incorporated into RAFT writing assignments. In Table 11.1, Tchudi and Yates (1983) provide a representative listing of some of these forms for content area writing.

◀ Looking Back
Looking Forward ▶

In this chapter, we focused on writing to emphasize the powerful bonds between reading and writing. Content area learning, in fact, is more within the reach of students when writing and reading are integrated throughout the curriculum. The two processes, both rooted in language, are intertwined and share common cognitive and sociocultural characteristics. The combination of reading and writing in a classroom improves achievement and instructional efficiency. When students write to learn in content area classrooms, they are in-

volved in a process of manipulating, clarifying, discovering, and synthesizing ideas. The writing process is a powerful strategy for helping students gain insight into course objectives.

The uses of writing have been noticeably limited in content area classrooms. Writing has often been restricted to noncomposing activities such as filling in the blanks on worksheets and practice exercises, writing one-paragraph-or-less responses to study questions, or taking notes. The role of writing in content areas

TABLE 11.1   Some Discourse Forms for Content Area Writing

Journals and diaries (real
  or imaginary)
Biographical sketches
Anecdotes and stories:
  From experience
  As told by others
Thumbnail sketches:
  Of famous people
  Of places
  Of content ideas
  Of historical events
Guess who/what
  descriptions

Letters:
  Personal reactions
  Observations
  Public/informational
  Persuasive:
    To the editor
    To public officials
  To imaginary people
  From imaginary
    places
Requests
Case studies:
  School problems
  Local issues
  National concerns
  Historical problems
  Scientific issues
Songs and ballads
Demonstrations
Poster displays

Reviews:
  Books (including
    textbooks)
  Films
  Outside reading

Television programs
Documentaries
Historical "you are there"
  scenes

Science notes:
  Observations
  Science notebook
  Reading reports
  Lab reports
Written debates

Taking a stand:
  School issues
  Family problems
  State or national issues
  Moral questions

Books and booklets
Informational monographs
Radio scripts
TV scenarios and scripts
Dramatic scripts
Notes for improvised drama
Cartoons and cartoon strips
Slide show scripts
Puzzles and word searches
Prophecy and predictions
Photos and captions
Collage, montage, mobile,
  sculpture
Applications
Memos
Résumés and summaries
Poems
Plays
Stories
Fantasy
Adventure
Science fiction

Historical stories
Dialogues and conversations
Children's books
Telegrams
Editorials
Commentaries
Responses and rebuttals
Newspaper "fillers"
Fact books or fact sheets
School newspaper stories
Stories or essays for local
  papers
Proposals

Math:
  Story problems
  Solutions to problems
  Record books
  Notes and observations
Responses to literature
Utopian proposals
Practical proposals

Interviews:
  Actual
  Imaginary

Directions:
  How-to
  School or neighborhood
    guide
  Survival manual
Dictionaries and lexicons
Technical reports
Future options, notes on:
  Careers, employment
  School and training
  Military/public service

Source: From *Teaching Writing in the Content Areas: Senior High School* by Stephen Tchudi and JoAnne Yates. Copyright © 1983, National Education Association. Reprinted with permission.

should be broadened because of its potentially powerful effect on thinking and learning.

Because writing promotes different types of learning, students should have many different occasions to write. Students should participate in exploratory writing activities, keeping journals, and writing essays. Exploratory writing activities, such as the unsent letter, place students in a role-playing situation in which they are asked to write letters about the material being studied. Additional activities include biopoems, dialogues, and admit and exit slips. Journals, one of the most versatile writing-to-learn strategies, entail students' responding to text as they keep ongoing records of learning while it happens, in a notebook or loose-leaf binder. When students use response journals, double-entry journals, character journals, or learning logs, they soon learn to write without

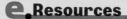

e.Resources

For additional readings related to the major ideas in this chapter, go to Chapter 11 of the Companion Website and click on Suggested Readings.

the fear of making mechanical errors. Students can also be assigned RAFTing activities that are task explicit. An explicit RAFT helps students determine the role, the audience, the form of the writing, as well as the topic.

The next chapter examines what it means to study. Studying texts requires students to engage in purposeful independent learning activities. Organizing information, summarizing chunks of information, taking notes, and conducting and reporting inquiry-centered research are examples of learner-directed strategies.

Minds On

1. Each member of your group should select one of the following roles to play: (a) a language arts teacher who believes that correct mechanics are the heart of good writing, (b) a science teacher who assigns students a variety of "writing-to-learn" projects, (c) a history teacher who believes that writing is the job of the language arts department, (d) a math teacher who uses math journals to aid in students' comprehension, and (e) an administrator who lacks a philosophical view and is listening to form an opinion.

   Imagine that this group is eating lunch in the faculty lounge at a middle school where you teach. The language arts teacher turns to the science teacher and says, "My students were telling me that in the writ-

ing assignment you gave, you told them not to worry about mechanics, that you were interested mainly in their content and form. I wish you wouldn't make statements like that. After all, I'm trying to teach these kids to write correctly." Continue the discussion in each of your roles.

2. What strategies do you believe would be most useful in making writing assignments meaningful for learning?

3. Your group should divide into two teams, one pro and one con. Review each of the following four statements, and discuss from your assigned view the pros and cons of each issue. After you have discussed all five statements, take an "agree" or "disagree" vote on each statement, and

discuss what you really believe about the issue.

a. We write to discover meaning (to understand) and to communicate meaning to others (to be understood).

b. Writing is an incidental tool in learning and relatively unconnected to reading.

c. Writing to learn is a catalyst for reading and studying course material.

d. Students need to know the writer's role, audience, and form, and topic for a writing assignment.

4. At the start of the chapter, we wrote, "When reading and writing are taught in tandem, the union influences content learning in ways not possible when students read without writing or write without reading." Drawing on your experience and the text, discuss some specific examples that support this thesis.

 ## Hands On

1. In the center of a blank sheet of paper, write the name of the first color that comes to your mind. Circle that color. Let your mind wander, and quickly write down all descriptive words or phrases that come to your mind that are related to that color word. Connect the words logically, creating clusters. Next, see what images these relationships suggest to you. Write a piece (a poem, a story, or an essay) based on your clusters. Exchange papers, and in pairs, comment on

a. The best phrase in your partner's piece

b. What needs explanation or clarification

c. The central idea of the piece

With your partner, discuss how this exercise illustrates the characteristics of writing to learn.

2. Work with a partner. Your task is to observe the other during the following activity and to record the characteristics of the other's approach to writing. For example, you might describe the writer pausing, sighing, gazing off, writing hurriedly, scratching out, and erasing. At the end of the activity, share your written description with the partner you observed to see if your observations match the writer's own perceptions.

For this activity, write down seven pairs of rhyming words, and then recopy the pairs, alternating words (e.g., *hot, see, not, me*). Next, give your list of rhymes to your partner, and have him or her write lines of poetry, using each word on the list as the final word in a line of the poem.

What did you learn from both observing and being observed as a writer?

3. Take part in the following activities:

a. Brainstorm by clustering associations with the topic "writing in school."

b. Use this cluster to write a first draft of your experiences with writing in school.

c. Meet with a small group. Share your draft by reading it aloud to your group. Receive formative evaluation on your piece, and respond to the writing presented by others in your group. Make notes about possible changes that might be made in a second draft of your piece.

d. Revise your draft.

e. Describe for the entire class your experiences during this activity. Was this a helpful process? Discuss implications for your own teaching.

e.Resources extra

- Go to Chapter 11 of the Companion Website (**www.ablongman.com/vacca8e**) and click on Activities to complete the following task:

    The following site contains thousands of story problems for enhancing critical thinking and problem solving skills: **www.mathstories.com/**. Many of the problems are based on children's literature. Browse the site and, working in small groups, write your own story problems based on content area topics of interest.

- Go to the Companion Website (**www. ablongman.com/vacca8e**) for suggested readings, interactive activities, multiple-choice questions, and additional Web links to help you learn more about writing to learn.

expect the world®

The New York Times
nytimes.com

Themes of the Times

Extend your knowledge of the concepts discussed in this chapter by reading current and historical articles from the *New York Times*. Go to the Companion Website and click on eThemes of the Times.

c h a p t e r 12

Studying Texts

The process of reading is not a
half-sleep, but in the highest sense,
an exercise, a gymnast's struggle . . .
—WALT WHITMAN

Organizing Principle

Walt Whitman, the great American poet, says in a few words what we have been illustrating throughout this book: Learning with text is as demanding mentally as gymnastics are physically. Reading is not a passive activity, a "half-sleep," but an active process, an exercise that takes place inside the head. The mental gymnastics that readers engage in help them use text to construct meaning. A reader who works with a text is as skillful as a gymnast who works on a balance beam or the parallel bars.

Looking for and using text structure helps students to study texts in order to make connections and think more deeply about ideas encountered during reading.

Students who study texts are self-directed, deliberate in their plans and actions, and conscious of their goals. They have reasons for studying, whether their purposes involve acquiring, organizing, summarizing, or using in-

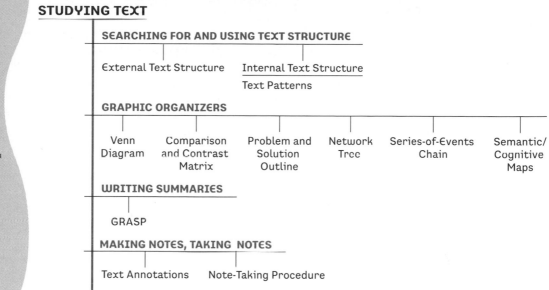

STUDYING TEXT

SEARCHING FOR AND USING TEXT STRUCTURE

External Text Structure   Internal Text Structure
                           Text Patterns

GRAPHIC ORGANIZERS

Venn   Comparison   Problem and   Network   Series-of-Events   Semantic/
Diagram   and Contrast   Solution   Tree   Chain   Cognitive
              Matrix   Outline   Maps

WRITING SUMMARIES

GRASP

MAKING NOTES, TAKING NOTES

Text Annotations   Note-Taking Procedure

STUDY GUIDES

formation and ideas. Studying a text is hard work, just as building the body through gymnastic activity is hard work. It requires readers to be disciplined and patient with print. But because they are deliberate in their plans and actions and conscious of their goals, students who study texts not only know how to work hard but also know how to work smart.

To work smart, students need to develop strategies for studying. Putting study strategies to good use is directly related to students' knowledge and awareness of what it means to study. As they become more aware of studying

texts, students look for *structure*—how the important information and ideas are organized in text—in everything they read. The organizing principle suggests that one important aspect of studying is to show students how to use the structure of ideas in text to their advantage: **Looking for and using text structure helps students to study texts in order to make connections and think more deeply about ideas encountered during reading.**

Frame of Mind

1. What does it mean to study?

2. How is internal text structure different from external text structure?

3. What are text patterns? How can they be used to develop study guides?

4. How do graphic organizers help students make connections among important ideas?

5. How can you show students how to summarize information?

6. How can you show students how to take and make notes?

The poster caught our attention immediately. It had just gone up on the bulletin board in Julie Meyer's classroom. "School Daze: From A to Z" defined significant school activities in the lives of students, each beginning with a letter of the alphabet. The entry for the letter *S* just happened to be the subject of this chapter. It read, "STUDY: *Those precious moments between soap operas, movies, sports, video games, food, personal grooming, and general lollygagging when one opens one's school books— and falls asleep.*"

Response Journal

How is studying a text different from reading it?

Though some students might agree that study is a quick cure for insomnia, few of us would deny that studying texts is one of the most frequent and predominant activities in schools today. The older students become, the more they are expected to learn with texts.

It's not uncommon to find a teacher prefacing text assignments by urging students to "study the material." And some students do. They are able to study effectively because they know what it means to *approach* a text assignment: to *analyze* the reading task at hand, to *make plans* for reading, and then to *use strategies* to suit their purposes for studying. Students who approach texts in this way achieve a level of independence because they are in charge of their own learning.

Other students, less skilled in reading and studying, wage a continual battle with texts. Some probably wonder why teachers make a big deal out of studying in the first place. For them, the exhortation to "study the material" goes in one ear and out the other. Others try to cope with the demands of study. Yet they are apt to equate studying texts with rote memorization, cramming "meaningless" material into short-term memory.

Whenever teachers urge students to study, they probably have something definite in mind. Whatever that something is, it shouldn't remain an ambiguous or unattainable classroom goal. All too often, the problem for students is that they aren't aware of what it means to study, let alone to use study strategies.

Studying is an intentional act. Students need to establish goals for studying. Nila B. Smith's (1959) straightforward definition of study captures what it means to study. She explains studying as strategies that we use when our purpose is to do something with the content we have read. "Doing something" means putting strategies to good use by applying them toward purposeful ends.

Students will tell you that they study to pass tests. Fair enough. They are quick to associate studying with memorizing information. A concept of study that includes retention has merit. But too many students spend too much time using up too much energy on what often becomes their only strategy: rote memorization. Rote memorizing leads to short-lived recall of unrelated bits and pieces of information. Alternatives to rote memorization should be taught and reinforced when and where they count the most: in a content area classroom.

Studying text *is* hard work. Cultivating a repertoire of study strategies to "get the important ideas straight in your head" is essential. Showing students how to distinguish important from less important ideas is one of the key aspects of studying texts effectively.

Searching for and Using Text Structure

Authors impose structure—an organization among ideas—on their writing. Perceiving structure in text material improves learning and retention. When students are shown how to see relationships among concepts and bits of essential information, they are in a better position to respond to meaning and to distinguish important from less important ideas.

Educational psychologists from Thorndike (1917) to Kintsch (1977) and Meyer and Rice (1984) have shown that text structure is a crucial variable in learning and memory. Likewise, for more than fifty years, reading educators have underscored the recognition and use of organization as essential processes underlying comprehension and retention (Herber 1978; Niles 1965; Salisbury 1934; Smith 1964).

The primary purpose of many content area texts is to provide users with information. To make information readily accessible, authors use external and internal structural features. *External text structure* is characterized by a text's overall instructional design—its format features. Its *internal text structure* is reflected by the interrelationships among ideas in the text as well as by the subordination of some ideas to others.

External Text Structure

Printed and electronic texts contain certain format features—organizational aids— that are built into the text to facilitate reading. This book, for example, contains a *preface,* a *table of contents, appendixes,* a *bibliography,* and *indexes.* These aids, along with the *title page* and *dedication,* are called the *front matter* and *end matter* of a book. Of course, textbooks vary in the amount of front and end matter they

BOX 12.1

What about . . .
Content Standards and Assessment?

The word *student*, derived from Latin, means "one who pursues knowledge." Certainly the goal of all content standards is to ensure that today's children and adolescents become *students* in the truest sense of the word. To pursue knowledge, learners not only must develop and use strategic knowledge and skills in text study situations but they also must build a positive attitude toward studying academic texts. A true student—one who pursues knowledge—develops the attitude of searching for meaning in everything that he or she reads—and knows what to do with it!

Considerate authors help with this search by the way they organize information in the *text structures* they use to communicate with readers. Many of today's content standards for reading include provisions for the proficient use of *graphic organizers*, *summaries*, and other study strategies for organizing, interpreting, and remembering information. State content standards, such as the *Ohio Academic Content Standards for English Language Arts* (ELA) with which we are most familiar, recognize the importance of creating and using study strategies, such as *graphic organizers* and *summaries*, as tools for comprehension and learning. For example, the following content standard embodies the Informational, Technical and Persuasive Text Standard of the *Ohio Academic Content Standards for ELA* (Ohio Department of Education 2003):

Students gain information from reading for purposes of learning about a subject, doing a job, making decisions, and accomplishing a task. Students need to apply the reading process to various types of infor-

mational texts, including essays, magazines, newspapers, textbooks, instruction manuals, consumer and workplace documents, reference materials, multimedia, and electronic resources. They learn to attend to text features, such as titles, subtitles and visual aids, to make predictions and build text knowledge. They learn to read diagrams, charts, graphs, maps, and displays in text as sources of additional information. Students use their knowledge of text structure to organize content information, analyze it, and draw inferences from it. Strategic readers learn to recognize arguments, bias, stereotyping, and propaganda in informational text sources. (p. 7)

In addition to the content standards, the Ohio Department of Education (ODE) provides *benchmarks*—guidelines for academic progress and development related to the standard—to guide instructional and assessment decisions. The following benchmarks are from the ODE's Website for Academic Content Standards and Benchmarks for ELA (www.ode.state.oh.us/academic_content_standards/acsenglish.asp).

BY THE END OF THE K–3 PROGRAM:

A. Use text features and structures to organize content, draw conclusions, and build text knowledge.

B. Ask clarifying questions concerning essential elements of informational text.

C. Identify the central ideas and supporting details of informational text.

D. Use visual aids as sources to gain additional information from text.

E. Evaluate two- and three-step directions for proper sequencing and completeness.

BY THE END OF THE 4–7 PROGRAM:

A. Use text features and graphics to organize, analyze, and draw inferences from content and to gain additional information.

B. Recognize the difference between cause and effect and fact and opinion to analyze text.

C. Explain how main ideas connect to each other in a variety of sources.

D. Identify arguments and persuasive techniques used in informational text.

E. Explain the treatment, scope, and organization of ideas from different texts to draw conclusions about a topic.

F. Determine the extent to which a summary accurately reflects the main idea, critical details, and underlying meaning of original text.

BY THE END OF THE 8–10 PROGRAM:

A. Evaluate how features and characteristics make information accessible and usable and how structures help authors achieve their purposes.

B. Identify examples of rhetorical devices and valid and invalid inferences, and explain how authors use these devices to achieve their purposes and reach their intended audiences.

C. Analyze whether graphics supplement textual information and promote the author's purpose.

D. Explain and analyze how an author appeals to an audience and develops an argument or viewpoint in text.

E. Utilize multiple sources pertaining to a singular topic to critique the various ways authors develop their ideas (e.g., treatment, scope, and organization).

BY THE END OF THE 11–12 PROGRAM:

A. Analyze the features and structures of documents and critique them for their effectiveness.

B. Identify and analyze examples of rhetorical devices and valid and invalid inferences.

C. Critique the effectiveness and validity of arguments in text and whether they achieve the author's purpose.

D. Synthesize the content from several sources on a single issue or written by a single author, clarifying ideas and connecting them to other sources and related topics.

E. Analyze an author's implicit and explicitly philosophical assumptions and beliefs about a subject.

As you read this chapter, you will understand the rationale and strategies needed to ensure that students meet these standards, not only in English language arts but also in all content domains. You may also want to conduct a Web search for the academic content standards in your state related to the study of informational texts and compare them with Ohio's. You will probably find these in the content domain of ELA, but you may also come across references to the strategies in state content standards in your academic area.

contain. These aids can be valuable tools for prospective users of a textbook. Yet the novice reader hardly acknowledges their presence in texts, let alone uses them to advantage.

In addition, each chapter of a textbook usually has *introductory or summary statements, headings, graphs, charts, illustrations,* and *guide questions.*

Organizational aids, whether in electronic or printed texts, are potentially valuable—if they are not skipped or glossed over by readers. Headings, for example, are inserted in the text to divide it into logical units. Headings strategically placed in a text should guide the reader by highlighting major ideas.

Within a text, authors use an internal structure to connect ideas logically in a coherent whole. Internal text structure might vary from passage to passage, depending on the author's purpose. These structures, or patterns of organization, within a text are closely associated with informational writing.

Response Journal

Why do some students ignore external organizational aids as tools for studying?

Internal Text Structure

Content area texts are written to inform. This is why exposition is the primary mode of discourse found in informational texts. This is not to say that some authors don't, at times, attempt to persuade or entertain their readers. They may. However, their primary business is to *tell, show, describe,* or *explain.* It stands to reason that the more logically connected one idea is to another, depending on the author's informative purpose, the more coherent the description or explanation is.

Skilled readers search for structure in a text and can readily differentiate the important ideas from less important ideas in the material. Research has shown that good readers know how to look for major thought relationships (Meyer, Brandt, & Bluth 1980; Taylor 1980). They approach a reading assignment looking for a predominant *text pattern* or organization that will tie together the ideas contained throughout the text passage.

Text patterns represent the different types of logical connections among the important and less important ideas in informational material. A case can be made for five text patterns that seem to predominate in informational writing: *description, sequence, comparison and contrast, cause and effect,* and *problem and solution.* Here are descriptions and examples of these text structures.

Description

Providing information about a topic, concept, event, object, person, idea, and so on (facts, characteristics, traits, features), usually qualifying the listing by criteria such as size or importance. This pattern connects ideas through description by listing the important characteristics or attributes of the topic under consideration. Niles (1965) and Bartlett (1978) found the description pattern to be the most common way of organizing texts. Here is an example:

There were several points in the fight for freedom of religion. One point was that religion and government should be kept apart. Americans did not want any form of a national church as was the case in England. Americans made sure that no person would be denied his or her religious beliefs.

Sequence

Putting facts, events, or concepts into a sequence. The author traces the development of the topic or gives the steps in the process. Time reference may be explicit or implicit, but a sequence is evident in the pattern. The following paragraph illustrates the pattern:

> John F. Kennedy was the Democratic candidate for president when in October 1960 he first suggested there should be a Peace Corps. After he was elected, Kennedy asked his brother-in-law, Sargent Shriver, to help set up a Peace Corps. In March 1961, Kennedy gave an order to create the organization. It wasn't until September that Congress approved the Peace Corps and appropriated the money to run it for one year.

Comparison and Contrast

Pointing out likenesses (comparison) and/or differences (contrast) among facts, people, events, concepts, and so on. Study this example:

> Castles were built for defense, not comfort. In spite of some books and movies that have made them attractive, castles were cold, dark, gloomy places to live. Rooms were small and not the least bit charming. Except for the great central hall or the kitchen, there were no fires to keep the rooms heated. Not only was there a lack of furniture, but what there was was uncomfortable.

Cause and Effect

Showing how facts, events, or concepts (effects) happen or come into being because of other facts, events, or concepts (causes). Examine this paragraph for causes and effects:

> The fire was started by sparks from a campfire left by a careless camper. Thousands of acres of important watershed burned before the fire was brought under control. As a result of the fire, trees and the grasslands on the slopes of the valley were gone. Smoking black stumps were all that remained of tall pine trees.

Problem and Solution

Showing the development of a problem and one or more solutions to the problem. Consider the following example:

> The skyrocketing price of oil in the 1970s created a serious problem for many Americans. The oil companies responded to the high cost of purchasing oil by searching for new oil supplies. This resulted in new deposits being found in some Third World nations, such as Nigeria. Oil companies also began drilling for oil on the ocean floor, and scientists discovered ways to extract oil from a rock known as *oil shale*.

Signal Words in Text Structure

Authors often showcase text patterns by giving readers clues or signals to help them figure out the structure being used. Readers usually become aware of the pattern if they are looking for the signals. A signal may be a word or a phrase that helps the reader follow the writer's thoughts. Linguists call these words *connectives,* or *ties,* because they connect one idea to another (Halliday & Hasan 1976).

Figure 12.1 shows connectives that authors use to call attention to the organizational patterns just defined.

Awareness of the pattern of *long stretches* of text is especially helpful in planning reading assignments. In selecting from a passage of several paragraphs or several pages, teachers first need to determine whether a predominant text pattern is contained in the material. This is no easy task.

Informational writing is complex. Authors do not write in neat, perfectly identifiable patterns. Within the individual paragraphs of a text assignment, several kinds of thought relationships often exist. Suppose an author begins a passage by stating a problem. In telling about the development of the problem, the author *describes* a set of events that contributed to the problem. Or perhaps the author *compares* or *contrasts* the problem under consideration with another

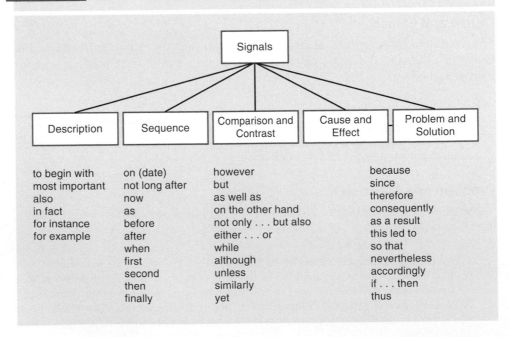

FIGURE 12.1 **Signal Words and Phrases Used in Various Text Structures**

Signals

Description	Sequence	Comparison and Contrast	Cause and Effect	Problem and Solution
to begin with	on (date)	however	because	
most important	not long after	but	since	
also	now	as well as	therefore	
in fact	as	on the other hand	consequently	
for instance	before	not only . . . but also	as a result	
for example	after	either . . . or	this led to	
	when	while	so that	
	first	although	nevertheless	
	second	unless	accordingly	
	then	similarly	if . . . then	
	finally	yet	thus	

problem. In subsequent paragraphs, the *solutions* or attempts at solutions to the problem are stated. In presenting the solutions, the author uses heavy description and explanation. These descriptions and explanations are logically organized in a *sequence*.

The difficulty that teachers face is analyzing the overall text pattern, even though several types of thought relationships are probably embedded in the material. Analyzing a text for a predominant pattern depends in part on how clearly an author represents the relationships in the text.

Several guidelines follow for analyzing text patterns. First, survey the text for the most important idea in the selection. Are there any explicit signal words that indicate a pattern that will tie together the ideas throughout the passage? Second, study the content of the text for additional important ideas. Are these ideas logically connected to the most important idea? Is a pattern evident? Third, outline or diagram the relationships among the superordinate and subordinate ideas in the selection. Use the diagram to specify the major relationships contained in the text structure and to sort out the important from the less important ideas.

Students must learn how to recognize and use the explicit and implicit relations in the text patterns that an author uses to structure content. When readers perceive and interact with text organization, they are in a better position to comprehend and retain information.

Graphic Organizers

Graphic organizers are visual displays that help learners comprehend and retain *textually important information*. When students learn how to use and construct graphic organizers, they are in control of a study strategy that allows them to identify what parts of a text are important, how the ideas and concepts encountered in the text are related, and where they can find specific information to support more important ideas.

An entire family of teacher-directed and learner-directed techniques and strategies is associated with the use of graphic organizers to depict relationships in text: word maps, semantic maps, semantic webs, flowcharts, concept matrices, and tree diagrams, to name a few. Although it is easy to get confused by the plethora of labels, a rose by any other name is still a rose.

e.Resources

Find out more about graphic organizers by going to Web Destinations on the Companion Website and clicking on Professional Resources. Search for Graphic Organizers.

What these techniques and strategies have in common is that they help students interact with and outline textually important information. For example, when students read a text with an appropriate graphic organizer in mind, they focus on important ideas and relationships. And when they construct their own graphic organizers, they become actively involved in outlining those ideas and relationships.

Outlining helps students clarify relationships. Developing an outline is analogous to fitting together the pieces in a puzzle. Think of a puzzle piece as a separate idea and a text as the whole. A completed puzzle shows the separate identity of each idea as well as the part each idea plays in the total picture (Hansell 1978). Outlining strategies can be used effectively to facilitate a careful analysis and synthesis of the relationships in a text. They can form the basis for critical discussion and evaluation of the author's main points.

Problems arise when students are restricted by the means by which they must depict relationships spatially on paper or on a screen. The word *outlining* for most of us immediately conjures up an image of the "correct" or "classic" format that we have all learned at one time or another but have probably failed to use regularly in real-life study situations. The classic form of outlining has the student represent the relatedness of information in linear form:

I. Main Idea

    A. Idea supporting I
      1. Detail supporting A
      2. Detail supporting A
        a. Detail supporting 2
        b. Detail supporting 2

    B. Idea supporting I
      1. Detail supporting B
      2. Detail supporting B

II. Main Idea

This conventional format represents a hierarchical ordering of ideas at different levels of subordination. Roman numerals signal the major or superordinate concepts in a text section; capital letters, the supporting or coordinate concepts; Arabic numbers, the supporting or subordinate details; and lowercase letters, the subsubordinate details.

Some readers have trouble using a restricted form of outlining. Initially, at least, they need a more visual display than the one offered by the conventional format. And this is where graphic organizers can play a critical role in the development of independent learners.

To show students how to use and construct graphic organizers, begin by assessing how students usually outline text material. Do they have a sense of subordination among ideas? Do they have strategies for connecting major and minor concepts? Do they use alternatives to the conventional format? Make them aware of the rationale for organizing information through outlining. The jigsaw puzzle analogy—fitting pieces of information together into a coherent whole—works well for this purpose. Assessment and building awareness set the stage for illustrating, modeling, and applying the strategies. Box 12.2 outlines the steps used to build strategic knowledge and skills related to students' use of graphic organizers.

RESEARCH-BASED BEST PRACTICES

BOX 12.2

Graphic Organizers

To introduce students to various kinds of graphic organizers that may be applicable to texts in your content area, Jones, Pierce, and Hunter (1988–1989) suggest some of the following steps:

1. *Present an example of a graphic organizer that corresponds to the type of outline you plan to teach.* For example, suppose that a text that students will read is organized around a cause and effect text pattern. First, preview the text with the students. Help them discover features of the text that may signal the pattern. Make students aware that the title, subheads, and signal words provide them with clues to the structure of the text. Then ask questions that are pertinent to the pattern—for example, "What happens in this reading? What causes it to happen? What are the important factors that cause these effects?"

2. *Demonstrate how to construct a graphic outline.* Suppose that math students have completed a reading about the differences between isosceles triangles and isosceles trapezoids. Show them how to construct a *Venn diagram* to map how they are alike and different. Next, refer to the comparison

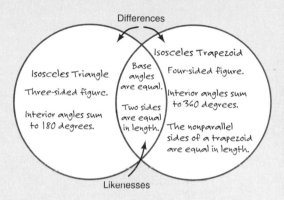

and contrast questions you raised in the preview. Guide students through the procedures that lead to the development of the Venn diagram: First, on an overhead transparency, present an example of a partially completed Venn graphic. Second, have students review the text and offer suggestions to help complete the graphic. The accompanying graphic display shows a class-constructed rendering of the Venn diagram. Third, develop procedural knowledge by discussing when to use the Venn graphic and why.

3. *Coach students in the use of the graphic outline and give them opportunities to practice.* If other texts represent a particular text pattern that you have already demonstrated with the class, encourage students individually or in teams to construct their own graphic outlines and to use their constructions as the basis for class discussion.

e.Resources

Find more examples of graphic organizers by going to Web Destinations on the Companion Website and clicking on Professional Resources. Search for Graphic Organizer Index.

Using Graphic Organizers to Reflect Text Patterns

Students can be shown how to construct maps and other types of visual displays to reflect the text patterns authors use to organize ideas. According to Jones, Pierce, and Hunter (1988–1989), "A fundamental rule in constructing graphic organizers is that the structure of the graphic should reflect the structure of the text it represents" (p. 21).

Jones and her colleagues recommend a variety of possible graphic organizer representations that reflect different text patterns. These "generic" outlines are illustrated in Appendix C. What follows are classroom examples of how some of these outlines might be developed in content area classrooms.

Comparison and Contrast Matrix

In addition to the Venn diagram and graphic organizers, a teacher can show students how a comparison and contrast pattern serves to organize ideas in a text through the use of a matrix outline. A comparison and contrast matrix shows similarities and differences between two or more things (people, places, events, concepts, processes, etc.). Readers compare and contrast the target concepts listed across the top of the matrix according to attributes, properties, or characteristics listed along the left side. Study the two examples of a comparison and contrast matrix in Figure 12.2. High school students used the biology example to outline the likenesses and differences of fungi and algae. Precalculus students used the matrix outline to compare and contrast conic sections (parabola, ellipse, and hyperbola).

Problem and Solution Outline

This graphic representation depicts a problem, attempted solutions, the results or outcomes associated with the attempted solutions, and the end result. It works equally well with narrative or informational texts to display the central problem in a story or the problem and solution text pattern. Noden and Vacca (1994) show how a world history teacher used the problem and solution outline in conjunction with a text assignment related to Wat Tyler's Rebellion, which took place in England in 1381. Wat Tyler's Rebellion was one of the first popular English movements for freedom and equality. The teacher introduced the outline in Figure 12.3 as a tool for organizing the information in the text relevant to the problem. Students first worked in pairs to complete the outline and then shared their work with the whole class. The completed outline in Figure 12.3 illustrates the thinking of two "study buddies."

Network Tree

The network tree is based on the same principle as the graphic organizers introduced in Chapter 8 and used in the chapter organizers in this book. That is to say,

FIGURE 12.2	**Comparison and Contrast Matrices for Biology (a) and Precalculus (b)**

	Fungi	Algae
Body structure		
Food source		
Method of reproduction		
Living environment		

(a)

(continued)

FIGURE **12.2** **Continued**

	Parabola	Ellipse	Hyperbola
Sketch two examples			
Equation in standard form			
Special characteristics			
Foci (focal points)			
Line(s) of symmetry			

(b)

FIGURE 12.3 **Problem and Solution Outline for Wat Tyler's Rebellion**

Problem

> Who has the problem?
>   Peasants of England
>
> What was the problem?
>   Unfair taxes and harsh labor laws
>
> Why was it a problem?
>   Peasants were treated as serfs and were the lowest class of people in England.

Solutions

Attempted Solutions	Outcomes
1. Riots	1. Property destroyed People killed
2. Protest march on London to force a meeting with king	2. King's advisers desert him; King agrees to protesters' demands
3. Tyler refuses to give in —makes more demands	3. Tyler killed by mayor of London

End Result
King broke his promises Peasants' demands forgotten, but the rebellion inspired other popular movements for freedom and equality

Source: From Harry Noden and Richard Vacca, *Whole Language in Middle and Secondary Classrooms.* Copyright © 1994 by Allyn & Bacon. Reprinted by permission.

it represents the network of relationships that exists between superordinate concepts and subordinate concepts. It can be used to show causal information or to describe a central idea in relation to its attributes and examples. Notice how math students explored relationships in the quadratic formula by using the network tree illustrated in Figure 12.4.

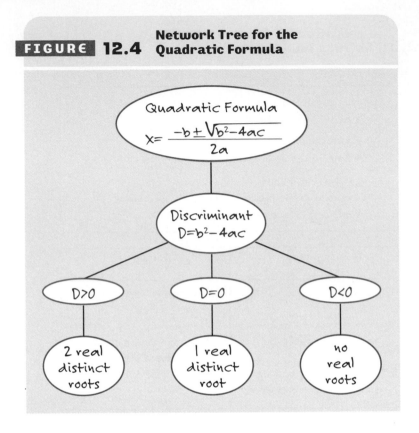

FIGURE **12.4** Network Tree for the Quadratic Formula

Series-of-Events Chain

The series-of-events chain may be used with narrative material to show the chain of events that lead to the resolution of conflict in a story. It may also be used with informational text to reflect the sequence pattern in a text. It may include any sequence of events, including the steps in a linear procedure, the chain of events (effects) caused by some event, or the stages of something. Scientific and historical texts are often organized in a sequence pattern and lend themselves well to this type of graphic display. A science class, for example, might be asked to map the sequence of steps in the scientific method by using a series-of-events chain. After reading about the scientific method, students might make an outline similar to the one in Figure 12.5.

In an English class, students read an excerpt from *My Bondage and My Freedom,* by Frederick Douglass, the famous American slave, abolitionist, and journalist. Douglass writes about the reasons for and purposes of the Negro spirituals that slaves sang and the effects that these songs had on his life. The teacher assigned the text selection to be read in class and then divided the students into

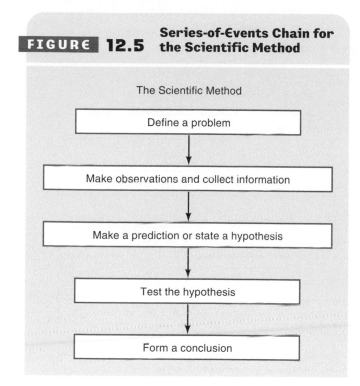

FIGURE **12.5** **Series-of-Events Chain for the Scientific Method**

The Scientific Method

Define a problem

Make observations and collect information

Make a prediction or state a hypothesis

Test the hypothesis

Form a conclusion

learning circles (four-member teams) to work through the sequence of events that had led to Douglass's hatred of slavery. The series-of-events chain in Figure 12.6 illustrates the work of one of the learning circles.

Appendix C illustrates additional types of graphic organizers that may be adapted to different content areas. Closely associated with the use of graphic organizers is an instructional scaffold that involves questioning.

Using Questions with Graphic Organizers

Graphic organizers are closely associated with key questions that parallel the text patterns used by authors (Armbruster & Anderson 1985). Skilled readers are aware of these key questions, and they study texts with the expectation that the authors have organized the content within the text patterns that are associated with a content area.

Along with the graphic organizers, introduce students to the key questions associated with each of the major text patterns. Beuhl (1991), for example, lists the types of questions associated with the problem and solution, cause and effect, and comparison and contrast patterns.

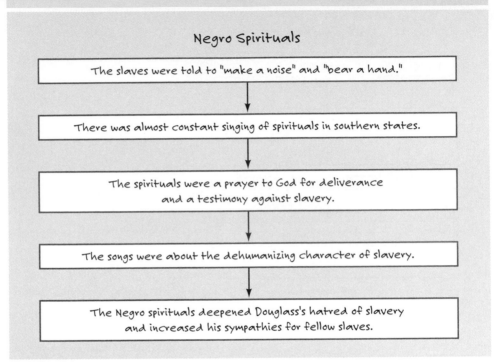

FIGURE 12.6 **Series-of-Events Chain for an Excerpt from *My Bondage and My Freedom***

Negro Spirituals

The slaves were told to "make a noise" and "bear a hand."

There was almost constant singing of spirituals in southern states.

The spirituals were a prayer to God for deliverance and a testimony against slavery.

The songs were about the dehumanizing character of slavery.

The Negro spirituals deepened Douglass's hatred of slavery and increased his sympathies for fellow slaves.

PROBLEM AND SOLUTION

1. What is the problem?

2. Who has the problem?

3. What is causing the problem?

4. What are the effects of the problem?

5. Who is trying to solve the problem?

6. What solutions are attempted?

7. What are the results of these solutions?

8. Is the problem solved? Do any new problems develop because of the solutions?

CAUSE AND EFFECT

1. What happens?

2. What causes it to happen?

3. What are the important elements or factors that cause this effect?

4. How are these factors or elements interrelated?

5. Will this result always happen from these causes? Why or why not?

6. How would the result change if the elements or factors were different?

COMPARISON AND CONTRAST

1. What items are being compared and contrasted?

2. What categories of attributes can be used to compare and contrast the items?

3. How are the items alike or similar?

4. How are the items not alike or different?

5. What are the most important qualities or attributes that make the items similar?

6. What are the most important qualities or attributes that make the items different?

7. In terms of the qualities that are most important, are the items more alike or more different?

Additional questions are provided in Appendix C. There are many benefits to learning how to use and construct graphic organizers, not the least of which is that they make it easier for students to find and reorganize important ideas and information in the text.

Another type of graphic display has been called a *semantic map* or *cognitive map*. Maps are based on the same principles as graphic organizers.

Semantic (Cognitive) Mapping

A popular graphic representation, often called a *semantic map* or a *cognitive map*, helps students identify important ideas and shows how these ideas fit together. Teachers avoid the problem of teaching a restricted, conventional outline format. Instead, the students are responsible for creating a logical arrangement among key-words or phrases that connect main ideas to subordinate information. When maps are used, instruction should proceed from teacher-guided modeling and illustration to student-generated productions. A semantic map has three basic components:

1. *Core question or concept.* The question or concept (stated as a keyword or phrase) that establishes the main focus of the map. All the ideas generated for the map by the students are related in some way to the core question or concept.

2. *Strands.* The subordinate ideas generated by the students that help clarify the question or explain the concept.

3. *Supports.* The details, inferences, and generalizations that are related to each strand. These supports clarify the strands and distinguish one strand from another.

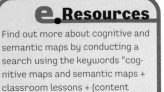

Students use the semantic map as an organization tool that illustrates visually the categories and relationships associated with the core question or concept under study. To model and illustrate the use of a semantic map, a middle school social studies teacher guided students through the process. The class began a unit on Ohio's early settlements. As part of the prereading discussion, four questions were raised for the class to ponder: What do you think were the three most important early settlements in Ohio? What do you think these settlements had in common? How were they different? In what ways might the location of a settlement be important to the survival of the settlers? Predictions were made and discussed and led naturally to the text assignment.

The teacher assigned the material, directing the students to read with the purpose of confirming or modifying their predictions about the early settlements.

After reading, the students formed small groups. Each group listed everything its members could remember about the settlements on index cards, with one piece of information per card.

In the center of the chalkboard, the teacher wrote "The First Ohio Settlements" and circled the phrase. She then asked students to provide the main strands that helped answer the question and clarify the concept "What were Ohio's most important early settlements?" The students responded by contrasting their predictions to the explanations in the text assignment. The teacher began to build the semantic map on the board by explaining how strands help students answer the questions and understand the main concept.

Next, she asked the students to work in their groups to sort the cards that had been compiled according to each of the settlements depicted on the semantic map. Through discussion, questioning, and think-aloud probes, the class completed the semantic map depicted in Figure 12.7.

Some teachers prefer to distinguish strands from supports through the use of lines. Notice that in Figure 12.7, a double line connects the strands to the core concept. Supports are linked to each web strand by single lines. With younger students, some teachers also recommend using different-colored chalk to distinguish one strand from another.

With appropriate modeling, explanation, and experience, students soon understand the why, what, and how of semantic maps and can begin to develop maps by themselves. We suggest that the teacher begin by providing the core question or concept. Students can then compare and contrast their individual productions in a follow-up discussion. Of course, text assignments should also be given in which students identify the core concept on their own and then generate the structures that support and explain it.

FIGURE **12.7**   **Semantic Map: The First Ohio Settlements**

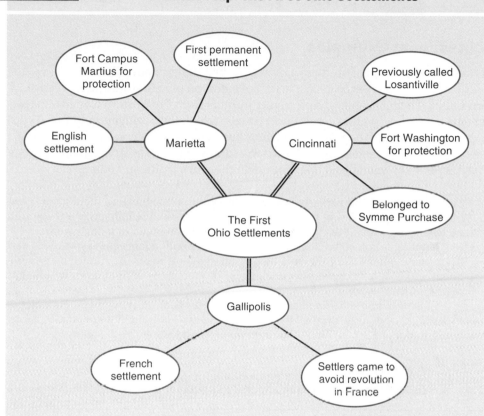

In addition to using graphic outlines, teachers can develop study guides to help students discern text patterns.

Study Guides Based on Text Patterns

Text patterns are difficult for some readers to discern, but once students become aware of the importance of organization and learn how to search for relationships in text, they are in a better position to use information more effectively and to comprehend material more thoroughly.

A study guide based on text patterns helps students perceive and use the major text relationships that predominate in the reading material. As you consider developing a study guide for text patterns, you may find it useful first to read through the text selection and identify a predominant pattern; and second, to develop an exercise in which students can react to the structure of the relationships represented by the pattern.

Classroom Examples

An eighth-grade social studies class read a text assignment, "Today's Stone Age Elephant Hunters" (Beebe 1968), as part of a unit on primitive cultures in the modern world. The text explains how pigmy hunters from the western Congo hunt elephants for food as well as for cultural rituals associated with young hunters' rites of passage into manhood. To get a feel for how a study guide scaffolds the reader's recognition of text relationships, read the following excerpt from "Today's Stone Age Elephant Hunters" and then complete the study guide in Figure 12.8.

Some pigmies of the western Congo use a system of concealing their scent when hunting elephants. Few of these little jungle dwellers hunt elephants but those who do have chosen about the most dangerous way to secure food in today's world.

Hunting is done by a single man using a spear with a large metal spearhead and thick shaft. After taking the trail behind an elephant herd, the hunter pauses frequently to coat his skin with fresh elephant droppings for several days until he has lost all human scent.

Closing on the herd the pigmy selects his prey, usually a young adult. He watches this animal until he is aware of its distinctive habits—how often it dozes, eats, turns, wanders out of the herd, and other individual behavior.

FIGURE 12.8 A Study Guide for the Sequence Text Pattern

Directions: The pigmy hunter follows ten steps in hunting and killing an elephant. Some of the steps are given to you. Decide which steps are missing, and write them in the spaces provided. The pigmy hunter

1. takes the trail of an elephant herd.

2. _____

3. selects the elephant he will kill.

4. _____

5. moves in for the kill.

6. _____

7. _____

8. pulls out the spear.

9. _____

10. cuts off _____

Then he moves toward his prey, usually at midday when the herd is dozing while standing. The little hunter moves silently between the elephant's legs, braces himself and drives the spear up into the stomach area for several feet. The elephant snaps to alertness, screaming and trying to reach his diminutive attacker. Many pigmy hunters have lost their lives at this moment, but if the little hunter is fast enough he pulls out the spear to facilitate bleeding and ducks for safety.

Death does not come for several days and the hunter must follow his wounded prey until it stops. When the elephant falls the pigmy cuts off the tail as proof of his kill and sets off for his village, which may be several days away by now.

The study guide in Figure 12.8 reflects a sequence pattern. Note the variations in the next two classroom examples of pattern guides developed for the cause and effect pattern.

> **Response Journal**
> How did the study guide help you to think about the text as you reconstructed the sequence of events used by the hunters?

Auto Mechanics

The students in an auto mechanics class—part of a high school vocational arts program—were described by the teacher as "nonreaders." Most activities in the course were hands-on, as you might expect, and although the students had a textbook, they seldom used it. But the auto mechanics teacher believed that the textbook section on transmissions warranted reading because of the relevance of the material. To help the students follow the author's ideas about causes and effects, the teacher constructed the pattern guide in Figure 12.9.

The students worked in pairs to complete the guide. When some had trouble locating certain effects in the assignment, the teacher told them what page to study. As a result of the guided recognition of cause and effect, the teacher believed that the students would be better able to handle interpretation and application through class discussion followed by a hands-on activity.

Social Studies

A middle school teacher prepared a matching activity to illustrate the cause and effect pattern for students who were studying a unit titled "The American Indian: A Search for Identity." One reading selection from the unit material dealt with Jenny, an adolescent member of the Blackfoot tribe, who commits suicide.

The teacher asked, "Why did Jenny take her life?" The question led to a before-reading discussion. The students offered several predictions. The teacher then suggested that the reading assignment was written in a predominantly cause and effect pattern. He discussed this type of pattern, and the students contributed several examples. Then he gave them the study guide in Figure 12.10 to complete as they read the selection.

The class read for two purposes: to see whether their predictions were accurate and to follow the cause and effect relationships in the material. Notice that the social studies teacher included page numbers after the causes listed on the guide. These helped students focus their attention on the relevant portions of the text. First, the students read the selection silently; then they worked in groups of four to complete the study guide.

FIGURE **12.9** **Cause–Effect Study Guide for Power Mechanics**

Directions: In your reading assignment on transmissions, find the causes that led to the effects listed. Write each cause in the space provided.

1. Cause:_____
   Effect: Grinding occurs when gears are shifted.
2. Cause:_____
   Effect: Car speed increases but engine speed remains constant while torque is decreasing.
3. Cause:_____
   Effect: Car makers changed over to synchronizing mechanisms.
4. Cause:_____
   Effect: Helical gears are superior to spur gears.
5. Cause:_____
   Effect: Some cars cannot operate correctly with three-speed transmissions and require extra speeds.
6. Cause:_____
   Effect: Most manuals have an idler gear.
7. Cause:_____
   Effect: All cars require some type of transmission.

English/Language Arts

A final example, the comparison and contrast study guide in Figure 12.11, shows how the format of a guide will differ with the nature of the material (in this case, narrative) and the teacher's objectives. In Figure 12.11, juniors in an English class used the study guide to discuss changes in character in the story "A Split Cherry Tree."

Adapting guide formats to match the major text structures in your content materials will help students develop the habit of searching for structure in everything they read. Another strategy that will help them use text structure involves showing students how to write a summary. Well-written summaries distinguish main ideas from details implicit in various text patterns.

Writing Summaries

Summarizing involves reducing a text to its main points. To become adept at summary writing, students must be able to discern and analyze text structure.

FIGURE 12.10   **Cause–Effect Study Guide for "The American Indian: A Search for Identity"**

Directions: Select from the causes column at the left the cause that led to each effect in the effects column at the right. Put the letter of each effect next to its cause in the space provided.

Causes

_____ 1. Jenny takes an overdose of pills (p. 9).
_____ 2. The buffalo herds have been destroyed, and hunger threatens (p. 10).
_____ 3. Native Americans remain untrained for skilled jobs (p. 10).
_____ 4. The temperature reaches 50 degrees below zero (p. 10).
_____ 5. There are terrible living conditions (no jobs, poor homes, and so on) (p. 10).
_____ 6. Pride and hope have vanished from the Blackfeet (p. 11).
_____ 7. Because we're Native Americans (p. 12)
_____ 8. The old world of the Native Americans is crumbling and the new world of the whites rejects them (p. 13).
_____ 9. The attitude of the Bureau of Indian Affairs (p. 13).

Effects

a. Unemployment rate for the Blackfeet is about 50 percent.
b. The first victim of this life is pride.
c. Blackfeet have become dependent on whites' help for survival.
d. Blackfeet turn to liquor.
e. Native Americans are robbed of their self-confidence.
f. They are always downgraded.
g. Eighty percent of the Blackfeet must have governmental help.
h. *Hope* is a word that has little meaning.
i. She kills herself.

If they are insensitive to the organization of ideas and events in expository or narrative writing, students will find it difficult to distinguish important from less important information. Good summarizers, therefore, guard against including information that is not important in the text passage being condensed. Immature text learners, by contrast, tend to *retell* rather than condense information, often including in their summaries interesting but nonessential tidbits from the passage. Good summarizers write in their own words but are careful to maintain the author's point of view and to stick closely to the sequence of ideas or events as presented in the reading selection. When important ideas are not explicitly stated in the material, good summary writers create their own topic sentences to reflect textually implicit main ideas.

Box 12.3 outlines the "rules" to follow in developing a well-written summary.

e.Resources

Find out more about writing summaries by going to Web Destinations on the Companion Website and clicking on Professional Resources. Search for Writing Summaries.

FIGURE 12.11   **Comparison–Contrast Study Guide for "A Split Cherry Tree"**

Directions: Consider Pa's attitude (how he feels) toward the following characters and concepts. Note that the columns ask you to consider his attitudes toward these things twice—the way he is at the beginning of the story (pp. 147–152) and the way you think he is at the end of the story. Whenever possible, note the page numbers on which this attitude is described or hinted.

Characters and Concepts	Pa's Attitude at the Beginning of the Story	Pa's Attitude at the End of the Story
Punishment Dave Professor Herbert School His own work His son's future Himself		

Using GRASP to Write a Summary

Teachers can show students how to summarize information through the guided reading procedure (GRP) as explained in Chapter 10. After students have read a text passage, they turn the books face down and try to remember everything that was important in the passage. What they recall is recorded by the teacher on the chalkboard. Seize this opportune moment to show students how to delete trivial and repetitious information from the list of ideas on the board. As part of the procedure, the students are given a chance to return to the passage, review it, and make sure that the list contains all of the information germane to the text.

When this step is completed, the teacher then guides the students to organize the information using a graphic outline format. Here is where students can be shown how to collapse individual pieces of information from a list into conceptual categories. These categories can be the bases for identifying or creating topic sentences. The students can then integrate the main points into a summary.

Hayes (1989) shows how to adapt the GRP to summarizing information. As part of his instructional framework, he modeled the development and writing of an effective summary by guiding students through a procedure he labeled GRASP (guided reading and summarizing procedure). After following the initial steps of the GRP, Hayes illustrates, in Figure 12.12, the information that his students remembered based on their first recollections after reading an article on the Rosetta Stone and their additions and corrections after rereading.

RESEARCH-BASED BEST PRACTICES

BOX 12.3

Writing a Summary

Kintsch and van Dijk (1978) were among the first to formulate a set of basic rules for summarization based on analyses of how people summarize effectively. Others have modified and adapted these rules, but generally, students must follow these procedures:

1. *Include no unnecessary detail.* In preparing a summary, students must learn not to include trivial and repetitious information from a text passage.

2. *Collapse lists.* When a text passage includes examples, details, actions, or traits, students must learn how to condense these into broader categories of information. With frequent exposure to instructional activities, such as graphic organizers, vocabulary categorization exercises, and outlining strategies, students soon become aware that similar items of information can be encompassed by more inclusive concepts. They must learn to summarize information by collapsing a list of details and thinking of a keyword or phrase that names its concept. Study the examples that Hare and Borchardt (1984) give: "If you saw a list like eyes, ears, neck, arms, and legs, you could say 'body parts.' Or, if you saw a list like ice skating, skiing, or sledding, you could say 'winter sports' " (p. 66).

3. *Use topic sentences.* Expository text sometimes contains explicit topic sentences that preview a paragraph. However, if a paragraph doesn't have a topic sentence, students must learn to create their own for a summary. This is probably the most difficult demand placed on maturing learners.

4. *Integrate information.* Summarizers must learn how to use keywords, phrases, and explicit and invented topic sentences to compose a summary. The first three rules help students do the basic work of summarizing. In other words, the rules *prepare* students for writing the summary. Yet when they actually put ideas into words, they must integrate the information into a coherent piece of writing.

5. *Polish the summary.* Because writing often follows a composing process, students must learn to revise a *draft* of a summary into a more organized, natural-sounding piece of writing. While rethinking a summary, students will get a firmer grasp on the main points of the material and will state them clearly.

The students then organized the information into the following categories: importance of the Rosetta Stone, its discovery, its description, its decipherment, and the result of having made the discovery. These categories, along with the subordinate information associated with each, became the basis for writing the summary. Hayes walked the students through the summary-writing process as a whole class. First, he asked students to contribute sentences to the summary

FIGURE 12.12 **Details Remembered from an Article on the Rosetta Stone**

Students' First Recollections	Additions and Corrections
Found by an officer in Napoleon's army	Engineering corps
1799	Taken to British Museum, where it is today
Key to language of Egypt	Ancient
Forgotten language of Egypt	Champollion published a pamphlet
Found in mud near Rosetta	The pamphlet a tool scholars use to translate ancient Egyptian literature
Black basalt	Ancient language of Egypt had been a riddle for hundreds of years
3' 9" tall	The stone half buried in mud
Inscriptions in hieroglyphics	Demotic, the popular Egyptian language at the time
	Written with Greek letters
Jean Champollion deciphered the inscription	Champollion knew Coptic
Compared Greek words with Egyptian words in same position	Proper names
Coptic was the Egyptian language	Coptic was last stage of Egyptian language
Decree to commemorate birth of an Egyptian king	Crowning
2' 4½" wide	Carved by Egyptian priests
He knew Greek	Ptolemy V Epiphanes 203–181 B.C.

Source: From David A. Hayes, "Helping Students Grasp the Knack of Writing Summaries," *Journal of Reading,* November 1989. Copyright © 1989 by the International Reading Association. All rights reserved. Used by permission of the author and the International Reading Association.

based on the outline of information that was organized on the chalkboard. Then he invited their suggestions for revising the summary into a coherent message. Figure 12.13 displays the completed summary, as revised by the class.

Polishing a Summary

As you can see from the revised summary in Figure 12.13, a good summary often reflects a process of writing *and* rewriting. Teaching students how to write a polished summary is often a neglected aspect of instruction. When students reduce large segments of text, the condensation is often stilted. It sounds unnatural. We are convinced that students will learn and understand the main points better and retain them longer when they attempt to create a more natural-sounding summary that communicates the selection's main ideas to an audience—for example,

FIGURE 12.13 The Completed Rosetta Stone Summary, as Revised

The Rosetta Stone provided the key for reading the ancient ~~language of Egypt. The~~

~~ancient~~ Egyptian language, which had been a riddle for hundreds of years. (An officer in

Napoleon's engineering corps) ~~found~~ the Rosetta Stone ~~half buried in the~~ was found in 1799

the Egyptian city of — by
~~mud near~~ Rosetta. The black basalt stone bore Inscriptions in ancient Egyptian

in   in
hieroglyphics, Demotic, and Greek. The inscriptions were deciphered by Jean

Champollion, who with knowledge of Greek and Coptic (the last stage of the Egyptian

in the Greek text   in the Egyptian texts   had been
language) compared ~~Greek~~ words with ~~Egyptian~~ words. The inscription ~~were~~ carved

by Egyptian priests to commemorate the crowning of Egyptian king Ptolemy Epiphanes,

203–181 B.C. In 1822 Champollion described the decipherment in a pamphlet which

has since been used as a tool for translating ancient Egyptian literature. The Rosetta

preserved
~~kept~~
Stone is in the British Museum.

Source: From David A. Hayes, "Helping Students Grasp the Knack of Writing Summaries," *Journal of Reading,* November 1989. Copyright © 1989 by the International Reading Association. All rights reserved. Used by permission of David A. Hayes and the International Reading Association.

the teacher or other students. Rewriting in a classroom is often preceded by *response* to a draft by peers and teacher. We dealt in much more detail with responding and revising in Chapter 3. Here, however, let us suggest the following:

- *Compare a well-developed summary that the teacher has written with the summaries written by the students.* Contrasting the teacher's version with the student productions leads to valuable process discussions on such subjects as the use of introductory and concluding statements; the value of connectives, such as *and* and *because,* to show how ideas can be linked; and the need to paraphrase—that is, to put ideas into one's own words to convey the author's main points.

- *Present the class with three summaries:* One is good in that it contains all the main points and flows smoothly. The second is OK; it contains most of the main points but is somewhat stilted in its writing. The third is poor in content and form. Let the class rate and discuss the three summaries.

- *Team students in pairs or triads, and let them read their summaries to one another.* Student response groups are one of the most effective means of obtaining feedback on writing in progress.

- *In lieu of response groups, ask the whole class to respond.* With prior permission from several students, discuss their summaries. What are the merits of each one, and how could they be improved in content and form?

The real learning potential of summary writing lies in students' using their own language to convey the author's main ideas.

Making Notes, Taking Notes

Effective study activities for acting on and remembering material involve making notes as well as taking notes. Notes can be written on study cards (index cards) or in a learning log that is kept expressly for the purpose of compiling written reactions to and reflections on text readings.

Note making should avoid verbatim text reproductions. Instead, notes can be used to paraphrase, summarize, react critically, question, or respond personally to what is read. Whatever the form notes take, students need to become aware of the different types of notes that can be written and should then be shown how to write them.

Text Annotations

Eanet and Manzo (1976) underscore the importance of making text annotations as a means of helping students learn what they read. They describe the different kinds of notes students can write. Several are particularly appropriate for middle grade and secondary school students. For example, read the following passage. Then study each of the notes made by a high school student, shown in Figures 12.14 through 12.17.

> Unpleasantness for those trading illegally in wild animals and their products is escalating around the world. Within the past decade government after government has passed laws to restrict or prohibit the sale of wildlife seriously depleted by hunting and habitat destruction. With legal channels pinched, animal dealers have resorted to nefarious schemes to continue the flow.
>
> Wildlife is big business. Exotic-bird collectors will pay $10,000 for a hyacinth macaw. . . . In New York I tried on a pair of trendy western boots trimmed in lizard skin. The price? "Two hundred thirty five," the clerk said, with an archness suggesting that most of his customers didn't bother to ask. . . .
>
> These items are being sold legally. But somewhere in the dim beginnings of their trail through commerce, they may have been acquired illegally. . . .
>
> This fascination with wildlife within the affluent nations of the world adds to the disappearance of animals in the less developed countries. In between stand the illegal traders willing to circumvent the wildlife-protection laws to satisfy the demand and their own pocketbooks. . . .
>
> Wildlife smuggling is costing the U.S. millions of dollars to control and is denying income to the treasury of any nation that would otherwise receive duty from legal imports. It has spread diseases that would have been detected in legal quarantine periods. . . . An irreversible effect of illegal trade could be the extinction of animal species that are finding fewer and fewer places to hide. (Grove 1981)

The *summary note,* as you might surmise, condenses the main ideas of a text selection into a concise statement. Summary notes are characterized by their brevity, clarity, and conciseness. When a note summarizes expository material, it should clearly distinguish the important ideas in the author's presentation from supporting information and detail. When the summary note involves narrative material, such as a story, it should include a synopsis containing the major story elements. Examine the example of a summary note from a student's note card in Figure 12.14.

The *thesis note* answers the question, "What is the main point the author has tried to get across to the reader?" The thesis note has a telegramlike character. It is incisively stated yet unambiguous in its identification of the author's main proposition. The thesis note for a story identifies its theme. Study the example in Figure 12.15.

The *critical note* captures the reader's reaction or response to the author's thesis. It answers the question, "So what?" In writing critical notes, the reader should first state the author's thesis, then state the reader's position in relation to the thesis, and finally, defend or expand on the position taken. See Figure 12.16.

The *question note* raises a significant issue in the form of a question. The question is the result of what the reader thinks is the most germane or significant aspect of what he or she has read. See Figure 12.17.

FIGURE 12.14 A Summary Note

> The illegal trading of wildlife and their products is a profitable business in affluent countries around the world. The continuation of such trade threatens both developed and underdeveloped nations economically and ecologically. More recent laws are making this illegal trade much more difficult to carry out.

FIGURE 12.15 A Thesis Note

> Illegal wild animal trade is a very profitable business. Illegal wildlife trade is a threat to humans and their environment. More laws throughout the world can restrict this activity.

Showing students how to write different types of notes begins with assessment; leads to awareness and knowledge building, modeling, and practice; and culminates in application. First, assign a text selection and ask students to make whatever notes they wish. Second, have the class analyze the assessment, share student notes, and discuss difficulties in making notes. Use the assessment discussion to make students aware of the importance of making notes as a strategy for learning and retention.

Third, build students' knowledge for note making by helping them recognize and define the various kinds of text notes that can be written. Eanet and Manzo (1976) recommend the following strategy: Assign a short selection to be read in class; then write a certain type of note on the board. Ask students how what they read on the board relates to the passage that was assigned. Through discussion, formulate the definition and concept of the note under discussion.

As part of a growing understanding of the different types of notes, students should be able to tell a well-written note from a poorly written one. Have the class

FIGURE 12.16 A Critical Note

The trading of wildlife for high profits is something all of us will pay for ultimately. Countries are being cheated out of needed revenues. Even more important, the future of species of animals is being threatened. The money-minded traders also give little thought to the spread of disease that could be avoided by legal quarantines. All nations need to cooperate to pass stricter laws to control or prohibit the trade of wildlife for temporary luxury

FIGURE 12.17 A Question Note

(Should illegal wildlife trade be allowed to continue or, at least, be ignored, after unsuccessful attempts to stop it?) The author says that it is becoming more unpleasant for illegal traders of wildlife and their products because of more laws instituted by governments around the world. He also cites serious economic and ecological reasons not to give up the fight.

read a short passage, followed by several examples of a certain type of note, one well written and the others flawed in some way. For example, a discussion of critical notes may include one illustration of a good critical note, one that lacks the note maker's position, and another that fails to defend or develop the position taken.

Modeling and practice should follow naturally from awareness and knowledge building. Teachers should guide students through the process of making different types of notes by sharing their thought processes. Show how a note is written and revised to satisfaction through think-aloud procedures. Then have students practice note making individually and in peer groups of two or three. Peer-group interaction is nonthreatening and leads to productions that can be duplicated or put on the board, compared, and evaluated by the class with teacher direction.

To facilitate application to classroom reading tasks, we suggest that students write notes regularly in a learning log, on study cards, or on their computers. Save note-making activities in learning logs for the latter half of a class period. The next class period then begins with a review or a sharing of notes, followed by discussion and clarification of the text material.

Notes written on study cards are an alternative to the learning log. Direct students to make study cards based on text readings. One tactic is to write questions on one side of the cards and responses to the questions on the other side. For example, ask students to convert the major subheadings of a text selection into questions, writing one question per card. The responses will probably lend themselves to summary or critical notes, depending on the questions posed. Later, students can use the study cards to prepare for a test. As part of test preparation, a student can read the question, recite the response aloud, and then review the note written earlier. Lester (1984) offers the following tips for making notes on cards:

1. *Use ink.* Penciled notes smudge easily with repeated shuffling of the cards.

2. *Use index cards.* Index cards are more durable and can be rearranged and organized more easily than large sheets of paper.

3. *Jot down only one item per card.* Don't overload a card with more than one type of note or one piece of information.

4. *Write on one side of the card.* Material on the back of a card may be overlooked during study. (One exception is question-and-response cards.)

A Note-Taking Procedure

Walter Pauk's response to the question "Why take notes?" is profound in its simplicity: Because we forget (1978). More than 50 percent of the material read or heard in class is forgotten in a matter of minutes. A system for taking and making notes triggers recall and overcomes forgetting.

A popular note-taking procedure, suggested by Palmatier (1973), involves the following steps: First, have students use only one side of an 8½-by-11-inch sheet of loose-leaf paper with a legal-width margin (if necessary, the student should add a margin line 3 inches from the left side of the paper). Second, have the students take lecture notes to the right of the margin. Although no specific format for taking notes is required, students should develop a format that uses subordination and space to illustrate the organization of the material; for example, they can indent to show continuation of ideas or enumerate to show series of details. Third, have the students put labels in the left margin that correspond to units of information recorded in the notes. The labels help organize the welter of information in the right column and give students the chance to fill in gaps in the notes. The labeling process should be completed as quickly as possible following the original taking of notes. (See Figure 12.18.)

> **Response Journal**
> What kind of note-taking procedures do you use?

Once notes are taken and the labeling task is completed, students can use their notes to study for exams. For example, in preparing for a test, the student can spread out the note pages for review. One excellent strategy is to show students how to spread the pages, in order, in such a way that the lecture notes are hidden by succeeding pages and only the left-margin labels show. The labels can then be used as question stems to recall information—for example, "What do I need to know about (*label*)?" Accuracy of recall, of course, can be checked by referring to the original notes, which were concealed by overlapping the pages.

Students need to learn how to work smart. Working smart involves knowing when and when not to take shortcuts; it's knowing how to triumph over the everyday cognitive demands that are a natural part of classroom life.

Knowing how to work smart requires time and patience. Studying is a process that is learned inductively through trial and error and the repeated use of different strategies in different learning situations. And this is where teachers have a role to play. Through the instructional support you provide, students discover that some strategies work better for them than others in different learning situations.

> **e.Resources**
> For additional readings related to the major ideas in this chapter, go to Chapter 12 of the Companion Website and click on Suggested Readings.

◀ Looking Back
Looking Forward ▶

Teaching students how to study texts involves showing them how to become independent learners. In this chapter, we used the role that text structure plays to illustrate how you can teach students to use learner-directed strategies that involve constructing graphic organizers, writing summaries, and making and taking notes.

How authors organize their ideas is a powerful factor in learning with texts. Because authors write to communicate, they organize ideas to make them accessible to readers. A well-organized text is a considerate one. The text patterns that authors use to organize their ideas revolve around description, sequence, comparison and contrast, cause and effect, and

FIGURE 12.18 Note-Taking Procedure That Uses Labels and Notes

Labels	Notes
Neurons are detectors that signal messages to the brain	Our eyes, ears, nose, tongue, and skin pick up messages and send them to the brain. 1. The lens of the eye focuses light on the retina, and neurons change it into a message that's carried by the optic nerves. 2. The tongue and nose work together to detect chemicals and send a message to the brain. – tongue has areas for sweet, salty, sour – each area has neurons 3. The skin has neurons that detect pain, pressure, touch.

problem and solution. The more students perceive text patterns, the more likely they are to remember and interpret the ideas they encounter in reading.

Graphic organizers help students outline important information that is reflected in the text patterns that authors use to organize ideas. The construction of graphic organizers allows students to map the relationships that exist among the ideas presented in text. This strategy is a valuable tool for comprehending and retaining information.

Students who engage in summarizing what they have read often gain greater understanding and retention of the main ideas in text. Students need to become aware of summarization rules and to receive instruction in how to use these rules to write and polish a summary.

Notes are part of another useful strategy for studying text. Making notes allows students to reflect on and react to important ideas in text.

 Minds On

1. A member of the board of education has been quoted as saying that she is opposed to "spoon-feeding" high school students. After a board meeting one evening, you have an opportunity to talk with her. You explain that there is a difference between "spoon-feeding" students and scaffolding instruction. As a group, discuss how you might justify supporting students' studying through the use of techniques such as graphic organizers, summaries, and note taking.

2. Following an in-service program on using graphic organizers, you notice that some teachers in your building are preparing a semantic map for every assignment, whereas others, who say they don't have time, never use them. Your principal asks you, as a member of a team, to prepare a one-page sheet of guidelines for the use of graphic organizers in which you suggest when, why, and how various graphic displays should be used. What would you include in this guide?

3. Imagine that your group is team-teaching an interdisciplinary unit on the Civil War. Each member of your group should select (a) a content area and (b) one of the text patterns described in this chapter (sequence, comparison and contrast, problem and solution, cause and effect, or description). After reviewing some materials on the art, history, music, politics, science, mathematics, and literature of the Civil War, discuss how you might make use of a selected text pattern to teach a concept.

4. As part of an effort to improve school achievement in content area subjects, the curriculum director of your school system has suggested implementing a mandatory study skills course for all high school first-year students. As a team, compose a memo explaining why and how studying can be effectively taught when content area teachers are also involved in the delivery of instruction.

Hands On

1. Design a semantic map for a science lesson on the characteristics of the planets. Create what you consider the most effective design for that specific content.

2. Using either problem and solution, cause and effect, or comparison and contrast, construct a graphic for a passage from an informational text. Share your representation with members of your group, and discuss how some topics seem appropriate for one specific organizational pattern, whereas others might be organized in a variety of ways.

3. Distribute one card to each member of the class. Ask the students to write down the name of an individual they believe has made a significant contribution to society. Emphasize that the contribution may be in either a specific area of knowledge (art, music, science, literature, politics) or a nonspecific area such as acts of humanitarianism or environmental activism.

   Next, announce that the task of the class will be to create clusters of cards with names that have a common focus. Give each student in the class three minutes to find one partner whose card name relates to his or her own. Then have each team of partners locate another team whose names can be classified together. Explain that, if necessary, groups may redefine their common focus to create clusters. As a whole class, share the focus categories developed by each group.

   Finally, repeat the process, but do not allow any group to use the same common focus. Discuss how this activity relates to the process of outlining.

4. Imagine that one of your colleagues asks students to write summaries of what they are reading in class but does not provide explicit instruction on how to summarize a text effectively. You have observed that many of your colleague's students are frustrated by the task or are simply copying summaries written by other students. With a member of your group, create a dialogue in which you discuss some instructional alternatives that will lead students' writing summaries effectively. As a group, discuss the suggestions you found effective and recommend some others that might have been included.

5. In a small group, read a short selection from a current news story, magazine article, textbook selection, or electronic media source. Write examples of the different kinds of notes that can be made from the text. Compare your group's notes with those of other groups, and discuss the different thinking tasks each type of note required, as well as the further use of each note in a classroom teaching situation.

6. In a small group, compile a list of study strategies that the group members use as well as the purposes for which they are used. Categorize the strategies into different groupings according to their perceived purposes. Display the strategies on an overhead or a chalkboard for a discussion of commonalities and suggestions for studying texts.

e.Resourcesextra

- Go to Chapter 12 of the Companion Website (**www.ablongman.com/vacca8e**) and click on Activities to complete the following task:

  The following site contains information on how to study in elementary through high school: **www.how-to-study.com**. Browse the site and share your findings in small groups. As part of the small-group discussion, model one study strategy, describing how teachers could adapt it for use in a content area.

- Go to the Companion Website (**www. ablongman.com/vacca8e**) for suggested readings, interactive activities, multiple-choice questions, and additional Web links to help you learn more about studying texts.

expect the world®

The New York Times

nytimes.com

Themes of the Times

Extend your knowledge of the concepts discussed in this chapter by reading current and historical articles from the *New York Times*. Go to the Companion Website and click on eThemes of the Times.

Affixes with Invariant Meanings

AFFIX	MEANING	EXAMPLE
Combining Forms		
anthropo-	man	anthropoid
auto-	self	autonomous
biblio-	book	bibliography
bio-	life	biology
centro-, centri-	center	centrifugal
cosmo-	universe	cosmonaut
heter-, hetero-	different	heterogeneous
homo-	same	homogeneous
hydro-	water	hydroplane
iso-	equal	isometric
lith-, litho-	stone	lithography
micro-	small	microscope
mono-	one	monocyte
neuro-	nerve	neurologist
omni-	all	omnibus
pan-	all	panchromatic
penta-	five	pentamerous
phil-, philo-	love	philanthropist
phono-	sound	phonology

photo-	light	photosynthesis
pneumo-	air, respiration	pneumonia
poly-	many	polygon
proto-	before, first in time	prototype
pseudo-	false	pseudonym
tele-	far	television
uni-	one	unicellular

Prefixes

apo-	separate or detached from	apocarpous
circum-	around	circumvent
co-, col-, com-, con-, cor-	together or with	combine
equi-	equal	equivalent
extra-	in addition	extraordinary
intra-	within	intratext
mal-	bad	malpractice
mis-	wrong	mistreatment
non-	not	nonsense
syn-	together or with	synthesis

Noun Suffixes

-ana	collection	Americana
-archy	rule or government	oligarchy
-ard, -art	person who does something to excess	drunkard, braggart
-aster	inferiority or fraudulence	poetaster
-bility	quality or state of being	capability
-chrome	pigment, color	autochrome
-cide	murder or killing of	insecticide
-fication, -ation	action or process of	classification, dramatization

-gram	something written or drawn	diagram
-graph	writing, recording, drawing	telegraph, lithograph
-graphy	descriptive science of a specific subject or field	planography, oceanography
-ics	science or art of	graphics, athletics
-itis	inflammation or inflammatory disease	bronchitis
-latry	worship of	bibliolatry
-meter	measuring device	barometer
-metry	science or process of measuring	photometry
-ology, -logy	science, theory, or study of	phraseology, paleontology
-phobia	fear	hypnophobia
-phore	bearer or producer	semaphore
-scope	instrument for observing or detecting	telescope
-scopy	viewing, seeing, or observing	microscopy
-ance, -ation, -ion, -ism, -dom, -ery, -mony, -ment, -tion	quality, state, or condition; action or result of an action	tolerance, adoration, truism, matrimony, government, sanction
-er, -eer, -ess, -ier, -ster, -ist, -trix	agent, doer	helper, engineer, countess, youngster, shootist, executrix

Adjective Suffixes

-able, -ible	worthy of or inclined to	debatable, knowledgeable
-aceous, -ative, -ish, -ive, -itious	pertaining to	impish, foolish, additive, fictitious
-acious	tendency toward or abundance of	fallacious
-est	most	greatest
-ferous	bearing, producing	crystalliferous
-fic	making, causing, or creating	horrific

-fold	multiplied by	fivefold
-form	having the form of	cuneiform
-ful	full of or having the quality of	masterful, useful, armful
-genous	generating or producing	androgenous, endogenous
-ic	characteristic of	seismic, microscopic
-less	lacking	toothless
-like	similar to	lifelike
-most	most	innermost
-ous, -ose	possessing, full of	joyous, grandiose
-wise	manner, direction, or positions	clockwise

Commonly Used Prefixes with Varying Meanings

PREFIX	MEANING	EXAMPLE
ab-	from, away, off	abhor, abnormal, abdicate
ad-	to, toward	adhere, adjoin
ante-	before, in front of, earlier than	antecedent, antediluvian
anti-	opposite of, hostile to	antitoxin, antisocial
be-	make, against, to a great degree	bemoan, belittle, befuddle
bi-	two, twice	biped, bivalve
de-	away, opposite of, reduce	deactivate, devalue, devitalize
dia-	through, across	diameter, diagonal
dis-	opposite of, apart, away	dissatisfy, disarm, disjointed
en-	cause to be, put in or on	enable, engulf
epi-	upon, after	epitaph, epilogue, epidermis
ex-	out of, former, apart, away	excrete, exposition
hyper-	above, beyond, excessive	hyperphysical, hypersensitive
hypo-	under, less than normal	hypodermic, hypotension
in-, il-, im-, ir-	not, in, into, within	inept, indoors
inter-	between, among	interscholastic, interstellar
neo-	new, young	neophyte, neo-Nazi
ortho-	straight, corrective	orthotropic, orthopedic

per-	through, very	permanent, perjury
peri-	around, near, enclosing	perimeter, perihelion
post-	after, behind	postwar, postorbital
pre-	before, in place, time, rank, order	preview, prevail
pro-	before, forward, for, in favor of	production, prothorax, pro-American
re-	again, back	react, recoil
sub-, sur-, sug-, sup-	under, beneath	subordinate, subsoil, substation
super-	above, over, in addition	superhuman, superlative, superordinate
syn-	with, together	synthesis, synchronize
trans-	across, beyond, through	transatlantic, transconfiguration, transaction
ultra-	beyond in space, excessive	ultraviolet, ultramodern
un-	not, the opposite of	unable, unbind

Graphic Organizers with Text Frames

Graphic organizers are visual illustrations of verbal statements. Frames are sets of questions or categories that are fundamental to understanding a given topic. Here are shown nine "generic" graphic forms with their corresponding frames. Also given are examples of topics that could be represented by each graphic form. These graphics show at a glance the key parts of the whole and their relations, helping the learner to comprehend text and solve problems.

Spider Map

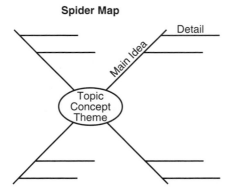

Used to describe a central idea: a thing (a geographic region), process (meiosis), concept (altruism), or proposition with support (experimental drugs should be available to AIDS victims). Key frame questions: What is the central idea? What are its attributes? What are its functions?

Used to describe the stages of something (the life cycle of a primate); the steps in a linear procedure (how to neutralize an acid); a sequence of events (how feudalism led to the formation of nation-states); or the goals, actions, and outcomes of a historical figure or character in a novel (the rise and fall of Napoléon). Key frame questions: What is the object, procedure, or initiating event? What are the stages or steps? How do they lead to one another? What is the final outcome?

Series-of-Events Chain

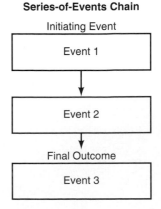

Used for time lines showing historical events or ages (grade levels in
school), degrees of something
(weight), shades of meaning (Likert
scales), or ratings scales (achievement in school). Key frame questions: What is being scaled? What
are the end points?

Continuum/Scale

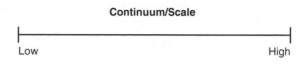

Low   High

Compare/Contrast Matrix

	Name 1	Name 2
Attribute 1		
Attribute 2		
Attribute 3		

Used to show similarities and
differences between two things
(people, places, events, ideas,
etc.). Key frame questions: What
things are being compared? How
are they similar? How are they
different?

Problem/Solution Outline

Used to represent a problem, attempted solutions, and results (the
national debt). Key frame questions: What was the problem? Who
had the problem? Why was it a
problem? What attempts were
made to solve the problem? Did
those attempts succeed?

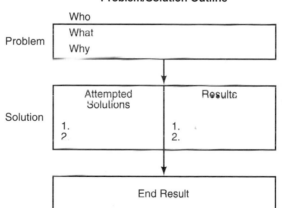

Network Tree

Used to show causal information
(causes of poverty), a hierarchy
(types of insects), or branching procedures (the circulatory system).
Key frame questions: What is the
superordinate category? What are
the subordinate categories? How
are they related? How many levels
are there?

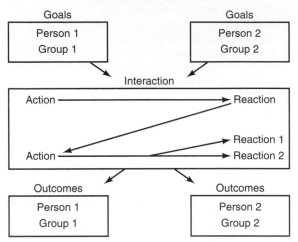

Used to show the nature of an interaction between persons or groups (European settlers and Native Americans). Key frame questions: Who are the persons or groups? Did they conflict or cooperate? What was the outcome for each person or group?

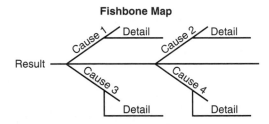

Used to show the causal interaction of a complex event (an election, a nuclear explosion) or complex phenomenon (juvenile deliquency, learning disabilities). Key frame questions: What are the factors that cause X? How do they relate? Are the factors that cause X the same as those that cause X to persist?

Used to show how a series of events interact to produce a set of results again and again (weather phenomena, cycles of achievement and failure, the life cycle). Key frame questions: What are the critical events in the cycle? How are they related? In what ways are they self-reinforcing?

Source: © 1988 North Central Regional Educational Laboratory. Reprinted with permission.

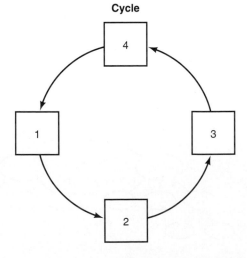

Ackerman, N. (1990). *The tin heart.* Ill. M. Hays. New York: Atheneum.

Adolescent literacy position statement. (1999). Newark, DE: International Reading Association.

Aliki. (1983). *A medieval feast.* New York: Crowell.

Aliki. (1986). *A medieval feast.* New York: Harper-Collins.

Aliki. (1999). *William Shakespeare and the Globe.* New York: HarperCollins.

Allington, R., & Johnston, P. H. (Eds.). (2002). *Reading to learn: Lessons from exemplary fourth-grade classrooms.* New York: Guilford.

Allington, R. L. (2001). *What really matters for struggling readers: Designing research-based programs.* New York: Longman.

Allington, R. L., & Strange, M. (1980). *Learning through reading in the content areas.* Lexington, MA: Heath.

Alvarez, M. C. (1996). Explorers of the universe: Students using the World Wide Web to improve their reading and writing. In B. Neate (Ed.), *Literacy saves lives* (pp. 140–145). Herts: United Kingdom Reading Association.

Alvermann, D. E. (1991). The discussion web: A graphic aid for learning across the curriculum. *Reading Teacher, 45*(2), 92–99.

Alvermann, D. E., & Moore, D. W. (1991). Secondary school reading. In P. D. Pearson, R. Barr, M. L. Kamil, & P. Mosenthal (Eds.), *Handbook of reading research* (2nd ed., pp. 951–983). New York: Longman.

Ames, L. J. (1986). *Draw fifty cars, trucks, and motorcycles.* Garden City, NY: Doubleday.

Anderson, D. L. (1999). *Using projects in the mathematics classroom to enhance instruction and incorporate history of mathematics.* Paper presented at the National Council of Teachers of Mathematics, San Francisco, CA.

Anderson, L. (2000). *Fever 1793.* New York: Simon & Schuster.

Anderson, R. C., & Freebody, P. (1981). Vocabulary knowledge. In J. T. Guthrie (Ed.), *Comprehension and teaching: Research perspectives* (pp. 77–117). Newark, DE: International Reading Association.

Anderson-Inman, L., & Horney, M. (1997). Electronic books for secondary students. *Journal of Adolescent and Adult Literacy, 40*(6), 486–491.

Anno, M. (1970). *Topsy-turvies: Pictures to stretch the imagination.* New York: Weatherhill.

Anno, M. (1982). *Anno's counting house.* New York: Philomel.

Anno, M. (1989). *Anno's math games II.* New York: Philomel.

Applebee, A. N. (1991). Environments for language teaching and learning: Contemporary issues and future directions. In J. Flood, J. M. Jensen, D. Lapp, & J. R. Squire (Eds.), *Handbook of research on teaching the English language arts* (pp. 549–558). New York: Macmillan.

Armbruster, B. B., & Anderson, T. H. (1981). *Content area textbooks.* Reading Education Report No. 23. Urbana: University of Illinois Center for the Study of Reading.

Armbruster, B. B., & Anderson, T. H. (1985). Frames: Structure for informational texts. In D. H. Jonassen (Ed.), *Technology of text* (pp. 331–346). Englewood Cliffs, NJ: Education Technology Publications.

Armstrong, J. (1998). *Shipwreck at the bottom of the world: The extraordinary true story of Shackleton and the* Endurance. New York: Crown.

Armstrong, L., & Jenkins, S. (2001). *It's not about the bike: My journey back to life.* New York: Berkley Books.

Aronson, E. (1978). *The jigsaw classroom.* Beverly Hills, CA: Sage.

Aronson, M. (1998). *Art attack: A short cultural history of the avant-garde.* New York: Clarion Books.

Artley, A. S. (1975). Words, words, words. *Language Arts, 52,* 1067–1072.

Ashabranner, B. (1988). *Always to remember: The story of the Vietnam Veterans Memorial.* Ill. J. Ashabranner. New York: Putnam.

Atkin, S. B. (1993). *Voices from the fields: Children of migrant farmworkers tell their stories.* Boston: Little Brown.

Atwell, N. (1990). Introduction. In N. Atwell (Ed.), *Coming to know: Writing to learn in intermediate grades* (pp. xi–xxiii). Portsmouth, NH: Heinemann.

Atwell, N. (1998). *In the middle: New understandings about writing, reading, and learning* (2nd ed.). Portsmouth, NH: Heinemann.

Au, K. H. (1981). Social organizational factors in learning to read: The balance of rights hypothesis. *Reading Research Quarterly, 17*(1), 115–152.

Au, K. H. (1993). *Literacy instruction in multicultural settings.* Orlando: Harcourt Brace.

Baker, J. (1991). *Window.* New York: Greenwillow.

Baker, L. (1991). Metacognition, reading, and science education. In C. M. Santa & D. E. Alvermann (Eds.), *Science learning: Processes and applications* (pp. 12–13). Newark, DE: International Reading Association.

Baker, L., & Brown, A. (1984). Cognitive monitoring in reading. In J. Flood (Ed.), *Understanding reading comprehension* (pp. 21–44). Newark, DE: International Reading Association.

Ballard, R. D. (1988). *Exploring the* Titanic. New York: Scholastic.

Bamford, R. A., & Kristo, J. V. (Eds.). (1998). *Making facts come alive: Choosing quality nonfiction literature K–8.* Needham Heights, MA: Christopher Gordon.

Bandura, A. (1986). *Social foundations of thought and action: A social cognitive theory.* Englewood Cliffs, NJ: Prentice Hall.

Bank, J. A. (2001). *Cultural diversity and education: Foundations, curriculum, and teaching* (4th ed.). Boston: Allyn & Bacon.

Barnes, D. (1995). Talking and learning in the classroom: An introduction. *Primary Voices K–6, 3*(1), 2–7.

Barnes, D., Britton, J., & Rosen, H. (1969). *Language, the learner, and school.* New York: Penguin.

Barrentine, S. J. (1999). *Reading assessment: Principles and practices for elementary teachers.* Newark, DE: International Reading Association.

Barron, R. F. (1969). The use of vocabulary as an advance organizer. In H. L. Herber & P. L. Sanders (Eds.), *Research in reading in the content areas: First report* (pp. 29–39). Syracuse, NY: Syracuse University Reading and Language Arts Center.

Barron, R. F., & Earle, R. (1973). An approach for vocabulary development. In H. L. Herber & R. F. Barron (Eds.), *Research in reading in the content areas: Second report* (pp. 51–63). Syracuse, NY: Syracuse University Reading and Language Arts Center.

Barron, R. F., & Stone, F. (1973, December). *The effect of student constructed graphic post organizers upon learning of vocabulary relationships from a passage of social studies content.* Paper presented at the meeting of the National Reading Conference, Houston, TX.

Bartlett, B. (1978). *Top-level structure as an organizational strategy for recall of classroom text.* Unpublished doctoral dissertation, Arizona State University.

Bartoletti, S. C. (2001). *Black potatoes: The story of the great Irish famine, 1845–1850.* Boston: Houghton Mifflin.

Barton, J. (1995). Conducting effective classroom discussions. *Journal of Reading, 38*(5), 346–350.

Beaman, B. (1985). Writing to learn social studies. In A. R. Gere (Ed.), *Roots in sawdust: Writing to learn across the disciplines* (pp. 50–60). Urbana, IL: National Council of Teachers of English.

Beatty, P. (1987). *Charley Skedaddle.* New York: Morrow.

Beck, I. L., McKeown, M. G., Hamilton, R. L., & Kucan, L. (1997). *Questioning the author: An approach for enhancing student engagement in text.* Newark, DE: International Reading Association.

Beebe, B. F. (1968). *African elephants.* New York: McKay.

Beil, K. M. (1999). *Fire in their eyes: Wildfires and the people who fight them.* San Diego: Harcourt Brace.

Berger, M. (1986). *Atoms, molecules, and quarks.* New York: Putnam.

Berliner, D.C. & Biddle, B. (1995). *The manufactured crisis.* New York: Longman.

Berlyne, D. E. (1965). *Structure and direction of thinking.* New York: Wiley.

Bernhardt, B. (1977). *Just writing.* New York: Teachers and Writers.

Betts, E. (1950). *Foundations of reading* (Rev. ed.). New York: American Book Company.

Beuhl, D. (1991, Spring). Frames of mind. *The Exchange: Newsletter of the IRA Secondary Reading Interest Group,* pp. 4–5.

Biggs, A. L., Emmeluth, D. S., Gentry, C. L., Hays, R. I., Lundren, L., & Mollura, F. (1991). *Biology: The dynamics of life.* Columbus, OH: Merrill.

Bitton-Jackson, L. (1997). *I have lived a thousand years: Growing up in the Holocaust.* New York: Simon & Schuster.

Blachowicz, C. (1986). Making connections: Alternatives to the vocabulary notebook. *Journal of Reading, 29,* 643–649.

Blachowicz, C., & Fisher, P. (1996). *Teaching vocabulary in all classrooms.* Columbus, OH: Merrill.

Bleich, D. (1978). *Subjective criticism.* Baltimore: Johns Hopkins University Press.

Bode, J. (1989). *New kids in town: Oral histories of immigrant teens.* New York: Franklin Watts.

Bracey, G. W. (2003). April foolishness: The 20th anniversary of *A Nation at Risk. Phi Delta Kappan, 84*(8), 616–621.

Brashares, A. (2001). *Sisterhood of the traveling pants.* New York: Delacorte.

Britton, J. (1970). *Language and learning.* London: Allen Lane.

Britton, J. (1975). *Language and learning.* London: Allen Lane.

Brown, A. L. (1978). Knowing when, where, and how to remember: A problem of metacognition. In R. Glaser (Ed.), *Advances in instructional psychology* (pp. 117–175). Hillsdale, NJ: Erlbaum.

Brown, A. L., Bransford, J. W., Ferrara, R. F., & Campione, J. (1983). Learning, remembering, and understanding. In J. Flavell & E. Markham (Eds.), *Handbook of child psychology* (pp. 393–451). New York: Wiley.

Brown, A. L., & Palinscar, A. S. (1982). Inducing strategic learning from texts by means of informed, self-control training. *Topics in Learning and Learning Disabilities, 2,* 1–17.

Brown, A. L., & Palinscar, A. S. (1984). Reciprocal teaching of comprehension-fostering and comprehension-monitoring activities. *Cognition and Instruction, 1,* 117–175.

Brown, D. (1987). *Principles of language learning and teaching.* Englewood Cliffs, NJ: Prentice Hall.

Brown, M. W. (1949). *The important book.* Ill. L. Weisgard. New York: Harper & Row.

Brozo, W. G. (1989). Applying a reader response heuristic to expository text. *Journal of Reading, 32,* 140–145.

Brozo, W. G. (1990). Learning how at-risk readers learn best: A case for interactive assessment. *Journal of Reading, 33,* 522–527.

Brozo, W. G., & Tomlinson, C. M. (1986). Literature: The key to lively content courses. *Reading Teacher, 40,* 288–293.

Bruner, J. (1961). The act of discovery. *Harvard Educational Review, 31,* 21–32.

Bruner, J. (1970). The skill of relevance or the relevance of skills. *Saturday Review, 53.*

Bruner, J. (1986). *Actual minds, possible worlds.* Cambridge, MA: Harvard University Press.

Bruner, J. (1990). *Acts of meaning.* Cambridge, MA: Harvard University Press.

Bruner, J., Goodnow, J., & Austin, G. (1977). *A study of thinking.* New York: Science Editions.

Bunting, E. (1994). *Smoky night.* Ill. D. Diaz. Orlando: Harcourt Brace.

Burgess, J. (1988). *The heart and blood (How our bodies work).* Englewood Cliffs, NJ: Silver Burdett.

Burleigh, R. (1997). *Hoops.* Ill. S. T. Johnson. San Diego: Silver Whistle.

Calabro, M. (1999). *The perilous journey of the Donner Party.* New York: Clarion Books.

Camp, G. (1982). *A successful curriculum for remedial writers.* Berkeley: National Writing Project, University of California.

Canfiled, J. (2000). *Chicken soup for the sports fan's soul: 101 stories of insight, inspiration and laughter in the world.* Deerfield, FL: HCI.

Carter, B. (2000). *Best books for young adults.* Chicago, IL: American Library Association.

Carter, B., & Abrahamson, R. F. (1990). *Nonfiction for young adults: From delight to wisdom.* Phoenix, AZ: Oryx Press.

Chang, I. (1991). *A separate battle: Women and the Civil War.* New York: Scholastic.

Chekhov, A. (1991). *Kashtanka.* Trans. R. Povear. Ill. B. Moser. New York: Putnam.

Clark, R. P. (1987). *Free to write: A journalist teaches young writers.* Portsmouth, NH: Heinemann.

Collins, J. L. (1997). *Strategies for struggling writers.* New York: Guilford Press.

Cone, M. (1992). *Come back, salmon: How a group of dedicated kids adopted Pigeon Creek and brought it back to life.* Photo. S. Wheelwright. San Francisco: Sierra Club Books for Children.

Congressional Digest. (1999). The federal role in education: 1999–2000 policy debate topic. *Congressional Digest,* August–September, 193.

Conrad, P. (1992). *Pedro's journal.* New York: Scholastic.

Cooney, T., Bell, K., Fisher-Cauble, D., & Sanchez, W. (1996). The demands of alternative assessment: What teachers say. *Mathematics Teacher, 89,* 484–487.

Coville, B. (1997). *William Shakespeare's* Macbeth. Ill. G. Kelly. New York: Dial.

Crue, W. (1932, February). Ordeal by Cheque. *Vanity Fair.*

Crutcher, C. (1989). *Athletic shorts.* New York: Greenwillow.

Cummins, J. (1981). The role of primary language development in promoting educational success for language minority students. In J. Cummins (Ed.), *Schooling and language minority students: A theoretical framework* (pp. 3–49). Los Angeles: Evaluation, Dissemination, and Assessment Center, California State University at Los Angeles.

Cummins, J. (1994). The acquisition of English as a second language. In K. Spangenberg-Urbschat & R. Pritchard (Eds.), *Kids come in all languages: Reading instruction for ESL students* (pp. 36–62). Newark, DE: International Reading Association.

Cunningham, R., & Shablak, S. (1975). Selective reading guide-o-rama: The content teacher's best friend. *Journal of Reading, 18,* 380–382.

Curry, J. (1989). The role of reading instruction in mathematics. In D. Lapp, J. Flood, & N. Farnan (Eds.), *Content area reading and learning: Instructional strategies* (pp. 187–197). Upper Saddle River, NJ: Prentice Hall.

Daisey, P. (1994). The value of trade books in secondary science and mathematics instruction: A rationale. *School Science and Mathematics, 94,* 130–137.

Daisey, P. (1997). Promoting literacy in secondary content area classrooms with biography projects. *Journal of Adolescent and Adult Literacy, 40,* 270–278.

Dale, E. (1969). Things to come. *Newsletter, 34,* 1–8.

Dash, J. (2000). *The longitude prize.* New York: Frances Foster.

Davey, B. (1983). Think aloud: Modeling the cognitive processes of reading comprehension. *Journal of Reading, 27,* 44–47.

Davidson, J. L., & Wilkerson, B. C. (1988). *Directed reading–thinking activities.* Monroe, NY: Trillium Press.

Davis, O. (1978). *Escape to freedom: A play about Frederick Douglass.* New York: Viking Penguin.

Deighton, L. (1970). *Vocabulary development in the classroom.* New York: Teachers College Press.

Delpit, L. D. (1986). Skills and other dilemmas of a progressive black educator. *Harvard Educational Review, 56,* 379–385.

Delpit, L. D. (1988). The silenced dialogue: Power and pedagogy in educating other people's children. *Harvard Educational Review, 58,* 280–298.

Diaz, C. F. (2001). *Multicultural education for the twenty-first century.* New York: Longman.

Diaz-Rico, L. T. & Weed, K. Z. (2002). *The crosscultural, language, and academic development handbook: A complete K–12 reference guide.* Boston: Allyn & Bacon.

DiBacco, T. V., Mason, L. C., & Appy, C. G. (1992). *History of the United States: Vol. 2. Civil War to the present.* Boston: Houghton Mifflin.

Dillon, D. R. (1983). Showing them that I want them to learn and that I care about who they are: A micro-ethnography of the social organization of a secondary low-track English-reading classroom. *American Education Research Journal, 26,* 227–259.

Dolciani, M. P., Graham, J. A., Swanson, R. A., & Sharron, S. (1992). *Algebra 2 and trigonometry.* Boston: Houghton Mifflin.

Donelson, K. L., & Nilsen, A. P. (1997). *Literature for today's young adults* (5th ed.). New York: Longman.

Duffy, G. G. (1983). From turn taking to sense making: Broadening the concept of reading teacher effectiveness. *Journal of Educational Research, 76,* 134–139.

Duke, N. K. & Pearson, P. D. (2002). Effective practices for developing reading comprehension. In A. E. Farstrup & S. J. Samuels (Eds.), *What research has to say about reading instruction* (3rd ed., pp. 205–242). Newark, DE: International Reading Association.

Dyer, D. (1997). *Jack London: A biography.* New York: Scholastic.

Eanet, M., & Manzo, A. V. (1976). REAP: A strategy for improving reading/writing/study skills. *Journal of Reading, 19,* 647–652.

Echevarria, J. & Graves, A. (2003). *Sheltered content instruction: Teaching English-langue learners with diverse abilities* (2nd ed.). Boston: Allyn & Bacon.

Echevarria, J., Vogt, M., & Short, D. J. (2000). *Making content comprehensible for English language learners: The SIOP model.* Boston: Allyn & Bacon.

Education Commission of the States. (2001). *ECS state notes: Reading: Common state strategies to improve student reading.* Retrieved September, 2003, from www.ecs.org.

Edwards, P. (1967). *Equiano's travels: The interesting narrative of the life of Olaudah Equiano or Gustavus Vassa, the African.* New York: Praeger.

Egan, K. (1989). Layers of historical understanding. *Theory and Research in Social Education, 17,* 280–294.

Eisner, E. W. (1985). *The educational imagination: On the design and evaluation of school programs* (2nd ed.). New York: Macmillan.

Eisner, E. W. (1991). The celebration of thinking. *Maine Scholar, 4,* 39–52.

Epstein, S., & Epstein, B. W. (1978). *Dr. Beaumont and the man with a hole in his stomach.* New York: Coward McCann & Geoghegan.

Erickson, B. (1996). Read-alouds reluctant readers relish. *Journal of Adolescent and Adult Literacy, 40*(3), 212–215.

Farr, R. (1992). Putting it all together: Solving the reading assessment puzzle. *The Reading Teacher, 46,* 26–37.

Farr, R., & Tone, B. (1998). *Assessment portfolio and performance* (2nd ed.). Orlando: Harcourt Brace.

Feelings, M. (1971). *Moja means one: Swahili counting book.* Ill. T. Feelings. New York: Dial.

Feelings, T. (1995). *The middle passage: White ships, black cargo.* New York: Dial.

Fetterman, D. M. (1989). *Ethnography step by step.* Thousand Oaks, CA: Sage.

Flavell, J. H. (1976). Metacognitive aspects of problem solving. In L. B. Resnick (Ed.), *The nature of intelligence* (pp. 38–62). Hillsdale, NJ: Erlbaum.

Flavell, J. H. (1981). Cognitive monitoring. In P. Dickson (Ed.), *Communication skills.* Orlando: Academic Press.

Fleischman, J. (2002). *Phineas Gage: A gruesome but true story about brain science.* Boston: Houghton Mifflin.

Fleming, T. (1988). *Band of brothers: West Point in the Civil War.* New York: Walker.

Fox, M. (2000). *Feathers and fools.* Ill. N. Wilton. San Diego: Voyager.

Frank, A. (1967). *Anne Frank: The diary of a young girl.* New York: Doubleday.

Freedman, R. (2000). *Give me liberty! The story of the Declaration of Independence.* New York: Holiday House.

Freeman, E. B., & Person, D. G. (1998). *Connecting informational children's books with content area learning.* Boston: Allyn & Bacon.

Fry, E. (1977). Fry's readability graph: Clarifications, validity, and extension to level 17. *Journal of Reading, 21,* 242–252.

Fugard, A. (1984). *"Master Harold" . . . and the boys.* New York: Penguin.

Gallant, R. A. (1991). *Earth's vanishing forests.* New York: Macmillan.

Gambrell, L. B. (1980). Think-time: Implications for reading instruction. *Reading Teacher, 33,* 143–146.

Garcia, E. (2002). *Student cultural diversity: Understanding and meeting the challenge* (3rd ed.). Boston: Houghton Mifflin.

Garland, S. (1993). *The lotus seed.* Ill. T. Kiuchi. San Diego: Harcourt.

Gere, A. R. (Ed.). (1985). *Roots in the sawdust: Writing to learn across the disciplines.* Urbana, IL: National Council of Teachers of English.

Gersten, R. & Jimenez, R. (1994). A delicate balance: Enhancing literature instruction for students of English as a second language. *The Reading Teacher, 47,* 438–449.

Giblin, J. (1994). *Thomas Jefferson: A picture book biography.* Ill. M. Dooling. New York: Scholastic.

Giblin, J. (2000). More than just the facts: A hundred years of children's nonfiction. *The Horn Book, 76,* 413–424.

Giblin, J. (2002). *The life and death of Adolf Hitler.* New York: Clarion Books.

Giblin, J. C. (1995). *When plague strikes: The Black Death, smallpox, AIDS.* New York: HarperCollins.

Giblin, J. C. (2000). *The amazing life of Benjamin Franklin.* Ill. M. Dooling. New York: Scholastic.

Gillet, J., & Kita, M. J. (1979). Words, kids, and categories. *Reading Teacher, 32,* 538–542.

Glenn, M. (1991). *Class dismissed! High school poems.* New York: Clarion Books.

Goble, P. (1991). *I sing for the animals.* New York: Bradbury.

Golenbock, P. (1990). *Teammates.* Ill. P. Bacon. San Diego: Harcourt Brace Jovanovich.

Gonick, L. (1991). *Cartoon history of the United States.* New York: HarperCollins.

Goodall, J. (1979). *The story of an English village.* New York: Atheneum.

Goodall, J. (1987). *The story of a main street.* New York: Macmillan.

Goodall, J. (1990). *The story of the seashore.* New York: Macmillan.

Goodlad, J. (1984). *A place called school.* New York: McGraw-Hill.

Goodman, K., & Goodman, Y. (1978). *Reading of American children whose language is a stable rural dialect of English or a language other than English.* Washington, DC: National Institute of Education. (ERIC Document Reproduction Service No. ED173754)

Greenberg, J., & Jordan, S. (1998). *Chuck Close: Up close.* New York: DK Inc.

Greenlee-Moore, M. E., & Smith, L. L. (1996). Interactive computer software: The effects on young children's reading achievement. *Reading Psychology, 17,* 43–64.

Grove, N. (1981, March). Wild cargo: The business of smuggling animals. *National geographic, 159,* 287–315.

Guthrie, J. T., & McCann, A. D. (1996). Idea circles: Peer collaborations for conceptual learning. In L. B. Gambrell & J. F. Almasi (Eds.), *Lively discusssions! Fostering engaged reading* (pp. 87–105). Newark, DE: International Reading Association.

Guthrie, J. T., & Wigfield, A. (2000). Engagement and motivation in reading. In M. Kamil, P. Mosenthal, P. D. Pearson, & R. Barr (Eds.), *Handbook of reading research, Vol. III* (pp. 403–424). Mahwah, NJ: Erlbaum.

Hadaway, N. L., Vardell, S. M., & Young, T. A. (2002). *Literature-based instruction with English language learners.* Boston: Allyn & Bacon.

Haggard, M. R. (1986). The vocabulary self-collection strategy: Using student interest and world knowledge to enhance vocabulary growth. *Journal of Reading, 29,* 634–642.

Hahn, A. (1984). Assessing and extending comprehension: Monitoring strategies in the classroom. *Reading Horizons, 24,* 225–230.

Hakim, J. (1999). *A history of US.* New York: Oxford University Press.

Halliday, M., & Hasan, R. (1976). *Cohesion in English.* London: Longman.

Hamilton, V. (1985). *The people could fly: American black folktales.* New York: Knopf.

Hamilton, V. (1988). *In the beginning: Creation stories from around the world.* Orlando: Harcourt Brace.

Hancock, M. R. (1993). Exploring and extending personal response through literature journals. *Reading Teacher, 46,* 466–474.

Hancock, M. R. (2000). *A celebration of literature and response: Children, books and teachers in K–8 classrooms.* New York: Prentice Hall.

Hansell, T. S. (1978). Stepping up to outlining. *Journal of Reading, 22,* 248–252.

Hansen, J. (1986). *Which way freedom?* New York: Walker.

Hare, V. C., & Borchardt, K. M. (1984). Direct instruction of summarization skills. *Reading Research Quarterly, 20,* 62–78.

Harvey, S. (1998). *Nonfiction matters: Reading, writing, and research in grades 3–8.* Portland, ME: Stenhouse.

Harvey, S., & Goudvis, A. (2000). *Strategies that work.* York, ME: Stenhouse.

Hayes, D. A. (1989). Helping students grasp the knack of writing summaries. *Journal of Reading, 33,* 96–101.

Healy, M. K. (1982). Using student response groups in the classroom. In G. Camp (Ed.), *Teaching writing: Essays from the Bay Area writing project* (pp. 266–290). Portsmouth, NH: Boyton-Cook.

Herber, H. L. (1978). *Teaching reading in content areas* (2nd ed.). Upper Saddle River, NJ: Prentice Hall.

Hesse, K. (1997). *Out of the dust.* New York: Scholastic.

Hickam, H. (1998). *Rocket boys.* New York: Delacorte.

Hobbs, W. (1989). *Bearstone.* New York: Atheneum.

Hoffman, J. V. (1979). The intra-act procedure for critical reading. *Journal of Reading, 22,* 605–608.

Hoffman, J. V. (1992). Critical reading/thinking across the curriculum: Using I-charts to support learning. *Language Arts, 69,* 121–127.

Hoffman, J. V., Au, K. H., Harrison, C., Paris, S. G., Pearson, P. D., Santa, C. M., Silver, S. H., & Valencia, S. W. (1999). High-stakes assessments in reading: Consequences, concerns, and common sense. In Barrentine, S. J. (Ed.), *Reading assessment: Principles and practices for elementary teachers,* (pp. 21–34). Newark, DE: International Reading Association.

Holston, V., & Santa, C. (1985). RAFT: A method of writing across the curriculum that works. *Journal of Reading, 28,* 456–457.

Homer, C. (1979). A direct reading–thinking activity for content areas. In R. T. Vacca & J. A. Meagher (Eds.), *Reading through content* (pp. 41–48). Storrs: University Publications and the University of Connecticut Reading–Language Arts Center.

Hoose, P. M. (2001). *We were there, too! Young people in U.S. history.* New York: Farrar, Straus & Giroux.

Hoyt-Goldsmith, D. (1994). *Day of the Dead: A Mexican-American celebration.* Photo. L. Migdale. New York: Holiday House.

Huey, E. (1908). *The psychology and pedagogy of reading.* New York: Macmillan.

Hunt, I. (1964). *Across five Aprils.* New York: Follett.

Hymes, D. (1972). On communicative competence. In J. Pride & J. Holmes (Eds.), *Sociolinguistics.* Harmondsworth, UK: Penguin.

Hynd, C. R., McNish, M. E., Guzzetti, B., Lay, K., & Fowler, P. (1994). *What high school students say about their science texts.* Paper presented at the annual meeting of the College Reading Association, New Orleans.

Innocenti, R. (1985). *Rose Blanche.* San Diego: Creative Editions.

Innocenti, R. (1991). *Rose Blanche.* New York: Stewart, Tiboria, Chang.

International Reading Association. (1999). *High-stakes assessments in reading: A position paper of the International Reading Association.* Newark, DE: Author.

Irwin, J. W., & Davis, C. A. (1980). Assessing readability: The checklist approach. *Journal of Reading, 24,* 124–130.

Ivey, G. (2002). Getting started: Manageable literacy practices. *Educational Leadership, 60,* 20–23.

Ivey, G., & Broaddus, K. (2001). "Just plain reading": A survey of what makes students want to read in middle school classrooms. *Reading Research Quarterly, 36,* 350–377.

Jasper, K. C. (1995). The limits of technology. *English Journal, 84*(6), 16–17.

Jimenez, R. & Gamez, A. (1996). Literature-based cognitive strategy instruction for middle school Latina/o students. *Journal of Adolescent and Adult Literacy, 40*(2), 84–91.

Jimenez, R., Garcia, G., & Pearson, P. D. (1995). Three children, two languages, and strategic reading: Case studies in bilingual/monolingual reading. *American Educational Research Journal, 32,* 67–97.

Jimenez, R., Grcia, G., & Pearson, P. D. (1996). The reading strategies of bilingual Latina/o students who are successful English readers: Opportunities and obstacles. *Reading Research Quarterly, 32*(1), 90–112.

Johnson, D., & Pearson, P. D. (1984). *Teaching reading vocabulary* (2nd ed.). Fort Worth, TX: Holt, Rinehart and Winston.

Johnson, D. W., & Johnson, R. T. (1987). *Learning together and alone: Cooperative, conjunctive, and individualistic learning.* Englewood Cliffs, NJ: Prentice Hall.

Johnson, D. W., & Johnson, R. T. (1990). *Learning together and alone: Cooperative, conjunctive, and individualistic learning.* Upper Saddle River, NJ: Prentice Hall.

Johnson, D. W., Johnson, R. T., & Holubec, E. J. (1990). *Circles of learning: Cooperation in the classroom* (3rd ed.). Edina, MN: Interaction Book Company.

Johnson, D. W., & Steele, V. (1996). So many words, so little time: Helping college ESL learners acquire vocabulary-building strategies. *Journal of Adolescent and Adult Literacy, 39,* 348–357.

Jones, B. F., Pierce, J., & Hunter, B. (1988–1989). Teaching students to construct graphic representations. *Educational Leadership, 46*(4), 20–25.

June, R. (1995). Culturally appropriate books call for culturally appropriate teaching. *Journal of Reading, 38,* 486.

Kang, H. (1994). Helping second language readers learn from content area text through collaboration and support. *Journal of Reading, 37,* 646–652.

Kaplan, L. S., & Owings W. A. (2003). The politics of teacher quality. *Phi Delta Kappan, 84*(9), 687–692.

Kaywell, J. (1994). Using young adult fiction and nonfiction to produce critical readers. *The ALAN Review, 21,* 1–6.

Kennedy, B. (1985). Writing letters to learn math. *Learning, 13,* 58–61.

King, C., & Osborne, L. B. (1997). *Oh freedom! Kids talk about the civil rights movement with the people who made it happen.* New York: Knopf.

Kintsch, W. (1977). On comprehending stories. In M. A. Just & P. A. Carpenter (Eds.), *Cognitive processes in comprehension* (pp. 360–401). Hillsdale, NJ: Erlbaum.

Kintsch, W., & van Dijk, T. (1978). Toward a model of text comprehension and production. *Psychological Review, 85,* 363–394.

Kirby, D., Liner, T., & Vinz, M. (1988). *Inside out: Developmental strategies for teching writing* (2nd ed.). Montclair, NJ: Boynton/Cook.

Kitchen, B. (1993). *And so they build.* New York: Dial.

Klein, S. P., Hamilton, L. S., McCaffrey, D. F., & Stecher, B. M. (2000). *Issue paper: What do test scores in Texas tell us?* Santa Monica, CA: Rand.

Knoeller, C. P. (1994). Negotiating interpretations of text: The role of student-led discussions in understanding literature. *Journal of Reading, 37,* 572–580.

Koretz, D., & Barron, S. T. (1998). *The validity of gains in scores on the Kentucky Instructional Results Information System.* Santa Monica, CA: Rand.

Krogness, M. (1995). *Just teach me, Mrs. K: Talking, reading, and writing with resistant adolescent learners.* Portsmouth, NH: Heinemann.

Krull, K. (1993). *Lives of the musicians: Good times, bad times (And what the neighbors thought).* Ill. K. Hewitt. San Diego: Harcourt Brace.

Krull, K. (1995). *Lives of the artists: Masterpieces, messes (And what the neighbors thought).* Ill. K. Hewitt. San Diego: Harcourt Brace.

Krull, K. (1997). *Lives of the athletes: Thrills, spills (And what the neighbors thought).* Ill. K. Hewitt. San Diego: Harcourt Brace.

Krull, K. (2000). *Wilma unlimited: How Wilma Rudolph became the world's fastest woman.* Ill. D. Diaz. San Diego: Harcourt Brace.

Langer, J. A. (1981). From theory to practice: A prereading plan. *Journal of Reading, 25,* 152–156.

Langer, J. A., & Applebee, A. N. (1987). *How writing shapes thinking.* Urbana, IL: National Council of Teachers of English.

Langstaff, J. (1991). *Climbing Jacob's ladder.* New York: Macmillan.

Lapp, D., Fisher, D., Flood, J., & Cabello, A. (2001). An integrated approach to the teaching and assessment of language arts. In S. Hurley & J. V. Tinajero (Eds.), *Literacy assessment of second language learners* (pp. 11–26). Boston: Allyn & Bacon.

Lapp, D., & Flood, J. (1995). Strategies for gaining access to the information superhighway: Off the side street and on to the main road. *Reading Teacher, 48,* 432–436.

Lasky, K. (1994). *The librarian who measured the earth.* Ill. K. Hawkes. New York: Little Brown.

Lasky, K. (2003). *The man who made time travel.* Ill. K. Hawkes. New York: Farrar, Straus & Giroux.

Lauber, P. (1986). *Volcano: The eruption and healing of Mount St. Helens.* New York: Bradbury Press.

Lauber, P. (1996). *Hurricanes: Earth's mightiest storms.* New York: Scholastic.

Lawrence, L. (1985). *Children of the dust.* New York: HarperCollins.

Lester, J. (1968). *To be a slave.* New York: Dial Press.

Lester, J. D. (1984). *Writing research papers: A complete guide* (4th ed.). Glenview, IL: Scott, Foresman.

Leu, D. J., Jr. (1996). Sarah's secret: Social aspects of literacy and learning in a digital information age. *Reading Teacher, 50,* 162–165.

Leu, D. J., Jr. (2000). Literacy and technology: Deictic consequences for literacy education in an information age. In M. L. Kamil, P. M. Mosenthal, P. D. Pearson, & R. Barr (Eds.), *Handbook of reading research* (Volume 3, pp. 743–770). Mahwah, NJ: Erlbaum.

Leu, D. J., Jr. (2002). The new literacies: Research on reading instruction with the Internet. In A. E. Farstrup & S. J. Samuels (Eds.), *What research has to say about reading instruction* (pp. 310–336). Newark, DE: International Reading Association.

Leu, D. J., Jr., & Leu, D. D. (2000). *Teaching with the Internet: Lessons from the classroom* (3rd ed.). Norwood, MA: Christopher-Gordon.

Levine, D. S. (1985). The biggest thing I learned but it really doesn't have to do with science. . . . *Language Arts, 62,* 43–47.

Levstik, L. S. (1990). Research directions: Mediating content through literary texts. *Language Arts, 67,* 848–853.

Lewis, J. P. (1992). *The moonbow of Mr. B. Bones.* New York: Knopf.

Lindbergh, R., & Brown, R. (1992). *A view from the air: Charles Lindbergh's earth and sky.* New York: Viking.

Lindemann, E. (1982). *A rhetoric for writing teachers.* New York: Oxford University Press.

Linek, W. M. (1991). Grading and evaluation techniques for whole language teachers. *Language Arts, 68,* 125–132.

Lipsky, D. K. & Gartner, A. (1997). *Inclusion and school reform: Transforming America's classrooms.* Baltimore: Paul H. Brookes.

Llewellyn, C. (1991). *Under the sea.* New York: Simon & Schuster.

Long, R. (2003). Washington update. *Reading Today, 21*(1), 27.

Lowe, S. (1990). *Walden.* Ill. R. Sabuda. New York: Philomel.

Lowry, L. (1989). *Number the stars.* Boston: Houghton Mifflin.

Lyon, G. E. (1991). *Cecil's story.* New York: Orchard.

Macaulay, D. (1973). *Cathedral: The story of its construction.* Boston: Houghton Mifflin.

Macaulay, D. (1978). *Castle.* Boston: Houghton Mifflin.

Macaulay, D. (1982). *Pyramid.* Boston: Houghton Mifflin.

Macaulay, D. (1998). *The new way things work.* Boston: Houghton Mifflin.

MacGinitie, W. H. (1993). Some limits of assessment. *Journal of Reading, 36,* 556–560.

Maguire, K. (2001). *Governors find education bill faults.* Retrieved October, 2002, from http://speakout.com/cgi-bin/edt/im.display.printable?client.id=speakout&story.id=10037

Malinowski, B. (1954). *"Magic, science and religion" and other essays.* New York: Doubleday.

Manzo, A. V. (1969). The ReQuest procedure. *Journal of Reading, 11,* 123–126.

Manzo, A. V. (1975). Guided reading procedure. *Journal of Reading, 18,* 287–291.

Marol, J. (1983). *Vagabul escapes.* Mankato, MN: Creative Education.

Marsalis, W. (1995). *Marsalis on music.* New York: Norton.

Maruki, T. (1982). *Hiroshima no pika.* New York: Lothrop, Lee & Shepard.

Matthew, K. (1996). What do children think of CD-ROM storybooks? *Texas Reading Report, 18,* 6.

Maupassant, G. de. (1993). *The necklace.* Ill. G. Kelly. New York: Creative Editions.

McCullen, C. (1998). The electronic thread: Research and assessment on the Internet. *Middle Ground, 1*(3), 7–9.

McGinley, W. J., & Denner, P. R. (1987). Story impressions: A pre-reading/writing activity. *Journal of Reading, 31,* 248–253.

McGowan, T., & Guzzetti, B. (1991, January–February). Promoting social studies understanding through literature-based instruction. *Social Studies,* pp. 16–21.

McIntosh, M. (1991, September). No time for writing in your class? *Mathematics Teacher,* pp. 423–433.

McKinley, R. (1978). *Beauty: A retelling of the story of* Beauty and the Beast. New York: HarperCollins.

McKeon, C. (2001). E-mail as a motivating literacy event for one student: Donna's Case. *Reading Research and Instruction, 40*(3), 185–202.

McTighe, J., & Lyman, F. T. (1988). Cueing thinking in the classroom: The promise of theory-embedded tools. *Educational Leadership, 45*(7), 18–24.

Meltzer, M. (1988). *Starting from home: A writer's beginning.* New York: Viking Penguin.

Meltzer, M. (1994). *Nonfiction for the classroom.* New York: Teachers College Press.

Meyer, B. J. F., Brandt, D., & Bluth, G. (1980). Use of top-level structure in text: Key for reading comprehension of ninth-grade students. *Reading Research Quarterly, 16,* 72–103.

Meyer, B. J. F., & Rice, E. (1984). The structure of text. In P. D. Pearson (Ed.), *Handbook of reading research* (pp. 319–352). New York: Longman.

Miholic, V. (1994). An inventory to pique students' metacognitive awareness. *Journal of Reading, 38*(2), 84–86.

Mike, D. G. (1996). Internet in the schools: A literacy perspective. *Journal of Adolescent and Adult Literacy, 40,* 4–13.

Mikulecky, L. (1990). Literacy for what purpose? In R. L. Venezky, D. A. Wagner, & B. S. Ciliberti (Eds.), *Toward defining literacy* (pp. 24–34). Newark, DE: International Reading Association.

Miller, T. (1998). The place of picture books in middle-level classrooms. *Journal of Adolescent and Adult Literacy, 41*(5), 376–382.

Milton, J. W. (1982). What the student–educator should have done before the grade: A questioning look at note-taking. In A. S. Algier & K. W. Algier (Eds.), *Improving reading and study skills* (pp. 56–71). San Francisco: Jossey-Bass.

Moss, B. (1995). Using children's nonfiction tradebooks as read-alouds (Teacher's notebook). *Language Arts, 72,* 122–126.

Moss, B. (2003). *Exploring the literature of fact: Children's nonfiction trade books in the elementary classroom.* New York: Guilford Press.

Mraz, M. (2000). The literacy program selection process from the perspective of school district administrators. *Ohio Reading Teacher, 34,* 2, 40–48.

Mraz, M. (2002). Factors that influence policy decisions in literacy: Perspectives of key policy informants. Ph.D. Dissertation, Kent State University.

Mühlberger, R. (1993). *What makes a Monet a Monet?* New York: Metropolitan Museum of Art/Viking.

Murphy, J. (1990). *The boys' war: Confederate and Union soldiers talk about the Civil War.* New York: Clarion Books.

Murphy, J. (1992). *The long road to Gettysburg.* New York: Clarion Books.

Murphy, J. (1998). *The great fire.* New York: Clarion Books.

Murray, D. M. (1980). Writing as process: How writing finds its own meaning. In T. R. Donovan & B. W. McClelland (Eds.), *Eight approaches to teaching composition* (pp. 80–97). Urbana, IL: National Council of Teachers of English.

Murray, J. (1982). *Modern monologues for young people.* New York: Plays, Inc.

Myers, W. D. (1991). *Now is your time! The African-American struggle for freedom.* New York: HarperCollins.

Myers, W. D. (2002). *Patrol: An American soldier in Vietnam.* Ill. A. Grifalconi. New York: HarperCollins.

National Council of Teachers of Mathematics (NCTM). (2000). Principles and standards for school mathematics. Washington, DC: Author.

National Reading Panel. (2000). *Teaching children to read: An evidence-based assessment of the scientific research literature on reading and its implications for reading instruction* (National Institute of Health Pub. No. 00-4769). Washington, DC: National Institute of Child Health and Human Development.

NC Public Schools. (2003). *The ABC's accountability model.* Retrieved October, 2002, from www.ncpublicschools.org/abcs

Neal, J. C., & Moore, K. (1991). *The very hungry caterpillar* meets *Beowulf* in secondary classrooms. *Journal of Reading, 35,* 290–296.

Neill, M. (2003). Leaving children behind: How No Child Left Behind will fail our children. *Phi Delta Kappan, 85*(3), 225–228.

Neilsen, L. (1998). Playing for real: Performative texts and adolescent identities. In D. Alvermann, K. Hinchman, S. Phelps, & S. Waff (Eds.), *Reconceptualizing the literacies in adolescents' lives.* Mahwah, NJ: Erlbaum.

Nelson, J. (1978). Readability: Some cautions for the content area teacher. *Journal of Reading, 21,* 620–625.

Newell, G. (1984). Learning from writing in two content areas: A case study/protocol analysis. *Research in the Teaching of English, 18,* 205–287.

Niles, O. (1965). Organization perceived. In H. L. Herber (Ed.), *Developing study skills in secondary schools* (pp. 36–46). Newark, DE: International Reading Association.

Noden, H. R. (1995). A journey through cyberspace: Reading and writing in a virtual school. *English Journal, 84*(6), 19–26.

Noden, H. R., & Vacca, R. T. (1994). *Whole language in middle and secondary classrooms.* New York: HarperCollins.

Noyes, A. (1983). *The Highwayman.* Ill. C. Milolaychack. New York: Lothrop, Lee & Shepard.

Nye, N. S. (2002). *Nineteen varieties of gazelle: Poems of the Middle East.* New York: HarperCollins.

Nye, R. (1968). Beowulf: *A new telling*. New York: Hill.

Oakes, J. (1985). *Keeping track: How schools structure inequality*. New Haven, CT: Yale University Press.

O'Brien, R. C. (1975). *Z for Zachariah*. New York: Atheneum.

Ogle, D. M. (1992). KWL in action: Secondary teachers find applications that work. In E. K. Dishner, T. W. Bean, J. E. Readence, & D. W. Moore (Eds.), *Reading in the content areas: Improving classroom instruction* (3rd ed., pp. 270–281). Dubuque, IA: Kendall-Hunt.

Ohio Department of Education. (1999). *Model competency-based language arts program*. Retrieved September, 2003, from www.ode.state.oh.us/proficiency

Ohio Department of Education. (2002). *Ohio graduation tests: Frequently asked questions*. Retrieved September, 2003, from www.ode.state.oh.us/proficiency

Ohio Department of Education. (2003). *Ohio academic content standards for English language arts*. Retrieved September, 2003, from www.ode.state.oh.us/academic_content_standards/acsenglish.asp

Ohio Department of Education. (2003). *Ohio administrative codes and rules links: Rule 3301-13-01*. Retrieved September, 2003, from www.ode.state.oh.us/proficiency/rules.asp?pfv=True

Olsen, A., & Ames, W. (1972). *Teaching reading skills in secondary schools*. Scranton, PA: Intext Educational Publishers.

O'Neill, C. (1995). *Drama worlds: A framework for process drama*. Portsmouth, NH: Heinemann.

Palmatier, R. (1973). A notetaking system for learning. *Journal of Reading, 17*, 36–39.

Palmer, R. G., & Stewart, R. A. (1997). Nonfiction trade books in content area instruction: Realities and potential. *Journal of Adolescent and Adult Literacy, 40*, 630–641.

Papert, S. (1980). *Mindstorms: Children, computers, and powerful ideas*. New York: Basic Books.

Paris, S., & Meyers, M. (1981). Comprehension monitoring, memory, and study strategies of good and poor readers. *Journal of Reading Behavior, 13*, 5–22.

Parnall, P. (1984). *The daywatchers*. New York: Macmillan.

Parnall, P. (1991). *Marsh cat*. New York: Macmillan.

Parry, K. (1993). Too many words: Learning the vocabulary of an academic subject. In T. Huckin, M. Haynes, & J. Coady (Eds.), *Second language reading and vocabulary learning* (pp. 109–129). Norwood, NJ: Ablex.

Partridge, E. (2002). *This land was made for you and me: The life and songs of Woody Guthrie*. New York: Viking.

Pauk, W. (1978). A notetaking format: Magical but not automatic. *Reading World, 16*, 96–97.

Paulsen, G. (1987). *Hatchet*. New York: Viking Penguin.

Paulsen, G. (1989). *The winter room*. New York: Harcourt Brace.

Paulsen, G. (1990). *Woodsong*. New York: Macmillan.

Peacock, L. (1998). *Crossing the Delaware: A history in many voices*. Ill. W. L. Krudop. New York: Atheneum.

Pearce, D. L. (1983). Guidelines for the use and evaluation of writing in content classrooms. *Journal of Reading, 27*, 212–218.

Pearson, P. D. (1974–1975). The effects of grammatical complexity on children's comprehension, recall, and conception of certain semantic relations. *Reading Research Quarterly, 10*, 155–192.

Pearson, P. D. (1981). A retrospective reaction to prose comprehension. In C. M. Santa and B. L. Hayes (Eds.), *Children's prose comprehension: Research and practice*. Newark, DE: International Reading Association.

Pearson, P. D. (1982). *A context for instructional research and reading comprehension*. Urbana: University of Illinois Center for the Study of Reading, Technical Report No. 230.

Pearson, P. D., & Johnson, D. (1978). *Teaching reading comprehension*. Fort Worth, TX: Holt, Rinehart and Winston.

Pearson, P. D., & Spiro, R. (1982). The new buzz word in reading as schema. *Instructor, 89*, 46–48.

Peregoy, S. F., & Boyle, O. F. (2001). *Reading, writing, and learning in ESL: A resource book for K–12 teachers* (3rd ed.). New York: Longman.

Pichert, J. W., & Anderson, R. C. (1977). Taking different perspectives on a story. *Journal of Educational Psychology, 69,* 309–315.

Plato. (1966). Theatetus, 194c–195b. In E. Hamilton & H. Cairns (Eds.), *The collected dialogues of Plato.* New York: Pantheon.

Polacco, P. (1994). *Pink and say.* New York: Philomel.

Pradl, G. M., & Mayher, J. S. (1985). Reinvigorating learning through writing. *Educational Leadership, 42,* 4–8.

Pressley, M. (2000). What should comprehension instruction be the instruction of? In M. Kamil, P. Mosenthal, P. D. Pearson, & R. Barr (Eds.), *Handbook of reading research* (Vol. 3, pp. 545–562). Mahwah, NJ: Erlbaum.

Price, L. (1990). *Aida.* Ill. L. & D. Dillon. San Diego: Harcourt Brace.

Randall, S. N. (1996). Information charts: A strategy for organizing students' research. *Journal of Adolescent and Adult Literacy, 39,* 536–542.

Rand Reading Study Group. (2002). *Reading for understanding: Toward an R&D program in reading comprehension.* Santa Monica, CA: Science and Technology Policy Institute, Rand Education.

Ransom, K. A., Santa, C. M., Williams, C. K., Farstrup, A. E., Au, K. H., Baker, B. M., Edwards, P. A., Hoffman, J. V., Klein, A. F., Larson, D. L., Logan, J. W., Morrow, L. M., & Shanahan, T. (1999). High-stakes assessments in reading: A position statement of the International Reading Association. *Journal of Adolescent and Adult Literacy, 43*(3), 305–312.

Raphael, T. E. (1982). Question-answering strategies for children. *Reading Teacher, 36,* 186–191.

Raphael, T. E. (1984). Teaching learners about sources of information for answering comprehension questions. *Journal of Reading, 27,* 303–311.

Raphael, T. E. (1986). Teaching question-answer relationships. *Reading Teacher, 39,* 516–520.

Rappaport, D. (2001). *Martin's big words: The life of Dr. Martin Luther King, Jr.* Ill. B. Collier. New York: Hyperion.

Raschka, C. (1997). *Mysterious Thelonious.* New York: Orchard.

Ray, D. (1990). *A nation torn: The story of how the Civil War began.* New York: Scholastic.

Reeder, C. (1989). *Shades of gray.* New York: Macmillan.

Reeves, N. (1992). *Into the mummy's tomb: The real-life discovery of Tutankhamun's treasures.* New York: Scholastic/Madison.

Reinking, D. (1995). Reading and writing with computers: Literacy research in a post-typographic world. In K. A. Hinchman, D. J. Leu, Jr., & C. K. Kinzer (Eds.), *Perspectives on literacy research and practice* (pp. 17–33). Chicago: National Reading Conference.

Reinking, D. (1997). Me and my hypertext: A multiple digression analysis of technology and literacy. *Reading Teacher, 50,* 626–643.

Reinking, D. (1998). Synthesizing technological transformations of literacy in a post-typographic world. In D. Reinking, M. McKenna, L. D. Labbo, & R. Kieffer (Eds.), *Handbook of literacy and technology: Transformations in a post-typographic world* (pp. xi–xxx). Mahwah, NJ: Erlbaum.

Reinking, D. (2003). Multimedia and engaged reading in a digital world. In L. Verhoeven & C. Snow (Eds.), *Creating a world of engaged readers.* Mahwah, NJ: Erlbaum.

Rico, G. L. (1983). *Writing the natural way: Using right-brain techniques to release your expressive powers.* Los Angeles: Tarcher.

Ride, S., & Okie, S. (1986). *To space and back.* New York: Lothrop, Lee & Shepard.

Roberts, P. (1985). Speech communities. In V. Clark, P. Escholz, & A. Rosa (Eds.), *Language* (4th ed.). New York: St. Martin's Press.

Rodrigues, R. J. (1983). Tools for developing prewriting skills. *English Journal, 72,* 58–60.

Rose, B. (1989). Writing and mathematics: Theory and practice. In P. Connolly & T. Vilardi (Eds.), *Writing to learn mathematics and science* (pp. 19–30). New York: Teachers College Press.

Rose, S. A., & Fernlund, P. M. (1997). Using technology for powerful social studies learning. *Social Education, 13*(6), 160–166.

Rosenblatt, L. M. (1982). The literary transaction: Evocation and response. *Theory into Practice, 21*, 268–277.

Rumelhart, D. E. (1982). Schemata: The building blocks of cognition. In J. Guthrie (Ed.), *Comprehension and teaching: Research reviews* (pp. 3–26). Newark, DE: International Reading Association.

Ryan, P. M. (2000). *Esperanza rising.* New York: Scholastic.

Ryan, P. M. (2002). *When Marian sang: The true recital of Marian Anderson.* Ill. B. Selznikc. New York: Scholastic.

Rycik, J. A. (1994). *An exploration of student library research projects in seventh grade English and social studies classes.* Unpublished doctoral dissertation, Kent State University.

Rylant, C. (1982). *When I was young in the mountains.* New York: Dutton.

Rylant, C. (1984). *Waiting to waltz: A childhood.* Ill. S. Gammell. New York: Bradbury.

Salisbury, R. (1934). A study of the transfer effects of training in logical organization. *Journal of Educational Research, 28*, 241–254.

Samples, R. (1977). *The wholeschool book.* Reading, MA: Addison-Wesley.

Sansevere-Dreher, D., Dreher, D., & Renfro, E. (1996). *Explorers who got lost.* New York: Tor Books.

Santa, C. M., & Havens, L. T. (1991). Learning through writing. In C. M. Santa & D. E. Alvermann (Eds.), *Science learning: Processes and applications* (pp. 122–133). Newark, DE: International Reading Association.

Say, A. (1990). *El Chino.* Boston: Houghton Mifflin.

Say, A. (2002). *Home of the brave.* Boston: Houghton Mifflin.

Schoenbach, R., Greenleaf, C., Cziko, C., & Hurwitz, L. (1999). *Reading for understanding: A guide to improving reading in middle and high school classrooms.* San Francisco: Jossey-Bass.

Schumm, J. S., & Mangrum, C. T., II. (1991). FLIP: A framework for content area reading. *Journal of Reading, 35*, 120–124.

Schwartz, D. (1998). *G is for Googol.* New York: Tricycle Press.

Schwartz, R. M. (1988). Learning to learn: Vocabulary in content area textbooks. *Journal of Reading, 32*, 108–117.

Schwartz, R. M., & Raphael, T. E. (1985). Concept of definition: A key to improving students' vocabulary. *Reading Teacher, 39*, 198–204.

Sender, R. M. (1986). *The cage.* New York: Macmillan.

Service, R. (1986). *The cremation of Sam McGee.* Ill. T. Harrison. New York: Greenwillow.

Seuss, D. (1984). *The butter battle book.* New York: Random House.

Shanahan, T. (Ed.). (1990). *Reading and writing together: New perspectives for the classroom.* Norwood, MA: Christopher-Gordon.

Shanks, A. Z. (1982). *Busted lives: Dialogues with kids in jail.* New York: Delacorte.

Shulman, L. (1987). Learning to teach. *AAHE Bulletin, 5*–6.

Siegal, A. (1983). *Upon the head of the goat: A childhood in Hungary, 1939–1944.* New York: Signet.

Simon, R. (1990). *Oceans.* New York: Morrow.

Singer, H. (1978). Active comprehension: From answering to asking questions. *Reading Teacher, 31*, 901–908.

Slavin, R. E. (1988). Cooperative learning and student achievement. In R. E. Slavin (Ed.), *School and classroom organization.* Hillsdale, NJ: Erlbaum.

Smith, D. B. (1973). *A taste of blackberries.* New York: HarperCollins.

Smith, F. (1988). *Understanding reading* (4th ed.). Hillsdale, NJ: Erlbaum.

Smith, N. B. (1959). Teaching study skills in reading. *Elementary School Journal, 60*, 158–162.

Smith, N. B. (1964). Patterns of writing in different subject areas. *Journal of Reading, 7*, 31–37.

Soto, G. (1997). *Novio boy: A play.* San Diego: Harcourt Brace.

Spiegel, D. L. (1981). Six alternatives to the directed reading activity. *Reading Teacher, 34,* 914–922.

Spiegel, D. L. (1998). Reader response approaches and the growth of readers. *Language Arts, 76,* 41–48.

Spiegelman, A. (1986). *Maus: A survivor's tale.* New York: Pantheon.

Spier, P. (1978). *Bored—nothing to do!* New York: Doubleday.

Spivey, N. M. (1984). *Discourse synthesis: Constructing texts in reading and writing.* Newark, DE: International Reading Association.

Standards for English Language Arts. (1997). Newark, DE: International Reading Association/National Council of Teachers of English.

Stanley, D. (1996). *Leonardo da Vinci.* New York: Morrow.

Stanley, D. (2000). *Michelangelo.* New York: Harper-Collins.

Stanley, J. (1992). *Children of the dust bowl: The true story of the school at Weedpatch Camp.* New York: Clarion Books.

Staples, S. F. (1991). *Shabanu: Daughter of the wind.* New York: Random House.

Stenmark, J. K. (1991). Math portfolios: A new form of assessment. *Teaching Pre-K–8, 21,* 62–66.

Stephens, C. (2002). *Magnificent monologues for teens.* New York: Sandcastle.

Stewig, J. W., & Buege, C. (1994). *Dramatizing literature in whole language classrooms.* New York: Teachers College Press.

St. George, J. (2000). *So you want to be president?* New York: Philomel.

Sturtevant, E. (1992). *Content literacy activities in high school social studies: Two case studies in a multicultural setting.* Unpublished doctoral dissertation, Kent State University.

Suid, M., & Lincoln, W. (1989). *Recipes for writing: Motivation, skills, and activities.* Menlo Park, CA: Addison-Wesley.

Sutherland, Z., & Arbuthnot, M. H. (1986). *Children and books* (7th ed.). Glenview, IL: Scott, Foresman.

Taba, H. (1967). *Teacher's handbook for elementary social studies.* Reading, MA: Addison-Wesley.

Taylor, B. (1980). Children's memory of expository text after reading. *Reading Research Quarterly, 15,* 399–411.

Taylor, D. (1983). *Family literacy: Young children learning to read and write.* Portsmouth, NH: Heinemann.

Taylor, W. (1953). Cloze procedure: A new tool for measuring readability. *Journalism Quarterly, 30,* 415–433.

Tchudi, S., & Yates, J. (1983). *Teaching writing in the content areas: Senior high school.* Washington, DC: National Education Association.

Thimmesh, C. (2000). *Girls think of everything: Stories of ingenious inventions by women.* Boston: Houghton Mifflin.

Thorndike, E. (1917). Reading and reasoning: A study of mistakes in paragraph reading. *Journal of Educational Psychology, 8,* 323–332.

Tierney, R. J. (1998). Literacy assessment reform: Shifting beliefs, principled possibilities, and emerging practices. *Reading Teacher, 51,* 374–390.

Tierney, R. J. (2002). An ethical chasm: Jurisdiction, jurisprudence, and the literacy profession. *Journal of Adolescent and Adult Literacy, 45*(4), 260–276.

Tierney, R. J., Carter, M. A., & Desai, L. E. (1991). *Portfolio assessment in the reading–writing classroom.* Norwood, MA: Christopher-Gordon.

Tierney, R. J., & Pearson, P. D. (1983). Toward a composing model of reading. *Language Arts, 60,* 568–580.

Tierney, R. J., & Pearson, P. D. (1992). A revisionist perspective on "Learning to learn from texts: A framework for improving classroom practice." In E. K. Dishner, T. W. Bean, J. E. Readence, & D. W. Moore (Eds.), *Reading in the content areas: Improving classroom instruction* (3rd ed., pp. 82–86). Dubuque, IA: Kendall/Hunt.

Tierney, R. J., & Shanahan, T. (1991). Research on reading–writing relationships: Interactions, transactions, and outcomes. In P. D. Pearson, R.

Barr, M. Kamil, & P. Mosenthal (Eds.), *Handbook of reading research* (2nd ed., pp. 246–280). New York: Longman.

Tobias, S. (1989). Writing to learn science and mathematics. In P. Connolly & T. Vilardi (Eds.), *Writing to learn mathematics and science* (pp. 47–61). New York: Teachers College Press.

Tompkins, G. E. (1990). *Teaching writing: Balancing process and product.* Columbus, OH: Merrill.

Topping, D. H., & McManus, R. (2002). *Real reading, real writing: Content area strategies.* Portsmouth, NH: Heinemann.

Toppo, G. (2001). *Education bill could affect funding.* Available: http://speakout.com/cgi-in/udt/im.display.printable?client.id=speakout&story.id=9967.

Trueman, T. (2001). *Stuck in neutral.* New York: HarperTempest.

Tsuchiya, Y. (1988). *Faithful elephants: A true story of people, animals and war.* Trans. T. Kykes. Ill. T. Lewin. Boston: Houghton Mifflin.

Turner, A. (1987). *Nettie's trip south.* Ill. R. Himler. New York: Macmillan.

Ung, L. (2000). *First they killed my father: A daughter of Cambodia remembers.* New York: Perennial Press.

Vacca, J. L., Vacca, R. T., Gove, M. K., Burkey, L., Lenhart, L., & McKeon, C. (2002). *Reading and learning to read* (5th ed.). Boston: Allyn & Bacon.

Vacca, R. T. (1975). Development of a functional reading strategy: Implications for content area instruction. *Journal of Educational Research, 69,* 108–112.

Vacca, R. T. (1977). An investigation of a functional reading strategy in seventh-grade social studies. In H. L. Herber & R. T. Vacca (Eds.), *Research in reading in the content areas: Third report* (pp. 101–118). Syracuse, NY: Syracuse University Reading and Language Arts Center.

Vacca, R. T. (2002). Making a difference in adolescents'school lives: Visible and invisible aspects of content area reading. In A. E. Farstrup & S. J. Samuels (Eds.), *What research has to say about reading instruction* (3rd ed., pp. 184–204). Newark, DE: International Reading Association.

Vacca, R. T., & Padak, N. D. (1990). Who's at risk in reading? *Journal of Reading, 33,* 486–489.

Valdes, G. & Figueroa, R. A. (1994). *Bilingualism and testing: A special case bias.* Norwood, NJ: Ablex.

Valencia, S. (1990). A portfolio approach to classroom reading assessment: The whys, whats, and hows. *Reading Teacher, 43,* 338–340.

Valencia, S., McGinley, W. J., & Pearson, P. D. (1990). *Assessing reading and writing: Building a more complete picture for middle school assessment.* Champaign: University of Illinois, Center for the Study of Reading.

Van Allsburg, C. (1984). *Mysteries of Harris Burdick.* Boston: Houghton Mifflin.

Van Allsburg, C. (1990). *Just a dream.* Boston: Houghton Mifflin.

van der Rol, R., & Verhoeven, R. (1993). *Anne Frank: Beyond the diary.* New York: Viking.

Vardell, S. M., & Copeland, K. A. (1992). Reading aloud and responding to nonfiction: Let's talk about it. In E. B. Freeman & D. G. Person (Eds.), *Using nonfiction trade books in the elementary classroom: From ants to zeppelins* (pp. 76–85). Urbana, IL: National Council of Teachers of English.

Ventura, P. (1987). *Venice: Birth of a city.* New York: Putnam.

Walker, B. J. (1991, February–March). Convention highlights reading assessment changes. *Reading Today,* 20.

Wang, M. C., Reynolds, M. C., & Walberg, H. J. (1994–1995). Serving students at the margins. *Educational Leadership, 52*(4), 12–17.

Watson, J. (1968). *The double helix.* New York: Atheneum.

Webb, S. (2000). *My season with penguins: An Antarctic journal.* Boston: Houghton Mifflin.

Wehlage, G. G., & Rutter, R. A. (1986). Dropping out: How much do schools contribute to the problem? *Teachers College Record, 87,* 374–392.

Wilcox, S. (1997). Using the assessment of students' learning to reshape thinking. *Mathematics Teacher, 90,* 223–229.

Wilkinson, L. E., & Silliman, E. R. (2000). Classroom language and literacy learning. In M. Kamil,

P. Mosenthal, P. D. Pearson, & R. Barr (Eds.), *Handbook of reading research, Vol. III* (pp. 337–360). Mahwah, NJ: Erlbaum.

Williams, B. (1995). The Internet for teachers. Foster City, CA: IDG Books Worldwide.

Wisniewski, D. (1996). *Golem.* New York: Clarion Books.

Wixson, K. K., Boskey, A. B., Yochum, M. M., & Alvermann, D. E. (1984). An interview for assessing students' perceptions of classroom reading tasks. *Reading Teacher, 37,* 346–353.

Wood, K. D. (1987). Fostering cooperative learning in middle and secondary classrooms. *Journal of Reading, 31,* 10–18.

Wood, K. D. (1988). A guide to subject matter material. *Middle School Journal, 19,* 24–26.

Worthy, J. (1996). Removing barriers to voluntary reading: The role of school and classroom libraries. *Language Arts, 73,* 483–492.

Worthy, J., Broaddus, K., & Ivey, G. (2001). *Pathways to independence: Reading, writing, and learning in grades 3–8.* New York: Guilford Press.

Yokota, J. (1993). Issues in selecting multicultural literature for children and adolescents. *Language Arts, 20,* 156–167.

Yolen, J. (1992). *Encounter.* Ill. D. Shannon. San Diego: Harcourt Brace Jovanovich.

Young, T. A., & Vardell, S. M. (1993). Weaving readers theatre and nonfiction into the curriculum. *The Reading Teacher, 46,* 396–406.

Zarnowski, M. (1998). Coming out from under the spell of stories: Critiquing historical narratives. *The New Advocate, 11,* 345–356.

Zhensun, Z., & Low, A. (1991). *A young painter: The life and paintings of Wang Yani.* New York: Scholastic.

Name Index

Subject Index

ESL (English as a Second Language) programs, 116–117. *See also* English language learners (ELL)
Essays, 166
Evaluation, response versus, 98
Exit slips, 365–366
Expectation outlines, 313–314
Explanation, in strategy instruction, 79
Exploratory writing, 361–368
    admit slips, 365
    biopoems, 362–363
    brainstorming, 92–93, 366–368
    dialogues, 364–365
    in drafting stage of writing, 90, 91, 96–97
    exit slips, 365–366
    unsent letters, 361–362
Explorers of the Universe project, 210
External text structure, 393–396

Family and consumer studies
    magic squares in, 287–290
    OPIN exercise in, 287
Fiction books, 171–174
    multicultural books, 176
    reasons for using, 162
    teacher selection of, 164–165, 174
File transfer protocol (FTP), 203
FLIP strategy, 63–65
    described, 63–64
    example of, 64
Florida, 10
Flying Dutchman, The (Wagner), 239–243, 330–331
Folk literature, 173–174
Foreign languages
    dialogues in, 364–365
    text lesson in, 237–238, 240–241
    Web sites on, 211
"Forgotten" students, 107
Formal assessment. *See* High-stakes testing
Formal interviews, 48
Frames of reference, 299–300
Freewriting response journals, 375–378
Fry graph, 56–57, 58
Functional literacy, 7
Funds of knowledge, 113–114

Goals
    for classroom discussions, 150
    in cooperative learning groups, 257–258
Goals 2000, 37
Grade-equivalent-scores, 38
Graphic organizers, 271–276, 399–411
    in content areas, 402–407
    content standards for using, 394–395

defined, 271
introducing students to, 401
outlines as, 399–400
questions with, 407–409
to reflect text patterns, 402–407, 436–438
semantic (cognitive) mapping, 409–411
student-constructed, 275–276
teacher-constructed, 272–275
GRASP approach, 416–419
Great Society, 106
Group composition, in cooperative learning groups, 257
Group investigation, 254–255, 256
Group retellings, 255
Group roles, in cooperative learning groups, 259–260
Group size, in cooperative learning groups, 255–257
Guided discussions, 147–148
Guided imagery, 306–307
    example of, 306
    nature of, 306
Guided practice, in strategy instruction, 82
Guided reading procedure (GRP), 322, 331–335
    described, 331–332
    example of, 333–335
    GRASP approach to, 416–419
    procedures for, 332–333

Head Start, 106
Health science
    anticipation guides in, 309–310
    content standards for, 199
    intra-act in, 337–339
    three-level reading guides in, 343, 345
    Web sites on, 211
Heterogeneous grouping, 257
High-stakes testing, 32–39
    authentic assessment compared with, 34, 43
    basics of standardized testing, 37–39
    content standards and, 10, 108
    federal requirements for, 37, 108
    increasing use of, 33–34
    issues and concerns in, 33–35
    nature of, 32
    state standards in, 35, 36, 108, 394–395
Hispanic Americans. *See* Latinos
Historical fiction, 162, 168, 174, 178
History of the United States (DeBacco et al.), 158–159
Holistic scoring, 358–359
Homogeneous grouping, 257
Hyperlinks, 203–205
Hypermedia
    defined, 202
    learning with, 203–205

Credits